Research Methods
A Process of Inquiry
THIRD EDITION

ANTHONY M. GRAZIANO
State University of New York at Buffalo

MICHAEL L. RAULIN
State University of New York at Buffalo

LONGMAN

An imprint of Addison Wesley Longman, Inc.

New York • Reading, Massachusetts • Menlo Park, California • Harlow, England
Don Mills, Ontario • Sydney • Mexico City • Madrid • Amsterdam

For

Amy, Lisa, Michael, and Mark

For

Loren and Jean Chapman
Each a mentor, colleague, and friend to me

Acquisitions Editor: Catherine Woods
Project Coordination, Text and Cover Design: York Production Services
Cover Art: Vie No. 1, Auguste Herbin. Allbright-Knox Art Gallery, Buffalo, New York.
  Gift of Seymore H. Knox Foundation, Inc., 1966.
Art Coordination: York Production Services
Electronic Production Manager: Valerie Zaborski
Manufacturing Manager: Helene G. Landers
Electronic Page Makeup: York Production Services
Printer and Binder: R. R. Donnelley & Sons Company
Cover Printer: Phoenix Color Corp.

Library of Congress Cataloging-in-Publication Data

Graziano, Anthony M.
     Research methods: a process of inquiry / Anthony M. Graziano,
  Michael L. Raulin. — 3rd ed.
          p. cm.
     Includes bibliographical references and index.
     ISBN 0-673-98041-3
     1. Research—Methodology.   I. Raulin, Michael L.   II. Title.
  Q180.55.M4G7   1996
  001.4′2—dc20   95-48877
                                                           CIP

ISBN 0-673-98041-3

12345678910—DOC—99989796

Contents

To the Instructor

PEDAGOGICAL CONSIDERATIONS—TEACHING CONCEPTS OF RESEARCH

Research Methods: A Process of Inquiry has evolved over years of teaching. This text reflects our experience in teaching research methods, supervising student research, and conducting our own research. We worked hard to provide a solid text covering the expected content for a research methods course and also providing supportive material and organization to enhance students' learning. Pedagogical considerations guided every phase of the writing of this text and the preparation of the supplements.

This third edition builds on the success of the first two. Every change was designed to enhance the functioning, readability, and interest level of the text. We emphasize research concepts rather than cookbook-like strategies. We want students to develop an understanding of scientific research as an integrated process of thinking and an exciting enterprise and to appreciate that science involves the continuous interplay of rationalism and empiricism—a combination that makes stringent and unique demands on the nature of evidence and upon the methods used to arrive at conclusions about the universe. The first two chapters provide a basic foundation of scientific concepts and historical development to support the subsequent presentation of research methods.

PROGRAMMATIC NATURE OF THE TEXT

We assume that difficult or unfamiliar concepts are best taught programmatically. Thus, complex concepts (e.g., validity) are introduced and defined early in the text but only to the degree needed for that introductory discussion. Concepts are then systematically reexamined throughout the text, new facets are added, and related concepts are brought together into a coherent model, progressively building more complete and sophisticated conceptualizations. This programmatic development of concepts:

- provides students with systematic, progressive mastery of ideas, beginning with basic levels and building to more complex and more complete concepts;
- results in sequential rather than independent chapters, each chapter building upon earlier material;
- requires repetition—the same concepts are discussed several times but at progressively higher levels of sophistication.

The programmatic approach avoids the encyclopedic style of many texts, making complex material more accessible and understandable to students. We have included a complete glossary and a detailed index to help students quickly locate specific material and discussions.

TREATMENT OF STATISTICS

This text emphasizes that decisions regarding statistical analyses are an integral part of the design process and are not added after data collection. Basic statistical concepts are introduced early in the text (Chapters 4 and 5) and their integration into the design process is maintained throughout. Statistical procedures are presented conceptually with an emphasis on understanding what they can do, how to run them with computer analysis packages, and how to read and interpret the output. Choosing an appropriate statistical procedure often confuses students. We teach that the choice of appropriate statistical analyses follows systematically from the design characteristics of the study. Chapter 14 presents a unique addition to research methods texts—flowcharts that lead the student step-by-step through the characteristics of any basic research design to the choice of appropriate statistical analysis procedures.

In addition to Chapters 4, 5, and 14 (Measurement, Statistical Analyses, and Statistical Flowcharts), Appendix C lists statistical formulas, and Appendix D gives an introduction to the use of computerized statistical analysis packages (featuring *SPSS for Windows*). We have integrated computerized statistical analysis throughout the text. As the course instructor, you can determine how much of the statistical material to emphasize, depending upon the level and type of course you teach and whether your students have had a statistics course.

A COHERENT MODEL OF THE RESEARCH ENTERPRISE

Research is not presented in piecemeal fashion in this text. Rather, a coherent descriptive model of the universe of research is developed that integrates inductive and deductive reasoning, empirical observation, concepts of validity, and the phases in the conduct of a research project. The concept of levels of constraint is introduced. It refers to the degree of control that the researcher can exercise over the research process. Valuable research can be carried out at any level of constraint—a point on which we differ from some other textbook authors. Experimental research (Chapters 8-12) is the most rigorous and allows us to answer questions of causality. But other research questions are also important—questions about the strength and direction of relationships among variables, about differences between already-existing groups, about single individuals, or about observations leading to the formation rather than the testing of causal hypotheses. All are properly scientific approaches to study relationships among variables. It is important for students to learn that appropriate scientific research design is largely dependent upon the nature of the questions asked and that research at all levels—whether naturalistic, case-study, correlational, differential, quasi-experimental, or experimental—is appropriate and useful. The text builds conceptual foundations leading to experimental research by developing each of the other levels of constraint, thereby providing students with a full spectrum of research knowledge and skills. We have devoted three chapters (6, 7, & 13) to nonexperimental research procedures. Although we believe strongly that the nonexperimental designs are valuable tools for the psychologist, we take great care to emphasize their limitations and to impart an appropriate level of caution to students.

RESEARCH ETHICS

When we decide to use living organisms as subjects, we must be concerned with their welfare and must ensure that our procedures do not violate the health, safety, or rights of subjects. Because of the importance of ethical issues, this topic has been introduced early and, consistent with the text's general organization, returned to at later points for further discussions of the ethics of human and animal research.

LEARNING AIDS INTEGRATED WITHIN THE TEXT

Consistent with our pedagogical concerns, this text provides numerous learning aids for the student, including:

- Internal and end-of-chapter summaries
- A list of Key Terms and extensive Review Exercises at the end of each chapter (with answers to selected exercises provided in an appendix)
- Informational boxes set off from the chapter content
- A unique approach using diagrams to explain ANOVA procedures
- Unique decision-tree flowcharts to teach how to select appropriate statistical analyses
- A Pre-Data Checklist of items that must be completed before data collection (similar to the preflight checklists used by pilots)
- A Glossary with almost 400 terms defined for the student

- Suggested Readings for further study
- Appendices on:
  - Writing a Research Report in APA Style
  - Table of Random Numbers
  - Statistical Computation Procedures
  - Statistical Analyses Using *SPSS for Windows*
  - Selected Answers to Exercises
  - Conducting Library Research

In addition, as noted above, the text's organization includes:

- Programmatic development of concepts
- Presentation of a coherent model of research
- Extensive use of examples—several of which are repeated to provide continuity to the presentation

SUPPLEMENTS

The adoption package includes an Instructor's Manual, a Study Guide, and a Computerized Test-Item File with over 2,500 multiple-choice items. The Instructor's Manual provides:

- A brief outline of the focus of each chapter and the topics covered
- Identification of controversies in the field, with appropriate background reading
- A selected bibliography
- Over 2,500 multiple-choice test items, keyed to text pages where the material is discussed

The Study Guide provides for each chapter:

- A chapter summary
- A list of key terms
- Sample examination questions (fill-in blanks, true/false, multiple-choice, and essay)
- Chapter exercises
- Suggested Reading list
- Answers to sample examination questions

The computerized test-item file utilizes the TestMaster Program, which allows instructors to select from over 2,500 multiple-choice items, modify or write new items, and construct examinations.

THE THIRD EDITION

The first two editions of this text were very successful, and the same basic approach outlined above has been continued in this third edition. In addition, we have made the following improvements:

- A completely updated final chapter on new directions in research methodology
- A de-emphasis on manual computation of statistics in favor of emphasizing computerized statistical analysis
- An extensive revision of the appendix on using computerized statistical analyses (featuring *SPSS for Windows*)
- An expanded presentation of conducting library research
- Over 30 new figures to illustrate difficult concepts
- Addition of a pre-data checklist listing all the steps necessary before one begins to collect data
- New informational boxes throughout the text
- Updated examples and references
- More extensive integration of the role of theory in research
- Expanded treatment of research ethics
- More information on the history of psychology
- An introduction to regression
- A reorganization of the section on survey research
- An expanded glossary
- An expanded test-item file

INTERNET RESOURCES

We are now developing a World Wide Web (WWW) page for the text, which will contain additional materials for the instructor. These materials can be downloaded at will. The WWW will provide a repository for a constantly updated pool of teaching resources available to you as the instructor. We also want to maintain contact with the instructors who use this text. We have set up a list server to permit virtual discussions among the users of the text on any matter related to teaching research methods. Although we are both on this list, we hope that the conversations and exchange of ideas will be of the round-table variety. If you wish to be added to this list, send an e-mail request to raulin@acsu.buffalo.edu, and we will see to it that you are added immediately. Feel free to e-mail either of us at any time with questions, comments, and suggestions. The instructors using this text have been our single best source of ideas for improvement. Our e-mail addresses are:

Anthony Graziano: amgraz@acsu.buffalo.edu
Michael Raulin: raulin@acsu.buffalo.edu

ACKNOWLEDGMENTS

A project of this size and scope would not be possible were it not for the valuable assistance of many people. We have been fortunate to have many excellent reviewers for each edition. We would like to acknowledge the valuable feedback and suggestions of reviewers for the first edition (Vincent J. Adesso, University of Wisconsin, Milwaukee; Lawrence R. Gordon, University of Vermont; Burt R. Brown, Rutgers–The State University of New Jersey; Charles G. Halcomb, Texas Tech

University; Madeline Heilman, New York University; John P. Hostetler, Albion College; Daniel W. Leger, University of Nebraska; Daniel D. Moriarty, Jr., University of San Diego; James L. Pate, Georgia State University; Samuel L. Seaman, Baylor University; Robert M. Stern, The Pennsylvania State University; and Lois E. Tetrick, Wayne State University), second edition (Donald A. Czech, Marquette University; Stephen E. Edgell, University of Louisville; Gregory T. Golden, Immaculata College; Timothy E. Goldsmith, The University of New Mexico; Robert Grissom, San Francisco State University; Sherri L. Jackson, Jacksonville University; Richard G. Marriott, Lamar University; Linda Mealey, College of St. Benedict/St. John's University; Robert M. Murphey, University of California, Davis; and Patrick D. Slattery, Auburn University at Montgomery), and third edition (Mary Beth Gilboy, Immaculata College; Wendy Domjan, University of Texas, Austin; Peter Urcuioli, Purdue University; and Richard Hagen, Florida State University).

Several faculty colleagues provided valuable consultation, including Irving Biederman, B. Richard Bugelski, Jennifer Crocker, Edwin Hollander, Elaine Hull, Mark Kristal, Murray Levine, Kenneth Levy, Brenda Major, John Meacham, Dean Pruitt, James Sawush, and C. James Smith. Finally, we wish to thank the editorial staff of HarperCollins and York Production Services, including our sponsoring editor, Catherine Woods, her able assistant, Erica Smith, and our production editor, Susan Free.

To the Student

We often imagine scientists wearing white coats and spending time peering at complicated equipment in shining and mysterious laboratories. But scientific work can be done while sitting under a tree in the woods, thinking through a problem, and using apparatus no more technical than a pad and a pencil. This image is important, for it emphasizes that the essence of science is its logic—science is above all else *a way of thinking.* The laboratories, the equipment, the computers, and the hardware are just tools used to promote and support the scientist's central activity—creative, systematic thinking. That intellectual activity is incorporated into a process of inquiry in which the scientist asks and answers questions about nature. That process of inquiry is what we mean by scientific research, and it is the focus of this text.

People ask questions every day. We tend to rely on our hunches, already existing ideas, and respected authorities for answers to many questions. Seldom do we seek answers in the systematic manner of science. Although thinking scientifically is unfamiliar to most people, one can learn to think scientifically. This is the major challenge in this course. A research methods course is demanding, but the concepts are not difficult. The difficult part is learning to think critically and systematically, to phrase questions clearly, and to demand strong evidence for your ideas. Excitement, hunches, and flashes of insight are very much a part of science, and so are plodding hard work; rigorous, systematic thinking; and procedures that put our ideas to many demanding tests. All contribute to the creative and exciting endeavor of scientific research. You will learn to have more confidence in ideas that survive the rigors of scientific scrutiny and to discard those that do not.

This text has been designed for your *active* rather than passive use. Questions are posed in both the chapters and in the exercises at the end of each chapter. There is an index and a glossary. Work through the problems and exercises, consult the glossary when necessary, and if you need more information on a concept, use the index to direct you to additional discussion on that topic in the text. The chapter footnotes and the text's references are good sources for further reading.

A Study Guide is available to aid in your mastery of the material. The Study Guide organizes the information from each chapter and structures the studying of the material. The Study Guide starts by summarizing material and identifying key terms for each chapter, and then goes on to encourage you to test your knowledge with actual test questions. Answers are provided for all questions so that areas of confusion can be easily identified and corrected before the course examinations.

We welcome your comments and evaluation of this text and urge you to use the evaluation sheets that have been included in the Study Guide, or you can contact us through e-mail (amgraz@acsu.buffalo.edu; raulin@acsu.buffalo.edu). Our mailing address is: Psychology Department; SUNY at Buffalo; Buffalo, NY 14260-4110.

Anthony M. Graziano
Michael L. Raulin

Chapter
1

Curiosity, Creativity, and Commitment

SCIENCE IS A WAY OF THINKING

Scientists seek answers to their own questions. Their work is built on highly refined skills in asking and answering questions. Knowing how to ask questions is as important as knowing how to go about answering them. The essence of *science* is the process of forming questions and systematically seeking answers to gain a better understanding of nature. Science is a *process of inquiry,* a particular way of thinking.

From this process of inquiry many tools and useful products are created. These include laboratory equipment, statistical procedures, computers and computer programs, space flight, medicines, powerful detergents, and, unfortunately, even more powerful weapons. People too often mistake the tools and products of science for its essence. However, the essence of science is the scientist's ways of thinking—the logic used in systematically asking and answering questions. A scientist can operate scientifically while sitting under a tree in the woods, thinking through a problem, and using apparatus no more technical than paper and pencil. A scientific discipline such as chemistry is not made more scientific than another such as psychology by virtue of its bubbling liquids and laboratory equipment. Likewise, knowing how to use an electron microscope or how to run a computer program does not make a scientist out of a laboratory technician. Our modern television-sustained image of the white-coated laboratory worker surrounded by machines with blinking lights and computers fed by whirling tapes is an effective visual metaphor, but it does not validly portray the essence of science any more than, to use another metaphor, a skyscraper really scrapes the sky. *The essence of modern science is the way of thinking, the disciplined way in which questions are posed and answered in order to understand natural events. It is the logical processes and demands for evidence, and not the* technologies, *that characterize science. It is an intellectual process.* As discussed by Staddon and Bueno (1991), *the ultimate goal of this process of thinking is to understand the natural universe.*

ASKING QUESTIONS

Asking questions, of course, is not new. Socrates and his followers over 2400 years ago used a highly developed system for asking questions. As in a balanced equation, a question is one side of an idea; on the other side is an unknown quantity, a potential answer. Every question points to the existence of an unknown—to some area of human ignorance or uncertainty. Socrates knew, apparently to his delight, that by systematically posing sharp questions about religion, politics, and morality he could spear even the most dignified citizens, revealing their ignorance and uncertainties, and driving them to extreme discomfort. Unfortunately for Socrates, the good citizens were made so uncomfortable that they executed him as a subversive and corrupter of youth. It was thus established early in history that asking questions may be hazardous to one's health. But risk taking is part of any scientist's work. Numerous social and political strains have been caused by those who raise questions and expose ignorance, and these people often suffer serious reprisals. Leonardo da Vinci and Galileo posed serious threats to church dogma in the Renaissance; Charles Darwin, Alfred Russel Wallace, and a number of nineteenth-century geologists presented data that seriously questioned the biblical account of creation and the biblically derived age of the earth (see Box 1.1). Lest one believe that reprisals occurred only in the distant historical past, consider that "until 1965 anyone in the state of Arkansas who taught Darwinian evolution was subject to prosecution" (Bernstein, 1980, p. 4). The free *skepticism* of scientists cannot be tolerated in authoritarian states. Even in the United States, government officials have often interfered with the free pursuit and exchange of knowledge. Scientific knowledge has become so important in our modern world that competing governments impose constraints of secrecy on their own scientists to prevent the leaking of information. For example, in 1982, U.S. government agents forced the cancellation of 100 scheduled papers at the Annual International Technical Symposium of the Society of Photo-Optical Instrumentation Engineers held in San Diego. The Department of Defense was concerned that some of the information might be of military value to the Russians, whose scientists were also present.

An example of state censorship within the United States involved the massive Exxon Oil spill in Prince William Sound, Alaska, in 1989. A great deal of information, critically important for the clean-up efforts, had been gathered by government scientists and technicians. But, despite the urgent public need for the information, Alaska's attorney general ordered state scientists not to publish, publicly discuss, or otherwise disclose any data, fearing that such information might be of use to the Exxon Corporation in legal actions (Busch, 1991). Scientific information is often critical for the conduct of the affairs of nations and still, under some conditions, its dissemination makes many people uncomfortable.

Although scientists are not uncomfortable with uncertainties, they do attempt to resolve them, not by denying the questions and reasserting old beliefs, but by studying the questions and seeking new answers. The scientist is a pervasive *skeptic* who is willing to tolerate uncertainty (Sternberg & Lubart, 1992) and who finds intellectual excitement in creating questions and seeking answers about nature. Asking a question is a creative endeavor, bringing together ideas that, at least for the moment, pose something new. Creating new ideas provides scientists with the personal satisfaction of indulging their own curiosity and exercising their own creativity.

Scientists agree that sheer curiosity is one of their major motivators and a major component of their work. "What?" "How?" and "What if?" are among the scientist's most basic vocabulary. Curiosity may have killed the cat, according to the old saying, but curiosity also sustains the scientist. J. Robert Oppenheimer (1956), speaking about the commonalities of physics and psychology, notes that the sciences are "responsive to a primitive, permanent, pervasive human curiosity" (p. 128). According to Linus Pauling (1981), satisfying one's own curiosity is one of life's greatest sources of happiness. B. F. Skinner (1956) agrees, advising us: "When you run onto something interesting, drop everything else and study it" (p. 223).

The scientist's pursuit of curiosity follows unknown paths, sometimes resulting in dramatic and unanticipated discoveries that can appear to be accidental—a mat-

Box 1.1   # Charles Darwin and Alfred Russel Wallace

As happens often in science, important discoveries may be made simultaneously and independently by different researchers working from similar theoretical perspectives. Charles Darwin (1809–1882) was one of the most important scientists in history. His work *On the Origin of Species* (1859) has had profound effects on science, philosophy, religion, and even on political debate.

After completing his famous journeys, Darwin spent the next 21 years (1838–1859) in England, refining his ideas for publication. In June 1858, when his book was still far from completion, Darwin received a manuscript in the mail in which his own thesis had already been written. Darwin had been preempted by another naturalist, Alfred Russel Wallace (1823–1913).

According to Arthur Keith (1954), Wallace traveled and studied in the Amazon valley and in the South Pacific as Darwin had done many years before. Wallace was impressed by the diversity of life he found there, and he followed, completely independently, the same line of reasoning as Darwin in making sense out of the observed data. The result was Wallace's manuscript on the biological operation of natural selection in the origins of new species. Wallace mailed his discovery to Darwin for comment.

Who was to be the first to present this momentous discovery to the world? Darwin's associates arranged to have the two men's work presented simultaneously at a meeting of the Linnean Society of London on July 1, 1858. Thus, Wallace and Darwin are credited equally with the discovery. The Greeks had developed a concept of evolution over 2000 years earlier. However, it was Wallace and Darwin who gathered the mass of data and created the concept of natural selection that made their evolutionary theory so important. During the following year, Darwin completed *On the Origin of Species* and soon became the acknowledged originator of the idea of natural selection and the model that derived from it. Wallace, apparently content with this, made no great efforts to share in the subsequent acclaim, and the two men remained lifelong friends. Wallace outlived Darwin by 31 years and died in 1913. Wallace made important contributions to science and is recognized by biologists as an eminent naturalist. However, it is Darwin who is remembered for the great biological discovery.

ter of luck. But when scientists drop everything to indulge their curiosity, they do so with what has been called a "prepared mind"—a disciplined curiosity that makes them sharply alert to the possibility of unanticipated discovery. "A discovery," as Albert Szent-Gyorgi notes, "is said to be an accident meeting a prepared mind" (quoted in Bachrach, 1981, p. 3). Expressing the same point, George Nelson (1970) recounts a comment made by Louis Pasteur when he was the guest of honor at a large reception: "Isn't it extraordinary these days," someone asked Pasteur, "how many scientific achievements are arrived at by accident?" "Yes," replied Pasteur, "it really is remarkable when you think of it, and furthermore, did you ever observe to whom the accidents happen?" (p. 263). Scientists' curiosity is not idle, but active, leading to discoveries not through aimless luck but because it is embedded within a prepared mind and nurtured by long hours of research. It is a highly disciplined curiosity, sharpened and focused by labor and frustrations as well as by successes.

SCIENCE AND ART

Although we have attributed certain characteristics to scientists—curiosity, creativity, skepticism, tolerance for ambiguity, commitment to hard work, and a way of thinking that searches for answers to questions—these characteristics are equally well developed in poets, sculptors, painters, composers, philosophers, writers, and others. All engage in a mix of artistic and intellectual endeavors, indulge their own curiosity, and explore their worlds with skeptical questioning and sharp observations. They attempt to answer their own questions and to represent parts of the world through their own particular medium—whether it is color, shape, sound, language, the plasticity of clay, or the solidity of stone. Their representations of ideas become part of the public domain where they may be viewed, criticized, discussed, accepted, rejected, or worse, ignored. In each of these endeavors, we see people compelled by a combination of curiosity and creativity who delight in their discoveries of relationships in nature and in their created representations of nature. Their statements are tentative. Symphonies, paintings, and research investigations are presented not as fixed or complete truths but as tentative statements of their originators' understanding at a given point in time. This is not to argue that science and art are the same. They are not. Yet each employs variations of the same themes—human curiosity combined with a commitment to ideas, to disciplined processes of inquiry, and to producing the representations of their ideas. Although artists and scientists comprise only a small part of the world's population, they have created a large and enduring array of the ideas and products that have significantly affected the world.

There is a common belief that art and science are so totally different that artists and scientists must be thoroughly alienated from each other. We often hear suggestions that someone is the artistic type (poet, musician, or the like) and therefore has no aptitude for science or math, or that a scientist or mathematician cannot appreciate art and literature. These assumptions are most often false. For example, consider the 40 national winners of the annual Westinghouse Science Talent Competition. Many of these young people of high achievement in science, mathematics, and technology are also talented in other creative activities such as music, writing, and the visual arts. As we will see later in this chapter, art, science, and technology were all generated from the same pool of human skills and curiosity early in civilization. Art and science, although different from each other, share many characteristics.

COMMON METHODS OF ACQUIRING KNOWLEDGE

The essence of science is its systematic, disciplined way of thinking aimed at gaining *knowledge* about nature. Science places heavy demands on the adequacy of its information and on the processes applied to that information. However, science is not the only way of thinking about the world.

G. C. Helmstadter (1970) has labeled the common methods of acquiring knowledge as tenacity, intuition, authority, rationalism, empiricism, and science. These methods are ranked in the order of the demands made on the adequacy of the information that each is willing to accept and on the nature of the processing of that information. The methods of science, which include rationalism and empiricism, are the most demanding in these respects, whereas tenacity, intuition, and authority make few demands on information and require minimal processing.

Tenacity

Tenacity describes a willingness to accept ideas as valid knowledge because these ideas have been accepted for so long or have been so often repeated that they acquire an aura of unquestioned truth. We can see this principle of tenacity operating in modern political campaigns where ideas—often incorrect or distorted—are repeated so incessantly that the voters begin to accept them as true. Advertisers, especially in television commercials, successfully use this method, repeating the message over and over hoping consumers will accept it as truth. In modern politics, television advertising and political campaigning have combined to create a massive amount of accepted information based on tenacity. When tenacity operates, there is no demand to check on the accuracy of the ideas—there is no subjecting of those ideas to skeptical, critical, and objective review.

Intuition

Intuition operates, according to some, without any intellectual effort or involvement of sensory processes. Examples of such supposedly direct-access knowledge include extrasensory perception (a contradiction in terms), which has been claimed by self-styled psychics, and knowledge received directly from God, claimed by persons who have had powerful religious experiences.

Authority

Authority as a method of acquiring knowledge is the acceptance of an idea as valid knowledge because some respected source—such as religious writings, Aristotle, the United States Supreme Court, the president, the pope, or Sigmund Freud—claims it is valid.

Tenacity, intuition, and authority make few demands on their information and processes. In essence they assert that we know this is true because (1) it has always been so, (2) we feel it is so, or (3) the authority says it is so. They share an uncritical acceptance of the information and conclusions and have limited skepticism about their methods. All of us, even scientists, use some of these methods in everyday life and are willing to make some decisions based on an uncritical acceptance of information. Such methods have value in smoothing our personal lives. We might, for example, accept religious teachings intuitively or on authority, and experience personal satisfaction in sharing religious beliefs with others. We can easily act upon our strong urge that tells us we would rather have spaghetti than steak for dinner, accepting it as valid knowledge of what we really want, without any need for further evaluation of the information. But would we also uncritically agree to saunter across a six-lane freeway with our eyes closed because our companion tells us that he knows intuitively through his psychic powers that we will be perfectly safe in spite of the 360 cars per minute hurtling by at high speed from both directions? Clearly, for some kinds of decisions, we must demand that our information and the processes used to gather it be more adequate. In this regard, both *rationalism* and *empiricism* give us a much firmer basis for accepting information as knowledge.

Rationalism

Rationalism is a way of thinking in which knowledge is developed through reasoning processes alone. In the rationalistic approach, information is carefully stated and logical rules are followed to arrive at acceptable conclusions. Consider this classic deductive syllogism:

> All crows are black. (the major premise)
> This is a crow. (the minor premise)
> Therefore, this crow is black. (the conclusion)

The conclusion is logically derived from the major and minor premises. The same logic, however, would lead us to reject the following conclusion:

> All crows are black.
> This is black.
> Therefore, this is a crow.

In the rationalistic approach, the conclusion is reached through the logic of the procedure—which is a more reliable way to arrive at knowledge than tenacity, intuition, or authority. However, using rationalism alone has its limitations. Consider this syllogism:

> All 4-year-old children develop fears of the dark.
> Lisa is a 4-year-old child.
> Therefore, Lisa has developed fears of the dark.

The logic is clear and the conclusion is correct, unless of course Lisa has not developed fears of the dark. What is the limitation? Suppose it is not true that all 4-year-old children develop fears of the dark, or suppose Lisa is actually 7 and not 4 years old, or suppose Lisa is a yacht and not a child at all. Although essential, rationalism alone has its limitations in science; that is, *the premises must be true as determined by some other evidence* to arrive at the correct conclusions. Attaining knowledge, then, depends not only on the reasoning process but also on the accuracy of the premises. There is no provision for assessing their accuracy in the purely rationalistic approach.

The rationalistic approach allows us systematically and logically to develop a tentative statement (hypothesis) that can then be tested in some other manner. Each premise is a hypothesis, which, if shown to be true on the basis of external data, can be used rationally in drawing conclusions. In summary, the logic of rationalism is used in modern science to aid in developing hypotheses that can then be

TABLE 1.1   WAYS OF KNOWING

Tenacity	A willingness to accept ideas as valid because they have been accepted for so long or repeated so often that they seem true
Intuition	Accepting ideas as valid because they "feel" intuitively true
Authority	Accepting ideas as valid because some respected authority asserts that the ideas are true
Rationalism	A process that develops valid ideas using existing ideas and principles of logic
Empiricism	Gaining knowledge by observing the events around us
Science	A process that combines the principles of rationalism with the process of empiricism, using rationalism to develop theories and empiricism to test the theories

tested against external criteria. In order to perform this testing against external criteria, science must depend on still another way of knowing—empiricism.

Empiricism

Empiricism is a way of gaining knowledge through observation of real events—that is, *knowing by experiencing through our senses.* It is a method as old as civilization. For the empiricist, it is not enough to know through reason (or tenacity or intuition or authority) alone. It is necessary to experience events through the senses—to see, hear, touch, taste, and smell. "I won't believe it unless I see it!" is the empiricist's motto. Thales, Hippocrates, Galen, Copernicus, Galileo, and Darwin all based their important conclusions about nature largely on their observations of events. They rejected the more widely held, nonempirical conceptions provided by mythology, religion, appeal to authority, and rationalism. On a more modern and personal note, when we are ready to leave our home in the morning and we see that the sky is dark and filled with clouds and we hear approaching rumblings of thunder in the distance, we are good empiricists if we take a hat or umbrella—our senses are telling us something.

Empiricism alone, however, has its limitations. For example, suppose that a psychoanalyst concluded that all enuretic children (children over the age of 4 who do not control urination and who repeatedly wet their beds or clothing) suffer from unresolved Oedipal conflicts. These conflicts, according to this psychoanalyst, cause the enuresis and also cause all enuretic children to be highly anxious and phobic; consequently, all enuretic children need intensive psychoanalytic treatment to get to the basic causes of their problems. This psychoanalyst did not base her conclusions on an unthinking acceptance of Freud as an authority but on her own empirical observations made in more than 20 years of private practice. During that time, the analyst had treated more than 100 enuretic children and had viewed each child as being seriously troubled by the Oedipal conflict and as highly anxious and phobic. There was not a single exception to these observations and interpretations. With such consistent observations of so many cases over so many years of experience, the doctor was extremely confident in her conclusions. As carefully empirical as she tried to be, however, her conclusions about all enuretic children might still be resoundingly incorrect, as we will see in Chapter 2.

Science

Science brings together elements of both rationalism and empiricism, employing rational logic and checking each step with empirical observation. The scientist is constantly shuttling between empirical observation, abstract rational thought, and general principles, then returning again to further empirical observation of specific facts. It was this repeated return to empirical observation in an otherwise rationalistic process that marked the sixteenth century's apparently sudden surge into science. Much of the progress in scientific procedure since then has been to strengthen the empirical component by developing more precise methods of observation.

Science is a way of thinking that involves a continuous and systematic interplay of rational thought and empirical observation. Observed events—whether the movements of planets observed by an astronomer or the behavior of children observed by a psychologist—constitute the major facts of a discipline. But the empirical observation of events and the resulting identification or listing of facts is not sufficient in science. We must go beyond the immediately observable facts, using them in rational processes of abstract thought to construct general principles and understanding and to make new predictions about nature. The scientist remains curious, skeptical, and committed, using processes that identify or discover facts and that integrate those facts into coherent predictions, explanations, and general principles.

EMERGING MODERN SCIENCE

Modern science emerged in the fifteenth and sixteenth centuries. Readers are sometimes mislead into thinking that science was suddenly created and that there had been no science before Copernicus, Galileo, or Newton. That, of course, is not true. Science has been one of Western civilization's alternative methods of acquiring knowledge since the Greeks of 2400 years ago, and its antecedents date back still further, possibly 8000 years. It was not until the late Renaissance in the seventeenth century that science was able to acquire enough independence to begin its rapid acceleration into the powerful social movement it is today.

To understand the development of science, remember that it offers a way of thinking that integrates systematic rationalism with direct empirical observation. The latter allows testing prior observations and making new observations to serve as a basis for further rational development. Science is uniquely different from other ways of knowing. Its history suggests that empiricism developed first, followed by the emergence of rationalism, which, in turn, grew into a sophisticated and competing system. The two were integrated and the combined process—science—gained social support. Each step represented major changes, which do not occur quickly in history.

Early Civilization

Civilization is a process of human development from primitive hunter-gatherers, to the organized nomadic hunter's existence, to a settled and more socially organized cooperative lifestyle. Civilization operates on a broad array of collective human skills that evolved slowly over millennia and were taught to successive generations. Then, in the relatively short period from about 6000 to 4000 B.C., the long accumulation of human skills enabled a remarkable surge of progress from the late Neolithic period of polished stone tools into the age of metals. Urban settlements grew and the technological, social, and intellectual tools of early civilizations were integrated. Humans spread around the eastern Mediterranean and by about 6000 B.C. had established an astonishing array of skills. The magnificent civilizations of the Babylonians, Egyptians, and others had long flourished, and their people lived in complex, stable societies. Human skills and achievements that were passed on to the Greeks included architecture; agriculture; animal husbandry; preparing and preserving foods; mining, smelting, and refining metals and alloys; and manufacturing a great variety of stone and metal tools. Complicated business and commercial skills were developed that depended on long-distance land and sea navigation. People could weigh, count, do arithmetic, write and maintain permanent records, and monitor seasons with accurate calendars. By 4000 B.C., important books on astronomy, medicine, surgery, and mathematics were available. Early scholarly interests also included imaginative and mystical unified conceptions of the universe as filled with gods, demons, and spirits.

By 1000 B.C. there was a rich legacy of human skills. Benjamin Farrington (1949a, 1949b) emphasized two characteristics of that array of skills. First, they were practical skills aimed at the everyday demands of making a living. There was little value in knowledge for the sake of knowledge. By contrast, much value was placed on practical information about agriculture, manufacturing, and commerce. Practical skills and knowledge had been developed from long involvement in the direct, concrete, and objective manipulation of the environment. They were, in a word, *empirical* skills.

The second characteristic emphasized by Farrington is that from the long involvement in practical skills, there gradually developed more abstract, general ideas about nature. Agriculture and metallurgy are good examples of Farrington's point. In exercising their practical skills, the early farmers observed weather phenomena, floods, moon phases, and other changes in the sky for clues to help in farming. As a result they developed accurate calendars, learned about fertilizers and plant growth, and developed practical mathematics to measure plots and set boundaries. The Egyptians, for example, could accurately measure the annual fall of the Nile River within a few inches. With metallurgical knowledge, artisans could recognize types of ores and the best conditions under which to mine them. They knew, for example, about the action of heat in transforming solids into liquids. They were able to measure by weighing and to understand proportionality so as to reproduce reliably the particular mixes needed for various alloys. These skilled crafts required abstract, general information about nature, gathered and refined through generations of empirical observations and concrete manipulations. Such abstract knowledge was important only for carrying out practical tasks. The young apprentice did not study abstract astronomy, biology, chemistry, or mathematics; but embedded in the crafts were early elements of later, more abstract knowledge. Thus, in the early Mediterranean civilizations, the components of modern science were found in the arts and craftsmanship. Science, art, and technology were inseparable in practice.

Another important principle in the development of science is the *"orderliness belief"* (Whitehead, 1925). Science rests on the implicit belief that the universe operates in an orderly, lawful manner. If it did not or if we did not hold this belief, says Whitehead, there could be no science. If the universe were not orderly and predictable, it would not stay the same long enough to be studied. To apply their skills in a reliable manner, artisans in 1000 B.C. had to expect orderliness in the physical world. How else could they depend on *this* type of rock, when heated, to release *that* kind of metal, which will always have *these* particular properties, and to do so each time regardless of the different pieces of the rock used?

Greek Science

By 600 B.C. the components necessary for the emergence of science had been developed. There was as yet no articulate science to organize or to transmit skills or ideas. However, there were other social mechanisms: pragmatic skills and close-to-the-facts abstractions were transmitted by the artisans, tradesmen, and other practically oriented people; more imaginative, speculative, and less empirically based notions about the universe were transmitted through mythology, drama, and religion. In religion, gods and demons, humans and animals coexisted in a complicated universe that was both material and mystical but usually orderly. The artisans set their orderliness within pragmatic, concrete experiences; the priests set their orderliness within imaginative, abstract, and mystical cosmologies.

The pre-Socratic Greek period, about 600–400 B.C., was one of developing empirical science. Thales (ca. 640–550 B.C.) is credited as the first Greek philosopher to combine an empirical-rational view of the universe, a view that rejected religion and mysticism. Thales lived in Ionia, a Greek colony whose citizens developed a highly commercial level of skills and were pragmatic realists. The skills of artisans, farmers, and tradesmen were of great importance. Empirical knowledge was a basic part of their culture; and when some, like Thales, turned to philosophy, they developed a clearly empirical view of nature. Thales' philosophy stressed the observation of natural events in a natural universe and rejected the mysticism of gods, demons, or spirits. He speculated about a natural cosmology in which water was the basic substance from which all else developed and to which all will ultimately return. He learned about Babylonian astronomy and predicted accurately the solar eclipse that took place on May 25, 585 B.C. He developed an empirical-rational approach that was scientific, albeit in primitive form. His observations were based on empiricism and on what Whitehead (1925) terms "the painstaking attention to observational details." Thales is the founder of abstract geometry and Ionian philosophy, and is considered to be the "father" of science.

Thales' naturalistic rather than mystical speculations were continued by others. Anaximander's (611–547 B.C.) observations of a shark that had mammalian characteristics led him to develop the concept that higher-order creatures, including humans, developed from lower animals, specifically fishes, and gradually emerged from the seas to dry land. It is clear that a concept of the evolution of life on earth was an early development in Greek science. Empedocles (ca. 500 B.C.) created observable demonstrations of the existence of air by using inflated wine skins. Xenophanes (ca. 600 B.C.), having observed rock imprints of fish and seaweed high on mountains and in landlocked stone quarries, developed a systematic theory of geological change over time. Around 450 B.C., Hippocrates emerged with radical ideas for treating illness. At the time, most people believed that human illness was caused by demons and spirits invading the body, and treatment involved prayers, incantations, and exorcisms. Hippocrates attributed all mental and physical illness to natural events. For Hippocrates, no demon, spirit, or god played any part in disease, and no prayer, incantation, or exorcism could make a sick person well. The Hippocratic physician relied on careful, clinical observations of patients through the course of the disease, and on systematic, rational thought in trying to understand illness. Although Hippocratic teachings were a major alternative to mysticism and demonology, the Greeks had no science of anatomy, physiology, or chemistry, and therefore had few effective treatments.

In the Ionian development of science from Thales through Hippocrates, we see a major emphasis on the careful observation of events in natural, uncontrolled conditions. Thales' scientist and Hippocrates' physician were careful observers and systematic thinkers but not systematic manipulators of events. It would be a later Ionian, Strato, who would develop the next important step: making the scientist an active observer who manipulates and controls the conditions of observations. Strato developed Ionian science to the level of actual experimentation.

Strato, one of the last empirical philosophers, was a successor to Aristotle at the Lyceum from 287 to 269 B.C. He accepted the Ionian cosmology with its emphasis on natural events, its basic belief in the universe as orderly and knowable, and its rejection of mysticism. For Strato, the best method of acquiring knowledge was that of empirical manipulation and observation, that is, *experimentation.* He performed numerous experiments on air and water, demonstrating many of their properties and changes under different conditions. From his experimental work, Strato developed some general explanatory principles about nature.

By Strato's time, however, Ionian science was already in decline, overshadowed by other developments. By 400 B.C. a naturalistic, scientific view stood as an alternative to the generally accepted, mystical beliefs propounded by religion and, later, by philosophers such as Socrates and Plato. Then, as now, these models—empirical sciences versus mysticism—conflicted, leading to the near total suppression of one by the other. The early empirical science was virtually lost for the next 1900 years, until the late Renaissance. A condition that might have been partly responsible for the demise of empiricism in Greek science was the growing stratification of society into occupational and status classes. Manual labor and technological skills, with their pragmatic and empirical focus, became separated from the more socially desired and leisurely pursuits of priests, scholars, and ruling classes. Slavery became a major Greek institution for carrying out the manual labor and technical tasks necessary to maintain society. Plato and Aristotle, for example, defended slavery as a necessary and desirable institution, allowing people at higher levels to function in a more ideal manner.

After Socrates, the highest ideals were religion, politics, and rationalistic, mystical philosophy. The pursuit of practical goals was recognized as necessary and left to slaves, laborers, artisans, farmers, and tradesmen, whereas the pursuit of pure reason and abstract truths was reserved for upper social levels. As a result, theology and abstract philosophy were carefully taught and scrupulously preserved in writing; however, the technical, empirical skills and knowledge, not admitted into the realm of scholarship, remained in the oral tradition and were not as fully recorded or preserved. Although social stratification may have helped to separate empiricism from the mainstream of scholarship, more specific attacks on empiricism and naturalism also occurred. Religion was gaining social power, promulgating its mystical cosmology while attacking the natural philosophy of the Ionians as atheistic and therefore not only factually wrong but also a subversive danger.

The genius of the early Greeks had created empirical, rational science and generated the profound idea of searching for abstract and general principles to explain observed events. The later highly articulated rational philosophies culminating with Aristotle (384–322 B.C.) described an orderly universe that operated according to a few basic principles and in which all of the variety of specific, empirically observed events are but manifestations of these basic principles. This contribution of Greek philosophy is one of humanity's major intellectual developments. Greek philosophy transcended immediate, objective reality and conceptualized a universe of such magnificent orderliness that all of its seeming variation could be understood through discovery of a small number of basic principles. It has profoundly influenced modern thought.

The movement of scholars away from empiricism and pragmatism after about 400 B.C. was led by Socrates, Plato, and to some extent, Aristotle, despite his strong empiricism. The Greeks developed both rationalism and empiricism, but it was the pursuit of pure reason in which their philosophy culminated. As Farrington (1949a) commented, "When Plato died (about 347 B.C.) he left behind him a mystical view of the universe set forth in his dialogues in a unique combination of logic and drama. Its weakness was not that it lacked supports in argument, but that it was not open to correction from experience" (p. 13). After 400 B.C. Greek philosophy became increasingly abstract, rational, and mystical, relegating empirical knowledge to less importance and, eventually, joining the attacks on empiricism.

As philosophers became increasingly mystical in their pursuit of the ideal, there was a growing affinity of religion and philosophy. Universal orderliness, such as that observed in astronomy (e.g., it was believed that planets moved in perfect circles) and in the beautiful regularity of number relationships discovered by the Pythagoreans, was taken as evidence that nature was controlled by divine intelligence. An important shift in the goals of philosophy and science was occurring. Whereas the earlier investigators made observations of nature and rationally analyzed their observations to understand and control nature, the later philosophers began to observe and to think about nature to discover, understand, and illustrate the existence of divine intelligence. In other words, science was beginning to be used in the service of religion, a role that was to be continued and magnified in the Christian era for more than a thousand years, well into the Renaissance.

Medieval Science

After centuries of persecution, Christianity was accepted at the start of the fourth century as one of the Roman Empire's religions and, by the end of that century, was virtually the sole state religion. Christianity grew increasingly powerful as a religious-philosophical movement, a social institution, and a political power—pervading thought and action in Western Europe for the next 1000 years.

Although it has been said that Greek empirical science was suppressed by the medieval Christians, that suppression had actually begun with the later Greeks, long before Christianity. The Greeks' increasing reliance on intuition and pure reason rather than empiricism as methods of acquiring knowledge was continued by the medieval Christian scholars. They, like the Greeks, believed that divine intelligence controlled an orderly and knowable universe. Probably the most basic tenet in medieval thought was the powerful belief that the scriptures were the ultimate source of truth. In those instances where specific knowledge was not revealed in the Bible, the rational thought and/or intuition of church authorities substituted as truth. Theology was the reigning study; revelation, rationalism, and authority were its major methods of acquiring knowledge; and all other areas and methods of study were secondary. Empiricism had its place within medieval science, albeit a secondary one. While the Christian scholars continued empirical study in astronomy, optics, and zoology, their empiricism was in the service of religion (Nagel, 1948).

By the thirteenth century, however, some churchmen such as Thomas Aquinas and Roger Bacon, perhaps influenced by the rediscovery of early classical scholarship, recognized the value of using the senses for acquiring knowledge about God. Bacon and other medieval scientists repeated a number of optical experiments that had been performed earlier by Islamic scientists. A Dominican, Dietrich of Frieberg (ca. 1300), used water-filled glass balls to experiment with the visible spectrum, discovering that colors are reflected on the inside of spherical water drops. At about the same time, Jordanus DeNemore experimented with various types of levers and the equilibrium of weights on inclined planes. In 1269 Peter the Stranger of Maricourt published his empirical experiments with magnets. His work was "a model of the observational and experimental techniques in physics" (Clagett, 1948, p. 119). The increased influence of empiricism is illustrated by a comment attributed to Dietrich of Frieberg, which states that the usual appeal to authority notwithstanding, "one ought never to renounce what had been made manifest by the senses" (cited in Clagett, 1948, p. 119).

During the twelfth and thirteenth centuries, great secular changes occurred in politics, art, commerce, exploration, and even the technologies of warfare. People increased their interest and involvement in the present, real world and began to believe in values other than their belief in an afterlife. During this time there occurred a revival of the ancient Greek, Greco-Roman, and Islamic scholarship. As Western Europeans increased their explorations and trade around the Mediterranean world, they came into contact with Mohammedan scholars who had been part of the Moorish high civilization in Spain in the tenth century. The Mohammedans had brought with them Arabic versions of classical works. Over the next two centuries these were gradually translated into Latin; and by the end of the twelfth century, the medieval scholars were becoming familiar with Hippocratic and Galenic writings in medicine, Euclid's mathematics, Ptolemy's astronomy, Archimedes' physics, and a large variety of Hindu mathematical works. Under this influence, medical schools were established in southern Italy and, later, in other parts of Europe. In these new centers, the ancient, empirically based study of medicine, mathematics, and physics were revived. Empiricism and rationalism applied to the study of natural phenomena were again viewed as major ways of studying nature and acquiring knowledge. As empirical science grew in strength, it remained within the bounds of theology, where—for a while at least—there was room for science to grow. Soon, however, empirical science challenged these limits and, by the seventeenth century, began to escape from them.

Two major theological constraints on empirical science were set in place by the later Greeks and then adopted and strengthened by the Christian theologians for the next thousand years. First, and most importantly, empirical science was not allowed to contradict any theological dogma. If a dispute arose between knowledge gained through the senses and knowledge arrived at by revelation or from church authority, the resolution was simple: truth lay with theology, and any contradictory ideas were false. Second, when empiricism was used, it was in the service of religion. The value of empirical science for the medievals was to help illustrate divine workings. Both of these constraints were challenged by the reviving empirical sciences.

The second of those major theological constraints was challenged in the thirteenth century by the revival of classical and Islamic empirical science and its institutionalization in schools of medicine. Scholars asserted that the use of empiricism toward development of practical, applied knowledge for the betterment of humanity was a worthwhile goal (in this instance, the goal was to understand and combat sickness). The theological grip on empirical science was thus loosened as science began to focus more on service to humanity than on service to God. The church tolerated this application of science to humanity so long as it did not directly challenge church dogma. In time, of course, this challenge did occur in the revolutionary struggles of science in the fourteenth through seventeenth centuries.

The Scientific Revolution

The classical revival of the thirteenth century occurred when Western society was beginning major changes, shifting its focus of interest to greater concerns with the present life in this world. Given new strength by the developments of the thirteenth century, science became established in the new medical centers and a change of major significance began to occur. Scholars began to recognize and accept the potential value of science in the service of humanity. This theme was to become a major point in the development of science, a point that Francis Bacon would stress in the sixteenth century. By the beginning of the fourteenth century, although science began to focus more on human goals, it remained largely under the control of religious and political authorities. The growth of science into its independent status occurred during a seething 400 years of major social changes in virtually every area of human experience. The emergence of an independent science was but one of many areas in which old political and religious authority weakened, with people establishing new values and skills, particularly those aimed at achieving a better life.

During the thirteenth to sixteenth centuries, scientists made an increasing number of discoveries and developed new hypotheses about nature that conflicted with religious dogma and with some tenacious beliefs about nature. For example, one of the most important philosophers, René Descartes (1596–1650), was condemned by both Catholics and Protestants for his views. A philosopher and mathematician, Descartes was a major influence in moving thought away from theological and metaphysical analyses of the soul toward more objective observation and study of the operation of consciousness. Two of his ideas, which were critical in the development of psychology, are his concepts of mind-body dualism and his doctrine of ideas—that ideas arise both innately from processes within the mind and through experience in the external world. Established institutions fought what they perceived to be the scientists' attack on religious truth, just as they resisted most of the other social and intellectual pressures for change. Eventually, however, revolutionary changes did occur; by the beginning of the nineteenth century, science had not only been reestablished and strengthened but, for the first time since about 400 B.C., had achieved an independent status as an important alternative way of understanding nature.

By the eighteenth and nineteenth centuries, scientific centers for research and learning were established in universities; social resources were made available to support science; and the work of scientists became sought after by industries, universities, and governments. The science of psychology emerged in the latter part of the nineteenth century as an outgrowth of fields such as philosophy, biology, and physics. By the twentieth century, science had become an accepted institution and a major social movement.

Science has developed most rapidly in the latter part of the twentieth century. Building on its strong base, science has advanced enormously over the past several decades. For example, developments in high-energy physics have given us a view of the building blocks of matter; in biological science the ability to read and to manipulate DNA structure has led to creation of new variations of life forms; neuroscience is a new integration of psychology, biology, neurology, and biochemistry, leading to new understandings and applications; in medicine new technologies such as magnetic resonance imaging (MRI) allow us literally to look inside the body; and the current development of high-temperature superconducting materials has an enormous potential for future applications.

The current status of the scientific enterprise is dependent on a vast, heavily endowed social structure. This structure includes research centers, universities, industrial and private agencies, as well as many university departments created for the education and training of scientists. Large networks of scientific societies have been set up, with annual meetings in which scientists communicate their findings and lobby for greater public resources. The scientists also communicate with the general public in many different ways, including newspapers, magazines, radio, television, and books. Scientists and their contribution to our general information are supported by the general public, as well as by many special groups such as industry, government, and even some religious leaders.

Scientists have investigated many areas of physical and social phenomena and have created a large variety of special disciplines, each with its own content and procedures. The multiplicity of scientific disciplines is usually viewed as one measure of the complexity of the natural universe. The phenomena differ from one area to another, with observational and methodological procedures differing according to the kinds of questions being asked and the technologies associated with each area. These differences among scientific disciplines are primarily determined by the particular segments of nature that each area has chosen to investigate. But whatever their specialized differences, all sciences share not only a strong curiosity about nature but a commitment to science—combined empiricism and rationalism—as a way of thinking and a way to understand nature.

If modern science represents a way of thinking about nature, then people began thinking scientifically a very long time ago. However, the public's general conception of science appears to stress its recency and its marked differences from the less-enlightened, prescientific views of earlier times. The result is that science is popularly seen as a recent development. If science is so old, what makes it appear so new? Several factors may be involved. First, consider that in the eighteenth century science was still an obscure pursuit, barely known beyond a minority of educated people. But the general level of awareness of science has grown enormously, particularly in the past generation. This in itself may have fostered the perception of science as a recent development.

Second, science is only one of several ways of knowing. At any given time, we can find most or all of the ways represented—some ascendant and others muted. Some modes of thinking became associated with powerful political systems or became so generally socially accepted that they achieved controlling power, making it difficult for alternative views to develop. The social and political power of the medieval church is an example. With the decline of such power, the previously overshadowed scientific ideas became more visible, developed, and refined. Thus, one reason for the apparent recency of science may be the release of political and social constraints that allowed the further development of science.

A third possible factor is the closeness with which science and technology are perceived, and the general perception that because technology is always new, then so must science be new. Consider, for example, the development of the airplane. In 1903, after several years of research, Orville Wright took off from wooden rails and hopped through the air for 12 seconds in the world's first powered, piloted, heavier-than-air flight before losing control and crashing. He survived that crash and lived until 1948, missing by only 13 years being witness to the first manned flight into space by the Soviet cosmonaut Yuri Gagarin. Could he have imagined at the turn of the century, when he and

Wilbur were experimenting with their wind machines and models of wing surfaces, that a flight into space and back would occur almost within his lifetime? (See Box 1.2.)

Technological advances have helped to produce a world barely suggested at the beginning of this century. Such technological burgeoning overpowers us with its wonders, providing us with a continuing procession of new things and new procedures. Our sharp and constant awareness of new technology and our tendency to link technology and science may help to bolster the impression that science, too, is one of those new, marvelous developments. But, as we have noted, science has a long history and cannot accurately be considered a recent or modern occurrence.

THE SCIENCE OF PSYCHOLOGY

H. Ebbinghaus, an early German psychologist noted that "psychology has a short history but a long past," meaning that psychology has been an independent science for only a bit over a hundred years, but had been a part of philosophy for 2000 years. In this section we will introduce some of the major developments within psychology. It is not possible to review psychology's full history in a few pages, so this coverage will be selective. Several excellent texts are available for those interested in a more detailed coverage of psychology's history (Fancher, 1990; Hothersall, 1984; Madsen, 1988; Schultz, 1987).

There was a long period of prescientific psychology, dating at least to Aristotle. But it was not until the early nineteenth century, when laboratory procedures were developed in physiology, that psychological functioning could be studied objectively. *Psychology* evolved from earlier studies in philosophy, biology, mathematics, physiology, physics, and even astronomy. Weber (1795–1878) and Fechner (1801–1887), who developed the methods of *psychophysics,* were among the first researchers to demonstrate, as Descartes had suggested 200 years earlier, that perception could be studied objectively. Their methods consisted of presenting carefully measured stimuli to human subjects under controlled conditions and recording the subjects' responses.

Psychology as an independent scientific discipline is just over a hundred years old, having started with Wilhelm Wundt's psychological laboratory in Germany in 1879. Of course, there had been research and speculations about psychological phenomena long before that, but Wundt's was the first formal laboratory in the new discipline. Wundt's influence was multiplied by the fact that many of his students created psychology laboratories throughout much of the Western world, making him one of the most important psychologists in history. Wundt studied the structure of consciousness using introspection. He tried to infer the basic elements of consciousness on the basis of subjects' verbal reports of their experiences in the laboratory. Since Wundt was interested in the structure of consciousness, his work was known as *structuralism.*

Wundt's structuralism dominated psychology during the late nineteenth and early twentieth centuries. However, by the turn of the century, American psychologists, less interested in the German tradition of structuralism, shifted the focus to how the mind functions. They were interested in practical questions of education,

Box 1.2   # The Wright Brothers as Scientists

It is often supposed that the airplane was invented by the Wright brothers in a burst of Yankee ingenuity. They have been portrayed as independent, mechanical tinkerers in their bicycle shop, whose achievement had little to do with systematic scholarship and research. But in a 1906 interview, the Wrights complained about the way in which they were described in newspapers, noting, "Nearly every writer has characterized us as mechanics, and taken it for granted that our invention has come from mechanical skill. We object to this as neither true nor fair. We are not mechanics; we are scientists" (Oppel, 1987, p. 18). The Wright brothers were referring to their years of study of theoretical principles of flight, their knowledge of the many forms of aircraft, and the many attempts and successes of lighter- and heavier-than-air flight by their predecessors. The Wrights used careful development, experimentation, and testing in their Ohio workshop and on the windy sand dunes near Kitty Hawk, North Carolina.

The Wrights built on the work of several scientists and engineers. A hundred years earlier, in 1804, George Cayley had written a technical essay, *The Mechanic Principles of Aerial Navigation.* By 1857 Cayley had published his calculations for and descriptions of a future flying machine, including its lift surfaces, stabilizer, engine, and propellers. In 1889 Otto Lilienthal, a German engineer, published *Bird Flight as the Basis of Aviation.* Lilienthal became the first person to make controlled, heavier-than-air, flights. Between 1891 and 1896 he made more than 2000 successful glides in his biplanes and monoplanes. In 1896, with relatively light gasoline-powered engines available, Lilienthal was working on a design for a powered airplane but was killed in the crash of one of his gliders. Octave Chanute, a civil engineer, had followed Lilienthal's work and developed a number of gliders. In 1894 he published an important text, *Progress in Flying Machines.* In 1901 he gave the Wrights his expert advisement and enthusiastic support.

On hearing of Lilienthal's death, the Wrights increased their own efforts. They studied the technical writings of Chanute, Lilienthal, Langley, and others. As they perfected their gliders, based initially on Lilienthal's designs, and raced to achieve powered flight, they learned that Samuel Langley, a physicist at the Smithsonian Institution, was also close to success. Langley, backed by the U.S. government, had successfully flown a small-scale model of a steam-driven airplane in 1896, and a larger gasoline-powered model in 1902—the first (unpiloted) flights of powered, propeller-driven, heavier-than-air machines. All was set in December 1903 for Langley to test his full-sized, human-piloted, gas-powered airplane. The tests failed however, and the press concluded that heavier-than-air flight would not be developed for hundreds of years. But just nine days later the Wright Flyer I, propelled by a 12-horsepower engine and piloted by Orville, flew successfully at Kill Devil Hills.

A long process of scientific and technological advances led to the work of Lilienthal, Chanute, Langley, and the Wrights. That history included the early thinking and drawings of Leonardo da Vinci in the 1500s, the successful lighter-than-air flights from France to England shortly after the American Revolution, the improvement of propeller designs by Blanchard in 1797, several books on the mathematics and physics of mechanical flight published from 1780 to the 1890s, and the development of the gasoline engine. As can be seen, the Wright brothers developed powered flight within the context of a vast array of scientific and technical development. Building on the work of many others, they added the final developments that made powered flight possible. Their experimentation was neither mere tinkering nor their own solitary invention, but was based on knowledge of all of the preceding work. Their achievement is a good example of how science and technology builds upon previous discoveries to expand our knowledge base and to create new technologies.

training, treatment, and child rearing. This new *functionalism,* as it came to be known, was shaped not only by the cultural differences between the United States and Germany, but also by the scientific influences of Charles Darwin, Francis Galton (Darwin's cousin), and the study of animal behavior.

Darwin influenced psychology in many ways (Schultz, 1987). The concept of evolution suggested continuity of structure and function between humans and other animals. Religious and previous scientific and philosophical thought considered humans and animals to be qualitatively different. Darwin's work suggested that studying animal functioning could help us understand human functioning. Further, his emphasis on adaptation of organisms to their environments focused psychologists on the importance of studying function rather than just structure. Darwin's use of data from many sources (e.g., geology, paleontology, archeology, demography, naturalistic observations) legitimized the focus on multiple data sources and diverse methodologies that typified functionalism. His idea of natural selection helped focus psychology on individual differences, which helped set the stage for Galton's work on inheritance of intelligence, psychological testing, and the development of statistical techniques. The work of Darwin, Galton, and the early animal researchers profoundly influenced psychology. While structuralism has largely disappeared, the spirit of functionalism embodied in this early work continues today in the general orientation of American psychology toward practical applications and understanding functional processes.

Other important developments were Gestalt psychology and behaviorism, both emerging around 1912 and both critical of structuralism. *Gestalt psychology,* which originated in Germany, maintained that the structuralists' attempts to analyze consciousness into separate parts lost sight of the whole experience, which is greater than the simple sum of its parts. Gestalt psychologists focused their studies primarily on perception. *Behaviorism,* which emerged in the United States, criticized all of the previous human psychology as too mentalistic and subjective. Its chief spokesperson, John B. Watson (1878–1957), argued for a complete rejection of mentalistic concepts such as mind, consciousness, and image. Behaviorists would later reject psychoanalytic concepts such as ego, id, and unconscious, which Watson argued were meaningless carryovers from old, prescientific philosophy. The psychology of consciousness, according to Watson, needed to be replaced by an objective, modern psychology of observed behavior.

A major line of development within behaviorism was that of animal psychology. Researchers like Ivan P. Pavlov (1849–1936), E. C. Tolman (1886–1959), E. R. Guthrie (1896–1951), Clark Hull (1884–1952), and B. F. Skinner (1904–1990) believed that studying animal behavior was a way to unravel a complex concept such as learning. Previously, it was believed that animal behavior was largely instinctual. The animal psychologists, however, found that animal behavior is flexible, varied, and modifiable in a lawful manner.

An offshoot of the animal behaviorists' research was the development of behavior modification. It was reasoned that if animal behavior could be modified using behavioral techniques, such procedures might be applied to human behavior to treat neuroses, psychoses, drug dependency, depression, aggression, and so on. First studied in the 1920s, behavior modification became a major area of research and clinical application by the 1960s, growing to become a dominant model in the mental health field, a position it continues to hold today.

Another important development—*psychoanalysis*—occurred outside of the mainstream of academic psychology. There were many precursors to psychoanalysis in the early 1800s. Freud (1856–1938) popularized them and added his own observations from about 1900 to 1938. While other psychologists were studying human consciousness, Freud focused on unconscious processes. Psychoanalysis was the dominant clinical model of psychotherapy in the 1930s and 1940s, influencing not only psychology, psychiatry, and social work, but also sociology, literature, and history. Although it is no longer a dominant model, psychoanalysis continues as one of many treatment models.

World War II catapulted psychology from a primarily academic discipline into the arena of applied psychology. Although some psychologists were engaged in human testing and counseling, the applied mental health area was dominated by psychiatry and the major psychotherapeutic model was psychoanalysis. World War II brought academic psychologists into the armed forces to deal with issues of selection, training, rehabilitation, and treatment of military personnel. Many of these psychologists brought with them their objective, laboratory-based procedures and their behavioral orientations. The success of psychology during World War II challenged the dominance of psychiatry and psychoanalysis. With the value of mental health professionals established, the federal government became a major supporter of training programs in disciplines such as psychiatry and clinical psychology.

In the 1960s *humanistic psychology* developed from existential philosophies and now stands in opposition to both behaviorism and psychoanalysis. This approach emphasizes subjective experience, views humans as active, creative, and dynamic, with distinctively human qualities such as choice and self-realization. Humanists believe in self-actualization—the development of the potential that exists naturally in every person.

The modern discipline of *cognitive psychology* grew out of both the early work on human perceptual processes and efforts to study verbal learning in humans. A discipline that has always relied heavily on experimentation, cognitive psychology was once known as experimental psychology. Once almost exclusively an academic discipline studying perception, learning, and memory of humans, cognitive psychology now often addresses applied questions. The design of high-performance aircraft or modern computer software, to name two examples, rely heavily on cognitive psychologists' research. Cognitive psychologists employ sophisticated experimental methods and logic to infer cognitive processes. But this approach has not been without its critics. Skinner (1990), coming from a behaviorist's perspective, argued that cognitive psychologists speculated too much about what was going on inside a person's head, rather than focusing on the person's more objective and observable behavior. Modern cognitive psychology often crosses over into the broader discipline known as cognitive science. *Cognitive science* bridges once separate disciplines like psychology, behavioral neuroscience, computer science, neurophysiology, and linguistics, providing a unique integrated perspective on brain-behavior relationships.

Lest we leave the impression that the history of psychology has been one of warfare among various schools, we should point out that such controversy is more characteristic of the earlier years. By World War II, efforts to integrate ideas from different schools were evident. For example, social analysts, such as Karen Horney and Harry Stack Sullivan, applied sociological theory to psychoanalysis. Edward C. Tolman integrated concepts from Gestalt psychology, early cognitive psychology, and behaviorism in his theory of learning. Kurt Lewin integrated Gestalt concepts with social psychology and child development. John Dollard and Neil Miller (1950) modernized psychoanalysis by integrating it with Clark Hull's (1943) behavioral learning theory. In the last 20 years, *behavioral medicine* and *health psychology* have brought together behavior modification, medicine, nutrition, and health. Since the 1970s Albert Bandura, Frederick Kanfer, Donald Meichenbaum, and many others have integrated behavioral learning theory and cognitive psychology, essentially bringing "consciousness" back into behaviorism. The 1980s saw the development of integrated disciplines such as neuroscience, which incorporates many disciplines including cognitive and physiological psychology, neurology, and language development. Also in the 1970s and 1980s there has been a surge of interest by social psychologists in the issues of personality development and psychopathology, essentially bringing together aspects of social and clinical psychology.

Most psychologists today are not strong adherents of any particular school such as behaviorism, psychoanalysis, or Gestalt psychology. Rather, most are in what Madsen (1988) terms "mainstream psychology," which tends to be more integrative in nature. Madsen identifies at least four major areas of interest within mainstream psychology: learning, motivation, personality, and cognitive processes. Mainstream psychologists utilize concepts and methods from many earlier schools, integrating ideas rather than highlighting the differences between schools.

Throughout its history, psychology's unique contribution has been to extend our understanding of many dimensions of human and animal functioning. These include learning and motivation, memory, personality, physiological influences on behavior, sensation and perception, intelligence, language and problem solving, emotion, development, psychopathology, and social influences on behavior. Today, psychology is an independent scientific discipline, but in many areas it overlaps with other disciplines. For example, biopsychology combines biology and psychology; cognitive psychology overlaps with computer science and linguistics; the psychological study of the sensory processes of vision and hearing involves knowledge of the physics of light and sound.

Psychology is a large discipline, with more than 132,000 psychologists in the United States who are members of the major professional organization, the American Psychological Association (APA) (Fowler, 1995), and another 4000 psychologists who are members of the Canadian Psychological Association (Simner, 1995). In addition, many psychologists are members of other associations such as the American Psychological Society, the Association for the Advancement of Behavior Therapy, the Psychonomic Society, Society for Neuroscience, or the Society for Research in Child Development. The discipline of psychology, like science as a whole, is divided into a number of subdisciplines, each with its own focus. The diversity in psychology is reflected by the many divisions within the APA (see Box 1.3). Although all psychologists receive scientific education, many work professionally in applied settings such as hospitals, clinics, schools, industry, and government service, rather than in research settings.

Box 1.3   **Divisions Within the American Psychological Association (APA)**

The diversity of psychologists' interests is seen in the large number of special interest divisions within the organization. Listed here are the current active divisions of the APA, as of late 1995.

   1. General Psychology
   2. Teaching of Psychology
   3. Experimental Psychology
 * 5. Evaluation, Measurement, and Statistics
   6. Physiological and Comparative Psychology
   7. Developmental Psychology
   8. The Society of Personality and Social Psychology
   9. The Society for the Psychological Study of Social Issues
  10. Psychology and the Arts
 *12. Clinical Psychology
  13. Consulting Psychology
  14. The Society for Industrial and Organizational Psychology
  15. Educational Psychology
  16. School Psychology
  17. Counseling Psychology
  18. Psychologists in Public Service
  19. Military Psychology
  20. Adult Development and Aging
  21. Applied Experimental and Engineering Psychologists
  22. Rehabilitation Psychology
  23. Consumer Psychology
  24. Theoretical and Philosophical Psychology
  25. Experimental Analysis of Behavior
  26. History of Psychology
  27. The Society for Community Research and Action: Division of Community Psychology
  28. Psychopharmacology and Substance Abuse
  29. Psychotherapy
  30. Psychological Hypnosis
  31. State Psychological Association Affairs
  32. Humanistic Psychology
  33. Mental Retardation and Developmental Disabilities
  34. Population and Environmental Psychology
  35. Psychology of Women
  36. Psychology of Religion
  37. Child, Youth, and Family Services
  38. Health Psychology
  39. Psychoanalysis
  40. Clinical Neuropsychology
  41. The American Psychology-Law Society
  42. Psychologists in Independent Practice
  43. Family Psychology
  44. Society for the Psychological Study of Lesbian and Gay Issues

Continued

Box 1.3-1 *Continued*

45. Society for the Psychological Study of Ethnic Minority Issues
46. Media Psychology
47. Exercise and Sport Psychology
48. Peace Psychology
49. Group Psychology and Group Psychotherapy
50. Addictions
51. Society for the Psychological Study of Men and Masculinity

*There are no divisions 4 and 11.

Psychology is often considered to be a social science, as are anthropology, economics, history, and sociology. However, as noted above, psychology is grounded in natural sciences such as biology and physics. In fact, many would argue that the research methods used in psychology are primarily drawn from the natural sciences. There are many areas of research within psychology, each with its own particular interests, content, and methods. But in all areas of psychology, the scientific model is used to study the behavior of living organisms. In the remainder of this book, we will focus on the use of scientific research methods in psychological inquiry.

SUMMARY

Common to all art and science is the essential activity of asking questions. Science may be thought of as a systematic way of asking and answering questions, a disciplined curiosity, a set of procedures by which we make inquiries about the universe.

Basic ways in which people have accepted information as being true are tenacity, intuition, authority, rationalism, empiricism, and science. Science combines rationalism and empiricism. Scientists order their thinking rationally and seek facts through empirical observations. It is the inclusion of empiricism that enables scientists to verify their rational conclusions through external validation.

This combination of rationalism and empiricism was first developed in ancient Greece but was later weakened by a shift to more rational and abstract approaches to knowing the world, particularly as influenced by Plato. Later, medieval Christian scholars maintained science, but as a method science was secondary to theology. Scientific thought increased through the Renaissance, emerging by the seventeenth century as largely independent from religion. Science was becoming increasingly important as human beings turned more to concerns about understanding and controlling the physical world and the human position in it.

In the twentieth century, science has developed into a major, increasingly powerful way of thinking about the universe. Our contemporary lives are largely organized by modern advances in many scientific fields.

Psychology is a relatively recent scientific discipline that studies the behavior of organisms. By combining rational thinking and empirical observations, psychologists create ideas of how organisms function, and those ideas are then used as bases for further study and discovery.

REVIEW EXERCISES

1.1   **Define the following key terms. Be sure you understand them. They are discussed in the chapter and defined in the glossary.**

scientist	Scientific Revolution
science	psychology
process of inquiry	psychophysics
technology	structuralism
skepticism	functionalism
knowledge	Gestalt psychology
tenacity	behaviorism
intuition	psychoanalysis
authority	humanistic psychology
rationalism	cognitive psychology
logic	cognitive science
empiricism	behavioral medicine
orderliness belief	health psychology
experimentation	

1.2   **Briefly answer each of the following questions. Check your answers in the chapter.**

1. Explain this statement: For some types of decisions, most of the common ways of knowing are not sufficient, and we need the precision of science.
2. What is meant by the statement that "science involves a process of thinking"?
3. Science and technology are overlapping but different. Explain this statement.
4. What is creative about science?
5. What is meant by "a prepared mind" and how does that concept help to explain the so-called accidental discoveries made by scientists?
6. What are some of the major characteristics of scientists as a group?
7. In what ways are science and art similar?
8. Define the different ways of knowing or bases on which we accept information as valid knowledge and give two or three examples of each.
9. What are the limitations of rationalism? Of empiricism?
10. What is the orderliness belief? What has it to do with modern science?
11. What is the relationship of the early crafts, such as metallurgy, to the later emergence of abstract science?
12. How did science survive under the domination of the religious thinkers?

1.3   **Think about and work the following problems.**

1. Your friend asserts that scientists "can't make up their minds—they argue with each other over their different views, and they even change their views from one time to another. So how can they claim they know what they are talking about

when they can't even stick to their views or agree with each other?" How would you answer this?

2. A common belief is that scientists and artists are fundamentally different types and that they have little in common. A scientific person supposedly cannot appreciate art, and the artistic person cannot understand science and math. If you were talking to someone who asserted this, how would you respond?

3. Suppose you are in a discussion or a debate and the topic is hard sciences versus soft sciences. It is argued that psychology is not a true science at all. How would you defend the proposition that psychology is a true science?

4. If you were discussing science with your friend, how would you explain that the person sitting under a tree and just thinking could be operating scientifically?

Chapter
2

Research Is a
Process of Inquiry

Research is a systematic search for information, a process of inquiry. It can be carried out in libraries, laboratories, schoolrooms, hospitals, factories, in the pages of the Bible, on street corners, or in the wild watching a herd of elephants. Indeed, research can be carried out anywhere, on any phenomena in nature, and by many different people. Scientists, rabbis, and head chefs can all carry out systematic inquiry in their own domains. Although all research is a systematic process of inquiry, not all research is scientific. A religious scholar might study and research religious writings. The scholar's research is a serious, systematic process of inquiry, but it is not, and it is not meant to be, scientific. What distinguishes scientific research from other research is the emphasis in science on using both empirical and rational processes.

BASIC ASSUMPTIONS OF SCIENCE

Every discipline, including science, is built on a series of assumptions—ideas that are tentatively accepted as being true without further examination. These assumptions are articles of faith, not unlike the articles of faith found in most religions. In science, we try to make few assumptions, preferring to subject the majority of our ideas to the rigorous demands of rational and empirical challenges; but the assumptions provide a strong platform for expanding our understanding of nature. Whatever their particular discipline, scientists share several basic assumptions about nature and the role of science in understanding it:

1. A true, physical universe exists.
2. While there may be randomness and thus unpredictability in the universe, it is primarily an orderly system.
3. The principles of this orderly universe can be discovered, particularly through scientific research.
4. Our knowledge of the universe is always incomplete. New knowledge can, and should, alter current ideas and theories. Therefore, all knowledge and theories are tentative.

These assumptions may seem minimal, but they form the bases of all science. We assume a real, mostly orderly universe, and that the principles by which this universe operates can be discovered. The assumption that theories and knowledge are tentative is as much an admonition to scientists as an assumption. Not even the best scientists possess the godlike wisdom to create the perfect theory. In time, the flaws and limitations of every theory will be exposed.

It is instructive to note what is not in our list of scientific assumptions. We do not assume that all of the universe is visible. In fact, scientists would argue that some of the most interesting aspects of the universe may not be detectable with our senses. As scientists, we may hypothesize about invisible, but presumably real, forces such as gravity. However, even concepts about unseen factors like gravity must conform to the twin constraints of rationalism and empiricism. As we will see in the next section, science is built partly on concepts that are not directly observable. Yet we are confident in using concepts about unseen events because we constantly challenge their validity. Only concepts that have survived repeated empirical challenges reach the level of "generally accepted scientific theory." Even then, some hotshot young scientist may poke holes in an accepted theory by either (1) exposing its flaws with a single well-designed study, or (2) proposing a better theory, one that explains current data and goes further to predict and explain new phenomena that have yet to be studied.

OBSERVATION AND INFERENCE: FACTS AND CONSTRUCTS

At minimum, scientific research involves:

1. Posing a question.
2. Developing procedures to answer the question.
3. Planning for, and then making, appropriate empirical observations.
4. Rationally interpreting the empirical observations.

Scientists carefully observe events, try to reason about why things occurred, and then try to make predictions based on the ideas developed during the reasoning process. The elements of observation and rational abstraction are brought together to create a coherent understanding of the phenomenon.

In scientific research, empirical observations constitute the facts of research. In a somewhat circular fashion, *facts* are those events that can be directly, empirically, and repeatedly observed. Each scientific discipline has its particular kinds of facts. In psychology, observed facts include the physiological structures of the subjects, the physical conditions around them, the behavior of other organisms (including the researcher), and, of course, the subject's own behavior. Most facts observed in psychology are *behaviors*. The behaviors observed can include verbal behavior, nonverbal communication such as gestures, physiological activity, social behavior, and so on. We can observe the behavior of children at play, shoppers in stores, subjects responding to various perceptual stimuli, clients talking about their inner feelings, parents describing their children's problems, workers at machines, or senators in debate. We can also study animal behaviors in the laboratory and in the natural environment. All these behaviors can be objectively observed and recorded. *Observation* is the empirical process of using our senses to recognize and record factual events.

In addition to studying behavioral facts, psychologists also study memory, emotion, intelligence, attitudes, values, creativity, thinking, perception, humor, and so on. These are not behavioral events. They are not directly observable, and thus are not facts. We cannot directly observe intelligence or thinking or perception, but we can observe behavior that we believe to be related to those nonobservable concepts. For example, in some early work with autistic children (Graziano, 1974), we observed that the children frequently exhibited highly disruptive behavior in which they injured themselves and others and caused upheaval in their therapy program. Their behavior was a *fact;* it was repeatedly and clearly observed by many people, was measured by observers, and its sounds and forms were recorded on audio- and videotape. Initial treatment reduced both the intensity and duration of the disruptive behavior, but not its frequency. That is, the children were "blowing up" just as often as before treatment, but the episodes were shorter and less intense. We therefore posed the question, "Having reduced the intensity and duration of these outbursts, can we now reduce their frequency?" Continued careful observation revealed a subtle but observable change in the child's behavior just prior to the disruptive behavior: activity stopped, facial expressions became contorted and mobile, limbs stiffened, and the severe behavior "exploded." We looked carefully to see if there was anything external to the child that could cause this observed reaction and found nothing. We therefore inferred that just prior to their outbursts, something was happening inside the children. They may have been feeling some intense internal arousal, which might have served as the major cue for the emission of the outbursts. Thus, we reasoned, to reduce the frequency of the outbursts we would have to control the internal arousal. But how were we to accomplish this? From our knowledge of the behavior therapy research literature, we selected an approach developed by Joseph Wolpe (1958, 1990), systematic desensitization, which employs relaxation training as a first step. Although used with adults, it had not to our knowledge ever been applied to children. But in light of our inference that the aroused state of the children lead to their outbursts, it seemed a reasonable approach to try. We trained the autistic children in relaxation, and in time the frequency of their outbursts decreased to zero.

What is important here is the distinction between our observations of behavior (the outbursts) and our inferences of an internal condition (arousal). The internal condition is not observable. It is inferred, and those inferences are drawn from the observations of behavior—from the facts. Note that drawing an *inference* is an intellectual process in which conclusions are derived from observed facts or from other ideas.

From empirical observations, events are inferred that cannot be observed; such as the inferred condition of internal arousal. Most of the psychologists' work deals with inferences. When we study the anxiety of a client, the intelligence of a student, or the memory of a subject, we are working with inferences. It is important for students to recognize that inferences are largely drawn from empirical observations (the facts). Unless the observations are carefully made, little confidence can be placed in any inference drawn from them. In research, precisely defined empirical methods are used to develop a factual, observational base for drawing inferences about events that cannot be directly observed. Inferences can also be drawn from other inferences, but in science an important starting point for making inferences is careful observation. In general, the better the observational base and the more ties our inferences have to that base, the more confidence we have in the inference. When making inferences, we are cautioned to stay close to the data. As Detective Sergeant Joe Friday used to say to the witness in the old *Dragnet* television series, "Just give us the facts, ma'am." He might have added, "We'll draw our own inferences."

When a researcher draws an inference, the inference resides in the researcher and not in the subject. The process involves the researcher's rational activity of tentatively accepting the sensory data (the observations) as true and then drawing from them an idea (inference) about nonobservable events. With the autistic children, we used the inferential process and concluded that a state of arousal existed. The inferred state of arousal was not a fact; it was an idea that we inferred. In other words, the inference of an internal arousal was not in the child; it was an idea we created. We have no direct observation of what was really going on in the child. Our hypothesis of an internal arousal, although plausible, is an explanatory idea—not reality. It helped to explain the behavior observed, and it helped us to generate a possible course of action that proved to be effective. This is an important point. Nonobservable inferred events—such as gravity, electricity, intelligence, memory, anxiety, perception, id, and ego—are all rational ideas that have been constructed by researchers. They are not facts! Not surprisingly, the ideas constructed in this way by the researcher are called *constructs.* Once these ideas are constructed by the researcher, they are used analogically—that is, *as if* they exist in fact and *as if* they really have a relationship with observable events. With the autistic children, we never observed the reduction of their internal state of arousal. We operated *as if* the inferred state actually existed and would be reduced if we trained the children to relax. Further, we predicted that if the inferred state were reduced, then we would observe a reduction in the frequency of the disruptive behavior. To repeat, psychological constructs are ideas constructed by the researcher through a rational process of inference. These constructs are based on empirical observation as well as on other constructs. The constructs are used in further thinking and research *as if* they exist and *as if* they have observable effects.

An important caution is needed. The analogical nature of constructs must never be forgotten. Too often a construct becomes so commonly used that people begin to think of it as a fact—a directly observed event—and they lose sight of its very tentative, analogical nature. For example, some people may believe there really is an id, an ego, and a superego inside each of us. These constructs take on a reality they were never meant to have. Confusing a construct for a fact is a logical error known as *reification of a construct.*

CONCEPTUAL MODELS IN SCIENCE

In the above example of autistic children, note the relationship between the construct of internal arousal and the observed facts. First, the construct was inferred from observed behavior. Then the construct was used as a basis for predicting some new behavior that could be observed. We predicted that if the internal arousal were reduced, we would then observe a reduction in disruptive behavior. Thus, the construct is related to observed facts in two ways: it was derived from the observations, and it served as a basis for predicting future observations. We use the construct, in effect, to show and explain a relationship between two sets of facts. In this instance, the two sets of facts were observations of behavior—one made before relaxation training and the other made after training. This use of constructs to explain relationships among two sets of observed facts is an important part of the thinking process in science. Recall that a critical characteristic that makes the scientific thought process different from other ways of gaining knowledge is the continual, interactive movement between empirical observation and rational abstractions. Now you can see that this interactive movement is between observations and constructs. The scientist moves from one to the other and back again, at each step refining constructs from observations and predicting observations from constructs. During that process, we build up limited descriptions or explanations of relationships among facts and constructs. With the autistic children, the relationship between the observations and the constructs provided a description or partial explanation of an observed phenomenon—in this case, the disruptive behavior. We then used the description *as if* it adequately represented what was really happening, even though we could not observe all the parts. We call such descriptive and explanatory ideas *models.*

Any phenomenon can be represented by models, which help us organize our knowledge about the full reality each model represents. The word *model* derives from the Latin *modulus,* meaning a small measure of something. It has come to mean in science a miniature representation of reality. A model is a description or analogy to help understand something usually unseen and/or more complex.

A model airplane is a good example. It clearly is not equivalent to a real airplane. It has the general form and many of the characteristics of a real airplane, such as wings, propellers, wheels, and so on. Although these characteristics may correspond faithfully to those of a real airplane, the model is not an exact replica of the real airplane. It is smaller, does not have all the working parts, and may be constructed of balsa wood or plastic instead of aluminum. If the model airplane could be improved to make it progressively more like the real one, then eventually it would be a full-sized, fully operational airplane, a replica of the original and fully equivalent to it.

But the model only *represents* reality, it does not duplicate it. Models are useful because constructing and examining a model helps us organize knowledge and hypotheses about the reality represented by the model. We can examine a model, observe relationships among its parts, and observe how it operates. We can generate from the model new ideas about how the real world is constructed and how it operates. For example, a model airplane in a wind tunnel can give us ideas about how the real airplane might behave and lead us to new ideas or hypotheses about design and operation of the real airplane. Likewise, our model of the relationship of internal arousal and disruptive behavior in autistic children led us to new applications of behavior therapy.

Models can be constructed to represent any aspect of the universe that we wish to study. We can build models of airplanes or the solar system, of an atom or a bacterium, of wave motions, neurons, memory, thinking processes, or genetic structure. Our knowledge of any phenomenon can be organized into models to represent reality. Further, the models need not be physical in their construction, such as a balsa wood airplane. They can be abstract or conceptual models, constructed of ideas and expressed in verbal and/or mathematical language. The classical model of human memory is a good example of an abstract model. It assumes multiple levels of memory, each having its own characteristics. The sensory store is assumed to hold information for a very short period of time (about 1 second), but it is able to hold a very large amount of information. The short-term memory holds information longer (about 15 seconds) but has a much more restricted capacity. The long-term memory provides the long-term, high-capacity storage that we usually think of when we think about memory. Few cognitive psychologists believe such structures exist or that their model is the way we process and store information. But a model does not have to be real or true to be useful. It needs only to make accurate predictions about relationships between observable events. The classical model of memory is a strong one because it is based on hundreds of independent observations of behavior and the relationship of behavior to other observable events. In other words, the model is closely tied to the observational base on which it was first developed. Further, the model proved useful in that it correctly predicted a number of new observations that were confirmed by careful scientific study. It is not a perfect model of memory and will be replaced by better models as research identifies behavioral relationships that cannot be predicted or explained by it. In fact, this model of memory has already been seriously challenged. Nevertheless, it is convenient and useful and has contributed enormously to our understanding of how we remember things.

All models share the following characteristics:

1. Models are constructed representations of parts of the real universe, which have point-to-point correspondence with some of the characteristics of the reality being represented.
2. Models provide a convenient, manageable, and compact representation of the larger, complex, and mostly unknown reality.
3. Models are incomplete, tentative, and analogical.

Models are extremely useful. Manipulating models helps us to organize information, to illustrate relationships among parts, and to create new ideas and predict new observations.

The ancient religious cosmologies were models of the universe. Some of them pictured a flat earth riding on the back of a massive turtle paddling across a large lake. The lake was in turn held in place by the arching coils of a huge snake, whose body defined the arc of the sky across which the gods rode each day in a blazing chariot. We are now reasonably certain that while there was some point-to-point correspondence between those models and reality (both include water, the earth, and the heavens), and while they may have predicted and explained many observable events (such as the apparent daily movement of the sun across the sky), those ancient models were not accurate representations of reality. An example of an early Renaissance scientific model is the Copernican model of the solar system. An elaborate and elegant model, it was constructed in mathematical terms. The resulting model represented the solar system and its parts, spatial and temporal relationships among them, as well as the phenomena of regularity and change in the solar system. Using his model, Copernicus and others developed hypotheses about the operation of the solar system. Some of the hypotheses conflicted with religious dogma, creating difficulties not only for Copernicus but for others, such as Galileo 85 years later. Copernicus delayed publication of his work for 13 years, from 1530 to 1543, because he feared reprisals from the church. In time, the Copernican model proved to be a reasonably accurate model of the solar system and was important in later astronomy and physics. The Copernican model, though incomplete and in some ways inaccurate, nevertheless provided far more accurate point-to-point correspondence with the real solar system than had any model before it. As such, it allowed more accurate predictions of several phenomena that previously could not be predicted with any consistency.

"This is Gronski's new model of the synaptic transmission mechanism. Nobody understands it, but it won third prize in the campus art competition."

INDUCTIVE AND DEDUCTIVE THINKING

Sherlock Holmes buffs will probably argue that the great detective never said it, but the statement attributed to Holmes—perhaps first voiced in a movie version—has entertained and perhaps misled us for some time. We all know the scene: at the site of the crime Holmes inspects the room, his keen eyes darting and his nose alert to the lingering tobacco smoke. Suddenly, with an explosive "Aha!" he pounces on a partially burnt matchstick cracked in the middle with a small flake of tobacco stuck to its tip. Holmes examines it closely and then announces, "Our culprit, Watson, is 44 years old, 5 feet 8 1/2 inches tall, 183 pounds. He is right-handed, a veteran of the India conflicts, and still carries a lead ball in his right calf. He is a gentleman, Watson, and had no intention of committing a crime when he entered this room. He left hurriedly by way of that window when he heard us at the door, and, if I am not mistaken, he will return here to confess his crime and will knock on that door precisely . . . now!"

A tentative knocking is heard at the door. Watson opens it revealing the gentleman so precisely described by Holmes.

"Egads 'Olmes!" says Watson, wide-eyed. "'Ow did you ever know that?"

"Deduction, my dear Watson," says Homes. " A simple process of deduction."

Actually, it was not deduction alone. Holmes had confused two terms, and what he should have said was, "Induction-deduction my dear Watson. A simple process of induction-deduction!" Assuming that the great Holmes could in fact have drawn such complete conclusions from such limited evidence, his process was one familiar to all of us. He observed some specific clues and inferred (the induction) something he could not directly observe (i.e., the type of person who would have committed such a crime, leaving those clues). Holmes then made the prediction (the deduction) that the man would return. When we reason from the particular to the general, we are reasoning inductively; when we use the more abstract and general ideas to return to specifics (i.e., to make predictions about future observations), we are reasoning deductively (Copi & Cohen, 1990).[1] Induction and deduction are rational processes used constantly by the scientist. In terms of our earlier discussion, it is the combination of these two kinds of thinking—induction and deduction—that characterizes science. A researcher who begins with empirical observations and then infers constructs is engaged in *inductive reasoning.* Using the constructs as the basis of making predictions about new, specific observations is *deductive reasoning.* A scientist must use both processes to build and validate conceptual models.

Inductive-deductive reasoning is not unique to science; we use these processes constantly in our everyday behavior. When I return from work on a cold winter day and find the front door left partly open and a single muddy sneaker on the hall rug, I *inductively* infer that "the kids are home from school." Knowing a good deal about these kids, I can also *deductively* predict that "right now Lisa is upstairs talking on the telephone with one of her friends," and I can go upstairs to make observations and check the accuracy of my predictions. From the specific observation to the general idea; from the general idea back to the more specific observation; induction and deduction. In everyday affairs, people have been thinking inductively and deductively all of their lives, although probably not with the precision of the scientist. We would like to emphasize this last point. Although the scientist uses the same kind of reasoning process used in everyday life, he or she must use the process with a precision rarely seen in everyday life. Indeed, the entire scientific research enterprise can be seen as the development of a framework within which the scientist can carry out inductive and deductive reasoning under the most precise conditions. Here we can add to a point made early in Chapter 1: the essence of science is its process of thinking, and that process entails systematic inductive-deductive logic. Science, more than any other way of gaining knowledge, bases its inductive reasoning on carefully observed facts (i.e., empirical observations). Making the observations or getting the facts is one of the critical components of scientific research. Thus, the

[1]In psychology, we tend to use the concepts of induction and deduction as discussed above. However, philosophy students will recognize this distinction as being incomplete, distinguishing only one kind of induction from one kind of deduction (Reese, 1980).

enterprise of scientific research uses facts to fuel the inductive-deductive process and obtains the facts with the greatest precision possible. Making empirical observations is the focal point around which the inductive-deductive process revolves. The observations provide the data on which theories are inductively produced. Data are gathered later to test the predictions deduced from the theory as part of the process of theory validation.

MODELS AND THEORIES IN SCIENCE

Scientists study many phenomena, sometimes solving practical problems like building bridges and curing disease and sometimes making new discoveries about nature. However, regardless of the phenomena studied or the goals of the research, scientists develop and use theories. It has been said that the major aim of science is theory and that there is nothing as useful and practical as a good theory.

What is theory? For purposes of this text, let us consider a *theory* to be a formalized set of concepts that organizes observations and inferences and predicts and explains phenomena. A great deal of research must go into the development of theory. In order for a theory to be a scientific theory it must be testable—that is, it must make specific predictions that can be tested empirically. Scientific theories allow the possibility that empirical evidence will contradict them. A good theory demands a solid empirical base of evidence and a set of carefully developed constructs, neither of which can be created offhandedly. Thus, scientists do not create theories out of mere guesses and hunches, nor are their theories flimsy and ephemeral flights of fancy. They are carefully constructed from empirical observations, constructs, and inductive and deductive logic. In building theories, the scientist brings together and integrates what has been learned about the phenomena under study. To develop an adequate theory that will organize, predict, and explain natural phenomena is a major goal of scientists.

It is often difficult for a beginning student to appreciate the importance of theory to science. Without theory, we could still use most of the procedures described in this text to discover new facts, but the facts we discovered would be much less useful without the organizing framework of theory. Theory provides a blueprint that organizes our facts into ideas and ideas into an understanding of our world. We can think of facts as the bricks and mortar that will eventually make up a building. A good building needs quality bricks if it is to remain strong and functional, but it also needs to be well designed. A theory is the conceptual equivalent of a building's design. If we are constructing a building, we want it to be functional, strong, and beautiful. A well-designed and constructed building will have all of these characteristics. Scientists want their theories to be functional, strong, and beautiful. A functional theory works; it explains how variables are related to one another. A strong theory makes specific predictions—predictions that are confirmed by empirical observation. The strongest theories make unique predictions—predictions that other theories do not make—which are consistent with subsequent observations. A beautiful theory, like a beautiful building, has a simple elegance. Scientists prefer *parsimony;* a simple, straightforward theory is preferred over a complex theory if the theories provide equivalent predictive validity. A single theory that explains several different phenomena is preferred over a collection of theories that collectively explain the same phenomena. The principle of parsimony, however, never supersedes the concept that the theory must be valid (i.e., must make specific testable predictions that are confirmed by observation).

There is a continuing debate in psychology about the value of formal theory. Marx (1963) describes four types of theories used in psychology—inductive theory, deductive theory, functional theory, and models. All theories involve both induction and deduction, but they often differ in the degree to which they emphasize one or the other.

An *inductive theory* begins with a solid data base of empirical observations and builds up to more abstract levels of explanations in the theory. The inductive theorist follows the data wherever they may lead. Skinner epitomizes this inductive method of theory construction. Skinner (1972) built his theories on extensive observational data and was very careful not to extend the theory beyond the data. In an eloquent presentation only days before his death, Skinner (1990) continued to argue that there are serious risks associated with postulating theories that go well beyond the data and that involve processes not directly observable.

A *deductive theory* is the more traditional, formalized theory in which constructs are of major importance. The constructs (the ideas) guide the researcher in making and testing deductions from the constructs. The deductions are empirically tested through research, and thus support or lack of support for the theory is obtained. The now classic learning theory of Clark Hull (1943) is an example. A more recent example is Paul Meehl's (1990) theorizing about the underlying cause(s) of schizophrenia. Meehl's approach has been to postulate strong theories that make specific predictions. The theory is tested every time a prediction is investigated and should be rejected when a prediction is not confirmed. Although Meehl's theorizing is not purely deductive (e.g., his theories take into account the information we know about schizophrenia), his theories go well beyond the data, challenging us to make new observations. It may be worth noting that Skinner and Meehl were colleagues during their early careers at the University of Minnesota. Their discussions on the role of theory in science must have been intense and dynamic.

Most psychological theories are *functional theories* involving about equal emphasis on induction and deduction. All three types of theories have the characteristic functions of organizing knowledge, predicting new observations, and explaining relationships among events. Constructing theories is critical if we are to develop a coherent understanding of nature.

The fourth type of theory discussed by Marx (1963) is the *model*. Remember that we described a model as an analogical representation of reality. It is not a duplicate of reality but only a representation. We use models analogically, as if they correctly represent reality. As we discussed earlier, models, like theories, organize existing information. A model is somewhat less developed than a formal theory, and consequently models are sometimes referred to as "mini-theories." Models are often used as steps in the development of theory.

A final point should be made here: we do not usually think of a theory just in terms of whether it is *right* or *wrong*. A safe assumption is that every theory is wrong; it is only a matter of time before we find the data to disprove it. But we do not judge a theory only on whether it is right or wrong. We judge theories by how useful they are in organizing information, explaining phenomena, and generating accurate predictions. For example, the theory of Newtonian Mechanics, which you probably learned in high school physics, is clearly wrong. When objects move very fast (i.e., near the speed of light), they do not behave the way Newtonian Mechanics would predict. Einstein's general theory of relativity describes objects more accurately regardless of how fast the object is traveling. But, Newtonian Mechanics survives and is taught extensively in high school and college. Why? The reason is simple. Everyday objects hardly ever travel at speeds close to the speed of light. Therefore, the theories developed by Newton describe the motion of such ordinary objects accurately. The theory survives because it is useful and accurate in a wide range of situations.

Internal Summary: The Process of Science

Based on assumptions about the nature of the universe and of knowledge, scientists proceed through a highly interactive, inductive-deductive process of making observations and inferences. Through systematic procedures scientists observe facts (events that are empirically and reliably observed) and they infer constructs (ideas and concepts about the relationship among observed facts). In this process models are constructed. These are useful representations of reality, and they are used to guide further thinking and research. Models are useful in constructing theories, which are larger organized sets of facts and constructs that predict and explain parts of nature. Theories are based on facts as well as inferences, and they are judged in terms of how useful they are in making predictions and in explaining events.

A MODEL OF THE RESEARCH PROCESS

Almost any phenomenon can be studied scientifically, and a model can be developed to represent the phenomenon. One purpose that a model can serve is to help organize the activities of the person using the model. We will present a model in this section to serve as an outline for the text—a model that we will call "psychological research methods." We will propose a model of the universe of the research enterprise.[2] Like any model, this model is not a complete representation of reality. The model tries to simplify the complexity of psychological research to help emphasize some of the most important aspects of research process. We will label our model *Research: A Process of Inquiry.*

Phases of Research

Psychological research usually proceeds in an orderly manner, through successive phases, from the beginning to the end of a particular project. However, this se-

[2]The model of research presented here is a variation of a model presented by Hyman (1964).

TABLE 2.1   THE PHASES OF A RESEARCH STUDY

Idea-generating phase	Identify a topic of interest to study.
Problem-definition phase	Refine the vague and general idea(s) generated in the previous step into a precise question to be studied.
Procedures-design phase	Decide on the specific procedures to be used in the gathering and statistical analysis of the data.
Observation phase	Using the procedures devised in the previous step, collect your observations from the subjects in your study.
Data-analysis phase	Analyze the data collected above using appropriate statistical procedures.
Interpretation phase	Compare your results with the results predicted on the basis of your theory. Do your results support the theory?
Communication phase	Prepare a written or oral report of your study for publication or presentation to colleagues. Your report should include a description of all of the above steps.

quencing of phases can vary under special conditions. The most general sequence of research events is described here.

Table 2.1 presents each of the phases of research. The concept of *phases of research* provides one dimension of the conceptual model on which this text is based. Note in Table 2.1 that research begins with ideas, and flows through the successive, overlapping phases of the research process. Each phase has its own characteristics, and different work is accomplished in each, preparing for the next phase.

Idea-Generating Phase   All research must begin with an idea, sometimes vague, in which the researcher has interest. The interest of the researcher is critical, particularly in the beginning phases of research. For example, a researcher may have interest in children's reasoning but no further idea for a research project. The interest, however, is enough to point the researcher to an area within which more defined ideas can be developed. For the new researcher in particular, interest in the area to be studied is critical in helping to sustain the long, hard work to follow. This, of course, repeats a point made in Chapter 1 that the scientist's curiosity is a basic component in research, both in helping to generate research ideas and in sustaining the researcher's efforts.

The idea phase can begin with vague thoughts, and initial ideas can emerge in very nonscientific ways. Archimedes is supposed to have had a flash of creative thought while sitting in a bath. Ideas can be generated while in conversations, reading novels, watching television, walking in the woods, buying a hamburger, crossing the street, or even while dreaming. They can be born of vaguely perceived fleeting thoughts. Lest we leave the impression that getting research ideas is always so unsystematic, we should stress that most research ideas are generated in a systematic fashion from other research results. Research ideas vary from unsystematic hunches to highly systematic and precise steps in logical thinking. The former are most characteristic of exploratory research, which occurs in the early history of a research area; whereas the latter are characteristic of research at more advanced levels of the research area.

In the early idea-getting activities, we ought not to be too critical of our relatively unformed ideas because premature criticism might serve to destroy an emerging good idea. The early ideas ought to be nourished, thought about, and taken seriously. Critical ingredients are curiosity, interest, and enthusiasm for an area under study. Once an area of interest is identified, it is useful to dive right in by reading articles and books, talking with people who work in the area, and thinking about it.

There is a general lack of information and understanding about the processes involved in the creative idea-generating phases of research. Indeed, here is a good area for research—how are creative ideas generated? Can you think about this and generate some interesting research questions? Perhaps somewhere in one of these research methods classes there is a student who will eventually make important contributions to the scientific understanding of generating creative ideas. What seems clear is that productive scientists have many ideas. When asked in a television interview, "Where does a scientist get a good idea to study?" the Nobel Prize winner Linus Pauling replied, "Well, you have lots of ideas, and you throw out the bad ones."

Problem-Definition Phase   Identifying an area of interest and generating ideas for study begin the research process. Vague ideas alone are not sufficient however. In good scientific tradition, we must clarify and refine ideas. In this part of the process, the scientist examines the research literature and learns how other researchers have conceptualized, measured, and tested these and related ideas. The scientist continues working on the ideas—clarifying, defining, specifying, and refining them. The goal is to produce one or more clearly posed questions based on a well-developed knowledge of previous research and theory as well as on the scientist's own ideas and speculations.

How carefully we conceptualize and phrase a research question is important, because everything we do in the remainder of the research process will be aimed at answering that research question. Think of it this way: the questions we ask will largely control the way we conduct the rest of the research process. The questions might involve highly specific and precisely drawn hypotheses, or they might be phrased in a much more general manner typical of exploratory research. The way we ask the question will often determine how we should carry out the study.

The activities that make up the problem-definition phase are highly rational, abstract processes that manipulate and systematically develop ideas toward the goal of refining them into researchable questions. This rational process is used to prepare for the next phase, in which we design the procedures to make the observations.

Procedures-Design Phase   Before any data are collected, the researcher must determine which observations are to be made and under what conditions, what methods will be employed for recording the observations, what statistical methods to use for analyzing the data, and so on. We also make decisions about who the subjects will be in this phase. Since we are making decisions about how we will use living organisms in research, we must consider our ethical responsibilities. The ethics of scientific research include guidelines for humane, sensitive treatment of subjects. Before we contact a single subject, we must be sure the research plan survives ethical evaluation. The plan must be modified whenever ethical guidelines are not met. Only when the plan can stand up to ethical demands do we proceed with the next phase—making the observations. The ethics of psychological research is a major area that every researcher must know, understand, and apply. (Ethics will be discussed in more detail in later chapters.)

As can be seen, the design phase is active, systematic, and complex. Much of the content of research methods courses focuses specifically on this phase.

Observation Phase   Making the observations (getting the data) is the most familiar phase to beginning students, who often see this as "actually doing the research." In this phase the researcher carries out the procedures that were selected in the previous phase, making observations of the subjects' behavior under the conditions specified in the earlier phase. The observation phase is central in all science. Note that the earlier phases serve as preparation for making the empirical observations, and the remaining phases focus on using those observations (i.e., processing, understanding, and communicating them). Scientific research can thus be seen as a process of inquiry that revolves around its most central aspect—making empirical observations.

Empirical observations constitute the facts of the research. When the researcher records observed facts, the record constitutes the *research data.* When a subject answers "yes" to an item on a questionnaire or shows an increase in physiological activity when a specific stimulus is presented, this information becomes part of the data. In the remainder of the research process, the data are processed, interpreted, and communicated.

Data-Analysis Phase   By the data-analysis phase of research, the empirical observations have been made and recorded as data. Remaining are the primarily abstract, rational tasks of processing and making sense out of these data and communicating the results. The data-analysis procedures, like the observation procedures, are selected in the design phase to be carried out in the data-analysis phase. It is often confusing to students that data analysis procedures are selected before we gather the data (in the design phase). As we will see later in this text, many design decisions (e.g., sample size) will follow from the choice of data-analysis procedures. In almost all psychological research, the data will be in the form of a numerical record representing the observations made. The numerical data must be organized and analyzed. Statistical procedures are used to describe and to evaluate numerical data and to help determine the statistical significance of the observations. The statistical procedures might be as simple as counting responses and drawing graphs to show response changes over time, or they may be as complex as a two-way analysis of variance (described in Chapter 12). Whatever the statistical procedures may be, the important point here is that the researcher must choose statistical procedures appropriate to the question being asked and to the observational procedures being used. As we will see in Chapter 14, the choice of statistical procedure is not difficult to make. It is determined by the nature of the question and the observational procedures.

Interpretation Phase   Having statistically analyzed the data, we continue to make sense out of them by interpreting the statistical results in terms of (1) how they help answer the research question and (2) how this answer contributes to the knowledge in the field. Here we put our findings into a context that helps to relate them not only to the original questions but also to other concepts and findings in the field. This stage represents the flip side of the problem-definition phase. When defining the research problem, we use theories to guide us to important questions. Now we use the answers we have generated to those questions to determine how accurately our theories predict new observations. In the problem-definition phase, we use deductive reasoning—from the general theory to the specific prediction. In the interpretation phase, we use inductive reasoning—from the specific results of the study back to the generality of the theory. In many cases, the results of a study will suggest ways to expand or modify the theory to increase its usefulness and accuracy.

Communication Phase   Science is a public enterprise. A critical component of science is communication of research findings. Scientific communication occurs through presentations at scientific meetings and through publication in journals and books. Note that not only the results are communicated, but also the procedures used in all phases of the research and the rationales behind them. Specific guidelines are used to organize in a concise manner all of the information needed in a research report. Such guidelines are provided by the *APA Publication Manual* (1994). (A discussion of how to write a research report is presented in Appendix A.)

Scientific publications should describe procedures in detail, not only so that other scientists can understand the research, but also to allow them to *replicate* (repeat) it if they wish. Replication is very important. If a research finding cannot be replicated, then considerable doubt is placed on the genuineness of that finding. By presenting full accounts of research rationales, procedures, findings, and interpretations, the researcher is contributing to public scientific activity, and the work can be fully evaluated by others, even to the point of replicating the research. (Further discussion of the importance of replication will be presented in Chapter 9.) The writing of a research report should be clear and concise. Avoid the pretentious style illustrated in the adjacent cartoon.

Each finished project can serve as the basis for further questions and further empirical research. Now we have come full circle, back to the beginning phase of

Calvin and Hobbes   by Bill Watterson

Source: Calvin and Hobbes copyright © 1995 Watterson. Distributed by Universal Press Syndicate. Reprinted with permission. All rights reserved.

Figure 2.1   An Example of the Process of Conceptualizing and Carrying Out a Research Project

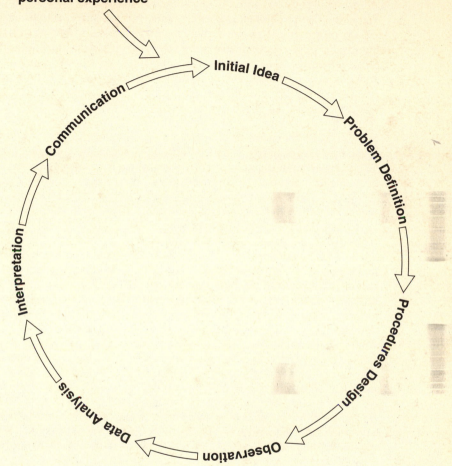

Ideas for research are generated from sources outside of the specific research project, as well as from ideas generated within the research process.

generating ideas. In a developing field of research, the ideas for asking new questions and making new observations are mainly ideas that have been generated systematically by previous research. Scientists are stimulated by the work of their colleagues and derive research questions from them. In turn, their own work stimulates others. Figure 2.1 illustrates this process.

Scientists use two major avenues for communicating their work. The most formal is written communication in books and scientific journals. These reports become a permanent record, part of the archives of a scientific discipline. They are preserved and can be retrieved and studied by colleagues soon after publication or

Box 2.1   # Scientific Communication in the Information Age

The "information superhighway" is changing the way that research is conducted as well as increasing the availability of information about science. Simple changes, like computerized databases for research articles and books, have dramatically reduced the time needed to locate key materials during the planning phase of research. But much more profound changes are occurring. *Electronic mail* (*e-mail*) makes it almost as easy to communicate and collaborate with a colleague across the country (or even around the world) as a colleague down the hall. E-mail is very inexpensive. The Internet—the electronic highway that carries these messages all over the world—can be used to transmit a short note or an entire book. The *list server* (a program that takes messages that are sent to the list server and sends a copy of the message to everyone on the list) has also changed the way professionals communicate and share ideas. List servers make it possible for hundreds of scientists to carry on extended conversations, literally brainstorming with the best people in the field. In rapidly developing fields, such as the recent work in high-temperature superconductivity, these electronic mail networks virtually took over the process of disseminating information. List servers also provide an opportunity for students to "listen in" on these high-level discussions, receiving electronic mail almost daily from the best minds in the field. List servers can even be used to generate extended discussion among students of topics raised in classes (Meacham, 1994, 1995), creating a virtual classroom where ideas can be exchanged at any time day or night. But the most exciting development is the increasing availability of almost unlimited information in an electronic form, permitting instant location and access to critical material. The World Wide Web provides Internet access to unbelievable amounts of information, and the Web is growing by the hour. Journals in Chemistry (Krumenaker, 1993), Physics (Taubes, 1993), and Psychology (e.g., the *Journal of Behavior Analysis and Therapy* published at http://rsl.cc.und.nodak.edu/misc/jBAT) are now being published in electronic form accessible through the Internet. In addition, many articles that have been accepted for publication in traditional research journals can now be accessed months before publication through the Internet (Holden, 1995). Soon books may be just as easily accessible. Both books and journals are now available on CD-ROM. You may soon be able to have the equivalent of the Library of Congress at your fingertips from your own living room. The invisible college, not to mention the library, is increasingly electronic in this information age.

many years later. A minor disadvantage of written reports is that the publication process usually takes a year or more after the research has been completed before written reports are available in journals and books.

More immediate and more interactive communications are oral and graphic presentations researchers make at scientific meetings and informal communication among colleagues. Scientists visit each other's laboratories, talk on the telephone or during parties or poker games, exchange letters, and so on. This informal, highly interactive network of communication has been called the "invisible college," and it serves the important function of keeping scientists in communication with each other. Indeed, some believe it is the most critical means of communication among scientists. It is important for the young researcher, seriously interested in a research career, to become involved actively in this invisible-college network of communications (Osberg & Raulin, 1989). The nature of this invisible college has been changing rapidly in the Information Age, as illustrated in Box 2.1.

The research process we have briefly described is common to all sciences. The particular observations made in the various disciplines vary from one to the other because each discipline is interested in observing and understanding quite different phenomena. But the basic processes and the systematic way of studying problems are common elements of science, regardless of each discipline's particular subject matter. It is the process and not the content that distinguishes science from other ways of knowing, and it is the content—the particular phenomena and facts of interest—that distinguishes one scientific area from another.

Although it is generally true that research proceeds in the sequence described (from the initial idea phase through the communication phase), the sequencing of the phases is not rigid. New ideas might occur while the researcher is involved in the data-analysis phase, and he or she might design and run another study before interpreting and communicating the results of the first. It is also common for some of the phases (such as data-analysis and interpretation) to overlap as the researcher moves back and forth between them.

The empirical observation phase is the center of the research process. We first generate and refine ideas, sharpening them into answerable questions. We then carefully make many decisions about what procedures we will use to answer the questions. All of that work is in preparation for the central activity—making empirical observations. The remaining phases are then focused on analyzing the empirical observations and determining and communicating their importance. That central activity—making empirical observations within a systematic rational process—is what characterizes science as a method that is different from other ways of seeking knowledge. Notice that in this process the scientist moves through a systematic, successive cycling of rational thinking, empirical observations, back again to rational thinking, and so on. Science combines the interactive processes of rationalism and empiricism.

Research in psychology, as in any other science, revolves around that empirical component. Observed facts are the most basic unit in psychological research. It should be clear then, that the more systematically and carefully we make the observations, the more solid will be the database on which we can continue to build a greater understanding of psychological phenomena.

Levels of Constraint

Recall that in Chapter 1 we noted the various ways people have used to pursue knowledge—tenacity, intuition, authority, rationalism, empiricism, and science. In the order listed, these approaches range from low to high demands on the adequacy of the information each is willing to accept and on the nature of the processing of that information. Of all these approaches, science is the most demanding.

Now let us add to that idea: within science itself, already at the high-demand end of this continuum, there are many approaches to gaining knowledge. Some approaches place little demand on the adequacy of the information and the nature of the processing of that information; other approaches place high demands. Thus, within scientific research, some methods are more demanding than others, but they all have their useful place in the scientific research scheme.

Within each phase, the researcher must make decisions about how to develop the research. The decisions may be fairly general, leaving the ideas, questions, and procedures relatively unrefined—as in some of the exploratory research undertaken early in the investigation of some phenomenon. On the other hand, the decisions might involve highly specific and refined ideas, with precise hypotheses, detailed procedures, complex statistical analyses, and so on. In each of these two extremes, the researcher moves through all of the phases but each is obviously at a different level of refinement. Exploratory research makes relatively few demands for structure or precision on the procedures in each phase. In contrast, the highly refined research project demands a great deal more structure and precision in its procedures.

For example, suppose we are operating a special training program for exceptional children and have just admitted some children diagnosed as moderately mentally retarded. In order to plan adequately, we might want to know, among other things, whether children with moderate retardation behave aggressively. Answering that question would not be difficult; we could ask the parents or we could go into a room with several moderately retarded children and simply watch them for a few hours. Both are observational procedures designed to answer the question. From those observations of parents and/or children, we can arrive at some tentative ideas about children with moderate retardation and their aggressive behavior. Continuing the research process, we can report our observations to our colleagues in the program, perhaps in a staff meeting. The point is, that as simple and imprecise as this seems, we have gone through a process of empirical research from original idea to communication of results. It was not highly detailed or structured, but it was research nonetheless. Note that because of the noncomplex nature of the question and the observational procedures, there was little demand that the question or procedures be precise, complex, or highly structured. If, while watching the children, we had decided to change the observation procedure, that change in procedure for that particular research would have been acceptable. Here, the activities in each phase are very flexible. As the research questions become more complex and precise, the activities in each phase of research must become correspondingly more demanding, precise, and controlled. Increased control is most readily seen in the observation phase of the process. As noted above, in some research the observations are made in a very flexible low-control manner; whereas in other research greater control over the conditions of observation is demanded. As we increase control over the conditions and methods of observation, we are imposing constraints on our freedom to be flexible. In essence, in the search for precision, we give up flexibility. In almost all research decisions, we are required to make certain trade-offs, and every design decision we make has a price associated with it. Beginning students often believe that the best way to conduct research is always to be precise and controlled. But precision and control may not always be the ideal, because sometimes the loss of flexibility is too great a price to pay for the increase in precision and control.

The idea of constraint provides a second dimension for our model of the research enterprise. The two dimensions are as follows:

1. **The phases of research.** Each complete research project proceeds along this dimension from original ideas to communication of new ideas.
2. **The levels of constraint.** This dimension is one of precision, structure, and control. Projects of the highest precision demand the greatest constraint on activities in each phase, the constraint being seen most clearly in

the controls imposed in the observation phase. By *"levels of constraint"* we mean *the degree to which the researcher imposes limits or controls on any part of the research process.*

When combined, these concepts of phases of research and levels of constraint form a two-dimensional descriptive model of research, which is outlined in Figure 2.2. Notice in Figure 2.2 that we have given names to the successive levels of constraint, ranging from the lowest constraint (naturalistic observation) to the highest constraint (experimental research). With the exception of the label *differential research,* we have employed commonly used labels for the levels of constraint. We have adopted the term *differential* from Hyman (1964) because it represents a broad class of research often overlooked in research methods texts. All the constraint levels represent scientific research and combine observation and rational inference. Some researchers hold an unfortunate view that only the high-constraint methods can properly be considered scientific. In our model, all are proper scientific methods and all can be effective when properly used. The use is determined by the nature of the question being asked and the precision of the existing knowledge about it; when it is a low-constraint question, then low-constraint methods are appropriate, and so on. When Jane Goodall (1971) was interested in learning about the social behavior of chimpanzees, naturalistic observation methods were the most appropriate methods to use, even though they were at a low-constraint level. Her research resulted in new knowledge about those animals. Her questions were general and flexible, so the level of research had to be equally general and flexible. High-constraint research would not have been appropriate and could not have given the information sought. The general nature of Goodall's questions was not a flaw in her work. Any scientist breaking new ground might very well start with just such low-constraint questions.

It is important to understand that all levels of research are properly scientific when used appropriately and that the nature of the question helps to determine the level of constraint used in answering it. Problems arise when researchers inappropriately mix constraint levels, such as when they try to interpret low-constraint data

Figure 2.2   A Two-Dimensional Model of Scientific Research

	Phases of Research						
	(1) Idea- Generating	(2) Problem Definition	(3) Procedures Design	(4) Obser- vation	(5) Data Analysis	(6) Interpre- tation	(7) Commu- nication
Levels of Constraint							
Naturalistic observation							
Case-study method							
Correlational research							
Differential research							
Experimental research							

in highly precise, predictive, and/or generalized ways. This is essentially the problem in the hypothetical example given in Chapter 1 of the psychoanalyst who observed enuretic children. She employed low-constraint, case-study observations but tried to apply her conclusion to all enuretic children, a step that properly requires high-constraint sampling methods to be certain subjects adequately represent the total population of enuretic children about whom the generalization is to be made.

Consider the researcher who applies highly complex and sophisticated statistical techniques to low-constraint research under the mistaken belief that in good research, high-powered statistical analyses must always be used. This idea is not correct. In fact, there are many important research questions that are most appropriately and most correctly investigated with low-constraint, relatively simple methods, including simple statistical analyses. What is important to impress on the beginning researcher is this: in doing research, we should refine our question so it can be answered using the highest constraint level possible, given both current knowledge in that field and practical and ethical constraints on the researcher. Once the constraint level of the question has been determined, then the remainder of the research process must be carried out at that same level of constraint. When we mix constraint levels, we run the serious risk of distorting or losing important information.

Notice that Figure 2.2, which describes our two-dimensional model of the research process, is blank except for the labels of the phases of research and the levels of constraint. This figure is essentially the outline for the remainder of the text. In later chapters, we will provide the information that defines each of the implied cells in this two-dimensional model. For now, we just want you to appreciate the organization of this model of research activity and to recognize that the activities in each phase of the research process may differ depending on the level of constraint of the research.

How can we ever move from low- to high-constraint research? Conclusions drawn from well-executed, low-constraint research can serve as the starting points for high-constraint questions and research methods. For example, when a clinical psychologist observes a consistent pattern of reported childhood trauma in patients with panic disorder, she might ask: "Now that I have observed these consistencies in my clinical sample, do the same consistencies hold in the general population of panic-disorder patients or is this some peculiarity of my sample?" This question could lead to research utilizing careful sampling procedures in selecting subjects who adequately represent the general population of panic patients. In this example, it would be unwarranted to conclude that childhood trauma is associated with panic disorder, based only on a single clinical sample. The patients of this psychologist may be unusual in some way, thus creating the impression that childhood trauma is typical of patients with panic disorder. Concluding that all panic-disorder patients have some childhood trauma, based only on her own clinical sample, would be a large leap from her low-constraint data to higher constraint conclusions. By asking the question as posed above, she could have moved from low- to higher-constraint research.

We should mention here that we do not always move from low-constraint to high-constraint research. There are times when we want to move in the other direction. As we will discuss later, it is sometimes useful to test findings from high-constraint research in low-constraint, naturalistic settings.

Like the phases of research, the constraint levels in our model are overlapping rather than being sharply categorical. This constraint dimension should be understood as forming a continuum and the labels (naturalistic, case study, and so on) as indicating bands or portions of the continuum. The number of levels we choose to identify in our model of research is not critical in understanding the research activity that the model seeks to represent. The important concept is that constraint ranges from low to high, and the five labels and their descriptions given below are adequate for describing most of the various kinds of psychological research. In later chapters, we will discuss the levels of constraint in more detail. Here we will define briefly each level.

Naturalistic Observation   The *naturalistic observation* level of constraint requires the researcher to observe the behavior of subjects in their natural environment. We are using the term *naturalistic observation* more narrowly than some authors. Our use of the term describes procedures where there is no attempt made to change or limit the environment or the behavior of the subjects. The only constraints that do exist are those that researchers impose on their observational methods. However, the researchers usually are not bound by strong hypotheses that demand a particular set of observational procedures. Therefore, they are free to shift their attention to any behaviors that seem interesting. This kind of flexible research is common in the early stages of research on a given topic and in exploratory research in general. Such flexible techniques are replaced by higher-constraint procedures as we develop a basic familiarity with the area. It is important here to make the distinction between naturalistic observation as we define it and higher-constraint research in naturalistic settings. As we will see in Chapters 6 and 13, research in naturalistic settings need not be low-constraint research; in fact, it often involves detailed and precise procedures.

Case-Study Method of Observation   *Case-study* research is somewhat higher-constraint because the researcher does intervene with the subject's functioning to some degree. Case-study research might include, for example, asking questions of a subject. Even though slightly more constrained than naturalistic observation, the case-study method still allows the researcher flexibility to shift attention to whatever behaviors seem most interesting and relevant at the time. In our usage, case-study research is *not* limited to research on psychopathology or psychotherapy. Rather, it is a set of methods that can be applied to many human issues.

Correlational Research   The *correlational* level of constraint requires much greater constraint on the procedures used to measure behavior. In this method, the setting can range from a naturalistic one to the highly constrained setting of a scientific laboratory. However, because we are interested in quantifying the relationship between two or more variables in the correlational method, we must use precise (constrained) procedures for measuring each variable. As we will see later in the text, knowing the relationship between variables allows us to predict the value of one variable from knowing the value of another, related variable.

Differential Research   The *differential* level of constraint involves a direct comparison between two or more groups of subjects. To make the comparison meaningful,

TABLE 2.2   THE LEVELS OF CONSTRAINT OF SCIENTIFIC RESEARCH

Naturalistic observation	This involves the observation of subjects in their natural environment. The researcher should do nothing to limit or change the environment or the behavior of the subjects.
Case-study	This involves moving the subject into a moderately limiting environment, intervening to a slight degree, and observing the subject's responses.
Correlational research	Here, the focus is on quantifying the degree of relationship between two variables. The measurement procedures must be carefully defined and precisely followed.
Differential research	Here two or more preexisting groups of subjects are compared. The setting is usually highly constrained, and the measurement procedures must be carefully defined and precisely followed.
Experimental research	Similar to differential research except that the subjects are randomly or in some other way assigned without bias to the various groups or conditions in the study. This is the highest constraint level of research.

the dependent variable must be measured in exactly the same way in each group. (The classification of independent and dependent variables will be discussed in Chapter 3.) That is, the settings and observational procedures must be constrained across groups. If done properly, the only thing that is not identical across the groups is the variable that defines the groups. In differential research, the variable that defines the groups is a *preexisting variable* not under the researcher's control. Such preexisting variables can include clinical diagnoses, age, IQ, sex, socioeconomic class, and so on. For example, research comparing adults born and raised in the United States with adults born and raised in England is differential research utilizing preexisting groups.

Experimental Research   *Experimental* research is the highest constraint research. In experimentation, comparisons are made between subjects under different conditions. A major difference between differential and experimental research is the way subjects are assigned to the groups or conditions. In experimental research, subjects are assigned to the groups or conditions in an unbiased manner, such as with random assignment. In contrast, in differential research, assignment of subjects is based on some preexisting variable not within the researcher's control.

The concept of level of constraint does not represent a single, simple dimension. Some levels differ on the basis of the constraint applied to the setting in which the observation takes place, some differ on the basis of the constraint placed on the measurement procedures, and others differ on the basis of the constraint placed on the subject-assignment procedures. But as we move from low-constraint methods to high-constraint methods, more constraint is placed on more aspects of the research study. In pure naturalistic observation, the only constraint is that placed on the observer. In pure experimental methods, every aspect of the study is planned in advance and explicit procedures must be followed throughout the study. Table 2.2 summarizes these various levels of constraint. A particular research study may not fit neatly into one of these five categories because there is much overlap between categories. We present this model only as a way of conceptualizing the many kinds of research studies that can be carried out.

A final point about levels of constraint should be introduced here. It is a point we will discuss again in later chapters. All research involves the study of relationships among events, but the types of relationship that can be discovered vary from one constraint level to another.

SUMMARY

Scientists use a combination of empirical observations and rational thinking to study natural phenomena. Based on specific empirical observations, the researcher employs a rational intellectual process of inductive inference to develop more general constructs that represent events that cannot (yet) be observed. Using the more general constructs as bases, the researcher can then make deductive inferences or predictions about future specific observations. The inductive-deductive process (specific-to-general-to-specific process) is highly interactive, and it ties together the empiricism and rationalism basic to scientific thinking.

Research is a process of inquiry in which the researcher carefully poses a question and proceeds systematically to gather, analyze, interpret, and communicate the information necessary to answer the question. The central part of this research process is making empirical observations. All activities that take place prior to the observation phase are designed as preparation for the actual gathering of data (making observations). All activities following the observation phase focus on analyzing, interpreting, and communicating those observations.

We have presented a two-dimensional model of the research enterprise to help organize knowledge about research. The two dimensions are (1) the phases through which each research project progresses and (2) the levels of constraint that distinguish the severity of the demands made on the information and the procedures used in each research project.

REVIEW EXERCISES

2.1   **Define the following key terms. Be sure you understand them. They are discussed in the chapter and defined in the glossary.**

assumptions of science
facts
behaviors
observation
inference
constructs
reification of a construct
model
inductive reasoning

deductive reasoning
theory
parsimony
inductive theory
deductive theory
functional theories
phases of research
idea-generating phaseinductive
problem-definition phase

procedures-design phase
observation phase
data-analysis phase
interpretation phase
communication phase
research data
replicate
electronic mail
e-mail

list server
levels of constraint
  naturalistic observation
  case-study
  correlational
  differential
  experimental
preexisting variable

2.2   Answer each of the following. Check your answers in the chapter.

1. Comment on this statement: "Only scientists can do research."
2. What are the basic assumptions of science?
3. What are facts? What is the major category of facts in psychology?
4. Distinguish between observation and inference. Give examples of each.
5. Distinguish between facts and constructs. Give examples of each.
6. Explain this statement: "Well-accepted ideas such as gravity, anxiety, and super-ego do not refer to facts at all."
7. Explain the two ways in which constructs are related to facts.
8. What are the major characteristics of scientific models?
9. What kinds of information do scientific models provide?
10. Explain this statement: "Models are used analogically."
11. In what ways are inductive and deductive reasoning commonly used in everyday life?
12. Explain this statement: "Making empirical observations is the focal point around which the inductive-deductive process revolves."
13. Identify and describe the phases of a research project.
14. What is meant by *data* in research? How are data obtained?
15. Explain this statement: "In the problem-definition phase we are engaged in deductive reasoning; in the interpretation phase we are engaged in inductive reasoning."
16. Distinguish between inductive theories, deductive theories, and functional theories.

2.3   Think about and work the following problems.

1. As an exercise, think of common issues or events in your life and try to generate as many general research ideas as you can. You might begin some of your questions with "I wonder what would happen if . . . ?" or "I wonder why . . . ?" For example: I wonder why I wake up every morning just a moment or two before my alarm rings? Do I have some inner time sense?
2. A professor asserts that only high-constraint, highly controlled experimental research is worth doing. You bravely raise your hand and are recognized. Now, how do you respond to that assertion?
3. Generate some examples of the inappropriate mixing of constraint levels in a research project.
4. Some brief descriptions of research follow. For each one, identify the level of constraint.
   a. A therapy researcher has several clients with very similar problems. He compares their statements in therapy to see what might be common among all of the cases.

b. A researcher compares subjects' reaction times to visual stimuli in a laboratory setting.

c. Two groups of rats are compared for their accuracy in running a maze. One group was fed just before the comparison, and the other had not been fed for 4 hours.

d. A third-grade class and a sixth-grade class are compared on their taste preferences.

e. A researcher observes prairie dog colonies to learn more about their behavior.

f. A researcher analyzes data on the relationship between the number of calories consumed and weight.

5. Following is a repetition of a question you were asked at the end of Chapter 1. Now you should be able to give a more complete answer: In a discussion or debate it is argued that social sciences such as psychology are not true sciences at all, as are sciences like chemistry and physics. How would you defend the proposition that psychology is a true science?

Chapter
3

The Starting Point: Asking Questions

ASKING QUESTIONS

Asking a question is the usual starting point for research. A question is a problem or statement in need of a solution or answer. "How can we reduce the disruptive behaviors of autistic children?" "Do whales communicate vocally?" "How can we get drunk drivers off the road?" Such questions have served as starting points for research. But where do we find such questions? Beginning students are often at a loss for research ideas and often believe formulating such ideas is more difficult than it really is. Questions are all around us; all we have to do is observe and be curious! As we shall see, research ideas in psychology are readily derived from a variety of sources.

Sources of Questions

Researcher's Personal Interests and Observations   Our own interests and observations are important because they point to directions for research that are personally relevant to us. Personal relevance can sustain our work, particularly when the going gets tough. Most of us can identify interests in psychological questions, which can serve as starting points for research. For example, we might be interested in emotion or, more specifically, in positive emotions like love or joy; we might be interested in memory, creativity, musical ability, social processes; or we might wonder about some aspect of ourselves or our family members. We may be puzzled by something we observe, asking ourselves "Why did that happen?" Any of these interests or observations can serve as the starting point for research.

Other Investigators' Theories and Research   An interesting thing about research is that it often raises more questions than it answers, and these new questions can serve as starting points for more research. Examples of theories and research that have generated a great deal of study are Freud's psychoanalytic theory, Skinner's (1938, 1972) research on learning, Miller's (1971) work on physiological influences on motivation, Bandura's (1969) research on modeling, Festingers's (1957) theory of cognitive dissonance, Lovaas's (1973) research with autistic children, Seligman's studies of learned helplessness and depression (Abramson, Seligman, & Teasdale, 1978; Seligman, 1974), Gleick's (1987) discussion of chaos theory, and the controversy around repressed memory (Bass & Davis, 1988; Loftus & Ketcham, 1994). To derive ideas from other research, scientists communicate with each other at scientific meetings, over the phone, or through the Internet, and by studying published research literature. The more knowledge we have of a research area, the stronger base we have for generating new research ideas. For beginning students, it is difficult to read journals and recognize what new questions are explicitly and implicitly being posed. Therefore, secondary sources such as textbooks or review chapters (e.g., *Annual Review of Psychology*) are more useful. These sources, designed to teach about a particular area, devote considerable space to explaining ideas. In contrast, research journals have severe space restrictions, and most articles are condensed and difficult to understand unless one already has a good background in the area under study. As one gains sophistication in research and in a particular area of research, journal articles become more useful and eventually become your major source of information.

Fortunately for researchers, libraries have well-organized systems of journal abstracts and cross-referencing systems by topics and authors, which allow us to locate quickly most relevant research. In psychology, the *Psychological Abstracts* are the primary source of such data. Other abstracts often used by psychological researchers include *Index Medicus* and the *Social Sciences Citation Index.* In most university and research-center libraries, these abstracts are part of a computer database, which makes it even easier to locate appropriate references. It is important for the researcher to become thoroughly familiar with these abstract systems. Reference librarians are very helpful to students seeking to learn how to search abstract systems. We have included an appendix that covers the basics of library research.

Theories and research raise questions for further research in two general ways—heuristically and systematically. Heuristic influence occurs when a theory or research finding such as the work of Darwin or Freud generates a great deal of interest, or even disbelief and outright antagonism, and in that process also suggests further areas of study. The impact of such theories on furthering research is enormous, but not necessarily in a systematic manner. The systematic influence occurs when theories or research make explicit, testable propositions as the next step for further research. Research in respondent and operant conditioning, for example, has systematically generated considerable research. Both influences, heuristic and systematic, are important in the continued development of science.

Seeking Solutions to Practical Problems   Much of psychology is *applied psychology,* and much of the research is therefore *applied research,* in which the goal is to provide solutions to practical problems. Two applied questions were mentioned earlier, one concerning autistic children and the other concerning drunk drivers. Both questions are derived from practical issues: therapy for children and public safety. Applied research questions in psychology are fairly easy for the beginning student to generate. Table 3.1 lists some more examples. Try generating some of your own.

Research can be categorized as applied or basic research. *Basic research* (also known as *fundamental* or *pure research*) is carried out to add to our understanding and store of knowledge, but without any particular practical goals. Basic research

TABLE 3.1   SOME EXAMPLES OF APPLIED RESEARCH QUESTIONS

1. How can we better train people to be good drivers?
2. What can department stores do to reduce shoplifting?
3. How can we help an underachieving child to improve academically?
4. What are the best placements of dials and levers on machines so as to reduce worker fatigue?
5. What is an effective approach to calming children before and after surgery so as to improve their recovery?
6. How can we design nuclear power plant control rooms to minimize the chance of operator error?
7. How can we change human behavior on a large scale so as to reduce the incidence of diseases such as lung cancer and AIDS?
8. How can we promote better parenting to reduce child abuse?

Box 3.1   **Sensory Deprivation: Applied Research Becomes Basic Research**

Although basic research often leads to applied research, sometimes it can be the other way around as, for example, the research on sensory deprivation. Funded by the Canadian government and conducted at McGill University (Heron, Doane, & Scott, 1956), this research was stimulated by reports that communist countries were using brain-washing techniques involving sensory deprivation.

At McGill, subjects in a sensory deprivation chamber wore translucent goggles and soft cuffs over their hands to reduce sensory stimulation. College students were paid $20 per day to remain in the chamber as long as they were willing. (This was conducted in the early 1950s, and $20 per day was comparable to approximately $120 per day now.) Even with this incentive, however, over half of the students quit the experiment within 48 hours. Almost all of them found the experience unpleasant, and many began to have vivid hallucinations.

These powerful findings created interest and excitement, and special laboratories were set up in Canada and the United States. Knowledge about sensory deprivation accumulated, but real understanding came only when scientists started relating the findings to other findings within the scientific literature and to integrate them into a coherent scientific theory. The research stimulated new ideas and new ways of thinking about phenomena that had been studied for years. Basic research on sensory processes was alive with a new excitement and new sets of ideas.

Applied research, born out of the Cold War tensions of the late 1940s and early 1950s, stimulated basic research in many other areas, which made valuable contributions to understanding human sensory processes, stimulating basic research that has since been used in dozens of applied research projects.

---

findings are often incorporated into applied research. For example, basic research findings about the language development of children might be used to develop training methods for language-deficient, disturbed, or retarded children. Unfortunately, it is often more difficult for basic researchers to obtain support than it is for applied researchers, perhaps because those who allocate funds do not realize the importance of basic research as necessary background for most applied research. It is difficult for even the most creative of individuals to imagine what applications an area of research might have until some basic understanding of that area is achieved (see Box 3.1). In many cases, research does not break down neatly into either applied or basic research. Instead, the findings of a study contribute both to an immediate application and to our basic understanding of a problem.

REFINING QUESTIONS FOR RESEARCH

Research projects begin with a question. Perhaps first only vaguely considered, the question is gradually examined and refined until it becomes specific enough to provide the researcher a clear direction for answering it. The initial question, once developed, is much more than just a point from which to begin research; its nature determines much of how we carry out the rest of the research process. Thus, developing the initial question is of considerable importance. Beginning students may wonder at what level of constraint they should carry out a particular research project, how to determine the observational methods to use, or how to select the right statistical test from the confusing array of available statistics. At least part of the answer to those and similar issues lies in the nature of the question asked. Once we refine the initial question, then many of those other decisions will follow.

Suppose that a psychologist studying animal behavior is interested in the parenting behavior of elephants in the wild and wants to know how long baby elephants are dependent on their parents or other adults. The psychologist also wants to know whether and to what degree male and female elephants engage in parenting and whether the baby's care is shared by other adult elephants. If we refine these questions further, we might restate them as follows:

1. In their natural habitat, which (if any) adult elephants assist in the birth and early care of the infant elephants and in the primary care of the growing young?
2. At what age do young elephants raised in their natural habitat become independent from the parents and/or caretakers?

Having posed those questions, the first thing to do is search the literature for previous work on these and related questions. This will determine whether the questions have already been answered and, if not, what methods have been used by other investigators in answering similar ones. Let us assume that these particular questions had not yet been studied so that we may proceed with the example.

Notice two important points about the initial questions. First, the questions themselves have begun to specify the behavior we are going to observe (parenting behavior of the adults and independent behavior of the young). Second, the conditions under which the observations are to be made (the elephants' natural habitat) have also been identified in the question. These specific elements could vary in many ways.

A *variable* is any set of events that may have different values. Height can be a variable because people, other organisms, and inanimate objects exist at different heights. Biological sex is a variable because there are two sexes. Behavior is a variable because a great number of behaviors can be performed. Any specific behavior (such as aggression) can be a variable because it can occur in different degrees or not occur at all. Some variables can be easily manipulated (e.g., the amount of food eaten). Manipulating a variable such as the amount of food eaten might change other variables such as one's weight (at least that's our hope when we go on diets). In the study of elephants' behavior, two variables of interest are (1) the setting under which we observe the elephants and (2) the behavior of the elephants. We could observe elephants in many different settings. We have chosen to exercise some control by saying that we are interested only in settings that qualify as the "natural habitat of the elephant." We will not observe elephants in a zoo or circus. But there will still be variability in the observational settings. The elephants' natural behavior is likely to be so variable and complex that we will want to simplify it by establishing broad categories into which it can be classified.

Note that the initial questions have also begun to narrow the choices of just how we are going to design and conduct this research. By specifying the natural habitat as one variable, we will have to make observations in low-constraint natural settings. But more is involved. Because we have posed a question about the normal flow of behavior under natural conditions, we do not want to manipulate or control any of the variables. Instead, we will use naturalistic observation of the animals without any manipulation of the animals' behavior on our part.

In formulating initial questions, researchers proceed through an often lengthy process of thinking about their area of interest, posing loosely defined questions at first, studying their own previous work and the work of others reported in the literature, and gradually refining their ideas into initial research questions. This process might take them far from their starting point, and their refined questions might be quite different from where they began. We are guided in this process of refining our ideas into researchable questions by the theories and research of other investigators. Theories are particularly important in this enterprise because good theories organize and structure vast amounts of information into a few general concepts. Theories often act like a map of the research area, revealing which areas are well understood and which areas could benefit from additional research.

The process of refining originally vague or general ideas does not stop when we arrive at an initial question. Rather, the question is further refined into a specific *statement of the problem* that we wish to investigate; that statement is further refined into a specific *research hypothesis,* which we then test in a specific research project. Developing the statement of the problem and the research hypothesis are formal processes that will be more fully discussed in Chapter 8 as we approach the experimental level of constraint. The important point here is that the starting point for research may be vague or general ideas; these are refined into initial questions, which in turn are further refined into problem statements and research hypotheses.

Once refined, the initial question implicitly helps to identify the major variables of interest and to structure the ways in which we will design and carry out the research. The level of constraint of a research project—and therefore the degree and types of controls, the kinds of observations, the type of data and measurement, and even the kinds of statistical analyses to be used—all depend to some extent on the nature of the question asked. In general, we try to develop the initial question to the highest level of refinement possible, given the state of knowledge about the particular area of interest. The more we know about an area, the more refined the question will be and the more likely that high-constraint research methods will be used to answer it. In areas where we know little about a phenomenon, the initial question will be correspondingly unrefined and less specific, and the procedures will therefore be carried out at lower constraint levels. In the example of elephants' parenting behavior, the question was general rather than highly detailed because we assumed that little was known about such behavior in elephants. We were unable to define exactly what behavior we were going to focus on because we were not sure what behaviors might be included in the broad category of parenting. We would not want to constrain our observations by trying to be overly specific about what behaviors to observe and how and when to observe them, for fear we might miss something important that we had not expected. In this case, we want to maintain maximum flexibility in the research, so we place no constraints on the behavior of the subjects (the elephants) and we place few constraints on the researcher other than that we not manipulate or interfere with the subjects. Had we known more about elephants before beginning the research, our questions would be more specific and our behavior as researchers would be more constrained by our specific focus. The nature of the question determines much about how we carry out our research project.

TYPES OF VARIABLES IN RESEARCH

There are several important ways of classifying variables in psychology.

Behavioral Variables

Any overt (i.e., observable) response of an organism is a *behavioral variable.* This includes a rat running a maze, a chimpanzee opening a puzzle box, a child playing with a toy, a subject pressing keys in an experiment, a person playing the piano, people talking to each other, and so on. Behavioral variables can range from simple behavior, such as a single keypress, to complex responses, such as social and verbal behavior. Because psychology is defined as the study of behavior, behavioral variables are of particular importance. *The variables most often observed in psychological research are behavioral variables.*

Stimulus Variables

Behavior always occurs in a context. The context is the total situation surrounding the behaving organism and all of the factors that make up the situation. The factors that have an actual or potential effect on the organism's response are *stimulus variables.* Stimulus variables may be specific and easily measurable or controllable, such as a flashing light as a signal for the subject to respond. They also may be more general, such as the total situation surrounding the subject being observed. An example of a stimulus variable is the habitat in which we observe elephants' behavior or the condition of a classroom in which we observe a child. Stimulus variables range from simple, such as a light signal, to complex, such as a controlled, contrived, social situation to which we assign subjects. In psychological research it is the stimulus variables that we control and the response variables that we observe. As we move from lower to higher levels of constraint (see Chapter 2), we apply greater degrees of control over stimulus variables.

Some stimulus variables, however, are internal to the subject and are difficult or impossible for the experimenter to manipulate directly. For example, stimuli for balance, sympathetic nervous system activity, and so on are internal stimuli. Although procedures may affect internal conditions, and therefore internal stimuli such as mood or anxiety, those variables are difficult to manipulate and are generally not under the direct control of the experimenter. Nevertheless, these variables are still a part of the subject's environment and can affect behavior.

Organismic or Subject Variables

Organismic or *subject variables* are the characteristics of the subjects, such as age, sex, height, weight, intelligence, neuroticism, racial attitudes, musical ability, psychiatric diagnosis, socioeconomic class, educational level, and so on. Some of the subjects' characteristics, such as weight, height, and sex, can be directly observed and are referred to as *observed organismic variables.* Other subject characteristics, such as neuroticism, racial attitudes, and intelligence, cannot be directly observed but are inferred from the subject's behavior. These are called *response-inferred organismic variables.* (You may recognize that response-inferred organismic variables are also constructs, which were discussed in Chapter 2.) Organismic variables can be used to classify subjects. For example, we might measure the anxiety level of subjects and then divide the subjects into three groups (high, moderate, and low anxiety) based on their scores.

It should be noted that some variables can be classified under more than one of the above categories depending on the way they fit into the research situation. For example, educational level would normally be thought of as an organismic variable—it is a characteristic of subjects. But educational level could also be a stimulus variable if the researcher provided an educational experience for subjects as part of a study. It might also be a behavioral variable if we are interested in the behavior of obtaining more education and what factors might influence that behavior. Thus, it is not just the characteristics of the variable itself that allow us to classify it as behavioral, stimulus, or organismic, but also how the variable fits into the research project.

Independent and Dependent Variables

Variables can also be classified as independent and dependent variables. The *independent variable* is what the experimenter manipulates; the *dependent variable* is the subject's response. In the research with autistic children, disruptive behavior (a behavioral variable) changed from a high frequency of occurrence when there was no relaxation training to a low frequency of occurrence after relaxation training. The researchers manipulated relaxation training (a stimulus variable) and observed the presumed effects of that manipulation on disruptive behavior. Because disruptive behavior was thought to be dependent upon the manipulation of relaxation training, it is therefore labeled the *dependent variable.* In experimental research, it is the independent variable that is manipulated by the experimenter; the changes that occur in the dependent variable are observed and measured. The dependent variable is not directly manipulated by the experimenter, but we hypothesize that it will be affected by the independent variable manipulation. The independent variable in the above research was the relaxation training. It was hypothesized that the independent variable would have a measurable effect on the dependent variable.

There are two kinds of independent variables: (1) manipulated independent variables and (2) nonmanipulated independent variables.[1] *Manipulated independent variables* are those that the experimenter controls by actively manipulating them, such as the relaxation training in the above study. *Nonmanipulated independent*

---

[1]There are some who would disagree with using the term *nonmanipulated independent variable,* arguing that an independent variable by definition is manipulated. In general usage, however, the term *independent variable* is used more broadly to include organismic variables as possible independent variables. We have made the distinction between manipulated and nonmanipulated independent variables explicit to minimize confusion for students while acknowledging the broad and somewhat inaccurate general usage of the term.

variables are classification variables, where subjects are assigned to the groups by the researcher on the basis of preexisting characteristics. The largest category of nonmanipulated independent variables in psychology are organismic or subject variables; that is, those variables that are preexisting characteristics of the subjects, such as IQ, religious affiliation, age, motor coordination, political affiliation, and so forth. The researcher does not actively manipulate such variables but assigns subjects to groups based on the organismic variables. For example, suppose we wanted to test the hypothesis that moral problem-solving skills are related to religious affiliation. We would assign subjects to groups based on their identified religious affiliation. Subjects would then take the Moral Problem-Solving Test, and we would compare the test scores of the religious-affiliation groups to determine whether there were significant differences between them.

Researchers often hypothesize a causal relationship between independent and dependent variables. A causal relationship between two variables exists when changes in one variable result in a predictable change in the other. However, as we will discuss in later chapters, it is difficult to draw a causal conclusion without the control provided by actively manipulating the independent variable. Thus, conclusions about causal relationships in a study with organismic independent variables (subject variables) are tentative conclusions. We will discuss manipulated and nonmanipulated variables more in later chapters. For now, it is important that you be able to make two distinctions: (1) between the independent and the dependent variable and (2) between manipulated and nonmanipulated independent variables. The independent-dependent variable distinction is most important in high-constraint experimental research where a major assumption is that the experimenter's manipulations of the independent variable are *causally related* to the observed changes in the dependent variable. It is important in experimental research, if one is to have any confidence in the assumption of causality, to distinguish between the two and to apply carefully all of the operations necessary to ensure that the independent variable will be as precisely defined and fully controlled as needed and that the dependent variable will be adequately measured.

In lower-constraint research, such as correlational research, there is usually no assumption of a causal relationship. Thus, the independent-dependent variable distinction is not needed. In some research, such as naturalistic observation, there may be no clearly defined independent variable because the behavior being observed is not properly a dependent variable. It is simply a variable of interest—an observational variable. In differential research, the independent variable is not manipulated by the experimenter but rather is a variable that already characterizes the subjects. It serves as a guide for observing and interpreting the changes in the dependent variable. Thus, although the independent-dependent variable distinction is most importantly applied in higher-constraint experimental research, the term is used in lower-constraint research, often as a convenience to distinguish between the two variables of interest.

The independent variable in psychological research is usually a stimulus variable (in the case of manipulated independent variables) or an organismic variable (in the case of nonmanipulated independent variables). The dependent variable is usually a behavioral variable. Also note that an independent variable in one study may be a dependent variable in another. For example, in a learning study, the researcher might manipulate as the independent variable the amount of time that visual stimuli are presented to subjects. The dependent variable in this study might be the accuracy of the subjects' recognition of the stimulus. In another study, the researcher might manipulate as the independent variable the complexity of visual stimuli presented. The dependent variable in this second study might be the amount of time needed by the subjects to identify the stimuli. Thus, in the first study, the amount of stimulus presentation time is controlled by the researcher and is an independent variable. In the second study, the amount of stimulus presentation time required by the subjects to identify the stimuli is the dependent variable. It can be confusing at times, but do not despair; in a few weeks all these distinctions will be second nature to you.

Variables as Constants

Now that we have discussed what a variable is, let us briefly consider what a *constant* is. Essentially, a constant is a variable that is prevented from varying. For example, suppose that we are using animals in research on the effects of hormones on learning. Earlier research leads us to suspect that age and sex may cause some variability in response to specific hormones. Thus, we decide to hold those two variables constant. We then use laboratory rats that are all males and all 10 months old. Sex and age are *constants* in this research. By holding those variables constant, they do not affect the outcome of the research. If they were not held constant or otherwise controlled, then the results of the experiment might be due to those uncontrolled variables and not to the variable(s) that we manipulated. As discussed below, the uncontrolled variables of age and biological sex could affect the results (i.e., they could be *extraneous variables* which might *confound* the results).

VALIDITY AND THE CONTROL OF EXTRANEOUS VARIABLES

Validity is one of the most important concepts in research and a central theme throughout the remainder of this text. Validity is a complex idea, and there are many types of validity. When we ask, "Does this study really answer the question it posed?" or "Does this test really measure what we want it to measure?" or "What does this laboratory study tell us about the 'real world?'" we are asking questions about validity. *Validity* refers to how well a study, a procedure, or a measure does what it is supposed to do. One of the fundamental tasks of research is to ensure the validity of the procedures by applying controls.

We have referred several times to *control* or *controlled research* but have not yet defined what we mean by those terms. Let us begin to think of control in research by recognizing that empirical observation is a central point in the scientific research process. Observations in psychological research are usually observations of the behavior of organisms. Behavior may be influenced by many factors, some of which are known and many of which are unknown to the researcher. Further, some of the factors may be of theoretical interest to the researcher, whereas others may be extraneous and even interfering factors. If the extraneous factors are numerous or powerful in the research, then their interference might make it impossible for the researcher to draw meaningful conclusions about the operations of the variables of interest. In effect, the influence of extraneous variables can reduce the methodological soundness, or validity, of the research findings. That is, *extraneous variables* are threats to the validity of the study. Thus, it is important to reduce the influence of extraneous variables on the behavior being observed. However, it is not only the behavior of subjects that can be influenced by extraneous variables but also the behavior of researchers doing the observing. Extraneous influences on researchers might so powerfully bias their observations as to invalidate the research or at least make it difficult to draw clear conclusions from the results. Therefore, it is necessary in research to reduce the effects that extraneous variables might have on the behavior of subjects being observed and on that of researchers doing the observation.

The procedures used to reduce such extraneous influences are what we mean by controls in research. Thus, the concept of *control in research* refers to the *systematic methods employed by the researcher to reduce threats to the validity of the study posed by extraneous influences on the behavior of both the subjects and the observer.* Although detailed systematic control methods become most important in higher-constraint research, they are nevertheless part of the procedures at all levels. For example, in a case-study research project, we might want to observe the solutions of some problems by children working individually. It would be important to prevent the child from being interrupted in the problem-solving tasks by other children who might make distracting noises or perhaps become interested themselves and volunteer their own solutions. These would be extraneous factors, and we would arrange to test the children individually in a quiet room, separated from the rest of the class, to reduce their potential influence on the child's behavior. In effect, we would exert some control over the observational setting as a means to reduce the effects of those and perhaps other extraneous variables.

There are two ways of controlling extraneous variables. One is to use higher-constraint research designs whenever possible. Another is to use *general control procedures,* which can be incorporated in research at many different levels of constraint. These general control procedures (discussed in Chapter 9) can compensate for some of the controls that are not available in lower-constraint research. Table 3.2 briefly summarizes the different ways in which we classify variables.

Internal Summary: Developing the Research Questions

There are several sources of research questions—personal interest and curiosity, current theories and research, and the need to solve practical problems. Initial research questions are refined into a problem statement and that, in turn, is refined into a specific research hypothesis, which is tested in the research. Both the problem statement and the research hypothesis include the variables to be studied. There are several types of research variables: behavioral, stimulus, organismic, independent and dependent, and extraneous. If not controlled, extraneous variables can confound research results. One way of controlling extraneous variables is by holding the variables constant. Other control procedures will be discussed later in the text.

TABLE 3.2   CLASSES OF RESEARCH VARIABLES

Behavioral variable	Any observable response of an organism
Stimulus variable	The specific features that make up the context in which behavior occurs
Organismic variable (or subject variable)	A characteristic of the organism that can be used to classify the organism for research purposes
Independent variable	A variable that is actively manipulated by the researcher to see what its impact will be on other variables
Dependent variable	The variable that we hypothesize will be affected by the independent variable manipulation
A constant	Any variable that is prevented from varying (i.e., held constant)
Extraneous variable	Any variable other than the independent variable that might affect the dependent measure and might confound the results

RESEARCH ETHICS

The research process involves a series of decisions that must be made by the researcher before observing even a single subject. These decisions include subject selection and assignment, controls, definition and measurement of variables, the statistical analyses to be used, and so on. One important set of decisions involves *research ethics.* Researchers make decisions about how they will use living organisms, human and nonhuman, for research purposes. This demands that ethical concerns be included in the decision process. The ethical guides extend to both human and nonhuman research (the latter is referred to as "animal research") and emphasize humane, sensitive treatment of subjects who are often put at varying degrees of threat or risk by research procedures. Before the researchers contact a single subject, they must be sure that the research plan stands up to ethical evaluation. Ethical concerns, therefore, are an integral part of the pre-observation decision-making process in research.[2]

Ethical Guides for Human Research

Concern over inhumane treatment of subjects was generated by post–World War II revelations of what German researchers did to people, including children, in the name of science. Organizations such as the American Psychological Association and the American Medical Association began to examine their own research practices. Although no inhumanities were found to approximate those of the Germans, concern developed that even in the United States some research subjects might be treated badly. In the 1950s and 1960s, there were growing criticisms of some of the methods used in biomedical research, which placed human subjects at risk without subjects' knowledge of the risks, and the discussions continue today as evidence by Rosenthal's (1994) lead article in a special section of *Psychological Science.* In

---

[2]Our discussion will focus on research ethics, but ethical concerns also apply to other activities of psychologists such as testing, psychotherapy, and teaching.

some instances, live disease organisms were injected into subjects, or new surgical techniques were practiced on patients who were undergoing surgery not related to the new techniques, without subjects' or patients' knowledge or permission. Researchers were careful to provide the best-known medical safeguards, but the point remains that the procedures were carried out without subjects' knowledge and consent. To tell subjects only that they were to be given a test of biological resistance, while withholding the information that the substance injected into them contained live cancer cells, is at least a serious deception. Many writers maintained that research subjects must be protected against deception, dangerous procedures, and invasion of privacy. Subjects, they said, have a right to know what is going to be done to them and to be given enough clear information that they can freely consent to or refuse to participate.

Psychological research with human subjects is rarely physically intrusive, and the risks to subjects are not as great as in some biomedical research. Nevertheless, issues of *deception, invasion of privacy,* and *subjects' rights* to be informed so as to be able to make a free choice still apply to psychological research. Potential invasions of privacy occur when researchers examine highly personal and sensitive areas of psychological adjustment, such as sexual behavior, private thoughts and fears, or relationships between couples. Social scientists often gain access to confidential records of patients in hospitals or of children in schools for research purpose. Deception in psychological research has become standard in some areas of study, although in nearly all instances the deception is mild. (When a social psychologist tells a group of children he wants to see how well they can judge the length of lines drawn on the blackboard, but in fact really wants to know how much the least and most popular child influence the other children's judgments, he or she is practicing a mild form of deception.)

At the center of these issues lies a genuine conflict of interests and a moral problem. On one hand, society demands scientific solutions to a large array of problems. On the other hand, there are times when searching for such solutions may violate individuals' rights to privacy and to proper treatment. If we are going to meet society's demands for new knowledge and treatments for physical illness such as AIDS and cancer, to solve social problems such as psychosis or aggression, or to improve teaching, we must be able to carry out scientific research, and that requires the cooperation of subjects. It is in the long-term interests of society for individuals to contribute to scientific efforts. One way is by participating as subjects in research. Responsible people will consider donating their time, effort, and information as subjects to promote scientific knowledge for its potential benefits to society—even when they do not personally benefit. Of course, the decision is up to each individual.

A moral dilemma arises because research, even with its potential benefits to society, sometimes exposes subjects to potential risks. In attempting to solve this dilemma, most research agencies, universities, and professional organizations have adopted a position that accepts the following basic ideas:

1. Scientific research offers potential benefits to society in general as well as to specific scientific disciplines.
2. It is reasonable to expect that individuals will behave in a socially responsible manner and contribute to knowledge by participating as subjects in research.

3. Subjects have basic rights when they elect to participate in a research study—rights to privacy and to protection from physical and psychological harm. They must also be given clear and sufficient information on which to base their own decision as to whether they will serve as subjects in any research project.

4. It is the responsibility of the researcher to conduct research in such manner as to respect subjects' rights and to protect subjects from possible physical and/or psychological harm.

The American Psychological Association (APA) was one of the first professional organizations to develop ethical guidelines for research, recognizing both the need for research and the rights of subjects. This position recognizes that in order to obtain information, some research employs deception, makes subjects uncomfortable, or pries into personal areas. These and other conditions of research place the *subjects at risk.* To say that a subject is at risk means that the potential exists for that individual to suffer physical or emotional harm as a result of participating in the study. The ethical principles are an attempt to help researchers conduct research while at the same time minimizing risks to subjects. Federal policy regarding human subjects in research is detailed in the *Federal Register* (1991).

Perhaps the most important safeguard built into these guidelines is this: it is the *subject* who decides to participate in research. The subject has the right to refuse or to discontinue participation at any time, even after having agreed to participate. The ethical researcher is bound to honor this right and can neither coerce subjects into participating nor prevent subjects from withdrawing. Researchers may not proceed to gather data until they have received the unequivocal consent of the subjects. *Informed consent* is an important safeguard; that is, the researcher must provide subjects with enough information about the research to enable them to make informed decisions about their participation.

When the subjects are children or are in some way incapacitated, as is the case with persons with mental or emotional disorders, they may have difficulty in understanding the information or in giving consent. Under those conditions, greater responsibility is placed on both the researcher and some designated person (e.g., parents, school administrators, or other institutional officials) who acts on behalf of the subjects to ensure that subjects' rights and well-being are protected.

Deception is frequently employed in some types of psychological research. Although nearly always innocuous, the use of any deception places the subject at risk. Therefore, if even mild deception is used, safeguards must be employed. The most common safeguards are (1) the researcher's judgment that the deception poses no serious or long-term risks and (2) explaining the true nature of the deception to the subject in a postexperimental debriefing. The subject is informed about the procedures and why they were used, which should counter any lingering misconceptions, possible discomfort, or risk that may have been generated by the research.

Another important safeguard concerns the responsibility of the researcher to maintain strict *confidentiality* of information gathered about subjects. This is particularly important when the research deals with sensitive personal information about the subjects, or information derived from normally confidential personal records such as hospital or school records. Researchers commonly use numerical codes rather than subjects' names on any records that contain sensitive information. The researcher is responsible for ensuring that such information does not become known to others.

The major ethical responsibility falls on the researcher. In planning research with human subjects, the researcher must judge the research in terms of its value, the amount of risk it poses, whether the potential benefits outweigh the risks, and whether adequate safeguards have been included to minimize the risks. Should the risks to the subjects outweigh any potential benefits of the research, the ethical researcher must redesign or discontinue the project.

A point seldom made, but one we believe to be of considerable ethical importance, concerns the potential value of the research. If the research is badly designed or carried out so that its results are of little or no scientific value, then (1) the potential informational value to society and to the discipline will be minimal, and (2) subjects will have wasted their time and perhaps been exposed to some risks in a largely valueless endeavor. Thus, in addition to all the other values in good research design, it is also an ethical responsibility of the researcher to develop well-designed projects and execute them with care.

Ethical Checks   Assume that we are designing a research project with human subjects. We have identified an area of interest and refined the initial question. We have also identified and defined the major variables and determined the nature of the subjects, how they will be selected, and how we propose to observe them. At this point it is necessary to make *ethical checks* by asking the questions in Table 3.3. By subjecting the research plan to ethical checks, we can identify and correct most of the potential ethical problems. When the study has been completely designed, repeating the ethical checks is necessary as a final test before submitting the proposal to the Institutional Review Board.

Institutional Review Boards (IRBs)   To assist researchers and help protect subjects, *Institutional Review Boards* consisting of the researchers' peers and members of the community at large have been set up in universities, research institutes, hospitals, and school systems—wherever research on human subjects is carried out. The task of an IRB is to review whether a research proposal meets the ethical guidelines determined by the IRB, and if it does not, to suggest appropriate changes. Every institution that receives federal funding is required to submit all human-subject research proposals to a review board. Members of the board are usually appointed by the president or other administrator of the institution. It is the responsibility of the individual researcher to be sure that his or her proposal is submitted to the appropriate IRB and is approved by the IRB before gathering any data.

When it functions well, the IRB is a helpful advisory group of colleagues that expedites the research, advises the researcher, and suggests improvements. The IRB is an additional safeguard, assisting researchers in clarifying and solving potential ethical issues. It does not, however, replace or reduce the researcher's ethical responsibility to design acceptable research. *The final ethical responsibility always rests with the researcher.*

Ethical principles in research continue to evolve as psychologists debate larger issues involving social values and scientific research (Kendler, 1993; Prilleltensky, 1994). As this text went to production, the American Psychological Association has appointed a task force to update ethical principles in research with human subjects

TABLE 3.3   THE ETHICAL CHECKS TO MAKE BEFORE TESTING ANY SUBJECTS

1. Is the proposed research sufficiently well designed to be of informational value?
2. Does the research pose any risks to subjects such as physical or psychological harm, by such means as the use of deception, obtaining sensitive, personal information, or using minors or others who cannot readily give consent as subjects?
3. If risks are placed on subjects, does the research adequately control those risks by including such procedures as debriefing, removing or reducing risks of physical harm, guaranteeing through the procedures that all information will be obtained anonymously or if that is not possible, guaranteeing that it will remain confidential, and providing special safeguards for minors and subjects who may have impairments?
4. Have I included a provision for obtaining informed consent from every subject or, if subjects cannot give it, from responsible people acting for the benefit of the subject? Will sufficient information be provided to potential subjects so they will be able to give their informed consent? Is there a clear agreement in writing (the *informed consent form*) between the researcher and potential subjects? The informed consent should also make it clear that the subject is free to withdraw from the experiment at any time.
5. Have I included adequate feedback information, and/or debriefing if deception was included, to be given to the subjects at the completion of the study?
6. Do I accept *my full responsibility* for the ethical and safe treatment of all subjects by myself and *all research assistants.*
7. Has the proposal been reviewed and approved by the appropriate review board?

(APA, 1995). Box 3.2 illustrates with a controversial example how the evolution of scientific technology requires a parallel evolution of ethical principles.

Ethical Principles in Research with Animals

In our view, concern for the ethical and humane treatment of animal subjects in research is just as important as the concern for human subjects. A great deal of animal research is being conducted in many biomedical disciplines, and large numbers of animal subjects are used each year. The APA estimated in 1985 that over 3,000 psychologists used animals in their research.

The major ethical concerns in animal research involve two basic issues: (1) animals are captive subjects and, of course, are not capable of providing informed consent and (2) the nature of the research carried out on animals is generally more invasive than that carried out on humans. Thus, there are many more serious risks to individual animal subjects than there are in human research. Therefore, much more responsibility is placed on the researcher to ensure that animal subjects are treated humanely.

For years, professional and governmental organizations have followed ethical guidelines in the use of animal subjects. The APA, for example, has had ongoing professional committees since 1925 to address issues of animal research. That early concern has evolved into a set of standards and principles in animal research, which are periodically reviewed. Most scientific societies whose members use animals in research have their own policy statements (e.g., Society for Neuroscience,

Box 3.2 **Information, Knowledge, and Ethical Questions**

Some questions are of a moral or ethical nature and cannot be answered through rational and empirical study alone. Consider the question "Should children be conceived specifically for the purpose of providing fetal tissues, organs, blood transfusions and bone marrow, or tissues from infants to give to people with illness?" Certainly the technology exists to conceive children, abort them at certain optimal points, and take the needed tissues to treat ill persons. But should we use the technology just because it exists? How can this question be answered by science? Science and technology can tell us if the procedures *can* be carried out and if they can be successful in medical treatment. But science cannot tell us if it *should* be done.

An example is the case of a child who was conceived in order to provide bone marrow transplant for her 16-year-old sister, who was suffering from myelogenous leukemia (Tomlinson, 1990). The girl's brother and both parents were not suitable donors because of conflicting blood types, and the girl was expected to live only a few more years if a donor was not soon found. The parents decided to conceive another child, based on odds of one in four that the child would be a suitable match. A girl was born, the match was successful, and the older daughter received the bone marrow transplant from her new infant sister. At this point both of these girls are doing well and are enjoying a very loving family life.

Should such procedures be done? How do you answer such questions?

1991, 1995; National Institutes of Health, 1985, 1986, 1991; Canadian Council on Animal Care, 1993; Foundation for Biomedical Research, 1987). Anyone who publishes in APA journals and who uses animals as research subjects must attest that the research was conducted in accordance with APA guidelines (APA, 1986). All researchers who submit studies to the Journal of Neuroscience or to Neuroscience meetings must attest that they have complied with animal use standards and policy as set out by the National Institutes of Health (1985, 1986, 1991) and the Society for Neuroscience (1991, 1995). The guidelines cover areas such as appropriate selection of animals, adequate and humane housing, preoperative and postoperative care, concerns about inflicting as little pain and discomfort as possible, and the need to have as much confidence as possible that the proposed research is necessary and is well designed.

In addition to the policies demanded by various professional groups (see above), animal research is also constrained in a number of ways that are similar to the controls applied to research with human subjects. Every animal laboratory in the United States, Canada, and Mexico must abide by their respective federal, state, and local laws governing the use and care of animals. In the United States all laboratories that receive federal funds must have a *Laboratory Animal Care Committee,* which serves the same function as the IRBs for human research. These committees include veterinarians and nonprofessional community representatives, as well as the researcher's professional colleagues. They review for approval all proposed animal care and use procedures, focusing not only on the specifics of humane care for the animals, but also on the relevance of the proposed research for human and animal health, the advancement of knowledge, and the gains to society. Thus, animal researchers must proceed in much the same way as those using human subjects;

they must thoroughly review the ethical animal-use issues in their planned research, must assume full responsibility for the ethical conduct of the research, and must submit the research plan to their local Laboratory Care Committee for evaluation and approval.

There is increased interest in reducing the number of live animals used in experimentation and research training. These reductions are being accomplished by sharpening the designs of experiments so that fewer animals are needed, substituting computer simulation for live animals, and using cells cultured in laboratories rather than live animals. The number of live animals used in training researchers and practitioners in schools of veterinary medicine has been reduced by substituting realistic models of animals. However, it is much more difficult to develop alternatives to live animals in the behavioral studies conducted in psychology. Intact, functioning animals are needed if we are to observe changes in their behavior.

Recently there has been considerable controversy about the use of animals in research. Some have argued that animal research is unnecessary and does not contribute meaningful information. However, as Neal Miller (1985) pointed out, animal research has not only contributed to the understanding of disease processes, improved services, and reduced risks for human beings, but has often lead to more effective and humane care for animals and solutions to problems that animals face in natural environments. For example, behavioral research on taste aversion has led to humane alternatives to shooting or poisoning animals, such as deer, coyotes, geese, crows, and others, that destroy crops or attack livestock. Behavioral and biological research has led to improved habitat preservation for wildlife, to successful reintroduction of Atlantic salmon and other fish to areas where they had been killed off, and to successful treatment for and vaccination against many diseases of pets, livestock, and zoo animals. Animal research has also led to successful medical and psychological treatments of human disorders, such as enuresis and encopresis, scoliosis (a severe curvature of the spine), anorexia, life-threatening vomiting in infants, retraining use of limbs following accidents or surgery, and many other disorders. Miller's article is highly recommended reading.

Concern for humane and ethical treatment of animals in research is legitimate, and few researchers deny the importance of that concern. Ulrich (1991), for example, argued that misuse and overuse of animals does occur in research, and that scientists, like everyone else, are thoughtlessly guilty of our culture's propensity to consume anything, without regard to ecological issues. Ulrich, an animal researcher for many years, writes thoughtfully about scientists' responsibilities to other life forms and the necessity to consider seriously the ethical issues involved in animal research. Like Miller's article noted above, Ulrich's is also recommended reading. Research with animals has made enormous contributions to our understanding of nature. As with all research, the costs in terms of risks to the subjects must be balanced by the potential benefits to society.

SUMMARY

The starting point for research is finding an area of interest and generating a researchable question. Research questions can be readily developed from our own personal experiences and interests, from the published theoretical and empirical work of others, and from attempts to solve practical problems. New research can be generated from current research both heuristically (by stimulating interest and even opposition) and systematically (by making precise predictions about the needed next step in the research process).

Psychological research can be categorized as (1) basic research in which we attempt to develop new information without any particular practical goals and (2) applied research in which we attempt to answer questions to help solve practical problems.

Initial research ideas may be quite vague and must be refined and sharpened until we have attained the most precise questions possible given the state of knowledge in that particular area. The refined question is of considerable importance because it will influence how we will proceed with the remainder of the research. Refining the initial question implicitly helps to identify the major variables of interest and structure the ways in which we will proceed to design and carry out the research. The level of constraint of the research project—and therefore the degree and type of controls, the observational procedures, the methods of measurement, the type of data, and the statistical analyses to be used—all depend to a great extent on the nature of the question.

It is important to identify not only the variables of interest but also variables in which we have no interest but which might affect the outcome of research. These extraneous variables must be identified so that appropriate procedures can be developed for controlling or minimizing their effects on the variables we do want to study.

One category of important pre-observational decisions concerns ethics. The rights of the individual must always be balanced against society's need for scientific information. Ethical guidelines have been developed by the APA for psychological research with human subjects. The basic focus of the guidelines is to ensure that subjects are not coerced into cooperating in research, that such research is meaningful, and that it poses no undue hazards to subjects. It is the responsibility of individual researchers to see that risks to subjects are minimized and to have each project reviewed by an appropriate Institutional Review Board for their department or agency. However, the ultimate responsibility for insuring subjects' rights lies with the researcher.

Ethical concerns in the use of animal subjects are equally important. The guidelines for animal research focus on the adequacy of housing and general care of laboratory animals and on minimizing pain or other discomfort that might result from the research procedures, and on the need for and value of the proposed research. Animal researchers must submit their research plans to their local Laboratory Animal Care Committee for review and approval.

REVIEW EXERCISES

3.1 **Define the following key terms. Be sure that you understand them. They are discussed in the chapter and defined in the glossary.**

applied psychology
applied research
basic research
variable

statement of the problem
research hypothesis
variables
behavioral variables

stimulus variables

organismic variables

subject variables

observed organismic variables

response-inferred organismic variables

independent variables

dependent variables

manipulated independent variables

nonmanipulated independent variables

constants

extraneous variables

validity

control

controlled research

control in research

general control procedures

research ethics

deception

invasion of privacy

subjects' rights

subjects at risk

informed consent

confidentiality

ethical checks

informed consent form

Institutional Review Boards (IRBs)

Laboratory Animal Care Committee

3.2   Answer each of the following. Check your answers in the chapter.

1. Explain this statement: "Freud's research was of considerable heuristic value."
2. Name and briefly describe the three main starting points for research.
3. To review an earlier concept, what is meant by "levels of constraint"?
4. Name and define the classes of variables discussed in this chapter.
5. For each of the following variables, determine the class of variables to which it belongs: academic achievement; aggressive behavior; number of correct answers on a test; giving one group of rats sugar and another group saccharine; height of subjects; socioeconomic class of subjects; subjects' general health status; amount of light at a desk in research on office working conditions; psychiatric diagnosis of subjects.
6. Distinguish between an independent and a dependent variable.
7. In the research on autistic children described in the chapter, identify the independent variable and the dependent variable.
8. Distinguish between the two types of independent variables.
9. Explain this statement: "The independent-dependent variable distinction is most important in high-constraint experimental research."
10. Exactly what is meant by "manipulating the independent variable"?
11. What is the major assumption about the relationship between variables in experimental research?
12. Distinguish between basic and applied research. Give examples of each.
13. What are extraneous variables? Give some examples.
14. What is deception in research with human subjects, and what is the major safeguard for deception? Give examples of deception in research.
15. Identify and explain the moral problem that lies at the center of research ethics.
16. If proposed subjects are minors or are mentally incapacitated, what is the standard ethical procedure to safeguard their rights?

3.3   Think about and work the following problems.

1. At the end of Chapter 2 we asked you to generate some research questions. Now we want you to generate more, but this time try to refine them further by clearly identifying the major variables included in the questions. For example:

   Question: How much does alcohol affect driving?

   Variables: Alcohol, driving.

2. Some brief descriptions of research follow. For each one, you are to (i) identify the variables, (ii) indicate the class of variables to which each belongs, and (iii) identify any potential extraneous variables.

   a. You are investigating the relationship between children's ethnic prejudices and their socioeconomic status.

   b. In a study on the effects of alcohol on driving, subjects are randomly assigned to seven conditions of alcohol consumption: 0.0, 0.5, 1.0, 1.5, 2.0, 2.5, and 3.0 ounces, respectively. Subjects in each condition are tested in a driving simulator, and the number of driving errors is measured. The hypothesis is that higher consumption of alcohol will cause greater driving errors.

   c. Shoppers are asked to compare two laundry products while being videotaped for a television commercial. During the comparison the products' labels are covered, supposedly so the subjects cannot identify them. The subjects know they are not supposed to see the labels. However, the covering on one product, the sponsor's product, is thinner than the other, and the subjects can actually see what the label says. Will the sponsor's product be chosen more than the other as the superior product?

   d. You are investigating the relationship between size (a height-weight measure) and peer status in sixth-grade children.

3. Some research situations follow. What are the potential ethical problems in each? Where you can, indicate what safeguards you would use.

   a. A researcher is going to test third- and fourth-graders to compare boys and girls on their interest in math problems.

   b. A study of small-group interactions is being conducted with adults as subjects. The subjects, observed in groups of five people, do not know that three of the five subjects in their group are actually assistants of the researcher and that their behavior during the small-group meeting has been planned ahead of time.

   c. A researcher wants to examine the files on hospitalized schizophrenics to obtain basic information about their families.

4. Suppose you have designed a research project using human subjects, written a research proposal, and submitted it to your Institutional Review Board for clearance on ethical issues. The board returns your proposal as "ethically unacceptable" because the design is so flawed that the information from the study would be meaningless. There is no other issue raised. Why is this criticism of your proposed design an ethical issue and not just a design problem?

5. Think of several examples of variables that could be independent variables in one study and dependent variables in another.

Chapter
4

Data and the Nature of Measurement

In Chapter 2 we developed the idea that observation is the pivotal phase in the research process. In Chapter 4 we will take a closer look at observations, noting some of the critical issues associated with the observation process in research.

RESEARCH VARIABLES

As introduced in Chapter 3, every research project, whatever its level of constraint, includes one or more sets of variables that the researcher manipulates and/or observes and measures. A *variable* is any characteristic that can take more than one form or value (e.g., anxiety, intelligence, height, reaction time). Because scientific research methods can be used to study any natural phenomena, any varying event or set of events can become a research variable. Intelligence as measured by a standard IQ test can be a variable in research because in any group of subjects the scores will vary from one subject to another. The number of correct answers on a memory test can also be a variable because that number will differ from one subject to another and can change from one condition to another. Suppose, for example, we measure the number of correct answers on an achievement test given by one group of students under quiet classroom conditions and the number given by another group under noisy classroom conditions. In each example, the variable (intelligence, memory, or academic achievement) is a complex event that varies from one subject to another and/or from one condition to another. If the events of interest are static with no variation, they cannot serve as research variables. Simply put, a variable must vary. The major task in measurement is to represent the research variables numerically.

In research there are usually at least two variables of interest: (1) the independent variable (which is manipulated by the researcher) and (2) the dependent or response variable (which is observed and measured by the researcher). The distinction between independent and dependent variables is often blurred or not wholly necessary in some low-constraint research, and the terms are used largely for convenience. But at higher-constraint levels, particularly at the experimental level, the distinction becomes critical.

MEASUREMENT

In scientific research variables must be measured. To measure a variable is to assign numbers that represent values of the variable. The measurements of the variable for each subject constitute the numerical or quantitative data. These data are the basic units for subsequent data analyses and interpretation. Further, the particular statistical analyses chosen by the researcher will be determined largely by the way the dependent variables are measured. Beginning students are often confused when faced with the question "What statistical procedures should be used in this study?" As we will see later (in this chapter and in Chapter 14), choosing appropriate statistical procedures is often relatively simple once the observational procedures have been designed and the ways in which we will measure the dependent variable have been determined.

Measurement of a variable is essentially the process of assigning numbers to that variable. In assigning numbers to a variable, the researcher works with two major sets of information. The first set is the abstract number system with all its characteristic rules and procedures. The second set is the variable to be measured with all of its particular characteristics. The task for the researcher is to bring the two systems together, applying one to the other so the numbers accurately represent the variable. The task becomes complicated because the two systems do not necessarily function according to the same rules. The abstract number system has specific and well-defined characteristics and rules. However, variables in psychology, as in many sciences, are not usually so well defined and well understood, and they do not necessarily function according to the same clear rules as the abstract number system. Thus, the two systems cannot always be easily matched. It is necessary for the researcher to determine how the characteristics of a particular variable might fail to match those of the abstract number system, so as to construct appropriate measures of the variable and to use the appropriate statistical methods of analysis. Serious errors in data analysis and interpretation can occur when the researcher misapplies the number system.

The characteristics or properties of the abstract number system are identity, magnitude, equal intervals, and a true zero. Identity means that each number has a particular meaning. Magnitude means that numbers have an inherent order from smaller to larger (5 is of greater magnitude than 3). Equal intervals means that the difference between units is the same anywhere on the scale (the difference between 2 and 3 is the same as the difference between 99 and 100). The zero on the abstract number scale is a true zero. Because of these properties, we can add, subtract, multiply, and divide the numbers. However, if we apply the abstract number system to a psychological variable such as intelligence, we find that the abstract number system and intelligence do not match exactly. The number system has a true zero point, but the psychological variable—intelligence—does not have a zero point. That is, in the unlikely event that a person were to score zero on an intelligence test, we could not conclude that he or she had zero intelligence. Thus, the score zero does not indicate zero intelligence on the psychological variable. In this situation, the number system and the psychological variable do not match exactly. In the abstract number system, 100 is exactly twice as much as 50, but because the psychological variable has no zero point, we cannot say that an intelligence test score of 100 shows twice as much intelligence as a score of 50.

Suppose we were doing a study of taste preferences. We give our subjects samples of solutions to taste and ask the subjects to rank them according to which one they liked the most, which one second, third, and so on. We assign numbers to the ranks (1, 2, 3, etc.) and report that number 1 was most preferred, 2 was second, and so on. But it would not make sense to report that the difference in preference between 1 and 2 is the same as between 2 and 3. Suppose, for example, you were asked to rank Coke, Pepsi, and vinegar from most to least preferred. Now, unless you have strange tastes, your rankings would probably be either 1-2-3 or 2-1-3 for Coke, Pepsi, and vinegar. Clearly, the difference in preference between Coke and Pepsi is much smaller than between either of those drinks and vinegar, even though the difference in rank orderings is the same. Similarly, it makes no sense to say that the drink ranked 1 is three times as preferred as the drink ranked 3. In these examples, the characteristics of the variables as they are measured do not match the

TABLE 4.1   FREQUENCY OF QUESTIONS ASKED IN THE CLASSROOM BY TEN CHILDREN OVER FIVE CONSECUTIVE DAYS

Subjects	Days					Total
	Mon	Tues	Wed	Thurs	Fri	
01	1	2	1	1	1	6
02	0	0	1	0	1	2
03	4	2	3	3	3	15
04	6	4	5	3	4	22
05	1	3	1	0	2	7
06	2	0	2	1	0	5
07	2	3	1	2	2	10
08	2	0	1	1	0	4
09	1	1	0	2	1	5
10	4	3	5	3	3	18
Totals	23	18	20	16	17	94

characteristics of the real number system, and so we are limited in the type of mathematical operations we can perform on the data.

In some cases, however, the variable and the number system can be matched. Let us consider an example. Suppose that a developmental psychologist wanted to observe classroom behavior of a group of children. One of the behaviors of interest was asking questions of the teacher. Each question asked by a student was observed and recorded for each child. At the end of each school day, the total number of questions asked by each child in each school day was computed. Table 4.1 shows sample data for five days of observation for ten children.

The data in Table 4.1 give us considerable information. Because of the nature of the data, we can apply all of the mathematical operations to them. We can add the number of daily questions for each child and arrive at each child's total number of questions for that week. If you look across each row in Table 4.1 at the totals for each child, you will see that child 02 asked a total of only two questions, whereas child 04 asked a total of 22 questions. This large difference suggests that the children are quite different from each other with regard to their willingness to ask questions in class. We can subtract the totals or divide one by the other and report that in this particular week of observation, subject 04 asked 20 more questions or 11 times as many questions as subject 02. We also can divide the total for the week by the number of children and report the children's average number of questions for the week. The point is that when we have a dependent variable such as the number of responses made by a subject, it provides a good match with the real number system. The variable shows a magnitude in the same direction as the real number system so that 22 responses are more than 20 responses. This particular dependent measure also has equal intervals so that the difference in response between 4 and 6 is the same as the difference between 10 and 12. Finally, the dependent variable in this study has a true zero point, which means that a child with a score of zero asked no questions during the observation period. Because of this match of the characteristics of the dependent variable with those of the real number system, we are able to perform all mathematical operations on the data—we can add, subtract, multiply, and divide. This in turn allows us to use some of the more powerful statistical tests, which cannot properly be used with dependent variables not as well matched with the real number system.

SCALES OF MEASUREMENT

Some of the variables used in psychological research (such as the number or duration of responses, the number of items answered correctly on a test, the amount of weight a subject can lift) have characteristics that closely match those of the real number system. Other variables (e.g., scores on intelligence or personality tests, academic standing in class, attitudes) are not so well matched with the number system. To help identify the closeness of match, Stevens (1946, 1957) classified variables into four levels or scales of measurement.[1] The scales, arranged from least to most matching with the real number system, are the nominal, ordinal, interval, and ratio *scales of measurement.* For more complete discussions, see Coombs, Raiffa, and Thrall (1954) and Roberts (1979).

Nominal Scales

Nominal scales are at the lowest level of measurement, the scales least matching to the number system. As their name suggests, nominal scales are naming scales, and their only property is the property of identity. Dependent variables such as place of birth (Chicago, Boston, Nyack), brand name choice (Ford, Honda, Volvo), political affiliation (Democrat, Republican, Socialist, Independent), diagnostic category (panic disorder, schizophrenia, bipolar disorder), sex of the subject, or any other way of categorizing subjects are all nominal scales of measurement. The differences between the categories of nominal scales (e.g., Ford, Honda, Volvo; Republican, Democrat; male, female) are qualitative and not quantitative. We can assign numbers to represent different categories. For example, we could label Chicago as 1, Boston as 2, and Nyack as 3, but the numbers are only arbitrary labels for the categories. Except for identity, these numbers have none of the properties of the real number system, and therefore we cannot meaningfully add, subtract, multiply, or divide them. Is Chicago with its assigned number of 1 to be understood as only one-third of Nyack with its assigned number of 3? Nominal scales have no zero point, cannot be ordered low to high, and make no assumption about equal units of measurement. In other words, they are not numbers at all, at least not in the sense that we usually think of numbers. Nominal scales of measurement classify or categorize each subject, and we work with the number or frequency of subjects who fall into each of the categories. The data of nominal scales are called *nominal data* (also sometimes called *categorical data*). Various forms of chi-square are the most commonly used

[1]There are those who disagree with Stevens (Gaito, 1980; Michell, 1986), challenging his distinction between scales of measurement on mathematical grounds. Although we are sympathetic to these arguments, we believe that Stevens' original presentation is still the best teaching and organization tool for a textbook at this level.

statistical tests for nominal data. Some common uses of nominal scales are a number on an athlete's jersey, a social security number, or a telephone area code.

Ordinal Scales

Ordinal scales, as their name suggests, measure a variable in order of magnitude. Thus, ordinal scales have the property of magnitude as well as identity. In ordinal scales, numbers are assigned to categories or groupings that are arranged in order so that some numbers represent more of the variable than others. For example, using socioeconomic class as a variable, we could categorize subjects as belonging to the lower, middle, or upper socioeconomic class. There is a clear underlying concept here of order of magnitude, from low to high. Other examples of ordinal scales are measurements by rankings, such as a student's academic standing in class, a subject's taste preferences, or children ranked by height in a nursery school; or measurements by ranked categories, such as low, medium, or high anxiety; low, medium, or high artistic ability; or grades of A, B, C, D, or F. We refer to data measured on ordinal scales as *ordered data.*

Ordinal scales tell us about the relative order of magnitude (nominal scales do not), but they do not give us any information about the differences between categories or ranks. If we rank students on class standing, for example, we can determine from the data which student is first, second, and so on, but we cannot determine how much higher the first ranked student is compared to the second. That is, the numbers tell us about ranks or relative positions but not about the distances or intervals between ranks. The difference in academic achievement between students ranked 1 and 2 might be very small (or large) compared with the difference between students ranked 12 and 13. As illustrated in the example of ranking preferred taste of Coke, Pepsi, and vinegar, the intervals in ordinal scaling are not necessarily equal. In fact, it is usually assumed that they are unequal. Therefore, it is inappropriate to try to analyze ordered data with statistical procedures that implicitly require equal intervals of measurement. The most commonly used statistical tests with ordered data are nonparametric tests, such as the Mann-Whitney *U*-test or the Wilcoxon matched-pairs signed-rank test.

Interval Scales

When the measurement conveys information about the ordering of magnitude of the measures and about the distance between the values, we have interval scaling. *Interval scales* have the properties of ordinal scales and the property of equal intervals between consecutive values on the scale. Thus, interval scales come close to matching the real number system but still do not have a true zero point. The most commonly used example of an interval scale is the measurement of temperature on either the Fahrenheit or Celsius scale. The units of the thermometer are at equal intervals representing equal volumes of mercury. We know that 90° is hotter than 45°. We also know that the difference in temperature between 60° and 70° is the same as the difference in temperature between 30° and 40°. However, the zero point on the scale is arbitrary and not a true zero point. Zero degrees on the scale does not indicate a total absence of heat. Interval scales thus give us order and equal intervals but no true zero point. Most variables in psychology are measured in interval or near interval scales (e.g., IQ test scores, neuroticism scores, attitudes). With an IQ test, for example, we can report that the measured IQ difference between two people with IQs of 60 and 120 is 60 IQ points. However, because there is no true zero point on the IQ scale, we cannot say that the first person is half as smart as the other. We refer to data measured on interval scales as *score data.*

Ratio Scales

Ratio scales have all of the properties of the preceding scales (identity, magnitude, and equal intervals) as well as a true zero point. Thus, ratio scales provide the best match to the real number system, and we can carry out all of the possible mathematical operations (addition, subtraction, multiplication, and division) on such scales. When the variable is some physical dimension, such as weight, distance, length, volume, number of responses, or time duration, we can use a ratio scale of measurement. We refer to such scales as ratio scales because dividing a point on the scale by another point on the scale (taking a ratio of values) gives a legitimate and meaningful value. For example, a person who runs 10 miles is running twice as far as a person who runs 5 miles and five times as far as someone who runs 2 miles. It is the true zero point that gives the ratio scale this property. Just as with interval scales, we refer to the data measured on a ratio scale as *score data.* A variety of statistical techniques are typically used for score data, including *t*-tests, analysis of variance (ANOVA), and product-moment correlations. The statistical procedure used with score data will depend both on what question is asked and on the design of the study. Although some variables in psychology can be measured on ratio scales, most variables can be measured only on ordinal or interval scales of measurement. The characteristics of the various scales of measurement are summarized in Table 4.2, along with examples and the statistical procedures most commonly used.

TABLE 4.2   SOME ASPECTS OF SCALES OF MEASUREMENT

	Levels of Measurement			
	Nominal	**Ordinal**	**Interval**	**Ratio**
Examples	Diagnostic categories brand names; political or religious affiliation	Socioeconomic class; ranks	Test scores; personality and attitude scales	Weight; length; reaction time; number of responses
Properties	Identity	Identity; magnitude	Identity; magnitude; equal intervals	Identity; magnitude; equal intervals; true zero point
Mathematical operations	None	Rank order	Add; subtract	Add; subtract; multiply; divide
Type of data	Nominal	Ordered	Score	Score
Typical statistics used	Chi square	Mann-Whitney *U*-test	*t*-test; ANOVA	*t*-test; ANOVA

Note: Many more examples of the various scales and additional appropriate statistical procedures could be given.

MEASURING AND CONTROLLING VARIABLES

Now that we have defined different types of variables, scales of measurement, and types of data, we should consider how to measure and manipulate variables. Let us start with a fairly simple problem so that we can easily follow the steps required to solve it. Assume that we are interested in the effects of food intake on weight for human subjects. In this example, food intake is the independent variable (the variable to be manipulated in the study). We want to know what effect manipulations of food intake will have on subjects' weight, so weight is the dependent variable. We are hypothesizing that weight fluctuations will be dependent on the manipulations of food intake.

Measurement Error

Consider the problem of measuring weight. Suppose we have the subject stand on a standard doctor's scale. If the subject were to lean against the wall, the weight measurement would be distorted. If the subject were weighed at one time while wearing a heavy coat and boots and the next time while in bare feet and no coat, the two weights would not be comparable. Factors such as these are sources of *measurement error.* Measurement error can distort the scores so that the observations no longer accurately reflect reality. Measurement error can also attenuate (reduce) the observed strength of a relationship between variables, giving the impression that two variables are unrelated when in fact they are related to one another.

Another source of measurement error is the problem of *response-set biases.* One of the most powerful response-set biases is social desirability. *Social desirability* is the tendency of many subjects to respond in what they believe to be the most socially acceptable manner. For example, suppose we were studying the relationship between level of food intake and weight in a weight-loss program. Have you ever cheated when you were on a diet? If you did, would you always be willing to admit it to people? There is a good chance that you would not admit it because you would find it embarrassing. In this case, some subjects might not be willing to report their true level of food intake because they do not want to admit to socially undesirable behavior such as cheating on a diet. This social desirability response set would obviously affect the validity of the measurement and create measurement error in the study.

In research it is important to minimize measurement error. This is best accomplished by developing a well thought out operational definition of the measurement procedure and by diligently using the operational definition in the research.

Operational Definitions

Most of us measure our own weight periodically by standing on a scale and reading the weight from a dial or a balance scale. Measuring one's weight is easy because the scales are already developed and readily available. However, consider the process of weighing ourselves. What we are doing is operationally defining the measurement of weight. An *operational definition* is a definition of a variable in terms of the procedures used to measure or manipulate the variable. That is, an operational definition specifies the activities of the researcher in measuring and/or manipulating a variable (F. N. Kerlinger, 1986). In research, even for such simple measures as weight, every step of the measurement procedure should be carefully planned in order to avoid confusion.

Measuring a variable such as food intake requires a scale different from the weight scale. We know from past research that food intake is measured in terms of calories and that foods differ in their level of calories. If we know the calorie level of each type of food, we can compute the total calorie intake for each subject without much difficulty. This process of measuring food intake is based on a good deal of research and theory. We can be reasonably sure that this approach to measuring food intake is effective because it has worked well for researchers in the past—a fact we can confirm by reading earlier research.

In many psychological studies, the researcher wants to create a particular response in subjects, such as increasing their levels of motivation, anxiety, or alertness. These are factors that are within the subject and are therefore difficult to measure or manipulate. But such variables can be studied by operationally defining the set of procedures for manipulating the variables. In a study discussed earlier, the relaxation level of autistic children was manipulated to see whether it would have any effect on the level of disruptive behavior. The manipulation was defined in terms of a set of explicit procedures that was followed by the researcher. The following example of some of the specific procedures used in the study of autistic children shows how much detail and specificity is needed to define such a manipulation effectively:

A specific area of the room was selected and for three days prior to the initiation of relaxation training the children were told about "relax time" and shown the "quiet spot" where the training would occur. Characteristically, they asked no questions nor exhibited any reaction to the announcements. The first training session was announced simply: "O.K. kids, now it's relax time." The lights were turned out, and the children were led to the "quiet spot" and instructed to lie down on a clearly defined blanket on the floor. The therapist gently, quietly, and in a soft, almost "lullaby" cadence, told them, ". . . Close your eyes, now, just like when you're in bed, nice and comfortable. That's it, eyes closed. Breathe slow and easy, slow and easy, that's it, good job, nice and easy, nice and slow, nice and relaxed, good job, calm, slow, easy, relaxed. That's right. That's it. Real good, real relaxed!" The therapist continued her quiet instructions to breathe easily and be calm, settled and relaxed. After two minutes of quiet cooperation, Cathy got up and walked away. The therapist then ended the training session, and the children resumed their usual program.

The training sessions occurred once daily, always following snack time, and just prior to resuming the academic session. The children continued to experience relaxation not only lying down, but gradually also sitting and standing. The therapist continued her soothing, quiet instructions and paired the gentle manipulation of arms, legs and necks, with the verbal instructions to relax. Any sign of approximating relaxed behavior was given immediate verbal reinforcement and, eventually, the children learned to relax on verbal instruction alone. (Graziano, 1974, p. 170)

The first training session was about one minute in duration, increasing daily until a criterion of five consecutive minutes of relaxation had been reached for 12 consecutive training sessions. Relaxation involved the child's being quiet, without talking or squirming, and with no perceptible rigidity or tension in the muscles of the arms, legs, shoulders, and stomach.

The operational definition above gives a description of the procedures used with the subjects and the criteria to be achieved. Although wordy, this operational definition does serve the purpose of giving researchers a clear set of operations or instructions to define the independent variable. Once the independent variable is operationally defined, we refer to it simply as "relaxation training" with the understanding that it refers to the entire set of procedures. A good operational definition of a procedure defines the procedure so precisely that another researcher could perform the same procedure by simply following the description. Good operational definitions make replication of research possible.

In the study of disruptive behavior in autistic children, an operational definition for the dependent variable of disruptive behavior was also needed. In a staff-training manual, disruptive behavior had been defined in terms of its frequency, duration, and intensity, as follows:

> Disruptive behavior is any observed, sudden change in a child's behavior from calm, quiet, cooperative, and appropriate behavior to explosive, loud, screaming and tantrums, including sudden attacks on people, smashing and throwing objects, throwing oneself into walls, or on the floor, self-abuse such as head-banging, biting, scratching, picking sores and so on, all carried out in rapid, near "frenzied" manner. Each disruptive behavior incident will be considered to have ended when the child has returned to the previous level of calm, appropriate behavior for at least three consecutive minutes.
>
> **Frequency**—Each occurrence of disruptive behavior is recorded as a single event. The frequency score per child is then the total number of events.
>
> **Duration**—Each disruptive event is timed by stopwatch from the observed beginning to its end, as defined above.
>
> **Intensity**—Each disruptive event is rated by the observers on a three-point scale of intensity: low, moderate, high. The rating is made immediately after the event is over and is made for the perceived peak of intensity for the incident.

It is important to note that developing an operational definition involves a combination of drawing on the wisdom reflected in past research and making some arbitrary decisions. The arbitrary decisions should be based on an analysis of how best to measure a variable from both a theoretical and a practical sense. For example, the decision to set the relaxation criterion at five consecutive minutes for 12 consecutive sessions is partly judgmental. Instructions to use a "soft, gentle, calm, voice" leave some margin for interpretation by other researchers who may want to replicate the study. Perhaps with more research on the use of relaxation with autistic children, we will be able to define the variables operationally in a more precise manner. The point is that operational definitions used in research vary in constraint. Under some conditions, such as in nonlaboratory settings, it is more difficult to create precise op-

---

Box 4.1   **Some Examples of Operational Definitions**

Independent and dependent variables should be defined in terms of how they are to be measured (i.e., defined operationally). A variable can be operationally defined in different ways depending upon the particular questions being asked in any research project. Different operational definitions of the same concepts lead to different procedures and thus to different studies. Several examples follow.

Variable	Operational Definition
Anxiety	1. A physiological measure such as heart rate
	2. A self-rating score of anxiety
	3. Behavioral observation of avoidance behavior
Aggression in children	1. Ratings of aggressive behavior made by the child's teacher
	2. Direct observation during play period of the number of times a child hits, pushes, or forcibly takes toys from other children
	3. Child's rate of hitting a punching doll in an experimental situation
	4. The number of acts of aggression in stories created by subjects in response to pictures in an experimental situation
Obesity	1. The Pinch Test—a measures of fat folds at waist
	2. Water Immersion—volume of water displaced by submerged subject
	3. Subject's height/weight ratio compared with standard charts
Intelligence	1. Score on a standardized IQ test
	2. Judgment by others of person's ability to solve social problems
	3. Grades in school

---

erational definitions for the variables. Under other conditions, such as in measuring physiological responses to a series of carefully constructed visual stimuli in a laboratory, we can operationally define both variables far more precisely. In any study, the researcher should operationally define the independent and dependent variables as clearly and precisely as possible. The completeness and detail of operational definitions will depend to a great extent on the nature of the issues being investigated, the subjects used, and the settings in which the observations are made.

It should be noted that if we are not careful, we could create operational definitions that do not work or are not very useful. For example, suppose that students in their first research project tried to measure intelligence using a short test that they constructed. This test can be their operational definition for intelligence, but is it a valid one? Unless we have some indication of the validity of the measure, it might not be a very useful operational definition.

As shown in Box 4.1, most concepts may be operationally defined in several ways. Each one can lead to different procedures and thus different research projects. For example, in studies of obesity in children (e.g., Epstein, Valoski, Wing, & McCurley, 1994), a number of different measures of obesity could be used (Wang, Heshka, Pierson, & Heynsfield, 1995). In this way, many aspects of a problem statement can be investigated.

Reliability, Effective Range, and Validity

Whatever we wish to measure, it is important that we do so in such a way that the measure would agree with anyone else's measure of the same variable measured in the same way. The reproducibility factor of the measure is referred to as the *reliability* of the measure. In measuring weight, for example, a scale is said to be reliable if it always gives the same reading when measuring the same object, assuming the object remains constant in weight. Because a person's weight fluctuates, we might want to use some standard that is unlikely to fluctuate (e.g., a 100-pound lead weight) to test the reliability of the scale. If the scales are of the type that can be adjusted, we can also use a standard weight to standardize the measuring instrument so that it reads the correct weight for any standard we put on the scale.

The same procedure can be used to establish the reliability of many other kinds of psychological measures. If the measure involves some sort of rating of behavior by a human observer, it is necessary to have at least two observers independently rate the same sample of behavior to see how well they agree with one another. To rate independently of one another, both raters must be blind to the ratings of the other. This type of reliability is referred to as *interrater reliability* and should be evaluated whenever a rating or judgment is required of the researcher. A measure is not wholly reliable or unreliable but, rather, varies in its degree of reliability. If two raters always agree with one another, then the interrater reliability is perfect. If their ratings are unrelated to one another, then the interrater reliability is zero. However, the actual level of reliability is likely to be somewhere in between. The concept of interrater reliability is illustrated graphically in Figure 4.1. A correlation coefficient can be used to quantify the degree of reliability—although other, more sophisticated indices are also available (see Nunnally & Bernstein, 1993).

If we measure variables that should be stable over time, then a reliable measure of the variables should give the same reading at different points in time. Measuring a group of subjects on that variable at time 1 and then remeasuring the same subjects at some later point in time requires the measures to be consistent. This type of reliability is known as *test-retest reliability*. Like interrater reliability, test-retest reliability is not an all-or-nothing phenomenon and is usually quantified with a correlation coeffi-

Figure 4.1   Illustration of Interrater Reliability Concept

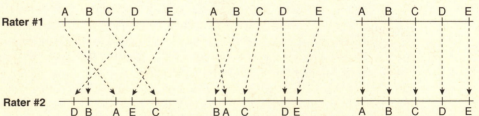

There are two raters (#1 and #2) and five subjects (A, B, C, D, and E) in this illustration. Each horizontal line represents a scale on which the subjects were rated by one of the raters. Note that in the third example, where there is perfect interrater reliability, the two raters independently rated the five subjects the same on this scale. The more disagreement that is shown in the ratings, the lower the interrater reliability.

cient. If you change the labels in Figure 4.1 of Rater #1 and Rater #2 to Time #1 and Time #2, you will have a graphical representation of test-retest reliability.

Another type of reliability is referred to as *internal consistency reliability,* which is relevant when we make several observations to obtain a score for each subject. This might be the case if we had subjects complete a test with several items or if we observed their behavior under several different conditions. Internal consistency reliability is high if each of the items or behavioral observations correlates with the other observations—that is, if all of the items are measuring the same thing. A measure that is internally consistent measures one construct with several independent observations or items. Discussing all the ramifications of internal consistency reliability is beyond the scope of this book, but one principle important in research should be mentioned. Generally speaking, *the more observations we make to obtain a score for a person, the greater will be the reliability of that score.* Take for example the typical tests that are used in courses to determine the grade for each student. The test could be considered an operational definition of the level of knowledge of the students in that particular course. A test with many questions covering all of the different topics in the course should give a consistent indication of how much students know. Asking only one or two questions, on the other hand, will not provide the same level of consistency, because it is possible that students will misinterpret any given question and answer it incorrectly even though they know the material. This same principle holds for behavioral observations as well. It is better to have several observations of behavior on which to base the measurement of a construct than to rely on only a few.

The concept of reliability of measures is critical in research because if the measures we use in a study are not reliable then the study cannot produce useful information. The factors that contribute to reliability include (1) the precision and clarity of the operational definition of the construct, (2) the care with which we carry out the measures and the precision with which we follow the procedures outlined in the operational definition, and (3) the number of independent observations on which the score is based. [Discussion of all the potential issues in measuring and improving the reliability of measures is beyond the scope of this book. See Anastasi (1988) for further discussion.]

Another factor to consider in measuring variables is the *effective range* of the scale. If we are interested in weight changes in people, a normal bathroom scale will usually have sufficient range because it typically can weigh objects between 0 and 300 pounds. But weighing very large or very small objects (like elephants or mice) would require different scales, scales capable of accurately measuring weight in whatever range necessary. Although the concept of weight is the same for both mice and elephants, it is unlikely that a scale constructed to measure one can also measure the other. The heavy duty construction required of a scale to measure an elephant would make the scale quite insensitive to the relatively light weight of a mouse. The same is true of most psychological measures. A test of mathematical skills sensitive enough to detect different skill levels in college math majors would be too difficult to detect differences in math skills among third-grade students. A measure of social skills designed for use with children would probably not be appropriate for use with adults. A measure of memory ability challenging enough to detect differences in college students would be too difficult to detect memory ability differences in retarded adults. Procedures designed to effect some change with one group of subjects, such as inducing anxiety or relaxation, may not be appropriate for other subjects. The procedures lack the range to work with any and all subjects. When designing or selecting measures for research, therefore, we must keep in mind who the subjects will be so that we can select measures that will be sensitive to the differences in the variables the subjects are likely to show.

The third factor that must be considered is the *validity* of the measure. When we say that the scale to measure weight is valid, we mean that the scale does indeed measure what it is supposed to measure—weight. Validity is not the same as reliability, which refers to how consistently the weight is measured. A scale for measuring weight, for example, might not be properly adjusted, thereby giving a reading 10 pounds lighter than the object really is. The scale is reliable if it consistently gives the same weight, but it is not valid because that weight is not the true weight. It is important to note that *a measure cannot be a valid measure unless it is a reliable measure, but a measure can be reliable without being a valid measure of the variable of interest.* It is also important to realize that validity, like reliability, is not an all-or-nothing concept. There are degrees of validity from none to perfect validity. Once again, a correlation coefficient is used most often to quantify the degree of validity.

As we will see in Chapter 8, validity can also be used in a more general way. We can evaluate the ability of a measure to predict some other variable. For example, we might want to know if SAT scores really do predict performance in college. We call the variable that we are predicting the *criterion;* we call the measure used to predict the criterion the *predictor measure.* Figure 4.2 illustrates graphically levels of validity. Notice the similarity between Figure 4.1 (illustrating reliability) and Figure 4.2 (illustrating validity). When we use the concept of validity in the broader sense, we must always specify the criterion measure. For example, the SAT score may be a valid predictor of freshman college grades. It probably is a less valid predictor of whether a student completes college because many factors besides ability determine this criterion. Finally, the SAT is probably not a valid predictor of the number of friends a student has or how happy the student is.

Figure 4.2   Illustration of Validity Concept

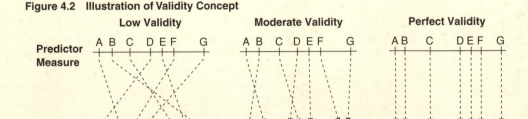

There are two measures (the predictor and the criterion) and seven subjects (A, B, C, D, E, F, and G). The top horizontal line represents the scale for the predictor measure, and the bottom horizontal line represents the scale for the criterion measure. Note that in the third example, where there is perfect validity, the ordering of the seven subjects is identical on the predictor and criterion measures. The more disagreement that is shown in the rank ordering of subjects on the predictor and criterion measures, the lower the validity.

Scale Attenuation Effects

A problem related to the effective range of a measure is *scale attenuation effects.* In this context, *attenuation* refers to restricting the range of a scale. Using a measuring scale with a restricted range—not ranging high enough or low enough or both—can result in data showing subjects bunched up near the top or bottom of the scale. For example, suppose that we are conducting a study on changing high school students' attitudes toward tobacco use. For obvious health reasons, we hope to bring about more negative attitudes. We administer our pretest of negative attitudes toward to-bacco use, and we find that virtually all subjects score very near the top of the scale. The subjects show at pretest, at least as measured by that scale, already high nega-tive attitudes toward tobacco use. Suppose we then proceed to apply the attitude change intervention and take post-intervention measures of attitudes. The posttest results cannot possibly show much change toward greater negative attitudes even if the intervention is highly effective. The subjects, already at the top of the scale be-fore the intervention, simply have no room to show change toward still higher scores. This direction of scale attenuation is called a *ceiling effect.* It should be clear that such a restricted scale will have serious effects on the research findings.

A scale can also be attenuated by having a restricted lower range, thus creating a possible *floor effect.* In this situation, subjects would tend to score near the bottom of the scale only because the scale does not allow a sufficiently low range. A floor effect would occur if an instructor gave an examination that was too difficult for the class and almost all students scored low. That is, if the scale had a greater lower range, the stu-dents' scores might be more spread out rather than bunched at the bottom of the scale.

Ceiling and floor effects are illustrated graphically with a simple example in Fig-ure 4.3. The true weights of each of ten people are illustrated in the first panel by the height of a bar. The second and third panels illustrate what would happen if there were a ceiling or floor effect, respectively. In this example a ceiling effect occurs if the scale read weights up to only 200 pounds. A floor effect occurs if the needle stuck so that it never read below 120 pounds, for example, even if the person on the scale was lighter. Notice how the scores are compressed by both floor and ceiling effects and that scores for people outside the effective range are not accurate repre-sentations of reality.

Figure 4.3   Illustration of Floor and Ceiling Effects

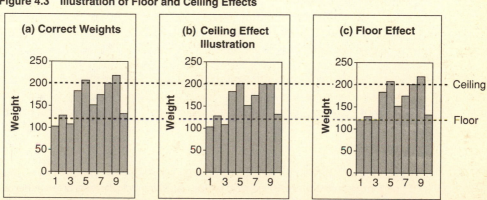

Ceiling and floor effects (scale attenuation effects) restrict the range of possible scores for subjects' responses—that is, they reduce the potential variability of the data. As we will discuss at some length in Chapter 10, restricting variability results in serious errors. Sufficient variability is essential in research.

THE NEED FOR OBJECTIVE MEASUREMENT

Every science stresses the need for objectivity, or *objective measures,* but often scientists do not make clear why objectivity is so important. Vague references to how objectivity is somehow more accurate than subjectivity are common, but *why* is it more accurate? One reason is that subjective measures are person-specific—that is, they represent the judgments of only one person. If other people in the same situation make different judgments, the findings will not be reproducible.

A hallmark of science is that the laws of nature should hold, no matter who tests them. There may be many reasons why two people disagree on their subjective impression of a phenomenon. If we take an example from physics, the judgment of temperature, Julie might judge a room to be hotter than Jenny because Julie is accustomed to cooler temperatures and so by comparison the room seems hot. Another reason for Julie and Jenny's disagreement about the temperature of a room might be a differential sensitivity to features other than heat, such as humidity. Yet another reason might be a physiological deficiency in the ability of one or both to sense temperature. Even with something as simple as temperature, subjective impressions pose many problems. If an objective measure of temperature (the thermometer) had not been developed, most of the physical laws relating temperature to other phenomena would have remained undiscovered. The thermometer measures temperature independently of other variables such as humidity. It can measure temperature reliably and across a much greater range than we could accomplish without such an instrument. Finally, the thermometer provides at least an interval scale of measurement of temperature. Although this concept may be difficult to grasp on the basis of our brief discussion, it is important to note that an interval scale greatly simplifies the mathematical description of the relationship of temperature to hundreds of other physical phenomena.

If so many problems can emerge with subjective measures when considering as relatively simple an issue as temperature, imagine the problems that might arise when trying to measure some complicated construct in psychology, such as self-esteem. Many phenomena that psychologists need to measure are events that all people have feelings about. These feelings can systematically distort perceptions of the phenomena. For example, a person who is easily upset by an angry outburst might be more sensitive to the presence of anger in an individual who is being frustrated as part of a study on frustration and aggression. Good research, therefore, demands objective measures that can be performed by anyone properly trained to use them and that give the same results regardless of who does the measuring.

Statistical Analyses

The use of mathematics and statistical procedures are central in modern research. They are powerful tools for accurately describing phenomena. They also provide objective ways of evaluating patterns of events by computing the probability of observing such patterns by chance alone. Insisting on the use of statistical analyses on which to draw conclusions is an extension of the argument that objectivity is critical in science. (In Chapter 5 we will discuss some basic statistical procedures.)

SUMMARY

In research we study relationships between variables. A variable is one or more sets of events that the researcher manipulates and/or observes and measures. To assess variables and their relationship to other variables, it is necessary to quantify our observations of the variables. The quantification process (measurement) involves application of the real number system, with all of its characteristics, to the variable, with all of its characteristics. The number system has many properties—identity, magnitude, equal intervals, and absolute zero. But the characteristics of variables seldom perfectly match the properties of the real number system. Consequently, in applying the real number system to variables (i.e., in measurement), we find that some variables match the number system well whereas others do not. Four levels of matching in measurement have been described: nominal, ordinal, interval, and ratio measurements.

After the observations have been quantified and the level of measurement determined, the selection of an appropriate statistical test is a fairly straightforward decision. (Selecting statistical tests will be discussed further in Chapter 14.)

The operational definition for a psychological variable describes precisely what operations will be performed to measure the variable. The specifications should be as precise as possible to reduce the likelihood of inaccurate measurement, to increase the reliability and validity of the measure, and to make replication of the research possible. The reliability of a measure is an index of how consistent the measure is. The validity of the measure is its effectiveness in tapping the characteristic measured. A measure cannot be valid unless it is first reliable, but a measure can be reliable without being valid.

Objectivity is essential in scientific research. Well-conceived operational definitions of variables can improve objectivity. Statistical procedures provide objectivity in the analysis of data. Objectivity will normally improve reliability and make it more likely that researchers can discover valid relationships between variables.

REVIEW EXERCISES

4.1   **Define the following key terms. Be sure you understand them. They are discussed in the chapter and defined in the glossary.**

variable	nominal data
scales of measurement	categorical data
nominal measurement	ordered data
ordinal measurement	score data
interval measurement	measurement error
ratio measurement	response-set biases
data	social desirability

operational definition
reliability
  interrater reliability
  test-retest reliability
  internal consistency reliability
effective range
validity

criterion
predictor measure
scale attenuation effects
  ceiling effect
  floor effect
objective measures

4.2   Answer each of the following. Check your answer in the chapter.

1. What is the major task in measurement?
2. Explain this statement: "In measuring variables, the researcher works with two major sets of information."
3. What are the important characteristics of the abstract number system?
4. Why is it important in measurement to match the characteristics of the dependent variable with those of the number system?
5. What type of data is generated by each level of measurement?
6. Define reliability and the different types of reliability.

4.3   Think about and work each of the following problems.

1. Following is a list of possible dependent variables. For each one, identify its level of measurement and the type of data it generates. Be sure that you understand why each is at the level you indicate.
   a. Number of disruptive outbursts
   b. Time needed (number of seconds) for a response to occur
   c. Place or position of each runner at the end of a race
   d. Speed of each runner during the race
   e. Annual income of subjects
   f. Car preference of each subject
2. Following are brief descriptions of research projects. For each one identify the (i) independent variable and type of independent variable it is, (ii) dependent variable(s), (iii) level of measurement and type of data for each dependent variable.
   a. In a study on the effects of television violence on aggressive behavior, schoolchildren are assigned to two conditions. In condition A, the subjects watch a typical half-hour of television in which eight violent acts are portrayed (aggressive TV condition); in condition B, the subjects watch a half-hour of television in which no violent acts are portrayed (nonaggressive TV condition). Following each TV condition, the subjects in each condition are observed in a playroom. Observers record all aggressive acts. The hypotheses are that the group exposed to aggressive TV (i) will have a greater number of aggressive acts and (ii) will perform acts rated as more highly aggressive in nature than the subjects in the nonaggressive TV condition. The rating will be done using a five-point rating scale in which the units are not equal intervals.
   b. College students are observed as they try to solve a series of puzzles. The subjects are compared on how many minutes it takes each to solve all the problems. One-third of the subjects are told they will be paid more if they solve the problems quickly; one-third are told they will be paid a fixed amount; and one-third are not told anything about being paid.
3. How would you explain to someone who does not know measurement that an IQ of 140 does not indicate twice as much intelligence as an IQ of 70?
4. Write an operational definition for each of the following variables:
   a. Racial attitudes
   b. Ego
   c. Intelligence

    d. Criminality
    e. Neurosis
    f. Hyperactivity
    g. Age
    h. Aggression
    i. Reading ability
    j. Creativity
    k. Fear
    l. Deafness

5. Identify at least 10 situations where one might experience problems with a dependent measure because the measure has a restriction of range problem.

6. For each of the following variables (i) write an operational definition for a subjective measure of the variable, (ii) write a second operational definition for an objective measure of the same variable, and (iii) identify potential problems with the subjective measure that might distort the data if it were to be used in an actual study:

the subject's ambivalence regarding their career goals

the degree of frustration experienced while engaging in a laboratory task

competitiveness

alertness.

7. Write three operational definitions for each of the following variables—one that produces nominal data, one that produces ordinal data, and one that produces score data:

a potential little league player's baseball skill

the strength of one's social support network

a rat's level of hunger

the level of conflict in an business environment.

Chapter
5

Statistical Analysis of Data

Once a decision on how to measure the research variables is made, the next step in designing research is to determine how to analyze the data statistically. *Statistics* are powerful tools for organizing and understanding sets of data. They provide ways to represent and describe groups, summarize results, and evaluate data. Without the use of statistics, little could be learned from most studies.

It is important to understand that statistical procedures and research design are interrelated: the plan for statistical analyses should be included as part of the research design. The decisions concerning which statistical procedures to use are made in the procedures-design phase as an integral part of the research design and are not something "tacked on" after data collection. Although this chapter review cannot replace a course in statistics, it is designed to introduce some basic statistical concepts (or refresh your memory of them) and to place statistical analyses in the context of research design. This chapter is supplemented by an appendix describing computational procedures (Appendix C) and a second appendix describing the use of a popular statistical analysis computer program (*SPSS for Windows*, briefly summarized in Appendix D). We will introduce many basic statistical concepts in this chapter, but will discuss more sophisticated statistical procedures in later chapters.

There are two major uses of statistical procedures: (1) *descriptive statistics*, which simplify and organize data, and (2) *inferential statistics*, which go beyond simple description to help us make inferences about the population represented by the data. Both descriptive and inferential statistics are important tools for the research scientist.

INDIVIDUAL DIFFERENCES AND STATISTICAL PROCEDURES

Statistical procedures depend on variability or differences in responses among subjects. No two subjects or groups will respond in exactly the same manner. Suppose, for example, we are studying the effects of memory training. We predict that subjects given special training will perform better on a memory task than those who are not trained. In a study designed to test the hypothesis, subjects are assigned to one of two conditions: (1) memory training or (2) no training. The dependent measure is a memory test. Let us suppose the test yields scores from 0 to 100. Hypothetical data are shown in Table 5.1. We see in Table 5.1 that there is a difference in mean (average) scores between the groups. There is also considerable variability of scores within each group. That is, the scores in Group A range from 66 to 98 and those in Group B range from 56 to 94. The variation within each group illustrates that there are *individual differences* in memory skills. Some people, with or without training, remember well; others remember very little; most people fall somewhere in between. All subject variables that we study in psychology—anxiety, intelligence, reaction time, social skills, hormonal levels, and so on—show individual differences. Therefore, in the study of the hypothesized effects of memory training on memory, we cannot be sure whether the memory training is the reason for the apparent differences

TABLE 5.1   HYPOTHETICAL DATA AND DESCRIPTIVE STATISTICS FOR TEST RE-
SULTS FROM TRAINED AND NONTRAINED SUBJECTS

	Group A (trained)	Group B (nontrained)
	98	94
	93	88
	90	82
	89	77
	87	75
	87	74
	84	72
	81	72
	78	67
	71	61
	66	56
Median	87	74
Mode	87	72
Mean	84	74.36

between the groups, or whether the subjects in the training group have better memories and would have performed better regardless of the training. Most of the variables manipulated in psychology make only small differences in how people perform, compared with the individual differences that already exist between people. Statistics help us decide whether differences on our dependent measures between groups are due to the research manipulations or are merely the result of existing individual differences.

Research studies generate many measures or scores, which will typically vary from subject to subject. With so many measurements and so much variability, a way is needed to organize and simplify the numbers. *Descriptive statistics* summarize, simplify, and describe a large number of measurements. *Inferential statistics,* on the other hand, help us interpret what the data mean. For example, in the study on memory training, the means (a descriptive statistic) of the two groups are different, with the trained group showing a higher mean score than the nontrained group (as predicted by our hypothesis). But we want to know whether that mean difference is large enough so that we suspect it is due to more than chance variation among subjects. That is, is the difference we found between the groups so large that the difference probably did not occur by chance? Inferential statistics are used to help answer such questions.

DESCRIPTIVE STATISTICS

There are three important groups of descriptive statistics: (1) frequency counts and frequency distributions, (2) graphical representations of data, and (3) summary statistics. Each of these descriptive statistics will be illustrated with the hypothetical

TABLE 5.2   DATA FROM 24 RANDOMLY SELECTED SUBJECTS

Subject	Age	Income	Number of Times Voted in Last Five Years	Sex	Political Affiliation
1	28	17,000	6	M	R
2	46	34,000	4	M	D
3	33	28,000	0	F	D
4	40	29,000	5	M	R
5	21	14,000	1	M	R
6	26	19,000	0	F	O
7	39	26,000	6	M	O
8	23	17,000	0	F	D
9	20	11,000	1	M	O
10	26	15,000	2	M	R
11	29	23,000	6	F	R
12	24	18,000	2	M	D
13	34	28,000	2	M	O
14	35	29,000	3	M	O
15	52	30,000	8	M	O
16	31	23,000	4	F	D
17	30	27,000	6	M	R
18	45	31,000	7	F	D
19	18	12,000	0	M	O
20	29	28,000	7	M	R
21	26	22,000	6	F	D
22	23	21,000	3	M	O
23	47	32,000	7	M	D
24	53	35,000	8	M	D

data in Table 5.2, which represent responses from 24 subjects, aged 18 and above, selected at random from the population of a moderate-sized city. The researchers are interested in variables that may relate to voting patterns. The information gathered from each subject included (1) the subject's age, (2) the subject's income, (3) the number of times he or she had voted in the last five years, (4) the subject's sex, and (5) the political affiliation of the subject (coded as Democrat, Republican, or other).

What type of data do each of these variables generate? The subject's age, income, and the number of times voted are measured on a ratio scale (score data). Each of these variables has the property of magnitude (34 is older than 25, $20,000 is more than $15,000, and so on). All three variables have the property of equal intervals (e.g., the difference in age between 25 and 20 is the same as the difference between 38 and 33). The variables are measured on ratio scales because they have

TABLE 5.3   FREQUENCY OF MALES AND FEMALES IN OUR SAMPLE

	Males	Females	Total
Frequency	17	7	24
Percentage	71%	29%	100%

not only the property of equal intervals but they each have a true zero point. A person who is zero years old is just being born; a person whose income is zero doesn't earn anything; a person who has voted zero times in the last five years has not voted in that time. The other two variables, sex of the subject and political affiliation, are measured on nominal scales. These data are nominal or categorical, and there is no logical way of ordering the categories. (See the discussion in Chapter 4 on identifying scales of measurement.)

Frequency Counts and Distributions

Nominal and Ordinal Data   For most kinds of nominal or ordinal data, statistical simplification involves computing *frequencies* (i.e., the number of subjects who fall in each category). Table 5.3 shows the distribution of frequencies of biological sex for the data from Table 5.2. This *frequency distribution* was constructed using a statistical analysis package called *SPSS for Windows.* We will be using this program throughout this chapter and at several points later in the text. Appendix D describes the procedures for data entry and computation of these and other descriptive and inferential statistics.

Note that in any frequency distribution, when we sum across all categories, the total should always be equal to the number of subjects initially measured. It is often helpful to convert frequencies to percentages. This is done by dividing the frequency in each cell by the total number of subjects and multiplying each of these proportions by 100, as has been done in Table 5.3.

Sometimes it is useful to categorize subjects on the basis of more than one variable at the same time. This is called *cross-tabulation.* For example, subjects can be categorized on the basis of each subject's sex and political affiliation. Cross-tabulation can help us to see relationships between nominal measures. In our example, we have two levels of the variable sex (male and female) and three levels of the variable political affiliation (Democrat, Republican, and other) giving a total of six (2×3) possible joint categories. The data are arranged in a 2×3 matrix in Table 5.4 where the numbers in the matrix are the frequency of people in each of the joint categories. For example, the first cell represents the number of male Democrats. Note that the sum of all the frequencies in the six cells equals the total number of subjects. Also note that the row and column totals represent the *univariate* (one-variable) frequency distribution for the political affiliation and biological sex variables, respectively. For example, the column totals in Table 5.4 of 17 males and 7 females represent the frequency distribution for the single variable of sex and, not surprisingly, are the same numbers that appear in Table 5.3.

TABLE 5.4   CROSS-TABULATION BY SEX AND EXPRESSED POLITICAL AFFILIA-
TION FOR OUR 24 SUBJECTS

	Males	Females	Total
Democrats	4	5	9
Republicans	6	1	7
Other	7	1	8
Totals	17	7	24

TABLE 5.5   FREQUENCY DISTRIBUTION FOR THE VARIABLE OF THE NUMBER
OF TIMES SUBJECT VOTED IN LAST FIVE YEARS

Number of Times Voted	Frequency
8	2
7	3
6	5
5	1
4	2
3	2
2	3
1	2
0	4

Score Data   Different kinds of statistical procedures are used with score data. The simplest way to organize a set of score data is to create a frequency distribution. If we look at the variable "number of times a subject voted in the last five years" shown in Table 5.2, we will probably find it difficult to organize all 24 scores. Note that some of the subjects have not voted at all during that time, whereas two subjects voted eight times, but where do the rest of the subjects tend to fall? A frequency distribution will organize the data to answer a question like this at a glance. *Frequency distributions* list each possible score and the frequency of that score in a given group of subjects. There may be no subjects for some of the scores, in which case the frequency listed for the score would be zero. Table 5.5 shows the frequency distribution for the number of times subjects voted in the last five years.

If there is a large number of possible scores, such as 25 or more, between the lowest and the highest scores, then the frequency table will be very long and almost as difficult to read as the original raw data. In this situation, we use a *grouped frequency distribution,* which shortens the table to a more manageable size by grouping the scores into intervals, usually about 15 intervals. A grouped frequency distribution is required if you are working with a *continuous variable.* In a continuous variable there are theoretically an infinite number of possible scores between the lowest and the highest score. Table 5.6 shows a grouped frequency distribution for the variable of income. This is a continuous variable ranging from $11,000 to $35,000. Grouping the salary range into intervals of approximately $2,000 gives us about a dozen intervals. A grouped frequency distribution can be constructed easily

TABLE 5.6   GROUPED FREQUENCY DISTRIBUTION FOR THE VARIABLE
OF INCOME

Annual Income	Frequency
$34,000–35,999	2
$32,000–33,999	1
$30,000–31,999	2
$28,000–29,999	5
$26,000–27,999	2
$24,000–25,999	0
$22,000–23,999	3
$20,000–21,999	1
$18,000–19,999	2
$16,000–17,999	2
$14,000–15,999	2
$12,000–13,999	1
$10,000–11,999	1

from the frequency distribution generated by a statistical analysis package like *SPSS for Windows.*

Graphical Representation of Data

A Chinese proverb states "one picture is worth a thousand words" (Bartlett, 1980), and this is especially true when dealing with statistical information. Graphs often clarify a data set or help us to interpret a summary statistic or statistical test. Most people find graphic representations much simpler to understand than other statistical procedures. We strongly encourage the use of *graphs* and *tables* as supplements to other statistical procedures.

Frequency or grouped frequency distributions can be represented graphically by using either a *histogram* or a *frequency polygon.* Figure 5.1 shows both a histogram and a frequency polygon representing the voting data summarized in Table 5.5. These were generated in just a few seconds using *SPSS for Windows.* These figures are the actual output of the *SPSS for Windows* program as it would be seen on the computer screen. Both the histogram and the frequency polygon represent data on a two-dimensional graph where the horizontal axis (x-*axis* or *abscissa*) represents the range of scores for the variable and the vertical axis (y-*axis* or *ordinate*) represents the frequency of the scores. In a histogram, the frequency of a given score is represented by the height of a bar above that score as shown in Figure 5.1(a). In the frequency polygon, the frequency is indicated by the height of a point above each score on the abscissa. The frequency polygon is then completed by connecting the adjacent points, as shown in Figure 5.1(b). To aid in the interpretation of histograms and frequency polygons, it is important to label both axes carefully.

One can also graph two frequency distributions on the same graph. To compare the distributions, each is graphed independently with different colors or different types of lines (e.g., solid versus dotted) to distinguish one distribution from the other.

Figure 5.1   Examples of a Histogram and a Frequency Polygon

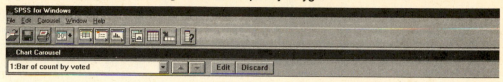

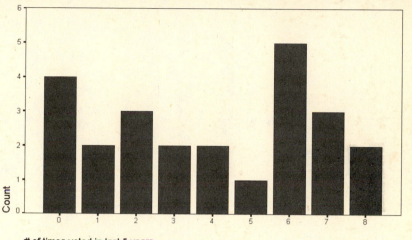

# of times voted in last 5 years

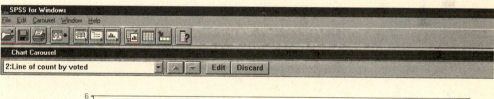

# of times voted in last 5 years

Figure 5.2   An Example of Using Histograms to Compare Two Distributions

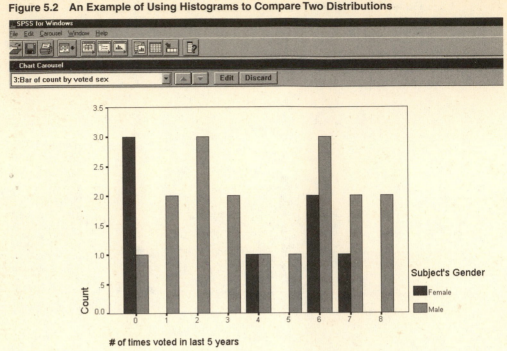

# of times voted in last 5 years

Figure 5.2 shows the distribution for the variable "number of times voted in the last five years" separately for males and females.

With small group sizes, the frequency polygon is usually jagged. There is an overall shape to the distribution, but the lines connecting the points will go up and down from one interval to another. The distributions graphed in Figure 5.1 and Figure 5.2 have this jagged appearance. As the group size increases, the frequency polygon tends to look more like a smooth curve. Data in textbooks are often described by drawing smooth curves, even though such curves are seen only when the group sizes are extremely large.

Figure 5.3 represents several different smooth-curve drawings of frequency polygons illustrating various distribution shapes. Figure 5.3(a) shows a common shape for a *symmetric distribution,* a bell-shaped curve. In a bell-shaped curve, most of the subjects are near the middle of the distribution. Distributions with this shape are referred to as normal curves or *normal distributions.* The normal curve is actually a mathematical curve defined by an equation, but many variables in psychology form distributions similar in shape to a true normal curve. Figure 5.3(b) and Figure 5.3(c) represent *skewed distributions.* In a skewed distribution, the scores tend to pile up on one end of the distribution. The direction of the skewness is indicated by the tail of the curve. In Figure 5.3(b) the curve is *positively skewed,* with most of the scores piled up near the bottom (the tail points toward the high or positive end of the scale, thus the distribution is positively skewed). Figure 5.3(c) is *negatively skewed.* Note the tail is toward the negative end of the scale. We might see

Figure 5.3   Examples of Symmetric and Skewed Distributions

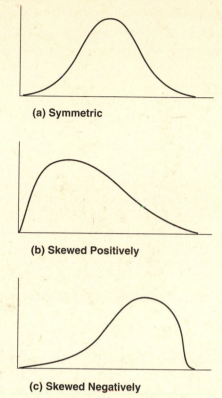

(a) Symmetric

(b) Skewed Positively

(c) Skewed Negatively

such distributions on an easy classroom test where almost everyone does well and only a few people do poorly.

These are the distribution shapes most likely seen when variables of interest to psychologists are measured. In addition to the shape of the curve, we describe distributions in terms of the location of the middle of the distribution on the *x*-axis (the *central tendency* of the distribution) and their horizontal spread (the *variability* of the distribution).[1]

Summary Statistics

Summary statistics serve two purposes. The first is to describe the data with just one or two numbers, which makes it easier to compare groups. The second is to provide a basis for later analyses in which inferential statistics will be used. Normally, a measure of central tendency and a measure of variability are computed.

Measures of Central Tendency: Mode, Median, and Mean   Measures of central tendency describe the typical or average score—that is, they summarize the data. They are called measures of central tendency because they provide an indication of the center of the distribution where most of the scores tend to cluster. There are three measures of central tendency used in describing psychological data: the

[1]An excellent book on graphical presentation of data is Tufte (1983).

TABLE 5.7 MEASURES OF CENTRAL TENDENCY

Mode	The most frequently occurring score in a distribution
Median	The middle score in a distribution; the score at the 50th percentile
Mean	The arithmetic average of the scores in a distribution; computed by summing the scores and dividing by the number of scores

mode, the median, and the mean, which are summarized in Table 5.7. The *mode* is the most frequently occurring score in the distribution. In the example shown in Table 5.1, the mode for Group A is 87 and for Group B is 72. If the data are more complicated and a frequency distribution like the one in Table 5.5 has been prepared, the mode can be computed by finding the largest number in the frequency column and noting the score with that frequency. In Table 5.5 the mode is 6. A distribution may have more than one mode. If there are two, then the distribution is *bimodal;* if there are three, it is *trimodal.* The mode has the advantage of being easily computed but the disadvantage of being unstable, which means that it can be affected by a change in only one or two scores. The mode can be appropriately used with all scales of measurement.

A second measure of central tendency is the *median.* This is the middle score in a distribution where the scores have been arranged in order from lowest to highest. The median is also the 50th percentile, which means that half the scores fall below and half above the median. The median can be easily computed if there are few scores and they have been ordered from lowest to highest. With an odd number of scores, the median is the $(N + 1)/2$ score where N is the number of scores. In Table 5.1 there are 11 scores. Therefore, the sixth score $[(11 + 1)/2]$ will be the median. Note that the sixth score in a group of 11 scores will be exactly in the middle, with 5 scores above it and 5 scores below it. In Table 5.1 the median for Group A is 87; in Group B it is 74. When there are an even number of scores, there will be two middle scores; the median is the average of the two middle scores. The median can be appropriately used with ordered and score data but not with nominal data.

The most commonly used measure of central tendency is the *mean*—the arithmetic average of all of the scores. The mean is computed by summing the scores and dividing by the number of scores as follows:

$$Mean = \overline{X} = \frac{\sum X}{N} \tag{5.1}$$

The term $\overline{X}$ (read "X bar") is the notation for the mean. The term $\sum X$ (read "sigma X") is the summation notation and simply means to add all the scores. Table 5.8 shows a sample computation of a mean. The mean is appropriately used only with score data.

The mean and the median are frequently used to describe the average score. The median gives a better indication of what the typical score is if there are some deviant scores in the distribution (i.e., unusually high or low). This property is shown in the example given in Table 5.9. The mean, on the other hand, is more useful in other statistical procedures such as inferential statistics.

Measures of Variability: Range, Variance, and Standard Deviation In addition to measures of central tendency, it is also important to determine the variability of

TABLE 5.8   SAMPLE COMPUTATION OF A MEAN

Compute the mean for the following ten scores: 12, 7, 8, 5, 10, 8, 9, 13, 9, 6

1. Start by listing the scores in no particular order in a column labeled X at the top.
2. Sum the column.
3. Use the computational formula below to compute the mean.

X
12
7
8
5
10
8
9
13
9
6

$$\sum X = 87$$

Computing the mean

$$\bar{X} = \frac{\sum X}{N} = \frac{87}{10} = 8.7$$

TABLE 5.9   AN ILLUSTRATIVE EXAMPLE OF THE EFFECTS OF A SINGLE DE-
VIANT SCORE ON THE MEAN AND THE MEDIAN

Assume we have two companies (Company A and Company B), each with five
employees. Listed below are the salaries of each employee in each company.

Company A	Company B
$16,000	$16,000
$18,000	$18,000
$20,000	$20,000
$22,000	$22,000
$24,000	$124,000

The salaries of the employees in both companies have been ordered for ease of
comparison between companies. Note that four of the salaries paid out to employees
are exactly the same in both companies. Only the top salary is different in the two
companies. In Company A the top salary is $24,000 where as in Company B the top
salary is $124,000. The mean salary is $20,000 in Company A and $40,000 in
Company B. The median (or middle) salary is the same for both companies ($20,000).
Which measure gives the most typical salary in each company?

Figure 5.4   An Example of Two Distributions with the Same Central Tendency but Different Levels of Variability

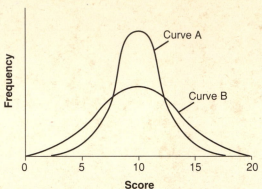

the scores. The concept of variability of scores is illustrated in Figure 5.4, which shows two distributions with identical means. However, curve A is narrower—the scores are bunched closer together. Curve B is more spread out than curve A; that is, the scores in curve B are more variable, have greater dispersion, or have a greater spread or range than does curve A. All of these are different ways of saying the same thing—variability of scores is greater in curve B than in curve A. Let us consider an example. If we compare the ages of people who attend county fairs and those who attend rock concerts, we would probably find that county fair–goers range from infants to people over 90 while rock concert–goers are mostly in their teens and early twenties, with few preteens and people over 30. Clearly, there is far more variability in the age of attendees at a county fair than at a typical rock concert.

Variability is one of the most important concepts in research. It is also a fact of life. Individuals differ from one another, and they differ in their responses to different stimuli. But this natural variability among subjects can often mask the effects of variables under study. Most of the sophisticated research designs and statistical procedures used in research were developed to control or minimize the effects of natural variability of scores.

But as critically important as the concept of variability is, it is an easy concept to understand. Subjects differ from one another, and those differences are reflected in differences in scores on whatever variable we are measuring. On some variables, there are large differences between subjects; on other variables, there are only small differences between subjects. For any given variable, there may be numerous reasons why scores among subjects vary as they do, but we need not worry about the reasons for the variability at this point. The important points to remember for now are that the scores do vary and that the degree of variability can be quantified.

Measures of variability—the *range,* the *average deviation,* the *variance,* and the *standard deviation*—are summarized in Table 5.10. The simplest measure of variability is the *range,* which is the distance from the lowest to the highest score. Although the range is easy to compute, it is too unstable to describe the variability in data because it depends on only two scores—the highest and the lowest. A single deviant score can dramatically affect the range of scores. For example, in Figure

TABLE 5.10   MEASURES OF VARIABILITY

Range	The distance from the lowest to the highest score in a distribution; may be specified by either giving both the lowest and highest scores or by subtracting the lowest from the highest score and reporting that value
Average deviation	The arithmetic average of the distance that each score is from the mean
Variance	Essentially the average squared distance from the mean; the variance is computed by summing the squared distances from the mean and dividing by the degrees of freedom (equal to the number of scores minus 1)
Standard deviation	The square root of the variance

5.4, the scores for curve A range from 4 to 16 (a range of 12) and the scores for curve B range from 1 to 19 (a range of 18). However, if one more score were added to curve A (a score of 22), the range for curves A and B would be equal. Still, even with the addition of this one deviant score, the scores are more tightly clustered or less variable in curve A than in curve B.

A better measure of variability is the *variance*. The variance utilizes all of the scores (instead of just the lowest and highest scores) in quantifying the degree of variability in the data, and it has the statistical properties that make it useful in inferential statistics. To begin our discussion of the variance, suppose that you have a set of scores (a sample), and you have calculated the mean of that sample. Now suppose that you ask a reasonable question about variability, "On average, how much do the scores in the sample differ from the mean of the sample?" It is a simple matter to find this value; just subtract the mean from each score (deviation), add up those deviations (ignoring the + and − signs), and find their average by dividing the sum of the deviations by the number of scores, as shown in the example in Table 5.11. We ignore the sign when adding the deviations because if the sign is not ignored the average deviation from the mean will always be zero no matter how variable the scores are—which would make the index useless. When you divide this sum by the number of scores, you get an *average deviation*. In Table 5.11, the scores differ from the mean by an average of 1.9 units. If we had a second sample in which the average deviation was 5.0, this second sample would clearly have greater variability compared with the sample in Table 5.11.

The average deviation is included here only to help explain the concept of deviation. It is never used in statistical analyses because it lacks the statistical qualities that would make it useful. Instead, the *variance* and *standard deviation* are used, both of which are based on the same concept of variability of scores from the mean. The variance is arrived at by squaring the deviations of the scores from the mean. That is, just as the average deviation measures the average deviation of each score from the mean, the *variance* measures the average squared deviation of each score from the mean. We square the deviations from the mean to make them all positive. The notation s^2 refers to variance. The formula for variance is:

$$s^2 = \frac{SS\ (Sum\ of\ Squares)}{df\ (Degrees\ of\ Freedom)} = \frac{\sum (X - \overline{X})^2}{N - 1} \tag{5.2}$$

TABLE 5.11 A COMPUTATIONAL EXAMPLE OF THE AVERAGE DEVIATION, THE
VARIANCE, AND THE STANDARD DEVIATION

Compute the average deviation, the variance, and the standard deviation for the data
from Table 5.8

Steps in computing the average deviation
1. Start by listing the scores in no particular order in a column labeled X at the top.
2. Compute the mean as was done in Table 5.8.
3. Label another column $|X - \bar{X}|$.
4. Compute the values of $|X - \bar{X}|$ then add up the numbers in the column. This total is
   the numerator of the average deviation formula.
5. Divide by the number of scores to get the average deviation.

Steps in computing the variance and standard deviation
1. Start by listing the scores in no particular order in a column labeled X at the top.
2. Compute the mean as was done in Table 5.8.
3. Label another column $|X - \bar{X}^2|$.
4. Compute the values of $|X - \bar{X}^2|$, then add up the numbers in the column. This total is
   the numerator for the variance computation.
5. Use Equation 5.2 to compute the variance and Equation 5.3 to compute the standard
   deviation.

X	$|X - \bar{X}|$	$(X - \bar{X})^2$
12	3.3	10.89
7	1.7	2.89
8	.7	.49
5	3.7	13.69
10	1.3	1.69
8	.7	.49
9	.3	.09
13	4.3	18.49
9	.3	.09
6	2.7	7.29
$\sum X = 87$	$\sum |X - \bar{X}| = 19.0$	$\sum (X - \bar{X})^2 = 56.10$

Formulae for computing the mean, average deviation, and variance

$$\bar{X} = \frac{\sum X}{N} = \frac{87}{10} = 8.7$$

$$Average\ Deviation = \frac{\sum |X - \bar{X}|}{N} = \frac{19.0}{10} = 1.9$$

$$s^2 = \frac{\sum (X - \bar{X})^2}{N - 1} = \frac{56.10}{10 - 1} = \frac{56.10}{9} = 6.23$$

$$s = \sqrt{s^2} = \sqrt{6.23} = 2.50$$

Box 5.1   **Degrees of Freedom**

Degrees of freedom, a basic statistical concept needed in many computations, refers to the number of scores that are free to vary. Suppose you are asked to pick any three numbers. There are no restrictions, and the numbers are completely free to vary. In standard terminology, there would be three degrees of freedom; that is, three numbers are free to vary. Now suppose you are to choose any three numbers, but they must total 15; now there is one restriction on the numbers. Because of the restriction, you will lose some of the freedom to vary the three numbers you choose. If you freely choose the numbers 5 and 1 as the first two numbers, you must choose 9 as the third number to arrive at the total of 15. If instead you freely choose the numbers 8 and 11 as the first two numbers, the third must be –4 in order to total 15. In both examples, two numbers are free to vary but one is not free to vary. In standard terminology, there are two degrees of freedom—that is, two numbers are free to vary. In comparison to the first example where there was no restriction on what the total had to be and all the scores could be freely selected, we now can freely select only two scores. We have lost a degree of freedom.

Now suppose that you are to choose three scores where (1) the total must be 15 and (2) the first score must be 7. Notice there are two restrictions placed on these scores: the total and the value of the first score. Because of the two restrictions, two degrees of freedom have been lost, leaving only one degree of freedom. The only score that can vary freely is the second score.

In statistics, the restrictions imposed on data are not arbitrary as they are in our examples. Instead, they are determined by the demands of the statistical procedures used. Many statistical procedures require that estimates be made of certain values, such as the mean. These estimates constitute restrictions. The more such restrictions there are, the more degrees of freedom are lost. In the computation of the variance, one such restriction is imposed and consequently the degrees of freedom are reduced by one. Hence, the denominator is $N - 1$.

That is, variance equals the sum of the squared differences of each score from the mean (the *sum of squares*), divided by the number of scores (N) minus 1 (the degrees of freedom). The *degrees of freedom* is an important concept in statistics, referring to the number of scores that are free to vary (see Box 5.1). To use Formula 5.2, we first compute the mean of the scores. We then subtract the mean from each score and square that difference. We then sum the squared differences to calculate the numerator of Formula 5.2, which is called the sum of squares. The sum of squares is short for "the sum of squared deviations from the mean" and is often abbreviated in formulas as SS. We then divide the sum of squares by $N - 1$, the degrees of freedom, to obtain the variance. In Table 5.11, the variance is computed for the data presented in Table 5.8.

The variance is an excellent measure of variability and is used in many inferential statistics. Notice that the variance is expressed in squared units, whereas the mean is expressed in the original units of the variable. A measure called the standard deviation can be computed to transform the variance back into the same units as the original scores. The *standard deviation* (written *s*) is equal to the square root of the variance. Like the mean, the variance and standard deviation are appropriately used only with score data.

$$s = \sqrt{s^2} = \sqrt{Variance} \qquad\qquad (5.3)$$

Measures of Relationship (Correlation and Regression) Measures of central tendency and variability are basic descriptive statistics that summarizes the distribution of a variable. At times, however, we need to know more about a variable, such as what relationship it has to other variables. This *relationship* or association between variables is best indexed with a *correlation coefficient.* A *correlation* is a descriptive statistic in that it describes some aspect of the data. However, it is different from the other descriptive statistics in that it always involves at least two variables. There are different correlation coefficients for different types of data. With score data, the Pearson product-moment correlation should be used; with ordered data, the Spearman rank-order correlation should be used.

The *Pearson product-moment correlation* is the most widely used correlation index. (The computational procedures of the Pearson product-moment correlation are detailed in Appendix C.) The product-moment correlation can range from –1.00 to +1.00. A correlation of +1.00 means that the two variables are perfectly related in a positive direction—as one variable increases, the other variable will increase by a predictable amount. A correlation of –1.00 represents a perfect negative relationship—as one variable increases, the other decreases by a predictable amount. A correlation of zero means that there is no relationship between the variables. The strength of the relationship is indicated by the absolute value of the correlation coefficient. For example, a correlation of 0.55 indicates a stronger relationship between two variables than a correlation of 0.25, and a correlation of –0.85 indicates an even stronger relationship. Remember, the sign of the correlation indicates only the direction of the relationship and not the strength of the relationship.

The Pearson product-moment correlation is an index of the degree of *linear relationship* between two variables. What that means is best illustrated if we look at *scatter plots*—a graphic technique used to represent the relationship between two variables. To construct one, standard *x*- and *y*-axes are labeled with the names of the two variables of interest. Each axis is divided into a sufficient number of equal intervals to handle the range for the variable represented by that axis. A scatter plot for the relationship between age and income using data from Table 5.2 is graphed in Figure 5.5. As indicated in the figure, subject #1 is 28 years old and earns $17,000 a year. The point representing subject #1 is directly above $17,000 on the *x*-axis and directly across from 28 on the *y*-axis. To complete the scatter plot, each person's set of scores is plotted in the same way.

The pattern of scores in the scatter plot can tell us a great deal. For example, in Figure 5.5 the people with the highest incomes are all older; young people tend to have lower incomes. One could draw a straight line through the middle of the dots from the lower left to upper right of the graph, with most of the dots falling close to that line. This is a good example of a *linear relationship;* the points in this scatter plot cluster around a straight line. It is a *positive correlation* because incomes are higher for older subjects. It is not a perfect correlation. In a *perfect correlation,* all the dots form a straight line.

The scatter plots in Figure 5.6 illustrate other types of relationships. Figure 5.6(a) and Figure 5.6(b) illustrate a strong positive and a strong *negative correla-*

Figure 5.5   A Sample Scatter Plot of the Relationship Between Age and Salary

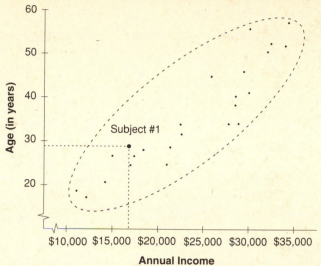

tion, respectively. Notice that the points cluster close to a straight line. Figure 5.6(e) illustrates a perfect positive correlation, with the points all falling on a straight line. Figure 5.6(c) and Figure 5.6(d) illustrate zero correlations. When the variance is approximately equal for the two variables, the scatter plot is roughly circular as in Figure 5.6(c). When the variance of the variables differ, the scatter plot is elongated either vertically or horizontally as shown in Figure 5.6(d). Figure 5.6(f) illustrates the effect of a single deviant score on the distribution. This scatter plot is similar to Figure 5.6(c) except that one point (at $X = 5$ and $Y = 2$) has been moved to $X = 11$ and $Y = 11$. Changing this single score changes the correlation from zero to +.77. Finally, Figure 5.6(g) and Figure 5.6(h) illustrate *nonlinear relationships.* In Figure 5.6(f) through Figure 5.6(h), the product-moment correlation coefficient does not represent the data well. In fact, in these cases the correlation would mislead us. That is one reason why it is always advisable to produce a scatter plot to see how the scores cluster instead of relying on a single number like a correlation coefficient to summarize the relationship between variables. With modern statistical analysis computer packages, it takes just a few seconds to create a scatter plot.

If either or both variables are ordinal (and neither variable is nominal), the appropriate coefficient is the *Spearman rank-order correlation* (the computational procedures are included in Appendix C). The Spearman rank-order correlation is interpreted like the product-moment correlation: a correlation of –1.00 is a perfect negative relationship; a correlation of +1.00 is a perfect positive relationship; and a correlation of zero means that no linear relationship exists. Scatter plots can be drawn using the ranking of each subject on each variable.

Note that a correlation coefficient provides a measure of the degree and direction of relationship between variables. Finding such relationships is a major goal of science as we try to understand natural events. In addition to discovering relationships among variables, another goal of science is to make predictions about events. The correlation coefficient is an important part of this because when we find a

Figure 5.6 Several Examples of Scatter Plots and Regression Lines

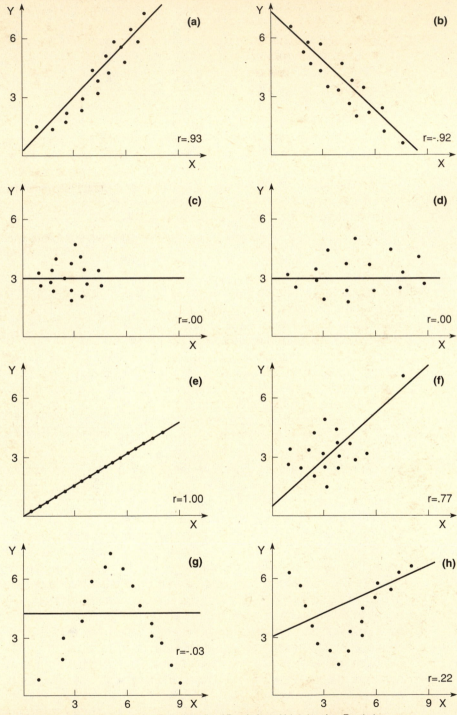

Source: Coleman, A.C. (Ed.) Companion Encyclopedia of Psychology, *Vol. 2. London: Routledge.*

strong relationship between two variables, we have information that will help us predict one variable by knowing the values of the other. For example, if we find a significant correlation between test scores and later job performance, then we have information that may help us predict future job performance.

The prediction of the value of one variable from the value of another is called *regression.* We typically assume that the variables have a linear or straight line relationship.[2] You may have noticed that a line has been drawn in each of the scatterplots in Figure 5.6. This line is the linear regression line for predicting the variable *Y* from the variable *X.* In Figure 5.6(a, b, and e), the points cluster close to the line, suggesting a strong linear relationship. When the correlation is zero, as in Figure 5.6(c and d), the line is horizontal; when the correlation between *X* and *Y* is zero, our best prediction for *Y* will always be the same regardless of the value of *X* (predict the mean of *Y*). For Figure 5.6(f, g, and h), the regression line, like the correlation, is misleading (i.e., it does not reflect the data well). The computational procedures for simple linear regression are included in Appendix C. Statistical analysis packages, such as *SPSS for Windows,* can compute a regression line easily for any data set. However, you should always request a scatterplot so that you can see how well the data fit a straight line function.

Standard Scores   The *standard score* (written *Z;* also called the *Z-score*) is a useful transformation frequently used in research. The standard score is computed by subtracting the sample mean from the raw score and dividing the difference by the sample standard deviation as shown in Formula 5.4. This is referred to as a *relative score* because it tells how the subject scored relative to the rest of the subjects. If the subject scores above the sample mean, the standard score is positive; if the subject scores below the sample mean, the standard score is negative. The size of the standard score indicates how far from the mean the subject scored. Many tests convert the standard score to avoid negative numbers and decimals. For example, the standard score on the IQ test is converted into an IQ by multiplying the standard score by 15 and adding 100, producing an IQ distribution with a mean of 100 and a standard deviation of 15. The SAT scores have similarly been converted from standard scores to a distribution with a mean of 500 and a standard deviation of 100.

$$Z = \frac{(X - \overline{X})}{s} \tag{5.4}$$

The standard score is useful in many situations. Converting several different measures taken on each subject to standard scores before summing them gives each measure the same weight in the total. Instructors often use this principle in computing grades—summing the standard scores for each exam rather than the raw scores. Many statistical procedures use an implicit conversion to standard scores, including most advanced regression procedures. Finally, if your distribution is approximately normal in shape, the standard score can be easily converted into a percentile rank by using a table found in any statistics textbook. A person's *percentile rank* tells what percent of the sample scored below the person.

---

[2]Nonlinear regression is possible, but the procedures are well beyond the level of this text. The interested student is referred to Cohen and Cohen (1983) or Myers and Well (1991).

Internal Summary: Descriptive Statistics

Descriptive statistics help us to summarize and describe data with just a few numbers. They are a vital first step in interpreting research data. Even with complicated research designs, describing data will always be the first step in any data-analysis procedure. Frequency distributions and graphical representations of data are often helpful. Summary statistics simplify data further. There are summary statistics to indicate the typical score (measures of central tendency), including the mean, the median, and the mode. There are summary statistics to indicate the variability of the scores, including the range, the variance, and the standard deviation. There are descriptive statistics to indicate the degree of relationship between two or more variables (correlations), which aids in prediction. Finally, the standard score is a useful transformation that puts each score in a context relative to all other scores. One common use of the standard score is to put all of a student's test scores on the same scale so that they will be equally weighted in arriving at a final grade.

INFERENTIAL STATISTICS

Using statistics to describe data is only the first step in analyzing the results of a research study. The rest of the analysis is concerned not so much with the specific subjects we have tested (the sample), but with what those subjects can tell us about a larger group of people (the population). That is, we use statistical analysis of the data obtained from the sample to draw inferences about a larger group—the population. These statistical methods are called *inferential statistics*.

Populations and Samples

Although we are usually interested in large populations of subjects, it is rarely possible to observe whole populations. Therefore, we observe samples from populations. In human research, a *population* is the larger group of all the people of interest from which the sample is selected. The *sample* is a subset of people drawn from that population. For example, a researcher might be interested in the population of high school students in a county, but the population is too large to include in a study. Therefore, the researcher selects a sample of students from the population. A sample is used as if that sample adequately represents the population. In research, we want to draw conclusions about the population on the basis of a small sample from that population. However, no two samples drawn from the same population will be exactly alike. For example, one sample of subjects from the general population may have a mean IQ of 101.2, whereas another sample from the same population will have a mean IQ of 100.3. Most samples are reasonably representative of the population from which they are drawn, but sometimes samples are unrepresentative of the population even though the sampling procedure may have been carried out flawlessly. The variation among different samples drawn from the same population is referred to as *sampling error*. In a sense, the term *sampling error* is misleading in that it does not represent a mistake. Rather, sampling error refers to the small variability among samples due to chance. Because samples are not perfectly representative of the population from which they are drawn, we cannot be sure that the conclusions drawn from the samples will generalize to the entire population. In fact, we can never be sure that inferences drawn from a sample are valid for the population; the best we can do is calculate probabilities about potential inferences. Probability is a critical concept in inferential statistics.

Suppose, for example, we were interested in reaction time in patients with schizophrenia and in nonpsychiatric control subjects. The variable, reaction time, is measured by recording how quickly subjects press a button in response to an auditory signal. The samples used would be drawn from the population of patients with schizophrenia and from the population of nonpsychiatric individuals. Suppose we found that mean reaction time from the samples was 0.278 seconds for the patients with schizophrenia and 0.254 seconds for the controls. Clearly, the sample means are different but not very different. However, we are actually interested in the population of patients with schizophrenia and the population of nonpsychiatric individuals. That is, we want to draw conclusions about characteristics of the populations from the results of the samples. Would the observed difference in mean reaction time in the samples lead us to believe that a similar difference exists between the populations, or could the observed difference simply be a result of sampling error? This question (comparing population means) is the type most often raised in such research. Suppose for the moment that the reaction time means for the populations were not different. In this case, samples drawn from the populations should have approximately equal mean reaction times. Returning to our example, are mean reaction times of 0.278 and 0.254 approximately equal? Are they close enough to infer that the populations' means (unknown to us) are also approximately equal? Here we are testing the null hypothesis, which in this case is that the population means are not different from one another.

The Null Hypothesis

The *null hypothesis* is a general hypothesis that can be applied to many types of comparisons. In the situation discussed above, it is the population means that are being compared. *Null* is from the Latin *nullus,* meaning "not any." Thus, the null hypothesis in this situation is that there is "not any" statistical difference between the population means. Inferential statistics are used to test the null hypothesis. If the observed sample means were very different, then we would reject the null hypothesis and conclude that the population means are not equal. But how different is "very different"? Inferential statistics give a probabilistic answer to this question.

Before proceeding further, let us distinguish between a population parameter and a sample statistic. If we compute a characteristic of the population (such as the mean) by testing everyone in the population, we refer to the value as a *population parameter.* If we compute the same characteristic on a sample drawn from the population, we refer to the value as a *sample statistic.* Our task is usually to estimate population parameters and to draw conclusions about population parameters on the basis of sample statistics.

Statistical Decisions and Alpha Levels

Inferential statistics are used to compute the probability of obtaining the observed data if the null hypothesis is true. If the probability is small, then it is unlikely that the null hypothesis is true. We would therefore conclude that the null hypothesis is false. A somewhat arbitrary cutoff point called the *alpha level* (written α) is used for making this decision. Traditionally, we set alpha to a small value such as 0.05 or 0.01. To clarify these difficult but important concepts, let us refer back to our example. We are interested in the reaction time of patients with schizophrenia and nonpsychiatric individuals. The null hypothesis is that the mean reaction times are the same in these two populations. The inferential statistical procedure evaluates the size of the observed mean difference between the samples. If the sample means are so different that it is unlikely the samples could have come from populations with equal means, then we reject the hypothesis that the population means are equal (the null hypothesis).

Type I and Type II Errors

The alpha level that we select guides us in rejecting or not rejecting the null hypothesis—the hypothesis that there is no difference between the means. When the probability exceeds the alpha level, we retain the null hypothesis; when the probability is at or below the alpha level, we reject the null hypothesis.

Of course, there is always the chance that the researcher's decision might be wrong. For example, the researcher might reject the null hypothesis and conclude the population means are not equal when, in fact, they are equal. In this case, the researcher has made a *Type I error*. The probability of this error occurring is equal to the alpha level we set. If an alpha of 0.05 is used, Type I errors will occur 5 percent of the time. If the alpha is 0.01, Type I errors will occur 1 percent of the time. The *alpha level* is the proportion of Type I errors one could expect to make if the study were repeated many times.

If alpha is the level of Type I error and the researcher decides what alpha to use, why not set alpha to zero to avoid all Type I errors? The reason is that there is another possible error known as a Type II error. A *Type II error* occurs when we fail to reject the null hypothesis when it is false. We use the term *beta* (β) to refer to the probability of making a Type II error. We want to avoid both errors, but because we can never be sure what the real state of nature is, there is always the chance for error in our decision. It is important to realize that decreasing the Type I error rate (without doing anything else), we will automatically increase the Type II error rate. Therefore, the two types of error have to be balanced against one another. Table 5.12 summarizes the definitions of Type I and Type II errors.

Testing for Mean Differences

Inferential statistics are used most frequently to evaluate mean differences between groups. Such statistical techniques are valuable because we often can specify the research hypothesis in terms of mean differences. There are a number of tests for evaluating mean differences in two or more groups, including the simple *t*-test, correlated *t*-test, and analysis of variance (ANOVA).

TABLE 5.12   TYPE I AND TYPE II ERRORS

		Researcher's Decision	
		Reject the Null Hypothesis	Retain the Null Hypothesis*
True state of nature	**Null hypothesis true**	Type I error	Correct decision
	Null hypothesis false	Correct decision	Type II error

*Technically, we never actually accept the null hypothesis. Instead, we retain or fail to reject the null hypothesis. The interested student should consult an introductory statistics textbook for the reasoning behind this subtle distinction.

Simple *t*-Test   The *simple* t-*test* (sometimes referred to as the t-*test for independent groups*) is typically used with score data from two *independent samples* of subjects. The samples are independent if different subjects appear in each sample and if the subjects in the two samples are not matched in any way. The null hypothesis is that there is no difference in the two population means—that is, the observed difference between the sample means is due only to sampling error. The test statistic is called *t*. Computational formulas for *t* can be found in Appendix C. The general procedure in this and most other inferential statistics is to compute the test statistic and the probability (p *value*) of obtaining this value of the test statistic if the null hypothesis is true. If the *p* value is less than our chosen alpha level, we reject the null hypothesis and conclude that the population means are different.

Correlated *t*-Test   In some research designs we do not have independent samples. One such design is called a *within-subjects design,* where the same subjects appear in each group. In this design, the groups represent different conditions under which the subjects are tested. Another design is the *matched-subjects design,* where all subjects are matched in pairs and then randomly assigned so that one member of the pair goes into one group and the other member goes into another. (We will discuss these designs in Chapter 11.) In either case, a *correlated* t-*test* would be the appropriate test to use to analyze the results of the study. (The computational procedures for the correlated *t*-test are included in Appendix C.)

Analysis of Variance (ANOVA)   When we have more than two groups and want to test for mean differences among the groups, an *analysis of variance (ANOVA)* is the appropriate test. The term analysis of variance is confusing because the test actually compares the means of the various groups, but it compares the means by computing and comparing different population variance estimates. (Explaining how this is accomplished is beyond the scope of this book; we will focus only on the conceptual basis of ANOVA in this section. Standard terminology and interpretation will be discussed in Chapters 10–12, and computational procedures are included in Appendix C.)

One reason analysis of variance is so useful a tool for analyzing the results of research is that it is flexible. We can analyze the results of studies that use one independent variable and of studies that use two or more independent variables. If we have more than one independent variable, the independent variables are referred to as *factors* and the research design is said to be *factorial.* We refer to the analysis of a study with only one independent variable as a *one-way ANOVA,* with two independent variables as a *two-way ANOVA,* and so forth. Each factor can have many levels or groups. Also, ANOVAs can be used to analyze data from studies where different subjects appear in each condition (a between-subjects design) or where the same subjects appear in all of the conditions (a within-subjects design). An ANOVA used to analyze data from a within-subjects design is referred to as a *repeated measures ANOVA.*

The Power of a Statistical Test

The term *power* or *statistical power* refers to the sensitivity of the statistical procedure to the differences being sought. Thus, the concept of the power of a procedure refers to the sensitivity of that procedure to provide a basis for correctly rejecting the null hypothesis. Power is the ability to reduce Type II errors. It is equal to $1 - \beta$. It is important to realize that power is not a function of the statistical procedure alone, but also depends on the precision of the research design. The traditional way of increasing power is to increase the sample size. However, any improvement in a research design that increases sensitivity will increase power, including sampling more precisely, using more precise measures, better standardization of all procedures, and controlling individual differences through your choice of a research design (see Chapter 11).

Statistical Versus Practical Significance

A statistically significant finding is impressive and usually pleases the researcher, especially if it is in the predicted direction. But the mere fact of finding statistical significance can be misleading, and we have to be careful not to conclude that because a finding is *statistically significant,* it is therefore important or of *practical significance.*

Suppose, for example, that we compare two groups of seriously obese adults. The experimental group attends a weight-reduction program and the control group is put on a waiting list. After six months, the treated group has lost a mean of 3.4 pounds whereas the control group has gained a mean of 1.2 pounds, and the difference between the groups is statistically significant. Despite the statistical significance, the question must be asked, "Is the loss of just over three pounds after six months of dieting, exercise, and group meetings of any personal importance or significance to those obese people who wanted to lose weight?" Most of those dieters would probably say "No!" Thus, when evaluating the effectiveness of the weight-reduction program in practical terms, we have to be careful not to let the statistically significant findings blind us to the fact that the program was simply not practically or personally successful for those people.

SUMMARY

Statistics are tools that help us interpret the results of experiments and observational studies. The interpretations made on the basis of statistical calculations are limited by (1) the quality of the data gathered, (2) the appropriateness of the statistic, and (3) the accuracy with which we compute and interpret the statistic. Some statistical procedures are designed solely to describe the data from a study (descriptive statistics). Other statistics (inferential statistics) are designed to help interpret the data. Whatever our purpose in using statistics, the appropriate statistic(s) will depend on the nature of the data and of the questions we ask.

In this chapter, we have discussed the most commonly used statistics. Computational procedures for frequently used statistics are included in Appendix C. Appendix D outlines procedures for computing statistics using a popular statistical analysis package. In addition, Chapter 14 presents a flowchart for selecting the appropriate statistical technique based on the research design.

REVIEW EXERCISES

5.1 **Define the following key terms. Be sure you understand them. They are discussed in the chapter and defined in the glossary.**

statistics
descriptive statistics
inferential statistics
individual differences
frequencies
frequency distribution
cross-tabulation
univariate
grouped frequency distribution
continuous variable
graphs
tables
histogram
frequency polygon
x-axis or abscissa
y-axis or ordinate
symmetric distribution
normal distribution
distribution skewed
positively skewed
negatively skewed
central tendency
variability
summary statistics
mode
bimodal
trimodal
median
mean
range
average deviation
variance
sum of squares

degrees of freedom
standard deviation
relationship
correlation coefficient
correlation
Pearson product-moment correlation
linear relationship
scatter plot
positive correlation
perfect correlation
negative correlation
nonlinear relationship
Spearman rank-order correlation
regression
standard score
Z-score
relative score
percentile rank
population
sample
sampling error
null hypothesis
population parameters
sample statistics
alpha level
Type I error
Type II error
beta
t-test
t-test for independent groups
independent samples
p value
within-subjects design

matched-subjects design
correlated *t*-test
analysis of variance (ANOVA)
factors
factorial design
one-way ANOVA

two-way ANOVA
repeated measures ANOVA
power
statistical power
statistical significance
practical significance

statistical symbols: Σ (sigma); $\overline{X}$; $\underline{N}$; $\underline{s}$; $\underline{s}^2$; SS; α (alpha); β (beta); *t*; *F*

5.2   Answer each of the following. Check your answers in the chapter.

1. With what kind of data do we use frequency distributions?
2. Draw a graph showing a negatively skewed distribution and one showing a positively skewed distribution.
3. What are the different kinds of summary statistics?
4. Name and define the measures of central tendency and of variability.
5. Is it possible for a distribution of scores to have more than one mode? More than one mean?
6. Suppose you are the teaching assistant in this course. How would you present and explain variability and its measures to students?
7. Why is the variance a better measure of variability than the range?
8. Why is the mean a better measure of central tendency than the mode?
9. How does a correlation differ from other descriptive statistics?
10. Which correlation coefficient would you calculate for each of the following: (a) age and height; (b) class rank and IQ; (c) grade (number correct) on two different exams?
11. How do inferential statistics differ from descriptive statistics?

5.3   Think about and work the following problems.

1. For each of the following data sets, (i) draw a descriptive graph, (ii) compute the measures of central tendency, and (iii) compute the measures of variability.
   a. 20 scores: 8; 6; 4; 3; 9; 5; 7; 8; 6; 7; 9; 5; 9; 8; 9; 7; 4; 8; 7; 9
   b. 15 IQ scores: 104; 121; 94; 107; 81; 96; 100; 96; 102; 115; 87; 101; 91; 114; 111
2. In the following research projects, identify (i) the independent variable and the type of independent variable (manipulated or nonmanipulated); (ii) the dependent variable(s); (iii) the level of measurement and the type of data for each dependent variable. (Refer to Chapter 4 if you have difficulty with this exercise.)
   a. Thirty rats are randomly assigned to one of three groups (10 rats per group). Each group of rats is under a different duration of food deprivation (4 hours; 8 hours; 12 hours). The rats are then tested to see how many trials are required to learn a standard maze.
   b. Twenty 2-year-olds and twenty 3-year-olds are compared on their enjoyment of toys. Each child is allowed to play for a period of 30 minutes in a playroom. An observer rates each child on a five-point scale on the child's enjoyment.
   c. Birth records of 250 schizophrenic patients and 250 randomly selected individuals are compared on the frequency of birth complications in each group. The birth record for each subject is categorized as normal (no complications) or abnormal (complications reported).

Chapter
6

Field Research
I. Naturalistic Observation and Case-Study Research

*F*ield research is a term that applies to a variety of research methods, ranging from low to high constraint. They share a focus on observing naturally occurring behavior under largely natural conditions (i.e., "in the field"). Although definitions vary, we include each of the six techniques shown in Table 6-1 in the category of field research.

We will divide the topic of field research into two chapters. Lower-constraint field research (naturalistic observation, archival research, case studies, and surveys) will be discussed in this chapter. In Chapter 13, after we have covered higher-constraint research, we will return for a second look at field research (program evaluation, field experiments).

In this chapter, we will discuss naturalistic observation, archival research (which is a special case of naturalistic observation), case-study research, and surveys, including when to use them, the information they provide, their limitations, and procedures for minimizing their limitations. These low-constraint field research methods are not necessarily inferior to higher-constraint research. The appropriate level of constraint in any research depends upon a number of factors, the most important of which is the nature of the research question. For some questions, low-constraint research procedures, such as naturalistic observation and case studies, are most appropriate.

In the low-constraint naturalistic and case-study methods, researchers observe the behavior of subjects in a flexible manner, which allows them to take advantage of unexpected occurrences and new ideas developed during the observations. Low-constraint research focuses on the natural flow of behavior—a flow of events that occurs without the imposition of controls or intervention by the researcher. The investigator imposes few, if any, controls or constraints on subjects' behavior. Naturalistic research is carried out in the subject's natural environment (e.g., an animal's habitat, a schoolroom, a workplace, an urban park, and so on). Case-study research is slightly higher in constraint because the researcher does intervene to some degree. Surveys can be thought of as more formalized case studies, where the researcher asks standardized questions of a carefully drawn sample of subjects. Naturalistic research methods have been used by ethologists and comparative psychologists studying the behavior of animals in their natural habitats and by sociologists and social psychologists interested in the natural behavior of human groups under various conditions that cannot be duplicated in the laboratory. Case-study research methods have been used to study subjective processes such as thinking and problem solving in children and personal adjustment in both adults and children. Most often case-study research is carried out with one subject at a time, usually in an interactive or face-to-face situation. Surveys have been used to quantify preferences, values, and reported behavior of large segments of the population.

THE CHALLENGE OF LOW-CONSTRAINT RESEARCH

It is tempting to think that, because the researcher imposes few controls and can make observations in a flexible manner, low-constraint methods such as naturalistic observation and case-study research are easy to carry out. As in all research, however, considerable care and effort is required, even at low-constraint levels. Indeed,

TABLE 6.1   CATEGORIES OF FIELD RESEARCH

Naturalistic observation	Direct observation of events as they occur in natural settings
Archival research	Studying information from already existing records made in natural settings
Surveys	Asking direct questions of persons in natural settings
Case study	Making extensive observations of a single group or a person
Program evaluation	Conducting evaluations of applied procedures in natural settings
Field experiments	Conducting experiments in natural settings where causal inferences are sought (discussed in Chapter 13)

the very lack of high-constraint controls and procedures adds to our burden because we cannot depend on the supports found in laboratory settings.

To illustrate the particular difficulties faced in low-constraint research, suppose you want to study the mating, nesting, and rearing behaviors of a certain rarely seen bird. Before going into the field, you must search the literature and communicate with other ornithologists to learn what is known about the species and the best methods by which to study it. Assume also that you have identified the bird's natural habitat, outfitted your expedition, and traveled there. You probably have with you audiotape and videotape recording equipment, camping supplies, food, and so on. If your research grant permits it, you have an assistant to help carry the load. If not, you do it yourself. There are long hours of searching for this rare bird and when you find it, you spend long days, perhaps weeks, waiting for opportunities to observe and record the behavior you wish to study. Because you are not in control of the bird's behavior, you have to "take it as it comes," which results in a long enterprise, often carried out under difficult and uncomfortable conditions. After the observations have been successfully made, you must analyze your data—often a mammoth task in naturalistic research—then interpret the data, and finally communicate the results.

Researchers face the same problems, although perhaps not quite so dramatically, when they observe human behavior in natural settings. Because you are a passive observer, you must make yourself as unobtrusive as possible and then wait for your subjects to display the behavior you want to observe. Naturalistic observation of some human behaviors may be difficult or impossible. Few people would be upset if you observed the mating behavior of some rare bird. On the other hand, unobtrusively observing the mating behavior of human beings is more likely to lead to a jail sentence than to a scientific publication. Even public behavior, such as leadership styles, may be difficult to observe because so much of it is done in private meetings. Some settings lend themselves to naturalistic observation. Most behavior in schools, hospitals, and many industrial settings occurs in public or semipublic settings where it could be observed and recorded as part of a research project.

Note that in naturalistic and case-study research the constraints are primarily on the observer, and little control is placed on the behavior of the subject. As we move to higher-constraint levels, more controls are placed on subjects to specify and delimit their behavior. As we will discuss in Chapter 13, controlled experiments can be conducted in the field. Martin and Bateson (1986) provide an excellent introductory discussion of field research—from naturalistic observation to field experiments.

EXAMPLES OF NATURALISTIC OBSERVATION

A classic example of naturalistic observation is the research of Charles Darwin, who voyaged five years on the HMS *Beagle.* Darwin gathered specimens and compiled descriptive data in the form of notes and drawings. He carefully observed animals and plants in natural settings, as well as weather and geological formations. He began to see patterns in the data and to form ideas about how the variety of life might have developed. Over a number of years, Darwin integrated his observations and ideas and formulated his theory of evolution. However, Darwin was not the first person to propose the idea of biological evolution. Over 2000 years earlier, Greek philosophers had developed concepts of biological evolution. In addition, Alfred Russel Wallace proposed the concept of natural selection just prior to Darwin's publication of *On the Origin of Species.* But it was Darwin who was most influential in bringing the data and the interpretations to the attention of other scientists and the public (Dennett, 1995).

Another example is Jane Goodall's (1971, 1986) study of chimpanzees in their natural habitat in Tanzania. Beginning in the early 1960s, Goodall persisted two years in the forests under difficult conditions before she was able to begin making substantial observations. Her research, primarily low-constraint and naturalistic, presents a remarkable picture of the chimpanzee as a highly social creature. Thirty years later, Goodall has shifted her focus to applying her knowledge to the conservation of these now endangered animals.

Observations by Goodall and others illustrate the range of adaptive behavior in the chimpanzee. Boesch and Boesch-Acherman (1991) observed chimpanzees using stones to crack open nuts. The stones were carefully selected according to the type and size of nuts to be opened and were used with great skill. This was the first observation of stone hammer-and-anvil use by nonhuman primates. Goodall (1986) observed that chimps hunt, kill, and eat monkeys, antelopes, and wild pigs. Boesch and Boesch-Acherman (1991) added to those observations that chimps hunt cooperatively—a behavior considered by many to be a major step in social evolution.

A similar example of naturalistic research is the work of Dian Fossey, who for years studied the mountain gorilla in its natural habitat in Africa. In her book, *Gorillas in the Mist* (1983), Fossey described her discovery that the gorilla is a complex, highly social, responsive, and even gentle animal—far different from the earlier, distorted beliefs about the gorilla's ferociousness and danger to humans.

Naturalistic methods are also applied to human behavior. Anthropologists often live among people of different cultures, observing and recording everyday behavior. They organize and interpret their observations to produce a detailed account of how the people function. From the descriptive data, inferences are drawn about each culture's values, religious and other beliefs, power status, organization, and so forth.

The detailed descriptions are valuable in understanding a variety of processes, including parenting, divisions of labor, and conflict resolution.

Adeline Levine's (1982) sociological study of the Love Canal disaster in Niagara Falls, New York, is another example of naturalistic research. Just after World War II, the city built a grammar school on top of a toxic dump site, and the area was developed for residential use. Unknown to the residents, thousands of metal drums were slowly and quietly corroding underground, releasing their toxins into the surrounding soil. Over the next two decades, the toxins spread into the cellars of nearby homes and percolated up to the surface. There were unaccountable small explosions in the area and "brown ooze" that clung to the legs of schoolchildren. The "ooze" and the odors became so bad that the school playground was closed after heavy rains. Pets began to die and several children were burned by the chemicals. The residents gradually realized that there was an unusually high occurrence of cancer, miscarriages, and intestinal and respiratory disease among their children. By 1978, more than 25 years after the toxic dump had been covered up, the residents suspected that their entire area was contaminated with dangerous toxins. They were in peril, and many hundreds of families had to abandon their homes.

Levine (1982) and her students studied the Love Canal disaster using naturalistic methods. They reviewed historical records, met with residents, attended public meetings, talked to officials, read newspaper reports, and monitored local television and radio broadcasts. Using this mass of observation, Levine documented the disaster and its psychological, social, and financial impacts. Levine's investigation is a major sociological study with important implications for federal and state policy making and could not have been carried out in any way other than through the use of naturalistic research methods.

Rosenhan (1973) investigated the use of psychiatric diagnoses and the experiences of mental patients in hospitals. Rosenhan asked eight "pseudopatients"—normal people—to admit themselves to various mental hospitals with feigned complaints of hearing voices saying "thud," "hollow," and "empty." They were instructed to display no other signs of mental disorder during their hospital stays. In fact, once admitted to the hospital, the pseudopatients behaved in their normal manner and gave no indication of their supposed hallucinations. The patients (actually Rosenhan's researchers) made observations of the hospital conditions, of their treatment, and of the staff and patients. Much like an anthropologist in a strange culture, each researcher made naturalistic observations and kept detailed notes on what he or she observed. The eight researchers were admitted to 12 different hospitals, and apparently none of the hospitals' staff ever discerned that they were not real patients. In fact, the only people who did realize it were some of the other patients. These researchers, like anthropologists, were more than neutral observers; they were participant-observers. As in the Levine study, the use of naturalistic methods was not only appropriate for the investigation but was probably the best way to investigate the issue. Box 6-1 reviews this study in more detail, including several challenges to Rosenhan's interpretation of his data.

Naturalistic methods are used in psychology to study a variety of human behavior in public places. Researchers have studied smoking, eating, and drinking behavior in restaurants and bars, drivers' behavior at intersections, children on school grounds or in class, shoppers in stores, and so on. There are many examples in the

---

Box 6.1   # Interpretation of the Rosenhan Data

Rosenhan's naturalistic study (1973), demonstrated that it is quite easy to be admitted to a psychiatric hospital, and it created quite a stir inside and outside of psychiatry. According to his report, one need only go to a hospital and report hearing voices. It apparently matters little what the voices say or whether there are any other symptoms. Furthermore, once a diagnostic label is given as part of an admission procedure, the label prevents the professional staff from recognizing the person does not really have symptoms. All of his "pseudopatients" continued to be diagnosed at discharge, usually with the notation "in remission."

Few of Rosenhan's critics argued with his data; instead, the arguments centered on the interpretation of the data. Rosenhan's interpretation seems persuasive, but other interpretations are possible, and some of those alternatives are more reasonable given other available data. For example, Rosenhan argued that it is unreasonable to make a diagnosis of schizophrenia (11 out of 12 admissions received this diagnosis) on the basis of one symptom (hearing voices). Weiner (1975) notes, however, that by Rosenhan's own admission (1973, pp. 365–366), the pseudopatients showed "concomitant nervousness" and apparently were truly in serious distress because they went to a psychiatric hospital and requested admission. This pattern, plus the fact that the pseudopatients would likely have denied other symptoms and experiences that might have indicated alternative explanations for the auditory hallucinations (Spitzer, 1975), makes schizophrenia the most likely diagnosis. Spitzer goes even further in his criticism of Rosenhan's conclusions about diagnosis. Rosenhan interpreted the discharge diagnoses as indicating that the doctors never detected that the patients were not psychotic. Spitzer notes, however, that Rosenhan reported that all the patients were diagnosed as "in remission" at discharge. The qualification "in remission" is almost never used in clinical practice, and therefore the data on discharge diagnosis clearly indicates that every patient was determined by the professional staff to be symptom free at discharge. Others (e.g., Crown, 1975) even questioned the ethics of deceptive research of the type done by Rosenhan.

Rosenhan's research is still widely quoted. His was a powerful study with interesting findings, but there are some who argue that his interpretation of the findings were scientifically wrong. Rosenhan drew strong conclusions from this low-constraint research, conclusions that seem unreasonable when you compare his results with other research data (e.g., typical discharge diagnoses). His study illustrates both the strengths (i.e., studying a natural phenomenon in its natural setting) and the weaknesses (i.e., the hazards implicit in interpreting naturalistic data) of low-constraint, naturalistic research.

---

research literature; the interested student is encouraged to find and examine these reports.

EXAMPLES OF CASE-STUDY RESEARCH

Like naturalistic observation, case-study research falls near the low-constraint end of our continuum, and the two areas overlap. Case-study research is naturalistic observation but with some mild constraints imposed on the procedures. What are those constraints? First, case studies are not typically carried out in natural environments; instead, they are carried out in a setting that is usually selected by the researcher. Second, case-study research is typically focused on individuals. Finally, case-study research usually looks at limited classes of behavior rather than the total context and natural flow of behavior. Thus, we can see that case studies, by imposing a few constraints, narrow the focus somewhat but retain their essential interest in subjects' natural behavior.

The best-known example of case-study research is that of Sigmund Freud. Beginning in the late nineteenth century, Freud accumulated observations from which he formulated psychoanalytic theory and treatment. He interviewed patients intensively, not in their natural environments but in the mild constraints of his office. Freud and his many followers believed their clinical observations were more useful than laboratory observations in studying the highly subjective events that seemed to be critical for understanding their patients' psychological dysfunction. Freud focused on the psychology of unconscious processes, and his work had an enormous impact on early psychology, popularizing an alternative to the then current laboratory-based psychology of consciousness. Freud established case-study methods in psychology as a major way of studying human subjective phenomena. His influence was not only substantial at the time but has endured, continuing to be powerfully evident even today.

Freud's case-study methods consisted of interviews with his patients in which they free-associated, telling of their early lives, dreams, fears, current and past fantasies, and so on. From this mass of verbal behavior Freud began to see patterns in his work, much as Darwin had in his observations, and he drew inferences about patients' subjective functioning. These inferences eventually were integrated into his psychoanalytic theory and techniques.

Another early proponent of the case-study method was a psychologist, E. L. Witmer, who had studied with Wundt in Germany. Witmer began teaching at the University of Pennsylvania in 1896, where he founded the first psychological clinic [see Boring (1950) and Brotemarkle (1966)]. His clinic treated children with learning and behavioral problems. Witmer used careful medical and psychological examinations of each child in an effort to determine whether the child's problems were due to brain pathology or to inadequate teaching and learning. He developed a treatment-educational approach to children, which became known as "psychoeducation." He applied psychological procedures, many based on those used in the laboratory, in a highly individualized, intense, single-case-study method that he called the new "clinical psychology."

Jean Piaget's work provides us with another example of the use of case-study methods in research. Freud and Witmer used case-study methods to provide services to persons with psychological problems, as well as bases for inferences about human psychological functioning in general. Piaget's case-study methods, on the other hand, were aimed at research into children's normal cognitive development. Studying one child at a time in mildly controlled settings, Piaget asked questions and presented tasks to the children and observed how they answered. He did not follow any carefully detailed set of procedures; rather, his procedures were flexible. This allowed him to alter the methods to take advantage of ideas or observations that occurred during the interviews or to follow up on something new the child might say or do. Piaget did impose some mild constraints. The interviews were usually carried out in simplified settings where there would be little interference. Piaget presented tasks to the child. He then observed the child's responses, both verbal and

motor. His approach had a bit more constraint than that found in naturalistic observation. Piaget used his observations of children to develop hypotheses about their
cognitive development. His theories have been examined in higher-constraint research by other psychologists, with most of them holding up well under scientific
scrutiny. His flexible case-study methodology resulted in important knowledge about
children's intellectual development and might not have been discovered if Piaget
had insisted on high-constraint, experimental research.

Low-constraint research, when done well, can be enormously valuable, but it
must be done as carefully as any level of research. To illustrate this we need to look
at the conditions under which low-constraint research should and should not be
used, the kinds of information it can generate, its strengths and weaknesses, and
the procedures involved in carrying out low-constraint research.

THE VALUE OF LOW-CONSTRAINT METHODS

Conditions for Using Low-Constraint Research

The above examples illustrate the conditions under which low-constraint research is
useful. When the question concerns the natural flow of behavior in natural settings,
then low-constraint observational research is appropriate. For example, if we are interested in studying the peak hours of aircraft takeoffs and landings at an airport,
the flow of traffic in certain kinds of intersections, the patterns of seating in theaters,
the flow of events in a disaster or crisis, or the relative amounts of positive and negative feedback given to students by teachers, then the best methods will involve direct observations of those events as they occur in their natural settings.

Another condition under which low-constraint research is appropriate is at the
beginning stages of research in a new area. For example, we know adults can organize their behavior with reference to time, but can children do so? The researcher
might be well advised to begin studying this question at a low-constraint level by observing young children in a normal setting such as a nursery school or playground.
Such observations might stimulate the researcher to develop ideas or hypotheses
for higher constraint research. Thus, low-constraint research is useful in new areas
to generate ideas for further, presumably higher-constraint, research.

Naturalistic observation is also an excellent way for researchers to familiarize
themselves with subjects or settings that are new to them, although not a new research area. For example, you might be interested in replicating or extending some
part of Piaget's work on conservation in young children. You know the previous research but have had little experience working with young children as subjects. It
would be useful for you to spend a few hours familiarizing yourself with young children by observing a nursery school class.

Low-constraint procedures also can be used to demonstrate a new research or
treatment technique. Here the only question is whether the technique is feasible.
The researcher is not attempting to test a prediction or develop new hypotheses but
only to see whether some method can be carried out.

An often overlooked use for case-study and naturalistic research is their potential contributions to *generalizability* of research findings. This is a problem faced constantly by psychologists who conduct most of their research in highly constrained

Box 6.2   # The Therapist as Scientist

Case-study methods can be used in settings not normally thought of as research. For example, a therapist must gather information and generate hypotheses about the reasons for the client's behavior and about ways in which problem behaviors can be modified or replaced. The effective use of research methods, especially methods of inference, can greatly improve the therapist's effectiveness. The phases of research presented in Chapter 2 are applicable to the therapy session. The therapist is faced with a variety of information about the client from which the therapist generates ideas about what problems the client has, how they developed, and how they might be corrected. At first the information may be vague, allowing several possible ideas to be developed. The clinician then translates these ideas into specific hypotheses and develops plans for testing them. The observation phase may be no more than asking the client specific questions, or it may involve closely observing how the client responds to particular actions by the therapist or others. The analysis phase relies less on statistics and more on rational inferences, and the analysis and interpretation phases are difficult to separate. Most therapists record their observations in progress notes so that the information will be available to them or to other clinicians who might work with the client in the future. The important point is that a clinician, in gathering the information necessary for treatment planning, is operating much like a research scientist. It is no accident that the most widely accepted model for the training of a clinical psychologist is the *scientist-practitioner model*. Understanding the way scientists gather information and draw conclusions can sharpen the clinician's skills in information gathering and treatment planning.

laboratory settings. The advantages of laboratory research are enormous, and it is therefore not surprising that so much of it is conducted. But a problem is that we cannot be sure that the behavior we see in the laboratory is representative of the behavior we would see in the natural environment. Naturalistic research methods, and to some degree case-study research, can be used to test the generalizability of the theories developed or refined on the basis of laboratory studies. The most useful laws of behavior are those that predict behavior in the real world. Thus, naturalistic observation is not only useful in the early stages of research on a particular topic, but can also be helpful in establishing the generalizability of findings during the later stages of research.

The most common justification for case-study research is when the question being asked concerns the specific individual or case who is the object of the study, such as when psychological tests are administered to a client to learn more about that particular person. Under such conditions, there is no concern for developing inferences and concepts that can be generalized to a population (see Box 6-2).

While naturalistic and case-study observation procedures constitute low-constraint research, the observational methods might nevertheless employ highly sophisticated instrumentation. In the naturalistic observation of the rare bird in its habitat, for example, the investigator might use advanced, lightweight equipment, including telephoto lenses and sensitive microphones. In case-study research, we might employ computerized psychophysiological testing equipment. The research is still naturalistic or a case study; the technological equipment does not define the level of constraint.

Information Gained from Low-Constraint Research

Naturalistic and case-study research can provide only certain kinds of information. First, observation of relatively unconstrained subjects can give us new, descriptive information. For example, Goodall (1978) observed that one group of chimpanzees in the wild attacked and killed another group. This was the first observation of behavior that resembled warfare among chimpanzees, and as such, it was new information. These observations could not explain the event or tell us what caused it or whether it is a commonly occurring behavior among chimpanzees. But, Goodall's observations did establish a new fact never before observed.

Evidence from naturalistic and case-study research can be used to negate a general proposition. Suppose that prior to Goodall's observation some naturalist had stated the general proposition that "chimpanzees are known to act aggressively toward each other in individual conflicts, but they do not engage in any concerted or group aggression resembling warfare seen in certain insects and in man." Goodall's observations show that this general proposition is incorrect; she observed at least some chimpanzees engaging in warlike behavior. Another example involves the statement, "Man's superiority over other creatures is due to the fact that man is the only tool-making and tool-using animal." Again the naturalistic observations of Goodall effectively refute this general proposition. She observed chimpanzees select and pull twigs from a bush or tree and strip off the leaves so as to fashion a slender flexible rod. The chimps then carefully inserted the twigs into the narrow tunnels of a termite nest, waited a moment, then withdrew the twig and licked off the termites clinging to it. This was not accidental behavior; it was purposeful, sophisticated, and performed repeatedly. The chimpanzees selected and then modified a natural object, preparing it for use as a food-gathering tool.

A final example involves some of our early research with autistic children (Graziano & Kean, 1968). Psychologists who had pioneered the use of relaxation in behavior therapy had noted that neither children nor psychotic adults could be taught relaxation. Ignoring the general proposition, we succeeded in training four autistic children in relaxation skills, procedures that have since been repeated many times with other children. This research was low constraint with no experimental controls and only four subjects. However, like the examples above, this case study successfully negated the general proposition that children cannot be taught relaxation skills.

Low-constraint research can negate a general proposition, but can it establish one? The answer is no. We cannot conclude from Goodall's observations that chimps, in general, engage in warfare; or from the Graziano and Kean study that all autistic children can be taught relaxation skills. We do not know whether those single observations are truly representative or whether they are one-shot phenomena. This limitation is related to issues of sampling, which we will discuss in more detail later in this chapter and again in Chapter 9.

Another important kind of information provided by naturalistic and case-study research involves observations about the relationships among variables. All research seeks to identify and understand relationships among variables. The type of relationship that is studied varies from one level of constraint to another. In experimental research we apply systematic controls and we manipulate variables so that we can identify causal relationships among variables. In low-constraint research, however, such causal inferences cannot be made, but we can obtain other useful information about relationships among variables. For example, the ethologist Niko Tinbergen (1951, 1963) observed that the parent herring gull readily provides food for its chick when the young bird pecks on or near a particular red spot on the adult's bill. The observation is that when the spot appears, the chick will most likely peck at it; when the chick pecks at the spot, the parent will most likely provide food (i.e., when X occurs, then Y will probably occur). Note that this does not state that X causes Y but only that there is a high probability of one occurring when the other is present. It is a statement of probability, and it helps to identify and describe a relationship between two variables. The chick's pecking is a stimulus for the parent's feeding behavior; further, a red spot on the parent's bill seems to be a stimulus for the chick's pecking behavior. When the young bird pecks on the parent's bill, there is a high probability that the parent will provide food.

In the above example, the relationship among the variables is one of probability; given X, then Y is probable. This kind of relationship is referred to as a *contingency;* feeding is contingent on pecking; pecking is contingent on the presence of a red spot. Naturalistic and case-study research can reveal many such contingent relationships among observed variables, and these contingencies can then become the bases for higher-constraint research. This is exactly what Tinbergen did once he noticed the contingent relationship between the chick's pecking and the adult's feeding behavior: having made the observation in relatively uncontrolled situations, he later carried out experimentation in which conditions were systematically varied. Contingent relationships observed in low-constraint research can be a great source for hypotheses to test with higher-constraint research, which is one of the major values of low-constraint research. Notice in the above example that flexibility is an advantage of both naturalistic and case-study research. Unlike the formal, high-constraint experiment, the researcher in low-constraint studies is free to vary procedures during the study, changing the focus on the basis of the obtained data or the changing interests of the researcher.

To summarize, low-constraint naturalistic and case-study research is useful and often the only way to proceed, and it can yield important information when used carefully and appropriately. In general, low-constraint research is appropriate for low-constraint questions: questions about unconstrained behavior in natural settings. Table 6-2 lists some of the conditions when low-constraint research is useful.

PROBLEM STATEMENTS AND HYPOTHESES IN NATURALISTIC OBSERVATION AND CASE-STUDY RESEARCH

In Chapter 3 we noted the importance of developing a statement of the problem for each research project. Although problem statements and their ultimate development into one or more research hypotheses are most formalized and best developed at the experimental level of constraint, they represent important steps in the research design process at *all* levels of constraint. Problem statements help us to organize our thinking, to specify how we are going to carry out our research, and to focus on

TABLE 6.2   THE VALUE OF LOW-CONSTRAINT RESEARCH

Naturalistic and case-study research is useful:

1. When we are beginning to investigate a new area in which little information is available
2. When the researcher wishes to gain familiarity with typical characteristics of settings or subjects before planning high-constraint research for similar settings or subjects
3. When the questions specifically focus on the natural flow of behavior and/or on the behavior in the natural environment
4. When the study is of a single individual, group, or set of events, and the questions are specific to those people, settings, or events
5. For demonstrations or illustrations, such as demonstrating a new procedure
6. As a way of discovering contingencies that can then be used as a basis for higher-constraint questions and research
7. When, on completing high-constraint research, we want to know if the relationships we have discovered and demonstrated under laboratory conditions hold true for behavior in the natural environment

Further, naturalistic and case-study research can provide

1. Descriptions of events, including events never before observed
2. Identification of contingent relationships among variables
3. Bases for hypotheses to be used in higher-constraint research
4. Observations to negate general propositions; low-constraint research cannot establish general propositions or causal inferences

the kinds of inferences we can confidently make based on data obtained in the research. The inferences we are able to make with confidence are different at different constraint levels: at the experimental level, problem statements and research hypotheses are focused on questions of causality; in differential studies, they are focused on determining differences between groups; at the correlational level, they are focused on the direction and strength of relationships between two or more variables; at the naturalistic and case-study levels, problem statements and research hypotheses are focused on identifying contingencies (i.e., on what variables seem to go together). Research hypotheses can be tested at any level of constraint, but those concerning causality can be tested with confidence only at the experimental level, where the most complete controls are applied.

Problem statements in low-constraint research are often general or vague. The reason is that we may have no basis for generating more specific questions. Problem statements also change readily in low-constraint research as the researcher begins to grasp the issues through observation and starts to focus attention on specific behavior. Suppose that an industrial/organizational psychologist is called in to evaluate a "communication problem" in a company. The psychologist is knowledgeable about the dynamics of business organizations and strategies that might be applied to specific problems, but the psychologist has no way of knowing what the "communication problem" really represents. The initial problem statement in this case might be "I wonder what is wrong." Interviewing several key people will likely provide some insight into the problem, but just as likely the psychologist will find several different opinions on it. Careful observation of interactions between members of the company might suggest an underlying defensiveness, commonly referred to in business circles as "CYA" (cover your ass). The consultant might narrow the problem statement to focus more on this attitude, suspecting that it may be a key to understanding the "problem." But further observation and discussion with employees and managers seems to suggest that the "cover your ass" mentality is more likely an effect of problems in the company, rather than a cause. At this point the consultant may begin to work with two or three more narrow problem statements, which are based in part on the consultants knowledge of what types of situations could create the scenario observed. Each of these might be independently evaluated through continued observation, fact gathering, and interviewing. All of this may occur in just the first day of the consultant's visit or it may take several days or even weeks to get this far. Any consultant who came in and immediately suggested that communication problems should be handled, for example, with a reorganization of the company, an integrated computer network with Electronic and Voice Mail, and sensitivity training for middle-level managers would not be doing the job very well. There is no guarantee that the problem really is communication. That would be no different than a doctor prescribing open heart surgery five minutes after a patient reports experiencing chest pain. This example illustrates the strength of low-constraint research—being able to move flexibly from one area to another depending on what you find. Of course, eventually the consultant will need to focus in on key elements, gather relevant data, and make specific suggestions. But an early narrow focus can blind you to critical issues and lead to poor recommendations.

The above example illustrates key features of problem statements in low-constraint research. The problem statements tend to start out general and become more focused as the researcher learns more about the problem. Problem statements will gradually evolve into more specific hypotheses, which will guide the researcher in gathering detailed information relevant to the hypothesis. Finally, there is an inherent limitation in this process. Low-constraint research can provide only so much information. If we want to know with confidence what is causing what, we must translate our hypotheses into higher-constraint research questions. It is often tempting to try to draw causal inferences from low-constraint research when we observe some clear contingency in which variable Y seems to occur whenever we also observe variable X. But as we have emphasized here and will discuss again later in this chapter, we cannot confidently draw causal inferences from low-constraint research.

USING NATURALISTIC OBSERVATION AND CASE-STUDY METHODS

As noted earlier, the central phase of any research project is the observational or data-gathering phase. This is especially true in the naturalistic and case-study methods. In some higher-constraint research, before we do any observation, we make detailed and highly specific plans of how to observe and record the data and how to analyze the data once it has been collected. In lower-constraint research, planning is much less formal and plans are much more fluid. The researcher is free to change hypotheses and modify procedures in the middle of the observations. It is not unusual, for example, for the observer conducting naturalistic and case-study research to design a whole new study based on some of the initial observations made by the researcher.

Making Observations

Unobtrusive and Participant Observation   There are two ways to gather data in naturalistic observation—as an unobtrusive observer or as a participant observer. As an *unobtrusive observer,* the researcher tries to avoid responding to or influencing in any way the subject under observation. As a *participant-observer,* the researcher becomes a part of the situation being observed and even contributes to it. The contribution might be the normal contribution almost anyone would make in that situation, or it might consist of carefully planned and executed changes in the researcher's behavior as a way of tentatively testing specific hypotheses the researcher has generated. Dr. Levine's work, discussed earlier, utilized participant observation in parts of her study of the Love Canal crisis.

One advantage of participant observation is that by manipulating your own behavior as an observer, you are able to test hypotheses by creating situations that are unlikely to occur naturally. The case-study method often uses participant observation. For example, Piaget did not passively observe children. Instead, he asked questions, created test situations, interacted with the children, and observed their responses. Another advantage of the participant-observer method is that it often makes the observer less obtrusive and in so doing can reduce the likelihood that the observer will influence the subject to behave in particular ways. The term *measurement reactivity* refers to the phenomenon of subjects behaving differently than they might normally because they know they are being observed. Some measures (*reactive measures*) are particularly prone to such distortions, while others (*nonreactive measures*) are not affected by the subjects' knowledge that they are being observed. Measurement reactivity is not unique to social science research. In physics, for example, simply measuring the movement of an electron changes the motion of that electron so that a physicist can never observe continuously the motion of so small a particle. In psychology and other social sciences, the reactivity is often a function of what the subject believes is the appropriate behavior in that particular situation. All of us have a tendency to behave in ways we think are appropriate when we know we are being observed. How much more likely is it that you will use a fork and knife to eat your chicken if you are dining in a restaurant than if you are eating chicken at home with no one else present?

Unobtrusive Measures and Archival Records   The problem of reactivity in social science research has spawned a variety of interesting concepts, the best known of which is the unobtrusive measure. *Unobtrusive measures* are measures of behavior that are not obvious to the person being observed and, consequently, are less likely to influence the person to behave in particular ways. Webb, Campbell, Schwartz, and Sechrest (1966) described a number of clever ways of measuring phenomena without appearing to. Some of their measures were designed to provide information about phenomena that had already occurred. These *archival records* are often readily available in libraries, schools, or town halls and may include school records, marriage and divorce records, driving records, or census data. Many such records are protected from unlawful use even by well-intentioned researchers.

It might appear that using archival records (records that already exist) is a sloppy way to measure a phenomenon. But that need not be the case. Some of the most sophisticated research on genetic influences in psychopathology were archival studies (Kety, Rosenthal, Wender, & Schulsinger, 1968; Wender, Kety, Rosenthal, Schulsinger, Ortmann, & Lunde, 1986). These investigators used records from many sources to track the rates of psychopathology in both the adoptive and biological families of severely disturbed adults who were adopted as infants.

Governments gather archival data routinely to identify nationwide problems quickly. Statistics computed from such archival data, such as the Index of Leading Economic Indicators, can be accurate predictors of future events. Data gathered from hospitals about diseases under treatment have allowed officials to identify new diseases like toxic shock syndrome or AIDS and even narrow the range of possible causes of the diseases. The key to the effectiveness of using archival data is the quality of the data and the degree of its relevance to the question being asked.

Archival records are only one type of unobtrusive measure available to psychological researchers. Webb et al. (1966) describe several clever ways of measuring constructs of interest to the psychologist. For example, suppose you want to measure the level of interest of particular museum exhibits. You first need an operational definition of level of interest. (Remember from Chapter 4 that an operational definition is a statement of the procedures or operations an investigator will perform to measure a specified variable.) One operational definition of "interest level" is the average of many people's interest ratings. You might ask each of the first 200 people who walked by an exhibit to rate how interesting it is on a ten-point scale. This measure would not be unobtrusive because each subject would be well aware that something about them—their level of interest in an exhibit—was being measured. The measure would therefore have the potential for being reactive because subjects might behave differently because they know they are being measured. Another operational definition of the level of interest is the number of people who choose to view a particular exhibit. One way to measure this is to ask each person who viewed the exhibit to sign a log. This measure would be obtrusive, and the person would know that something about them (their presence) was being recorded. A less obtrusive measure would involve having someone standing off to the side count the number of people who approach the exhibit. One advantage of having an observer do the counting is that the observer can code other information, such as how long people observe the exhibit, the subject's sex, approximate age, and so on. We could automate the counting procedure by using an electric eye and an electronic counter. But there are also simpler yet effective measures that might give us the information we desire. One procedure suggested by Webb et al. (1966) is to note the degree of wear on the tiles of the floor surrounding the exhibit. In some museums, the tiles around popular exhibits need to be replaced every few weeks, whereas the tiles around other exhibits will last for several years. Another method suggested by Webb et al. is the nose-print approach. In this approach, the exhibit is put in a glass display and arranged so that people can get the best view by putting their faces right up to the glass. The glass is cleaned at the start of each day. At day's end the glass is dusted with fingerprint powder, and the number of nose prints is counted. Of course, not everyone will leave a nose print, and some people will press their nose to the glass in several places, so this method will not give an accurate count of how many people viewed the display. But remember, we want to measure how "interesting" the exhibit is, and the number of people who viewed the exhibit is an operational definition of "interest." The number of nose prints is also a reasonable operational definition of interest level and may in some ways be superior to our head-count method.

The above examples are not intended to be specific suggestions for research measures; rather, they are designed to make you think more creatively when you develop your own measures. There is nothing wrong with asking people to rate how interesting museum exhibits are, but it is often valuable to get some independent data to substantiate the ratings.

Ethical Issues

Ethical considerations are important when using unobtrusive measures. Each potential subject should be made aware of the procedures of the study in order to make an informed decision, and thus give their informed consent. The principle is not absolute, however. If it were, unobtrusive measures could never be used. But to justify unobtrusive measures in a study, the researcher must show that nondeceptive measures would not work, and that there is no significant risk of harm from use of the measure. These judgments, often difficult to make, are one reason for having a formal review process of all studies using human subjects.

Sampling of Subjects

Deciding on the best way to observe subjects is an important matter. An equally demanding task is to decide what subjects will be observed. The term *sampling* refers to the selection of subjects. Sampling is important in any research but is particularly so in higher-constraint research. (We will discuss sampling in more detail in Chapters 9 and 13.) The issue of sampling that we need to understand now is the concept of *representativeness* and its relationship to generalizability.

In naturalistic and case-study research, sampling may not be under the researcher's control. In many cases we do not actually select the sample of subjects for study. If we are psychotherapy researchers, the clients who come to us for treatment constitute the sample. If we are investigating behavior of human beings during a natural disaster, the people unfortunate enough to be present when the disaster occurs represent the sample. In both cases, however, we must address the question of how well the samples represent the larger population. In the psychotherapy example, we might expect that people who come to a therapist for help may well be different from people in general. They probably have more psychological problems and are more concerned with those problems than is the typical person. They may be wealthier than the typical person since they can afford the cost of psychotherapy or have insurance that will cover the cost. To the extent that there are differences between the sample and the general population, the sample is said to be unrepresentative of the population. Whenever a sample is not representative of the general population, we must be careful in generalizing the findings. *We generalize the findings when we assume that what we observed in the sample of subjects would also be observed in any other group of subjects from the population.* We want to be able to generalize the findings, but we can do so only if the sample is truly representative of the population in which we are interested. In our psychotherapy example, suppose we found that most of the male clients expressed hatred for their mothers. Could we then conclude that most men hate their mothers? We certainly could not, because the sample is not representative of all men. It may be that men who hate their mothers are more likely to develop psychological problems or that people with psychological problems tend to hate their mothers. Could we generalize the findings to a more narrow population? Could we conclude that most men who have psychological problems hate their mothers? We cannot even draw that conclusion safely, because there may be many people with psychological problems who do not seek therapy and who may be different from those people who do.

We rarely have the opportunity to select our own samples in case-study and naturalistic research. Therefore, we must make some judgment of how well the sample represents the population to which we want to generalize the results. The more representative of the population a sample is, the more confident we can be in making generalizations. However, with low-constraint research, we should always be cautious in making generalizations. We should think of such generalizations as tentative hypotheses that can be tested with higher-constraint research methods. As we will see later in the text, when we are allowed to control the sampling procedures, we can almost guarantee the representativeness of the sample.

Sampling of Situations

The sampling of situations also can affect generalizability. Suppose, for example, we want to study work habits in factories. As part of the study, we install a television camera to monitor employees' behavior. From the previous section's discussion, we know that the presence of the camera may be reactive; that is, the subjects may behave differently because they know they are being watched. But we can view this same problem from another perspective, that of sampling. Our sample of behaviors comes from a situation that is different from the situations to which we want to generalize (i.e., the typical factory). Because closed circuit TV is not used to monitor employees in most factory settings, this situation is not representative of the population of settings to which we wish to generalize our results, and so we cannot generalize our findings with confidence.

The sample of situations can be distorted in numerous ways. Some variables are beyond our control and others can be controlled only at great cost or inconvenience. Suppose we want to study animals in the wild. Many animals behave differently during different seasons of the year, being active during some seasons and inactive during others. Most animals show the same kind of fluctuations in activity level on a daily basis. If we observe the animals only during the morning hours of spring and summer, because these were convenient and comfortable times to make such observations, we might get a distorted picture of the behavior of the animals under study. An even worse violation of this principle would be to study only animals in zoos because they are close and easy to find. The situation in even the best of zoos is dramatically different from the natural environment to which we want to generalize our findings. Therefore, a good rule of thumb in early study of any population is to sample as widely as possible the many situations the subjects are likely to face in their daily existence. The broader the sample of situations studied and the broader the sample of subjects, the more confidence we can have in the generalizability of the findings.

Sampling of Behaviors

A related issue is the importance of adequately sampling behaviors within any given situation. In any particular situation, organisms may behave in many different ways. Therefore, a single observation of behavior in a particular situation could lead to an incorrect conclusion about how the organism behaves in that setting. However, by sampling behaviors repeatedly in each situation, it is possible to identify whatever behavioral variability actually occurs.

EVALUATING AND INTERPRETING DATA

Once observations are made and data are gathered, we need to evaluate and interpret the results of the study. This step usually involves statistical analyses. In many low-constraint studies, direct statistical analysis is not possible until some coding of the data is accomplished. In low-constraint studies, we often observe and record everything that happens. The record might be a verbal description of everything we observed or it might be a video- or audiotape of the action. For example, if we were studying the process of labor contract negotiation, the data set might be the transcripts of all negotiation sessions. In analyzing the data, we might code the interactions in terms of categories such as hostile comments, requests for information, suggested solutions, and so forth. Dean Pruitt and his colleagues (Kimmel, Pruitt, Magenau, Konar-Goldband, & Carnevale, 1980; McGillicuddy, Welton, & Pruitt, 1987; Welton, Pruitt, & McGillicuddy, 1988; Rubin, Pruitt, & Kim, 1994) have used similar categories in a series of studies of the negotiation process. Once the data have been coded, we can count the numbers of each type of interaction. For lower-constraint studies, the statistical procedures used may be no more complicated than means and standard deviations or frequency counts. There may be some natural comparisons to be made, such as between different groups of subjects or among the same subjects under more than one condition. In the above example, we might want to compare the verbal statements of the labor and management negotiators, or the negotiation sessions that were fruitful with sessions that were not. If such comparisons are needed, we would use the appropriate inferential statistic. (Procedures for selecting the appropriate statistical test are reviewed in Chapter 14.)

Regardless of the statistical procedures used, it is important to realize that we must be cautious when interpreting the data from a low-constraint research study. By its very nature, low-constraint research employs few controls. The purpose of control is to eliminate alternative explanations for results, making it easier to draw a single strong conclusion. Because those controls are absent from this level of constraint, we will seldom be able to draw strong conclusions from a low-constraint study. Further, these limitations cannot be corrected by applying sophisticated statistical analyses. *No statistical analysis will create controls that were not part of the original study.*

LIMITATIONS OF NATURALISTIC AND CASE-STUDY METHODS

We have noted the positive values of low-constraint research, but it also has limitations. Consider some of the limitations of one example already given—Freud's psychoanalytic theory and the observational methods on which it was based. Freud's case-study methods exemplified so well many of the strengths and weaknesses associated with this level of research. As noted earlier, psychoanalytic ideas generated by Freud and his early followers have had a creative, heuristic impact on many areas of research. Today, more than half a century after Freud's death and a full century since his early work, researchers are still investigating his concepts and methods. However, there are weaknesses in the research on which psychoanalytic theory is based, many of which have yet to be corrected.

Poor Representativeness

One of the major weaknesses in the use of low-constraint methods is poor representativeness. Recall that one use of low-constraint research is in answering questions about the particular group or person. The conclusions in low-constraint studies almost always must be limited to those individuals who are directly studied and cannot be generalized to a wider population. But Freud drew inferences from his limited sample, which were presented and accepted as universally applicable to all people of all ages in all cultures and across all time. The phrase "sweeping generalization" certainly applies here. Freud studied a limited sample of adult, neurotic, well-to-do, turn-of-the-century Europeans, and he rarely, if ever, directly studied children. The unwarranted overgeneralizations led, for example, to the remarkable situation in which psychoanalytic theory was enthusiastically accepted by many professionals as the major and most definitive theory of child development, even though Freud never directly treated a child during the theory's development. If psychoanalytic theory is to be generalized to all children, then a sample of children who adequately represent the population must be studied. Indeed, more recent psychoanalytic investigators have tried to do this. The late Anna Freud's work, for example, focused primarily on children. But even in Anna Freud's work, her low-constraint case studies of children do not allow us to generalize the findings beyond the individuals studied unless they have been carefully selected as representative samples. We do not know, for example, how Freud's patients might have been different from people in general. They may have been more troubled than most people because they sought psychological help, or they may have been simply more willing to seek psychological help. We know they were more wealthy because they could afford treatment. (There were no insurance reimbursements at the time.) Any clinical sample, including Freud's, is going to be a biased rather than a representative sample because the

---

Box 6.3   # For What Is a Scientist Remembered?

Sigmund Freud and E. L. Witmer provide a contrast for students interested in studying the sociology of science. Freud and Witmer were contemporaries in the early 1900s. Both emphasized and developed case-study methods applied to people with psychological problems. Both pushed their colleagues to seek new directions and applications in their professions. They also contrasted sharply. Whereas Freud worked with adults and never directly studied or worked with children, Witmer focused his clinical work almost exclusively on children. Freud based his inferences on his clients' verbal self-reports; Witmer included self-reports but also used more objective medical and psychological testing approaches. Freud never went beyond the clients' self-reports for any corroborating evidence; Witmer sought information from parents, teachers, and others to provide some degree of external validation for his inferences. Freud worked with individual adults, virtually all of whom were economically well-to-do; Witmer worked with individual children across all social classes. Both men emphasized case-study methods, but Witmer was more scientifically sophisticated than Freud. Given the apparent superiority of Witmer's approach, the final comparison leaves us with a puzzle. Freud's influence on anthropology, drama, literature, psychiatry, psychology, social work, sociology, and on popular culture generally has been enormous and sustained; Witmer is ordinarily accorded a footnote here and there. It was Freud's enormous contribution to theory, and not his prowess in validating that theory with sophisticated research, that made him such a powerful figure. Some of Freud's inferences were clearly wrong, and he routinely went far beyond the data while developing his theory; but his ideas were stimulating, relevant, and often scientifically testable (see Masling & Bornstein, 1994)—even if they were not always right.

---

subjects have selected themselves for therapy and not every person in the population is equally likely to seek therapy. Therefore, generalization of findings from clinical samples to any group other than those who seek therapy is unwarranted without additional research with representative samples (see Box 6-3).

Poor Replicability

Another limitation of low-constraint research is related to the very characteristic that gives it its greatest strength—flexibility. Because observations of naturally occurring behavior are made in settings where the observer has imposed few if any constraints on the behavior of the subject, it is often difficult to replicate (repeat) such research. Different investigators studying the same phenomenon through low-constraint methods may make different observations and therefore draw different inferences. In order for *replication* to be possible, the researchers must clearly state all details of their procedures. Freud, for example, never made his methods of observation and inference explicit, so it is impossible to replicate them. In addition, Freud published a total of only six psychoanalytic case studies (two of which were not his own cases). This is another weakness, because the small number of cases cannot adequately represent the true variability among human beings. Many more cases would be necessary.

Causal Inference and Low-Constraint Research: The Ex Post Facto Fallacy

As mentioned earlier, drawing causal inferences from case studies is virtually impossible. Freud listened to his clients talk about their subjective experiences. He noted that certain past experiences seemed to be associated with current functioning, and he drew *causal inferences* about these relationships (i.e., that specific past experiences helped to bring about or cause current problems). Ex post facto ("after the fact") reasoning is a major part of Freud's research approach; he observed events after the fact, such as current neurotic symptoms, and then searched the client's reported history for clues about what earlier events might be causally related. This type of speculative and tentative identification of contingencies is useful in suggesting hypothetical relationships. However, as a research procedure, it does not provide the controls needed to rule out the possibility that other factors may have influenced the observed symptoms. Therefore, we cannot properly state that we have demonstrated a causal relationship. Case studies are by their nature ex post facto approaches. Case studies lack control over independent variables and are unable to rule out the possible effects of other variables. For this reason we cannot have confidence in any causal inference we might be tempted to draw. Such inferences must be treated as no more than speculative hypotheses for further research. For that purpose—stimulating higher constraint research—case-study methods can be useful.

The *ex post facto fallacy* is a common and serious error because it can mislead investigators into severe misinterpretation of data. Table 6-3 gives some common examples of ex post facto fallacies. You should note the logical fallacy is obvious in some of the statements, whereas other, exactly parallel statements seem quite reasonable. There may even be some assertions in the list that you have heard many times before and may have accepted without giving them much thought.

If the statements in Table 6-3 are taken as speculative hypotheses rather than confident statements of causality, then they can be useful for further research. In this case, we view them as tentative statements to be tested rather than as already established conclusions. When we interpret and use low-constraint results as if they were equivalent to high-constraint research results, we not only draw conclusions

---

TABLE 6.3   SEVERAL EXAMPLES OF POSSIBLE EX POST FACTO FALLACIES

---

1. Hard drug users all smoked marijuana before turning to hard drugs; therefore, marijuana use leads to hard-drug addiction.
2. Alcoholics started with beer and wine; therefore, beer and wine lead to alcoholism.
3. Child-abusing parents were abused themselves as children; therefore, being abused as a child leads to becoming an abusive parent.
4. Most of the inmates in urban jails are black; therefore, being black leads to crime.
5. Nearly all institutionalized juvenile delinquents are from urban backgrounds; therefore, growing up in cities leads to juvenile delinquency.
6. Aggressive children watch a great deal of television; therefore, watching a great deal of television leads to aggressive behavior in children.

Note: The relationships noted above might have some validity, but we can never establish the validity through ex post facto reasoning.

that are likely to be false but we might also damage the credibility of other research, even well-designed high-constraint research.

Limitations of the Observer

Another issue in low-constraint research concerns the limitations of the observer. When Freud listened to his clients, were they giving spontaneous verbalizations or were they saying what they thought Freud wanted to hear? Did he influence their verbalizing, perhaps by emitting an interested "mm-hmm" whenever the client touched on some sexual fantasy? The issue is one of *experimenter reactivity* or *experimenter bias* (Rosenthal, 1976). To obtain natural behavior, the observer must be uninvolved. In case studies, it is difficult for observers to control their own reactivity—to control the many possible subtle influences they might have on the subject. In higher-constraint research, controls can be used to minimize the observer's possible reactivity, which might influence the results.

It is important for researchers to understand the limitations of low-constraint methods. Knowing the limitations will allow us to use the methods appropriately. When used appropriately, naturalistic and case-study methods are valuable. The dangers are more in our temptations to infer causality erroneously, to generalize beyond the subjects studied, to consider the findings certain rather than tentative, and to fail to recognize how the observer may be reactive, thereby influencing the behavior of the subjects. These and other limitations are adequately dealt with in higher-constraint research by the careful addition of controls. With controls in place, we are able to use high-constraint experimental research as a basis for making causal inferences and for generalizing the results from the research subjects (sample) to the larger group (population).

Internal Summary: Naturalistic Observation and Case Studies

These are low-constraint research methods. They can be used to discover contingencies, can negate general propositions, and provide descriptions of the natural flow of behavior in natural or slightly constrained environments, but they cannot establish causality. They tend to be used in early stages of a research area and as bases for developing hypotheses that can later be tested with higher-constraint research. When carried out well, low-constraint procedures can provide important information.

SURVEY RESEARCH

Survey research is not a single research design (Schuman & Kalton, 1985). Rather, it is an area of research that utilizes several basic procedures to obtain information from people in their natural environments. It is because of the emphasis on measures in natural environments that survey methods are introduced in this chapter on field research.

The basic instrument used in this research is the *survey,* a set of one or more questions presented to subjects. A survey asks people about their attitudes, beliefs, plans, health, work, income, life satisfactions and concerns, consumer preferences, political views, and so on. Virtually any human issue can be surveyed. The researcher using survey methods does not manipulate variables but, rather, imposes some constraints on subjects by virtue of using a specific survey instrument. As will be seen below, the survey may be used to test relationships among variables. This, plus its emphasis on the natural environment, makes survey research similar to both case studies and correlational research, making it somewhat of a transition between them.

Types of Surveys

Status Survey   A survey can be relatively simple, such as a *status survey,* in which the information sought is a description of the current status of some population characteristic. For example, surveys to determine what proportion of voters are Republican, Democrat, Liberal, or Independent, or what proportion of teachers are satisfied with their professions, are status surveys. Status surveys were in use as long ago as the 1830s in England, when the working conditions of young children and adults in mines and factories during the Industrial Revolution were first investigated.

Survey Research   In contrast to simple status surveys, *survey research* is relatively new, having been developed by social scientists in the twentieth century. It is also more complex than status surveys, as it seeks not only the current status of population characteristics but also tries to discover relationships among variables. In this sense, it is a variation of a correlational research design. (Correlational research will be discussed in Chapter 7). For example, survey research could be conducted to determine whether teachers' job satisfaction is related to teacher training, income, age, type of school, grade level taught, and so on. An example is a large-scale survey carried out by Campbell, Converse, and Rodgers (1976) in which they measured the perceptions, evaluations, and satisfactions of Americans to assess the quality of American life. They examined the relationships among demographic variables, such as age, education, income, social class, and the sense of satisfaction that Americans have with critical domains of their lives, such as marriage, jobs, and housing. The researchers were not primarily interested in the status of the variables they measured but in the relationships among the variables.

Steps in Survey Research

Surveys are the most ubiquitous form of research in social science and are familiar to most of us. Surveys are commissioned by Congress, are carried out by manufacturers, retailers, health agencies, lobbyists, churches, private organizations, political parties, foreign governments—by anyone who wants to find out what people are thinking or feeling about specific issues or events.

At first glance, it may appear an easy task to conduct surveys; after all, surveys are based on the idea that if you want to know what people are thinking, just ask

TABLE 6.4   MAJOR STEPS IN SURVEY RESEARCH

1. Determine what area of information is to be sought.
2. Define the population to be studied.
3. Decide how the survey is to be administered.
4. Construct the first draft of the survey instrument; edit and refine the draft.
5. Pretest it with a subsample; refine it further.
6. Develop a sampling frame and draw a representative sample.
7. Administer the final form of the instrument to the sample.
8. Analyze, interpret, and communicate the results.

them! But as we will see, the same carefully detailed planning is necessary for surveys as for any good research (see Table 6-4).

The major goal of a survey is to learn about the ideas, knowledge, feeling, opinions, attitudes, and self-reported behavior of a defined population of people by directly asking them. Therefore, to carry out a survey the researcher must identify the content area, construct the survey instrument, define the population, draw a representative sample, administer the survey instrument, analyze and interpret the data, and communicate the results. Those steps are overlapping, and each step demands careful work.

Among the first tasks of the researcher is to determine the informational area to be studied, the population to be surveyed, and how the survey instrument is to be administered. Those decisions guide the construction and administration of the survey instrument. The survey instrument might be an *interview schedule* for surveys done in person or by telephone. The instrument could also be a *questionnaire* for group and self-administered surveys. For example, Milbrath, Hausbeck, and Enright (1991) wanted to determine the knowledge and attitudes of New York State high school students (the population) about environmental problems (the area of information), using an in-class, group-administered questionnaire (the form of the survey). In the Campbell et al. (1976) survey, the area studied was American's perceived quality of life, the targeted population was Americans over 18 years of age, and the form was a personal interview schedule.

The Form of the Survey Instrument

The survey instrument may be in the form of a questionnaire or an interview schedule. In a mailed survey or group-administered *questionnaire,* the respondents read the instructions and write or mark their answers to the questions. In group-administered questionnaires, such as might be carried out in a classroom, the researcher might read and clarify the instructions to the respondents. In telephone or in-person interviews, the instrument is called an *interview schedule,* and the researcher reads the questions to the respondent and records the answers. The survey instrument (questionnaire or interview schedule) lists the questions in the order in which they are to be answered and provides instructions and means for answering them. If it is a self-administered questionnaire, it must be a clear and unambiguous guide for the respondent. If it is to be administered by a researcher, as with an interview schedule, then it must be a clear guide for the interviewer as well. In either event, the questions are listed in a fixed order for all respondents. The language must be clear and concise and must be appropriate for the population being studied. Overall, a questionnaire should have an uncluttered and orderly appearance and must be well within the reading and comprehension abilities of the respondents. The questionnaire must include clear instructions and uncomplicated means for answering.

Questionnaires and interviews begin with an introduction, which explains the purpose of the survey and gives instructions to the respondent. The questions then fall into two main categories—demographic and content questions. The demographic questions seek information about the respondents such as age, sex, occupation, family status, and so on. These are factual items, and they can be verified independently. Most of the items are content items, dealing with the subject being surveyed. Content items ask about the respondents' opinions, attitudes, knowledge, and behavior. People's opinions and attitudes are subjective, vary among individuals, and are not evaluated independently as right or wrong. Questions about what people think of particular political parties or where they stand on issues such as animal rights, abortion, or environmental versus business values are attitude and opinion items.

Frequently, surveys ask about the respondents' knowledge, such as high school students' knowledge of geography, history, or science. Questions that ask, "What is the capital of Afghanistan?" or "What percentage of paper products in the United States is made of recycled paper?" are tests of knowledge. Answers to those questions can be evaluated independently and objectively as right or wrong.

Content items can also focus on the overt behavior of the respondent. For example, the question "How many times in the past month have you taken newspapers to the campus recycling center?" asks about the person's actual behavior. Theoretically, behavior-focused items can be objectively verified, but only if there are dependable observers of the behavior. The fact is that in surveys, the information is the self-report of the respondent. While self-report data may be relatively convenient to obtain, there are obvious concerns over their reliability and validity.

Surveys typically include all types of items—demographic, attitude, opinion, knowledge, and behavior items. In the Milbrath et al. (1991) questionnaire of eleventh graders, for example, the content focused on the respondents' knowledge, attitudes, opinions, and behavior with reference to environmental issues.

Developing the Survey Instrument

The instrument is developed in several steps, always keeping in mind the content area and the nature of the respondents. The researcher must determine exactly what questions are to be asked, in what form, and in what order. The instrument must be constructed so that it adequately covers the area of information sought and is appropriate for the targeted population. Construction of the survey instrument also depends on the procedure that is going to be used to administer it. A face-to-face interview generally requires a much more detailed survey instrument than is typical for a telephone survey, which usually includes a few simple items in a one- or two-minute conversation. In contrast, personal interview surveys can include many questions, many opportunities for the interviewer to probe for more information, and may require several hours to complete.

Construction of the survey instrument is one of the most time-consuming steps in the survey research process. The researcher must have a clear understanding of the nature of the information desired, and the questionnaire should be kept well focused on that area. Sometimes researchers try to cover too many areas or they attempt a "shotgun" approach in which clear reasons for the questions are lacking. These approaches make the questionnaire hard for the respondent to answer and difficult to analyze and understand later. A basic rule in survey research is that the instrument should have a clear focus and should be guided at least in part by hypotheses and expectancies held by the researcher. This means that survey research is not well suited to early exploratory research, because it does require some orderly expectations by the researcher.

Constructing Items   Let us suppose that we want to survey local school teachers (the population) on their views about the use of corporal punishment by parents and teachers to discipline children (the area of information), and we are going to use a self-administered, mailed questionnaire (the form of administration). Having determined the general area of inquiry, the population to be surveyed, and the form of administration, the next step is to develop the instrument.

The researcher writes the items, carefully ensuring that they cover the area of information desired (use of corporal punishment) and that the items are in language appropriate for the population (teachers). The items should be clearly written, unambiguous, fairly short, and should be preceded by clear instructions and explanations for the respondent. After the items are written, they are edited for clarity and meaning and are pretested, usually on a small sample from the population to be surveyed. Based on the pretesting, the items may be further refined, and the final form of the instrument is then prepared.

The items in the questionnaire or interview schedule can take several forms—open-ended items, multiple-choice items, and Likert-scale items. In our hypothetical questionnaire, we might ask the open-ended question:

What do you think of using corporal punishment in disciplining children?

If this were a questionnaire, we would leave sufficient space for the respondents to write their answers. In an interview, we would tape-record their answers for later coding and scoring. An example of a multiple choice question is:

Approximately what proportion of parents use corporal punishment to discipline their children?

a. 10%   b. 25%   c. 50%   d. 75%   e. 100%

In Likert scales, the items are arranged on a continuum, with extreme positions at the end points. Respondents are typically asked to indicate the degree to which they agree with a statement, such as:

Corporal punishment is necessary in raising children.

Strongly Agree   Agree   Uncertain   Disagree   Strongly Disagree

This item could be scored from 1 to 5 (strongly agree = 1). The respondent would answer all of the items on the questionnaire, and the overall score would be the total of the scores on each item. [Other scaling methods such as the Thurstone, Guttman, and Semantic Differential Scales are also used, but a detailed discussion of all of the scaling formats is beyond the scope of this text. The interested student is referred to Dawis (1987) and Kerlinger (1986).]

A single questionnaire might include items in each format (open-ended, multiple-choice, Likert). If so, it is good procedure to keep those of the same format together.

The Subjects in a Survey: Populations and Samples

Obtaining an adequate sample is one of the most important factors in conducting surveys. When the population about which we seek information is very large and diverse, it is impossible to question every member (element) of that population. The U.S. census is an example of such an attempt. We know that the census is expensive and time-consuming and that there are many problems and much incomplete information. Instead, in most surveys we draw a sample of the population and then generalize the findings from our sample to the population.

The population in a survey is the larger group about whom we wish to obtain information. Some examples of survey populations are eligible voters for a presidential election, high school teachers in New York State, readers of the *National Review,* middle-school children in Milwaukee, students at the State University of New York at Buffalo, Chevrolet owners, and so on.

In our example, we have taken the first step by tentatively identifying the population as local school teachers. Now we must be more precise, specifying a geographic area or specific school systems and other characteristics of the population, such as the grade levels of the teachers or their areas of teaching expertise (science, social studies, English, etc.). The survey might include all school teachers or be limited to grammar school or full-time teachers. We would have to decide whether to include teachers in private schools or limit the population of study to only public school teachers. Suppose that we decide our population for study will be all full-time, state-certified, public school teachers (grades 1 through 12), whose primary task is classroom teaching in Arkright, Frankston, Transville, and Wellbourne counties. Note the variability among the population: some will be male and some female; some will be special-education teachers; others will have specialized areas such as music and shop; their ages will vary considerably from the early 20s to the late 60s; their experiences and abilities as teachers will also vary greatly.

Sampling Considerations   Having constructed and tested the survey instrument and identified the population to be studied, the researcher must also specify the sampling procedures. The essential approach of survey research is to draw a sample of people from a known population and then to administer the survey directly to each subject. The survey can be administered by mail, telephone, or personal interview. The most information and generally best results are obtained when the survey is administered in a personal, face-to-face interview. In the Campbell et al. (1976) study, each of 2164 people was personally interviewed. The personal interview is effective but also time-consuming and expensive.

Survey information is obtained from a sample, but the goal is to learn about the population from which the sample is drawn. The survey researcher wants to draw inferences from the data obtained from the sample in order to describe characteristics of the population. Using the terminology developed earlier in the text, whenever we use a sample as a basis for generalizing to a population, we are engaging in a process of inductive inference (from the specific sample to the general population). It should be clear that inductive reasoning is the general process involved in use of inferential statistics. It should also be obvious that, if we are to have confidence in inductive inferences from sample to population, then the sample must be carefully drawn to *represent adequately the population to which we want to infer.* The heart of survey research is the careful selection of representative samples. Without it, the results of survey research can tell us only about the sample and are not meaningful or useful in learning about a larger population.

Sampling Procedures   Sampling procedures fall into two major categories: (1) nonprobability sampling and (2) probability sampling.

Nonprobability sampling methods include, for example, carrying out a survey by interviewing the first 50 people whom you meet on the street or as many people as you can interview who are coming out of a polling place at election time. Newspaper, TV, and radio surveys are often carried out in this way to obtain a quick public response to an issue while it is still a current news item. The advantage of nonprobability sampling is the ease with which it can be carried out. Its weakness is that the first 50 people, or whatever other nonprobability sample is obtained, might not be a representative sample of the total population, and the survey results might therefore be biased.

Probability sampling procedures give us greater confidence that the sample adequately represents the population to which we want to infer. In probability sampling, each population element (i.e., each person) has some known, specifiable probability of being included in the sample. The two major probability sampling methods are simple random sampling and stratified random sampling.

In *simple random sampling,* every member of the identified population has an equal chance of being selected. There is no systematic bias in simple random sampling that can lead to persons with certain characteristics having a higher probability of being selected than persons without those characteristics. Simple random sampling, however, requires that we have a list of all members of the population. Clearly this would be difficult to obtain if the population is large, such as all people living in the United States or all children and youth enrolled in primary and secondary schools. With such large populations, we cannot use simple random sampling. If the population is more limited, such as all children in a specific school or all psychologists in private practice in a certain city, an initial list (called a *sampling frame*) is much more feasible. We could randomly select from such sampling frames without much difficulty. Thus, simple random sampling is used for survey research in which population size allows a workable sampling frame from which individuals can be randomly selected. For example, suppose we want to survey 50 of the 317 families in a town who have a mentally retarded child in a special class. The sampling frame would consist of the names of all 317 families.

Each would be assigned a number from 1 to 317, and we would use a table of random numbers to select randomly the sample of 50 families. However, as careful as we may be to obtain an accurate sampling frame, it may be incomplete. Changes might occur between the time we obtain the list and begin selecting the sample. Families may move into or away from the town, people may become ill or die. Thus a sampling frame is almost always incomplete and is an approximation of the true population.

Stratified random sampling procedures are used when it is important to ensure that subgroups within a population are adequately represented in the sample. In essence, the researcher divides the population into subgroups or *strata* and a random sample is taken from each stratum. Suppose we want to conduct an in-person, detailed survey on 100 of the 1737 students in McKinley High School. We would not want to bias the results by over- or underrepresenting any groups (e.g., freshmen, sophomores, juniors, seniors, minority students, males, females, and so on). A stratified random sample, drawing randomly from each of the strata, would be used. The number drawn from each stratum would be based on the proportion of students in that stratum in the population. In this way, we can have confidence that the sample accurately represents the population, at least on the dimensions on which we stratified the sample.

Sample Size and Confidence Intervals   Having developed the survey instrument and determined the sampling procedure, the researcher must also determine the size of the sample that will be needed. In general, larger samples represent populations better than do smaller samples. But exactly how large a sample should be must be determined for each project. Costs and time are important considerations in determining how large a sample can be handled in a project. But more importantly, the size of the sample needed to represent a population adequately depends on the degree of *homogeneity* in the population. A *homogeneous* population is one where the members are similar to one another. In general, if the population is homogeneous, then smaller sample sizes are possible. On the other hand, the more *heterogeneous* the population, the more diversity there is that must be represented in the sample. Therefore, the sample must be larger to represent that diversity accurately. Thus, in determining how large a sample must be to be representative of the population, we must make an estimate of the variability of the characteristics of the population; that is, we estimate the size of the standard deviation of the population for the characteristic we want to measure. With this we can then determine the confidence limits for estimating population characteristics based on the measured sample characteristics. For example, if we computed a sample mean of 10.50, we expect that the population mean is close to this figure. How confident we are that our sample mean is close to the population mean depends on the sample size. The larger the sample size, the more confidence we have. We express our confidence with something called a *confidence interval.* For example, we could compute that we are "95 percent confident that the population mean is between 9.75 and 11.25" (our confidence interval). [Methods for calculating required sample size and confidence intervals are beyond the scope of this text; interested students are referred to Rossi, Wright, and Anderson (1985).]

Research Design of Surveys

Having developed and tested the survey instrument, determined the population to be surveyed, and drawn the sample, the researcher must also determine the research plan or design to be used in gathering the survey data. Two basic designs are used in survey research: (1) the cross-sectional design and (2) the longitudinal or panel design.

Cross-Sectional Design   A *cross-sectional design* involves administering the survey in "one shot" (once) to a sample, yielding data on the measured characteristics as they exist at the time of the survey. The information can be completely descriptive, such as a status survey, or can involve testing relationships among population characteristics. A variation of the cross-sectional design allows comparisons to be made of population characteristics at different points in time, such as surveying Americans' perceived quality of life in 1965, 1975, and 1985 to determine whether there have been changes over time. If the successive surveys use independent samples of respondents, the design is cross-sectional.

Longitudinal Design   The *longitudinal* or *panel design* is a within-subjects survey research design in which the same group or panel of subjects is surveyed successively at different times. Longitudinal surveys make it possible to assess changes within individuals over time. It is often difficult, however, to obtain subjects who are willing to be surveyed several times, and often large numbers of subjects drop out of the study before it is completed.

Internal Summary: Survey Research

Survey research is the type of social research most familiar to the public. A good deal of important information on a variety of human issues has been gathered through surveys. Because of the central importance of representative sampling, survey researchers have contributed much to the procedures for drawing representative samples from populations. Surveys are usually in the form of questionnaires or interviews, which may be conducted face-to-face, over the phone, or through the mail. Virtually any issue or question can be the topic of a survey.

SUMMARY

This chapter has discussed field research, focusing on low-constraint research (naturalistic observation and case studies) and survey research. In naturalistic and case-study research, little constraint is placed on the behavior of subjects. Although the behavior of the observer may be tightly constrained by the observational techniques employed, it need not be by these methods. In fact, one of the biggest advantages of lower-constraint research methods in general is the flexibility they allow the researcher. Survey research is not a single method, but a range of methods, which do reach into higher-constraint research.

The most common error in interpreting low-constraint research (naturalistic observation and case studies) is to overinterpret the results—either to generalize the results to a broader population than actually sampled in the study or to draw a causal inference from the observed relationships in the study. Even though we cannot easily generalize to other populations or draw causal inferences, naturalistic and case-study methods can provide useful information. These methods can help us describe events not previously observed. They can inform us about relationships and contingencies. We can then speculate about the causal bases of these relationships and test those speculations with higher constraint research methods. And, finally, they can negate a general proposition if an appropriate counterexample can be observed. Some kinds of research can be done only with naturalistic research methods, such as the study of the unconstrained behavior of subjects in their natural surroundings.

The key issue in low-constraint research is the observation of behavior. Whether that observation is made with only our senses or with highly sophisticated equipment, the same general principles apply. We should make observations in ways that will allow us to generalize to the population of interest. The way the measures are taken will influence the validity of the data. Neither the actions of the researcher nor the process of measurement should affect the behavior of subjects if we want to measure their natural behavior validly. As with any research project, ethical issues in low-constraint research are important and must be considered carefully during every phase of the study. Low-constraint methods of naturalistic observations and case studies are of great importance in psychological research. Among the many important uses are observing contingencies, developing new hypotheses for later testing, and testing the generalization of laboratory findings.

Surveying (status surveys and survey research) is a large and growing area of research in the natural environment. Researchers directly ask questions of subjects concerning virtually any issue, attempting to learn the presence or absence and the value of factors in the population and correlations among them. The heart of the survey is the sampling methods used to ensure a representative sample. Surveys can be carried out as longitudinal or cross-sectional studies.

REVIEW EXERCISES

6.1   **Define the following key terms. Be sure you understand them. They are discussed in the chapter and defined in the glossary.**

field research	unobtrusive measure
generalizability	archival records
scientist-practitioner model	sampling
contingency	representativeness
unobtrusive observer	replication
participant-observer	causal inference
measurement reactivity	ex post facto fallacy
reactive measures	experimenter reactivity
nonreactive measures	experimenter bias

survey

status survey

survey research

interview schedule

questionnaire

nonprobability sampling

probability sampling

simple random sampling

sampling frame

stratified random sampling

strata

homogeneous

heterogeneous

confidence interval

cross-sectional design

longitudinal (panel) design

6.2   **Answer each of the following. Check your answers in the chapter.**

1. What are the two essential characteristics of low-constraint research?
2. Differentiate between case-study and naturalistic research methods.
3. Explain and discuss this idea: "In naturalistic research, the constraint or controls are placed on the researcher."
4. Under what conditions do we use low-constraint research methods?
5. Sometimes naturalistic research allows greater generalization than does laboratory research. How?
6. Explain how naturalistic research can negate a general proposition but cannot establish a general proposition.
7. What kind of relationship among variables is sought in naturalistic research?
8. Explain the concept of measurement reactivity.
9. What are the major criticisms of Freud's research methods?
10. What is experimenter reactivity?
11. How do status surveys and survey research differ?
12. What are the major steps involved in developing surveys?
13. What are the different forms a survey might take in terms of presenting questions to respondents?
14. Compare open-ended, multiple-choice, and Likert scales in surveys.
15. What is a sampling frame? How does it relate to populations and samples?

6.3   **Think about and work the following problems:**

1. Explain this statement: "Freud's case-study research had poor validity."
2. You are in a discussion about research, and someone asserts, "The only worthwhile research is high-constraint experimentation!" You jump into the discussion and explain how low-constraint research can be valuable. Develop your argument, making it as strong as you can.
3. What is the ex post facto fallacy? Develop ten examples of research conclusions in which the ex post facto fallacy occurs.
4. For each of the following research areas, assume that you will perform some of the ground-breaking research. Because there is no prior research in the area to draw on, you will need to utilize the flexible naturalistic and case-study approaches to identify critical variables, formulate initial hypotheses, and so on. Develop an initial research plan to accomplish these goals.
   a. Some people are concerned about the possible effects of televised wrestling on viewers and on society in general. How would you begin to study such an issue?
   b. Studies have shown that seat belts dramatically reduce the risk of injury or death in the event of an accident. In spite of this, many people continue to avoid the use of seat belts. The issue of concern to you is how one might increase seat belt use among average drivers.
   c. Many naturalists and others are concerned about the welfare of animals in the natural environment because of increasing incursions of human activity.

Most people seem to be little concerned with the fate of wildlife or with the effects of hunting, habitat destruction, environmental pollution, and so on. You are to develop ways to sensitize people to greater concern for wildlife and greater efforts to reduce human incursions. What research would you develop toward these goals?

   d. Shoplifting costs retail businesses and consumers billions of dollars annually. You have been hired by a national retail consortium to study shoplifting and make recommendations toward control of this problem. How would you begin such a study?

5. Explain this statement: "Survey research can be correlational in nature."

6. Think of some issue of interest to college students and develop ten scaled items to survey college students. Use 5-point Likert scales.

Chapter
7

Correlational and Differential Methods of Research

In naturalistic research we observe the behavior of organisms in natural settings. Case-study methods limit the setting but do little to constrain the reactions of subjects. This chapter on correlational and differential methods of research will focus on the measurement of relationships between variables (correlational) and differences between groups defined by preexisting variables (differential). As we will see, correlational and differential methods, although operationally different, are conceptually similar.

CORRELATIONAL RESEARCH METHODS

In *correlational research* the strength of a relationship between two or more variables is quantified. The variables must be quantifiable and usually represent at least an ordinal scale of measurement. For example, we may want to know if adolescents' current self-esteem is related to their earlier experiences of being punished by their parents. We can administer a test of self-esteem and a questionnaire to each of the subjects about the amount of their past punishment. By calculating a correlation between the two measures we can determine to what degree and direction the two measures are related.

The correlational research approach can be conceptualized as an extension of naturalistic observation. As in naturalistic observation, variables are not usually manipulated in correlational research, and there is usually a single group of subjects sampled from a larger population. However, there are important differences between correlational and naturalistic research. The correlational research design always measures at least two variables, and plans for measuring variables are formalized prior to any actual measurement.

Statistics and research methods textbooks caution that a correlation cannot imply causality. We will discuss this issue later in this chapter. But you might be wondering what is the value of an observed correlation if it cannot be used to determine causality? Knowing the correlation between two variables serves two useful functions in science. The first is that any consistent relationship can be used to predict future events. Prediction is possible even if we have no idea why the observed relationship exists. It is not unusual in science to become accurate at predicting events long before we understand why the events occur. For example, as early as 140 A.D., Ptolemy developed a complicated system to predict the movements of the planets. Although his predictions were remarkably accurate, he had little understanding of how the planets actually moved. In fact, his model of planetary movement—that all celestial bodies revolve about the earth—was clearly wrong. But the inaccuracy of his assumptions does not diminish the accuracy of the predictions that could be made using his system.

A second valuable function of correlational research is to provide data that are either consistent or inconsistent with some currently held scientific theory. A study, correlational or otherwise, cannot prove a theory correct, although it can negate a theory. For example, the question of what intelligence is and how it should be measured has been debated for most of this century. British psychologist Charles Spearman (1904) proposed that there is a dominating general intellectual trait that governs performance in all areas of cognitive functioning. He referred to this trait as a *g* (general) factor. Spearman's theory can be validated or invalidated by research data. The process of validating a theory requires the scientist to derive predictions from the theory, predictions that can then be tested by gathering the appropriate data. One prediction that could be derived from Spearman's *g* factor theory is that there should be a strong correlation between different cognitive abilities, because each ability is affected primarily by the dominant *g* factor. Suppose we decide to test a randomly selected sample of subjects on both math and vocabulary skills and find the two to be highly correlated; that is, people who score high on the math skills measure also tend to score high on the vocabulary measure. Do the data confirm Spearman's theory? No, they do not. The data show only that one relationship out of thousands of possible predicted relationships exists. To prove the theory one would have to test every possible prediction from it—usually an impossible task because many theories make an almost infinite number of predictions. The data are consistent with the theory and as such provide a small increment in the confidence that we place in the theory. Suppose we also test reading ability, abstract reasoning, short- and long-term memory, and the ability to solve riddles, and we find that all possible correlations between the measures are large and positive. Have we then proved the theory correct? The answer is still no because there remain other predicted relationships that we have not tested. However, we do have considerably more confidence in the theory because all predictions of the theory we tested are confirmed. But suppose we find that memory and math ability are virtually uncorrelated. What do these data mean? If the procedures were done correctly, we have to conclude that Spearman's *g* factor theory is incorrect. In other words, *a correlation cannot prove a theory but can negate a theory.* Notice that this function of correlational research is similar to a function of naturalistic and case-study research discussed in Chapter 6. In naturalistic and case-study research, we cannot establish a general proposition but we can negate one.

As noted earlier, research involves studying relationships among variables. In correlational research, we measure the strength of relationships among variables so that one variable can be predicted from the other. Thus, the relationship sought in correlational research can be described as a predictive relationship.

DIFFERENTIAL RESEARCH METHODS

In *differential research* we observe two or more groups that are differentiated on the basis of some preexisting variable. For example, using sex as the preexisting variable, we may want to compare men and women on their knowledge of current political events. We administer a "Current Politics Test" to 100 men and 100 women, with the two groups matched for age, education, and socioeconomic class. By comparing the test scores of the two groups, we can see if there is a significant difference between them. (What statistical test would you use to test the significance of that difference?) Groups can be determined by some qualitative dimension (such as the subject's sex, religion, political party, or psychiatric diagnosis) or by some quantitative dimension (such as the subject's age or number of years of education). Whether the variable that differentiates the groups is qualitative or quantitative, the group differences *existed before any research study was conducted.* The researcher measures the variable and assigns subjects to groups based on their scores. This classification variable is called the *independent variable,* and the behavior measured in the different groups is called the *dependent variable.* Independent variables in differential research are *nonmanipulated independent variables* rather than *manipulated independent variables* (see Chapter 3). In differential research, the independent and dependent variables are measured by the researcher and neither is directly manipulated. In experimental research, the independent variable is actually manipulated by the researcher. Because differential research involves only measuring, and not manipulating, variables, we are actually studying relationships between them. Thus, differential research is conceptually similar to correlational research. This conceptual similarity means that the same general principles will be used in interpreting the results from each of these approaches. We should avoid drawing causal conclusions from either differential or correlational research studies. The structural similarity of differential research to experimental research (that is, there are different groups defined by an independent variable with a dependent measure taken on all subjects in each group) means that we will use essentially the same statistical procedures to evaluate the data from these two approaches (see Table 7.1). Thus, differential research is similar to both correlational and experimental research.

There is a special case of differential research that is used extensively in developmental psychology. In studying developmental processes, psychologists often use a *cross-sectional design,* where groups of subjects at different ages are compared on some set of variables. For example, cognitive development might be explored by giving groups of 3-, 5-, and 7-year-olds a set of carefully constructed problems or puzzles. Differences between the younger and older children in performance on the task would likely give us insight into the development of certain reasoning processes. This is a differential research design because subjects are assigned to groups on the basis of a preexisting characteristic—in this case, age. As with all differential research, there is always the possibility of confounding, and therefore care is needed in drawing conclusions from cross-sectional studies. For example, if we wanted to study the aging process, we could look at groups of people in their 40s, 50s, 60s, and 70s. Differences between these groups might give us insight into expected changes as one ages. However, we must be careful in our interpretation because some of the observed changes may be due to other variables. For example, subjects in their 70s would have lived through the Great Depression, while subjects in their 40s grew up during relatively prosperous years. If we found that older people were more cautious about going into debt, we could not assume that this represented a developmental process, because it could just as easily be explained by differences in life experiences between the groups. The concept that because of shared life experiences people of a given age in a given culture may behave similarly throughout their lives but differently from people of other ages is known as the *cohort effect.* Those who grew up during the Depression shared an experience powerful enough that it likely shaped much of their thinking, their expectations, and even their emotional responses. As we will see later, developmental psychologists have other research designs at their disposal, such as *longitudinal designs* and *time-series designs* (discussed in Chapters 10 and 13, respectively). These designs, as opposed to cross-sectional designs, follow the same people over time to observe developmental changes, thus controlling confounding due to cohort effects in developmental research. However, longitudinal designs have the disadvantage of

TABLE 7.1   THE APPARENT SIMILARITY OF A SIMPLE EXPERIMENTAL DESIGN
(A) AND A SIMPLE DIFFERENTIAL DESIGN (B)

A. An Experimental Design

Group 1 Short Time Interval	Group 2 Moderate Time Interval	Group 3 Long Time Interval
Subjects	Subjects	Subjects
1	1	1
2	2	2
•	•	•
•	•	•
•	•	•
N	N	N

B. A Differential Design

Group 1 Caucasian	Group 2 Black	Group 3 Asian
Subjects	Subjects	Subjects
1	1	1
2	2	2
•	•	•
•	•	•
•	•	•
N	N	N

An experimental design and differential design can look the same, but there are critical differences. In the experimental design, subjects are randomly assigned to conditions and the conditions are manipulated by the experimenter. In the differential design, the subjects are included in conditions based on their preexisting characteristics—in this case, ethnic identity. Because of this, we cannot infer causality from the differential design.

taking a long time to complete (sometimes years). The aging study described above would take 40 years to complete with a longitudinal design.

Artifacts and Confounding Variables

Adding one or more additional groups forces the researcher to standardize (i.e., constrain) the observational methods. In the naturalistic methods, we could easily change our observational method or focus of observation to study any phenomenon that captured our interest. In differential research, we compare observations in one group of subjects with observations in one or more other groups. We can legitimately compare observations from two or more groups only if the observations are made in the same way in each group. If we use different methods to observe and measure a phenomenon in two groups, any difference we observe between the groups may be real or a function of the different observational methods. We would have no way of knowing which of these possibilities is correct. In such a case, we speak of the two variables as being *confounded*. The two variables in this case are the group the subjects were in and the different methods of observing and measuring in the two groups. When we say they are confounded, we mean that they both vary at the same time—as the group variable changes, the method of observation variable also changes. Because the two variables change together, we can never know which of them is responsible for any observed difference in the dependent variable. The only way to avoid confounding two variables is to make sure that they vary independently of one another, and the simplest way of ensuring this is to hold one of the variables constant. *The variable that should be held constant is the variable we have less interest in, and the variable we want to focus our attention on is the variable we allow to vary.* In most differential research, we are not as interested in the effects of different observational procedures on the data recorded as we are in how the groups of subjects differ from one another. Therefore, we will hold the observational method variable constant and allow the group variable to vary. We must define in advance exactly what variables we will measure and how we will observe and measure them. Once the study starts, we are constrained by those design decisions, and we must use the same observational and measurement procedures throughout. As we will discuss later in this chapter, there are many sources of potential confounding other than measurement.

We gain power to answer research questions by using the higher-constraint differential research method instead of lower-constraint naturalistic and case-study observation methods. The additional power comes from the ability to compare groups of subjects who differ on important variable such as diagnosis. But a price is paid for this additional power—a loss of flexibility. When we have only one group, we can modify procedures easily. But when we have more than one group, we must use the same observational and measurement procedures in each group if we want to make valid comparisons between them. Failure to constrain the procedures can lead to *artifactual* findings. An *artifact* is any apparent effect of an independent variable that is actually the effect of some other variable not properly controlled (in this case, held constant). That is, an artifact is a result of confounding. Therefore, if we had used different measurement procedures for two groups, any observed difference between the groups might actually have been an artifact of changes in the measurement procedure rather than real differences in subjects' behavior.

In higher-constraint research, where precise and consistent observational procedures are required, more detailed planning is necessary prior to data collection. How can a researcher make such detailed plans before a study even begins? If the study is the first being conducted on a particular topic, the researcher usually cannot do so. Detailed planning is usually carried out when the phenomenon under study is already reasonably well understood. High-constraint research is thus seldom used in the early stages of studying a problem. Instead, the flexible low-constraint methods allow the researcher to explore the phenomenon and to gain a sense of what to expect. Such an understanding is necessary for any investigator to be able later to state hypotheses in explicit terms and to design procedures for measuring variables that will test hypotheses. Research on a particular topic often begins with low-constraint methods and proceeds to higher-constraint research only after a basic understanding of the phenomenon is achieved. Scientists often study topics that other people have already studied extensively and so may not need to start with low-constraint research. However, most researchers choose to do at least some low-constraint research to gain familiarity with the phenomenon that would be difficult to gain solely from the published accounts of other investigators.

WHAT MAKES DIFFERENTIAL RESEARCH HIGHER-CONSTRAINT THAN CORRELATIONAL RESEARCH?

Both correlational research and differential research measure relationships between variables. But for several reasons, we have listed differential research as higher-constraint in our model. One reason is that differential research is structurally similar to experimental research, where comparisons of two or more groups are made on a dependent measure. However, there are other, more relevant issues that define the level of constraint for differential research.

In many cases, the researcher conducting differential research is actually interested in addressing causal questions. Ideally, experimental research should be used to address a causal question, but often ethical or practical constraints prevent the use of an experimental procedure. For example, it is not possible to assign subjects randomly to groups of (1) patients with schizophrenia and (2) nonpatient controls. As we will see later, the advantage of random assignment of subjects to groups or conditions is that it will tend to equate the groups on potential confounding variables, so that the only consistent difference between the groups is the level of the independent variable. Consequently, it is relatively safe to conclude that any observed difference in the dependent variable is the result of the manipulation of the independent variable. With differential research, subjects are assigned to groups on the basis of some preexisting variable, and often the groups will differ on several variables other than the independent variable. For example, chronic patients with schizophrenia tend to be from lower social classes, have fewer relationships in adolescence and early adulthood, and spend more time in hospitals than a randomly selected group of people from the general population. These differences are predictable and are well established by past research. If we find differences between a group of chronic patients with schizophrenia and a general control group on some dependent measure (such as style of processing visual information), we have no way of knowing whether the differences are due to schizophrenia, to social class differences, to social experiences during adolescence, or to effects of hospitalization. In other words, all the group differences, other than diagnosis, are potential confounding variables; knowing which variable is responsible for the differences on the dependent variable is impossible.

As discussed later in this chapter, researchers using differential methods are rarely content with this state of affairs. Instead of selecting a general control group, the researcher might select one or more specific control groups using selection criteria that will assure that a given control group is comparable to the experimental group on some potential confounding variable. For example, a researcher suspecting that social class might affect the scores on the dependent variable might select a control group that is, on average, of the same social class as the patient group (see

Chapman & Chapman, 1973). Thus, social class could not confound the findings. The active control over sampling by the researcher is a form of constraint, which minimizes confounding and therefore strengthens the conclusions drawn from the study. There is no comparable control used in correlational research. Hence, differential research has more control procedures available and is higher-constraint than correlational research. The more controls that can be applied, the stronger the conclusions one can draw from the study.

WHEN TO USE CORRELATIONAL AND DIFFERENTIAL RESEARCH

Differential research designs are used most often in situations where the manipulation of an independent variable is impractical, impossible, or inappropriate. A psychologist who wants to know about the relative effectiveness of two theories of education in creating an environment to foster learning might set up two separate schools and for each school institute a different curriculum, randomly assign a pool of students, and then evaluate the amount the students learn. But the expense of setting up such a research program would make the study impractical. An alternative would be to use two existing schools that already have the kinds of curricula the researcher is interested in evaluating. Because these groups are naturally occurring instead of experimentally manipulated, this would be a differential research design. Differential designs are also used when an experimental manipulation is physically impossible to accomplish. That would be the case if we were interested in the social development of individuals with superior intelligence. There is no way that we could raise or lower the intelligence of newborns so that we could randomly assign them to normal and superior intelligence groups; but we could select children of high and average intelligence, assign them to two groups, and follow their social development. Finally, there are many cases in which experimental manipulation of a particular variable is possible but to do so would be unethical. We might hypothesize that a prolonged separation from one's parents during the first two years of life might lead to permanently retarded social development, but it would be unethical to select infants randomly and separate them from their parents to test the hypothesis experimentally. However, some children are separated from their parents for reasons beyond the researcher's control. Such a naturally occurring group might be a suitable population to study in order to explore the hypothesis.

Another field that uses correlational and differential research designs almost exclusively because of ethical considerations is the area of clinical neuropsychology. A neuropsychologist uses psychological measures of human behavior to infer the structural and functional condition of the human brain. The neuropsychologist administers tests to patients to determine what the patients can and cannot do. The patterns of such abilities and disabilities can often suggest where in the brain a particular problem, such as a tumor, might be located. The wealth of background data that neuropsychologists draw on when they evaluate a person is gathered from previous patients with neurological problems. If a particular pattern of abilities and disabilities is consistently found for patients later diagnosed as suffering from a specific type of problem in a designated location of the brain, then it is reasonable to predict that a new patient with that pattern might well be suffering from the same neurological dysfunction. The data gathering in this case is correlational, because the researcher is seeking to identify relationships between behavior and brain dysfunction. Granted, some of the relationships observed in neuropsychology are not easily quantifiable in terms of a simple correlation coefficient, but they are relationships nevertheless. Note that by mapping these relationships carefully and accurately we are able to obtain an accurate prediction of one of the variables (brain dysfunction) on the basis of knowing the other variable (the person's behavior). Accurate prediction is a principal goal of correlational research.

CONDUCTING CORRELATIONAL AND DIFFERENTIAL RESEARCH

Conducting correlational and differential research is among the most difficult tasks faced by the research scientist. Two factors contribute to this difficulty. On one hand, they are relatively high-constraint research approaches, which require the investigator to prepare detailed procedures prior to any data collection and then follow through on the procedures throughout the study. On the other hand, the investigator often is unable to use the powerful control procedures available in experimental research.

Conducting Correlational Research

In correlational research, we seek to quantify the direction and strength of a relationship between two or more variables. (Our discussion here will focus on the relationships between two variables only.)

Problem Statements for Correlational Research   Unlike the flexible and often initially vague problem statements of low-constraint research methods such as naturalistic observation and case studies, the problem statements for correlational research are much more specific. They typically take the form of "What is the strength and direction of the relationship between variable *X* and variable *Y?*" Sometimes, all we are interested in is this question. More often, we will want to know more, such as the best equation for predicting variable *Y* from variable *X* (termed the *regression equation*). By far the most frequent source of correlational research is the secondary statistical analyses commonly done in higher-constraint research to help explain findings or describe the samples under study. For example, a researcher might be doing a differential research project comparing urban and suburban groups on their fear of being victimized by crime. A good researcher would want to be able to describe accurately the samples and so would routinely collect data on demographic variables such as the age, education, and social class of each subject in the study. It is common to compare the groups to see if they are similar on these variables, but it is also common to compute the correlation of each of these variables with the dependent measure(s) in the study. These correlations can give considerable insight into our broader data set and are often highlighted in the research article. Here then the problem statement would likely be "What is the correlation of each of the demographic variables with our dependent variable(s)?" Traditionally, these correlations are computed separately within each group (in our example, the urban and suburban samples) because the relationship may be different in the groups (see our discussion of moderator variables in the section on sampling later in this section).

Measurement   Developing effective operational definitions of the variables is as important here as in any other kind of research. Measurement—the assignment of numbers to variables (see Chapter 4)—depends on the adequacy of operational definitions. The operational definition of a variable involves more than just selecting a measure to administer to subjects. We must consider every aspect of the measurement process including how the measurement will be taken. As in any other research, we want to avoid the possibility that the researcher might unintentionally influence the subjects. Ways to avoid influencing subjects include never allowing the same researcher to collect both measures on the subject and never allowing the researcher to know subjects' scores on the first measure until after the second measure is taken. Two effects need to be controlled: (1) the tendency of investigators to see what they expect to see (Chapman & Chapman, 1969) and (2) the tendency of investigators to influence the behavior of subjects. The first problem is referred to as *experimenter expectancy.* The latter problem is referred to as *experimenter reactivity* (see Chapter 6). The tendency of investigators to see what they expect to see is minimized by using objective measures whenever possible so that little subjective interpretation is necessary. The problem of experimenter reactivity may require the use of two independent researchers. The researcher's influence on the subject is particularly likely when the subject is being asked to give a voluntary response with the researcher present. (Experimenter effects on subjects will be discussed in more detail in Chapters 8 and 9.)

Another potential problem in correlational research is the subject's own influence on the measures. Subjects like to be consistent, especially when they believe they are being observed and evaluated. This is a variation on the *measurement reactivity* problem discussed in Chapter 6. Such contrived consistency can suggest strong relationships between variables when such relationships do not exist in real life. There are a number of ways of reducing this effect. One way is to disguise the self-report measures by including *filler items,* so that the subject is unsure of what the investigator is studying. Filler items are not meant to measure anything but rather to draw the subject's attention away from the real purpose of the test. A second method of controlling the subject's influence on the data is to rely on one or more unobtrusive measures. In this way subjects are unaware that they are being observed and are thus less likely to control their own behavior. A third method is to separate the measures from one another, which can be done by taking measurements at different times or by having different researchers take the measurements. Probably the best way to deal with the problem of measurement reactivity is to use measures beyond the control of the subject. If we want to measure anxiety, for example, we might rely more on psychophysiological measures than on self-reports or behavior as the index.

Sampling   A major concern in most research is obtaining a sample that is representative of the population to which we want to generalize. Another sampling issue important in correlational research is whether the relationship between the two variables is the same in all segments of the population under study. If we have any reason to believe that such differences exist, we might draw samples from separate subpopulations. For example, if we suspect that males and females demonstrate a different relationship between two variables, either in direction or strength, we should select samples of males and females separately and compute separate correlations for each group. In this example biological sex would be a *moderator variable*—that is, a variable that seems to modify the relationship between other variables. Biological sex is a commonly used moderator variable. If different sub-populations show different relationships between two variables, the relationships can be obscured if the variable that defines the subpopulations is not included in the study as a moderator variable. For example, if the variables dependency and hostility are positively correlated in males but negatively correlated in females, the correlation in a mixed group of males and females will probably be close to zero, suggesting no relationship. The opposite relationships in the two groups cancel each other. In this example, sex is a moderator variable in that biological sex modifies the relationship between the variables of dependency and hostility. Recognizing potential moderator variables requires a thorough knowledge of the area under study. When in doubt, it is always better to compute correlations for different subgroups. If the same relationship is found in all the groups, we can be more confident that the relationship will hold for the entire population sampled.

Analysis of Data   In correlational research, data analysis involves computing an index of the degree of relationship between variables under study. The correlation coefficient computed will depend on the level of measurement used for both variables. If both variables are measured on at least an interval scale of measurement (i.e., both measures produce score data), then a Pearson product-moment correlation coefficient should be computed. If one variable is measured on an ordinal scale and the other variable is at least ordinal, then the appropriate coefficient is a Spearman rank-order correlation. Both correlation coefficients accomplish the same thing; that is, they indicate the degree of linear relationship between two variables. Both range from −1.00 to +1.00. A −1.00 means a perfect negative relationship exists (as one variable increases, the other decreases in a perfectly predictable fashion). A +1.00 means a perfect positive relationship exists. A correlation of 0.00 means there is no linear relationship between the two variables. (See Figures 5-5 and 5-6 for examples of correlation scatter plots. The computational procedures for these correlation coefficients are shown in Appendix C, and Appendix D shows how to compute the correlations using a computer program.)

The most frequently used correlational procedures are the Pearson and Spearman correlations, both of which quantify the relationship between two variables. However, there are research situations that demand more complicated correlational analyses, such as correlating one variable with an entire set of variables (*multiple correlation*) or one set of variables with another set of variables (*canonical correlation*). It is also possible to correlate one variable with another after statistically removing the effects of a third variable (*partial correlation*). There are now analytical procedures (e.g., *path analysis*) that test the strength of evidence for a specific causal model using correlational data (Raulin & Graziano, 1995). Detailed discussion of these more sophisticated analytic procedures is beyond the scope of this book [see Nunnally & Bernstein (1993), Myers & Well (1991), or Loehlin (1992)]. However, it is important to realize that such procedures do exist to meet a variety of research needs.

Interpreting the Correlation   The first step in interpreting the correlation is to note its direction and size. Is the correlation a positive relationship between the variables or a negative relationship? Is the relationship small (close to 0.00) or relatively large (close to +1.00 or −1.00)?

The next step is to test for the statistical significance of the correlation; that is, test to see whether the observed correlation is large enough for us to believe there is a nonzero correlation between the variables in the population from which the current sample was drawn. To state it another way, we are testing the null hypothesis that there is a zero correlation between the variables in the population. Computer programs can give you the *p* value for each correlation computed. This *p* value is the probability of achieving a correlation this large or larger if the correlation in the population were actually zero. If that probability is low, it means that there is little chance that the population correlation is zero, and we conclude that there is a relationship between these variables in the population from which our sample was drawn. We say that the "correlation is significant" or that we have a *statistically significant correlation* to describe this situation. As we discussed in Chapter 5, we traditionally require that the probability be quite low (usually 0.05 or even 0.01) before we declare our finding "statistically significant." For example, if the correlation between two variables is 0.67 with a *p* value of 0.035, we would conclude that a significant relationship exists because the *p* value is less than our traditional alpha of 0.05 (see Chapter 5 for a more detailed explanation of this terminology).[1]

When using correlation coefficients one should calculate the *coefficient of determination* rather than just rely on the statistical significance of the correlation (Nunnally & Bernstein, 1993). The coefficient of determination is computed by squaring the obtained correlation. If the obtained correlation was 0.50, then $r^2 =$ 0.25. We can convert 0.25 to a percent by multiplying by 100 (100 x .25 = 25%). A correlation of 0.50 indicates that 25 percent of the variability in the first variable can be accounted for or predicted by knowing the scores on the second variable. We shorten this statement by referring to r^2 as the "proportion of variance accounted for." This procedure allows us to estimate how useful the relationship might be in prediction. However, it is appropriate to take r^2 seriously only if we have a good-sized sample (a minimum of 30 subjects).

Conducting Differential Research

Problem Statements for Differential Research   Problem statements for differential research are among the most challenging in all of research. At one level they are simple. The problem statement is in the format "Does Group A differ from Group B on our dependent variable(s)?" In theory you could create an infinite number of such problem statements by taking every possible group and comparing it with every other possible group. Why not ask, "Do balding college professors differ from laboratory rats in their preference for music?" One reason that you might not ask that question is that you do not care what the answer is. Although you can compare any group with any other group, it does not make sense to do so unless the comparison tells us something meaningful. Another way of saying the same thing is that we want to make comparisons that have theoretical significance. Unfortunately, research is

[1]We show how to compute correlations using *SPSS for Windows* in Appendix D.

done and published using a differential design and making comparisons that make about as much theoretical sense as our balding professor/lab rat example. Picking two groups and comparing them on something is easy; picking the right groups and the right thing to compare the groups on to advance scientific understanding of a phenomenon is much harder, but should always be our goal in differential research.

So what makes a comparison in differential research theoretically significant? A useful study will tell us something about factors that affect our dependent variable rather than just tell us about the difference between two groups. No one would be surprised if we found a difference in preference for music between balding college professors and lab rats. In fact, we would expect to find differences on lots of variables (weight, eye color, diurnal cycle, night vision, and social skills). Suppose we found differences on all these variables as well as our music preference variable. What would it mean? Who knows, or cares for that matter? The problem with this comparison is that the two groups (balding professors and lab rats) differ on so many variables that there is no way of even knowing which one(s) is(are) relevant. Our first rule of thumb, therefore, is to develop as much as possible problem statements that focus on comparing groups that differ on only one variable. If you are interested in sex differences, for example, do not compare balding professors (presumably male) with a group of fifth-grade girls. These groups differ not only on biological sex, but also on age, education, social class, and the types and range of experiences that they have had. If we found a difference, we could not even guess what caused it. A better comparison might be fifth-grade girls and fifth-grade boys. But we would not want to draw conclusions about the role of biological sex based on this one comparison either, which leads to our second rule of thumb. It is best to rely on several comparisons when trying to draw a conclusion about the role of a factor from differential research studies. If we find similar results in comparisons of fifth-grade girls and boys, college males and females, male and female business people, male and female college professors, and male and female truck drivers, we can be more confident in our hypothesis that there are sex differences that account for all of these findings. Even with this whole series of findings based on comparing groups that appear to differ only on biological sex, we have to be careful in drawing a causal conclusion as we will see later in this section. Finally, good problem statements focus on group differences in theoretically significant dependent measures. If you are interested in self-esteem, you may want to focus on variables like success, social support, childhood experiences, and internal cognitions. These variables could likely affect, or be affected by, self-esteem. Variables like hat size, finger tapping speed, visual acuity, and marital status are less likely to be theoretically relevant, although one could probably dream up some mechanism that could relate one or more of these variables to self-esteem.

In summary, good problem statements for differential research compare two or more theoretically relevant groups, which ideally differ on only a single dimension, on a theoretically significant dependent measure. Since we can never reach the ideal of the groups differing on only a single dimension, we rely on multiple comparisons in drawing conclusions about the role of group differences in influencing our dependent measure.

Measurement   In differential research, we distinguish between the independent variable and the dependent variable. The dependent variable is usually a continuous measure, but it might also be a discrete (categorical) measure. For example, it may be a measure of performance on a particular task, an index of anxiety level, or a physical characteristic such as a person's weight. All of the previously discussed issues of operationalizing the dependent variable are relevant here. It is important to select an operational definition for the dependent measure that can be clearly stated and communicated to other researchers.

In differential research the nonmanipulated independent variable is typically a discrete variable. For example, it might be a diagnostic category with two values such as manic patients and depressed patients. In differential research, the independent variable is measured rather than manipulated. In our example with psychiatric patients we need a procedure to measure the diagnosis of the patients. We might use a structured interview to gather information about symptoms from each patient and some clearly defined, easily replicable criteria for making the final diagnosis. This procedure would be our operational definition of diagnosis. Note that the issues that apply to creating operational definitions for the independent variable are the same issues that apply in defining operational procedures for measuring the dependent variable. We have noted that in differential research the nonmanipulated independent variable is usually a discrete variable. However, it is always possible to take a continuous variable, such as anxiety level, and break it into discrete intervals, such as high anxiety, moderate anxiety, or low anxiety, and thus convert a correlational research design into a differential research design.

Selecting Appropriate Control Groups   In differential research, we have to decide which groups to include in the study. In some cases, the decision is simple. If, for example, we are interested in sex differences, sex would be the independent variable, and there would be only two possibilities. Because the minimum number of groups required in differential research is two, we would use both a male and a female group. However, such is not the case with other independent variables. If we are interested in studying psychopathology, there are dozens of psychiatric disorders. Choosing which of those disorders to compare must be done within a theoretical framework. The theory in any research study should guide the researcher in selecting the appropriate comparisons and control groups. We use the term *control group* to refer to any group selected in differential research as a basis of comparison with the primary or *experimental group*.[2] In some cases, the experimental/control group distinction is irrelevant. With the example above of exploring sex differences, it makes little sense to say that one sex represents the experimental group whereas the other sex represents the control group. In other situations, the control group is arbitrarily defined as the group that has none of the characteristic that define the independent variable. For example, if the independent variable is college education and we had three levels (no-college, some college, college graduate), it would be customary to refer to the no-college group as the control group.

Recall that control groups are designed to reduce the effects of potential confounding factors. A variable can have a confounding effect in a differential study only if (1) it affects the scores on the dependent variable(s) and (2) there is a differ-

---

[2]Although the term *experimental group* is commonly used, it can be misleading in discussions of differential research. In spite of the common use of the term, differential research is *not* experimental.

ence between the experimental and control groups on the potential confounding variable. For example, suppose we want to study sex differences in the ability to perceive details in visual scenes. It is known that visual acuity will affect performance on the task. Therefore, visual acuity is a potential confounding factor. However, if males and females did not differ on visual acuity, then the potential confounding factor would not differentially affect performance in the two groups. If males and females did differ on visual acuity, then visual acuity would be a confounding factor.

In many differential research designs, the control group has to be selected with care if it is to be an effective control. *The ideal control group is identical to the experimental group on all variables except the independent variable that defines the groups.* For example, if we were studying the effects of exposure to toxic chemicals in the work environment on cognitive performance, the experimental group would consist of people who work in industries in which they are exposed to such toxins. An ideal control group would include workers of about the same age, social class, and education level, who do similar kinds of work but work in an industry that does not expose them to these toxins. A group of office workers from the same company as the plant workers in the experimental group might be a convenient control group, but it would *not* make a good control group. The office workers would probably differ from the plant workers on a number of important variables, such as education level, age, and the ratio of males to females. Any of these differences could affect how the subjects might do on the cognitive performance dependent measure and thus constitute potential confounding variables.

Let us consider another example of selecting a control group, this one from the research literature on psychopathology. Suppose we are interested in studying schizophrenia. The experimental group consists of patients with schizophrenia. What is a good control group to compare with this experimental group? Our choice will depend on the dependent measure and the confounding variables that might affect it. As noted earlier, a variable can have a confounding effect in a differential study only if (1) it affects the scores on the dependent variable(s) and (2) there is a difference between the experimental and control groups on the potential confounding variable. To select an appropriate control group, we must first identify factors that will affect the dependent measures. These represent potential confounding factors, but they will not actually confound the results unless the experimental and control groups differ on these factors. Therefore, we want to select a control group that is comparable to the experimental group on these potentially confounding factors. Let us assume that we are interested in measuring thought processes in patients with schizophrenia. We need to identify variables known to affect performance on the dependent measures. We can find answers to this question through careful library research. Past research using the same or similar dependent measures will often report correlations with potential confounding variables. Once the potential confounding variables are identified, we can identify a control group that will not differ from the experimental group on these variables. Potential confounding variables might include amount of education, age, and total amount of psychiatric hospitalization. To reduce the threat of these potential confounding variables, we select a control group as similar to the schizophrenics on these variables as possible. If we can accomplish this, the variables will not confound the results.

As mentioned earlier, it is rare to find an ideal control group. Instead, what we usually try to obtain is a control group that controls some of the most important and most powerful confounding variables. A confounding variable is powerful if it is likely to have a large effect on the dependent measure. In our hypothetical study of the thought processes of patients with schizophrenia, a powerful confounding variable might be education. We can identify education as a confounding variable because the research literature shows that education is highly correlated with measures of cognitive performance.

It is often difficult to find a single, ideal control group matched with the experimental group on all potential confounding variables. In fact, often when we select a group to control for a particular confounding variable, we confound other variables with the independent measure. Therefore, we commonly use more than one control group in differential research studies. Each of the comparison groups will typically control for one or more of the major confounding variables, but no group will control for all potential confounding variables. If each of the comparisons of the experimental group with the control groups gives essentially the same result and leads to the same conclusion, then the researcher can be reasonably confident that the independent variable and not one of the confounding variables is responsible for the observed effect. Most of the research in medicine and the social sciences, because of ethical and practical considerations, relies on such multiple comparisons. It is not always feasible to include all possible comparison groups in one study. Therefore, research often involves multiple studies by different researchers in different laboratories, each using slightly different procedures and control groups. If the phenomenon under study is stronger than the potential confounding variables, each researcher will come to the same conclusion.

The multiple-comparison approach was used in a study of schizophrenic ambivalence (Raulin, 1984). Ambivalence had long been considered to be a primary symptom of schizophrenia (Bleuler, 1911/1950). Surprisingly, in the nearly 90 years since this initial clinical observation, no one had actually tested the hypothesis with a high-constraint design. Raulin (1984) developed a self-report test of ambivalence that showed strong test-retest and internal consistency reliability. The test was then given to a sample of patients with schizophrenia and three control samples: hospitalized depressed patients, outpatient psychotherapy clients, and a nonpsychiatric control sample. Because this was the first measure of ambivalence, there was little existing information available about potential confounding variables. Therefore, three control groups were used and all groups were matched on demographic variables (age, education, social class) that were known to affect responses on other self-report measures. The nonpsychiatric control group controlled for demographic variables because it was matched with the schizophrenic group on these variables; the psychotherapy clients also controlled for psychological distress; the hospitalized depressed patients controlled for severe psychopathology and hospitalization. The results, illustrated in Figure 7.1, indicate the importance of the multiple-control-group approach. The patients with schizophrenia scored significantly higher than the nonpsychiatric controls on the ambivalence measure (consistent with the hypothesis). These patients, however, were not significantly different from the psychotherapy clients and scored significantly lower than the hospitalized depressed subjects on the ambivalence measure. Had the last two control groups been left out of the study,

Figure 7.1 Mean Scores on the Intense Ambivalence Scale for Patients with Schizophrenia and Three Control Groups (Patients with Depression, Clinic Clients, and a Normal Control Sample

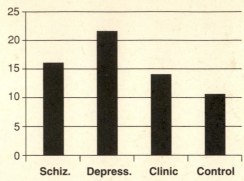

we might have mistakenly concluded that ambivalence is uniquely characteristic of schizophrenia.

We suspect that some students will find this discussion discouraging in that it seems no matter how hard we try, an ideal comparison cannot be found. This is, in fact, true and one of the reasons why it is so important to do multiple research studies. In Chapter 10 we will discuss experimental research designs in which groups are not defined on the basis of some preexisting variable, but instead subjects are randomly assigned to the groups. In this situation we will find that most of the problems described in the preceding discussion disappear and that, by and large, we are able on the basis of a true experiment to interpret findings with confidence. Our advice to students interested in studying areas where experimentation is unethical or impossible is to realize that drawing strong conclusions is very difficult at best—typically a long and intellectually demanding task.

Sampling Regardless of the type of research, the same issues of sampling always apply. To be able to generalize to a larger population, we must sample randomly from the population. Random sampling is a procedure for selecting subjects from a population, where each subject has an equal chance of being selected. To study patients with schizophrenia we should ideally utilize a procedure that samples randomly from all possible patients with this disorder. In practice that ideal is impossible to attain. It would be much too expensive, for example, to obtain a sample of 30 patients with schizophrenia from many different states and hospitals, because the cost of travel alone would be prohibitive. Usually a random sample is selected from all the subjects available to the researcher. Unless there is reason to believe that subjects from one part of the country are different from subjects from another part, the sample need not be from the whole country to be able to generalize to the whole country.

A serious threat to generalizability is the subtle kind of bias that can occur when a researcher has access to only certain groups. For example, if the researcher studying patients with schizophrenia obtained all the patients from one hospital, the sample might well be unrepresentative of schizophrenia because most psychiatric hospitals specialize in the kinds of patients they treat. Some hospitals handle chronic cases that require long-term hospitalization. Any sample from such a hospital would underrepresent those who recover fairly quickly. Private hospitals, because of their expense, serve patients from higher socioeconomic levels than state-funded hospitals. In fact, choosing patients only from hospitals may result in a biased sample. Many patients who might be cared for at home are in hospitals because they have no family or home to go to. A hospital sample of patients with schizophrenia might overrepresent patients from unstable homes.

Researchers studying other problems must also be sensitive to these subtle sampling biases. If we are sampling children from schools, we should recognize that a particular school may not have a representative sample of children. Depending on the location of the school, the children may come from higher or lower socioeconomic backgrounds than children in general. They may overrepresent or underrepresent certain ethnic or socioeconomic groups. They may be of higher or lower intelligence than the average child. Any of these variables might affect the results of a study.

Even when we appear to be sampling randomly, it is important to be sensitive to subtle biases. If, for example, we are surveying people randomly in a shopping center, we must still question the representativeness of the sample. A shopping center on the west side of town may have quite different customers than a similar shopping center on the east side of town. A shopping center in the city is likely to have different customers than one in the suburbs. To obtain a representative sample, it might be best to sample people from several locations. The time of day or day of the week also could affect the sample composition. If we sampled on a weekday afternoon, we would probably overrepresent homemakers; people who work evenings, weekends, or flexible hours; the unemployed; kids playing hooky; or people on vacation. Even if we take these exceptions into account, we might still have a biased sample. People who do not like shopping will probably be underrepresented. Finally, the researcher may be making subtle discriminations that could produce a biased sample. Because none of us likes to be turned away, we might choose to approach people who seem more likely to cooperate and avoid those who seem in a hurry. The point is that it is easy to obtain an unrepresentative sample that might threaten the generalizability of a study. This is a problem with any research and is particularly relevant in differential research studies. Because the groups in differential research already differ on some preexisting variable, the likelihood is high that they will differ on other variables that might affect the outcome of the research. The investigator must be careful in sampling subjects in differential research and must take measures to assure the representativeness of the sample. When a representative sample cannot be obtained, the researcher must use extra caution in interpreting the findings.

In differential research, especially differential research of diagnostic groups, sampling is usually not the primary factor in determining the generalizability of the study. Instead, the factor that most affects the generalizability of the study is the number of subjects who drop out. Using our hypothetical study of patients with schizophrenia, depending on the task, we might find that many patients would not or could not perform the task and hence would not be included in the study. To the extent that these patients are different from those who do perform the task, we cannot generalize to the larger population of patients with schizophrenia. If the patients who could not perform the task are more seriously disturbed than those who could, then we have not sampled all patients with schizophrenia. Instead, we have sampled the less severely disturbed patients with schizophrenia, and we can reasonably generalize the findings only to a population of these less seriously disturbed subjects. (Sampling will be discussed in more detail in Chapter 9.)

Analysis of Data   In some respects the data produced from differential research studies resemble the data from experimental studies. We will typically have scores from each subject in each group. We will want to compare the scores of the experimental group(s) with the scores of the control group(s). The type of statistical analysis used will depend on the number of groups and the scale of measurement of the dependent variable(s). If the dependent measure represents score data and we have two groups, a *t*-test for independent groups is typically used to compare the two groups. If we have more than two groups and score data, an analysis of variance (ANOVA) is typically used. (Both statistical procedures are described in Appendix C, and procedures for computer analysis are described in Appendix D.) If the data are ordinal or nominal, nonparametric statistics are typically used. With ordinal data, a Mann-Whitney *U*-Test is used; with nominal data, a chi-square is used (see Appendix C). (In Chapter 14 we will discuss the selection of the appropriate statistical analyses.)

Interpretation of Data   Regardless of what statistical test we perform, we interpret it in the same way. We always compare the probability value produced by the statistic with the predetermined alpha level to determine whether the null hypothesis should be rejected. The null hypothesis in this case is that the population means are equal, and rejecting that hypothesis suggests that at least one population mean is different from at least one other population mean.

Drawing the proper conclusion from the null hypothesis is the easy part of interpreting data in differential research design. The difficult part is taking into account all the possible confounding factors discussed previously. If we believe the groups may not be representative of the populations to which we hope to generalize, we must be especially cautious in making that generalization. If we think the control groups are inadequate to control for all the possible confounding variables, we should acknowledge this in the report of the study.

The possible confounding variables in most differential research make it difficult to draw solid conclusions on the basis of a single research study. Especially in differential research, results should be interpreted in the context of findings from other studies. Therefore, it is critically important for each investigator to describe the research procedures in detail. Whenever possible, confounding variables should be measured and reported. For example, if we were studying psychiatric patients, we would want to report the diagnoses of the patients and the procedures used to obtain them. We also should report variables such as subjects' average age, education, social class, amount of hospitalization, and any other patient variables relevant to the interpretation of the study. In this way, we communicate the information future investigators will need to interpret their studies in the context of our study.

LIMITATIONS OF CORRELATIONAL AND DIFFERENTIAL RESEARCH

Problems in Determining Causation

We must always be cautious in drawing conclusions from differential and correlational research. Remember, differential research is conceptually similar to correlational research. This means that causal conclusions cannot be safely drawn from either differential or correlational research. A correlation (i.e., an observed relationship) does not necessarily imply causality. Students may wonder why we keep repeating this point. In the abstract, the point is indeed simple. If *A* and *B* are correlated, then three possibilities exist: (1) *A* causes *B;* (2) *B* causes *A;* or (3) some third factor, *C,* causes both *A* and *B* (see Table 7.2). In the abstract, all of these are equally plausible. But in real-life situations, one or more of the possibilities may appear implausible and so we may feel justified in drawing a strong causal conclusion.

Suppose, for example, we find that reading and arithmetic abilities are highly correlated. How do we interpret such a finding? If we are testing Spearman's theory, we want to interpret the data to mean that some third factor (in this case the *g* factor) is responsible for both reading ability and arithmetic ability. However, there are other possible interpretations. Can arithmetic ability cause reading ability? It might, but it would be difficult to imagine a mechanism by which such a causal chain could proceed (i.e., how arithmetic skills could lead to better reading skills); therefore, we might be tempted to dismiss such an interpretation as unlikely. Consider the reverse causal chain. Can reading ability cause arithmetic ability? How did you learn about arithmetic? Your teacher in grammar school taught you basic arithmetic, *and* you read about it and practiced it from your arithmetic textbook. If you had poor reading skills, you might well have been less able to learn other skills including arithmetic. This is a plausible causal chain, which could explain how better reading skills can lead to better arithmetic skills.

Another explanation for a strong correlation between arithmetic and reading abilities should be considered. What does it mean when there is a strong relationship between reading ability and arithmetic ability? We are not trying to interpret this

TABLE 7.2   POSSIBLE DIRECTIONS OF CAUSATION WHEN TWO VARIABLES, *A* AND *B*, ARE FOUND TO BE CORRELATED

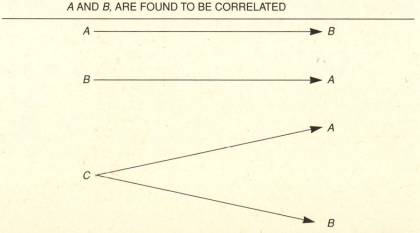

relationship but rather to define what it means in operational terms—that is, how we quantified this relationship. We asked a sample of people to take tests of reading ability and arithmetic ability. But what do the scores on the tests really mean? Suppose the arithmetic test includes the following question:

> *John goes to the market and buys five tomatoes. If tomatoes sell for $3 per dozen, how much change should John receive if he gives the clerk a $5 bill?*

Clearly, this question measures the ability to multiply, divide, and subtract. If tomatoes are $3.00 per dozen, they are $.25 each, and therefore five tomatoes would cost $1.25. The change John should receive (assuming no sales tax) is $3.75. It seems simple enough. But what other abilities would this question measure? Consider the following example:

> *Jean va au marche et il achègete cinq tomates. Si les tomates coute $3 la douzaine, combien de monnaie doit Jean recevoir s'il donne la vendeuse $5?*

Unless you read French, you probably found this question considerably harder to answer, yet it is the same arithmetic question. The example illustrates how important reading ability is in most tests regardless of the material being tested. Therefore, a correlation between reading ability and arithmetic ability may actually be an artifact of the phenomenon that reading ability is required to perform well on either test.

There is another point often overlooked when interpreting a correlation. When we say that both *A* and *B* may be caused by some third variable, *C,* we are not specifying what the third variable might be. In fact, variable *C* might be anything, so that we do not have three interpretations to choose from but rather hundreds. Suppose we believe that we can eliminate the possibility that arithmetic skills caused reading skills and the possibility that reading skills caused arithmetic skills. Could we then conclude that the third factor (Spearman's *g* factor) is responsible for both? No, we cannot. Spearman's general intelligence factor is only one of many possible third-factor variables that could account for the observed correlation. General test-taking ability might be a relevant factor. Anxiety level during the testing might be a relevant factor. (Have you ever taken an exam during which you panicked?) The amount of distraction during the testing session might be important or the level of motivation of the subjects or the general quality of their education or any one of a dozen other variables. Most likely, each of these variables contributes to the observed correlation. Yet, it is tempting to conclude that the one causal relationship being hypothesized is the one that led to the observed relationship.

Now that we have stated that causation cannot be implied by correlations, we want to acknowledge that not all theorists agree with this statement. There are sophisticated correlational designs that are well beyond the scope of this textbook. These designs are often used in disciplines such as medicine and clinical psychology where direct experimentation is often ethically irresponsible. There are some who argue that the right combination of correlational studies can so effectively exclude other interpretations of a complex data set that a causal interpretation is reasonable. Even though this may be true, the research literature is littered with hundreds of examples of top scientists drawing incorrect causal interpretations from complex correlational data. Therefore, we believe that the best rule for you to follow is "**Do not draw causal inferences from correlational data!**"

Confounding Variables

Another limitation of differential and correlational research methods is that it is often difficult or impossible to avoid confounding variables. Two variables are said to be confounded when they tend to vary together. Because they vary together, any observed relationships with other variables might be caused by either of the variables or both of them. In differential research in particular, confounding is more the rule than the exception. Some potential confounding variables may be controlled with a carefully selected control group, but rarely will we be able to eliminate confounding. Such problems will always make interpretation difficult, although some researchers choose to think of them as simply making the task more challenging.

SUMMARY

Our discussion has grouped together correlational and differential methods of research because they share the common characteristic that the measures studied are not systematically manipulated by the researcher. In correlational or differential research, the researcher measures, but does not manipulate, the variables of interest. By surrendering the opportunity to manipulate variables, the researcher surrenders a great deal of power in interpreting the data obtained. It is difficult to draw causal conclusions from data derived from correlational or differential research.

Correlational and differential research designs are appropriate when the researcher is interested in relationships between variables. Sometimes researchers are interested in a causal relationship but are unable to conduct a true experiment because practical or ethical concerns restrict them to measuring rather than manipulating a variable of interest. In such cases, a differential design is appropriate. The student should not view differential or correlational research methods as inferior to experimental research. It is true that experimental research is often easier to interpret and that causal conclusions are more safely drawn from experimental research, but many questions of interest in psychology and medicine cannot use experimental methods to answer questions posed by researchers. The effective use of correlational and differential research methods, coupled with a thorough knowledge of past research and a sophisticated use of logic, can often answer some of these difficult yet critically important questions.

REVIEW EXERCISES

7.1   **Define the following key terms. Be sure you understand them. They are discussed in the chapter and defined in the glossary.**

correlational research   dependent variable
differential research   nonmanipulated independent variable
independent variable   manipulated independent variable

cross-sectional design	filler items
cohort effect	moderator variable
longitudinal designs	multiple correlation
time-series designs	canonical correlational
confounding variable	partial correlation
artifact	path analysis
regression equation	statistically significant correlation
experimenter expectancies	coefficient of determination
experimenter reactivity	control group
measurement reactivity	experimental group

7.2   Answer each of the following. Check your answers in the chapter.

1. Explain this statement: "In many ways correlational research is an extension of naturalistic research."
2. In what ways are naturalistic research and correlational research different?
3. Why is it not advisable to try to infer causality from correlational research?
4. If causality cannot be inferred from a correlation, what information can be obtained from a correlation?
5. We keep noting that research at all levels of constraint seeks relationships between variables. What does this mean?
6. What are artifacts in research?
7. Under what conditions would we use differential research?
8. Why can we not infer causality in differential research?
9. What are moderator variables? Give examples.
10. What kind of variables are the independent variables in differential research?
11. What information is gained by squaring the correlation coefficient?
12. What kind of relationship among variables is sought in correlational research? In differential research?

7.3   Think about and work the following problems.

1. Interpret each of the following correlations (for statistical significance, proportion of variance accounted for, and conceptual interpretation):
   a. A product-moment correlation of 0.41 ($p = .007$) between age and height in grade-school girls.
   b. A rank-order correlation of 0.32 ($p = .074$) between ranks on a depression scale and rank order of activity level on the ward in a group of hospitalized psychiatric patients.
   c. A product-moment correlation of 0.20 ($p = .04$) between two different measures of assertiveness.
2. For each of the following experimental groups in a differential research study, list two to three possible control groups. For each control group, what possible confounding variables are likely to be controlled and which ones are likely to be left uncontrolled?
   a. Juvenile delinquent boys (aged 10–14) in a study of parenting style and its possible relationship to delinquency
   b. Data-entry clerks in a study of eye strain from working daily at CRT displays
   c. Residents of a neighborhood that is known to be contaminated by toxic chemicals in a study of health effects of exposure to such chemicals
   d. Mildly depressed individuals in a study of the number of negative events experienced in the last two months
3. We chose to include two apparently different types of research design in this chapter because we believe they are conceptually similar. What conceptual similarities exist between differential and correlational research?

Chapter
8

Hypothesis Testing, Validity, and Threats to Validity

In this chapter our main goal is to integrate concepts that have already been introduced into a more organized picture of the research process. Such integration is necessary to understand the experimental level of constraint—our focus in Chapters 8–13.

We have defined several levels of constraint (naturalistic, case-study, correlational, differential, and experimental), each with its own useful applications. Experimental research is at the highest constraint level, where high demands are placed on both the adequacy of the information and the methods used. In experiments, subjects are assigned to groups or conditions without bias, usually through random assignment. Dependent variables are observed and measured, and the independent variable is systematically manipulated to help answer questions about causality (i.e., "Does change in one variable cause change in another?"). Experimental manipulation helps to eliminate alternative hypotheses, giving us more confidence in our causal inferences. In summary, experimentation differs from other levels of constraint in (1) the high degree of control the experimenter exerts over the procedures in general and over the independent variable in particular, and (2) the focus on drawing causal conclusions from the results.

HYPOTHESIS TESTING

A crucial part of experimentation is developing and testing the *research hypothesis* (see Figure 8.1). The researcher carefully refines an initial, sometimes vague, idea into a *statement of the problem,* drawing on initial observations of the phenomenon and a thorough review of previous research. The statement of the problem is converted into a research hypothesis when the *theoretical concepts* in the problem statement are converted into specific procedures for measurement or manipulation, that is, into *operational definitions* of the concept. The research hypothesis is a specific prediction about the effects of the specific, operationally defined independent variable on the specific, operationally defined dependent variable.

Problem statements, operational definitions, and research hypotheses are important at all levels of research. Research hypotheses take different forms depending on the level of constraint. For example, a research hypothesis at the correlational level of constraint takes the general form "There is a significant (positive, negative) relationship between variables *A* and *B*." At the differential level, the general form of the hypothesis is "There is a significant difference between the groups on the dependent variable." At the experimental level, the research hypothesis is "Variable *A* will significantly affect variable *B*." Note the hypothesis might be directional (e.g., increase or decrease variable *B*) or it might be nondirectional (i.e., change variable *B* in either direction). We can test hypotheses at all levels of research, but the inferences we can confidently draw vary from one constraint level to another.

Starting the Research with an Initial Idea

A research study begins with initial ideas that are refined and developed into one or more specific questions and predictions. The researcher then designs the procedures to be used to answer the questions and test the predictions and only then pro-

Figure 8.1   A Model of the Generation of Research Hypotheses

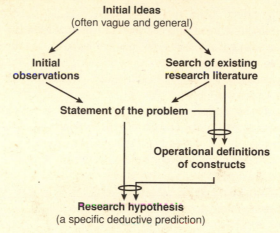

TABLE 8.1   EXAMPLES OF INITIAL RESEARCH IDEAS

1. Will children do better in school if they are given immediate feedback of examination results?
2. Is there any effect of cocaine on learning?
3. I wonder if nutrition affects schoolwork.
4. Is productivity better when employees own stock in their company?
5. Is it true that older people have poor memory?
6. Do men and women have different brain organization?

ceeds with the observations. Each step must be planned carefully, addressing many conceptual and procedural questions.

The experimental research process begins with one or more initial ideas, which are often phrased as questions. These ideas may come from reading the research literature, from one's own personal interests and observation, and from the general need for solutions to practical problems. The initial ideas begin to focus the research by identifying the major variables that are to be included. Some examples of initial ideas are listed in Table 8.1. Try to pick out the variables identified in each question in Table 8.1.

Having developed an initial idea, the researcher searches the literature to find research dealing with similar ideas and questions. It is common to find that one's "new idea" has already been studied by others. The published research provides a great deal of useful information such as how other researchers defined their variables and what procedures they used. Initial ideas are modified, discarded, or retained based on this examination of the literature. In essence, the literature search is the first of many "tests" of the ideas.

Statement of the Problem

Initial ideas that survive the evaluation of the literature search are refined into a statement of the problem, which will guide the researcher through the remainder of

TABLE 8.2   EXAMPLES OF PROBLEM STATEMENTS AT THE EXPERIMENTAL
LEVEL OF CONSTRAINT

1. Does the presence of male hormones increase the aggressive behavior of rats?
2. Does the presence of a mediator increase the likelihood of reaching a compromise in a negotiation setting?
3. Are words that are easily visualized more readily learned than words that cannot be easily visualized?
4. Does the presence of a stranger in the room increase the crying of an infant?
5. Does the administration of stimulants help hyperactive children control their behavior?
6. Does the presentation of contingent reinforcement increase the accuracy of maze running in mice?
7. Will frustrated people increase their level of aggressive behavior?
8. Will sensory deprivation lead to gross disturbance in thinking and emotional responsivity?
9. Will mandatory arrest and jail time reduce spouse abuse?

the research. In experimentation, the problem statement focuses on a causal predic-tion—"Does variable *A* cause a specific change in variable *B?*" For example, the ini-tial idea "I wonder if nutrition affects schoolwork" could become the problem state-ment "Will good breakfasts improve academic achievement?" Table 8.2 lists examples of other problem statements.

Problems are stated in the form of questions, which at the experimental level concern causality. Further, where possible the direction of the expected effects is clearly suggested (e.g., immediate feedback is expected to improve arithmetic skill, cocaine administration is expected to reduce learning, and so on). Most experimen-tal research questions are directional, but often a direction cannot be specified. For example, a researcher might be confident that some manipulation will bring about a change in racial attitudes, but cannot predict if it will make the attitudes more posi-tive or more negative. Therefore, in an experiment to test the hypothesis that the ma-nipulation will change attitudes, the experimenter cannot predict the direction of change. What will be tested is whether attitudes change in either direction. The statement of the problem at the experimental level includes (1) a statement about an expected causal effect, (2) identification of at least two variables, and (3) where pos-sible, an indication of the direction of the expected causal effects. Thus, formulating a clear statement of the problem points the researcher toward an effective design.

Developing a clear statement of the problem requires skill and creative thinking. As an example, consider the March 1964 murder of a young woman named Kitty Genovese. The most shocking aspect of this murder was that Ms. Genovese was at-tacked repeatedly in a parking lot over a 30-minute period while at least 38 of her neighbors heard her screams and/or watched the attack. No one came to her aid. No one even called the police until after she was dead. An incident like this raises questions such as "How could this happen?" or "Why didn't anyone help her?" These questions are important, but they are too vague to be tested scientifically. If, like Dar-ley and Latane (1968), we were interested in trying to find answers to these ques-tions, we would refine the questions into something more manageable. We would need to study reports of the attack and what the witnesses said about it and their behavior in not coming to the victim's aid. We would look for other similar occurrences in police files. We would look in the research literature to see if anyone had studied concepts that might explain what happened to Kitty Genovese. But in the end, we would need to focus our attention on only one or two factors to create a workable statement of the problem. A major issue in this case is that none of the 38 people who witnessed the attack or heard the screams came to the victim's aid. Common sense might lead us to believe that the more people present, the more likely it is that someone will help. But this incident suggests something contrary to common sense—that is, as the number of people present increases, the likelihood that someone will offer help decreases. This initial idea suggests that one variable (the number of people) may affect another variable (the likelihood of someone offering aid). We might develop the idea into the following problem statement: "Will bystanders be less likely to help a victim when there are many people present than when there are only a few people present?" The statement of the problem can lead to specific research studies. When Darley and Latane (1968) studied the problem, they found that people are less likely to help if there are other people present. People apparently assume that someone else will take the responsibility. Darley and Latane could have defined other problems from their initial ideas but chose to start with this particular issue.

The statement of the problem, then, is an important early phase in designing research. Kerlinger (1986, pp. 16-17) lists several characteristics of a good problem statement:

1. The problem should state the expected relationships between variables (in experimentation this is a causal relationship).
2. The problem should be stated in the form of a question.
3. The statement of the problem must at least imply the possibility of an empirical test of the problem.

In the research on the treatment of autistic children discussed in earlier chapters (Graziano, 1974), the major question was "Can relaxation reduce disruption in autistic children?" The independent variable was relaxation and the dependent variable was disruption. The expected effects were a decrease in disruption brought about by relaxation training. With the statement of the problem clearly defined—and, therefore, the major variables identified—the next step in the development of the research hypothesis is to define operationally the variables suggested by the problem statement.

Operational Definitions

Before the dependent variable can be measured or the independent variable can be manipulated, they must be defined. At all levels of research, variables are defined both conceptually and operationally. The independent variable in our treatment study of autistic children was relaxation. The concept of relaxation refers to an internal state—a condition in which people function evenly and without stress or anxiety. We have a fairly good idea of what we mean by relaxation, and we would probably agree that the concept refers to an internal, subjective condition. We cannot directly observe that internal condition but can infer it—that is, it is not an observed fact but an inferred *construct.* The conceptual definition of relaxation gives us an idea of what we want to manipulate. But how do we manipulate something that is internal to the subject and thus not directly accessible to the researcher? In this case, we need to define operationally how to manipulate the subjects' condition of relaxation. Unless we define precisely how we will manipulate relaxation, other researchers will not be able to repeat our studies. We define relaxation in terms of the procedures (the operations) we will use to manipulate, control, and measure it. The definition is spelled out clearly and may be several pages in length. It describes how the researcher should set up the room as well as what should be said and done to relax the subjects. Once the definition is created, the term "relaxation training" should be understood to mean all of the procedures. Because the definition provides detailed instructions, other researchers can replicate the procedure. The dependent variable in this study, disruption, must also be operationally defined. Disruption can be defined as any behavior that interferes with an existing activity of staff or other patients. Numerous examples of specific disruptive behaviors should be included in the behavioral description to clarify the concept and to simplify the task of recognizing which behaviors are classified as disruptive. (The actual operational definitions of relaxation and disruptive behavior used in this study are given in Chapter 4.) The operational definitions make it possible for the researcher to proceed a step closer to formulating the research hypothesis.

Research Hypothesis

To gain the information we seek about the effects of relaxation on the disruptive behavior of autistic children, we must test our hypothesis. To do that, we must develop the problem statement into a specific, testable prediction. The prediction becomes the research hypothesis. Notice that the problem statement has already suggested one basic way to test it: measure disruptive behavior before and after relaxation training and see whether there is a difference as predicted—a *pretest-posttest design* (see Figure 8.2). As we will see in later chapters, however, a simple pretest-posttest design has weaknesses, and there are better designs available to test the hypothesis. However, this simple design helps illustrate the use of operational definitions.

Having operationally defined both the dependent variable (disruptive behavior) and the independent variable (relaxation training), we can now combine the operational definitions and the statement of the problem into a specific prediction—the research hypothesis. The research hypothesis in this case is: "Following relaxation training, the frequency, duration, and intensity of disruptive behavior will be significantly less than at the pretraining baseline."

Figure 8.2   A Single-Group, Pretest-Posttest Research Design

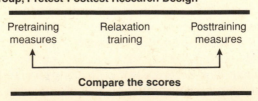

Pretraining   Relaxation   Posttraining
measures   training   measures

Compare the scores

TABLE 8.3   CHARACTERISTICS OF A RESEARCH HYPOTHESIS

A good research hypothesis

1. Is a declarative sentence.
2. Is brief and clearly stated.
3. Identifies at least two variables.
4. States an expected (predicted) relationship between at least one variable and at least one other variable.
5. States the nature of the relationship.
   [Example: "The amount of physical punishment they experienced as children will be positively correlated with parents' current use of physical punishment on their own children." (a correlational hypothesis)]
6. States the direction of the relationship.
   [Example: "Subjects in Group A will score significantly higher than subjects in Group B." (a directional prediction)]
7. Implies that the predicted relationship can be tested empirically.

A research hypothesis makes a statement about the relationship among variables and clearly implies that the relationship can be empirically tested. Notice that the research hypothesis is a declarative statement. Even though it is in this form, remember that it is only a tentative statement to be tested. Any research hypothesis is a tentative statement about the effects of one variable on another and is subject to verification by empirical testing. We have summarized the characteristics of a good research hypothesis in Table 8.3.

The Contribution of Theory to the Research Hypothesis

Theory plays a critical role in developing the research hypothesis. Even in a research area that has never been studied before, we usually have implicit theories about how things might relate. Most research involves studying constructs that have been studied extensively, and in such situations, explicit theories guide decisions about our research. Often several theories will guide our design decisions. Some of these theories will be mature, with hundreds of research studies providing empirical confirmation of the accuracy of the theory's predictions. Some of the theories will be new, with only limited validational evidence. It is possible that a theory may be brand new, being tested for the first time in your study, but that situation is rare. Theories are usually interconnected, and the typical study will provide evidence concerning the validity of more than one theory. This network of theories and established empirical relationships provides a critical foundation for a proposed study. We will illustrate the complex role of theory in formulating a research hypothesis with our example of using relaxation to control outbursts in autistic children. Admittedly, this review will be cursory, touching on only a few of the theoretical ideas that contributed to the study. A more complete review would take most of a chapter and is really not necessary to make our point.

Autism is a severely disabling condition that exists at birth and becomes increasingly evident with age. Autistic children are functionally impaired in emotional development, language, personal relationships, and general learning. Most researchers studying autism accept a diathesis-stress theory—that is, that the disordered functioning results from the interaction of (1) predisposing characteristics such as genetic/organic factors (the diathesis) and (2) environmental factors (the stress). The diathesis-stress model has been applied to virtually all psychological disorders (e.g., psychoses, anxiety disorders, autism, etc.). The relative contributions of diathesis and stress may be different for different conditions, but all of the functional problems are believed to result from the combination of these two factors. Data from hundreds of studies provide support for this general theory, which implies that an environmental manipulation may affect pathological behavior even if one believes that there is a strong biological component contributing to the pathology. The observation that the autistic children displayed a facial grimace just before each outburst suggested the existence of an internal, unobservable event. Both the facial expression and the nature of the outbursts suggested the presence of strong autonomic arousal. Arousal is a very complex construct that relates to many different theories—some physiological, some psychological, and some involving both systems. Some of those theories imply that arousal and relaxation are mutually exclusive constructs. Thus, inducing relaxation might well reduce the (inferred) state of autonomic arousal in these autistic children.

It is important to note that this brief review only scratches the surface of the role of theory in this one, relatively simple study. It is also important to realize that it is unlikely that all the theories that we drew on in developing this one study are valid (i.e., that they describe accurately all predicted relationships). The study provided an answer to the specific question we posed and information that helped us to evaluate the adequacy of many of the theories that guided the formulation of our question. One theory affected by this study was the theory that autistic psychopathology prevents the learning of new skills. Since these children were able to learn relaxation skills, the validity of this theory was seriously weakened. Research conducted since this study confirms that autistic children are able to learn many skills, although their pace of learning may be slower than other children (Koegel, O'Dell, & Koegel, 1987; Lovaas, 1987; Strain, 1983, 1984).

Testing the Research Hypothesis

The research hypothesis is a complex statement. It is not a single hypothesis but actually encompasses three hypotheses, each of which must be carefully checked: the null or statistical hypothesis, the confounding variable hypothesis, and the causal hypothesis.

Suppose we carry out the research with autistic children as follows: (1) we measure the frequency, intensity, and duration of the children's disruptive behavior during a four-week pretraining baseline period; (2) we then train the children in relaxation to the criteria specified (the training requires two months); and (3) after completion of training, we again measure the frequency, intensity, and duration of their disruptive behavior for a four-week posttraining period. This is an example of a simple pretest-posttest design. Now suppose that, as we predicted, there is less disruption after relaxation training. With such apparently clear results, can we conclude that the independent variable, relaxation training, reduced the children's disruptive

Figure 8.3 Flowchart Illustrating the Process of Evaluating a Research Study's Results

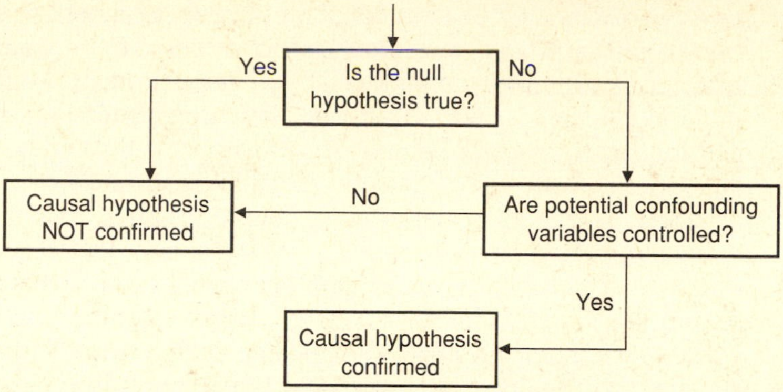

behavior? Not yet, because to answer the research question we must rule out two other hypotheses. Note again there are *three* hypotheses imbedded in the research hypothesis: (1) the null or statistical hypothesis, (2) the confounding-variable hypothesis, and (3) the causal hypothesis. Figure 8.3 illustrates the steps in this process.

Null Hypothesis   Before we can conclude that relaxation reduces disruptive behavior, we must determine that the posttraining measures of disruption are *significantly* smaller than the pretraining measures of disruption—that the differences observed are not merely due to chance variation. Thus, the first of the three hypotheses we must test is the *statistical hypothesis.* The *t*- or *F*-tests for correlated groups are appropriate here because the dependent measure yields score data and the measures are correlated because the same subjects were measured both before and after treatment.

The *null hypothesis* is what its name suggests; null means "none." The null hypothesis states that there is no difference between the two conditions beyond chance differences. If we find a statistically significant difference, we reject the null hypothesis; if we find the differences are within chance limits, we conclude there is not sufficient evidence to reject the null hypothesis. Suppose a *t*- or *F*-test discloses that the posttraining measures are significantly smaller than the pretraining measures—that the differences are not due only to chance. The differences are large enough to permit us to reject the null hypothesis. However, we are not yet ready to accept the hypothesis that relaxation training is responsible for the observed reduction in disruptive behavior.

Confounding-Variable Hypothesis   Although we have found statistically significant differences in the predicted direction, we still cannot be sure that the observed differences are due to the independent variable, relaxation. They may be due to some *extraneous variables* that have confounded the research. Rejecting the null hypothesis, while necessary, *is not sufficient to draw a causal inference.* We must also rule out the possibility that factors other than the independent variable may have had an effect on the dependent variable (i.e., that confounding variables are responsible for the observed effect). The task here is to rule out confounding variables as explanations of the results. It is best to rule out confounding variables during the design phase, when we anticipate possible confounding variables and design controls to eliminate their effect on the dependent variable.

The *confounding-variable hypothesis* suggests that the observed statistically significant differences may be due to extraneous factors that have systematic effects on the dependent measures. We accept the finding that there is a statistically significant difference as predicted, but being systematic scientists, we are not yet convinced that the difference we found is due to the independent variable. Rather, we consider the possibility that it may be due to the effects of confounding factors. For example, we have noted that relaxation training required two months to reach criterion, a long time in the life of a growing child. The children could have matured somewhat over these two months. The observed improvement might have been due to maturational factors and not to the independent variable, relaxation training. Thus, in this study, the independent variable may have been confounded with maturation. If we are not careful in our enthusiasm at having found a statistically significant difference, we might too readily conclude that relaxation training is the effective variable that brought about the improvement in disruptive behavior. But the confounding-variable hypothesis recognizes that the explanation of relaxation training being responsible for the improvement in disruptive behavior may be only one of several possible alternative explanations. To have confidence in our conclusions, we must carefully rule out all alternative explanations.

Note that, unlike the statistical hypothesis, the confounding-variable hypothesis is not directly tested. Rather, each confounding-variable hypothesis is ruled out by first anticipating potential confounding variables, reducing their likelihood by using appropriate research design, and later by inspecting the research design and procedures. This careful inspection shows where the design is weak and where it is strong. The researcher must then judge whether the design is strong enough to rule out the most likely potential confounding variables. As we will see in later chapters, some designs are so powerful that they can rule out most confounding variables.

The concern for ruling out alternative explanations in science is an important point for students to understand. Research is conducted not only to find evidence to support research hypotheses but also to rule out alternative explanations, which are also known as *rival hypotheses.* Every confounding variable is a threat to the validity of an experiment. We will discover that experimental designs often can rule out most of the confounding variables likely to occur in a research project.

Causal Hypothesis   The *causal hypothesis* states that the independent variable has the predicted effect on the dependent variable. Suppose we tested and rejected the null hypothesis and carefully ruled out *confounding variables.* (We will discuss how to control or rule out confounding variables in Chapter 9.) We are ready to return to the research hypothesis, "Following relaxation training, the frequency, duration, and intensity of disruptive behavior will be significantly less than at the pretraining baseline." Remember that when we first stated this research hypothesis it was a tentative statement to be tested with a research study. If we found in that study that there is significantly less disruption after training than before training and we can carefully rule out alternative hypotheses, we are then left with one hypothesis—that the independent variable affected the dependent variable as predicted. Note, however, that our assertion is not absolute but is a statement of probability. Our first hypothesis was the statistical hypothesis, which we tested in terms of probability. Even though the data may have been sufficiently persuasive to convince us to reject the null hypothesis of no difference, there is always the possibility that we have made a Type I error (see Chapter 5). It is wise to remember that there are so many complicated steps from initial conceptualization to running the study to interpreting the results that we must always be cautious in our interpretations. We can have confidence but not certainty in the results of a well-run study. Every finding in science is considered to be tentative, subject to change due to new observations.

Another important point about developing research hypotheses is that most problem statements can be developed into several different research hypotheses, each of which can then be tested. Thus, we can generate many different studies from the same problem statement. Recall that the problem statement in the research with autistic children is "Can relaxation reduce disruption of autistic children?" The essential question being posed here is whether there is a causal relationship between the child's relaxation and the degree of disruption. Relaxation was defined operationally in terms of procedures used to train the child to slow down, and disruption was operationally defined as the frequency, duration, and intensity of each disruptive behavior. These definitions led to the specific research hypothesis, "Following relaxation training, the frequency, duration, and intensity of disruptive behavior will be significantly less than at the pretraining baseline."

Now suppose that we want to study another aspect of the relaxation-disruption hypothesis and operationally define relaxation in terms of the pharmacological effects of a particular drug. We give each child a drug that is known to relax individuals. We also modify or redefine the dependent measure of disruptive behavior. The research hypothesis is similar to the original hypothesis, but, because we have defined variables in terms of different operations, we are actually testing a different research hypothesis. We conduct this second study using the same pretest-posttest design, only this time we use our redefined measures of disruption and we give the children specific drugs to induce relaxation instead of using a behavioral training approach to teach relaxation. We are still evaluating the same statement of the problem but with a different interpretation expressed as a different research hypothesis.

We can make other changes as well in the way we translate the statement of the problem into a research hypothesis. For example, we could use a different research design. Instead of using the pretest-posttest design, we may randomly assign each of the autistic children to one of two groups. One of the groups is relaxed with the drug, whereas the other group is not given the drug. We then measure the disruptive behavior of all subjects and compare the mean level of disruption in the two groups. This design is called a *two-group posttest-only design* and is illustrated in Figure 8.4. The research hypothesis in this study is stated differently from that of the previous example because the independent variable and the research design have been changed. The new research hypothesis is "Autistic children who are given drugs that relax them will show less disruptive behavior than autistic children who do not receive such drugs." Thus, the same problem statement can be combined with different operational definitions of the independent and dependent variables and different research designs. This results in the generation of several different research hypotheses and consequently several different studies. In essence,

Figure 8.4   A Two-Group, Posttest-Only Design

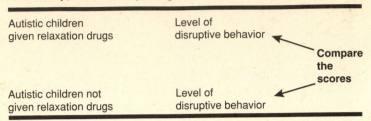

the researcher is able to investigate the same basic problem in different ways, testing different facets of the same issue. This allows us to *replicate* (repeat) systematically the study of the hypothesized relationship in several different ways, thus increasing confidence in the conclusions about that hypothesized relationship between relaxation and disruptive behavior. Replication is an extremely important part of research (see Chapter 9).

Internal Summary: The Research Hypothesis

Initial ideas are refined into the problem statement which, in an experiment, identifies variables, implies causality, and indicates the direction of the expected causal effect. The identified variables must then be operationally defined, and a research hypothesis is constructed by combining those operational definitions with the problem statement. The research hypothesis states a specific testable prediction—one that is directional or one that is nondirectional—about the relationship between specific variables.

Remember, testing the research hypothesis involves several hypotheses: the null or statistical hypothesis, the confounding-variable hypothesis (which is often a set of several hypotheses), and the causal hypothesis. We must consider and reject the null and confounding-variable hypotheses before accepting the causal hypothesis.

Statistical methods for testing null hypotheses rule out the possibility that the findings were due to chance. It is *equally important* to identify and rule out potential confounding variables in order to draw conclusions about causal relationships between the independent and dependent variables. Statistical tests tell us only whether there is a significant difference between groups but not whether the difference is due to the independent variable manipulation. To draw that conclusion we must identify and rule out competing interpretations. Finally, one problem statement can be developed into several research hypotheses that lead to several different studies, thus examining different facets of the problem and increasing our confidence through replication.

VALIDITY AND THREATS TO VALIDITY

A major concern in research is the validity of the procedures and conclusions. The term *validity* has several meanings, the most basic of which refers to methodological soundness or appropriateness. That is, a valid measure measures what it is sup-

TABLE 8.4   TYPES OF VALIDITY

Statistical	Accuracy of the conclusion drawn from a statistical test
Construct	Accuracy of the theory or theories behind the research study and the various procedures used to operationalize the variables addressed by the theory
External	Extent to which the results of a particular study generalize to real-world conditions
Internal	The extent to which we can be confident that the observed changes in the dependent variable were due to the effects of the independent variable and not to the effects of extraneous variables

posed to measure; a valid research design tests what it is supposed to test. In general, validity concerns whether the concepts being investigated are actually the ones being measured or tested.

At any level of constraint we must be concerned with issues of validity. At the experimental level we are concerned with answering specific questions about causality, such as "Does the independent variable have effects on the dependent variable?" We want to carry out the experiment so it will give us high confidence in the validity of the conclusions about that causal relationship. Because experimentation may involve many factors, all having effects on the outcome, there are likely to be many potential threats to the validity of any experiment. Therefore, the researcher must (1) anticipate all potential threats to validity and (2) create procedures to eliminate or reduce them. However, absolute accuracy or validity cannot be achieved, and validity must always be understood in relative terms.

Types of Validity

We follow closely the classic organization of Campbell and Stanley (1966) and Cook and Campbell (1979) in our discussion of four types of validity: statistical validity, construct validity, external validity, and internal validity (summarized in Table 8.4).

Statistical Validity   When we use statistical procedures to test the null hypothesis, we are making a statement about the *statistical validity* of the results—that is, are the results due to some systematic factor (ideally, the independent variable), or are they due merely to chance variations? Ruling out the null hypothesis is a necessary first step in testing the effects of the independent variable.

There are several possible threats to a study's statistical validity, and the researcher must carefully control them. One such threat is the possibility that the measures used to assess the dependent variable are unreliable. Unreliable measures threaten statistical validity. Another threat to statistical validity is the researcher's violations of the assumptions that underlie statistical tests. Each statistical procedure makes assumptions about the nature of the data. Using a statistical procedure in a situation where one or more of these assumptions are not true can threaten the study's statistical validity. Statistics textbooks normally list the assumptions of a test as part of their presentation of the test.

Construct Validity   Every hypothesis tested in research is constructed in a theoretical context of ideas. *Construct validity* refers to how well the study's results support the theory or constructs behind the research and asks whether the theory supported by the findings provides the best available theoretical explanation of the results. To help reduce threats to construct validity, the researcher uses clearly stated definitions and carefully builds hypotheses on solid, well-validated constructs. In brief, the theoretical bases must be clear and well supported with rival theories carefully ruled out.

As an example of dubious construct validity, consider the popular books by Erich von Daniken, *Chariots of the Gods* (1970) and *Gods from Outer Space* (1972). Millions of copies have been sold, and they have been translated into several languages. They present Daniken's proposition that an advanced race of extraterrestrials visited Earth thousands of years ago and started humans toward advanced civilization. Daniken presents an impressive array of evidence to support his hypothesis, including photographs of ancient objects that suggest technical skills far beyond the abilities of primitive humans. Many readers, impressed by his abundant evidence, are convinced of the validity of his theory. But Daniken's theoretical explanation of the observed artifacts is only one of at least two alternative explanations. The most plausible rival explanation is that humans, without extraterrestrial help, created the objects themselves. For example, Daniken presents a figure, which he interprets as a humanoid in a space helmet hundreds of years before space helmets were even thought of by humans. According to a rival hypothesis, the figure could be a religious symbol—a human figure with a halo of light around the head—or simply a stylized human figure. In other words, the evidence presented by Daniken does seem to support his theory, but it supports an alternative theory just as well. The construct validity of his theory is in doubt (see Figure 8.5).

An example from a continuing debate in psychology, the nature-nurture issue, further clarifies the concept of construct validity. The nature-nurture question has been raised in many different areas of psychological research from questions about the cause of schizophrenia to exploring the issue of why males usually score higher than females on math skill measures. On the latter issue, a lively debate has raged over how much of the difference is innate and how much is the result of environmental effects (Benbow & Stanley, 1980; Lubinski & Benbow, 1992; Parsons, 1980). Environmental variables alone could shape the differences if males receive more training than females in math or if males are more likely than females to be told that learning math is important to success. The issue is whether the data on this question support the idea of an innate, genetically determined characteristic (nature) as being responsible for the observed sex differences or whether the environment (nurture) could have shaped the relationships observed. In many cases, one is tempted to interpret data as consistent with our preconceptions and ignore the fact that the data are just as consistent with alternative conceptions. For example, the finding that men tend to take more math courses than women would seem to be consistent with the nurture hypothesis that males are better at math because they get more training in it. However, one could interpret that same finding to mean that men take more math courses because they tend to be good at math and are choosing courses in which they know they can excel. Therefore, the data are consistent with both a nature and a nurture hypothesis, and the construct validity of any one interpretation would be in doubt.

Figure 8.5 An Ambiguous Figure

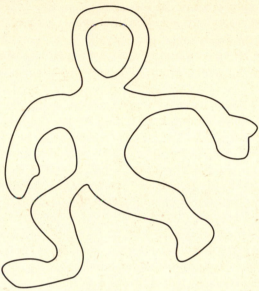

Here is an ambiguous figure. One could conclude that it depicts a spaceman floating in a space suit. But that conclusion is entirely speculative and tentative because there are many alternatives. Perhaps it is a child's drawing of a parent, a primitive culture's depiction of God, a stylized ballet dancer at the Bolshoi, a cartoon drawing of a Buffalo Bill's receiver during the Superbowl, or even a very flexible Gumby. How many alternatives can you develop?

External Validity   In its strictest sense, the results of an experiment are limited to those subjects and conditions used in the particular experiments. But when we test college students' memory ability, for example, are we really interested in how well these particular 20 freshmen in Dr. Perkins' introductory psychology class did on the morning of October 21? No, instead we are interested in memory functions in general. We want to generalize the results beyond the specific conditions and subjects to other, similar subjects and conditions. *External validity* refers to the degree to which we are able to generalize the results of a study to other subjects, conditions, times, and places.

To make statements about the overall population based on the findings of a particular sample, the sample must be selected from the population in such a manner that it adequately represents the population. Problems of *generalization* from a sample to a population are often best controlled by random selection of subjects from the population (controls are explained further in Chapter 9). In similar fashion, the researcher must be careful about generalizing across times, places, and conditions—to do so, one *must* sample across those times, places, or conditions. The term *ecological validity* is often used to refer to the appropriate generalization from the laboratory to real-life or natural environmental situations.

Internal Validity and Confounding Variables   *Internal validity* is of great concern to the researcher because it involves the very heart of the experimental goals—the demonstration of causality. In an experiment, internal validity concerns the question "Was the independent variable and not some extraneous variable responsible for the observed changes in the dependent variable?" An experiment is said to be internally valid when it can be concluded with confidence that the independent variable and not some other variable brought about the observed changes in the dependent variable. Any factor that weakens this confidence is a threat to the internal validity of the study.

In the next section we will describe several confounding variables, but before we do that, let's look at a couple of examples. Suppose, for example, we are interested in the ability of patients with schizophrenia to judge time duration. We predict that their time estimation will be significantly disrupted by intrusive auditory stimulation. We test patients for their time estimations of short intervals under two conditions: (1) a high-stimulation condition in which loud, rhythmic music is played during testing, and (2) a low-stimulation condition in which the testing room is kept quiet. Because of scheduling problems in the hospital, patients are available to us only on Monday and Thursday mornings, when the locked-ward and the open-ward patients, respectively, can be tested. We test the Monday patients under the high-stimulation condition and the Thursday patients under the low-stimulation condition. The research hypothesis is that patients with schizophrenia tested under the high-stimulation condition will make significantly more errors than those tested under the low-stimulation condition. We find, exactly as predicted, that significantly more errors are made under the high-stimulation condition and conclude that external auditory stimulation is a significant factor that affects time estimation in patients with schizophrenia. The major confounding variable in our study should be obvious: the subjects in the two conditions differ not only in terms of the independent variable—high- and low-auditory stimulation—but also because one group consists of closed-ward patients and the other group consists of open-ward patients. There is good reason to suspect that the closed-ward patients are more disturbed than the other group, and it is therefore not surprising that they perform more poorly on the time-estimation task. It would be unreasonable to attribute the difference between the two groups to the high- and low-stimulation conditions that we manipulated. That the results may be due to severity of illness rather than amount of auditory stimulation provides an alternative explanation. Until the alternative explanation is clearly ruled out, we cannot confidently conclude that auditory stimulation affected estimates of time duration. In our study the independent variable (amount of auditory stimulation) is confounded with an uncontrolled variable (severity of illness). When we use the term *confounded* we mean that the independent variable varies with at least one other variable. Because the two vary together, we cannot tell whether one or the other or both are responsible for the observed changes in the dependent variable. This confounding leaves us with an alternative explanation of the results. The confounding variable in this study should have been eliminated in the initial design of the study, long before testing any subjects.

Consider also the hypothesis concerning the effects of relaxation training on the disruptive behavior of autistic children and the research procedures used to test it. Can we conclude with confidence that the independent variable, relaxation training, is responsible for the observed reduction in disruptive behavior? Can we be confident about the internal validity of this study? Consider the basic design of the first study, which tested the research hypothesis, "Following relaxation training, the frequency, duration, and intensity of disruptive behavior will be significantly less than at the pretraining baseline." To test the hypothesis, we measured the disruptive behavior of the autistic children, then provided relaxation training, and then measured disruption again. It required two months for all the children in the study to reach the criterion of successful relaxation. We found that at posttraining the disruptive behavior was measurably less and the decrease was statistically significant. It is tempting to conclude that the relaxation training was responsible for the decrease in disruptive behavior, but what alternative explanations might there be for the results? What confounding variables might have been operating to have produced the results? As suggested earlier, the children might simply have improved over the two-month period through natural maturational processes with relaxation having little to do with the observed improvement. Maturation is a confounding variable in this study; it supplies us with an alternative explanation of the results so we cannot be confident that the results are due to the influence of the independent variable—relaxation training.

Another alternative explanation for the observed improvement is that some systematic factor in the research itself, other than relaxation, might have been responsible. After all, the children were in a full-day, five-day-a-week therapy program. Many procedures were used in addition to relaxation training. Might it not be possible that some other factor that was consistently applied to the children during the two months of relaxation training might have been responsible for the improvement? This is an example of the confounding variable of history; that is, during the course of the research, many variables besides the independent variable may have been operating.

A phenomenon called regression to the mean might also have been operating here. Any behavior will naturally vary in frequency or intensity, going through ups and downs of severity. Perhaps this research had been started at the peak of severity, perhaps begun even because the severity was so great. As time passed, the normal variation of the behavior returned to levels of severity closer to the mean, far lower than it was at the high, pretreatment baseline peak of severity. It was then that the posttraining measures were taken. If regression to the mean was operating, then the relaxation manipulation might have had little to do with the observed improvement in behavior.

There is yet another possible confounding variable that could explain findings of a decrease in disruptive behavior. In the course of the research, the staff making the observations of the children's disruptive behavior may have changed in the ways in which they observed and measured the behavior. They might have gradually become more accustomed to the children's severe behavior and, in time, tended to record it as less severe (i.e., their criteria for observations and not the behavior of the children might have changed during the course of the study).

There are many potential confounding variables in research, and there may be several in any given study. Their effects might all be in the same direction, thus compounding the errors, or in opposite directions countering one another. In any event, if we wish to draw valid, confident conclusions about the effects of one variable on another, we must carefully anticipate and control potential confounding variables to eliminate rival hypotheses, leaving the causal hypothesis as the most likely explanation for the results.

MAJOR CONFOUNDING VARIABLES

Cook and Campbell (1979) have summarized the major types of confounding variables that can affect experimental results and thus lead to erroneous interpretations. We will discuss each of them briefly. We have also summarized them in Table 8.5.

Maturation

In longitudinal research, especially with children, subjects grow older between the pretreatment and posttreatment measures. As they grow older, they may also become more sophisticated, experienced, bigger, stronger, and so on. Natural *maturational* changes can also occur in subjects other than children. Adults placed in a new environment tend to make predictable changes (adjustments) over time. Diseases tend to have a predictable course. Thus, observed changes over time may be due to maturational factors rather than to any effects of the independent variable. Researchers must be particularly alert to maturational factors when conducting research with children for whom change and growth are virtual certainties.

History

During the course of a study, many events that are not of interest to the researcher can occur and possibly affect the outcome. In general, threats to internal validity due

TABLE 8.5   MAJOR CONFOUNDING VARIABLES

Maturation	Changes in the dependent variable that occur during the course of a study that are due to the normal maturation of the subject
History	Changes in the dependent variable that are due to historical events that occur during the study but are unrelated to the study
Testing	Any change in a subject's score on the dependent variable that is a function of having been tested previously
Instrumentation	Any change in the calibration of the measuring instrument or procedure over the course of the study that affects the scores on the dependent variable
Regression to the mean	The tendency for subjects who are selected because they have extreme scores on a variable to be less extreme in a follow-up testing
Selection	Any factor that creates groups that are not equivalent at the beginning of the study
Attrition	The loss of subjects during a study; differential loss is problematic because the subjects who drop out are likely to be different from those who continue
Diffusion of treatment	Change in the response of subjects in a particular condition because of information the subjects gained about other research conditions from subjects in those other conditions
Sequencing effects	Effects on a subject's performance in later conditions that result from the experience the subject had in the previous conditions of the study

"OF COURSE I'VE BECOME MORE MATURE SINCE YOU STARTED
TREATING ME. YOU'VE BEEN AT IT SINCE I WAS 14 YEARS OLD."

Source: Reprinted by permission of S. Harris.

to *history* are greatest with longer times between pretest and posttest measurements. Historical factors are most important to consider when we are measuring dependent variables responsive to environmental changes. For example, weight is more affected by the amount of food intake than is height. Weight shows more natural variation within a subject over time than height. Therefore, historical factors are more likely to be a confounding variable for weight than for height. Most weight-control procedures would be lucky to hold their own if we evaluated them during the holidays, when people are constantly exposed to tempting high-calorie foods.

Testing

The effects of repeated *testing* of subjects may be a threat to internal validity because subjects may gain proficiency through repeated practice on the measuring instruments. Testing effects are most pronounced on measures where the subject is asked to perform some skill-related task. Tests of memory, IQ, or manual dexterity fall into this category. Most people will do better on the second administration of the test because of a practice effect.

Instrumentation

Apparent pre-post changes may be due to changes in the measuring *instrument* over time rather than to the experimental manipulation of the independent variable.

This is particularly true when the measuring instrument is a human observer. Observers might become more proficient in administering tests or in making observations or their criteria for judgments might change as they become familiar with the dependent variable being observed.

Regression to the Mean

The concept of *regression to the mean* suggests that whenever subjects are selected *because* their scores on a measure are extreme (either very high or very low), they will tend to be less extreme on a second testing (i.e., their scores will have regressed toward the mean). For example, consider the top 10 percent of a class based on the first of a series of exam scores. How should the top students perform on the second exam? We would expect them to do well, but would they do *as* well as on the first exam? Would they all be in the top 10 percent the second time around? Probably not. The reason is that some of the students did well on the first exam in part because they were fortunate to have known more about a significant number of questions. We might say they were "lucky." On the second test, however, many of the students who scored high on the first test because of good fortune might have found more questions on material they had not studied and thus would score lower. If we took the top 10 percent of students on the first test and computed their mean score on both the first and second tests, we would probably find that they scored (on average) lower on the second test—they regressed toward the mean. Similarly, if we took the bottom 10 percent of students on the first test and computed their mean score on both the first and second tests, we would find that they scored (on average) higher on the second test—again, they regressed toward the mean. How much regression occurs will depend on how much of the test performance is due to variable factors, such as "being lucky," and how much is due to consistent factors, such as skill and good study habits. The more that variable factors contribute to the score, the more regression we can expect to see.

Selection

Confounding due to *selection* can occur when care is not taken to ensure that two or more groups being compared are equivalent before the manipulations begin. Under ideal conditions, subjects are randomly selected and then randomly assigned to different groups. When random selection and assignment are not possible—as in most naturalistic, case-study, and differential research—then the possibility of confounding due to selection exists.

Attrition

In the normal course of a study, subjects drop out for different reasons; some go on vacation in the middle of the study, others forget their appointments, others decide they are not interested, some become ill, and so on. If there are no biasing factors, such dropouts will probably be evenly distributed across groups, and they will not differentially affect one group more than others. But confounding due to *attrition* can occur when subjects are lost differentially, such as when there are more dropouts from one group than from another or when subjects with certain characteristics are lost. When we plan research, we must be careful not to create situations or use procedures that will bias some subjects against completing the study, thus differentially affecting the outcome of the study. For example, suppose a researcher realized too late that nearly all of the seniors among the high school subjects failed to return for the second half of the experiment because it coincided with school parties, excitement, and general preparation for graduation. Their attrition left primarily underclass subjects in the second half of the study, thus biasing the sample and the results.

Sometimes procedures may tend to cause subjects with certain characteristics to drop out, leaving a biased sample. For example, in an unpublished study conducted many years ago by one of the authors, many sixth-grade boys dropped out of the study because they said the procedures were "too girlish." Perhaps in today's more egalitarian mood, this might be less likely. In any event, care must be taken to avoid confounding studies by allowing attrition of subjects to have a differential effect on the outcome.

Diffusion of Treatment

When subjects in different experimental conditions are in close proximity, such as children in the same classroom, and are able to communicate with each other, earlier subjects may "give away" the procedures to those scheduled later. Also, experimental subjects who receive a treatment may communicate with control subjects who supposedly do not receive that treatment or who may not have known they were in a control group. Such information exchanges may erode the planned experimental differences between groups. The groups become more similar because of the information exchange between subjects.

Diffusion of treatment can affect studies in many ways. For example, many psychologists use subjects from an undergraduate subject pool, where diffusion of treatment is likely. Students often hear about studies from other students and perhaps even select the study on the basis of what they hear. When they participate, the knowledge of what their friends experienced might affect how they respond regardless of the condition to which they are assigned. To compensate for this problem, many researchers try to make their study look the same to subjects in all conditions in an attempt to minimize diffusion of treatments.

Sequencing Effects

Much of the research in psychology is designed so that each subject is exposed to more than one of the experimental conditions. These are called *within-subjects designs.* Although they offer important advantages over other designs, they also introduce another confounding factor—*sequencing effects.* For example, if a study includes three conditions and each subject is exposed to all three, their experiences with earlier conditions of the study may affect their responses to later conditions. If the order of presentation of conditions for all subjects is always condition A followed by condition B followed by condition C, then systematic confounding effects can occur. To control for sequencing effects we would normally use more than one order of conditions. (Sequencing effects are discussed in more detail in Chapter 11.)

Internal Summary: Confounding Variables

The major objective of an experiment is to demonstrate that the manipulated independent variable is the primary cause of the observed changes in the dependent variable. When this causality is not clear because some variable other than the independent variable may have caused the effects, we have confounding, which threatens the internal validity of the study. Threats to internal validity reduce our confidence in the causal relationship between the independent variable and the dependent variable. Therefore, it is extremely important for the researcher to plan studies carefully, anticipating and controlling potential confounding.

SUBJECT AND EXPERIMENTER EFFECTS

There is a large category of threats to the validity of a study due to subject and experimenter effects. The expectations and biases of both the researcher and the subjects can systematically affect the results in subtle ways, thus reducing the study's validity.

Subject Effects

As discussed by Orne (1962), every psychological experiment is a social situation in which both subjects and researchers participate in a common undertaking—the experiment. Each behaves according to his or her understanding of how a subject or a psychological researcher should behave. When subjects enter an experiment, they are not entirely naive. They have ideas, understandings, and perhaps misunderstandings about what to expect in the experimental situation. Subjects enter with a variety of reasons for being subjects. Some do so because it is a course requirement. Others participate because of curiosity or because they will be paid for their participation. Some volunteer because they hope to learn something, perhaps about themselves. The point is that subjects enter and carry out their role with a variety of motivations, understandings, expectations, and biases, all of which can affect their behavior in the experimental setting. Furthermore, an experiment is an artificial, contrived situation, far removed from subjects' natural environments. When people know they are being observed, they are likely to behave differently than when they are in more familiar situations, which can lead to *subject effects.*

Most subjects do their best to be "good" subjects. They want to appear at their best for the researcher. This may lead some subjects to try to discern the research hypothesis so they will know how they are "supposed to behave." Subjects are often particularly sensitive to any real or imagined cues from the researcher. Furthermore, researchers, with their own expectations and biases, might inadvertently give such cues. Cues given to the subjects on how they are expected to behave are called *demand characteristics.* Demand characteristics usually occur unintentionally. They include not only characteristics of the setting and procedures but also information and even rumors about the researcher and the nature of the research.

A related phenomenon, the *placebo effect,* can occur when subjects expect a specific effect of an experimental manipulation. For example, some subjects in biofeedback studies of tension reduction or drug studies of pain control enter the study with the clear expectation that the procedures will help, and they actually report feeling better and even show physiological changes, all due to the suggestion that the procedure will work. In a number of studies, subjects have reported improvement when given a placebo treatment such as a pill that looks and tastes like the true drug being tested but lacks the drug's active ingredient.

Clearly there are many ways that subjects, bringing their own expectations and biases, can react in the experimental situation. Many of their reactions are not part of the experimental plan. Thus, the researcher should include controls for these and other possible subject effects to prevent confounding that can reduce the study's validity.

Experimenter Effects

Experimenter effects also can have significant impact on the outcome of a study. The researcher attempts to carry out the research plan as objectively and as accurately as possible. But researchers, too, are human and carry their own potentially biasing expectations and motivations into the study. The major expectation of the researcher is that the results will turn out as predicted and the hypothesis will be supported. But how can such expectations bias the results in an objective experimental situation? *Experimenter expectancies* might cause researchers to bias results in several ways: by directly influencing the subject's behavior toward support of the hypothesis; by selecting data that best support the hypothesis; by using statistical techniques that best show the particular effects predicted, but not other effects; and by interpreting results in a biased manner (i.e., by drawing conclusions that accept improbable explanations consistent with the research hypothesis while ignoring other, more probable and parsimonious explanations that do not support the hypothesis). Common to all of these ways of introducing bias is the idea that the researcher will tend to make decisions and choices that favor the hypothesis being tested. This is not to say that the researcher deliberately and knowingly falsifies data but, rather, behaves in ways that tend to support his or her own expectations and does so without being clearly aware of it. For example, suppose that a researcher has two groups of subjects. The subjects have been randomly assigned to the groups to avoid confounding due to selection. Subjects in each group are to be tested on a series of arithmetic problems and are timed by the researcher. The prediction is that, because of the difference in instructions to the two groups, the experimental group will take significantly longer than the control group to complete the problems. In this situation, there are several ways that experimenter bias can operate. If the researcher knows to which group each subject is assigned and knows the research hypothesis, then it is quite possible that the researcher might tend to time the experimental subjects in a way that would extend their times. The researcher also could influence the results by reading the same set of instructions in a slightly different tone to the two groups, emphasizing speed for the control subjects. In either case, the researcher would probably not be aware of this systematic bias and would deny it. However, the bias, accumulated over all of the subjects in the group, could very well affect the outcome toward support of the hypothesis.

Much of our understanding of experimenter expectancy effects is due to the research of Rosenthal and his colleagues. Rosenthal and Fode (1963a, 1963b) suggest several ways in which the experimenter might unintentionally affect a subject's responses and thus bias the results to favor the hypothesis. For example, the researcher might unintentionally present cues by variations in tone of voice or by changes in posture or facial expressions, verbally reinforce some responses and not others, or incorrectly record subjects' responses. Although such experimenter expectancy effects may occur, it has been difficult to demonstrate clearly that they do occur, leaving some researchers to conclude that although this may be a problem in a minority of studies, it does not characterize most research (Barber & Silver, 1968). But in any research where experimenter expectancy effects may occur, the effects provide an alternative explanation for the obtained results. When, for example, a journal editor reads a research manuscript that has been submitted for possible publication and determines that such expectancy effects may have occurred, just raising this possibility is sufficient to cast doubt on the validity of the experiment and lead to the rejection of the manuscript for publication. The editor need not provide data to support the alternative hypothesis that the obtained results were due to experimenter expectancy effects. If the rival hypothesis could be true, then we cannot accept the researcher's conclusions about the effects of the independent variable. The researcher would have to repeat the experiment, adding controls to eliminate the rival hypothesis. Thus, although Barber and Silver (1968) may be correct in doubting that such effects are as frequent as Rosenthal suggested, the simple existence of the rival hypothesis in a study is sufficient to cast doubt on a researcher's findings, and it is therefore important for the researcher to control for potential experimenter expectancy effects.

Internal Summary: Subject and Experimenter Effects

We have pointed out that not every confounding variable occurs in every experiment and, therefore, not all of the available controls are necessary in each experiment. However, subject and experimenter effects may occur in virtually any experimental situation; and the experimenter should, as a matter of course, take steps to avoid these biases. Note that *many of the most important threats to validity will be well controlled if the researcher designs into each experiment the random selection of subjects, the random assignment of subjects to conditions, and a proper control group* (see Chapter 9).

VALIDITY, CONTROL, AND CONSTRAINT

Validity, control, and constraint are closely related concepts. Control procedures are applied to increase the various kinds of validity in research, and constraint is largely a matter of the degree of control, precision, and structure applied in research. Thus, a large component of the difference between low- and high-constraint methods is the greater, more precise, and structured application of controls at high-constraint levels and the resultant increase in validity.

SUMMARY

Our focus has been on the development and testing of hypotheses, from initially vague and/or general ideas to specific research hypotheses. The careful construction of the research hypothesis is a critical step in all research, and it is most formalized and most fully developed at the experimental level of constraint. Testing the research hypothesis in any experiment actually involves three hypotheses—the null or statistical hypothesis, the confounding-variable hypothesis, and the causal hypothesis.

Also important are issues of validity and threats to validity in research. The researcher must be concerned with four types of validity—statistical validity, construct validity, external validity, and internal validity. Each type can be threatened in a number of ways, and the researcher must anticipate the potential threats and design appropriate controls into the research. The specific controls will vary according to the type of validity being threatened and the nature of the threats.

In addition, subject and experimenter expectations and biases can threaten validity, and these should be routinely controlled in any study. In general, the concepts of threats to validity and controls are two sides of the same conceptual coin. Of particular concern are threats to internal validity, because these affect the confidence with which we can conclude that there is a causal relationship between the independent and dependent variables. In Chapter 9 we will consider controls, paying particular attention to controls for threats to internal validity.

REVIEW EXERCISES

8.1 **Define the following key terms. Be sure you understand them. They are discussed in the chapter and defined in the glossary.**

research hypothesis	validity
statement of the problem	statistical validity
theoretical concept	construct validity
operational definition	external validity
construct	ecological validity
pretest-posttest design	internal validity
statistical hypothesis	generalization
null hypothesis	confounded
extraneous variables	confounding variables
confounding-variable hypothesis	maturation
rival hypothesis	history
causal hypothesis	testing
two-group posttest-only design	instrumentation
replicate	regression to the mean
replication	selection

attrition   demand characteristics
diffusion of treatment   placebo effect
sequencing effects   experimenter effects
within-subjects design   experimenter expectancies
subject effects

8.2   **Answer each of the following. Check your answers in the chapter.**

1. What is meant by "testing the research hypothesis actually involves three hypotheses"?
2. How do we deal with the confounding-variable hypothesis?
3. Explain why it is so important in experimental research to rule out the confounding-variable hypothesis.
4. What are the major types of validity in research?
5. For each of the following independent variables, indicate the number of levels of the independent variable and identify each:
   a. We study the effects of high- and low-audio stimulation on subjects' responses.
   b. We use six levels of room temperature in a working-conditions study.
   c. A researcher compares rats' running times. One group of rats is fed one hour prior to running, another group is fed two hours prior to running, and a third group is fed three hours prior to running.
   d. Four different arithmetic workbooks are tested in an elementary school.
6. Why is internal validity of such importance in experimentation?
7. What kind of relationships among variables are studied at each of the five levels of constraint?
8. What are the nine major confounding factors? For each one, develop at least three examples of research in which each confounding factor could occur.
9. What is meant by "subject and experimenter effects"? How do they threaten the validity of a study? Give several examples.

8.3   **Think about and work the following problems.**

1. Think of five or six experimental research ideas. Create them or obtain them from published reports of studies, such as in textbooks. For each of these research ideas:
   a. Develop each research idea into a clear statement of a problem.
   b. Identify and operationally define the variables suggested by the problem statement.
   c. Combine the problem statement with the operational definitions into a specific prediction and state the research hypothesis.
2. Take the problem statements you developed in the preceding exercise and develop different operational definitions. Then develop several research hypotheses that are different from those developed in the preceding exercise. Why is it important to be able to do this in research?
3. Explain, as if to another student in the course, how replication can be achieved in the process of varying the operational definitions when developing research hypotheses from problem statements. Give examples.
4. Develop a research project in which there are some clear experimenter and subject effects.

Chapter
9

Controls to Reduce Threats to Validity

Control procedures counteract threats to validity, allowing us to draw conclusions with greater confidence. Threats to validity and control procedures represent two sides of the same conceptual coin. In this chapter we will consider the major methods for controlling threats to the validity of experiments.

We define *control* more broadly than is usually done in research methods texts as any procedure used by the researcher to counteract potential threats to the validity of the research. There are many procedures available to control threats to validity, but not every threat to validity is likely to occur in every experiment; thus, not every control measure is needed in every experiment. Some control procedures are of general value and therefore applicable to nearly all studies. Other controls are relevant only in specific situations and should be carefully chosen to meet the particular threats to validity present in each study. Controls are necessary at all levels of research, but are most fully developed at the experimental level.

THREATS TO VALIDITY

In quality research, threats to statistical, construct, internal, and external validity must all be controlled. *Statistical validity* is threatened when unreliable dependent measures are used or when we violate the assumptions of statistical tests. *Confounding,* a term used earlier to refer to threats to internal validity, can also be applied to construct validity. Confounding exists when some factor allows a feasible alternative explanation of the experimental results or allows an alternative explanatory or basic construct to be used. With regard to *internal validity,* confounding exists when some factor other than the independent variable may be responsible for the results. With regard to *construct validity,* confounding exists when more than one theory could explain the obtained results. *External validity* is threatened whenever we cannot generalize the results beyond the study's particular subjects, times, and settings to other conditions. (See Chapter 8 for a review of these principles.)

Four types of controls are commonly used in experimentation to reduce threats to validity:

1. General control procedures
2. Control over subject and experimenter effects
3. Control through the selection and assignment of subjects
4. Control through specific experimental design

The four categories of controls are arranged from the more general control procedures applicable to most research to the most specific control procedures. We will focus on the first three categories of control in this chapter. The fourth category—specific *experimental design*—will be introduced here and discussed at length in Chapters 10–13.

GENERAL CONTROL PROCEDURES

Preparation of the Setting

The most general control procedures define the *research setting.* The advantage of the laboratory is that many extraneous variables can be eliminated, such as interfering visual and auditory stimuli, the influence of other people and of competing tasks, and so on. In the laboratory, we can eliminate competing variables, simplify the situation, and increase control over the independent variable, which increases our confidence in the results. Thus, control by preparation of the research setting helps to reduce threats to internal validity.

Increasing internal validity, however, may result in a reduction in external validity if we allow the lab setting to become so constrained and artificial that it is unlike the natural situation. But external validity need not be compromised if an effort is made to create a natural environment in the laboratory. For example, in a children's fear-reduction study (Graziano & Mooney, 1982), the laboratory was a living room setting in which children were trained in fear-control skills that they would use at home. This setting was similar to their own living rooms so as to enhance generalization (external validity). Thus, preparation of settings in laboratories can enhance external validity as well as internal validity.

Response Measurement

Another control procedure is the careful selection and preparation of the instruments used to measure the dependent variable. By using measuring instruments of known reliability and validity, we improve both statistical and construct validity. The care with which the researcher selects measuring instruments can have powerful effects on validity. Unfortunately, in our concern for operationalizing and manipulating the independent variable, we sometimes pay less attention to the dependent measures and therefore compromise the validity of the study.

Replication

Although some textbook authors do not consider *replication* to be a control procedure, we believe replication is an important general control procedure. By defining in operational terms and specifying the laboratory setting, conditions, procedures, and measuring instruments, we make it easier for ourselves and other researchers to replicate the research. Successful replication provides important information. If a phenomenon observed in one study can be reliably demonstrated a second or third time, confidence in the original observations increases; if the study cannot be replicated, confidence is shaken. Research in ESP (extrasensory perception—a contradiction in terms) is an example. Some researchers have reported statistically significant ESP phenomena that fail to replicate in later research, thus leaving the earlier reports open to serious question (see Edge, Morris, Rush, & Palmer, 1986). If a finding cannot be replicated, then it may be only a chance event and not an indication of a genuine phenomenon. In statistical terms, the researcher may have made a Type I error. If ESP phenomena cannot be reliably replicated, then we must ask whether they exist at all.

We distinguish between exact replication and systematic replication. *Exact replication* (repeating the experiment as nearly as possible in the way it was carried out originally) is rarely done in psychology. Journals seldom publish exact replication studies, and there are no career benefits to be gained by young researchers spending time to repeat other people's research. Although exact replication is rare, researchers often replicate earlier findings by testing some systematic theoretical or procedural modification of the original work, which is known as *systematic replication.* If, for example, Dr. Marlatt finds an interesting phenomenon in the alcohol research laboratory, a colleague might reason that a certain systematic modification will bring about a certain specific result. The second researcher uses Marlatt's initial work, making a systematic modification, which, if Marlatt's work was correct, should result in the predicted outcome.

There are still other ways to replicate. Recall that most problem statements can be developed into several different research hypotheses by combining the problem statement with various operational definitions of the research variables or using different research designs (see Chapter 8). Thus, many different studies can be generated from the same problem statement. In essence, the researcher is able to investigate different facets of the same issue. This kind of replication is sometimes referred to as *conceptual replication.*

Although replication increases confidence in the validity of findings, it does not guarantee validity. For example, suppose that confounding factors in a study brought about certain results. Then, if the procedures are replicated exactly without recognizing and controlling the confounding factors, the replication might well produce the same invalid results as in the initial study.

CONTROL OVER SUBJECT AND EXPERIMENTER EFFECTS

The behavior of both the subjects and the researcher may be influenced by factors other than the independent variable, thus threatening the validity of a study. Factors such as motivation, knowledge, expectations, and information or misinformation about the study can be powerful influences on behavior. Extra-experimental factors may significantly bias subjects' and researchers' behavior, affecting not only the experimental procedure but also the analysis and interpretation of data.

Uncontrolled experimenter and/or subject effects is sufficient to cast doubt on conclusions about causal relationships between the independent and dependent variables because these effects provide an alternative hypothesis. Subject and experimenter effects should be controlled in virtually all experimentation. Among the useful controls are

1. Single-blind and double-blind procedures
2. Automation
3. Use of objective measures
4. Multiple observers
5. Use of deception

Single- and Double-Blind Procedures

Experimenter effects arise from the experimenter's knowledge of (1) the hypothesis being tested, (2) the nature of the experimental and control conditions, and (3) the condition to which each subject is assigned. Such knowledge may subtly affect the ways in which the researcher interacts with each subject. To control for experimenter effects, we reduce the researcher's direct contact with and knowledge about the subjects. The researcher may employ an assistant who is trained to carry out the

"IT WAS MORE OF A 'TRIPLE-BLIND' TEST. THE PATIENTS DIDN'T KNOW WHICH ONES WERE GETTING THE REAL DRUG, THE DOCTORS DIDN'T KNOW, AND, I'M AFRAID, NOBODY KNEW."

Source: Reprinted by permission of S. Harris.

procedure with subjects but who does not know the condition to which each subject is assigned. If possible, the assistant should also be unaware of the hypothesis being tested. Thus, the assistant is *blind* to these factors and presumably cannot be biased by knowledge of the hypothesis or of the assignment of subjects to conditions. This is called the *single-blind control procedure.*

A more powerful control is the *double-blind control procedure* in which the researcher (i.e., the research assistant who is gathering the data) is blind to the assignment of each subject *and* subjects are blind to their assignments. The experiment is designed so that experimental and control procedures are indistinguishable to subjects and to the research assistants. Therefore, neither the research assistants nor the subjects know which subjects are in an experimental or a control group. The double-blind technique is often used in drug studies. The experimental group typically receives the drug in the form of a pill, while the control group receives a pill (a placebo) that is identical in appearance, weight, smell, and taste but lacks the actual drug. Neither the subjects who take the pill nor the experimental assistants who administer it and gather the data know which subjects are receiving the drug and which are receiving the placebo. The use of a placebo control group in research that is purely psychological in nature is more difficult and probably not as effective as in drug studies. For example, suppose a clinical researcher wants to study the effectiveness of exposure therapy on reduction of adult fears. Subjects are assigned in an unbiased manner to an experimental and a control group. The experimental group is given the exposure therapy and the control group is presented with a placebo treatment. The placebo treatment must be believable so that subjects do not know they are controls. The design problem is to create experimentally adequate, ethically acceptable, and believable placebo manipulations, a task that is often difficult.

In addition to design problems in the use of placebos, ethical issues must be considered. Can we ethically deny treatment to some subjects? For ethical reasons, subjects should be told they may receive a placebo treatment. For both design and ethical reasons, the use of true placebos in medical and psychological research is not recommended when an effective treatment is available. Instead of comparing a new treatment with a placebo, researchers usually compare the new treatment with the currently available treatment.

It is important to keep the research assistants who gather the data blind to the group or condition the subject is in and to the hypotheses of the study. It is equally important to maintain a blind condition during the scoring of data, especially when the scoring involves judgments. Knowledge of the hypotheses and of the conditions under which the subject is tested may affect judgments made during the scoring of data. In some cases, however, it is impossible for researchers to be blind during certain aspects of the study. For example, in a study of sex differences in aggression, the researcher testing subjects will know which subjects are male and which are female. In such a situation, the researcher should attempt to be blind in as many ways as possible, even if it is impossible at every stage. If, for example, the measure of aggression in the study is verbal behavior, someone otherwise not connected with the study should transcribe the tapes of subjects' verbal responses so that auditory cues of subject's sex are not used when the data are scored. Scoring should then be done by someone other than the person who tested the subjects in the study. Although in this case it may be impossible to test subjects blindly, the data can be scored as a separate procedure by researchers blind to the group membership of subjects. In this study, assistants testing subjects should also be blind to the hypothesis even if they cannot be blind to group membership. A general rule of thumb is to *test subjects and score data as blindly as possible to avoid experimenter biases.* Even though there are difficulties with single-blind techniques and double-blind placebo techniques, these methods can control a number of potentially biasing subject and experimenter effects and are good controls to employ in many studies.

Automation

Reducing experimenter-subject contact often reduces potential biases. One way to accomplish this is to standardize and *automate* instructions to subjects and procedures for obtaining and recording subjects' responses. Instructions to subjects can be tape-recorded, and the timing of instructions and recording of subjects' responses can be automated with electronic equipment. Removing the experimenter from the laboratory situation dramatically reduces the risk of effects due to experimenter bias.

Using Objective Measures

Using *objective measures* of dependent variables is critical. A measure is objective when it is based on empirically observable and clearly specified events about which two or more people could easily agree. In contrast, subjective measures involve the impressions of the observers, which are often based on poorly specified and/or unobserved events. An example of a subjective measure is an observer's feeling that a person is anxious in a public speaking situation. It is subjective because the observer does not specify what events were observed. Thus, it would be difficult for another observer to make the same observations and come to the same conclusions about the anxiety level of the speaker. In contrast, good objective measures precisely define the behaviors to be observed and require minimal judgments on the part of the observer. Consequently, objective measures are less prone to experimenter biases. Such measures usually produce impressive levels of interrater agreement and make replication by other researchers easier. For example, public speaking anxiety can be operationally defined in terms of empirically observable behavior, such as sweating, stammering, rapid speech, face flushing, and hands shaking. Each of these are observable behaviors. With objective measures, we know what a score means; with subjective measures, we are never sure.

Multiple Observers

In any research, especially when there may be questions about objectivity in making observations, a common control is to employ several observers to record subjects' behavior. Data obtained by *multiple observers* are compared for agreement using *interrater reliability coefficients* or an index of *percent agreement.* Suppose, for example, that two raters are simultaneously observing a videotape of children at play. At random intervals, an audio signal occurs and the observers rate the behavior occurring at that moment as either aggressive or not aggressive. The observers are separated in booths but are watching the same video monitor. Thus, the observers are independently rating exactly the same behaviors. Ten signals are given, and each observer rates ten instances of behavior as aggressive or not aggressive. The two observers' ratings can then be compared, as shown in Table 9.1, and a percent agreement computed. A more sophisticated index of agreement is *Kappa,* which takes into account the base rates of the ratings. The *base rate* of a rating is the relative frequency of that rating in your sample. It is generally easier to get high percent agreement between raters when one rating is appropriate almost all the time than when several ratings could apply. The Kappa takes this into account. Using Kappa is

TABLE 9.1   EXAMPLE OF COMPUTING PERCENT AGREEMENT BETWEEN TWO
OBSERVERS

Interval	Rater 1	Rater 2	Agree?
1	Aggressive	Aggressive	Yes
2	Aggressive	Aggressive	Yes
3	Not Aggressive	Aggressive	No
4	Not Aggressive	Not Aggressive	Yes
5	Not Aggressive	Not Aggressive	Yes
6	Not Aggressive	Not Aggressive	Yes
7	Aggressive	Aggressive	Yes
8	Aggressive	Not Aggressive	No
9	Not Aggressive	Not Aggressive	Yes
10	Aggressive	Aggressive	Yes

$$\text{Percent agreement} = \frac{\text{\# of agreements}}{\text{\# of observations}} \times 100 = \frac{8}{10} \times 100 = 80\%$$

beyond the scope of this textbook, but the interested student should consult Cohen (1960) and Neale and Oltmanns (1981) for more detail.

Using Deception

Perhaps the most common control for subject effects is to obscure the true hypothesis of the experiment. The researcher can deliberately misinform subjects about the nature of the experiment or withhold information that might reveal the hypothesis. This control, called *deception,* is almost always minor, but in some experiments deception can become quite elaborate.

In a procedure known as the *balanced placebo design,* used by G. Alan Marlatt and his colleagues to study the effects of alcohol on behavior, subjects were asked to drink a beverage that contained either tonic only or alcohol and tonic (Marlatt, Demming, & Reid, 1973; Rohsenow & Marlatt, 1981). The deception is that what subjects drank and what they were told they were drinking were not necessarily the same thing. Suppose the study included 100 subjects; 50 subjects were given vodka and tonic, and 50 were given tonic. Of the 50 subjects who drank tonic, half (25) were told they would be drinking tonic, and the other half (25) were told they would be drinking vodka and tonic. Similarly, half (25) of the 50 subjects who drank vodka and tonic were led to believe they were drinking tonic, and the remaining subjects (25) were told they were drinking vodka and tonic. Because vodka is tasteless, it is almost impossible to distinguish it from taste alone as long as the drink is not too strong. To reinforce the deception that subjects were drinking a vodka-tonic mixture instead of only tonic, the drinks were mixed in front of subjects. Vodka (actually water in the no-alcohol condition) was carefully measured from what appeared to be a new, unopened vodka bottle, with tonic added from a separate labeled bottle. This design is interesting in many respects. First, several ethical issues are raised by the deception. Therefore, appropriate safeguards must be included in the study. Second, it is equally desirable to have the experimenter blind to subject condition. To accomplish this an elaborate coding system is used on the bottles. The experimenter knows which bottle(s) to pour the drinks from but does not know what each bottle contains.

According to the ethical standards for research, the use of deception violates subjects' rights and places the subjects "at risk." Therefore, deception should be used only when truly necessary for the conduct of the study; and at the completion of the experiment, subjects should be debriefed (i.e., told about the deception and allowed to ask questions).

The balanced placebo design has been used to separate the pharmacological effects of alcohol from the expectations of the drinker. In several studies (cf. Lang & Sibrel, 1989) the behavior of the subjects was affected more strongly by whether they thought they were drinking alcohol than whether they actually were drinking alcohol. In other words, expectation effects were more potent than the pharmacological effects of alcohol. What makes the balanced placebo design work is that the subjects can be deceived. As long as the drinks are not too strong or the subjects do not drink too much alcohol, the taste and physiological cues are not strong enough to be detected. Identifying the parameters that make a deception like this work requires careful pilot testing. In some cases, a balance placebo or similar deception is possible with some subjects but not with others. For example, 10-year-old children with attention deficit/hyperactivity disorder apparently cannot tell whether they are taking stimulant medication used to treat the disorder or a placebo in spite of the dramatic effects of the medication on their behavior. In contrast, 15-year-old children can easily discriminate placebo and stimulant medication (Pelham, 1994: Pelham et al., 1992). In this case, a placebo deception is possible for the 10-year-olds but not for the 15-year-olds.

CONTROL THROUGH SUBJECT SELECTION AND ASSIGNMENT

Subject Selection

Appropriate *subject selection* enhances external validity, allowing us to generalize the results to a larger population. In nearly all psychological research, the investigator's interest is not limited to specific subjects but rather is focused on the larger, more general group—the population. For example, suppose that a poll is taken on Americans' attitudes toward (1) the animal rights movement, (2) hunting and trapping, and (3) gun ownership. The results of our hypothetical poll indicate that Americans are heavily opposed to animal rights (87 percent), are highly supportive of hunting and trapping (100 percent), and are strong opponents of gun control legislation (93 percent). A closer examination reveals that the poll was administered to licensed hunters in Montana and the Dakotas. Obviously, there is a major problem of sampling and of external validity. From this sample of active hunters living in western states, the pollsters drew conclusions about all Americans. Because the sample was not selected to represent all Americans, the findings of the study cannot be generalized to all Americans.

To understand subject selection, we must distinguish between (1) populations and samples, (2) general populations, target populations, and accessible populations, and (3) among representative samples, random samples, stratified random samples, and ad hoc samples. In general, the *population* is the larger group of all events of interest (people, rats, occurrences, and so on) from which a sample is se-lected. The *sample* is a smaller number of events (people, occurrences, rats, and so on) drawn from that population and used in a specific study as if the sample adequately represents the population of interest.

The *general population* is that large group of all persons, events, and so on. The *target population* is the subset in which we are ultimately interested. It is usually a naturally occurring population, such as all grammar school children, all diagnosed panic disorder patients, all registered voters, and so on. Target populations are typically not easily available. For example, suppose we are interested in the development of temporal concepts in 6-year-olds. We cannot readily sample from all of the 6-year-olds in the country. We do, however, have access to five local public schools that have a total of 400 6-year-old pupils. The 400 children become the *accessible population* from which we will draw (select) the sample. Thus, we must recognize that any generalizations from the results of our study can be made most confidently to the accessible population, but we must be cautious about generalizing to the larger, target population. Because nearly all psychological research is carried out by sampling accessible populations (e.g., introductory psychology students in a particular university), *we must always be cautious about generalizations made to the general population.* If we sample from an accessible population, then we may generalize the results only to that accessible population and not to a larger, target population. In this regard, replication is an important procedure. Each replication may be carried out on different accessible populations. If the results replicate in each accessible populations, our confidence in the generalizability of the findings is increased.

We almost never study populations directly. Instead, we select a sample from an accessible population. To generalize the findings to the accessible or target population, we must be careful to select a *representative sample* that adequately reflects population characteristics. The basic idea of representativeness is simple enough. If the sample is representative, then the characteristics found in the population (e.g., the distribution of sex, age, intelligence, socioeconomic class, ethnicity, attitudes, political affiliations, religious beliefs) will be found in the sample in the same proportions as in the target population. Although the concept is simple, actually obtaining a representative sample is a good deal more difficult. Further, small samples often do not adequately represent populations. In general, the larger the sample, the more likely the sample will adequately represent the population, because larger samples tend to reduce the effects of sampling error. Another issue is that most psychological research is conducted with samples drawn from accessible populations that are not necessarily representative of the larger, target population. The relationship between the general population, the target population, the accessible population, and the sample is illustrated in Figure 9.1.

An example might help to illustrate why small samples often fail to represent the population adequately. We will assume that we are sampling from a population of 1000 marbles in a large box. Half the marbles are red, 25 percent are blue, and 25 percent are green. In this case we know exactly what the population looks like; rarely will that be the case in real life. How big a sample do we need to represent the population adequately? Clearly, no sample of size $N = 1$ could represent the population. If we select just one marble, it will be either red or blue or green. The only general-

Figure 9.1   The Relationship of the General Population to the Target Population, the Accessible Population, and the Sample

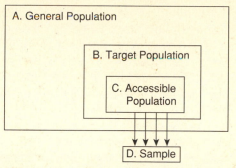

General population—All events, persons, animals, etc. (e.g., all children).

Target population—All events, persons, etc. of a particular class of interest to the researcher. This is the population to which we want to generalize our findings (e.g., all elementary school children).

Accessible population—That subset of a target population that is available to the research (e.g., elementary school children in the local school district).

Sample—The subset of an accessible population on which measures are taken. Note, occasionally a sample is drawn directly from a target population such as in national polls of voter preferences.

ization we could make from that sample of one marble is that all of the marbles in the population are the same color as the one we sampled—a clearly erroneous conclusion. A similar argument could be made for a sample of two marbles, which at best could represent only two of the three colors in the population. A sample of three marbles might represent the three colors, but no sample of three marbles could represent the three colors and the fact that red is twice as common as either blue or green. Furthermore, if you compute the probability of every possible sample of three marbles, you will find that less than 20 percent of the possible samples contain one red, one blue, and one green marble. The minimum sample that could accurately represent the population is four marbles (two red, one blue, and one green), but if you set up a box of marbles as described and try taking samples of four marbles, you will be shocked at how rarely that particular combination comes up. Even in this unreasonably simple example (a population varying on a single characteristic with only three different values), you would need samples of 30 or more marbles before the sample gave a reasonably accurate representation of the composition of the population most of the time.[1] In the far more complicated real world, where subjects vary on hundreds of potential variables, small samples almost never adequately represent the population.

In social science research, sampling of subjects is a critical issue. Many methods have been developed to solve the problems of obtaining representatives samples. Although some of the methods are beyond the scope of this text, we will consider three solutions to the problem of selecting a representative sample: (1) random sampling, (2) stratified random sampling, and (3) ad hoc samples.

---

[1]The mathematics of this computation is beyond the scope of this text. The interested student is referred to any introductory text on mathematical probability.

Random Sampling   Random selection of a sample from a target population or from an accessible population means drawing the sample so that (1) every member of the population has an equal chance of being selected for the sample and (2) the selections do not affect each other (i.e., they are independent). With *random sampling* there are no systematic biases that result in some members of the population having a greater chance than others of being selected. If the selection of subjects is truly random, then we assume that the distribution of characteristics of the population, such as age, ethnicity, and intelligence, will be distributed in the sample in the same proportion as in the population.

The best procedure for drawing an unbiased sample to represent a population adequately is to draw a random sample. This is rather like picking numbers out of a hat. In actual practice, numbers are usually drawn not from a hat but from a *table of random numbers* (see Appendix B) or a *random number generator* (a computer program for generating random numbers). Both random number tables and random number generators meet two criteria: (1) each number has the same chance of being selected and (2) each number is independent of the others. Suppose we want to draw a sample of 60 subjects from the accessible population of 400 6-year-old children in our local school system. We list all 400 children, assign each one a three-digit number such as 001, 002, 003, and so on up to 400. We then use the table of random numbers or a random number generator to get random numbers from 1 to 400 until we have a total of 60 nonduplicated numbers. Thus, 60 subjects will have been randomly selected from the accessible population. Random numbers are useful not only for selecting a random sample but also for making decisions based on the principle of randomness, such as assigning subjects to experimental conditions.

Stratified Random Sampling   In *stratified random sampling,* separate samples from each of several subpopulations are drawn. The subpopulations are defined in advance on the basis of one or more critical subject variables, such as age and socioeconomic status, that we expect will influence scores on the dependent measures. Therefore, small variations in the distribution of the variables in a sample can have a large effect on the results. For example, we might suspect that age is strongly correlated with the dependent measure of political preference. Therefore, the sample should approximate closely the distribution of age in the population studied. Rather than rely on random sampling, we divide the population into subpopulations on the basis of age. We then create a total sample by selecting the appropriate proportion of subjects from each of the subpopulations. If 16 percent of the population is between the ages of 20 and 25, then we select randomly from that subpopulation the number of subjects it would take to make up 16 percent of the total sample. If we want to draw a total sample of 200 subjects, we will need 32 subjects selected from the 20–25 age range. Stratified random samples are used extensively in sophisticated political polling operations. With this technique, samples as small as 1000 people can so closely represent the population that the outcome of elections involving several million actual voters can be accurately predicted.

Although random sampling is a major control for threats to external validity, psychological research rarely employs random sampling from a target population. Target populations are often difficult to access. For any large population, target or accessible, listing and numbering every individual to prepare for random selection is a sizable task. Random and stratified random sampling from a target population is important in some research, such as in large-scale political surveys, but most psychological research does not employ random selection. Rather, subjects are obtained from an accessible population, such as introductory psychology students, children from local schools, and so on. Furthermore, subjects are almost always volunteers. Those who do not volunteer are not included, and the sample is thus not representative of the target population. The ethical demand that subjects be volunteers makes it difficult for researchers to obtain a random sample of any population. For example, Graziano (Graziano, Lindquist, Kunce, & Munjal, 1992) surveyed young adults (18–23 years old) about their experience in having been spanked as children. The subjects were volunteers from large introductory psychology classes at a state university. Graziano, Hamblen, and Plante (1995) surveyed over 500 parents about their use of corporal punishment in child rearing. These subjects were volunteers from a local suburban middle-class population. Kraemer, Hastrup, Sobota, and Bornstein (1985) studied the crying behavior of children and their parents. To obtain subjects, they advertised in newspapers offering $20 for each volunteer family. In each of these projects, volunteer subjects with the required characteristics were obtained from accessible populations.

Ad Hoc Samples   How can we generalize results from samples that are not randomly selected from a target population? The answer is twofold: first, we generalize cautiously and conservatively; second, we generalize only to other people (or to laboratory animals or events or places) that have characteristics similar to those of the sample. That is, *we are careful not to generalize beyond the limits of the sample.* In the two examples given above, researchers may generalize their results only to people who are like those in their studies. In other words, the population to which we generalize is defined by the characteristics of the sample. This type of sample is called an *ad hoc sample,* which is used in most psychological research. In the spanking survey of college students cited earlier, it was found that 92 percent of the 600 subjects reported they had been spanked as children. The researchers should not suggest that 92 percent of the country's total population of young adults had been spanked as children. However, they could suggest that the findings do apply to people similar to the sample; that is, to other state university undergraduates from working and middle-class families in the northeastern section of the United States. The same research carried out at Columbia, Harvard, Princeton, Stanford, or Yale, with their student populations drawn largely from middle- to upper-socioeconomic classes, might have produced different results. In the Kraemer et al. (1985) study on children's crying, the generalizations are likewise limited. The selection procedure (in which subjects were volunteer families who knew they would receive a $20 fee) may have limited the sample to only certain subgroups. It may be that affluent families did not volunteer.

The point is that in most psychological research we do not have random sampling from a known target population; instead, we use ad hoc sampling. To generalize beyond the samples and yet maintain external validity, we must know the characteristics of the subjects and keep our generalizations within the limits of the characteristics. It becomes important in using ad hoc sampling to obtain descriptive data, such as subjects' age, physical and psychological characteristics, and family socioeconomic data. The more completely we describe subjects in the sample, the more secure we can be in establishing the limits of generalization and the more confidence we can have in making generalizations. When possible, it is valuable to obtain descriptive information on subjects who are invited but decline to participate in a study and subjects who drop out before the study is completed. Comparing these subjects with the subjects who agree and complete the study helps pinpoint potential biases in subject selection and attrition that would limit generalizability.

Thus, the researcher is advised to draw a random sample from a known target population whenever it is feasible to do so. In most instances that will not be feasible, and an ad hoc sample will be used. Here the researcher should obtain sufficient descriptive information about the subjects to establish the limits for generalization. In this way, threats to external validity can be reduced.

Subject Assignment

Once subjects are selected, we must then assign subjects to the conditions required by the experimental procedures. Unbiased *subject assignment* is critical in experiments. In experiments, the independent variable is systematically manipulated and the corresponding changes in the dependent variable are observed. For example, suppose we want to test the effectiveness of teaching arithmetic to third graders using a new video teaching program. In the experimental condition, third graders will have arithmetic lessons presented daily through videotapes. In the control condition, other third graders will have arithmetic lessons presented in the usual, nontelevised manner. In this experiment, there are two levels of the independent variable, video presentation and teacher presentation. Suppose that 60 children have been selected as subjects and we want to assign 30 children to each condition in an unbiased manner. We want to avoid, for example, assigning all female subjects to one condition and all male subjects to the other or assigning the best math students to the same condition. Take another example: in a study of office working conditions, six groups of typists are compared on their typing speed (number of words per minute) and accuracy (number of errors) under six different conditions of room temperature: 55°, 60°, 65°, 70°, 75°, and 80°. A sample of 48 typists is selected and assigned in an unbiased manner to the six groups (eight subjects per group). Random assignment makes it unlikely that all of the best typists would be in one group.

The ideal experiment would include (1) random selection of subjects from a known population and (2) random assignment of subjects to conditions. The ideal, however, is seldom achieved. As noted earlier, random selection is rare in psychological research. Therefore, we must be cautious in generalizing to other subjects, times, and conditions. *Of far greater importance in an experiment is random assignment of subjects to conditions.* Random assignment is a powerful control procedure that helps to reduce many known and unknown threats to internal validity—the central issue in experiments. Random assignment reduces the probability of biased assignment of subjects to conditions. Unbiased assignment of subjects to conditions can be accomplished by free random assignment or by matched random assignment.

Free Random Assignment *Free random assignment* of subjects to conditions is carried out using a table of random numbers or a random number generator. For example, in the experiment on working conditions, the 48 subjects can be randomly assigned to six conditions, eight subjects per condition. We number the subjects from 01 to 48, consult the table of random numbers or a random number generator, and assign the first subject number we encounter to the first condition, the next subject number to the second condition, and so on. The seventh subject would be assigned to the first condition, eighth to the second, and so forth. We continue in this way until all 48 subjects are assigned to the six conditions. The same random assignment procedure would be used in the experiment on teaching arithmetic to third graders to assign subjects to two conditions with 30 subjects in each condition.

Randomization is a control method used in subject selection and subject assignment to conditions. *Randomization is the most basic and single most important control procedure.* It has several major advantages: (1) it can be used to control threats to internal and external validity; (2) it can control for many variables simultaneously; and (3) it is the only control procedure that can control for unknown factors. When we randomly assign subjects to groups or conditions, subject variables are distributed without biases, even if we have not specifically identified the variables. Other control methods are effective with known extraneous variables that threaten the study, but randomization is effective in reducing the bias of unknown variables. A good general rule for the researcher is *whenever possible, randomize.*

Matched Random Assignment   *Matched random assignment* of subjects to conditions is often used in small-sample research. A good deal of psychological research is carried out with small numbers of subjects, and we are often faced with the task of assigning 20–30 subjects to two or three conditions. Free random assignment works best with large samples, but with a small sample of subjects to be assigned, randomized groups can be unequal on some important variable. For example, suppose that we are interested in investigating the effects of a study-skills training program on children in a specific school, but we only have the time and resources to study 12 children. Our research hypothesis is that those who receive the study-skills training (the experimental group), compared with those who do not (the control group), will display improved academic performance and possibly an increase in self-esteem. Free random assignment of so small a number might result in unequal groups on important variables. We might find, for example, that the children with the highest academic ability, or the oldest and thus presumably most socially capable, have been assigned to the same group. Thus, the experimental and control groups would not have been equivalent at the start of the study, and any results obtained may be due to the original differences between the groups rather than to the effects of the independent variable—study-skills training. That is, the independent variable may have been confounded by one or more extraneous variables.

To solve the problems of working with small numbers of subjects, we can use a matching procedure combined with randomization—*matched random assignment.* To do this, we must first decide what variables are the most important potential confounding factors. Suppose we decide that the age of the child is a potential confounding variable in this study and that the older children are more likely to learn the study-skills procedures more quickly and thoroughly than the younger children. We would then list the children ordered by age, as shown in Table 9.2, and match them on age by taking the children in pairs, successively, down the list. Kathy, the oldest,

TABLE 9.2   SEX AND AGE OF CHILDREN IN THE SAMPLE

Name	Sex	Age (in months)
Kathy	F	122
Robbie	M	120
Matt	M	119
Rick	M	115
Terri	F	108
Holly	F	104
Kevin	M	100
Miriam	F	98
Debbie	F	96
Randy	M	95
Jimmy	M	87
Tommy	M	86

TABLE 9.3   MATCHED CHILDREN RANDOMLY ASSIGNED TO TWO GROUPS

	Group 1			Group 2	
Name	Sex	Age (in months)	Name	Sex	Age (in months)
Robbie	M	120	Kathy	F	122
Matt	M	119	Rick	M	115
Holly	F	104	Terri	F	108
Miriam	F	98	Kevin	M	100
Debby	F	96	Randy	M	95
Tommy	M	86	Jimmy	M	87
% Females	3/6 = 50%		2/6 = 33%		
Mean age	103.8 months		104.5 months		

is matched with the next oldest, Robbie; Matt is matched with Rick, and so on. We can now assign the subjects to two groups by using a table of random numbers or by tossing a coin. Using the random number table, the first subject of each pair is assigned to Group 1 if the number is odd or to Group 2 if the number is even. If a coin toss is used, heads or tails determine group assignment. Whichever method is used, the second subject in each pair is assigned to the other group. This procedure might result in the assignment of subjects shown in Table 9.3.

As is seen in Table 9.3, the mean ages of the two groups (103.8 months and 104.5 months) are quite close. We have thus assured that Groups 1 and 2 are comparable on the age variable and that age will not be a confounding variable. Notice that Groups 1 and 2 do not have equal numbers of males and females. However, the differences are small, and biological sex is not considered to be a potential confounding variable in the study. (Our expectation, or course, may be incorrect, but given the state of knowledge at the time of the study, it is a reasonable expectation.)

Matching helps to make small-group research more sensitive to the effects of the independent variable by equally distributing known variables that are potentially confounding. We can even match for more than one variable. However, it is not feasible to match on several variables simultaneously because the task becomes so cumbersome and difficult that it is more efficient to assign subjects to groups randomly. Matching requires that we identify the variables to be matched and obtain a measure on the variables for each subject. Subjects can be matched on any measurable physical or psychological variables (e.g., age, weight, intelligence, neuroticism, biological sex, attitudes, performance on a pretest measure, and so on).

Other Matching Procedures   A number of other matching procedures are available. An alternative to subject-by-subject matching is to match characteristics of groups (see Chapman & Chapman, 1973). This procedure is more commonly used in differential research but can be useful in some experimental situations. In such a situation, we would first identify the variables on which the groups are to be matched and obtain measures on the variables for each of the potential subjects. Using a randomization procedure, we would assign subjects to one of the two groups and calculate that group's mean and standard deviation on each variable to be matched. We would then select the second group of subjects so that it has a comparable mean and standard deviation on the variables. The two groups would be equivalent on the matching variables, but individuals would not be matched as closely. The equal distribution of matching variables is thereby achieved and potential confounding avoided.

A variation of matching is to equate groups by holding the variable constant. For example, if we want to match on age we could use only subjects of approximately the same age. If there is little or no variability on this factor between the experimental and control groups, this factor cannot be a source of confounding. However, a disadvantage to matching by holding the variable constant is that it reduces the generalizability (i.e., it reduces external validity). For example, if we used only adult subjects, we would be unable to generalize with confidence to adolescents.

Matching by building the variable into the study is another of the many methods of control through matching. (This method creates what is known as a *factorial design,* which will be discussed in more detail in Chapter 12.) Suppose we want to test the effects of complexity of temporal stimuli on the time-duration estimates of 6-year-old children. The independent variable is the complexity of the temporal stimuli presented; the dependent variable is the time-duration estimates made by the subjects. However, we are concerned about differences in age of only a few months that may confound the results; that is, the older 6-year-olds might do better on the temporal tasks than the younger 6-year-olds. To control for this, we make the age variable a part of the study by grouping the 6-year-olds into four groups of three months each, as follows:

1. 6 years 1 month–6 years 3 months
2. 6 years 4 months–6 years 6 months

   3. 6 years 7 months–6 years 9 months.
   4. 6 years 10 months–6 years 12 months (i.e., 7 years)

The subjects in each group are of similar age, and we thus are able to determine the influence of the age variable.

CONTROL THROUGH EXPERIMENTAL DESIGN

An understanding of three major groups of methods for achieving control in experimentation—(1) general control procedures, (2) control of subject and experimenter effects, (3) control through subject selection and assignment—is necessary to an understanding of (4) control through experimental design. Because experimental design is a major topic, it is only introduced here, but will be discussed in detail in Chapters 10–13.

In any experiment, the protection of internal validity is of critical importance because it bears on the very essence of experimentation—the predicted causal relationship between the independent and dependent variables. The control methods we have chosen to list under experimental design primarily focus on protection of internal validity. By *experimental design* we mean the careful arrangement of all parts of the experiment so as to (1) test directly the effects of the independent variable on the dependent variable and (2) protect against threats to internal validity. In experimental design, control to reduce confounding and thus to protect internal validity is a key factor.

The True Experiment

A number of basic experimental designs are available to test hypotheses and protect internal validity (see Chapter 10). However, to introduce experimental design, let us consider a research design that is *not* a true experiment.

In an earlier discussion of confounding (see Chapter 8), a study of the effects of relaxation training on the disruptive behavior of autistic children was described (Graziano, 1974). Recall that a small group of autistic children was observed for disruptive behavior, trained in relaxation over a two-month period, and again observed for disruptive behavior. (The simple pretest-posttest design used in the study is illustrated in Table 9.4.) Suppose that the researcher found a statistically significant difference between the pretest and posttest measures—that is, the null hypothesis was rejected. That finding, however, is not sufficient for the researcher to conclude anything about causality—about the hypothesis that relaxation training brought about the improved behavior. Again, the conclusion cannot be drawn because of possible confounding. To avoid confounding variables (in this case, maturation and history), the experimenter would have to anticipate them and build suitable controls into the research design. In this instance a good control would be a no-treatment *control group* (i.e., an equivalent group of autistic children who do not receive relaxation training). Suppose there are 20 autistic children in the program. The researcher could randomly assign 10 of the children to the experimental condition and 10 to the control condition. All of the children would remain in the general program and receive the same general treatment. However, only the *experimental group*

TABLE 9.4   A SIMPLE PRETEST-POSTTEST DESIGN

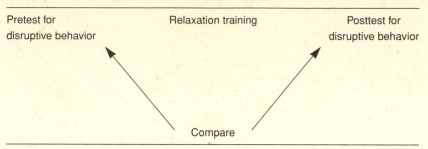

| Pretest for disruptive behavior | Relaxation training | Posttest for disruptive behavior |

Compare

TABLE 9.5   A PRETEST-POSTTEST, CONTROL-GROUP DESIGN

A. Experimental group	Pretest for disruptive behavior	Relaxation training	Posttest for disruptive behavior
B. Control group group	Pretest for disruptive behavior	No relaxation training	Posttest for disruptive behavior

would receive the relaxation training. This is a pretest-posttest, control-group design, as shown in Table 9.5. The critical comparison is to determine if the experimental group demonstrates significantly less disruptive behavior than the control group at the posttest. Suppose this is exactly what the researcher finds. Then the researcher can have considerably more confidence in concluding that relaxation is responsible for the difference because the confounding variables of maturation and history have been controlled. Maturation is controlled because, if the experimental and control groups are equivalent at the start of the experiment, the researcher can expect maturation to occur equally in the two groups. Confounding due to history is controlled in this design because both groups have received all other treatments in the general program. Thus, if some program factor other than relaxation is responsible for the posttest differences in disruptive behavior, it would affect both groups equally.

For the control-group design to be effective, it is *essential that the experimental and control groups be comparable at the start of the experiment.* If the experimental group has more of the most capable, older, or better-adjusted children, then confounding due to selection would occur. To control for possible confounding, the researcher must assign subjects to the two groups in an unbiased manner. Thus, in this example, unbiased subject assignment has controlled for confounding due to selection, and the inclusion of a no-treatment control group has controlled for confounding due to maturation and history. The two control procedures—unbiased assignment and a control group—provide a large measure of control in the experiment.

Routinely including three basic control procedures in between-subjects designs[2]—(1) unbiased subject selection or careful definition of subject characteristics to define an ad hoc sample, (2) unbiased assignment of subjects to conditions, (3) inclusion of appropriate control groups or conditions—controls most potential confounding.

[2]Between-subjects designs will be discussed in Chapter 10.

Note that in our relaxation study the independent variable of relaxation training is presented at two levels—all or none. The independent variable must vary in experiments; it must be actively manipulated so that it varies from one condition to another. There may be more than two levels; our hypothetical study earlier of typists' productivity at different room temperatures included six levels of the independent variable (room temperature). This design does not have one control group but six levels of the independent variable, each of which operates as a control for all other levels.

Scientific research generally is characterized by attention to details, such as developing carefully reasoned and clearly stated concepts, well-developed operational definitions, use of inductive-deductive logic, careful measurement of the observed variables, and careful use of appropriate statistical methods to analyze data. The *true experiment* shares these characteristics but also has the following five characteristics:

1. A clearly stated research hypothesis concerning predicted causal effects of one variable on another
2. At least two levels of the independent variable
3. Unbiased assignment of subjects to conditions
4. Specific and systematic procedures for empirically testing the hypothesized causal relationships
5. Specific controls to reduce threats to internal validity

In experiments, the task is to answer questions about causality and to control for threats to validity. To do so, the experimenter must carefully arrange all parts and procedures of the experiment—formation of a problem statement, operational definitions, and research hypotheses; subject selection and assignment; constructing different levels of the independent variable; creating measures for the dependent variable; creation of specific controls—in such a way as to answer the research question, "Does the hypothesized causal relationship between the independent and dependent variables exist?" The detailed task of arranging the components and procedures is what is meant generally by experimental design. In essence, experimental design gives us a detailed plan for the conduct of the experiment. In developing the experimental design, we specify the procedures. Once the design is formalized, we proceed through it step-by-step as planned. Remember that at the high-constraint level of experimentation we no longer have the flexibility to alter any part of the design once we begin making observations.

The essence of experimentation is to ask and answer questions about causality. In designing an experiment we must do so in such a way that we can clearly test the research hypothesis by ruling out various alternative hypotheses (i.e., the null hypothesis and the confounding-variable hypotheses). Our detailed procedural blueprint constitutes experimental design, the focus of the following chapters.

SUMMARY

Four major groups of control procedures used in research are defined: (1) general control procedures, (2) control of subject and experimenter effects, (3) control through subject selection and assignment, (4) control through experimental design.

General control procedures include careful preparation of the research setting, specification of measurement instruments, and replication. Subject and experimenter effects are controlled by keeping the researcher and subjects blind to both the hypotheses and the condition under which each subject is tested and by using automated procedures, objective measures, multiple observers, and deception when necessary. Appropriate subject selection (such as random sampling) helps control for threats to external validity, whereas random assignment of subjects to conditions helps to control for threats to internal validity.

The essential issue in experimentation is to develop, state, and test a hypothesized causal relationship between at least two variables and to do so in such way as to rule out alternative explanations of the results. Procedures to control for threats to validity are at the center of research design. The development of controls to their highest degree is a major factor that distinguishes experimentation from other levels of constraint in research. Control is a basic concept, and students must learn control procedures if they are to become scientific researchers—whether for a semester course or for a professional career.

REVIEW EXERCISES

9.1   **Define the following key terms. Be sure you understand them. They are discussed in the chapter and defined in the glossary.**

control	deception
statistical validity	balanced placebo design
confounding variable	subject selection
internal validity	population
construct validity	sample
external validity	general population
experimental design	target population
research setting	accessible population
replication	representative sample
exact replication	random sampling
systematic replication	table of random numbers
conceptual replication	random number generator
blind	stratified random sampling
single-blind procedure	ad hoc sample
double-blind procedure	subject assignment
automation	free random assignment
objective measure	matched random assignment
multiple observers	experimental design
interrater reliability coefficient	control group
percent agreement	experimental group
Kappa	true experiment
base rates	

9.2   **Answer the following. Check your answers in the chapter.**

1. Identify and define the types of validity in experimentation. For each type, identify and describe its major threats. (See Chapter 8.)

2. Explain this statement: "Confounding variables can threaten both internal validity and construct validity."
3. What is meant by "general control procedures"? Give examples of general control procedures and the threats they control.
4. Explain this statement: "Threats to validity and control procedures to reduce threats constitute two sides of the same coin."
5. How is replication a control procedure?
6. Describe single-blind and double-blind procedures.
7. Why is it important to use objective measures in research?
8. How can deception in an experiment be ethically justified?
9. What makes random sampling a powerful control technique?
10. Why is random assignment of subjects to conditions an important control procedure?
11. How is matching subjects a control?
12. Why is internal validity of such importance in experimentation?
13. What is a true experiment?
14. Why is it important in experimentation for experimental and control groups to be equivalent at the start of a study?
15. Why is it important that the independent variable is presented at least at two different levels?
16. What kind of relationship among variables is studied at each of the five levels of constraint?

9.3   Think about and work the following problems.

1. A researcher selects 30 children from among the 473 enrolled in an elementary school. On completion of the study, the researcher wants to discuss the results in terms of all elementary school children. Identify the various populations and samples involved in this study. What cautions must the researcher be aware of in generalizing the results?
2. If you were the teaching assistant for this course, how would you explain to students the concept of representativeness of a sample?
3. For each of the following independent variables indicate the number of levels and identify each level:
   a. We study the effects of bright and dark illumination on subjects' perception of stimuli.
   b. We vary the amount of noise using four levels in a study of classroom behavior.
   c. A researcher compares children's ability to solve riddles under different conditions. One group of children is given no extra clues, another group is given one extra clue, and a third group is given five extra clues.
   d. Five different kinds of pain relief medication are tested in a pharmaceutical laboratory.
4. Assume you have 60 subjects. Use the table of random numbers (Appendix B) to assign subjects randomly to three conditions with 20 subjects in each condition. Show which subjects are assigned to which conditions.

Chapter
10

Control of Variance Through Experimental Design:

Single-Variable, Independent-Groups Designs

EXPERIMENTAL DESIGN

Scientific research uses highly evolved procedures to provide answers to questions. It is at the experimental level of constraint that the design process is most important and most completely developed. *Experimental design* is thus a special case of the general concept of research design—a detailed customizing process for each specific study. True experiments share general research design characteristics and, in addition, have five specific experimental characteristics. The true experiment:

1. States one or more hypotheses about predicted causal effects of the independent variable(s) on the dependent variable(s).
2. Includes at least two levels of the independent variable.
3. Assigns subjects to conditions in an unbiased manner, such as through random assignment.
4. Includes specific procedures for testing hypotheses.
5. Includes controls for major threats to internal validity.

Planning the design is a critical element in experimental research. The researcher develops a problem statement, identifies and defines important theoretical constructs, identifies and operationally defines independent and dependent variables, formulates research hypotheses, identifies a population, selects and assigns subjects to conditions, specifies the details of observational procedures, anticipates threats to validity, creates controls, and specifies the procedures for data analysis—all of which are carried out before observing a single subject. The activity of planning and integrating these details and the resulting research plan for conducting the experiment is what we mean by experimental design. The term *experimental design* thus refers to both the activity involved in the detailed planning of the experiment and the product—the detailed plan itself. A well-developed experimental design provides a "blueprint" for the experimenter to follow. We cannot emphasize enough the importance of developing a clear experimental design *before beginning any observations.* Careful planning can build in all the controls necessary to have confidence in conclusions drawn from results. Therefore, *plan the experiment in careful detail and carry it out exactly as planned.* Furthermore, although planning at the experimental level is emphasized here, it should be noted that planning is a crucial ingredient in research at all levels of constraint.

VARIANCE

Variation is necessary to carry out experiments—without variation there would be no differences to test. When we conduct an experiment, we predict variation, and we hope to find that the variation between the experimental conditions is due to the manipulated independent variable(s). However, as much as we seek variation in experimental designs, we must be cautious about unwanted or extraneous variation. Experimental design is a blueprint for control of unwanted or extraneous variation. Unwanted variation can occur in any study and can threaten the validity of the study by allowing alternative explanations of results. This reduces confidence in drawing causal inferences, in generalizing beyond the sample, and in interpreting results. Experimental design controls many sources of unwanted, extraneous, and chance variation.

As introduced in Chapter 5, the most basic measure of variation is the *variance*.

$$\text{Variance} = \frac{\text{Sum of Squares}}{\text{Degrees of Freedom}} \qquad (10.1)$$

The variance is equal to the sum of squared differences from the mean (the sum of squares) divided by the degrees of freedom (equal to the number of scores minus 1). Using the concept of variance, the major goals of experimental design can be summarized succinctly by paraphrasing a statement made by Kerlinger: experimental design has two basic purposes: (1) to provide answers to questions by testing causal hypotheses and (2) to control variance so as to increase internal validity (1986, p. 280). Several concepts used throughout this text—levels of constraint, experimental controls, reducing threats to validity, control of variance—are closely related, all referring to similar issues of control but in different ways. Variance is a major underlying concept among these control issues.

Forms of Variance

Although a fairly easy idea, the concept of variance may seem difficult, and at times confusing, because it appears often and in different forms. We will focus on two sources of variance: (1) systematic between-groups variance and (2) nonsystematic within-groups variance (called "error variance"). These are important concepts in the logic of experimentation and in the analysis of data.

Systematic Between-Groups Variance   In an experiment we test the effects of an independent variable on the dependent variable(s). To do so we set up at least two levels of the independent variable and measure subjects' responses on the dependent variable(s). If, for example, the study included three levels of the independent variable, we would predict that the dependent measures will differ significantly among the three groups—that is, that there will be significant variability among the group means. By "significant variability" we mean that the variability among the means will be larger than the variability expected on the basis of *sampling error* alone. Recall from Chapter 5 that *sampling error* refers to the natural variation among samples drawn from the same population. In an experiment we seek a *significantly high variance between the groups.* If there is little between-groups variance—that is, if the groups are essentially the same on the dependent measures—then we have not observed an effect of the independent variable. Significant between-groups variance is necessary to support the research hypothesis that the independent variable has influenced the dependent variable as predicted.

However, if we find a significant difference between the groups (if the between-groups variance is high), we must be careful in drawing a causal inference. The significant difference may be due to either the systematic effects of the independent variable as predicted by the research hypothesis (*experimental variance*) or to the systematic effects of uncontrolled confounding variables (*extraneous variance*) or to a combination of the two. That is, the between-groups variance is a function of both experimental effects and confounding variables as well as the natural variability due to sampling error.

The systematic between-groups variance in the experiment might be statistically significant, thus tempting the researcher to conclude that there is a causal relationship between the independent variable and dependent variable. But, suppose the between-groups variance is high only because of systematic influence of confounding variables and not because of the independent variable. That is, suppose the observed differences were due to the extraneous variance and not to the experimental variance. Statistical tests will tell us only whether there is a significant difference between the groups but not whether the observed difference is due to experimental or extraneous variance. If there is any possibility that the differences between the groups are due to extraneous factors, then we cannot draw a causal inference. It is for this reason that we must anticipate possible confounding and plan controls to reduce the systematic between-groups variance due to extraneous variables.

To summarize, systematic, between-groups variance has two sources: (1) systematic between-groups variance due to the influence of the manipulated independent variables (experimental variance) and (2) systematic between-groups variance due to the influence of extraneous, uncontrolled variables (extraneous variance). High experimental variance is important for the experiment, but high *extraneous* variance is a serious problem, making it impossible to draw clear conclusions about causality. In testing hypothesized effects of an independent variable on a dependent variable, *we should seek to maximize the experimental variance and control the extraneous variance.* Even when we find a statistically significant difference between groups, if we have not used controls to minimize extraneous variance, we cannot conclude that the obtained difference was due to the independent variable. Note that extraneous variance cannot be measured directly; we try to minimize it by including careful control procedures.

Nonsystematic Within-Groups Variance   The term *error variance* is often used to denote the nonsystematic *within-groups variability.* Although systematic variance reflects influences on each group as a whole, error variance is due to random factors that affect only some subjects within a group. For example, some subjects may score as they do because they did not feel well or were anxious or excited that day. Error variance may also be increased by more stable factors, such as individual differences in motor coordination, personality, interest, and motivation. Error variance is also increased by experimenter errors or equipment variations that cause measurement errors for some subjects but not for others in the same group. In other words, *error variance* is the variation among individual subjects within a group that is due to chance factors. Because no two subjects are exactly alike and no procedures are perfect, there will always be some error variance—some noise in the system.

Nonsystematic within-groups influences are largely random and therefore will have random effects. There should be just as much chance that random errors will occur in one direction as in another and will have as much chance of affecting any one subject in the group as any other. Thus, if random errors cause some subjects to score lower than they ordinarily would, we expect that random error will also cause other subjects to score higher than they ordinarily would. That is, the effects of within-groups random errors tend to cancel each other. While some subjects score too high, others score too low, but the mean of the group as a whole is not affected; only the variance is affected. In contrast, systematic between-groups factors influence subjects in a group in one direction. The effects are not random; they do not cancel each other out within the group. As a result, the mean of the group as a whole is moved up or down by systematic between-group factors depending on the direction of their influence.

In summary, the distinction is made between

1. Systematic between-groups variance, which includes
   a. Experimental variance (due to independent variables) and
   b. Extraneous variance (due to *confounding variables*), and
2. Nonsystematic within-groups error variance (due to chance factors).

It is important to repeat that the between-groups variance is a function not only of the systematic between-groups variance (experimental and extraneous variance) but also of the nonsystematic effects that are due to sampling error. Even in situations where there is absolutely no systematic between-groups variance, there will still be small differences between groups due to sampling error. Systematic between-groups variance increases the between-groups variance beyond the small variance due to sampling error.

The relationship of the systematic between-groups variance and within-groups error variance is important. The way we analyze data is to compare the variation due to an experimental manipulation (between-groups variation) with the variation due to chance or error (within-groups variation) by computing appropriate measures of each and their ratio. As we will see later, the ratio defines the *F*-test:

$$F = \frac{\text{Measure based on between-groups variation}}{\text{Measure based on within-groups variation}} \qquad (10.2)$$

Without statistical detail, let us consider the principles involved in evaluating the relationship of the between-groups variation and the within-groups variation. Because of the way the numerator in analysis of variance is computed, the measure based on the between-groups variation is due to both the systematic effects (experimental variance plus extraneous variance) and the effects of sampling error (error variance). The measure based on within-groups error variation (the denominator) is due only to error variance. These terms are computed in such a way that the error variance is the same value in both the numerator and the denominator of the formula. Therefore, we could rewrite the above equation as

$$F = \frac{\text{Systematic effects} + \text{Error variance}}{\text{Error variance}} \qquad (10.3)$$

Suppose there are no systematic effects. In this case, both the numerator and the denominator would represent error variance only and the ratio would be 1.00. Whenever the *F*-ratio is near 1.00, it means there are no systematic effects present. In other words, the between-groups variation is no larger than would be expected by chance alone. On the other hand, suppose the measure based on the between-groups variation is substantially greater than the measure based on the within-groups error variation. This would suggest that the experimental manipulation may have had the predicted effects and caused differences between the groups that are greater than those due to chance alone. In this case, we would conclude the groups do differ. This is the basic idea behind the *F*-test.

Controlling Variance in Research

To show a causal effect of the independent variable on the dependent variable, the experimental variance must be high and not masked by too much extraneous or error variance. The greater the extraneous and/or error variance, the more difficult it becomes to show the effects of systematic, experimental variance. This idea leads to a general but important rule: *in experimentation each study is designed so as to maximize experimental variance, control extraneous variance, and minimize error variance.*

Maximizing Experimental Variance   Experimental variance is that variance due to the effects of the independent variable(s) on the dependent variable(s). In an experiment, there must be at least two levels of the independent variable. In fact, it is advisable to include more than two levels of the independent variable, because more information can then be gained about the relationship between the independent and dependent variable(s). To demonstrate a causal effect, we must be sure the independent variable really varies—that is, that the experimental conditions truly differ from one another. It is therefore necessary to design and carry out experiments so that the experimental conditions are clearly different from each other.

It is often useful when conducting a research study to evaluate the effectiveness of the manipulations of the independent variable by including a *manipulation check* to evaluate whether the manipulation actually had its intended effect on the subject. Suppose that, in an experiment to evaluate the effect of level of anxiety on performance of a coordination task, we plan to manipulate anxiety by changing the feedback given subjects during a training period. We reason that subjects who think they are doing poorly will be more anxious than subjects who think they are doing well. Therefore, we set up two conditions. In one, we tell subjects after the training period that they did quite well and should have no problems during the actual testing period (the low-anxiety group). A second group is told that they did badly during the training and that they must try harder if they want to avoid making themselves look foolish (the high-anxiety group). In this case, a manipulation check—such as a simple self-report measure of anxiety—would verify that the groups differ on their level of anxiety and, therefore, the anxiety manipulation was effective. A statistical evaluation would be conducted on the manipulation check. If we find that the groups do not differ statistically on anxiety, then we cannot be sure that the manipulation of anxiety was effective. Consequently, we would not be able to evaluate the effect of anxiety on the dependent measure.

Controlling Extraneous Variance   As discussed earlier, *extraneous variables* are those between-group variables other than the independent variables that have effects on whole groups and may thus confound the results. (Most of the common sources of extraneous variance are discussed in Chapter 8.) To demonstrate the effects of an experimental manipulation, it is necessary to control the extraneous variables and keep them from differentially affecting the groups. In this regard, two important ideas are basic in experimentation: we must be sure that (1) the experimental and control groups are as similar as possible at the start of the experiment and (2) that they are treated in exactly the same way except for the independent variable manipulation. Much of the discussion in Chapter 9 is devoted to controlling extraneous variables; the methods are summarized here:

1. The best way to avoid introducing extraneous variance during the study is to make sure that the independent variable manipulation is the *only* difference in the researcher's treatment of the experimental and control subjects.

The remaining methods for controlling extraneous variance are aimed at ensuring that the groups are equal at the beginning of the study.

2. The best general method of controlling for extraneous variance is by randomization, which decreases the probability that the groups will differ on extraneous variables. Thus, *whenever possible, randomly assign subjects to conditions.*

3. If a factor such as age, ethnic identification, social class, intelligence, or biological sex is a potential confounding variable, we may control it by *eliminating the variable as a factor by selecting subjects who are as homogeneous as possible on that variable.* For example, we can select only males or only females or select subjects who are within a few IQ points of each other. The cost of using this as a control is that we limit generalizability. By using only males or females, for example, we must limit our conclusions to only one sex.

4. A potential confounding variable also can be controlled by *building it into the experiment as an additional independent variable.* Thus, if biological sex is a potentially confounding variable, we could compare male and female subjects by adding sex as a nonmanipulated independent variable. There then would be two independent variables in the study, a design known as a "factorial design" (see Chapter 12). Note that biological sex is not actively manipulated, because it is a preexisting factor.

5. Extraneous variance can be controlled by matching subjects or by using a *within-subjects design* (see Chapter 11).

Minimizing Error Variance   Error variance is within-groups variance that is due to chance factors and individual differences and that affects individuals within a group rather than the group as a whole. One source of error variance is measurement error—that is, variations in the way a subject responds from trial to trial due to factors such as unreliability of the measurement instruments. To minimize this source of error variance we must *maintain carefully controlled conditions of measurement and be sure that the measuring instruments are reliable.*

Another major source of error variance is *individual differences.* Using within-subjects or matched-subjects designs (covered in Chapter 11) will minimize this source of error variance. There are problems in using within-subjects designs, such as sequencing and order effects. But the within-subjects design does effectively reduce error variance by eliminating the individual differences among subjects from one condition to another.

This brief discussion of maximizing experimental variance, controlling extraneous variance, and minimizing error variance is a summary of the earlier discussions of control. That is, when we discuss control in experimentation we refer to *the control of variance.* The general control procedures discussed in Chapter 9 deal with the control of error variance. Other control procedures help to control both error variance and extraneous variance. The most powerful control for extraneous variance is a properly selected experimental design in which subjects are randomly assigned to conditions. There are a number of useful experimental designs available as well as statistical tests for evaluating data generated by experimental designs.

NONEXPERIMENTAL DESIGNS

There are several true experimental designs, each with many variations. Earlier we listed five characteristics of true experimental designs. Research designs that do not meet the criteria are not true experimental designs capable of testing causal hypotheses. Unfortunately, some of the designs are still inappropriately used in social science research. To understand the limitations of these *nonexperimental designs,* we need to discuss those that are still sometimes used:

1. Ex post facto design
2. Single-group, posttest-only design
3. Single-group, pretest-posttest design
4. Pretest-posttest, natural control-group design

In this and the next section we will consider examples of designs, beginning with *nonexperimental designs* and progressing to the most highly controlled, high-constraint, *experimental designs:* As we progress along this continuum, notice that each successive design controls for more sources of extraneous variance. We will borrow heavily in the following discussion from the classic monograph of Campbell and Stanley (1966).

Ex Post Facto Design

In the *ex post facto design* ("after the fact" design), the researcher observes current behavior and attempts to relate it causally to some earlier factors. (The design is diagrammed in Table 10.1). A therapist might observe some difficulty in a client and conclude that the problem was caused by earlier life events that the therapist never directly observed or manipulated. For example, many people have concluded that abused children become abusive parents based on the observation that a large proportion of abusive parents report that they were themselves abused as children. The conclusion is arrived at in an ex post facto manner. As reasonable as the conclusion seems, we can have little scientific confidence in its validity because there were no controls for confounding factors. If we cannot control for confounding, such as by manipulating the independent variable, then we cannot eliminate rival hypotheses. Thus, we cannot infer a causal relationship between the independent and dependent variables.

TABLE 10.1 THE EX POST FACTO DESIGN

Group A	(Naturally occurring events) (No direct manipulation)	Measurement

For example, suppose a researcher suspects that food additives such as artificial colors, flavors, and preservatives stimulate hyperactive behavior in some children. Obtaining a sample of 30 hyperactive children, the researcher finds that 28 of them (93 percent) eat foods containing these additives every day. The number seems high to the researcher, and the findings are consistent with the researcher's suspicion that there may be a relationship between food additives and hyperactivity. The researcher can even formulate the hypothesis that food additives stimulate hyperactivity for future testing. But, because the researcher followed an ex post facto procedure, a valid conclusion that a causal relationship exists between food additives and hyperactive behavior cannot be made.

An ex post facto study, like all low-constraint research, can help us *generate* hypotheses to test with higher constraint studies, but is not itself capable of *testing* causal hypotheses. Because no independent variable is manipulated in ex post facto studies, controls to guard against confounding cannot be applied. Consequently, the researcher cannot know which variable(s) may have affected the results and is therefore *unable to eliminate rival hypotheses.* That is, any of several *confounding variables* may have been responsible. Any inferred causal relationship between an observed variable (such as a parent's current child abuse) and an assumed but never manipulated factor (having been abused as a child) is pure speculation. The ex post facto design should be used with great caution.

Single-Group, Posttest-Only Design

The *single-group, posttest-only* design is at a somewhat higher level of constraint than ex post facto procedures. Here an actual manipulation of a variable is included, but the design is still not a true experiment. In this design, a variable is manipulated with a single group and the group is then measured. The single-group, posttest-only design is diagrammed in Table 10.2.

Suppose, for example, a clinician wants to determine whether eliminating foods containing the additives thought to increase hyperactivity will help hyperactive children. She asks parents of 20 children diagnosed as hyperactive to eliminate the foods from their children's diets for four weeks. At the end of the period the children are tested for hyperactivity and only 4 out of the 20 children are found to be hyperactive. Here, there has been an actual manipulation in the form of the dietary change as well as measurement of posttreatment hyperactivity levels. But there are problems in the design that prevent the researcher from drawing causal inferences about the treatment's effect on hyperactivity. There are several confounding factors. Perhaps the children did not change at all, but because there was no pretreatment measurement we have no way of knowing this. Perhaps there was a change but it was a placebo effect—a change produced only by the expectation of improvement.

TABLE 10.2 SINGLE-GROUP POSTTEST-ONLY DESIGN

Group A	Treatment	Posttest

Note: The term *treatment* as used in these figures refers to any kind of manipulation of the independent variable.

Perhaps the children did improve but the improvement was due to some other uncontrolled factor, such as another program in which the children were involved. Perhaps the children matured over the four weeks of treatment and their low hyperactivity was actually due to their natural maturation and not to the dietary program at all. Perhaps they did become less active during the program but it was only a natural return to their normal activity level. In this case, it may have been a temporary peak in their activity level that prompted parents to bring their children in for treatment. In other words, the single-group, posttest-only design does not control for the confounding variables of placebo effects, history, maturation, or regression to the mean. The researcher cannot even be sure if there was any change in activity level.

Single-Group, Pretest-Posttest Design

Single-group, pretest-posttest designs are also frequently used, but they are weak designs for inferring causality. They are an improvement over the posttest-only design because they include a pretreatment evaluation (a pretest). The researcher studying hyperactivity, for example, might select a sample of hyperactive children and (1) observe them for rates of hyperactive behavior, (2) impose the four-week dietary restrictions, and (3) observe them again for hyperactivity at the end of the four weeks. This design is illustrated in Table 10.3.

Suppose the posttest measurement of hyperactivity is significantly less than the pretest measurement; the children clearly improved from pretest to posttest. Recall from our earlier discussion that the finding is not sufficient for us to conclude that dietary restrictions caused the decrease in hyperactivity. We cannot draw this causal conclusion because the single-group, pretest-posttest design fails to control for the same confounding variables as does the single-group, posttest-only design—primarily placebo effects, maturation, history, and regression to the mean. That is, the measured improvement might have occurred only because the children and parents expected improvement (placebo effect), because the children matured during the treatment period (maturation), because of some other factor in the program that was operating but was uncontrolled (history), or because the pretest measures of hyperactivity were at an abnormally high peak and they naturally returned in time to about their mean level (regression). To avoid these confounding variables, the researcher would have to anticipate them and build in suitable controls.

In the above discussion, we noted that the single-group, pretest-posttest design fails to control for the confounding variable of maturation. In some research,

TABLE 10.3 SINGLE-GROUP, PRETEST-POSTTEST DESIGN

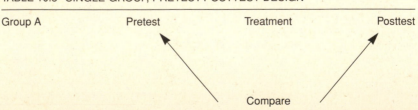

| Group A | Pretest | Treatment | Posttest |

however, maturation is not considered a confounding variable; rather, it is the phenomenon that we want to study. Developmental psychologists focus much of their research on the process of maturation. They often use designs similar to the pretest-posttest design described here but without the manipulation. As we discussed earlier, this is called a *longitudinal design,* where the same subjects are followed over time. Typically, multiple measures are taken over the course of a developmental study. Such a design is called a *time-series design.* In a developmentally focused longitudinal study we elevate maturation from confounding variable status to phenomenon of interest. However, it is important to realize that variables such as history can confound our study of maturation unless we include appropriate controls. We will discuss this in more detail in the section on time-series designs in Chapter 13.

Pretest-Posttest, Natural Control-Group Design

A good control to add to the above designs is a no-treatment control group. In the *pretest-posttest, natural control-group design* (illustrated in Table 10.4), subjects are not randomly assigned to groups as they would be in a true experimental design. Rather, naturally occurring groups are used, only one of which receives the treatment. For example, rather than randomly assigning students to two groups, we might use two intact classrooms. The students from one classroom are assigned to the first group, and the students from the other classroom are assigned to the second group. In the hyperactivity and food additives example, a control group of hyperactive children would not receive the dietary restriction treatment. Addition of this control group significantly strengthens the design.

With the natural control-group design, we begin to draw closer to true experimental design. However, this design still has a weakness in that there is no procedure (such as random assignment) to ensure that the two groups are statistically equivalent at the start of the study. For example, suppose that in forming the experimental and control groups the researcher asked parents if they were willing to try the four-week dietary restrictions. The children of those parents who were willing to expend the effort were put in the experimental group, and those who were not were put in the control group. The serious confounding in this procedure is that the experimental and the control groups are different from each other at the start of the study in terms of parents' willingness to try the dietary restrictions. In other words, the dietary restriction treatment is confounded with parents' willingness to cooperate. We might assume that parents who are willing to do everything necessary to change their child's diet in hope of decreasing their child's hyperactivity may be more motivated to help their child change. Any posttreatment differences between the groups on measures of hyperactivity might be due to either factor—dietary restriction or

TABLE 10.4 PRETEST-POSTTEST, NATURAL CONTROL-GROUP DESIGN

Group A (experimental)	Pretest	Treatment	Posttest	
Group B (control)	Pretest	No treatment	Posttest	Compare

parental willingness to cooperate. The children in the two groups may even have been different on the dependent measure (level of hyperactivity) before the experiment began. It may be that parents with the most hyperactive children are the most desperate and, therefore, the most likely to try *any kind* of treatment. Of course, the pretest in the design would allow us to check this possibility.

Remember that in a true experiment, when we compare groups of subjects at different levels of the independent variable, it is essential that the groups be equivalent on the dependent measures at the start of the study. Random assignment of subjects to conditions is one way of increasing our confidence that the groups are equivalent at the start of the study.

EXPERIMENTAL DESIGNS: TESTING ONE INDEPENDENT VARIABLE

Experiments maximize the control of variance, thus maximizing internal, external, statistical, and construct validity. Two critical factors that distinguish experimental designs from most nonexperimental designs, and through which many threats to validity are controlled, are *control groups* (or *conditions*) and *randomization.*

The addition of one or more control groups to nonexperimental designs can improve them considerably. Including proper control groups helps to control history, maturation, and regression to the mean. The experimental designs discussed here all include at least one control group. To make the control groups effective, subjects must be randomly assigned to conditions. Also, the random selection of subjects from a population is a valuable control that helps protect external validity. Randomization is a powerful tool. A good general rule to follow in designing research is to randomize whenever possible.

Because there are so many different experimental designs, we will divide our discussion into several sections. We will first discuss designs appropriate for evaluating a single independent variable using independent groups of subjects (the focus of the remainder of this chapter). Later chapters focus on designs for testing a single independent variable using correlated groups of subjects (Chapter 11), designs used for testing more than one independent variable in a single experiment (Chapter 12), and designs that test causal hypotheses in natural environments (Chapter 13).

Although many variations of experimental designs are possible, there are four basic designs used to test a single independent variable using independent groups of subjects (i.e., *single-variable, between-subjects designs*). These include:

1. Randomized, posttest-only, control-group design.
2. Randomized, pretest-posttest, control-group design.
3. Multilevel, completely randomized, between-subjects design.
4. Solomon's four-group design.

Randomized, Posttest-Only, Control-Group Design

Suppose we want to manipulate an experimental treatment to test the effects of relaxation training on disruptive behavior, a special tutorial program on reading skills, visual stimulus complexity on time estimation, or food additives on hyperactivity. In

TABLE 10.5   RANDOMIZED, POSTTEST-ONLY CONTROL-GROUP DESIGN

R Group A (experimental)	Treatment	Posttest	↖
R Group B (control)	No treatment	Posttest	↙ Compare

Note: The "R" in front of the group label means subjects are randomly assigned to groups.

each case, we wish to manipulate a variable and measure the effects, but we want to do it in such a way that unwanted variance is controlled and validity is protected. (Note that the terms *treatment* and *manipulation* are used interchangeably throughout this discussion.)

A basic experimental design that answers questions and protects validity is the *randomized, posttest-only, control-group design,* which includes randomization and a control group. In this design, we first randomly select subjects from a general or accessible population or carefully define an ad hoc sample. Our selected or ad hoc subjects are then randomly assigned to the experimental (treatment) and control (no-treatment) conditions. The resulting design, using "R" to indicate randomization, is illustrated in Table 10.5. The arrows denote the critical comparison to be made to test the hypothesis that the independent variable significantly affected the dependent measures.

The critical comparison is between the two levels of the independent variable (experimental and controls groups) on the dependent variable at posttest. Note that it is critical for this comparison that the two groups are equivalent at the beginning of the study. If they are not, then we cannot know if differences at the posttest are due to the independent variable or to preexisting differences between the groups. Random assignment of subjects to groups increases the probability that the groups are equivalent at the beginning of the study.

Several threats to validity are controlled by the randomized, posttest-only, control-group design. External validity (generalizability of the findings) is protected by random selection or ad hoc sample definition. Threats to internal validity from regression to the mean and from attrition are reduced by random assignment of subjects. Threats to internal validity from instrumentation, history, and maturation are reduced by the inclusion of the no-treatment control group. Random assignment helps to ensure statistical equivalence of the groups at the beginning of the study.

It is important to realize that this or any other experimental design will be effective only if the appropriate general control procedures are routinely applied (see Chapter 9 for review). A carefully prepared setting, using reliable dependent measures, applying single-blind or double-blind procedures where appropriate, and so on, will ensure that extraneous variance is controlled by the experimental design and that error variance is minimized. An experimental design alone, without using these general control procedures, is not sufficient for ruling out the effects of confounding variables. For example, a randomized, posttest-only, control-group design that does not keep the person who actually tests the subjects blind to the group

TABLE 10.6 RANDOMIZED, PRETEST-POSTTEST, CONTROL-GROUP DESIGN

R Group A (experimental)	Pretest	Treatment	Posttest
R Group B (control)	Pretest	No treatment	Posttest

Compare

each subject is in will allow the possibility of confounding due to experimenter effects. The control imposed by the design is forfeited by the failure to include the necessary general control procedures. In the food additive study, we should use a double-blind procedure because we anticipate placebo as well as experimenter effects. The no-treatment control group must be indistinguishable from the treatment group for the subjects. We might accomplish this by having the researcher provide specially packaged foods to all subjects regardless of what group they are in. The only difference would be that the food given to the experimental subjects would not contain the additives thought to increase hyperactivity. It is critical to remember throughout our discussion of experimental design (Chapters 10–13) that general control procedures must also be incorporated if the design is to be effective.

Randomized, Pretest-Posttest, Control-Group Design

Recall the pretest-posttest, natural control-group design discussed earlier in the chapter. That design is relatively weak but not far from a true experimental design. It is not a true experiment because it does not include a procedure, such as randomization, to ensure that the groups are comparable at the beginning of the study. In the *randomized, pretest-posttest, control-group design* (illustrated in Table 10.6), subjects are randomly assigned to experimental and control conditions. All subjects are then pretested on the dependent variable. The experimental group is administered the treatment and both groups are then posttested on the dependent variable. The critical comparison is between the experimental and control groups on the posttreatment measure of the dependent variable.

The randomized, pretest-posttest, control-group design improves on the randomized posttest-only, control-group design by adding a pretreatment measurement of the dependent variable (a pretest). By adding the pretest, we provide further assurance that the two groups are equivalent on the dependent variable at the start of the experiment. Random assignment of subjects to groups also helps to ensure the two groups' equivalence. Adding a pretest has advantages, but it also carries disadvantages, which are discussed later in the chapter.

Multilevel, Completely Randomized, Between-Subjects Design

More complex randomized designs are possible where several levels of a single independent variable are manipulated. The *multilevel, completely randomized, between-subjects design* is a simple extension of previously discussed designs. Instead of subjects being randomly assigned to two conditions, they are randomly assigned to three or more conditions (see Table 10.7). Pretests may or may not be included in this design depending on the questions the investigator wants to answer.

TABLE 10.7   MULTILEVEL, COMPLETELY RANDOMIZED, BETWEEN-SUBJECTS DESIGN

R Group 1	Pretest	Treatment 1	Posttest	
R Group 2	Pretest	Treatment 1	Posttest	
.	.	.	.	
				—— Compare
.	.	.	.	
.	.	.	.	
R Group N	Pretest	Treatment 1	Posttest	

Note: This design may or may not include a pretest.

Because this design is only an extension of earlier designs, it controls for the same confounding variables as the simple two-group designs.

Recall the description in Chapter 9 of a study in which room temperature was varied to test its effects on the speed and accuracy of typing. This study used a multilevel, completely randomized, between-subjects design in which 48 typists were randomly assigned to six groups of 8 typists each. Each group of typists was tested at a different room temperature (the independent variable), and their typing speed and accuracy were measured (the dependent variable).

Solomon's Four-Group Design

The addition of a pretest improves control in experimental design, but it also creates a new problem—the possibility that experiencing the pretest will affect subjects in some way. We might expect such pretesting effects to be the same in the experimental and control groups, but interaction effects might occur between the pretest and the experimental manipulation and constitute a potential confounding factor. By *interaction effect* in this situation we mean that the effect of the pretest will not be constant for the groups but will vary depending on the level of the independent variable. For example, suppose a researcher is interested in testing whether adolescents' attitudes toward cigarette smoking can be changed by presenting them with a videotape about the health hazards of tobacco use. One hundred subjects are randomly selected from a high school. They are given a pretest measuring their attitudes toward use of tobacco and are randomly assigned to two conditions—experimental and control. The pretests show that the subjects in the two conditions are statistically equivalent on attitudes toward tobacco use at the start of the study. The experimental group is then shown the videotape and the control group is not. Both groups are then retested on their attitudes toward tobacco use and the experimental and control groups' posttest measures are compared. As well designed as this study may appear, it is possible that the pretest of attitudes may sensitize the subjects to what the research is about. When the videotape is presented to the experimental group, this sensitization may interact with that new information and have some effect on subjects' responses. The experimenter might erroneously conclude that the observed difference is due only to the videotape, when it may actually be due to the interaction of the pretest and the videotape. If no pretest had been given, the videotape may have been less effective.

"Everything's been so completely randomized out there that we seem to have lost our research assistants among the subjects!"

In an attempt to control such effects, Solomon (1949) developed an "extension of control group design." *Solomon's four-group design* (illustrated in Table 10.8) combines the randomized, pretest-posttest, control-group design and the posttest-only, control-group design. Groups A and B in Table 10.8 constitute the pretest-posttest, control-group design component, and Groups C and D constitute the posttest-only design component. Groups A and B are the experimental and control groups, respectively, and they provide the basic comparison needed to test the hypothesis. Groups C and D represent a replication of this basic comparison but without the pretest. The critical comparison, of course, is between the posttest measures of Groups A and B. The random assignment of subjects to conditions ensures that the groups are statistically equivalent at the start of the study, and the pretest gives us the means to test their equivalence. Random assignment also controls for potential confounding due to statistical regression. The potential confounding due to history and maturation are controlled by the inclusion of the control group (Group B). Group C, which includes the treatment and posttest but no pretest, controls for the possible interaction effects of the pretest. By comparing the posttest measures of Group C and Group A, we have the basis for determining whether the pretest in Group A had an interactive effect. The final control, Group D, includes only the posttest and provides further control for the effects of maturation. The posttest measures for Group D should be similar to those of Group B and different from Groups A and C.

Solomon's four-group design is powerful, providing good controls and exceeding the minimum requirements for an experiment. However, because it requires the re-

TABLE 10.8 SOLOMON'S FOUR-GROUP DESIGN

R Group A	Pretest	Treatment	Posttest
R Group B	Pretest		Posttest
R Group C		Treatment	Posttest
R Group D			Posttest

sources of two experiments, it is not recommended for routine use. Rather, it is best used for experiments in a well-developed research program where the basic hypotheses have already been tested and supported using simpler designs and a test of greater rigor is desired. It is also used in situations where an interaction between the treatment and the pretest is expected.

Internal Summary: Basic Experimental Designs

Each of the four experimental designs discussed uses randomization to assign subjects to conditions. Actually, what is required is the *unbiased assignment of subjects to conditions,* which is achieved through free random assignment or matched random assignment (see Chapter 9). Thus, we can utilize matching procedures and still maintain a true experimental design. (Designs employing matching procedures are discussed in Chapter 11.)

The most basic experimental design is the randomized, posttest-only, control-group design. The other designs are more complex variations of this basic design and are used when more confidence or finer testing is needed. All of the experimental designs discussed in this section

1. Manipulate one independent variable.
2. Randomly assign subjects to conditions.
3. Compare subjects in one group with different subjects in another group, where the groups are independent of each other.

(We encourage you at this point to work problems 10.3.4 and 10.3.6 in the Review Exercises.)

STATISTICAL ANALYSES OF COMPLETELY RANDOMIZED DESIGNS

The statistical procedures used will depend on the level of measurement of the dependent variable (see Chapters 4–5). For example, if we test differences between groups and the data are nominal data, *chi-square* is typically used; if we have ordered data, a commonly used statistic for comparing two groups is the *Mann-Whitney U-test;* if we have score data, we would use either a *t*-test or an analysis of variance (*F*-test). Most dependent variables at the experimental level of constraint generate score data.

t-Test

The *t*-test evaluates the size of the difference between the means of the two groups. The difference between the means is divided by an *error term,* which is a function of the variance of scores within each group and the size of the samples. The t-test is easily applied, commonly used, and useful when we wish to test the difference between two groups. Its disadvantage is that it can compare only two groups at a time.

Analysis of Variance

Many studies are multilevel designs in which more than two groups are used. For those studies an *analysis of variance (ANOVA)* is preferred because it is flexible enough to handle any number of groups. In fact, ANOVAs are now so frequently used when there are only two groups that it is beginning to replace the *t*-test. In the typists study described earlier, there are six levels of the independent variable—room temperature. Because there are six groups, we would not use a *t*-test. Instead, we would use a one-way analysis of variance to test whether any of the six groups is statistically different from any of the other groups.

To introduce analysis of variance, it is necessary to review some of our earlier discussion of variance. Variance is a relatively simple concept, but it can seem confusing because, in analysis of variance, variance is calculated more than once based on different combinations of the same data. Analysis of variance uses both the within-groups variance and the between-groups variance. Within-groups variance is a measure of nonsystematic variation within a group. It is error or chance variation among individual subjects within a group and is due to factors such as individual differences and measurement errors. It represents the average variability within each of the groups. The between-groups variance is a measure both of the systematic factors that affect the groups differently and of the variation due to sampling error. The systematic factors include (1) experimental variance, which is variation due to the effects of the independent variables, and (2) extraneous variance, which is due to confounding variables. Even if there are no systematic effects, the group means are likely to be slightly different from one another by chance alone due to sampling error. The between-groups variance tells us how variable the group means are. If all groups in the experiment have approximately the same mean, the between-groups variance will be small. However, if the group means are quite different from one another, the between-groups variance will be large.

The researcher should arrange the experiment so as to maximize experimental variance, control extraneous variance, and minimize error variance. The reasoning behind this principle becomes apparent through knowing how the analysis of variance is computed. The variance is based on the *sum of squares,* which is the sum of squared deviations from the mean. In an analysis of variance, there is a sum of squares on which the between-groups variance is based, a sum of squares on which the within-groups variance is based, and a total sum of squares. In the ANOVA procedure, the sum of squares is calculated for each of these; that is, we *partition* the total sum of squares into the between-groups sum of squares and the within-groups sum of squares:

| Total sum of squares | = | Between-groups sum of squares | + | Within-groups sum of squares | (10.4) |

These principles can be illustrated by using the example described earlier, the study of the effects of room temperature on typing speed, in which 48 typists are randomly

TABLE 10.9   TYPING SPEED DATA FROM 48 TYPISTS RANDOMLY ASSIGNED TO ONE OF SIX ROOM TEMPERATURES

	55°	60°	65°	70°	75°	80°
	49	71	64	63	60	48
	59	54	73	72	71	53
	61	62	60	56	49	64
	52	58	55	59	54	53
	50	64	72	64	63	59
	58	68	81	70	55	61
	63	57	79	63	59	54
	54	61	76	65	62	60
Mean	55.75	61.88	70.00	64.00	59.13	56.50

TABLE 10.10 ANOVA SUMMARY TABLE FOR STUDY OF TYPING SPEED AND ROOM TEMPERATURE

```
- - - - - O N E-W A Y - - - - -
Variable   TYPSPEED    Typing Speed
By Variable            TEMP      Temperature

                  Analysis of Variance
                     Sum of        Mean        F         F
    Source     D.F.  Squares      Squares     Ratio     Prob.

Between Groups   5   1134.6667   226.9333    5.5054    .0006
Within Groups   42   1731.2500    41.2202
Total           47   2865.9167
```

assigned to six conditions defined by the temperature of the room in which their typing speed was tested. Table 10.9 shows the raw data and the mean scores for the typing-speed data for each group of typists. The first step in doing an analysis of variance of these data is to compute each of the sums of squares: the sum of squares between groups, the sum of squares within groups, and the total sum of squares. (The computational procedures for these values are given in Appendix C.) The results of the computations are recorded in an *ANOVA summary table* (see Table 10.10). The next step is to compute between-groups and within-groups variances, which are called *mean squares.* To compute the mean squares, we divide each of the sums of squares by the appropriate degrees of freedom (df). The between-groups sum of squares is divided by the number of groups minus 1 (in this case, 6 − 1 = 5). The within-groups sum of squares is divided by the total number of subjects minus the number of groups (in this case, 48 − 6 = 42). The between-groups and within-groups mean squares are then compared by dividing the between-groups mean square by the within-groups mean square. The result is the *F*-ratio, which we will interpret shortly. (The results of these computations are summarized in Table 10.10.) Note that the ANOVA summary table shows the sources of variation in column 1, the degrees of freedom associated with each source of variation in column 2, the sum of squares in column 3, the mean squares in column 4, the value of *F* (mean square between groups divided by mean square within groups) in column 5, and the probability value in column 6.

The statistical significance of the ANOVA is based on the *F*-test (named after its originator, Sir Ronald Fisher). Fisher's *F*-test involves the ratio of the between-groups mean square to the within-groups mean square:

$$F = \frac{\text{Mean square between groups}}{\text{Mean square within groups}} \tag{10.5}$$

Consider some of the possibilities we might find in this ratio. If there were no *systematic* between-groups differences, there would still be some *chance* differences between the groups. The group differences are due to the normal chance variation found among subjects and to sampling error in the formation of the groups. In fact, if there were no systematic between-groups differences, both the mean square between groups (based on between-groups variability) and the mean square within groups (based on within-groups variability) would be estimates of the same quantity—the within-groups variance. In that case, the *F*-ratio should have a value of approximately 1.00. However, if there are systematic between-groups differences, the ratio would have a value greater than 1.00. Consider also the conditions that would make the F-ratio larger or smaller. Any factors that increase the size of the numerator relative to the denominator will make the ratio larger; any factors that increase the size of the denominator relative to the numerator will make the ratio smaller. Thus, the ratio will be made larger by either increasing the between-groups mean square or by decreasing the within-groups mean square. We increase the between-groups mean square by maximizing the differences between the groups. We minimize the within-groups mean square by controlling as many potential sources of random error as possible. In other words, it is desirable to maximize experimental variance and minimize error variance.

Recall that within-groups variation is due to chance factors, and between-groups variation is due to both chance factors and systematic effects. Thus, if the mean square between groups is the same as the mean square within groups, the differences between experimental conditions are due solely to chance factors and the experimental manipulations have no additional effects. The between-groups mean square must be significantly larger than the within-groups mean square if we are to conclude that the experimental manipulations had effects beyond the chance differences.

The larger the *F*-ratio, the greater the difference *between* groups relative to the chance differences *within* groups. An *F*-value of 1.00 or less indicates there is no difference between groups relative to differences within groups. This is the concept that the *F*-test utilizes. A large *F* indicates that the experimental manipulations may have succeeded in causing a greater difference between experimental conditions than one would expect by chance alone (i.e., a significant difference between the conditions). In practice, if there are no systematic differences between groups, the *F*-ratio will sometimes by chance alone be larger than 1.00. Therefore, we do not reject the hypothesis that there are no systematic differences unless the *F*-ratio is larger than we would expect by chance alone. Statistical analysis programs routinely compute both the *F*-ratio and the *p*-value associated with it (termed *F*-probability in *SPSS for Windows*). If the *p*-value is less than the alpha level we have chosen, we reject the null hypothesis and conclude that at least one of the groups is significantly different from at least one other group.

It is relatively simple to compute either a *t*-test (if you have only two groups) or an analysis of variance (for two or more groups) using a statistical analysis program.

We will illustrate the procedures with *SPSS for Windows,* but there are several other commercially available programs that could do the same computations. We used *SPSS for Windows* to compute the ANOVA Summary Table shown in Table 10.10 (actual output shown). The key to doing this analysis is to structure the data file correctly. You must have a minimum of two variables—one variable indicates group membership and the second variable is your dependent measure. Of course in a real data set, you are likely to have other variables included such as basic demographic information on each subject (age, biological sex, education level, etc.) and you may have more than one dependent variable in a study. In this example, however, there is only one dependent variable and one independent variable. The first variable (temp) can take on values of 1 through 6 standing for 55 through 80 degrees, respectively. The second variable (typspeed) is the value on the dependent variable for each subject in this hypothetical study. Note that we have explicitly named these variables "temp" and "typspeed" using the "Define Variable" option on the Data Menu of *SPSS for Windows* (see Appendix D for details). Note that these are shorthand names because our variable name cannot exceed eight characters in *SPSS for Windows.* However, we have used the labels option to give a more complete label for each variable. We also labeled the meaning of each of the "temp" values (e.g., 1 is 55 degrees). Adding such labels is easy and will make it much easier to read and interpret the output.

Computing the analysis of variance with *SPSS for Windows* is easy, although there is one tricky part. We are comparing six independent groups (i.e., different subjects in each group). We use a one-way ANOVA to make this comparison. We select the "Statistics" Menu. The tricky part is that in *SPSS for Windows,* the one-way ANOVA is in the "Compare Means" submenu rather than the "ANOVA Models" submenu as you might expect (see Figure 10.1). Selecting the one-way ANOVA option gives you the screen shown in Figure 10.2. You need to define for the program what variable defines your factor (in this case, temp) and your dependent variable (in this case, typspeed). When you move the variable "temp" into the factor definition slot, it shows up as "temp (? ?)" because you also need to define the range for the program. Clicking your mouse on the Define Range button of this screen allows you to tell the program that the variable "temp" has values ranging from 1 to 6. All you need to do now to run the ANOVA is to click on the OK button and in a few seconds it is done. Table 10.10 shows the actual output for this analysis. Note that the *p*-value (.0006) in the last column is well below the traditional alpha level of .05. Therefore, we would conclude that at least one group is significantly different from at least one other group.

Specific Means Comparisons in ANOVA

Note that the *F*-test in the analysis of variance tells us if a significant difference among the groups exists but does not tell us which group or groups are significantly different from the others. This is not a problem when an ANOVA has only two groups to compare, because the significant *F*-ratio tells us that the two groups do differ. By simply inspecting their means, we can see whether the difference is in the predicted direction. But when we have three or more groups to compare, an additional step is needed; we must *probe* to determine where the significant difference(s) occurred.

Figure 10.1   Selecting a One-Way ANOVA from the *SPSS for Windows* Program

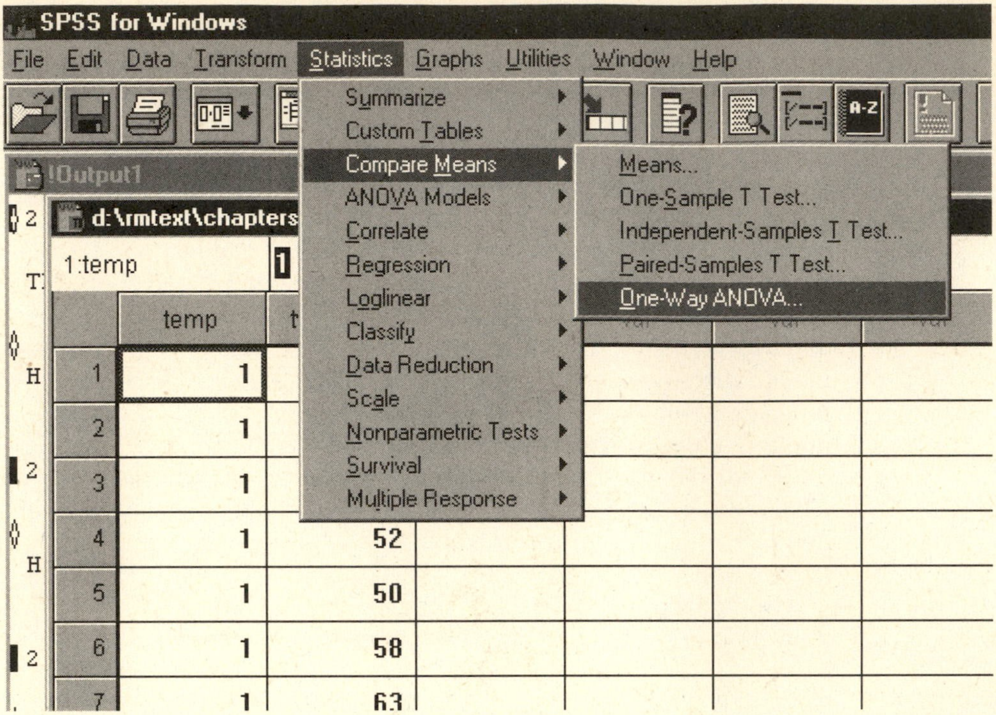

Probing is done by statistically testing the differences between the individual means. Specific comparisons are best carried out as a planned part of the research (i.e., a *planned comparison,* sometimes called an *a priori comparison* or a *contrast*) in which the experimenter makes predictions before data are collected about which groups will differ and in what directions based on theoretical concepts that underlie the experiment. (Computational procedures for a planned comparison are given in Appendix C.) At times we cannot make an a priori prediction and we carry out an ANOVA to answer the question of whether there are differences. Under these conditions, if a significant *F* is found, we compare the pattern of means using a *post hoc comparison* (also called *a posteriori* or *incidental comparison*). The scientific rigor and informational value is generally greater for the planned comparisons than for the post hoc comparisons. There are several statistical procedures that can be used for the specific comparisons, depending on whether they are planned or post hoc. Doing either planned comparisons or post hoc tests with *SPSS for Windows* or similar programs requires only a couple of extra mouse clicks. Notice in Figure 10.2 that there are buttons labeled "Contrasts" and "Post Hoc." Each of these opens menus that list available statistical tests for specific means comparisons.

It should be noted that a t-test is not an appropriate procedure for doing a post hoc comparison of means. The t-test used as a post hoc probe may indicate that significant differences exist where in fact they do not. Appropriate post hoc tests (e.g., Tukey, Newman-Keuls, Sheffe) have built-in procedures designed to deal with problems with the Type I error level. These problems are too complex to discuss ade-

Figure 10.2   Specifying the Variables in a One-Way ANOVA Using *SPSS for Windows*

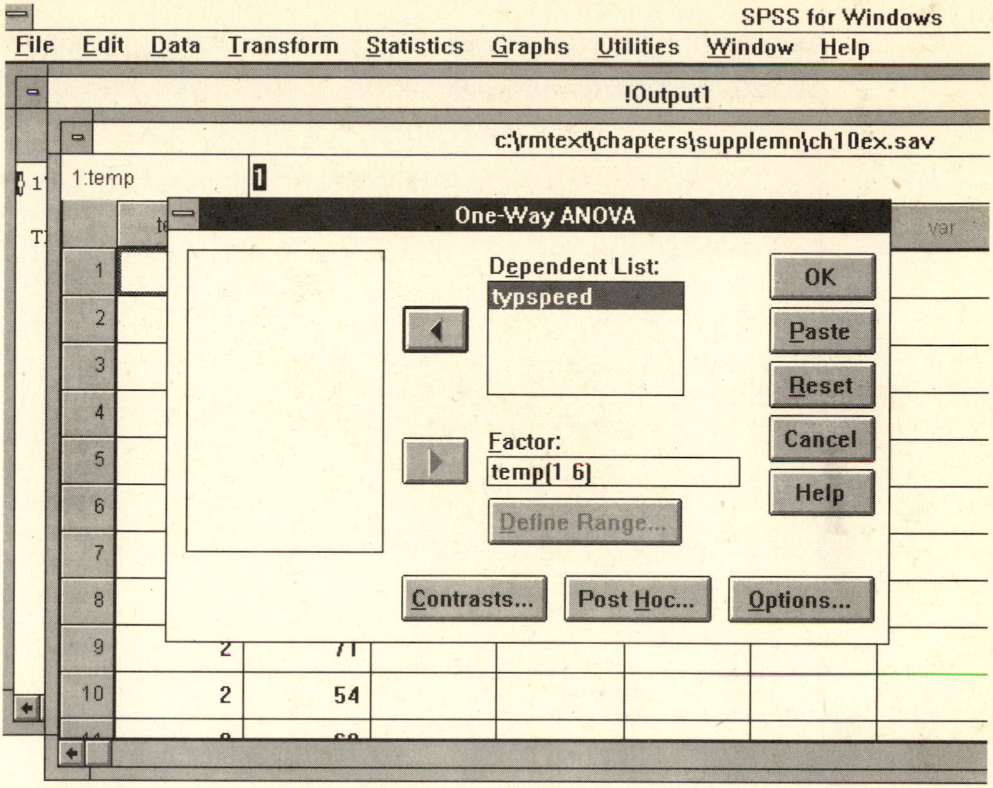

quately here. The interested student can consult Shavelson (1988) for computational procedures and the rationale.

Interpreting results is a process of making sense out of complicated findings, and a useful first step in the interpretation process is to look at the pattern of means. In the typing-speed example, we can inspect the means as they are listed in Table 10.9 and can organize the means into a graph as shown in Figure 10.3 (produced by *SPSS for Windows*). Graphs are usually easier to read than tables and are particularly helpful when there is more than one independent variable (i.e., factorial designs).

OTHER EXPERIMENTAL DESIGNS

The simple and multilevel, between-subjects, completely randomized designs have served researchers well. They are powerful, commonly used, and are appropriate where a single independent variable is to be manipulated and random assignment of subjects is used. However, there are three general conditions where these designs should not be used.

First, there are many research settings in which randomization is not possible. Here a lower-constraint design is necessary. Second, variables rarely operate singly; most often variables operate simultaneously to affect the responses of subjects. Further, variables may interact with each other. Thus, there are many research

Figure 10.3 Pattern of Mean Scores for the Study of the Effects of Room Temperature on Typing Speed

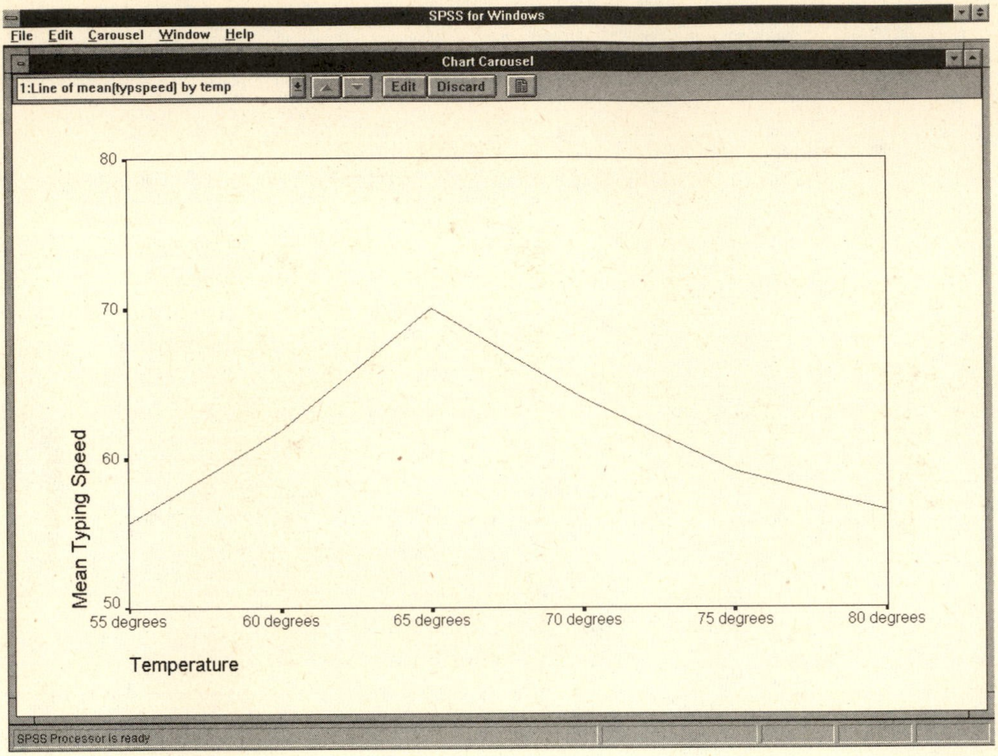

questions in which it may be useful to manipulate more than one independent variable in a study and to manipulate them in a way that enables us to assess whether the two independent variables interact with each other in producing their effects on the dependent variable. Here a *factorial design* is appropriate. Finally, there are research conditions in which it is desirable to have the same subjects tested under each condition. In this case, a *within-subjects design* is used.

We make two distinctions in our definition of experimental research designs. One distinction is between *independent-groups designs* (also called *between-subjects designs*) and *correlated groups designs* (either *within-subjects designs* or *matched-subjects designs*). In independent-groups designs, different subjects appear in each group. In correlated-groups designs, the same or closely matched subjects appear in each group. The second distinction is between *single-variable designs* (also called *univariate designs*) and *multivariable designs* (also called *factorial designs*). Single-variable designs have only one independent variable, while factorial designs have two or more independent variables in a single study. This chapter covered single-variable, independent-groups designs. Chapter 11 will cover correlated-groups designs, and Chapter 12 will cover factorial designs.

SUMMARY

Experimental design entails a highly detailed process of developing controls over unwanted variance to reduce threats to validity. Variance includes systematic between-groups variance and nonsystematic within-groups error variance. Between-groups variance is a function of both experimental variance and extraneous variance. A major principle in experimentation is to design the study in order to maximize experimental variance, control extraneous variance, and minimize error variance.

There are many experimental designs. We have organized these designs by making two distinctions: (1) between single-variable designs and factorial designs and (2) between correlated-groups and independent-groups designs. This chapter focuses exclusively on independent-groups, single-variable designs. Chapter 11 presents correlated-groups designs, and Chapter 12 presents factorial designs. Finally, Chapter 13 presents several specialized experimental designs used in field settings.

REVIEW EXERCISES

10.1   Define the following key terms. Be sure you understand them. They are discussed in the chapter and defined in the glossary.

experimental design	randomization
variance	experimental designs
sampling error	randomized, posttest-only,
sum of squares	control-group design
degrees of freedom	randomized, pretest-posttest,
between-groups variance	control-group design
experimental variance	multilevel, completely randomized,
extraneous variance	between-subjects design
within-groups variance	Solomon's four-group design
error variance	treatment
confounding variables	manipulation
manipulation check	interaction effects
extraneous variables	chi-square
within-subjects design	Mann-Whitney *U*-test
individual differences	*t*-test
nonexperimental designs	error term
ex post facto design	analysis of variance (ANOVA)
single-group, posttest-only	ANOVA summary table
design	mean squares
singled-group, pretest-posttest	*F*-test
design	specific means comparisons
pretest-posttest, natural	probe
control-group design	planned comparison
longitudinal design	a priori comparison
time-series design	contrast
control groups	post hoc comparison

a posteriori comparison   matched-subjects designs
incidental comparison   single-variable design
independent-groups designs univariate designs
between-subjects designs   multivariable design
correlated-groups designs   factorial design

10.2   Briefly answer the following. Check your answers in the chapter.

1. Review the concepts of deduction and induction.
2. What is extraneous variance? Why is it important to consider in research?
3. Why is it important to maximize between-groups variance?
4. If between-groups variance is high in an experiment, is that enough evidence to conclude that the independent variable has had the predicted effect on the dependent variable? Explain.
5. What are the two major sources of between-groups variance in an experiment?
6. What is the relationship between error variance and individual differences among subjects?
7. Why is it important to maximize experimental variance?
8. What is the relationship among these concepts: confounding variables, threats to validity, extraneous variance?
9. Why is randomization the single best way to control extraneous variance?
10. In terms of the *F*-test, why is it important to minimize the error variance?
11. Define *ex post facto studies* and explain why it is a weak design. What conclusions can you draw from this type of study?
12. Why is it important to be sure that the groups to be compared in an experiment are equivalent at the start of the study?
13. Almost all threats to validity are controlled if we include only two control procedures. What are they and what threats are controlled by their inclusion?
14. Why do we urge researchers to randomize wherever possible?
15. Why is it so important that the independent variable in experiments be presented at two or more levels?
16. Suppose we find a significant difference between groups in an experiment. Are we then justified in inferring that the experimental manipulation caused the difference? Explain.

10.3   Think about and work the following problems.

1. How do (a) random assignment of subjects to conditions and (b) the addition of a control group reduce threats to internal validity?
2. You are the teaching assistant for this course and you have to explain variability to your students. How would you explain the concept, its major measure, and its importance?
3. Explain this statement: "Error variance affects scores in both directions; systematic variance affects scores in only one direction." Why is this so important?
4. For each of the following designs (i) give an example, (ii) identify the major threats to validity, and (iii) state the limits on the conclusions that can be drawn.
   a. Single-group, posttest-only design
   b. Ex post facto design
   c. Single-group, pretest-posttest design
   d. Pretest-posttest, natural control-group design

5. As the course teaching assistant, you have the task of explaining the *F*-ratio. Define all of its components and explain the logic of the *F*-test.

6. For each of the following types of experimental design (i) give an example and (ii) indicate what threats to validity are controlled.

   a. Randomized, posttest-only, control-group design

   b. Randomized, pretest-posttest, control-group design

   c. Multilevel, completely randomized, between-subjects design

   d. Solomon four-group design

Control of Variance Through Experimental Design:

Single-Variable, Correlated-Groups Designs

In Chapter 10, we covered between-subjects designs where subjects are assigned randomly to groups. Random assignment of subjects increases our confidence that the groups are equivalent at the start of the study. The characteristics of randomized, between-subjects experimental designs are:

1. Each subject is exposed to only one level of the independent variable.
2. The groups are independent of each other.
3. Only one score per subject on the dependent variable is used in analyzing the results.
4. The critical comparison is the difference between independent groups on the dependent measures.

Randomized, between-subjects experimental designs have been a mainstay in psychological research. They are powerful designs used under many conditions to answer causal questions. Random assignment of subjects to conditions—a principle feature of the designs—is a powerful control and gives us confidence that the groups to be compared are equivalent at the start of the study.

CORRELATED-GROUPS DESIGNS

There are conditions in which a causal question must be answered but the researcher decides not to use random assignment of subjects to conditions. Given our emphasis on the importance of randomization, you might ask, "Is an experimental design possible when random assignment is not used?" There are designs that do not include random assignment but nevertheless provide equivalent groups at the start of the study and allow other controls to be applied when necessary. *Correlated-groups designs* allow us to test causal hypotheses with confidence and without randomization. Some researchers do not consider correlated-groups designs to be true experiments because they do not use random assignment; others believe they are true experiments because they meet the requirements of equivalence of groups and because most other controls are possible, thereby providing the bases for eliminating rival hypotheses and allowing systematic testing of causal hypotheses with confidence. Further, correlated-groups designs are generally more sensitive than between-subjects designs to the effects of the independent variable (for reasons discussed later in the chapter) and are often preferred by researchers to between-subjects designs. Therefore, correlated-groups designs are considered in this text as a category of experimental design.

Let us consider why these designs are called correlated-groups (or correlated-subjects) designs. Recall that random assignment helps to assure equivalence of groups at the start of the experiment. But there are other ways to assure equivalence. For example, suppose we have only five children and want to study their attention span for complex versus simple visual stimuli. We could measure the attention span of all five children under each of the two conditions (a within-subjects design). The independent variable—complexity of visual stimuli—is presented at two levels, simple and complex. The dependent variable—attention span—is measured under both conditions for all children. In this design, the subjects in level 1 of the experiment are the same subjects who are in level 2. Clearly, when the subjects in one group are the same individuals in the other group(s) then the groups are equivalent at the start of the study. Indeed, they are identical. Thus, by using the same subjects in all conditions we guarantee equivalence of groups at the start of the study. The groups are not independent of one another as they are in between-subjects designs but are correlated with each other. Note also that each subject is measured more than once in a within-subjects design (i.e., repeatedly measured). Hence, the term *repeated measures design* is sometimes used.

The strength of correlated-groups designs and the reason they are often preferred by experimenters is their power in assuring equivalence of groups. Thus, although random assignment of subjects to conditions is not used with correlated designs, we can still preserve the characteristics of experimental designs so as to have good control and reasonable confidence in testing causal hypotheses. The key idea in correlated-groups designs is that in seeking to ensure equivalence of groups, some correlation among subjects in different groups is introduced. There are two basic ways of introducing the correlation among subjects in correlated-groups designs. We can use either a within-subjects design (also called *repeated measures designs*) or a matched-subjects design, as discussed in the following pages.

Within-Subjects Design

In *within-subjects designs,* all subjects are exposed to all experimental conditions, thereby making the conditions correlated. *In essence, each subject serves as his or her own control.*

Using Within-Subjects Design   Suppose that in a time-perception experiment we want to test whether subjects' estimates of the duration of a standard time interval varies with the amount of information given during the interval. That is, we predict that the interval "filled" with information will be perceived as longer than the "partially filled" or "empty" intervals. Each of six subjects is presented with one filled time interval, one partially filled interval, and one empty interval, all identical in duration. Because each subject appears in each condition, each subject is measured more than once on the dependent variable. (The design of this study is illustrated in Table 11.1.) The characteristics of within-subjects designs are:

1. Each subject is exposed to all levels of the independent variable.
2. Therefore, the scores in each condition are correlated with the scores in the other conditions (i.e., performance in one condition is correlated with performance in each other condition).
3. Each subject is measured under each experimental condition on the dependent variable.
4. The critical comparison is the difference between correlated groups on the dependent variable.

TABLE 11.1   A WITHIN-SUBJECTS DESIGN IN WHICH EACH SUBJECT IS TESTED IN EACH OF THREE CONDITIONS

	Conditions		
	Filled	Partially filled	Empty
Group A	Measure	Measure	Measure

Compare

Note: The order of presentation of conditions will vary from subject to subject as shown in Table 11.2.

In within-subjects designs, subjects are sampled from a target or accessible population, and each subject is exposed to all conditions of the experiment. This design is similar to a single-group, pretest-posttest design (see Chapter 10) in that the same subjects are tested under each condition. In the single-group, pretest-posttest design, each subject responds to the pretest and the posttest in that order. In contrast, in within-subjects designs, each subject responds in two or more conditions and the order of presentation of conditions is not necessarily fixed as it must be in a pretest-posttest study. In the time-estimation study described earlier, each subject is measured under three conditions. Because it is similar to the single-group, pretest-posttest design, it also has many of the same weaknesses of that design. For example, because we have the same subjects in all conditions, the experience subjects have in one condition might affect how they respond in subsequent conditions. Thus, if we found differences between the conditions in an experiment, they might be due not to the independent variable manipulation but to the confounding effects of one condition on later conditions. This potential confounding, called *sequencing effects,* can occur in within-subjects designs and must be controlled by varying the order of presentation of conditions. A major control for sequencing effects is *counterbalancing,* in which the order of presentation of conditions to subjects is systematically varied. In complete counterbalancing, all possible orders of conditions occur an equal number of times. In that case, (1) each subject is exposed to all conditions of the experiment, (2) each condition is presented an equal number of times, (3) each condition is presented an equal number of times in each position, and (4) each condition precedes and follows each other condition an equal number of times. (Sequencing effects and their controls will be discussed more extensively later in the chapter.)

Table 11.2 shows the various orders of conditions for the hypothetical within-subjects experimental study of time estimation. Notice that all four conditions given in the previous paragraph are met with this set of orders. Hypothetical data for the experiment are also in Table 11.2. The data are the duration (in seconds) estimated by each subject in each condition. The first column lists the six subjects, the second column shows the order of presentation of the stimulus conditions to each subject, and the last three columns show the time estimations for each of the three experimental conditions.

Analyzing Within-Subjects Design   To analyze the results of within-subjects designs, we first organize and summarize the data, as shown in Table 11.2. As shown by the mean values of each condition in the table, the estimates are largest on average for the filled interval, next for the partially filled interval, and lowest for the empty interval. These results suggest that our hypothesis might be supported. But are the differences between conditions large enough for us to state with confidence that similar differences exist in the populations? In other words, are the differences statistically significant?

The most commonly used statistical analysis for the single-variable, within-subjects experiment is an ANOVA similar to the one discussed in Chapter 10. However, the difference is that in the present study the conditions are not independent of each other but are correlated. The ANOVA procedure must be modified to take this correlation into account. In this case the appropriate ANOVA to use is called a *repeated-measures ANOVA*.

The advantage of a within-subjects design is that it effectively equates subjects in different conditions prior to experimental manipulation by using the same subjects in each condition. Therefore, the single largest contributing factor to error variance—individual differences—has been removed. In the language of analysis of variance, we have removed the effects of individual differences from the error component. What effect do you think this would have on the *F*-ratio? Because the individual difference portion of the error term has been removed, the denominator in the *F*-ratio will be smaller and, therefore, the *F* will be larger. This means that the procedure will be more sensitive to small differences between groups.

In a repeated-measures ANOVA, the total sum of squares is computed in the same way as in a simple one-way ANOVA. What is called a between-groups sum of squares in a simple one-way ANOVA is in this case called a between-conditions or simply a between-sum of squares. Terminology is changed in the repeated-measures design because there is only one group of subjects. The within-groups sum of squares in the repeated-measures ANOVA is split into two terms—*subjects* and *error.* The subjects term is the individual differences component of the within-groups variability. The error term is what is left of the within-groups variability after the indi-

TABLE 11.2 HYPOTHETICAL DATA FOR THE TIME-ESTIMATION STUDY

Subjects	Order of Presentation	A (filled)	B (part filled)	C (empty)
		Condition (Time estimation in seconds)		
1	ABC	22	17	15
2	ACB	17	14	14
3	BAC	13	13	12
4	BCA	19	14	11
5	CAB	24	16	14
6	CBA	12	11	10
Mean scores		17.83	14.16	12.66

vidual differences component is removed. In the repeated-measures ANOVA, we test the null hypothesis that there are no differences between conditions by dividing the mean square between by the error mean square. As in the independent groups ANOVA, the ratio of mean squares is an *F*-ratio. The computational procedures for a repeated-measures ANOVA are given in Appendix C, although we recommend using a computer program like *SPSS for Windows* to do the computations.

We used *SPSS for Windows* to compute the repeated-measures ANOVA for the data listed in Table 11.2. Figure 11.1 shows the data file for this example as it would appear on the screen. Notice that, unlike the data file for a one-way ANOVA in a between-subjects design where only one dependent measure appears on each line, in the repeated-measures ANOVA each line contains a subjects scores on the dependent measure for each condition of the experiment. This difference in how the data file is set up can be confusing. However, there is an easy way to remember how to set up the file. Just remember that *SPSS for Windows,* and virtually every other statistical analysis package, will assume that each line (or record) represents that data from one subject. In a between-subjects design, each subject contributes one score; therefore, there is only one score per line. In a within-subjects design, each subject contributes scores in each condition; therefore, each line has the subject's score for each condition. Notice in Figure 11.1 that we have named the variables, which is a good habit to get into. Naming the variables makes it easier to interpret the output because we do not have to go back to figure out what each numbered variable (the default name) represents.

Figure 11.1 *SPSS for Windows* **Data File for the Time-Estimation Data from Table 11.1**

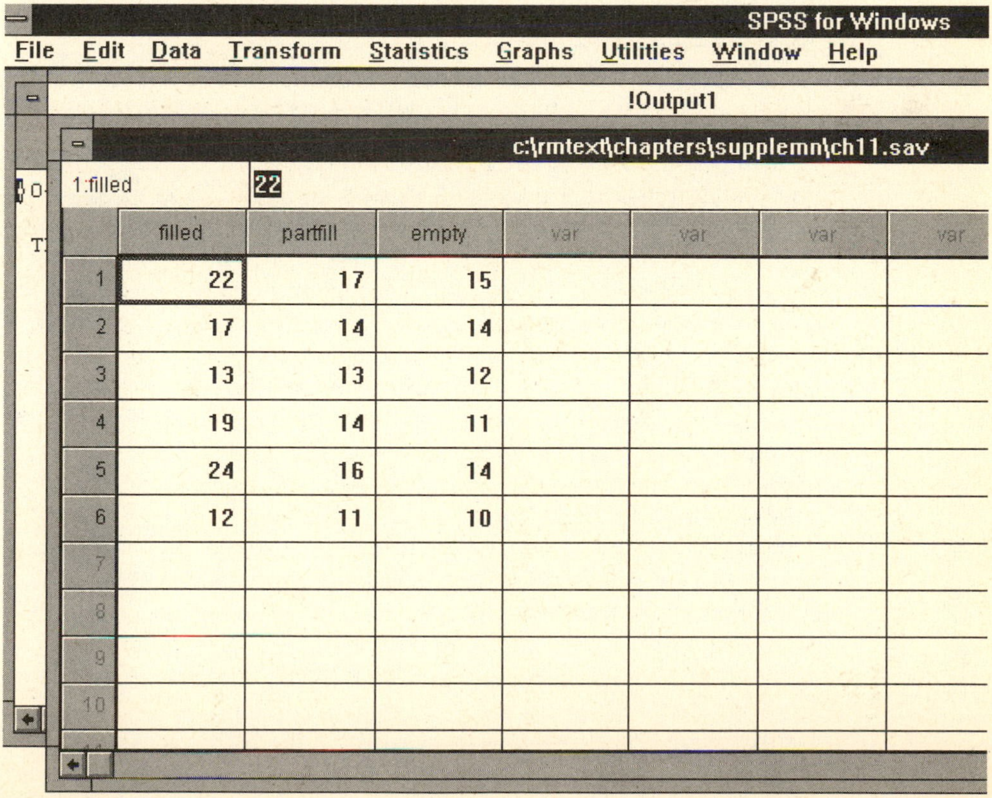

Figure 11.2   **Selecting the Repeated-Measures ANOVA from *SPSS for Windows***

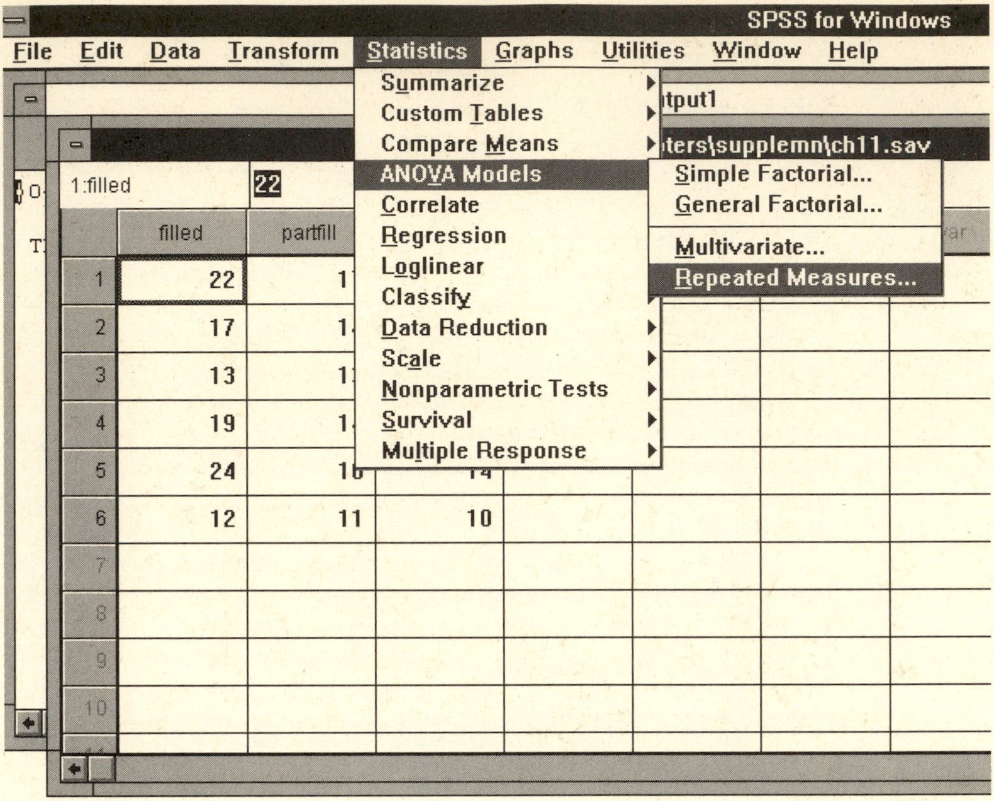

To compute the repeated-measures ANOVA in *SPSS for Windows,* we select the "Statistics" menu, the "ANOVA Models" submenu, and the "Repeated Measures" subsubmenu as shown in Figure 11.2, which will give us the screen shown in Figure 11.3. We will change the name of the factor from the default of "factor1" to something more descriptive (e.g., "fill_lvl") and will indicate that we have three levels of the factor where asked. Entering the number of levels activates (i.e., makes it operational) the Add button on the left, which adds this factor to the analysis. Simply click that button with the left mouse button, which will activate the Define button (upper right). Clicking the Define button brings up the screen shown in Figure 11.4 on page 260. This screen displays the variables in your data set by name in the left box. You tell the program which variable represents each of the three levels of your independent variable by highlighting the variable names (in the left box) and moving them across to the middle box by clicking on the arrow between the two boxes. Once that is done, clicking the OK button runs the analysis for you. Table 11.3 on page 261 shows selected sections of the output file produced by this analysis.[1] The *F*-ratio in this example is 10.99 with a *p*-value of .003. As with all statistical analyses, if the *p*-value is smaller than the alpha level we set (traditionally .05), we reject the null hypothesis.

[1]The part of the output in which we are interested is the test of our independent variable (which we named "fill_lvl").

Figure 11.3   Defining the Variables in a Repeated-Measures ANOVA in *SPSS for Windows*

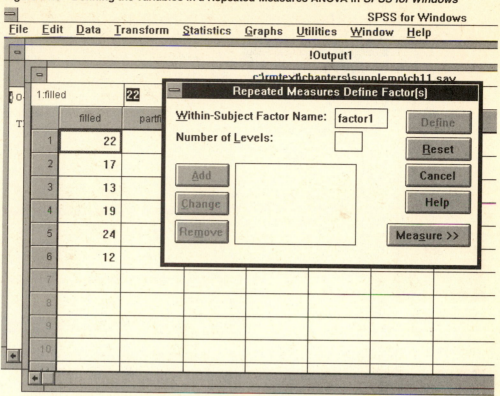

The analysis of variance tests the null hypothesis that there are no differences between any of the conditions. Therefore, a significant *F*-ratio indicates that at least one of the condition means is significantly different from at least one other condition mean. To determine which means are significantly different from which other means we must use one of the statistical tests to probe for specific mean differences. Computational procedures for the tests can be found in most advanced statistics textbooks (Keppel, 1991; Myers & Well, 1991). Most computerized statistical analysis packages include these tests as an option in the repeated-measures analysis.

Strengths and Weaknesses of Within-Subjects Design   When properly used, within-subjects designs have important advantages. First, because the same subjects are in each condition, there are no differences between groups due to subject variables. This guarantees that subjects in each condition are equivalent at the start of the study. If the conditions are not equivalent at the start of the study, we cannot know whether differences found are due to experimental manipulation or to preexisting differences between the conditions.

Another important advantage of within-subjects designs is that they are often a good deal more sensitive than between-subjects designs to the effects of the independent variable. Why is the sensitivity greater for within-subjects designs? Remember that the aim of an experiment is to show the effects of an independent variable

Figure 11.4 Defining the Levels of the Independent Variable in a Repeated-Measures ANOVA Analysis Using *SPSS for Windows*

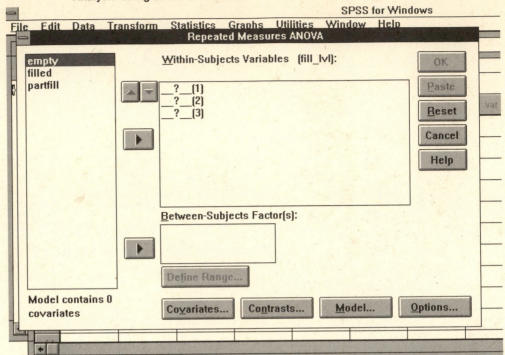

on a dependent variable. To show that effect, we try to maximize the experimental variance (variance due to the effects of the independent variable), control extraneous variance (variance due to confounding), and minimize error variance (variance due to individual differences and chance factors). A within-subjects design not only controls but *actually eliminates the variance due to subject differences, thereby reducing error variance.* The use of within-subjects designs decreases error variance by removing its major contributor—individual differences. The larger the individual differences in a population, the greater the benefit derived from using a within-subjects design. As the measure of within-conditions variance decreases, the value of *F* increases. The greater sensitivity of within-subjects designs to the effects of the independent variable leads many researchers to prefer within-subjects designs to between-subjects designs when given the choice.

Further, fewer subjects are needed in within-subjects designs. For example, an independent-groups design with 10 subjects in each of three conditions will require 30 subjects. Using a within-subjects design requires only 10 subjects, because each subject is tested under all conditions. In addition, because of its greater sensitivity, the within-subjects design might require even fewer subjects per condition. For example, 7 subjects in a within-subjects design might give us the same statistical power as 10 subjects per condition in a between-subjects design. Reducing the sample size reduces statistical power, but we can do it safely here because the greater sensitivity of the within-subjects design will balance the loss of statistical power from using fewer subjects.

TABLE 11.3 SUMMARY TABLE FOR THE REPEATED-MEASURES ANALYSIS RUN
USING *SPSS FOR WINDOWS*

```
      ***Analysis of Variance--design 1***

Tests involving 'FILL_LVL' Within-Subject Effect.

AVERAGED Tests of Significance for TIME EST using
UNIQUE sums of squares

Source of Variation   SS    DF   MS    F  Sig of F

WITHIN + RESIDUAL    38.56  10  3.86
FILL_LVL             84.78   2  42.39    10.99    .003
```

There is yet another advantage of within-subjects designs, one that further increases efficiency. Because the same subjects are tested under several conditions, instructions can be given only once instead of at the beginning of each condition, or the instructions may require only slight modifications for each condition. If instructions are long and/or complicated, or if a practice period is part of the instructions, time savings can be considerable.

Although within-subjects designs have many advantages, they also have some important disadvantages. The disadvantages all stem from the fact that in this design each subject is exposed to each condition. Therefore, subjects' experience in one condition may affect their responses to any or all of the conditions that follow. In other words, the major disadvantage of within-subjects designs are sequencing effects. If sequencing effects occur and are not properly controlled, any significant differences between conditions may be due to sequencing effects and not to the effects of the independent variable. In other words, there would be serious confounding in the study, and we could not confidently draw a causal inference about the effects of the independent variable. Sequencing effects obviously occur in experiments where a treatment has a permanent or long-lasting effect on subjects. Examples can be found in animal experimentation where chemical or surgical changes are implemented, or in human experiments where knowledge or attitudes are changed. A long-lasting or permanent effect of a condition certainly affects the subject's response to any other condition that follows it. A within-subjects design should not be used in such a situation. Even if the effects of conditions are temporary, there is always the risk of potential sequencing effects for at least some period of time following the treatment. There are a number of potentially confounding sequencing effects. The two most important are (1) practice effects and (2) carry-over effects.

Practice effects, as the term implies, are caused by subjects' practice and growing experience with procedures as they move through successive conditions. Practice effects are not due to influences of any particular condition, but rather to subjects' growing familiarity with the task. If, for example, the experiment includes five conditions and they are presented in the same order to each subject, then presumably because of practice effects many subjects might perform better in the last two or three conditions than in the earlier ones. This enhancement of performance on the later conditions constitutes a positive practice effect. On the other hand, if the procedure is lengthy or demanding, subjects might become fatigued as they continue in the experiment. Their performance in later conditions might therefore be reduced by fatigue. This is called a negative practice effect. Thus, practice effects may either enhance or reduce performance. In either case, they are a potential confounding variable and must be controlled. Note also that practice effects depend on subjects' experience as they move sequentially through the conditions. This means that practice effects occur regardless of the particular sequence of conditions.

In contrast, *carry-over effects* are sequencing effects due to the influence of a particular condition or combination of conditions on responses to the following condition(s). Carry-over effects may be greater for one condition than for the others. For example, there may be some aspect of condition A that produces an effect on any condition that follows it. Thus, wherever condition A appears in a sequence, the next condition will be influenced. Suppose that in the time-estimation study described earlier the conditions are always presented A, B, C, where A is the filled condition, B is the partially filled condition, and C is the empty condition. Each subject first responds to the two filled conditions before being presented with the empty condition. The sequence effect may be that when subjects reach the empty condition they are still responding to the details of the two filled conditions (i.e., conditions A and B might influence subjects to respond to condition C in a similar fashion). Thus, we might find no differences in response between the filled and empty conditions. On the other hand, experiencing the two filled conditions first and the empty condition last might set up a marked contrast, causing subjects to respond differently to the empty condition, not because of the empty condition itself, but because of the contrast with the prior filled conditions. Note that carry-over effects of one condition may be the same on all subsequent conditions or they might affect only some of the subsequent conditions; that is, carry-over effects may be differential. In either case, carry-over effects constitute an extraneous variable and must be controlled.

There are two general types of controls for sequencing effects: (1) holding the extraneous variable constant and (2) varying the order of presentation of conditions. In the time-estimation example presented earlier, to control for positive practice effects we might hold the practice variable constant by training all of the subjects to the same criterion of performance before the first condition begins. Thus, all subjects would be familiar with the procedures before they respond to any of the experimental conditions. A control for fatigue (negative practice effects) could be the inclusion of a rest period between the conditions, allowing fatigue that was building up to dissipate before going on to the next condition. Such procedures can minimize practice effects. However, control is best achieved by varying the order of presentation of conditions.

Carry-over effects can be controlled only by varying the order of presentation of conditions. For example, we should not use the same ABC sequence for all subjects in the time-estimation study. Varying the presentation can be accomplished by random order of presentations or by counterbalanced order of presentations. In *random order of presentation,* we randomly order the conditions to be presented to each subject. In this way, practice effects are not systematically maximized in one condition, and carry-over effects should occur as much to any one condition as to any other. Counterbalancing the presentation is more involved. In counterbalancing, we systematically arrange the order of presentations so that all possible orders are represented the same number of times. Counterbalancing controls for confounding due to both practice effects and carry-over effects.

In a study with three experimental conditions (A, B, C) there are six possible orders of presentation of conditions, as shown in Table 11.2. Subjects are assigned to orders of presentation with an equal number assigned to each order. If we have 30 subjects, for instance, we can assign 5 subjects to each of the six orders. Each condition appears in each position an equal number of times, and each precedes and follows every other condition an equal number of times. Clearly, counterbalancing is best used in studies with a small number of conditions. Counterbalancing procedures for many conditions can become extremely complicated. With two conditions—A and B—there are only two orders of presentation (AB and BA). With three conditions—A, B, and C—there are six orders of presentation. But with four experimental conditions—A, B, C, and D—there are 24 orders of presentation ($4 \times 3 \times 2 \times 1 = 24$). To meet the counterbalancing criteria noted above, we would need at least 24 subjects in the experiment. But suppose we have only 10 subjects and four experimental conditions and we still want to use a within-subjects design and control for sequencing effects? In experiments with three or more conditions, we can (1) randomize the order of presentation for each subject, (2) randomly select 10 of the 24 possible arrangements and then randomly assign subjects to those conditions, or (3) use a more formalized design known as a *Latin square design.* Latin squares are counterbalanced arrangements presumably named after an ancient Roman puzzle that required arranging letters in rows and columns so that each letter occurs only once in each row and once in each column. [The interested student should consult Keppel (1991) and Myers and Well (1991) for a discussion of Latin square designs.]

A word of caution is needed. If strong carry-over effects are expected, the within-subjects design is not recommended, even if the above controls are included. Carry-over effects tend to add error variance to scores, which can offset any increased sensitivity normally expected from a within-subjects design. If strong carry-over effects are expected, it is best to use either a between-subjects design or a matched-subjects design.

You might note that the within-subjects design introduced in Chapter 10 (the single-group, pretest-posttest design) is a nonexperimental design. The reason this design is nonexperimental, whereas the within-subjects designs discussed in this chapter are experimental, is that controls to reduce sequencing effects are not possible in the single-group, pretest-posttest design. We cannot counterbalance the order of presentation because the pretest must always precede the treatment and the posttest must always follow the treatment. The pretest-posttest design requires a separate control group to control confounding. Remember, the experimental level of constraint is defined in terms of the adequacy of control over potential confounding.

Internal Summary: The Within-Subjects Design

The within-subjects design is a type of correlated-groups design in which each subject is tested under each condition of the experiment. They are called correlated-groups designs because the subjects in each group have some important correlation with subjects in every other group (for example, as in the within-subjects design, they may even be the same subjects). The major strengths of the within-subjects design are that it *equates* groups prior to the experimental manipulation and is therefore sensitive to small effects of the independent variable. That is, the single largest contributing factor to error variance—individual differences—has been eliminated. The greater sensitivity of the within-subjects design leads many to prefer it to between-subjects designs. Its major disadvantage is that potentially confounding sequencing effects are likely. Sequencing effects must be controlled by varying the order of presentation of the conditions to the subjects.

Matched-Subjects Design

Matched-subjects designs have many of the strengths of within-subjects designs as well as some advantages of their own. Instead of using each subject as his or her own control by testing each subject under all conditions, the matched-subjects design uses different subjects in each condition but closely matches subjects before they are assigned to conditions. This process of matching before assignment to conditions is referred to as *matched random assignment* (see Chapter 9).

The characteristics of matched-subjects designs are:

1. Each subject is exposed to only one level of the independent variable.
2. Each subject has a matched subject in each of the other conditions so that the groups are correlated.
3. Only one measurement per subject on the dependent variable is used in analyzing the results, but the analysis also takes into account which subjects were matched with which other subjects.
4. The critical comparison is the difference between the correlated groups (i.e., where the correlation is created by the matching procedure).

Using Matched-Subjects Design   Matched-subjects designs are used when the researcher wants to take advantage of the greater sensitivity of within-subjects designs but cannot or prefers not to use a simple within-subjects design. Matched-subjects designs are most often used when exposure to one condition causes permanent or at least long-term changes in the subject, making it impossible for the subject to appear in the other conditions. For example, when surgical procedures are used in physiological studies, the procedures permanently alter the animal, making it impossible to use the animal in another condition that requires nonaltered subjects. When subjects learn a content area or behavior under one condition in a learning study, they are no longer suitable subjects for testing under other conditions. For example, suppose the Air Force wanted to compare two methods of teaching map reading to its navigation students. If one group of subjects were successfully taught map reading using method A, then those subjects could not be used for testing the effectiveness of method B. A separate group of subjects would have to be trained using method B, and then the two groups would be compared. These are examples of extreme forms of carry-over effects. It is best to avoid within-subjects designs if any large carry-over effects are anticipated and to consider instead a matched-subjects design.

There are other situations where a researcher might avoid a within-subjects de-sign. One situation is when the demands on subjects' time in each condition is ex-cessive so that it is unreasonable to ask subjects to be tested under all conditions. Researchers may also choose to avoid a within-subjects design if they are con-cerned that subjects who are tested under all conditions might discern the hypothe-sis of the study and thus influence the results through expectancy effects and/or de-mand characteristics (see Chapter 8).

Within-subjects designs can present problems for the researcher in certain situ-ations. To avoid them we can choose an independent-groups design and randomly assign subjects to each of the various experimental conditions. However, an inde-pendent-groups design relies on chance to equate the groups and, therefore, is not as sensitive to small effects of the independent variable as is a correlated-groups design. Statistical tests must take into account the possibility that independent groups of subjects may not be equal on the dependent measure before the study begins. Matched-subjects designs provide a solution to this problem; they make it more likely that the groups are equivalent at the beginning of the study by explicitly matching on the relevant variables.

How do we match subjects for a matched-subjects design? We want to match subjects on relevant variables, but what does that mean? Which variables are rele-vant? In the within-subjects design, these questions are irrelevant because each subject serves as his or her own control. Subjects in the various conditions are matched on all variables, whether relevant or not, because they are the same sub-jects. To obtain the same degree of control over all extraneous variables in a matched-subjects design, we would probably have to use only identical twins, and even then we would probably still not have perfectly matched groups. (Using only identical twins would also significantly reduce the pool of available subjects.) How-ever, many factors that differentiate one person from another may be irrelevant for a particular study. For example, eye color may be a relevant variable if we are studying ways of increasing attractiveness but is probably irrelevant if we are studying visual acuity. *A variable is relevant if it can have an effect on the dependent variable in a study.* Subjects' eye color may influence the ratings of their attractiveness but should not influence their level of visual acuity. The more powerful the effect of a variable on the dependent variable, the more important it is to match subjects on that variable to assure comparable groups of subjects. To use a matched-subjects design effec-tively, we must identify the relevant variables and match the groups subject-for-sub-ject on those variables.

The procedure for matching subjects on a given variable and assigning them to groups is described in Chapter 9 (see *matched random assignment*). In that exam-ple, we matched subjects on age. First we ordered subjects by age. Then we divided subjects into pairs by selecting the two oldest, then the next two oldest, and so on. Finally, we randomly assigned one member of each pair to one of the two available groups and automatically assigned his or her partner to the opposite group. The re-sult is two groups of subjects matched on the variable of age. It is legitimate during the pairing process to exclude subjects for whom a close age-mate is not available. One subject may be older than the rest of the children, with no other subjects of a comparable age. This subject would not be paired with any other subject and so would not be assigned to any condition. We could have extended this process to three or more conditions by matching in sets of three or more subjects. We would then randomly assign one member from the matched set to the first condition, randomly assign one of the remaining members to the second condition, and so on until there is only one member left in the matched set and only one condition left to which to assign that person. Of course, as we increase the number of experimental conditions to which we want to assign matched subjects, we also increase the likelihood that subjects will have to be excluded because we are unable to find enough close matches for them.

Extending the matching procedure to matching on more than one variable is even more complicated than extending it to matching more than two groups. For instance, matching on age and sex of the subject is relatively simple because one of the matching variables (sex) has only two levels. We could pair subjects just as we did before on age, except that we would pair the male children only with other male children and the female children only with other female children. That way, subjects in each pair will be similar to each other on both matching variables (i.e., they will be the same sex and approximately the same age). We might lose a few more subjects than before from the potential sample because appropriate matches could not be found, but the loss should not be too great.

However, if we match on two variables where both variables are continuous, matching can become tedious and subject loss can be large because an appropriate match for any given subject may be hard to find. For example, if we match on age and IQ, we would first want to order all of the subjects on one of the variables (e.g., age). We would then divide the subjects into small subgroups defined by having all of the subjects in each group within a narrow age range. Then within each of these subgroups we would order on the second variable—in this case, IQ. Within each group we would pair as many subjects as possible using as the criteria that each member of the pair must have similar IQs. We would probably find several people in each age group with no close match on IQ, and these people would have to be excluded from the potential sample. If the study required three conditions, we would have to match in triplets, which would make it even more likely that subjects would be excluded because appropriate matches could not be found. A general rule of thumb is that matching on more than one continuous variable is difficult to accomplish and will usually result in significant subject loss. If matching is used as a research strategy, it is best to match on only one or two of the most important and significant variables. Again, *important variables to match on are variables that are strongly related to performance on the dependent measure(s).* If age makes little difference in how well subjects perform on the dependent measure, it makes little sense to match subjects on age. Because age does not affect the dependent measure, it cannot confound the results. If we have several variables that could have strong effects on the dependent measure, matching on all of them simultaneously is usually not a workable solution. Instead, we should match on those variables that show the greatest natural variability (variance) in the population from which we are sampling. Characteristics that are more variable in the population are more likely to show large mean differences by chance in randomly selected groups if an explicit matching procedure is not employed. Therefore, they should be given the highest priority when deciding on which variables to match in a matched-subjects design. For example, with college students as subjects, age is probably not an important variable on which to match because there is little variability in age among college students and a difference of one or two years make little difference in students' behavior. However, when doing research with young children, age can be an extremely important variable. An age difference in children of even a few months can have major effects on their behavior. Therefore, matching on age may be an important control in many research studies with children.

Although it can be difficult to identify the critical variables on which to match, in many cases the needed information is already available in published studies by other investigators. These studies often report observed correlations of many potential confounding variables with their dependent measures. If we are using similar dependent measures, these correlations will help us decide on which variables to match in our study. Therefore, you should familiarize yourself with past research and with the population you are studying in order to make good design decisions. This is true regardless of the design being contemplated, but is particularly true in matched-subjects designs. However, even with the information from past research, we might not always be able to identify important confounding variables for matching. Therefore, it is necessary even in a matched-subjects design to assign each subject randomly in a matched set to one of the conditions. Random assignment within sets can control for unidentified confounding variables.

Analyzing Matched-Subjects Design   Designing a matched-subjects study can be complicated, but analyzing data from the design is no more complicated than analyzing data from a simple within-subjects design. The key is to maintain the ordering of data, from the matching of subjects at the beginning of the study through the analysis of data at the end. In the within-subjects design, the scores from each condition for a given subject are put on the same line, as shown in Table 11.2 and Figure 11.1. In the matched-subjects design, the scores on a given line represent the scores of different subjects tested under different conditions, but all the subjects in a given line are specifically matched with the other subjects on that line prior to the beginning of the study.

Once we have organized the data, we analyze them as if all the scores on a given line came from the same subject instead of from matched subjects. The same statistical procedures used in within-subjects designs are used for matched-subjects designs. The repeated-measures ANOVA is used to determine whether the observed mean differences between groups is large enough to assert that real differences exist in the populations (i.e., are the differences statistically significant?). If subjects are carefully matched on relevant variable(s), then their scores on the dependent measures in each condition should be correlated with one another. This design would have the same high statistical power to detect small differences between conditions as the within-subjects design but without some of the problems of the latter (such as carry-over or practice effects).

Strengths and Weaknesses of Matched-Subjects Design   The matched-subjects design has similar strengths to the within-subjects design but different weaknesses. Both designs have greater sensitivity to small differences between conditions than do between-subjects designs. While between-subjects designs rely on chance to equate groups, correlated-groups designs use selection and assignment procedures that almost guarantee that groups are equivalent. If we can be sure the groups are equivalent before the study begins, the groups do not have to show large differences after the manipulation for us to be convinced that treatment conditions and not chance differences account for the observed data.

Because matched- and within-subjects designs have greater sensitivity, we can use a smaller number of subjects and still be confident in our ability to detect population differences if differences exist. For example, for three conditions with 10 subjects in each condition, a between-subjects design will require 30 subjects. However, because of the greater sensitivity of the matched-subjects design, we may need only 8 matched subjects in each condition to test the null hypothesis with the same confidence that we would have using 10 subjects in each condition in the between-subjects design. This is a direct consequence of the increased *statistical power* or sensitivity of the designs. We can safely reduce the sample size because the design provides a balancing increase in sensitivity.

An advantage of the matched-subjects design over the within-subjects design is that there are no problems of practice and carry-over effects. Therefore, control procedures like counterbalancing are not needed. But there are disadvantages to the matched-subjects design. One disadvantage is that it requires extra work. We must decide on what variable(s) to match and must obtain measures of these variables from all potential subjects. The matching process is tedious, especially if we match on more than one variable simultaneously. Finally, the requirement of matching subjects in sets can eliminate many potential subjects because suitable matches cannot be found for them. We may need to pretest a large sample of subjects on the matching variables to obtain a modest sample of matched subjects. It may be more efficient to use large sample sizes in a between-subjects design.

Internal Summary: Matched-Subjects Design

Matched-subjects designs have many of the advantages of within-subjects designs while avoiding the problems of sequencing effects. In the simplest situation (two conditions), subjects are matched in pairs on one or more relevant variables. Then one member of the pair is randomly assigned to one condition and the other is automatically assigned to the other condition—a process known as matched random assignment. In a situation with three conditions, subjects are matched in triplets and each member of the triplet is randomly assigned to one of three conditions. The matched-subjects design is used when increased sensitivity is needed and when a within-subjects design is inappropriate.

SINGLE-SUBJECT DESIGNS

Single-subject designs are extensions of within-subjects designs. The same subject appears in all conditions, and as its name suggests, there is only one subject in the study. These designs are usually variations on time-series designs, where repeated measurements are taken over time and various manipulations are performed at different points. Single-subject designs have become highly developed and represent alternatives to some of the more traditional designs. They are especially useful in the evaluation of treatment effects and are used often in research on behavior modification. Time-series and single-subject designs are discussed in Chapter 13.

SUMMARY

Correlated-groups designs include both within-subjects design and matched-subjects design. In within-subjects designs, there is a correlation between the conditions because the same subjects appear in all conditions. In matched-subject designs, the correlation between conditions is created by carefully matching subjects on one or more relevant variables. Regardless of the method used, the result is the same—greater confidence in the comparability of groups before the start of the study. The correlation increases sensitivity when testing for differences between conditions.

Correlated-groups designs raise new issues not found in other designs. For example, in within-subjects designs, each subject is exposed to all conditions. This raises the possibility that the exposure to one or more of the conditions may affect the performance of the subject in later conditions (sequencing effects). Matching subjects and assigning one member of each matched set of subjects to each condition eliminates these problems but raises new issues. The most important issue in matched-subjects designs is the selection of the variable(s) on which subjects will be matched. Even when that question is answered, the actual matching of subjects can be a difficult and tedious task. Still, both within- and matched-subjects designs are used frequently in research and provide a powerful way to answer causal questions.

REVIEW EXERCISES

11.1   **Define the following key terms. Be sure you understand them. They are discussed in the chapter and defined in the glossary.**

correlated-groups design	carry-over effects
repeated-measures design	random order of presentation
within-subjects design	Latin square design
sequencing effects	matched-subjects design
counterbalancing	matched random assignment
repeated-measures ANOVA	statistical power
practice effects	single-subject design

11.2   **Answer the following. Check your answers in the chapter.**

1. What is meant by "independent-groups designs"?
2. Controversy exists over whether correlated-groups designs are true experiments. What are the arguments on this issue?
3. Under what conditions are correlated-groups designs used?

4. As the teaching assistant in this course, you have to explain the particular strength of correlated-groups designs. Explain it carefully so your students thoroughly understand it.

5. What is the essential feature of correlated-groups designs that distinguishes them from independent-groups designs?

6. What are the two major types of correlated-groups design? What are the characteristics of each?

7. What does it mean when we say that "within-subjects designs are experiments that are run on a single group of subjects"? How can this statement be reconciled with the requirement that in true experiments the independent variable must be presented at more than one level? Explain.

8. Here is a review of material from earlier chapters.
   a. What are the different kinds of samples used in research?
   b. Distinguish between internal and external validity.

9. Can ANOVA be used to test a null hypothesis in a within-subjects design? If not, why not? If so, are there any special steps that must be taken?

10. What are the major advantages of within-subjects designs over between-subjects designs? Explain how these advantages occur.

11. Explain this statement: "Once we complete an ANOVA and find a significant difference between groups, we still have more analyses to carry out."

12. What are the major disadvantages of within-subjects designs and how are they controlled?

11.3   Think about and work the following problems.

1. As a review of earlier material, you have 50 subjects to assign to two groups of 25 subjects each. Each subject is numbered (1–50). Using the table of random numbers, randomly assign the subjects to the two conditions.

2. Now assume you have 50 more subjects to assign to two groups but the 50 subjects are matched in pairs on IQ. Designate the first pair as subjects A_1 and A_2, the second pair as B_1 and B_2, and so on. Use the table of random numbers to assign the pairs to the two groups.

3. In counterbalancing, how many possible orders of presentation are there in an experiment with three conditions? With five conditions? With six conditions? Is counterbalancing the order of presentation feasible with a large number of conditions in an experiment?

4. What is meant by the phrase "match only on relevant variables"?

5. What is a major advantage of matched-subjects designs over within-subjects designs?

Chapter 12

Control of Variance Through Experimental Design:

Factorial Designs

The designs discussed in Chapters 10–11 have only one independent variable. However, we often design research to include two or more independent variables in the same experiment. These are called factorial designs. *Factorial designs* allow us to study both individual and interactive effects of the independent variables on the dependent variable.

FACTORIAL DESIGNS

Suppose we are working with children afraid of the dark and we wish to develop an effective treatment program. Through interviewing the children and their parents we determine that their fear reactions vary considerably from one night to another. On some nights the children do not seem afraid and go to sleep with no difficulty. But on most nights they are fearful and have difficulty sleeping. Thus it appears that, although the children's fears are related to darkness, other variables may also be operating. In further interviews we find that many of the children report vivid and frightening images of monsters, ghosts, vampires, burglars, and so on when they are put to bed and left alone in the dark. Can it be that darkness is a necessary but not sufficient condition for the fear reaction? Might the children's fears be triggered by a combination of being in the dark and having fearful images? That is, darkness alone or fearful images alone may not be sufficient to trigger the severe fear reactions, but the two in combination do trigger fear.

The question about the two variables having effects when they are in combination is a question about their *interaction.* As psychological research has become more sophisticated, we have realized that behavior is rarely determined by a single variable; instead, behavior is usually determined by several factors operating together in interaction. An interactive effect between two variables is an effect that is greater than summing the effects of the two variables; a true interaction is not simply additive—it is an enhancement.

In our hypothetical fear-of-the-dark research, a factorial design can be used to test two independent variables (illumination and frightening images) and their interaction. The independent variables in a factorial design are called *factors.* In this experiment, the dependent variable—the children's fear—can be measured by pulse rate, which has been shown in previous research to reflect fear arousal. Measured electronically, pulse rate can be taken under two conditions of illumination (lighted condition and dark condition) and two conditions of visual images (fear images and neutral images). That is, factor *A* (illumination) is presented at two levels (lighted and dark), and factor *B* (images) is presented at two levels (fear images and neutral images). The two independent variables (factors), each presented at two levels, will produce four treatment combinations called a *matrix of cells.* The result is a 2 × 2 (read "two-by-two") factorial design, as shown in Table 12.1.

The *design notation* for a factorial design (e.g., 2 × 2, 2 × 3, 3 × 3 × 2) shows how many independent variables and how many levels of each variable are in-

TABLE 12.1   A 2 × 2 FACTORIAL

	Factor A (Illumination)	
	Level A_1 (lighted condition)	Level A_2 (dark condition)
Factor B (images)		
Level B_1 (feared)	A_1B_1	A_2B_1
Level B_2 (neutral)	A_1B_2	A_2B_2

cluded. Each number in the notation represents one independent variable and denotes the number of levels for that variable. Thus, the notation 3 × 3 tells us that the design has two independent variables with three levels of each variable; a 2 × 3 × 2 notation tells us that the design has three independent variables with two levels of factor A, three levels of factor B, and two levels of factor C. As we make the designs more complex, more cells are produced and more subjects are required. Further, as factorial designs become more complex through the addition of independent variables, their results become increasingly difficult to interpret. Thus, although any number of factors and levels can be combined in factorial designs, there are practical limits to the complexity of the designs. They can become too unwieldy and too difficult to carry out and interpret, thus not serving the major purpose of providing clear answers to research questions. Table 12.2 diagrams several factorial designs.

Main Effects and Interactions

Factorial designs are used to test hypotheses involving more than one independent variable. We test two different kinds of hypotheses in a factorial design. We test the impact of each independent variable on the dependent variable (termed *main effects*) as well as the effect of any combination of two or more independent variables on the dependent variable (termed *interactions*).

Factorial designs, like single-variable designs, can be set up as independent- or correlated-groups designs. We will consider first the independent-groups, between-subjects factorial designs in which a different group of subjects is assigned to each of the conditions defined by the four cells. Each of these independent groups includes the scores of individual subjects on the dependent variable, and a mean of the scores is calculated for each group. Table 12.3 shows the 2 × 2 matrix for our hypothetical children's dark-fears study and includes a mean pulse rate for the group of subjects in each cell and the row and column means for each variable. Notice that the matrix is, in a sense, two separate studies that are combined. Figure 12.1(a) shows that the column means (factor A) can be compared, just as if one were the experimental and the other the control group in a completely randomized, single-variable design. For the dark-fears study, this comparison can answer the question "Is there a significant difference in fear reactions as measured by pulse rate between the darkness and the lighted conditions?" That is, are pulse rates different for

TABLE 12.2   EXAMPLES OF FACTORIAL DESIGNS

(a) 2 × 2 Design with Two Factors and Two Levels of Each Factor

	Factor A	
	A_1	A_2
Factor B		
B_1	A_1B_1	A_2B_1
B_2	A_1B_2	A_2B_2

(b) 3 × 2 Design with Two Factors; Three Levels of A, Two Levels of B

	Factor A		
	A_1	A_2	A_3
Factor B			
B_1	A_1B_1	A_2B_1	A_3B_1
B_2	A_1B_2	A_2B_2	A_3B_2

(c) 3 × 3 Design with Two Factors and Three Levels of Each Factor

	Factor A		
	A_1	A_2	A_3
Factor B			
B_1	A_1B_1	A_2B_1	A_3B_1
B_2	A_1B_2	A_2B_2	A_3B_2
B_3	A_1B_3	A_2B_3	A_3B_3

(d) 2 × 3 × 2 Design with Three Factors and Two Levels of A, Three Levels of B, and Two Levels of C

	Factor C			
	C_1		C_2	
	Factor A		Factor A	
	A_1	A_2	A_1	A_2
Factor B				
B_1	$A_1B_1C_1$	$A_2B_1C_1$	$A_1B_1C_2$	$A_2B_1C_2$
B_2	$A_1B_2C_1$	$A_2B_2C_1$	$A_1B_2C_2$	$A_2B_2C_2$
B_3	$A_1B_3C_1$	$A_2B_3C_1$	$A_1B_3C_2$	$A_2B_3C_2$

children tested under darkness conditions than for children tested under lighted conditions? This much of the matrix looks like a between-subjects, completely randomized, two-group comparison in which a single variable—in this case illumination—is manipulated.

TABLE 12.3 A 2 × 2 FACTORIAL DESIGN SHOWING CELL MEANS OF PULSE
RATES UNDER LIGHTED AND DARKNESS CONDITIONS (*A*) AND
FEAR AND NEUTRAL CONDITIONS (*B*)

Factor *B* (images)	Factor *A* (Illumination)		Row Mean
	Level A_1 (lighted)	Level A_2 (dark)	
Level B_1 (feared)	A_1B_1	A_2B_1	
	(98.3)	(114.1)	106.2
Level B_2 (neutral)	A_1B_2	A_2B_2	
	(98.1)	(99.9)	99.0
Column Mean	98.2	107.0	

In the same way, if we compare only the two levels of factor *B* (images), as shown in Figure 12.1(b), we see again a comparison of two independent groups. The question answered here is whether there is a significant difference in pulse rates between subjects in the fear-image condition and those in the neutral-image condition. Again, this much of the matrix is like a between-subjects, two-group comparison.

The comparisons illustrated in Figure 12.1(a) and Figure 12.1(b) are the tests of the *main effects* of the independent variables on the dependent variable. In the dark-fears study, we can test whether pulse rates differ under lighted and dark conditions (main effect of illumination) and whether they differ under fearful and neutral images (main effect of fear imagery). The factorial design is efficient in that it allows us to carrying out two studies in one. The questions about main effects could be answered by conducting two separate, single-variable studies. However, in order to answer a question about an interaction, the two variables must be combined in a single study. When we combine the two separate designs by crossing them, as shown in Figure 12.1(c), the original 2 × 2 matrix is formed with four cells within which are the data for testing interactions. This allows us to investigate not about main effects but also to address the more complex question "Are the effects of one variable different depending on the level of the other variable?" This question about the interaction is the major one posed in our hypothetical dark-fears study. In fact, in most factorial studies the primary focus is on the interaction.

Conducting the factorial experiment is similar to, but more complex than, conducting single-variable designs. The 2 × 2 factorial, because it is essentially two designs combined into a single study, contains more than one null hypothesis. A single-variable experimental design has only one null hypothesis for each dependent measure (i.e., there are no differences on the dependent measure between the levels of the independent variable). But in a 2 × 2 factorial there are three null hypotheses for each dependent measure: (1) there is no difference between the levels of factor *A* (no main effect for factor *A*); (2) there is no difference between the levels of factor *B* (no main effect for factor *B*); and (3) there is no significant interaction of factors *A* and *B*. With more complex factorial designs in which there are more than two factors, there will be more null hypotheses to test. In factorial designs, the null hypotheses are usually tested with an analysis of variance (as we will see later in the chapter).

Figure 12.1   A Factorial Design as a Combination of Two Separate Studies

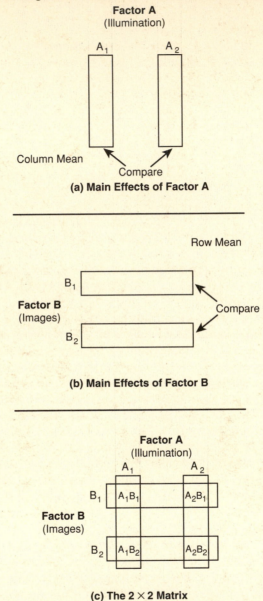

Factor A
(Illumination)

A_1 A_2

Column Mean

Compare

(a) Main Effects of Factor A

Row Mean

B_1

Factor B
(Images)

Compare

B_2

(b) Main Effects of Factor B

Factor A
(Illumination)

A_1 A_2

B_1 A_1B_1 A_2B_1

Factor B
(Images)

B_2 A_1B_2 A_2B_2

(c) The 2 × 2 Matrix

Because of the increased complexity of factorial designs, the potential threats to internal validity are more complex than in single-variable designs. Suppose that there are no significant main effects or interactions. We must conclude that the data fail to support the research hypotheses and thus fail to support the original idea that there is a causal relationship between the independent variables and the dependent variable. Although we cannot proceed further in interpreting the results in terms of the research hypotheses, it can be helpful to examine the procedures to detect possible errors that might help to account for the lack of support of the hypothesis and help to improve the design of the next study. If, on the other hand, one or more of the null hypotheses is rejected—if there are main effects and/or interactions—we must proceed to check for possible confounding so as to rule out alternative explanations of the findings. If satisfied that confounding variables are adequately anticipated and controlled, we can conclude that the data support the hypothesis that there is at least one causal relationship involving the independent and dependent variables.

The hypothesis-testing procedure in factorial designs is similar to the procedure used in single-variable designs. The reasoning is exactly the same. The major difference is that, because there are more independent variables in the factorial design, there are several null hypotheses to test rather than only one, and therefore there is more chance for confounding to occur. Further, the interpretation of interactions is more complex than the interpretation of differences in a simple, single-variable study (as you will see later in the chapter).

Possible Outcomes of Factorial Designs

There are many possible outcomes of a factorial design. There may be main effects for one or more factors but no interaction; there may be interactions but no main effects; there may be both interactions and main effects; there may be neither main effects nor interactions. Figure 12.2 illustrates several 2 × 2 and 2 × 3 factorial designs. The mean score for each cell is shown, and the combined means (*row means* and *column means*) for each level of each factor are also indicated. The means are simplified to show basic, general outcomes. For purposes of this discussion, we will assume that (1) the observed differences are sufficiently large to be statistically significant and (2) there are an equal number of subjects in each cell, which simplifies the computation of row and column means. For each matrix, the same information is shown in graphic form. Figure 12.2 shows a number of possible outcomes and their characteristic graphs.

In Figure 12.2(a), a 3 × 2 factorial design is shown using both a 3 × 2 matrix and a graph illustrating the same results. In this example, there are no significant main effects and no significant interaction. Around the margins of the 3 × 2 table are the means for each level of each variable (i.e., for level A_1, A_2, A_3, and level B_1 and B_2). Within each of the six cells is the mean score for the specific group in that condition (A_1B_1, A_1B_2, A_2B_1, A_2B_2, A_3B_1, A_3B_2). In this hypothetical experiment, the means are all equal and there are obviously no significant differences anywhere in the matrix. Thus, there are no significant main effects for factors A or B and no significant interactions. On the graph, the levels of variable A (A_1, A_2, A_3) are shown on the abscissa (the horizontal or x-axis) and the values of the dependent variable with a range sufficient to encompass the cell means are shown on the ordinate (the vertical or y-axis). Means for cells A_1B_1, A_2B_1, and A_3B_1 are all located on the graph at the value 50 and are identified on the graph with small circles. The points are connected to show graphically the overall effect of A on the dependent measure at the B_1 level of B, and that line is labeled B_1. Clearly there is no effect of A on the dependent measure at level B_1 because all values are the same (i.e., 50). The effects of A at level B_2 are plotted in the same way. In this case, they fall on the same points along the same line, all at the value 50. They are marked with stars to

Figure 12.2   Several Possible Outcomes of Factorial Designs

	A_1	A_2	A_3	Mean
B_1	50	50	50	50
B_2	50	50	50	50
Mean	50	50	50	

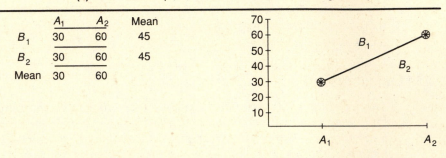

(a) 3 x 2 Factorial (A, B, and the interaction are not significant)

	A_1	A_2	Mean
B_1	30	60	45
B_2	30	60	45
Mean	30	60	

(b) 2 x 2 Factorial (A is significant; B and the interaction are not significant)

	A_1	A_2	Mean
B_1	70	70	70
B_2	40	40	40
Mean	55	55	

(c) 2 x 2 Factorial (B is significant; A and the interaction are not significant)

	A_1	A_2	A_3	Mean
B_1	10	30	80	40
B_2	30	50	100	60
Mean	20	40	90	

(d) 3 x 2 Factorial (A and B are significant; the interaction is not significant)

Figure 12.2 *Continued*

	A_1	A_2	A_3	Mean
B_1	40	50	60	50
B_2	60	50	40	50
Mean	50	50	50	

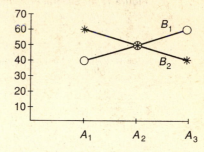

(e) 3 x 2 Factorial (the interaction is significant: *A* and *B* are not significant)

	A_1	A_2	A_3	Mean
B_1	30	40	50	40
B_2	40	40	40	40
Mean	35	40	45	

(f) 3 x 2 Factorial (*A* and the interaction are significant; *B* is not significant)

	A_1	A_2	A_3	Mean
B_1	30	40	50	40
B_2	70	60	50	60
Mean	50	50	50	

(g) 3 x 2 Factorial (*B* and the interaction are significant; *A* is not significant)

	A_1	A_2	Mean
B_1	40	40	40
B_2	40	60	50
Mean	40	50	

(h) 2 x 2 Factorial (*A*, *B*, and the interaction are significant) locate the B_2 level of B. Again, there is no effect of A at the B_2 level. By inspecting either the table or the graph, we can see that there are no main effects and no interaction.

Figure 12.2(b) illustrates a 2×2 factorial in which there is a significant main effect for factor A, no significant main effect for factor B, and no interaction. As shown on the graph, the B_1 and B_2 lines are the same line and, thus, B has had no effect. But the mean of A_2 is considerably greater than the mean of A_1, illustrating an effect for factor A. The 2×2 matrix shows the same results with the mean for levels B_1 and B_2 equal (at 45), whereas means for levels A_1 and A_2 are different (30 and 60). The interaction is most easily seen in the graph of the cell means. When there is an interaction, the lines are clearly not parallel. In this example, both lines show the same upward swing from left to right, so there is no interaction effect. Thus, there is a main effect for A, no main effect for B, and no interaction.

Figure 12.2(c) illustrates a 2×2 factorial design in which there is a main effect for factor B, no main effect for factor A, and no interaction. The means for levels A_1 and A_2 are the same, whereas the means for levels B_1 and B_2 are different. In the graph, the B_1 and B_2 lines are separated, showing that there is a difference between the levels. Because the lines are parallel, there is no interaction between A and B.

Figure 12.2(d) shows a 3×2 factorial in which there is a main effect for both factor A and factor B but no interaction. The means are different at each of the three levels of factor A and each of the two levels of factor B. As in Figure 12.2(c), the parallel lines indicate that there is no interaction.

A 3×2 factorial showing a significant $A \times B$ interaction but no significant main effects is illustrated in Figure 12.2(e). Note that the column means for the three levels of factor A are the same, thus indicating there is no main effect for factor A. The same is true for factor B, where the means at levels B_1 and B_2 are the same. Thus, there is no significant main effect for A or B. But when plotted on the graph, the two lines cross, giving an immediate clue that there may be a significant $A \times B$ interaction. Indeed, one of the values of drawing a graph is that interactions become readily apparent. Note in the graph of Figure 12.2(e) that the slope of line B_1 is from 40 to 50 to 60. Line B_2 changes in the opposite direction, decreasing from 60 to 50 to 40. Thus A, when paired with B_1, has a different effect on the dependent measure than when paired with B_2. The effects of A on the dependent variable are clearly influenced by the level of B. This is a classic interaction, where the effect of one variable is systematically influenced by the effect of a second variable.

Note also that the column means and row means in Figure 12.2(a) and Figure 12.2(e) are identical. However, in Figure 12.2(a) the pattern of means within the cells indicates no interaction, whereas the pattern of means in Figure 12.2(e) does indicate an interaction. This illustrates that the column and row means give us an indication only of main effects, and we must inspect the individual cells to see any pattern of interaction. Figure 12.2(f) shows a main effect for A and an $A \times B$ interaction. When both a main effect and an interaction occur, it is important to interpret the interaction first (the reasons for this are discussed in the next section). The remaining examples can be read in similar fashion. We also have included a number of exercises at the end of this chapter to provide additional practice with these difficult, but important, concepts and procedures.

An Example: Children's Dark-Fears Study

To illustrate a factorial design, let us return to our hypothetical children's dark-fears study, which used a 2×2 factorial design. Suppose that the subjects for this experiment include 40 children—20 boys and 20 girls—all afraid of the dark and drawn from an available population. Subjects are randomly assigned to the four conditions of the 2×2 matrix (10 children per condition). Random assignment helps to ensure the equivalence of the four conditions at the outset of the study.

There are two independent variables. Variable A (illumination) is presented at two levels—a lighted and a darkened condition. Variable *B* (images) is presented at two levels—fear images and neutral images. The dependent variable is the children's fear as measured by their pulse rates. The research hypotheses being tested are that there will be a main effect for factor *A,* a main effect for factor *B,* and a significant $A \times B$ interaction. That is, we predict that there will be higher pulse rates under dark conditions than under lighted conditions, higher pulse rates under the fear-images condition than under the neutral-images condition, and the greatest effects on pulse rates will occur when the two factors interact (i.e., under combined darkness and fear-images conditions).

Subjects are tested individually while seated comfortably facing a projection screen. A small sensor is placed on a finger to monitor pulse rate. Subjects are told they will be shown ten slides and will be asked questions about them later. Each slide is shown for 15 seconds with a 5-second pause between slides. Cell A_1B_1 represents the lighted-plus-fear-images condition. The lights are kept on in the room and the fear-image slides are presented (e.g., ghostly images, commonly feared animals such as snakes, a burglar entering a house, and so on). All 10 subjects in condition A_1B_1 are presented the fear images, and their pulse rates are recorded at each presentation. Cell A_2B_1 represents the dark-plus-fear-images condition. The lights in the room are turned off, and all 10 subjects in that condition are individually presented the fear images. Each subject's pulse rate is recorded at each presentation. Cell A_1B_2 represents the neutral-images-lighted condition, and cell A_2B_2 represents the neutral-images-dark condition. The general procedures in these two conditions are the same as described above except that the slide images presented are neutral (i.e., nonfearful). Thus, we have scores (pulse rates) for 40 subjects—10 subjects in each of four different conditions in the 2×2 design.

Table 12.4 shows hypothetical data for the 10 subjects in each of the four conditions of our study. Note the mean score, shown in parentheses for each condition, and the column and row means for each of the levels (A_1, A_2, B_1, B_2). Thus, the row mean, 106.2, is the mean for fear images; the row mean, 99.0, is the mean for neutral images; 98.2 and 107.0 are the column means for light and dark conditions. Further, the scores in cell A_1B_1 are presumably affected by the particular combination of light and feared images. Cell A_2B_1 reflects the combined effects of darkness and fear

TABLE 12.4 HYPOTHETICAL PULSE RATES FOR 40 DARK-FEAR CHILDREN

Factor B (images)	Factor A (illumination)		Row Mean
	A_1 (lighted)	A_2 (dark)	
B₁ (feared)	112	131	
	106	125	
	102	121	
	101	116	
	99	113	
	99	112	
	97	111	
	95	110	
	92	103	
	80	99	
	(98.3)	(114.1)	106.2
B₂ (neutral)	115	119	
	110	112	
	105	107	
	103	102	
	100	95	
	98	95	
	97	95	
	90	92	
	83	91	
	80	90	
	(98.1)	(99.9)	99.0
Column Mean	98.2	107.0	

images. Cell A_1B_2 reflects the combined effects of light and neutral images. Finally, cell A_2B_2 reflects the combined influence of darkness and neutral images.

The experiment is a completely randomized, between-subjects, 2×2 factorial. To test for main effects, we have to compare the means of the two levels of each factor. As shown in Figure 12.3(a), the means of the two levels of A (98.2 and 107.0) are compared to determine whether there is a main effect for illumination. This is essentially comparing two independent groups in a completely randomized, between-subjects, single-variable study. To determine whether there is a main effect for B, we compare the means of the two independent groups—fear and neutral images (106.2 and 99.0)—as shown in Figure 12.3(b). To determine whether there is an interaction, we compare means of the four cells to see whether the effects of one independent variable on the dependent variable are different depending on the level of the other independent variable. The essential issue in interaction is whether the two factors, when they occur together, influence the dependent variable differently than when they occur separately. The interaction is most easily seen in a graph of the data, such as the graph in Figure 12.4.

Figure 12.3 Testing for Main Effects

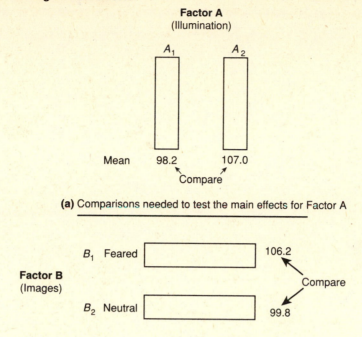

(a) Comparisons needed to test the main effects for Factor A

(b) Comparison needed to test the main effects for Factor B

The appropriate statistical test for factorial designs is an analysis of variance (ANOVA). However, before carrying out the ANOVA, it is helpful to graph the cell means, because it can be seen quickly whether an interaction might exist and whether the mean differences suggest the presence of main effects. We have graphed the data in Figure 12.4 using *SPSS for Windows.* Once the data have been entered and appropriate labels added to the data file, setting up the graph in Figure 12.4 takes less than a minute.

Let us examine the hypothetical results of our children's dark-fears study by inspecting the cell means and the row and column means in Table 12.4 and the graph in Figure 12.4. We can see that the subjects in the dark condition have a higher mean pulse rate (107.0) than the subjects in the lighted condition (98.2), suggesting that there may be a main effect for factor *A*—illumination. For factor *B*, the fear-images condition has a higher mean pulse rate (106.2) than the neutral-images condition (99.0), suggesting that there may be a significant main effect for factor *B*. Note that the two lines in Figure 12.4 are not parallel, alerting us to the possibility of an $A \times B$ interaction. The B_1 line slopes upward, moving from a mean of 98.3 to a mean of 114.1. The slope of that line appears to be due to the elevation of the A_2B_1 cell, where the dark condition and the fear images are combined. The mean of this cell is elevated when compared with the other three cells. Fear images produce high pulse rates but only in the presence of the dark condition. The B_2 line is nearly flat—that is, the amount of light has little effect when neutral images are used. This seems clearly

Figure 12.4 Graph of the Hypothetical Children's Dark-Fears Study

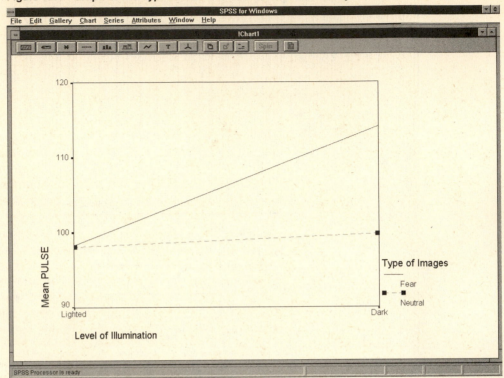

to be an interaction. Thus, we may have an $A \times B$ interaction, a main effect for *A,* and a main effect for *B.*

Inspecting the matrix and graph gives us only a suggestion of the results. The next step is to determine whether the differences we observed are large enough that they are unlikely to be only chance differences and instead reflect consistent differences in the response of the children in the different conditions. An analysis of variance is used to test for *statistically significant differences.* Before we can do this, however, another important point should be illustrated. Suppose that the statistical analysis does indicate an $A \times B$ interaction and a main effect for *A.* The important point here is that when we interpret the results of an analysis of variance in which we have found both an interaction and a main effect, *we always begin the interpretation with the interaction.* The reason for this becomes clear if we inspect the matrix and graph. Our hypothetical statistical analysis indicates a main effect for *A* (light versus dark condition). But by inspecting the matrix we can see that light or dark conditions have little effect (means = 98.1 versus 99.9) when the visual images presented are neutral. The effect seems to occur when the dark condition and fear stimuli are combined—that is, the main effect *actually seems to be due to the interaction* and can be best understood in terms of the interaction. We would have to interpret the findings as indicating that light and dark conditions by themselves do not seem to have an effect on fear, but the combination of darkness and fear images appears to have the effect of increasing the children's fear. To accept the finding of a main effect for *A* in our hypothetical study without interpreting it in terms of the interaction could lead us to an erroneous conclusion that the darkness itself causes increased fear. Again, *where we find both an interaction and a main effect, all effects must be interpreted in light of the interaction.*

Analysis of Variance in Factorial Designs

The appropriate statistical analysis for factorial designs is analysis of variance (ANOVA). The calculations for ANOVA are usually carried out by use of *computer-analysis programs,* such as the *Statistical Package for the Social Sciences (SPSS), Biomedical Programs (BMDP), Statistical Analysis System (SAS),* and *Minitab.* Many of these programs are available to run on your personal computer. Computer programs take the drudgery out of calculations, but the researcher still must understand experimental design, statistical principles and procedures, and how to use the computer to be able to set up and interpret the computer analysis. Knowledge of computer use is a virtual necessity for researchers, but that knowledge is not a substitute for understanding the principles of design and the concepts and procedures of statistical analysis. Remember our admonition in Chapter 1—a laboratory technician is not necessarily a scientist; it is not the technician's manipulation of laboratory equipment, including computers, that defines the science, but rather, the *process of systematic thinking* that guides the use of laboratory techniques.

Statistical computations for complex ANOVAs are beyond the scope of this text. In this section, our goal is an understanding of how to read an ANOVA summary table for a factorial design and how to interpret the results.

ANOVA Summary Table for Children's Dark-Fears Study   The results of an ANOVA are typically presented in an *ANOVA summary table.* Table 12.5 shows the results of an ANOVA carried out on our children's dark-fears data using *SPSS for Windows.*[1] The first column of the summary table lists the sources of variation—factors *A* (illumination), factor *B* (images), the *A* × *B* interaction, the within-groups variance (error variance), and the total variance. Each computer program will list these sources of variation somewhat differently, but it is not hard to tell what is what. In the *SPSS of Windows* output listed in Table 12.5, the factors are listed by name (up to eight characters) and the interaction is indicated by listing the independent variables involved (in this case, "IMAGETYP BY LIGHTLVL"). The error term is listed as "WITHIN + RESIDUAL."[2] The second column of the summary table lists the sum of squares (SS) that has been calculated for each source. Notice that the total sum of squares is, in fact, the total—the sum of all component sums of squares will equal the total sum of squares. In the third column, the degrees of freedom (df) associated with each source has been entered.

---

[1]We show how to set up both the data entry and the ANOVA analyses for this example in Appendix D.
[2]You can ignore the lines labeled "(model)," "R-squared," and "Adjusted R-squared" in this output. These are additional analyses, which can be helpful in interpreting the output, but are beyond the scope of this textbook.

TABLE 12.5 ANALYSIS OF VARIANCE SUMMARY TABLE FOR THE CHILDREN'S DARK-FEARS STUDY

```
**Analysis of Variance - design 1**

Tests of Significance for PULSE using UNIQUE sums of squares
Source of Variation      SS     DF    MS      F     Sig of F

WITHIN + RESIDUAL      3497.50  36   97.15
IMAGETYP                525.62   1  525.62   5.41    .026
LIGHTLVL                765.62   1  765.62   7.88    .008
IMAGETYP BY LIGHTLVL    497.02   1  497.02   5.12    .030

(Model)                1788.27   3  596.09   6.14    .002
(Total)                5285.78  39  135.53

R-Squared =    .338
Adjusted R-Squared =.283
```

Note that associated with the total variance there are 39 degrees of freedom (i.e., 1 less than the total number of subjects). The total degrees of freedom (39) are then apportioned to factors *A* and *B* [two levels of *A*, thus $df_a = (2 - 1) = 1$; two levels of *B*, thus $df_b = (2 - 1) = 1$; the degrees of freedom for the interaction ($A \times B$) is the product of the degrees of freedom for the main effects, thus $df_{a \times b} = df_a \times df_b = (2 - 1) \times (2 - 1) = 1$]. The remaining degrees of freedom (36) are associated with the within-groups or error variance and are calculated by taking the total number of subjects in the study and subtracting the number of cells. In the fourth column, each sum of squares has been divided by its associated degrees of freedom to yield the mean square (MS), which is the variance as it is calculated by the ANOVA procedure. In the fifth column, the mean square for each between-groups comparison has been divided by the within-groups mean square (the error term). This between-groups variance divided by the within-groups variance is the *F*-ratio. Thus, *F*-ratios for each factor and the interaction are calculated and recorded in the summary table. The probability of each *F*-ratio (*p*) is shown in column 6 of the summary table (listed as "Sig of F" in the *SPSS for Windows* output). If the *p*-value is less than the alpha level we set, we reject the null hypothesis and conclude there is an effect.

In our ANOVA, there is a significant interaction (*p* = .03 < alpha = .05). That is, fear as measured by pulse rate is highest when darkness and fear images are presented together. The summary table also shows significant main effects for both illumination level and image type, but they can be understood only in terms of the interaction. That is, as shown in the graph in Figure 12.4, under the neutral-images condition the light or dark condition does not make a difference; likewise, under lighted conditions, the fear images do not cause more fear than do the neutral images. The main effects are due to the interaction—to the condition A_2B_1, in which the fear images and darkness occur together. Remember, whenever a main effect *and* an interaction involving the significant factors occur, we interpret the interaction first and then interpret the main effects in light of the interaction. The main conclusion

Box 12.1 **Ethical Considerations in the Children's Dark-Fears Study**

In our hypothetical study of children who fear darkness, the children are exposed to the very conditions that may be frightening to them—darkness and fearful images. This immediately raises ethical concerns of placing the subjects at risk for potential harm.

What are the major concerns? First, the subjects are children. As such, they are presumed to be unable to understand all the implications of the procedure and, therefore, are unable to give their fully informed consent to participate. The standard ethical guidelines assume that children, by virtue of being under the age of consent, are automatically subjects at risk in any research. Therefore, steps must be taken by the researcher to reduce risks. One obvious safeguard is to obtain the informed consent of the children's parents, who presumably will be able to understand the situation and make an appropriate decision, thereby reducing the risks that result from using children as subjects.

Another issue is whether the children want to participate or whether they are being in some ways coerced by both the researcher and the parents. Thus, the ethical researcher will try to obtain the children's assent to participate by explaining the procedure to them and asking whether they want to take part. If a child says no or shows reluctance, the researcher must interpret that as a lack of assent. Further, in obtaining consent and assent the researcher should give a full account of the procedures, provide ample opportunity for questions, and answer all questions. Parents and children should also have the opportunity to ask more questions and to seek explanations after the conclusion of the experiment.

With parental informed consent and the child's assent included in the research procedure, the researcher must then consider other possible risks to the subject, such as undue anxiety and other psychological upset due to the procedures. For example, the children should be assured from the start that they may stop the procedure whenever they wish. Also, researchers and assistants should be sufficiently experienced with children to observe whether a child is becoming unduly upset so they can (1) soothe and reassure the child and/or (2) make a reasoned decision to discontinue the procedure for that child. Researchers must be as certain as possible that the procedures themselves are not unduly distressing and that only those procedures essential for the study are being used.

Finally, there is an ethical issue that bears directly on the adequacy of the experimental design itself: *it is the responsibility of the researcher to assure that the study is competently designed and carried out so that there can be a high degree of confidence in results and conclusions.* Why is this an ethical issue and not only a design issue? Because it is the researcher's responsibility to ensure that subjects' time, effort, expectations, and risk taking, however minimal, are given in an effort that will likely yield knowledge. The researcher must ensure that subjects do not make contributions to a research project that is poorly designed and from which little knowledge can be gained. Subjects' contributions must not be trivialized and wasted by an incompetent design.

Can you see other potential risks for the subjects in our experiment? If so, how would you reduce them?

that can be drawn from our hypothetical study is that neither fear images alone nor darkness alone appears to be sufficient to stimulate children's night fears, but the two together—darkness and fear images—is a sufficient condition for children's night fears (see Box 12.1).

Internal Summary: Factorial Designs

Factorial designs include two or more independent variables to test both their independent effects (main effects) and their interactive effects on dependent variables. They are more complex than single-variable designs, and they test at least three null hypotheses for each dependent measure (no main effect for factor *A;* no main effect for factor *B;* no *A* × *B* interaction). As the number of factors increases, so too does the number of null hypotheses to be tested. There are several possible outcomes in a factorial study (e.g., both main effects and an interaction; main effects but no interaction; interactions but no main effects; neither main effects nor interactions). Whenever you get both main effect(s) and an interaction, you should always interpret the main effect(s) in light of the interaction.

VARIATIONS OF BASIC FACTORIAL DESIGN

Among several important contemporary trends in psychological research, three are most important: the increased use of (1) factorial designs, (2) within-subjects designs, and (3) mixed designs.

The increased use of factorials has come about, not only because of their efficiency in testing several causal hypotheses in a single design, but also because by testing the effects on behavior of multiple variables in interaction factorials come closer than do single-variable designs to the multiply determined nature of behavior in natural environments.

The increased use of within-subjects designs reflects the growing recognition of their advantages over completely randomized designs. As discussed earlier, their major advantage is that they are generally more sensitive to the effects of the independent variable because they eliminate a major cause of error variance (individual differences between subjects). Within-subjects designs also require fewer subjects, which can be of enormous value when subjects are difficult to obtain or when considerable preparation per subject is required.

Mixed designs blend different types of factors into a single factorial study. This mixing can affect the statistical analyses and the restrictions placed on the interpretation of results. But mixing has its advantages as well. Many studies require the use of mixed designs to investigate the effects and interactions of most interest to the researcher.

Within-Subjects (Repeated-Measures) Factorial

We have already discussed randomized, between-subjects factorial designs in which subjects are randomly assigned to conditions. This basic factorial design was illustrated in the children's dark-fears study. With this design we meet the experimental requirements for unbiased subject assignment and can draw conclusions about causality with considerable confidence.

In factorial designs, as with single-variable designs, we may choose to employ a within-subjects design. This is called a *within-subjects* (or *repeated-measures*) *fac-*

torial. If we had employed it in the dark-fears factorial study, then each subject would have been measured under each of the four conditions. The ANOVA carried out to test for statistical significance is a *repeated-measures ANOVA,* which takes into account the correlated groups.

Recall from Chapter 11 that using a within-subjects design involves disadvantages that stem from the fact that each subject is exposed to each condition. This means that sequencing effects (practice and carry-over effects) are potential sources of confounding and must be controlled. Potential sequencing effects may be so strong that a within-subjects design is not appropriate. However, when not precluded by such strong potential sequencing effects, a within-subjects design has decided advantages over a between-subjects design. As with the single-variable design, use of a within-subjects design in a factorial experiment can (1) provide greater sensitivity to the effects of the independent variable by reducing the individual-differences component of the error term, (2) assure equivalence of groups at the start of the experiment because the subjects in each condition are identical, (3) require fewer subjects and (related to the third point) (4) be more efficient. In the dark-fears study, for example, if we want 10 subjects in each of the four conditions, then only 10 subjects in total are needed for a within-subjects design but 40 subjects are needed for a between-subjects design. This could be a major advantage when subjects are difficult to obtain or when considerable preparation is required for each subject. Many researchers prefer a within-subjects design over a between-subjects design because fewer subjects are required. This is true for both single-variable and factorial experiments.

Mixed Designs

When there is more than one factor, it is possible that the factors will be of different types. For example, one factor may be a within-subjects factor whereas the other may be a between-subjects factor. Subjects would respond to all levels of the within-subjects factor, but be randomly assigned to only one level of the between-subjects factor. This is a mixed design. Remember, each factor is like an individual study as we showed in Figure 12.1

The term *mixed design* is used in two different ways, which can lead to considerable confusion. In one meaning, mixed design refers to a factorial that includes a between-subjects factor and a within-subjects factor. In the other meaning, mixed design refers to a factorial that includes a manipulated factor and a nonmanipulated factor. It is important to distinguish between the two types of mixed designs.

Between-Subjects and Within-Subjects Factors   In this meaning of the term *mixed design,* where both *between-subjects factors* and *within-subjects factors* exist in the same study, the critical issue is a statistical one. For example, suppose a study has "level of distraction" as the within-subjects factor and the "amount of potential reward for success" as the between-subjects factor. Each subject would be assigned to one of the potential reward conditions (the between-subjects variable) and tested under all levels of distraction (the within-subjects variable). Of course, for

TABLE 12.6 SEVERAL EXAMPLES OF MIXED DESIGNS IN FACTORIAL
RESEARCH

(a) An Example of a One-Between, One-Within Factorial Design

		Level of distraction (within-subjects factor)		
		Low	Medium	High
Amount of reward (Between-subjects factor)	Small			
	Large			

(In this design, subjects are randomly assigned to either the small-reward or the large-reward condition and then are tested under all three levels of distraction.)

(b) An Example of a One-Manipulated Variable, One-Nonmanipulated Variable Mixed Design

		Level of crowding (between-subjects factor)		
		No Crowding	Slightly Crowded	Very Crowded
Sex of subject	Male			
	Female			

(In this design, male and female subjects are randomly assigned to one of the three levels of crowding. Both factors are between-subjects factors. Subjects are randomly assigned to the level of crowding [manipulated variable] and assigned to male or female based on their sex [nonmanipulated variable].)

(c) An Example of a Design That Is Mixed in Both a Statistical Sense (One-Between, One-Within) and in an Experimental Sense (One-Manipulated, One-Nonmanipulated)

		Type of words (within-subjects factor)	
		Neutral	Emotional
Diagnosis (Between-subjects factor)	Schizophrenic		
	Normal		

(In this design, diagnosis is a between-subjects factor whereas type of words is a within-subjects factor. This will affect the ANOVA formulas used. In addition, diagnosis is a nonmanipulated factor whereas the type of words is a manipulated factor. This will affect the confidence of our causal inference.)

---

the within-subjects factor, the order of presentation of conditions would be counterbalanced to control sequencing effects [see Table 12.6(a)].

The significance of the mixed design here is that the formulas used in the analysis of variance will differ depending on which factors are within-subjects factors and which are between-subjects factors. Recall that in analyzing within-subjects designs the statistical procedures must take into account the correlated nature of the data.

Computation of ANOVAs for mixed designs is beyond the scope of this text. In most cases, data from such designs are analyzed using statistical computer programs. It is critical to distinguish between-subjects and within-subjects factors to use the correct statistical procedure.

Manipulated and Nonmanipulated Factors   In this meaning of the term *mixed design,* where both *manipulated factors* and *nonmanipulated factors* are included, the essential issue is one of interpretation of results rather than statistical procedures. In a mixed design where one factor is a nonmanipulated variable and one factor is a manipulated variable, subjects are randomly assigned to conditions of the manipulated variable but are assigned to levels of the nonmanipulated independent variable based on their preexisting characteristics.

For example, if we are studying the effects of crowding on aggression, we might randomly assign subjects to one of three conditions: alone, slightly crowded, and crowded. We could observe the level of aggression of subjects in each of these conditions. The variable of crowding is a manipulated variable because the condition under which subjects are tested is actively manipulated by the researcher. Suppose we are also interested in sex differences in response to crowding. Here we are asking about an interaction between sex of subject and level of crowding on the dependent measure of aggression. Biological sex is the second factor—an organismic factor or subject variable that the researcher cannot manipulate. Instead, the researcher assigns subjects to the male or female group. The design shown in Table 12.6(b) is an example of the second type of mixed design—in which we are not concerned about whether factors are between-subjects or within-subjects but, rather, whether factors are manipulated or nonmanipulated.

The formulas for statistical analysis are not affected by whether the variables are manipulated or nonmanipulated as they are when we are dealing with between- and within-subjects factors. The importance of whether a factor is manipulated or nonmanipulated comes into play when we *interpret* the statistical analysis. Manipulated factors are experiments that effectively control confounding variables. We can therefore safely draw causal inferences based on analysis of the main effects of the variables. Research designs using nonmanipulated factors are *not* experiments. Instead, they represent differential research (see Chapter 7). Remember that in differential research, because subjects are not randomly assigned to groups, groups may differ on variables other than the independent variable. These potential differences may cause confounding; unless we can rule out all potential confounding, we cannot draw causal inferences with confidence. Therefore, interpreting the main effects of nonmanipulated factors must be done cautiously and with careful attention to likely confounding variables. In our example we cannot draw the inference that biological sex *caused* any observed differences in aggression. Random assignment of subjects in manipulated factors controls for such confounding and makes interpretation easier. If differences are found in the level of aggression shown at each level of crowding, we can confidently conclude that crowding causes changes in level of aggression. The same caution used in the interpretation of main effects for nonmanipulated factors should be used in the interpretation of any interaction involving a nonmanipulated factor. In our example, the interaction between biological sex and level of crowding on aggression should be interpreted as cautiously as the main effect of biological sex.

Finally, it is possible to have a mixed design that is mixed in both of the ways just described. Table 12.6(c) presents such a situation. In this example, we want to compare accuracy of recognition of neutral words compared with emotionally charged words in patients with schizophrenia and control subjects. We have arranged a factorial design in which both neutral and charged words are presented to the patients and controls for short intervals using a tachistoscope. Note that this is a factorial with one nonmanipulated variable (diagnosis) and one manipulated variable (type of words). Although subjects can be randomly assigned to the levels of factor *A* (type of words), we cannot randomly assign subjects to factor *B* (diagnosis). Diagnosis (schizophrenia or normal) is an organismic variable (i.e., a characteristic of the subject that preexists the experiment and cannot be manipulated by the researcher). In addition to being a mixed design in the above sense, this example is also a mixed design in that one factor (diagnosis) is a between-subjects variable whereas the other factor (types of words) is a within-subjects variable. We first classify each factor on the dimension of between-subjects versus within-subjects factors in order to select the appropriate ANOVA for statistical analysis. We then classify each factor on the dimension of manipulated versus nonmanipulated factors to interpret the results of the statistical analysis. Again, we must be especially cautious in drawing conclusions based on observed main effects and interactions with nonmanipulated factors because such factors represent differential research and do not have the controls of experimental research that makes causal inferences reasonably safe.

Internal Summary: Variations of Basic Factorial Designs

The basic factorial design has several variations. A factorial design can be either a between-subjects or a within-subjects design. As with single factor designs, the within-subjects factorial has advantages; its primary advantage is that it has increased sensitivity to the effects of the independent variables. A factorial can also be a mixed design. There are two meanings of the term *mixed design*. The first meaning affects the formulas we use in the analysis of variance. We label each factor as either a between-subjects factor or a within-subjects factor to identify the appropriate statistical analysis procedure. Once we have completed the analysis, we again label each factor, but this time on whether the factor is a manipulated or a nonmanipulated factor. These labels affect the confidence of the conclusions about the causal relationship between the independent variable(s) and the dependent variable.

ANOVA: A POSTSCRIPT

Analysis of variance (ANOVA) is one of the most flexible statistical tools available for the evaluation of data. The basic concept of ANOVA can be easily extended. ANOVA compares the variability of the means against a standard based on the variability of scores within each group. If the means are more variable than expected (based on the variability of scores within groups), we conclude that the independent variable had an effect. The concept of comparing the variability between groups to the variability within groups is constant in every ANOVA, no matter how complicated it becomes.

In an ANOVA with three or more groups, if the F is statistically significant, specific means comparisons must be made to find which group(s) differ significantly from the others. The specific means comparisons are carried out as a priori or as post hoc comparisons (see Chapter 10). In a repeated-measures ANOVA, the same subjects are tested under every condition, which the analysis of variance must take into account in computing the within-subjects variance. The repeated-measures ANOVA, a conceptual extension of the simple one-way ANOVA, adjusts for the effects of using the same subjects in each condition.

Finally, with factorial designs the analysis of variance is extended still further. Here the effects of each independent variable and the interactive effects of combinations of independent variables are examined. For example, if we have two factors (A and B), we have three possible effects: the A main effect, the B main effect, and the interaction between A and B. If we have three factors, we may have three main effects (A, B, and C), three two-way interactions (AB, AC, and BC), and one three-way interaction (ABC) for a total of seven different effects. With four factors, we have the following possible effects: A, B, C, D, AB, AC, AD, BC, BD, CD, ABC, ABD, ACD, BCD, and $ABCD$. Finally, the ANOVA can take into account which factors are within-subjects factors and which are between-subjects factors.

Although it can become complicated as factors are added to a study, extending the logic and the computational formulas of the analysis of variance to factorial designs is not difficult. The formulas themselves can become quite complex, but for the most part we rely on computers to perform the actual computation. Because there are many different effects, there are many different F-ratios, but each F-ratio represents a comparison of between-groups variability to within-groups variability. Further, we interpret the F-ratio in these complex designs in exactly the same way as in simpler designs: if the probability of obtaining the F or a larger F is small (i.e., less than the alpha level), we reject the null hypothesis that there are no group differences and conclude that the independent variable(s) had an effect on the dependent variable. The problem is not in the computation of complex ANOVAs but in the interpretation stage, where we have to visualize and explain complex interactions (see the cartoon). The combination of consistency in how the ANOVA is used and the flexibility of the procedure to analyze data from so many different designs make analysis of variance the most widely used statistical technique in psychology.

Given the diversity of ANOVA procedures, it is perhaps not surprising that analysis of variance procedures have been extended into still other designs. These more advanced procedures are generally beyond the scope of this book and are described here only briefly.

Analysis of Covariance (ANCOVA)

Another widely used technique is *analysis of covariance (ANCOVA)*. Unfortunately, ANCOVA is often misused (Lord, 1967). Analysis of covariance is used in the same way as analysis of variance with one addition. As part of the analysis,

"He wouldn't listen to me when he was designing the study — so now he has to interpret a five-way interaction."

the effects of a theoretically unimportant, but nonetheless powerful, variable are removed from the dependent measure scores. For example, if we want to study the effects of reinforcement strategies on learning in young children, we could set up a study with two or three levels of the independent variable. We could then randomly assign the sample of children to each condition and measure how well they perform on the measure of learning (the dependent variable). Of course, the age of the children will affect how quickly they learn material. However, we are not interested in the variable of age in our study. We could hold age constant by using only subjects who are in a narrow age range if we had enough subjects available in a single age range. We could use a matching procedure to make sure the groups are equivalent on age at the beginning of the study. On the other hand, we could randomly assign the subjects to groups and use analysis of covariance to remove statistically the effects of age from the dependent measure. Analysis of covariance would give us a more sensitive test of the hypothesis because unwanted variability due to an extraneous factor would be statistically removed as part of the analysis. We must caution, however, that ANCOVA is a complicated procedure, with many potential pitfalls. [For a detailed discussion of ANCOVA, consult Keppel (1991).]

Multivariate Analysis of Variance (MANOVA)

Another extension of analysis of variance, which is becoming much more popular as sophisticated computer analysis packages become more available, is *multivariate analysis of variance (MANOVA)*. The difference between a simple ANOVA and a MANOVA is in the dependent variable. In an ANOVA, we have only one dependent variable entered into the analysis. In a MANOVA, we have more than one dependent variable being analyzed at one time. Conceptually, it is similar to the extension from one-way (one independent variable) ANOVAs to factorial (more than one independent variable) ANOVAs, except that now we are looking at multiple *dependent* measures in the same study. The full power of MANOVA procedures is still being discovered. Just as in analysis of covariance, using MANOVA procedures correctly and interpreting the results accurately require an extensive understanding of the technique.

Clearly, analysis of variance techniques are flexible and powerful procedures for analyzing data from almost any design. With the aid of the computer and some well-written computer programs, the computations can be done quickly and easily. However, the researcher still has to understand research design in order to be able to set up the computer analyses correctly. Even more important, the researcher needs to understand when ANOVA procedures are appropriate to use. This is a reason why the requirements of Ph.D. programs in psychology include extensive course work in statistics. Finally, performing the appropriate statistical analysis is only the first step in the evaluation of data. The next step is interpreting the meaning of the results. Interpreting meaning requires evaluating the entire study on such issues as potential confounding and the adequacy of control procedures. The principles for such an evaluation are the primary focus of this text. Statistical procedures, even clever and useful ones such as ANOVA, do not impart meaning to data. Only the researcher well trained in science can take this last important step.

SUMMARY

Factorial designs include more than one independent variable. They are highly efficient and flexible designs in which we can combine information from the equivalent of two or more single-variable studies. Their greatest advantage is that they yield information about interactive effects of the independent variables.

Factorial designs can be of several types, in which the factors are (1) between-subjects variables or within-subjects variables, (2) manipulated variables or nonmanipulated variables, or (3) mixed factorials. A factorial with a within-subjects component must be analyzed with statistical procedures that take into account the correlated nature of the data. A factorial with a nonmanipulated component must be interpreted cautiously because causality cannot be properly inferred from nonmanipulated independent variables.

ANOVAs are used to analyze factorial designs. It is helpful to graph cell means and, by inspection of the graph, to note whether significant interactions and/or main effects seem likely. When the analysis indicates that both main effects and an interaction are significant, it is necessary to interpret the main effects in terms of interaction.

REVIEW EXERCISES

12.1 **Define the following key terms. Be sure you understand them. They are discussed in the chapter and defined in the glossary.**

factorial design	Statistical Analysis System (SAS)
interaction	Minitab
factors	ANOVA summary table
matrix of cells	within-subjects factorial
design notation	repeated-measures factorial
main effects	repeated-measures ANOVA
row means	mixed design
column means	between-subjects factors
statistically significant differences	within-subjects factors
computer analysis programs	manipulated factors
Statistical Package for the	nonmanipulated factors
Social Sciences (SPSS)	analysis of covariance (ANCOVA)
Biomedical Programs (BMDP)	multivariate analysis of variance (MANOVA)

12.2 **Answer the following. Check your answers in the chapter.**

1. What distinguishes factorial designs from designs discussed in Chapters 10–11?
2. Under what conditions would a factorial design rather than a single-variable design be used?
3. For each of the following (i) indicate how many factors are included and (ii) tell how many levels there are for each factor:
   a. 2×2
   b. 2×3
   c. $2 \times 3 \times 2$
   d. 4×3
   e. $4 \times 3 \times 2 \times 3$
4. For each of the above, draw the appropriate matrix and label the factors and levels.
5. Theoretically, we can handle any number of factors in a factorial design, but there are some important limitations to the number of factors we should include. Identify and explain the limitations.
6. It is noted that testing the research hypothesis in a factorial design is more complicated than in a single-variable design. What is (are) the complication(s)?
7. On completing an ANOVA and finding that there is a statistically significant difference, what other statistical procedures are needed? Why?
8. In a factorial design where both the interaction and main effects are significant, why is it important to interpret the interaction first?
9. What are main effects in factorials?
10. What is a mean square in an ANOVA table?
11. What are mixed designs? Explain the three types.
12. What are repeated-measures designs? What potential confounding variables are there in repeated-measures designs and what control must be used?
13. Explain the cautions in using mixed designs. That is, in one type of mixed design we must be cautious about statistical procedures; in the other, we must be cautious about the interpretation of results.
14. Carefully distinguish within-subjects designs and between-subjects designs. What are the major characteristics of each? Give an example of each.

12.3   Think about and work the following problems.

1. You are the teaching assistant for this course and are to explain the concept of interaction in factorial design. Organize your presentation by first making the distinction between main effects and interaction effects. Be sure to clarify for your students the distinction between additive and interactive effects.
2. You are the teaching assistant for the course and are to explain to the class that a 2×2 factorial study is, in a sense, two separate studies combined. How would you develop your explanation?
3. Given the following cell means and ANOVA summary table, how would you interpret the results?

Source	df	SS	MS	F	p	Matrix of Means		
							B_1	B_2
A	3	121.5	40.5	1.39	n.s.			
B	1	93.7	93.7	3.21	<.05	A_1	12.1	13.4
AB	3	288.6	96.2	3.29	<.05	A_2	9.5	15.7
Within	72	2102.4	29.2			A_3	7.5	17.5
Total	79	2606.2				A_4	5.9	18.9

4. Each of the following matrices shows group means of results of a factorial study. For each one, draw and label the appropriate graph. Indicate for each whether interactions and main effects are significant or not significant. (Assume that all differences are statistically significant.)

	A_1	A_2			A_1	A_2	A_3			A_1	A_2
B_1	10	15		B_1	10	15	10		B_1	14	22
B_2	10	15		B_2	15	20	15		B_2	26	18
B_3	10	15		B_3	25	30	25				

5. In the children's dark-fears study described in the chapter, suppose that we had found significant main effects for both level of illumination and fear images, but no interaction. Draw a graph to show how such results would look. How would you interpret the findings conceptually?
6. Assume in the dark-fears study that you got a significant main effect for fear images and a significant interaction. What would the graph of the results look like? How would you interpret these results?

Chapter
13

Field Research

II. A Second Look at Research in Natural Settings

CONDUCTING FIELD RESEARCH

Research in natural settings was introduced in Chapter 6, where our focus was on low-constraint *field research* (naturalistic observation, case-study, archival research, and survey research). Those methods are useful in gathering facts, observing contingencies, becoming familiar with selected phenomena, developing hypotheses that can be tested later at higher-constraint levels of research, and testing correlational hypotheses. But research in natural settings is not limited to low-constraint methods. In this chapter we will look again at field research, but now our focus will be on the higher-constraint levels. We will explore field research at several different levels of constraint including field experiments and program evaluation.

An important trend in psychological research is the increase in research, including experimental research, in natural settings. For example, there are increasing demands to evaluate the effectiveness of educational, clinical, and public health programs; to evaluate the effects of large-scale events, such as disasters and human-caused events (e.g., massive unemployment); and to determine employee reactions to changed work conditions and consumers' reactions to new products, procedures, or news about products they are using.

Naturalistic observation and case-study research allow us to identify contingencies and to form causal hypotheses that can be tested at higher-constraint levels. Survey research enables us to discover and to test relationships among variables (correlations). However, these techniques cannot easily answer questions about causality. Why? Primarily because they do not allow manipulation of the independent variable and therefore do not rule out alternative hypotheses. Conducting experimental research in natural settings is difficult because it is almost always limited by the demands and characteristics of the setting. We may not be able to obtain the number of subjects required to create experimental and control groups; random assignment of subjects to groups and precise measures of dependent variables are often impossible in the field; and manipulation of independent variables is usually difficult. Indeed, in some studies, such as a study of the psychological effects of a natural disaster, manipulating the independent variable is impossible. Finally, it is often difficult to maintain projects in the field because people, such as teachers and principals, who have decision-making responsibility for the field settings may cancel or curtail ongoing projects.

Reasons for Doing Field Research

There are three major reasons for conducting experiments in field settings:

1. To test the external validity of causal conclusions arrived at in the laboratory
2. To determine the effects of events that occur in the field
3. To improve generalization across settings

Experimental research conducted in the laboratory allows us to test hypotheses and infer causality under controlled conditions designed to maximize internal validity. However, high control and internal validity often mean a reduction of external validity. That is, the more precise, constrained, and artificial we become in the laboratory, the less natural are the procedures and findings. The result is that we sometimes have difficulty generalizing laboratory experimentation to the natural environment. As noted by Cook and Campbell (1979):

> The advantages of experimental control for inferring causation have to be weighed against the disadvantages that arise because we do not always want to learn about causation in controlled settings. Instead, for many purposes, we would like to be able to generalize to causal relationships in complex field settings, and we cannot easily assume that findings from the laboratory will hold in the field. (p. 7)

For example, suppose we have an experimental grammar school staffed by psychologists, teachers, and graduate student research assistants. We conduct a controlled experiment indicating that a new teaching method A is superior to methods B, C, and D, which are representative of the standard procedures used in schools throughout the state. No matter how much confidence we have in the internal validity of the results, can we assume that when the new teaching method is adopted in schools across the state, operating under a variety of conditions the method will still be just as effective? No, we cannot. Why? Because the field situations are different from the laboratory situation, and we cannot easily assume external validity of the laboratory findings. It is necessary to test new instructional procedures in field situations in order to have more confidence in the generalizability to other field settings. This is particularly important in applied research, where the goal is not only to understand phenomena but also to use the new understanding in practical ways.

The second reason for doing field research is to meet growing demands to test the effectiveness of social programs such as special educational programs, public health campaigns, crackdowns on drunk drivers, and programs that give tax incentives to corporations. Each of these programs has an implicit assumption: the large-scale educational program will lead to massive reduction of illiteracy; the public health program will reduce drug addiction; the drunk-driving crackdown will reduce highway fatalities; the tax incentives to corporations will increase economic growth. Unfortunately, such assumptions are seldom tested. Social programs, as well-meaning as they may be, are usually created through political inspiration and for political ends. Seldom are supporters committed to testing program effectiveness. Politically, it may be better not to subject such programs to testing than to find that one's costly and fine-sounding pet project does not work. Donald Campbell (1969) argued that developed countries should carry out social reforms as much like controlled social experiments as possible. The studies would be designed to maximize validity. We would make decisions about retaining, modifying, or ending programs in an objective manner, based on the data. There have been increased demands for careful evaluation of new programs, but such evaluations are not yet routinely carried out.

The third reason for conducting research in the field is to take advantage of the potential for greater generalizability of results to other conditions. To understand this, we must distinguish three types of generalization:

1. Generalization of results from the subjects in the study to the larger population
2. Generalization of the results of the study over time
3. Generalization of results from conditions of the study to other conditions or settings

The third type of generalization may be enhanced when we carry out research in naturalistic settings.

Consider the example given earlier in which we tested the effectiveness of a new elementary school teaching program in a university laboratory school. The high-constraint laboratory setting, although giving us confidence in the internal validity of the study, is not necessarily strong in external validity. To enhance its external validity, we should also carry out the research in real schools. If we find that in the natural setting the new program is superior to other teaching methods, we can have greater confidence in inferring that the results are generalizable to other, similar classroom settings.

Ulrich Neisser conducted a clever field study to verify the external validity of a phenomenon that had been well established in the laboratory. The work of Elizabeth Loftus and others has shown that memory is very fragile and subject to significant distortion (e.g., Loftus & Hoffman, 1989). Furthermore, we often are unaware of the distortion in our memory. Neisser (Neisser & Harsch, 1992) asked 44 college students the day after the Challenger space shuttle blew up in January of 1986 to write down how they heard about the explosion and what they did. Thirty months later he then asked them to do the same thing. None of these subjects was entirely accurate in recall at 30 months, and over one-third gave dramatically different accounts at day 2 and 30 months later of how they found out about the Challenger disaster. More striking is that his subjects were certain that their memories 2.5 years after the accident were accurate—often describing the memories as exceptionally vivid. Many were astonished, even flabbergasted, when confronted with their own handwritten accounts made the day after the disaster. Subjects could not beleive that memories that seemed so vivid and accurate could be so distorted over time and that they would have no realization that the memories were distorted. This field study of memory enhances our confidence in the external validity of the laboratory studies of the malleability of memory. It also suggests that these laboratory finding are relevant in real-world situations such as eye witness testimony in courts (Loftus & Ketcham, 1991).

Difficulties in Field Research

Ideally, we want to conduct experiments in the field so as to be able to draw causal inferences. However, doing so can be difficult. There are many field situations in which we cannot apply the laboratory controls completely or cannot assign subjects to groups at all. This is frequently the case in natural settings such as schools, hospitals, and neighborhoods, or in situations in which natural or contrived events occur and affect a large number of people.

Suppose some natural disaster has occurred, such as the near meltdown of a nuclear power plant, a powerful hurricane, or a major flood. We want to know how much the event has affected residents' psychological stability and/or their physical health. The natural event is the independent variable and the residents' behavior and/or health is the dependent variable. Note that we have no control over the independent variable—we cannot manipulate it. How then do we measure the reactions and draw causal inferences? To take another example, suppose that in studying children we cannot randomly assign subjects to different groups for treatment because subjects are all part of a single class following a common program. That is, they are always together, and whatever is applied to one child is applied to all others. Assigning the children to different groups for purposes of the experimental manipulation will seriously interfere with the ongoing program, and the program director will not allow it. We want to conduct research with as much control as possible in order to draw causal inferences, and yet we know that random assignment—or for that matter, any unbiased assignment of subjects to conditions—is not possible. Under these restrictions, how might we go about testing the new treatment? The essential question here is "How do we answer questions about causality in natural settings when we cannot utilize many of the usual manipulation and control procedures available in the laboratory?"

In this chapter we discuss several possible solutions to this question by way of three main topics: quasi-experimental designs, single-subject designs, and program evaluation. The first two topics cover research designs that have been developed to answer causal questions in natural settings. Program evaluation is not so much a method but a research area of growing importance.

QUASI-EXPERIMENTAL DESIGNS

The highest degree of control is obtained with experiments, which allow us to draw causal inferences with confidence. Thus, an experiment is the preferred procedure for answering causal questions. However, there are conditions under which we cannot meet all demands of a true experiment but still want to answer a causal question. In these situations we can use quasi-experimental designs. "Quasi" means "similar to." Thus, a *quasi-experimental design* is one that is like an experimental design but is not quite equal to it. Quasi-experiments have the essential form of experiments, including a causal hypothesis and some type of manipulation to compare two or more conditions. They do control for some confounding but do not have as much control as true experiments. Thus, we can draw causal inferences from quasi-experiments but not with the same confidence as when we use a true experimental design. Quasi-experimental designs are used in situations such as field research where full experimental controls cannot be used. Donald Campbell (1969) argues that when experiments cannot be carried out, quasi-experimental designs should be used. In many field situations, using quasi-experiments to draw causal inferences with somewhat less than high confidence *will still give us more useful information than not experimenting at all.* (Keep in mind that quasi-experimental designs are different from low-constraint methods in that they have many of the control procedures of true experiments.)

Quasi-experimental designs are similar to experiments but may lack some controls. Specifically, whereas quasi-experiments do include a comparison of at least two levels of an independent variable, the actual manipulation is not always under the experimenter's control. For example, if we compare health before and after a natural disaster, we obviously cannot manipulate the disaster but can compare the health records from the local hospital before and after it. Likewise, in many field situations we cannot assign subjects to groups in an unbiased manner; indeed, we often cannot assign subjects at all but must accept the natural groups as they exist. Thus, in quasi-experimental designs:

1. We state causal hypotheses.
2. We include at least two levels of the independent variable but cannot always manipulate the independent variable.
3. We usually cannot assign subjects to groups but must accept already existing groups.
4. We include specific procedures for testing hypotheses.
5. We include some controls for threats to validity.

[Compare these characteristics with the characteristics of an experiment (Chapter 10).]

There are a number of quasi-experimental designs, but this chapter focuses on two: the nonequivalent control-group design and the interrupted time-series design. Differential research, discussed in Chapter 7, is a variation on the nonequivalent control-group design. [Students who wish information about other quasi-experimental designs can consult Cook and Campbell (1979).]

Nonequivalent Control-Group Design

The best way to test causal hypotheses with confidence is to compare groups that are created by the researcher through random assignment. This makes it likely that the groups are equivalent at the beginning of the study. Recall that initial equivalence of groups is crucial in experimental design. However, there are conditions under which the subjects are not assigned randomly, and, therefore, the groups may not be equivalent at the beginning of the study. There are several designs in this category, all of which attempt to solve the problem of comparing two groups that we suspect are not equivalent at the beginning of the study. We introduced one design in this category in Chapter 10 (the pretest-posttest, natural control-group design).

In field research, we frequently have no choice but to use already existing groups, which means that subjects cannot be randomly assigned. Even though the groups appear to be similar, we cannot assume that they are equivalent at the start of the study. The groups may be different on the dependent variable at the beginning of the study. However, whether they are the same or different on the dependent variable, the groups may differ on other important variables that constitute potential confounding. Box 13.1 lists several examples of research using a *nonequivalent control-group design*.

Campbell and Stanley (1966) popularized the nonequivalent control-group design by suggesting that already existing groups can be similar to one another on most relevant variables even though there is no formal systematic assignment of subjects to groups. As they point out, the more similar natural groups are to one another, the closer the design approximates a true experiment and the more confidence we can have in conclusions. Later, Cook and Campbell (1979) extended these principles to even more extreme situations where there may be clear evidence that naturally occurring groups are not equivalent on potential confounding variables. What Cook and Campbell show is that, even in this extreme situation, it is sometimes possible to draw strong conclusions if the researcher carefully evaluates

---

Box 13.1   **Field Situations with Nonequivalent Groups**

1. We want to evaluate the effectiveness of an antismoking campaign using two different schools. We suspect that one school has a higher rate of smoking than the other.
2. A company wants to test their employees' attitudes toward work as they may be affected by new work rules. One department is selected as an experimental group, another as the control group. However, there is evidence that the first department has more positive work attitudes than the second.
3. A psychology professor wants to compare examination results in a research methods course based on two different textbooks. The professor teaches one section of the course at 8:00 A.M. on Monday, Wednesday, and Friday and the other at 4:00 P.M. on Tuesday and Thursday. It is suspected that students who chose the early section may be different from those who chose the later section.
4. A new treatment approach for hyperactivity is to be tested in a special school using three existing classes. The classes, however, are at different levels of hyperactivity.

---

all potential threats to validity. The ideal, of course, is a true experiment in which subjects are assigned to groups in a unbiased manner. If this is not possible, the best alternative is to use nonequivalent control groups where the groups give every indication of being similar on most of the relevant variables. But, as Cook and Campbell (1979) point out, even when that requirement cannot be met, careful analysis of the design and the results can sometimes allow the researcher to draw useful conclusions from what appears to be a weak research design.

There are two major problems with nonequivalent groups: (1) the groups may differ on the dependent measure(s) at the start of the study, and (2) there may be other differences between the groups that have not been controlled by random assignment. To address the first issue, the basic strategy in nonequivalent control-group designs is to measure the experimental and control group on the dependent measure both before and after the manipulation. Then, following the manipulation, the difference between the premanipulation and postmanipulation scores for each group is calculated. The *difference score* for each group is then taken as a measure of how much each group changed as a result of the manipulation. The pretest allows us to measure how similar the groups are on the dependent variable(s) at the beginning of the study. This similarity is important—the more similar the groups are, the greater control we have. Notice that as the similarity between groups at the beginning of the study increases, the design approaches the experimental designs discussed earlier.

To address the second issue—that groups may differ on variables other than the dependent variable—it is important to rule out each potential confounding variable. To do this, we must first identify potential confounding variables, measure them, and

TABLE 13.1   A NONEQUIVALENT CONTROL-GROUP DESIGN

Group A (experimental)	Pretest	Treatment	Posttest	Pretest-Posttest
Group B (control)	Pretest	No treatment	Posttest	Pretest-Posttest

Compare

carefully rule them out. This is the strategy we outlined in Chapter 7 when we discussed selecting control groups in differential research. In differential research, groups will potentially differ on several variables besides the variable that defined the groups. If we select the right control group(s), however, we can minimize confounding and thus move this nonequivalent control-group design closer to an experimental design. A typical nonequivalent control-group design is shown in Table 13.1.

Causality is inferred when the results show that the control group remains essentially the same from pretreatment to posttreatment measures but the experimental group changes markedly in the predicted direction. Cook and Campbell (1979) note that the nonequivalent control-group design controls for many potential sources of confounding but still must be interpreted carefully because some confounding variables may be uncontrolled. The confounding that can affect the outcome will vary from study to study.[1]

As noted, there are two major problems in nonequivalent control-group designs, both related to the fact that the groups exist prior to the study and subjects cannot be assigned to groups in an unbiased manner. The problems are (1) the experimental and control groups may differ on the dependent measures at the start of the study, and/or (2) there may be other differences between groups that were not controlled because unbiased assignment of subjects is not possible. Thus, there may be confounding due to selection. Figure 13.1 shows six possible outcomes of a nonequivalent control-group design. Figure 13.1(a) and Figure 13.1(b) show results where the experimental and control groups are equivalent on the dependent measure at the beginning of the study. Of course, the groups may be different on other important variables, in which case the major issue is to rule out confounding due to selection. In Figure 13.1(c) to Figure 13.1(f) the groups actually differ on the dependent measure at pretest. In these instances, we must rule out confounding due to selection to draw a causal inference, and we must also rule out confounding from regression to the mean, which results from the initial difference on the dependent variable. For purposes of illustration, it is assumed that all changes shown are in the predicted direction.

In Figure 13.1(a), both the experimental and control groups show an increase on the dependent measure from pretest to posttest. The groups are equivalent at the beginning and show equivalent change over time. Thus, there appears to be no effect of the independent variable. In Figure 13.1(b), the groups are equivalent on the dependent measures at the beginning of the study. The experimental group shows a large change, whereas the control group does not change from pretest to posttest.

[1]A complete discussion of the principles for identifying confounding variables and interpreting their likely effects on a nonequivalent control-group study is beyond the scope of this book. The interested reader is referred to Cook and Campbell (1979) for a more complete discussion.

Figure 13.1 Some Possible Outcomes for Nonequivalent Control-Group Designs

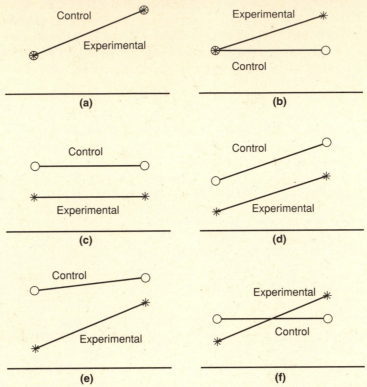

There does appear to be an effect of the independent variable. However, before drawing this conclusion we must still rule out possible confounding due to selection. In Figure 13.1(c), neither group changes from pretest to posttest. The obvious interpretation is that the manipulation had no effects. Figure 13.1(d) shows a similar change in both groups from pretest to posttest. With these results, we have to conclude that there is a pretest-to-posttest difference as predicted but, because both groups changed in the same manner, we cannot attribute the change to the independent variable. It appears more likely that some maturation process or historical event common to both groups may be responsible for the change in scores. Figure 13.1(e) shows a slight change in the control group but a marked change in the experimental group. With these results, we have some confidence in attributing the change to the effects of the independent variable. However, there is still the potentially confounding factor of regression to the mean, which limits our confidence in this interpretation. Recall from Chapter 8 that regression is a potential source of confounding whenever we begin an experiment with extreme scores. In Figure 13.1(e), the marked pretest difference between groups may well represent extreme scores for the experimental group. The scores for the experimental group may have returned to the mean level represented by the control group. Thus, the change in the experimental group may not be due to the independent variable. Consequently, we cannot be confident in attributing the results to the causal effects of the independent variable. In Figure 13.1(f), the control group does not change but the experimental group changes in the predicted direction, even going beyond the level of the control group. This is called a *crossover effect*. The results give us considerable confidence in a causal inference. Maturation is an unlikely alternative hypothesis because the control group presumably matured but did not change. If maturation were responsible, it is unlikely that the effect would be so different in the two groups. Regression to the mean is also an unlikely alternative hypothesis because the experimental group increased not only to the mean of the control group but beyond it. With these results, a quasi-experimental design gives us fairly good confidence in a causal inference.

The above examples represent reasonably interpretable data from nonequivalent control-group studies. Other situations can be more difficult—sometimes, impossible—to interpret. Using nonequivalent control-group designs and correctly interpreting data from them requires considerable expertise and is not recommended to beginning students. A true experiment is the best approach. When a true experiment is not possible, a quasi-experiment where groups are apparently equivalent is the best compromise. Only if neither of these alternatives is feasible should the researcher consider using a quasi-experimental design with a nonequivalent control group.

Interrupted Time-Series Design

In an *interrupted time-series design* a single group of subjects is measured several times both before and after some event or manipulation. Time-series designs are variations of within-subjects designs in which the same subjects are measured in different conditions. The time-series design is similar to a simple pretest-posttest design. However, instead of a single pretreatment measure and a single posttreatment measure of the dependent variable, a time-series design uses multiple measures taken at several points in time both before and after the manipulation. That is, a series of measures is taken over time, "interrupted" by the manipulation, after which another series of measures is again taken. It is the multiple measures over time that make this a useful design.

The simple pretest-posttest design is weak, leaving so many potential confounding factors uncontrolled that even if a statistically significant difference is found we cannot draw causal inferences (see Chapter 10). Recall the pretest-posttest study of the use of relaxation to reduce disruptive behavior of autistic children. Suppose this study is carried out by taking a pretreatment measure of disruption at one point in time, then applying the relaxation treatment, and then taking a posttreatment measure of disruption at another point in time. Even if we find a significant reduction in disruptive behavior, confounding due to history, maturation, and regression to the mean prevents us from drawing a causal inference.

A major potential confounding factor in the simple pretest-posttest study is *regression to the mean*. The disruptive behavior may naturally fluctuate over time, displaying considerable variability. The intervention might be applied only at a high point in that natural variation, just before the disruptive behavior decreased again. Thus, the observed reduction in disruption may not be due to the treatment but only to the natural variability of behavior; the reduction would have occurred at that time

Figure 13.2   An Interrupted Time-Series Design Showing the Effects of Relaxation Treatment for Four Autistic Children

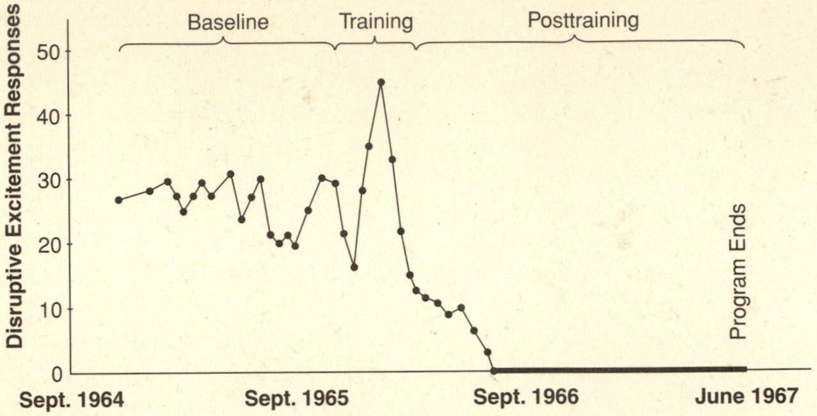

without the treatment. Multiple measures give several points of comparison over time, thus allowing us to recognize regression to the mean effects.

To apply the interrupted time-series design in the study of autistic children, we (1) measure disruption at several points in time during a baseline observation period prior to treatment, (2) apply the treatment, and (3) measure the same subjects on the disruptive behavior at several points in time after the intervention. The following example is from the actual results of the study of disruption in autistic children (Graziano, 1974). Disruptive behavior of four autistic children was measured and recorded for a full year as a normal part of the monitoring carried out in the program. The treatment (relaxation training) was applied, and the behavioral measures were again taken for more than a year following the treatment. Figure 13.2 shows the results. Inspection of the graph shows considerable variation during the one-year pretreatment baseline, but none of the variation is comparable to that which occurred after treatment. Following the treatment, the graph shows a marked decrease in disruptive behavior,[2] reaching zero and remaining there for a full year until the program ended. Because so long a pretreatment baseline was used, it is possible to see the magnitude of normal variations over a full year's time and compare it with the marked decrease following treatment. The results suggest that the decrease following treatment is not due to normal fluctuation or regression to the mean. It also seems unlikely to be due to maturation of all subjects during the same period of time. Although a good demonstration of the effects of relaxation training, there is still a major confounding factor remaining. Can you identify it? (We will return to this point soon.)

By using an interrupted time-series design with a single group of subjects, researchers can take advantage of data already gathered over a long period of time. It is a useful design in clinical or naturalistic settings where the effects of some

---

[2]Notice the peak of disruptive behavior immediately after training began. This peak is a common clinical phenomenon called a *frustration effect,* which occurs when new procedures are initiated with autistic children. *Frustration effects* are generally temporary. Note too that the disruption dropped dramatically following this short burst.

Figure 13.3 **Hypothetical Time Graph for an Interrupted Time-Series Design Showing the Number of Serious Auto Accidents Before and After Reduction of the State Speed Limit**

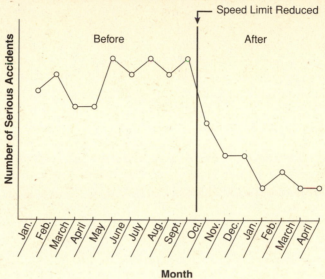

event—naturally occurring or manipulated—may be assessed by taking multiple measurements both before and after the event.

The interrupted time-series design can also be used in large-scale studies and is particularly useful when the presumed causal event occurs to all members of a population. For example, suppose a state government wants to reduce traffic accidents and their resulting injuries and deaths. To accomplish this, it reduces the state speed limit from 65 mph to 55 mph. It is important to determine whether the intervention (reduced speed) does result in fewer accidents. Because the new speed limit applies to every driver in the state, there cannot be an experimental group of state drivers for whom the new limit applies and a control group for which it does not. How then might the effects of the intervention be evaluated? One way is to use the interrupted time-series design. Figure 13.3 is a hypothetical time graph showing the number of accidents in the state that involved injury or death over a 16-month period, plotted for several months prior to implementing the new speed limit and for several more months during which the new speed limit is in effect. The time graph shows variation in the number of serious accidents during the preintervention phase, with an overall slight increase throughout the year. Following the new speed limit, there is a sharp reduction that eventually stabilizes at a new, lower level of accidents for the remainder of that year and into the next. Are these results sufficient for us to draw a reasonably confident conclusion that the reduced speed limit is effective in reducing the number of serious accidents? Let us consider the major potential confounding factors.

Selection is not at issue because this is essentially a within-subjects design and the two groups being compared—the state's drivers before and after the decreased speed limit—were thus equivalent at the start of the study. Testing effects are not critical because the measures taken are unobtrusive; that is, all measures are taken from traffic records and not directly from subjects. Maturation is not an issue because it is most unlikely that all of the state's drivers, of all ages, all became better drivers at the same time through some common maturational process. Regression to the mean is not an issue. Note that the post-intervention decrease in accidents is much sharper, lasts longer, and reaches a lower mean level than the pre-intervention normal fluctuations. Thus, the decrease does not seem to be due to regression to the mean. Primarily because of its multiple measures at pre- and posttreatment, the interrupted time-series design does control for most potential confounding. It is a far stronger design than the simple pre-post design where only one measure is taken at each phase.

With time-series designs, however, there are two potentially confounding factors: *history* and *instrumentation.* History can confound results in any procedure that requires a fairly long period of time, because any number of other events might occur to account for changes in the dependent variable. In our hypothetical speed limit example, there may be other factors that contributed to or are wholly responsible for the decrease. For example, the state might have also sharply increased the number of patrol cars, the number of speeding tickets, and the severity of penalties for speeding and for drunk driving. Any of these actions may have contributed to the decrease in accidents. Thus, when using the interrupted time-series design, the experimenter must be careful to identify potential confounding due to history and rule it out. In this example, we must be sure the state did not initiate these other actions at the same time it decreased the speed limit. (Recall a few paragraphs earlier when you were asked to identify the remaining major confounding factor in the time-series design for the experiment in relaxation training. If you identified it as *history,* you were correct.) Instrumentation is also a potential threat to validity in time-series designs. When people initiate new approaches or programs, there also may be accompanying changes in the way records are made and kept. The researcher must be careful to determine that the apparent reduction in accidents is not due to changes in measuring or record keeping.

In a time-series study, the change in the time graph must be quite sharp to be interpreted as anything other than only a normal fluctuation. Any post-intervention change that is slight or gradual is difficult to interpret as being due to the causal effects of the intervention.

Note two important points about the interrupted time-series design. First, it is a flexible design that can be used in many situations. With it we can evaluate events that are large- or small-scale, that have already occurred, and that are actually manipulated (such as the decreased speed limit) or uncontrolled (such as a natural disaster). Think about this and see whether you can determine how we might use this design to evaluate, for example, a large-scale natural disaster that has already occurred. Second, the time-series design is such that we can use data that already have been gathered and that are unobtrusive, such as data on auto accidents. This adds a great deal to the flexibility of the design.

The interrupted time-series design is powerful and useful in many naturalistic situations. However, it can be improved by adding one or more comparison groups. In our hypothetical study of the effects of a change in speed limit on the number of accidents, we can use comparable data from a neighboring state that did not reduce the speed limit. This would provide a comparison that helps to control for many potentially confounding variables such as history and maturation. For example, Guerin and MacKinnon (1985) studied the effects of the California Child Passenger Restraint Requirement. This law requires that children under 4 years of age be in federally approved child car seats while riding in cars. Using an interrupted time-series design, the authors examined the effects of the new law on child auto injuries. The number of injuries for children under 4 years was taken from state records for a period covering 48 months prior to the start of the new law and for 12 months following its initiation. The effect of the law should be evident in the pre-post comparisons on the interrupted time-series graph. As an added comparison, the researchers recorded auto injury data for children between 4 and 7 years of age (children not covered by the law). They predicted that there would be a significant decrease for the younger group but not for the older group of children. As shown in Figure 13.4, after the law went into effect there was a drop in injuries to the younger group but not to the older group, and the differences persisted over the next 12 months. Statistical analyses were also carried out that showed a significant reduction in injuries for the younger group but not for the older group. In addition, the younger group was compared with a group of young children from Texas, where no such child car seat law existed. The children in Texas did not show a decrease in injuries during the 12 months of comparison. They found a decrease in injuries for the young group covered by the new California law. By adding comparison groups of (1) over-4-year-olds in California (for whom the new law did not apply) and (2) the children in Texas (where there was no child car seat law), neither of which showed a decrease, the effect is further demonstrated. The comparison groups increase our confidence that the new law reduced auto injuries for children.

Interrupted time-series designs provide a good way of testing causal hypotheses under many field conditions in which we cannot apply all of the usual laboratory controls. Cook and Campbell (1979) discuss several variations of the time-series design, and interested students are urged to consult their work. Box 13.2 gives examples of published studies in which interrupted time-series designs were used. The references are given so the interested student can read the original reports.

Graphing the results of interrupted time-series studies provides considerable information. But in a time-series design, simply inspecting the graph does not address the null hypothesis—that the pretest and posttest data are not significantly different. Testing the statistical significance of pre-post differences in time-series designs requires sophisticated procedures that are beyond the scope of this book. The interested student is referred to Glass, Wilson, and Gottman (1975) or Kazdin (1992) for a more detailed discussion.

SINGLE-SUBJECT DESIGNS

Single-subject designs are experimental designs that are carried out using only a single subject. They were developed early in the history of experimental psychology and were used in both human and animal learning studies. Since the early 1960s they have become popular in clinical psychology, particularly in research on treatment effectiveness. Single-subject experimental designs should not be confused with the ex post facto, single-case study. Recall from our discussion in Chapter 6 that single-case

Figure 13.4   Time-Series Design Showing the Effects of a New Child Car Seat Law on Injuries in Young Children

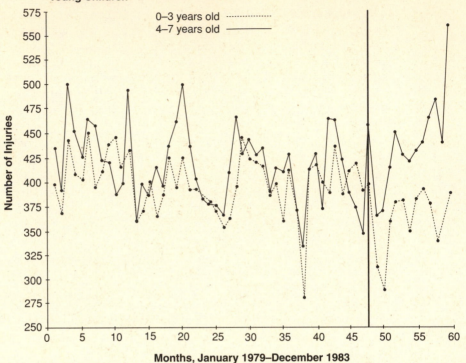

Months, January 1979–December 1983

Source: Guerin, D. and MacKinnon, D.P. (1985). "An assessment of the California child passenger restraint requirement."
American Journal of Public Health, 75, *142–144.*

studies using ex post facto analyses are frequently used in clinical research to provide in-depth descriptions of single individuals and to generate but not test hypotheses. The ex post facto, single-case study is weak, not because it has only one subject (the case), but because the researcher has no control over the independent variables, which are neither observed nor manipulated. Because the independent variable is not manipulated, *alternative hypotheses cannot be ruled out.* However, with single-subject, *experimental* designs, we are able to manipulate independent variables to observe their effects on dependent variables. The power of these designs is in the control of independent variables to eliminate potential confounding factors, enhance internal validity, and thus allowing us to test causal hypotheses.

Single-subject designs are a variation of time-series designs. They are within-subjects designs where the subject serves as his or her own control. There are several variations of single-subject designs, including reversal or ABA designs; multiple baseline designs; and single-subject, randomized, time-series designs.

There are two situations where a single-subject design is preferable to a group comparison: (1) when we want to evaluate change in a single subject and (2) when we want to obtain information that might otherwise be lost in a group comparison. Obviously, such designs are appropriate when we have only one subject such as when we want to evaluate the effectiveness of a clinical treatment for a particular client. Sin-

Box 13.2   **Examples of Research Using Interrupted Time-Series Design**

1. D. T. Campbell (1969) describes a study of the effects on traffic fatalities of a highway speeding crackdown. The program was initiated by the state of Connecticut after a year of particularly high traffic fatalities. Traffic deaths prior to and following the crackdown are compared.

2. Lawler and Hackman (1969) used time-series designs to test the effects of having employees participate in the planning of an employee bonus incentive plan for reducing absenteeism. Rates of absenteeism were recorded at several points prior to and following the new incentive plan.

3. Using time-series designs, Caporaso (1974) studied the effects of the formation of the European Economic Community (EEC) on the subsequent development of international economic cooperation and interdependencies among the member nations. The EEC was formed in 1958. Caporaso compared a number of measures of dependencies before the EEC was formed (1950–1957) and following the start of the EEC (1958–1970).

4. The on-task school behavior of three overactive preschoolers was improved by Bornstein and Quevillon (1976), who used a time-series design to study the effects of teaching self-instruction skills.

5. Mazur-Hart and Berman (1977) studied the effects of a new no-fault divorce law in the state of Nebraska. They compared the recorded number of divorces for the 3.5 years prior to the new law and the 2.5 years following it. The time-series analyses show that the number of divorces increased prior to the new law and continued to increase at the same rate following it. The new law had no apparent effect on the divorce rate.

6. McSweeny (1978) used a time-series design to study the effects of introducing a small fee for telephone directory assistance (information) on the public's use of the information service. Carried out in Cincinnati with a million telephone users as subjects, McSweeny found that following the introduction of the 20-cent fee, the number of calls for information dropped by nearly 70,000 each day.

7. Phillips (1983) used time-series designs to investigate the effects of televised violence on homicide rates. Using broadcasts of heavyweight boxing matches as the independent variable and homicide rates as the dependent variable, Phillips found a 12.4 percent increase in homicide rates following telecasts of the boxing matches.

gle-subject studies are useful in education, where we might want to know whether an intervention improves a child's academic performance. Thus, when we want to study an individual rather than a group, single-subject designs are useful. In this situation we are not usually interested in generalizing to a population but wish to limit the conclusions to the individual. Clearly, a single-subject experiment is weak in external validity but may give us valid and reliable information about a single individual.

Sidman (1960) argues for a second advantage of single-subject designs. The basis for his argument is that group-comparison procedures compare groups by summarizing each group's performance. In the process of summarizing, we may lose important information about the ways in which individuals perform. For example, suppose we have pretested 20 phobic subjects on the intensity of their fears and then randomly assigned them to a treatment and a control condition. We find at posttesting that the treated group has a lower mean fear score than the control group, and the difference is statistically significant. Assuming that all confounding has been controlled, we can conclude that the treatment is effective—that the independent variable did, indeed, have an effect on the dependent measure of fear. However, if we examine the scores of individual subjects, we might find that although the treated group as a whole had lower fear measures than did the control group as a whole, there is considerable variability within each of the two groups—some of the treated subjects may have fear scores that are higher than those of the untreated subjects. Further, if we examine the subject's pretreatment and posttreatment scores, we might find that although most of the control subjects did not improve, some did improve, and, although most of the treated subjects did improve, some did not and some got worse. In other words, individuals respond differently to the same treatment. Although the treatment may be effective when we consider an overall group comparison, it may not be effective for some subjects. This information would be more readily apparent if we had used single-subject procedures rather than between-subjects, group comparisons (Sidman, 1960).

Such considerations became particularly important in clinical psychology in the 1950s and 1960s. Researchers were becoming increasingly critical of traditional psychotherapy because much of the research failed to support the effectiveness of traditional psychological treatment. Bergin (1966), Bergin and Strupp (1970), and others, using the argument proposed by Sidman (1960), recognized that group-comparison studies of psychotherapy failed to support the hypothesis of the effectiveness of treatment. However, on closer inspection of the data, it was clear that some clients improved, some remained the same, and some became worse. When taken together as a group, they tended to cancel each other out, and the overall finding was that psychotherapy was not effective for the group as a whole. Obscured by group-comparison designs was the improvement of some clients following psychotherapy. Bergin suggested studying those individuals who improved to determine whether their improvements were due to some systematic effects of the treatment rather than to chance variation. This might allow us to identify characteristics of clients that make them more responsive to therapy. That is, can we discover whether there are factors that make psychotherapy effective for some people but not for others? Sidman (1960) and Bergin (1966) argued for the development of methods for the controlled study of single individuals.

The intensive experimental study of individuals had a prominent place in psychology until the late 1930s when psychologists began adopting new research designs and statistical procedures for making group comparisons. A major factor in this shift was Sir Ronald Fisher's *The Design of Experiments* (1935), which created the groundwork for multisubject, group-comparison designs. Researchers soon followed Fisher's lead. B. F. Skinner (e.g., 1953) was an influential exception.

He continued to develop methods for the intensive, systematic, and controlled study of individual subjects. The experimental analysis of behavior, as these methods became known, was expanded and refined by researchers influenced by Skinner.

The controlled study of a single individual has become particularly important in clinical psychology. Modern clinical psychology is now heavily reliant on behavioral treatment methods, which utilize single-subject research designs refined from Skinner's work. There are many single-subject designs. Three of the most frequently used are (1) reversal or ABA designs, (2) multiple baseline designs, and (3) single-subject, randomized, time-series designs. [For more information on single-subject designs, see Sidman (1960), Barlow and Hersen (1984), and Kratochwill (1978).]

Single-subject experimental designs are variations of within-subject designs because the same subject is exposed to all manipulations. They are also variations of time-series designs. Recall that in time-series designs we have no control group, and we take dependent measurements of the same subjects at different points in time. This allows us to compare measures taken before and after some naturally occurring event or an experimental manipulation. Single-subject designs are similar. Multiple measures are taken from a single subject over time—both before and after a manipulation. The basic comparison is between the same subject's own pretreatment and posttreatment responses. Note that at its simplest level, this resembles the pretest-posttest comparison—a relatively weak nonexperimental design. Causal inferences cannot be drawn from the pretest-posttest design because so many potential confounding variables are left uncontrolled. The simple use of two conditions alone, pretest and posttest, is not sufficient basis for drawing causal inferences. The addition of a control group allows for the control of many potential confounding variables but a control group is not possible when we have only one subject. Single-subject designs improve on the pre-post designs not by adding a control group but by adding more measures to the experiment. If the dependent variable changes in the predicted direction at each subsequent manipulation, then we have a more confident basis for inferring that the manipulation is responsible for the observed change in the dependent variable.

Reversal Design (ABA Design)

In *reversal designs,* also referred to as *ABA designs,* the effects of an independent variable on a dependent variable are demonstrated by measuring the dependent variable over three or four time periods. At a minimum, there is a no-treatment baseline period during which the dependent behavior is only observed, a treatment period in which the manipulation is carried out, and a return or reversal to the no-treatment condition. The effects of the independent variable (the treatment) on the dependent variable (the behavior to be changed) is demonstrated if the behavior changes in the predicted direction whenever the conditions are reversed. There are numerous published reports of the ABA reversal procedure. The following hypothetical study concerns self-stimulatory behavior that is often engaged in by retarded, autistic, or brain-injured children. It includes head-banging, self-biting, gouging, screaming, violent head shaking, and so on. This behavior interferes with treatment programs for the child and for other children in the group. Such behavior may be maintained, at least in part, by the responses of staff members. For some children, being ignored seems to help maintain the self-stimulatory behavior; for others, the staff's attention to the episodes may help maintain it.

Suppose that a retarded child, Betty, displays a complex self-stimulatory behavior that consists of loud, piercing shrieks, grotesque facial grimacing, and rapid, energetic arm-flapping. The three behaviors occur together, are maintained for as long as 25 minutes, and occur many times each day. The behavior, not only interferes with Betty's learning, but also with the progress of the other children. After observing the child, a psychologist forms the tentative hypothesis that the teacher's attention is the major reinforcement that maintains the behavior. That is, when Betty does not receive attention, she begins self-stimulation, which brings the teacher to the child to try to soothe and comfort her. The teacher does not realize that it may be her efforts to help Betty control the behavior that are actually helping to maintain it.

To test the hypothesis, the psychologist sets up an ABA reversal design, in which condition A, the baseline, involves the teacher's usual approach of attending to Betty whenever she displays the behavior. Condition B is the treatment—a differential reinforcement procedure in which the teacher provides attention and support for Betty whenever she refrains from the self-stimulatory behavior but withdraws all of her attention from Betty whenever she begins or maintains the disruptive behavior. The child is carefully observed, and the self-stimulating behavior is recorded during each condition. The observations are carried out for one hour at the same time each day. Figure 13.5 shows the behavioral changes as the A and B conditions are sequentially reversed, which suggests there may be a causal relationship between teacher attention and Betty's self-stimulatory behavior. Notice in Figure 13.5 that another reversal was added at the end for an ABAB procedure. The ABA sequence is sufficient to suggest causality. Why do you think the psychologist added that extra reversal, back to the B condition? (Think about this. We will return to it shortly.)

Figure 13.5   An ABAB Reversal Design Showing the Effects of Contingent Reinforcement on Self-Stimulatory Behavior on a Single Child

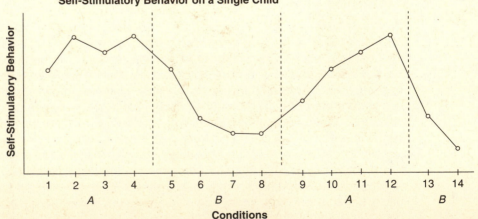

In reversal designs we test a causal relationship between an independent variable and a dependent variable. In this case the independent variable is the teacher's attention. It is presented at two levels, baseline (A) in which teacher's attention is given when the self-stimulation occurs and the intervention (B) in which teacher's attention is withdrawn when self-stimulation occurs. The experimental manipulation is the sequential reversal of levels A and B. The dependent variable is Betty's self-stimulatory behavior and is operationally defined in terms of the number of minutes per day in which it occurs. The question being asked is one of causality: "Does the teacher's attention affect self-stimulation for Betty?" When we find that behavior changes in the predicted direction, increasing or decreasing each time the reversal occurs, then we have a compelling demonstration that the independent variable, and not some confounding variable, has affected the dependent variable.

In this hypothetical example, an intervention was tested for reducing undesirable behavior. But the same reversal design has often been used to test the effectiveness of interventions to increase the strength of positive behaviors. For example, Correa, Poulson, and Salzberg (1984) used a reversal design in their study of blind retarded children. Because of multiple handicaps, the children have difficulty reaching for and grasping objects, and hence their general development can be markedly impaired. The researchers set up a treatment procedure to train the children to reach for and to grasp objects accurately. This was the first step in a more general developmental training program. The researchers used a reversal procedure for one child, Cory. They observed Cory's reaching and grasping under both a baseline condition and a treatment condition and repeated the reversal from baseline to treatment one more time. As shown in Figure 13.6, Cory's reaching and grasping increased from baseline to treatment at each reversal. Again, why is the last treatment condition included? In this case and the example presented earlier, the behavior under the B condition was preferable to the behavior under the A condition. Once we have demonstrated the causal relationship between an independent variable and the dependent variable with an ABA design, it is appropriate to use that relationship to return the subject to the best possible position—that is, to reinstate condition B. If you think about this, you should see that in many situations we would have an ethical obligation to do so.

Multiple Baseline Design

Although the ABA reversal design is a powerful demonstration of the effect of one variable on another, there are situations in which reversal procedures are not feasible or ethical. For example, suppose the self-stimulatory behavior of a child is injurious, such as severe head-banging, or suppose we succeed in improving the academic performance of a child in school. In both cases, we would be unwilling to reverse conditions once we achieved improved functioning. For the first child, a return to baseline could risk injury; for the second, it could risk disruption of the improved academic performance. Thus, the ABA reversal design used in the last example might not be acceptable. Instead, we could use a multiple baseline design.

In the *multiple baseline design* the effects of the treatment are demonstrated on different behaviors successively. To illustrate, we will use an example similar to the previous example of an ABA design. Suppose that a fifth-grade boy is doing poorly

Figure 13.6   A Study of Percentage of Trials in Which Cory Reached and Grasped Objects in Baseline and Treatment Conditions

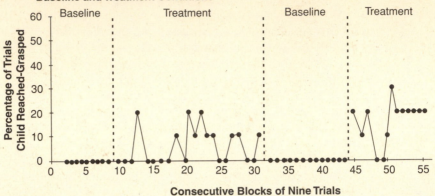

Source: Correa, V.I., Poulson, C.L., and Salzberg, C.L. (1984). *"Training and generalization of reach-grasp behavior in blind, retarded young children."* Journal of Applied Behavior Analysis, 17, *57–69.*

in both math and reading, although he appears to have the ability to achieve at a high level. He is also a class disrupter, continually interrupting and generally failing to attend to the academic work. A psychologist observes the class and notes some apparent contingencies regarding the boy's behavior—the teacher, attempting to control the boy, pays a good deal of attention to him whenever he is disruptive. The teacher scolds, corrects, and lectures him, draws the attention of the class to his antics in an effort to make him feel embarrassed, and makes him stand in a corner of the class. The psychologist notes that the boy seems to accept the attention with a good deal of pleasure. However, on those rare occasions when he does his academic work, the teacher ignores him. "When he is working, I leave well enough alone," the teacher says. "I don't want to risk stirring him up."

Based on these observed contingencies, the psychologist hypothesizes that the contingent teacher attention to the boy's disruptive behavior may be a major factor in maintaining the disruptive behavior, whereas the teacher's failure to attend to the boy's good academic work may account for its low occurrence. The psychologist sets up a multiple baseline design to test the hypothesis about the importance of teacher attention on both disruptive and academic behavior. Note that the independent variable here is teacher attention and the dependent variables are the child's (1) disruptive behavior, (2) math performance, and (3) reading performance. The independent variable is presented at two levels—presence of contingent teacher attention and absence of contingent teacher attention. Figure 13.7 shows the sequence of phases of the hypothetical study. During baseline, all three dependent variables are measured while the teacher continues the usual procedure of trying to punish the disruption and ignoring the effective academic behavior. Disruptive behavior is high, and math and reading performance are low in this phase. In the second phase, the teacher's attention to disruptive behavior is withdrawn and is instead focused on reading performance. In the third phase, both reading and math performance receive the teacher's attention whereas disruption continues to be ignored. The measured changes in the dependent variables associated with the indepen-

Figure 13.7   **Hypothetical Results of a Multiple Baseline Design Showing Improvement in Disruptive Behavior, Math Performance, and Reading Performance for a Single Child Contingent upon Teacher Attention**

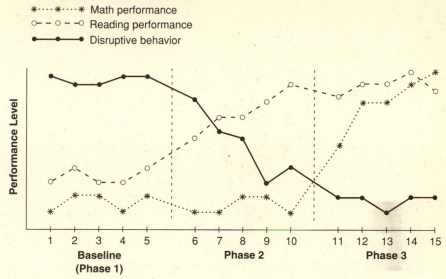

Single-Subject, Randomized, Time-Series Design

The multiple baseline procedure is effective in situations where a reversal design is not appropriate, but sometimes even this design is not feasible, such as when there is only one behavior at issue. The *single-subject, randomized, time-series design* is used to overcome these limitations. This design is an time-series design for a single subject with one additional element—the randomized assignment of the manipulation in the time-series.

The single-subject, randomized, time-series design could be applied to the single-subject experiments described above, but let us take another example. Suppose that Joey, another child in the special class, does not complete his daily work. During the 15-minute lesson periods in which he is supposed to be responding to a workbook lesson and marking answers on the page, Joey looks around the room or just closes his eyes and does no work. Frequent reminders by the teacher might rouse him briefly but not enough for him to complete the lessons. The teacher is convinced that Joey has the skills to do the academic work, but how can the teacher help him to show it?

An effective motivational intervention with children is a token reinforcement system in which paper or plastic tokens are given to the child whenever he engages in the desired behavior. The tokens serve as immediate secondary reinforcement for the desired behavior, and the child saves them and cashes them in for items and privileges that he or she prizes. If we are to employ a single-subject, randomized, time-series design, we might decide to measure the child's arithmetic achievement

"Hey, Dad! Who sez you guys could play with my tokens!"

for six weeks (30 school days), which would yield a time graph of 30 measurements. We devote a minimum number of days, perhaps the first 5 and the last 5 (1–5 and 26–30) to measure his pretreatment and posttreatment arithmetic achievement. This ensures adequate pretreatment and posttreatment measures. We then use a table of random numbers to select randomly one of the middle 20 days as our point for introducing the manipulation. The manipulation is the use of token reinforcement for arithmetic achievement. Suppose that we selected the number 9 from the table of random numbers, thus the beginning of the ninth day becomes our point for introducing the token reinforcement. The beginning of the manipulation is preceded by 8 days of arithmetic achievement measured under the usual nontoken condition followed by 22 days of measurements of the dependent variable under the token reinforcement condition. If the time graph shows a marked improvement in arithmetic achievement coincident with the ninth measurement, as shown in Figure 13.8, we have a convincing illustration of the effects of the token reinforcement. Note that it is highly unlikely that such marked improvement would occur by chance at exactly the point at which we have *randomly* introduced the treatment. It is also unlikely that this particular time-series pattern would have occurred because of maturation or history.

PROGRAM EVALUATION

The task in *program evaluation research* is to evaluate how successfully a program meets its goals. For example, we may need to evaluate a food stamp program, a state highway speed-control program, or the effectiveness of rehabilitation programs for criminal offenders. In these days of budget deficits, a key word is *accountability*. The goal of a good program evaluation is to provide evidence on whether the money being spent on the program is accomplishing the goals intended.

Program evaluation is not a set of research designs distinct from the designs discussed earlier in the text. Instead, these designs are modified to meet the constraints of the situation. We always want to use the best possible research design— the design that permits us to draw causal inferences with the greatest degree of confidence. However, program realities frequently restrict our choice of design.

Practical Problems in Program Evaluation Research

Perhaps what separates program evaluation research from many other types of research are the unique practical considerations involved. In lower-constraint research, we observe subjects in natural or only slightly constrained settings even though we realize it is difficult to impose effective controls in such settings. We normally are restricted to observing the public behavior of subjects. An unobtrusive study of the sexual behavior of married couples would be unethical—not to mention illegal. In higher-constraint research, we bring subjects into laboratory settings, allowing us to exercise more control over the situations. Again, we are usually ethically restricted to studying public behavior, although in theory we could get the permission of the subjects to study normally private behavior. Masters and Johnson (1966),

Figure 13.8   Hypothetical Results of a Single-Subject, Randomized, Time-Series Design Showing Improved Math Achievement by a Single Child

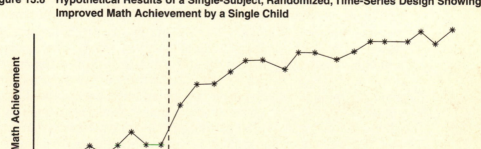

for example, obtained subjects who agreed to allow the researchers to observe and measure details of their physiological response during sexual activity—a normally private behavior. In program evaluation research, we evaluate the effectiveness of a program that operates in a complex and often uncontrolled natural setting. Further, we are often interested in how effective the program is in meeting the needs of clients—often a private and personal matter for each client. Finally, in most cases, the participants in the program generally are not people who have volunteered for a research study. Rather, they have become involved in the program because they have needs addressed by the program. Therefore, the program evaluator is faced with difficult practical and ethical considerations that few other researchers face.

Ethical constraints are common in program evaluation. Often the program is designed to meet an urgent need that cannot be ignored. The ideal research design from the perspective of internal validity would randomly assign subjects to one of two conditions—the program group and the no-program group. But is it ethical to deny food stamps to some randomly selected individuals to see whether they really suffer malnutrition more than individuals who are given food stamps, or to deny some children access to a special education program designed to overcome learning disabilities so we can evaluate the program? Sometimes, more than ethical concerns restrict the researcher. In our earlier example, one could argue that the learning disabilities program is experimental and may not work at all. In fact, it may do more harm than good in spite of the effort that went into designing it. Therefore, denying some subjects access to the program to allow a cleaner evaluation of its effectiveness is reasonable from an ethical perspective. However, it may not be acceptable from a political perspective. Depending on the perceived value of the program by the parents of children who might benefit from it and on the availability of other programs, the school board may believe that it is politically impossible to deny some students access to such a program. Any of these issues can prevent use of a randomly assigned control-group design in the evaluation.

Another ethical issue affecting program evaluation research is that of informed consent. Voluntary consent to participate in research is the cornerstone of most ethical guidelines. But people being served by a particular program may feel obligated to participate even if they do not wish to. They may fear that some of the benefits they receive from the program will be cut off if they do not cooperate. The program evaluator must be careful to minimize this kind of subtle coercion.

There are also practical issues that make program evaluations more challenging. Unlike controlled studies, which are conducted in the laboratory where the researcher can control most aspects of the study, the program is in a natural setting and usually not under the control of the evaluator. Staff members are interested in doing the best job they can in running the program, and evaluating it is often secondary. A good program evaluator needs excellent political skills to convince staff to cooperate in the evaluation and to maintain their cooperation throughout. Often when staff are involved in an evaluation, they resent the time that is taken away from their important work of providing services. If the evaluator is not sensitive to these realities, the relationship between the evaluator and staff in a program can become hostile. The program evaluator must be aware of potentially biasing factors in the data being gathered. A staff is generally interested in showing the program in its best possible light, not only because it is theirs but because a program that appears to be ineffective might not get continued funding. Clients may have a vested interest in the program if they believe it has been helpful, and they may therefore inflate their ratings of its effectiveness. On the other hand, some clients may believe that better programs could be implemented; therefore, they deflate their ratings of effectiveness. Such potential biases make it especially important that the evaluator rely on many data sources, at least some of which are objective measures.

Issues of Control

Control in program evaluation research is as important as in any other research. Because of the more naturalistic nature of the program evaluation setting, it is often more difficult to apply all the controls that would be ideal. However, many controls can be applied—three of which are discussed here.

Selecting Appropriate Dependent Measures   Most programs are developed with several goals in mind. Therefore, the program evaluator needs to use several dependent measures to evaluate the effectiveness of the program in meeting each of the intended goals. Some of the measures will focus on actual change in the individuals served by the program, and some will focus on changes outside the program (such as enhanced economic activity in the community). It is useful to include satisfaction measures, both from the people served by the program and from the community in general. Although satisfaction measures do not indicate the program's actual effectiveness, they are factors that can influence future effectiveness. An effective but politically unpopular program will need to work to address this issue or continued funding will be jeopardized.

Minimizing Bias in Dependent Measures   In any research, it is essential to minimize measurement bias. This is particularly important in program evaluation research, where the possibility of bias is high because data are often collected by the same people who run the program. Program evaluators try to minimize such bias by using objective rather than subjective measures and by using people who are not involved directly in the administration of the program to gather data. Many broad-based programs are intended to have community-wide effects that can be monitored using routinely available data such as census data. No technique for minimizing bias will be completely effective in all situations. One of the better approaches is to use several dependent measures. If each is a valid measure and they all point to the same general conclusion, we can be confident of the results.

Control Through Research Design in Program Evaluation   As with any research project, the major controls are incorporated into the research design. In program evaluation, the strongest research design is an experimental design with random assignment of subjects. When this cannot be done, the strongest alternative design should be used.

Typical Program Evaluation Designs

Dozens of research designs have been used for program evaluations, but two or three designs account for most of this research.

Randomized Control-Group Design The ideal design to use in program evaluation is a control-group design with random assignment of subjects to conditions. This design provides maximum control. The control group may be either a no-treatment control, a waiting-list control, or some alternative treatment strategy. Ethical considerations often dictate the nature of the control group. For example, under some conditions, it might not be ethical to assign some subjects to a no-treatment control group. In such situations, we may use the best treatment currently available as a control against which we compare the experimental procedure.

Nonequivalent Control-Group Design If a randomized control-group design is impossible, the best alternative is a nonequivalent control-group design. It is often possible to identify a natural control group that is likely to be very similar to the group you are evaluating. Our example earlier in this chapter of evaluating the California Child Passenger Restraint law used this design with time-series data. The researchers (Guerin & MacKinnon, 1985) selected two control groups—(1) children in the same age range from another state and (2) slightly older children (4–7 years old) from California. Children were not randomly assigned to these groups, but there was no reason to believe that the groups were different on variables likely to affect risk of death or injury from automobile accidents. So even though this was not a true experiment, it came very close to an experiment in its ability to rule out confounding variables. Remember, when an experiment is not possible, Campbell (1969) argued that we should consider a quasi-experimental design such as a nonequivalent control-group design.

Single-Group, Time-Series Design If a control group is not possible, the best alternative strategy for evaluation is a time-series design. Repeated measures on the dependent variables before, during, and after the program can control many threats to internal validity. Depending on the funding source, pretest measures may be difficult to obtain because there is often pressure to begin services as soon as funds are released. Still, this design is flexible and useful in many situations. In fact, even when a control group is possible, using a time-series strategy with repeated preprogram and postprogram measures would increase confidence in the evaluation of the program's effectiveness.

Pretest-Posttest Design The pretest-posttest design is weak. Unfortunately, it is used much too often in program evaluation research. With only two measures and no control group, almost none of the threats to internal validity are controlled. The simple pretest-posttest design is not recommended.

Program Evaluation: An Example

Managed care is a concept that has quickly become a part of health insurance coverage in this country. With managed care, the insurance company or an organization hired by the insurance company attempts to control health care expenditures by monitoring health care and authorizing each procedure according to the principle of whether it is "medically necessary." The promise is that managed care will provide quality health care at lower cost by reducing waste and eliminating unnecessary procedures. Critics charge that managed care reduces costs by denying patients the treatment that they require. In a debate of this magnitude, it is surprising that almost no data exist on the effectiveness of managed care programs in meeting their stated goals.

Raulin and his colleagues (Raulin, Brenner, deBeaumont, & Vetter, 1995; Raulin, deBeaumont, Brenner, & Vetter, 1995) used a nonequivalent control-group design to evaluate the effectiveness of a program to manage mental health benefits. Stratified random samples were selected from two insurance plans operated by the same insurance carrier—one that included management of mental health benefits and one that represented the standard insurance policy. The samples were stratified on age, sex, and severity of diagnosis—factors that are known to affect the outcome and cost of psychological treatment. Subjects were selected from health insurance plans that were matched on their total mental health coverage. Although subjects were not randomly assigned to groups, the selection procedure produced groups from the same geographical area that were closely matched on key demographic variables and had equivalent health care insurance coverage.

Subjects selected by the above procedures were recruited by letter to participate. To increase the likelihood of participation, subjects were offered a payment equivalent to $40 per hour for participation in a phone interview. As is often the case in program evaluation studies, initial procedures had to be modified because they did not work well. Face-to-face interviews were replaced with a phone interview (to make it more convenient for subjects) and an initial $25 per hour reimbursement rate was raised to $40 per hour. Of course, not all subjects that were contacted by letter chose to participate. It would be unethical to insist that everyone selected participate. Therefore, we have to accept that our sample may not be perfectly representative of the population because of self-selection biases for subjects. Approximately one-fourth of the subjects selected for the study did agree to participate, and there were no differences between the subjects who agreed to participate and those who refused on key demographic variables.

The managed care program evaluated in this study was designed to accomplish several things. Therefore, several dependent measures were needed in the evaluation to evaluate adequately how well the program was functioning. Patients were evaluated on (1) symptom level using several well validated symptom measures, (2) mood, also using measures with established validity, and (3) satisfaction with their care and their insurance coverage. In addition, cost data were obtained from the insurance carrier for both mental health coverage and for other medical care. (Previous research had suggested that skimping on mental health coverage increases general medical costs because the patients take their concerns to their family physician.)

The data suggest that the management of mental health benefits did not decrease the quality of care as measured by the standardized symptom and mood scales and the patient satisfaction measures used in the study. The mental health care costs were reduced by approximately 50% in the managed care group, and there were no differences between the groups on medical costs.

This was not a perfect study; no program evaluation ever is. Compromises have to be made when testing programs because of ethical and practical constraints. But this study did provide useful data on the effectiveness of a particular program relative to an alternative program. Caution is necessary in generalizing from this study to managed care programs in general. This study involved only the management of mental health benefits and therefore could tell us little about whether managing general medical benefits would work as well. The managed care firm evaluated was relatively small, operated locally, and run by an unusually well qualified clinical director. It is not clear that we could generalize the findings of this study to other managed care operations—usually much bigger and operated out of regional or national centers. But even with these limitations, this study provides useful data for making critical policy decisions on how to spend our health care dollars.

Interal Summary: Program Evaluation

In program evaluation, the researcher faces the major problem of attempting high-constraint research in low-constraint naturalistic settings. Compromises are often forced on the evaluator by limitations of the setting. However, program evaluation is a valuable tool in the management of limited resources, because ineffective programs consume dollars that might have been spent on effective programs. Program evaluation is both a science and an art. One needs good research skills and excellent political and communication skills to conduct program evaluations successfully. More than any other kind of research project, program evaluation depends on the ability of the researcher to gain the cooperation of people who are not necessarily committed to the cause of maximizing internal and external validity.

SUMMARY

Low-constraint research enables us to observe the natural flow of behavior in natural settings, try out new procedures, initiate research in new areas of inquiry, negate general propositions, and most importantly, observe contingencies and develop hypotheses that can be tested at higher constraint levels. With low-constraint methods, however, we cannot rule out alternative hypotheses and, therefore, cannot test causal hypotheses. In this chapter, we returned to a discussion of research in naturalistic settings that was first presented in Chapter 6. Here, however, we discussed higher-constraint research, including experimental research in naturalistic settings. Three major topics were discussed: quasi-experimental designs, single-subject designs, and program evaluation.

Specific quasi-experimental and single-subject designs, as well as their strengths and weaknesses, were discussed. Program evaluation involves the use of many of the designs to evaluate the practical effectiveness of programs carried out in naturalistic settings, such as education and therapy programs, public health programs, traffic control, and so on. Although program evaluation is difficult because of many constraints imposed by the natural setting on the researcher, it has become a major area of applied research in the social sciences.

REVIEW EXERCISES

13.1   **Define the following key terms. Be sure you understand them. They are discussed in the chapter and defined in the glossary.**

field research
quasi-experimental design
nonequivalent control-group design
difference scores
crossover effect
interrupted time-series design

single-subject designs
  reversal (ABA) design
  multiple baseline design
  single-subject, randomized,
    time-series design
program evaluation

13.2   **Answer each of the following. Check your answers in the chapter.**

1. Naturalistic research is the focus in Chapter 6, and research in naturalistic (field) settings is the focus in this chapter. How do the research discussed in Chapter 6 and that discussed here differ?
2. What are the reasons why naturalistic research, as discussed in Chapter 6, cannot answer questions of causality?
3. Why would we want to conduct experiments in field settings?
4. Distinguish between applied and basic research. Give at least two examples of each.
5. What are quasi-experimental designs? Under what conditions would we want to use these designs? Give an example.
6. What are the major characteristics of experiments?
7. Name and define the two kinds of quasi-experimental designs discussed in this chapter. Give at least two examples of each.
8. As a review, define ex post facto research and discuss its limitations.
9. Under what conditions do we use single-subject designs?
10. What is the major weakness of single-subject designs?
11. What types of single-subject designs are there? Name and define each.
12. What is meant by "program evaluation"?
13. What is the importance of program evaluation?
14. What are the major difficulties in doing program evaluation?

13.3   **Think about and work the following problems.**

1. The following graphs represent results in several nonequivalent control-group designs. How do you interpret each? (Assume that the differences are statistically significant.)

✳ = Control Group
○ = Experimental Group

(a)   (b)   (c)

2. How would you interpret the following results of time-series designs?

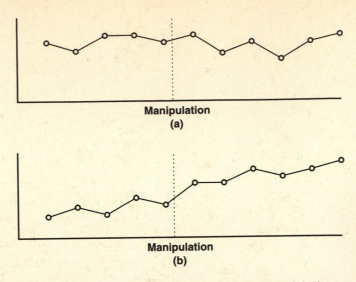

Manipulation
(a)

Manipulation
(b)

3. Explain how we determine causality from single-subject designs.
4. You are the teaching assistant in this course, and you have to explain to the class that there are important tradeoffs in doing highly controlled experimental research in the laboratory, rather than doing research in field settings. What are the tradeoffs? Explain this carefully to the class.

Chapter 14

Final Preparations Before Data Collection

In this chapter two important ideas will be discussed—the selection of appropriate statistical procedures and the necessity for the pre-data check. In both discussions we will summarize much of the material presented earlier in the text, but the ideas are so important that this entire chapter has been devoted to them.

SELECTING APPROPRIATE STATISTICAL PROCEDURES

Research is a systematic process of inquiry proceeding across all phases from initial ideas through problem definition, design, observation, data processing, interpretation, and communication. At each phase the researcher makes important decisions to design and carry out the research. One decision made in the design phase is what statistical procedures to use in analyzing the results. The decision about how to analyze data should be made *before* data collection. This demand is relaxed somewhat at the more flexible naturalistic level but becomes increasingly important at higher levels of constraint. We must select statistical tests that are appropriate and valid for the data we plan to collect and the questions we are asking. It would be a most unpleasant surprise to find after six months of data collection that there is no way to analyze the data to answer the questions that we posed.

Choosing an appropriate statistical procedure is often a difficult task for the beginning student. Because there are so many research designs, a large array of questions that can be asked in each design, and a variety of statistical procedures, students sometimes are overwhelmed by the data-analysis process. As illustrated in the accompanying cartoon, sometimes the vast amount of information with which one is faced makes it difficult to know where to focus. But like everything else in research, careful systematic steps can simplify the decisions and bring the process under control. This set of decisions—how to select appropriate statistical analyses—is the major focus in this section.

An Initial Example

As in most aspects of research, a systematic approach is needed to select the appropriate statistical procedure. Chapters 5 and 10–12 laid the groundwork, describing several research designs and illustrating appropriate statistical procedures. Appropriate statistical procedures are determined by the characteristics of the research such as the number of independent variables, type of question, and level of measurement for each dependent variable. Let us take an example of a relatively simple study and determine how to analyze it statistically. Remember, the first step is to describe the research carefully so as to identify its important characteristics.

Incidental Learning in Rats

An experimenter has hypothesized that laboratory rats can learn incidentally without specific rewards. Twenty rats are used in the experiment. As a control, all rats are first exposed to several different mazes for two hours.

"You don't often see a real silk lining, these days. . . ."

Source: Drawing by Spencer, copyright © Punch/Rothco. Reprinted by courtesy of Punch.

After the exposure, none of the animals shows any signs of stress when placed in new mazes. The 20 maze-adapted animals are randomly assigned to two conditions—10 animals per condition. The experimental group is allowed to explore the test maze for one hour without any rewards. The control group does not explore the test maze. All animals are then given learning trials in the test maze, and each successful trial is reinforced with food reward. The experimental and control groups are compared on the number of learning trials needed to reach a learning criterion of five successive correct trials. The research hypothesis is that the experimental group, having explored the test maze prior to their reinforced learning trials, needs significantly fewer learning trials to reach criterion than does the control group.

Our task is to determine the appropriate statistical procedure to use in the research on learning in rats. The preceding description provides all the information we need. Remember that the characteristics of the research determine what statistical procedures to use. Thus, we need to refer to the description and ask questions that will identify the characteristics of the research.

1. **What is the level of constraint for the research?** Experimental.
2. **What are the independent variables?** There is one independent variable—exploration of the maze prior to learning trials.
3. **What are the levels of the independent variable?** There are two levels—prior exploration and no prior exploration.
4. **What type of design is the research** (i.e., independent-groups, correlated-groups, mixed, and so on)? Independent-groups design.
5. **What are the dependent variables?** There is one dependent variable—maze learning (i.e., operationally defined as the number of trials needed to reach criterion).
6. **What is (are) the dependent measure(s)** (i.e., how is the dependent variable to be measured)? There is one dependent measure—number of maze-running trials needed to reach criterion.
7. **What is the level of measurement of each dependent measure?** Ratio.
8. **What type of data is generated for the dependent measure?** Score data.
9. **What is (are) the research hypothesis (hypotheses)?** There is one research hypothesis—The experimental group will require fewer learning trials than the control group to reach criterion.
10. **What kind of test is needed** (e.g., a test of relationship, a test of differences, etc.)? A test of differences (i.e., a test of the null hypothesis of no differences between the experimental and control groups).

We have now determined that our example study is an independent-groups experimental design in which a hypothesized difference between two groups is tested. There is only one dependent variable—maze learning—and measuring it yields score data. The appropriate statistical procedure is one that can test differences between independent groups with score data. Recall from earlier discussions that the t-test for independent groups or the one-way ANOVA are appropriate. We also routinely include descriptive statistics to summarize data and help us interpret the results.

In our simple example, the decision about what statistical procedure to use is easily made. In more complex research, where there may be several research hypotheses and several dependent measures, we may need a number of statistical procedures, perhaps a different one for each hypothesis. In such complex research the decisions are not so readily apparent, but the procedure to arrive at them is essentially the same. First we describe the research; then we ask a number of questions to identify its important characteristics; finally, we use the characteristics identified and proceed to make decisions to arrive at the appropriate statistical procedures. This sequence of steps has been incorporated into the following discussion of a decision-tree model.

A Decision-Tree Model

The remainder of this section describes a decision-making model for determining the appropriate statistical procedure(s) for research designs. We use a *decision tree* where we follow a line of thinking, reach a decision point, make the decision, and then branch off in appropriate directions based on the decision. These lines of think-

Figure 14.1 Selecting Statistical Analyses: Initial Flowchart

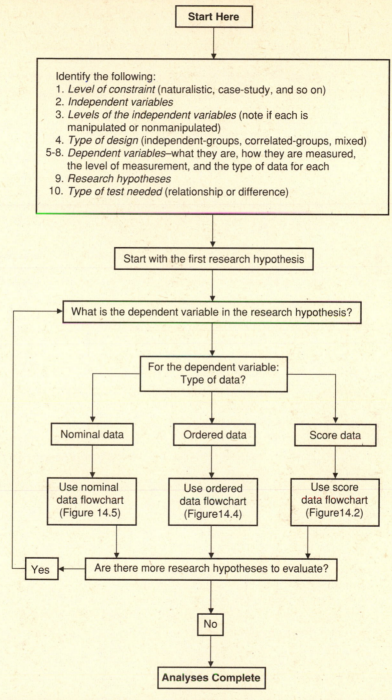

ing and the branching-off process are organized in five decision-tree flowcharts, which are shown in Figures 14.1 through 14.5.[1]

[1]The flowcharts are also provided as tear-out sheets in the Study Guide.

Figure 14.2   Selecting Statistical Analyses: Score Data Flowchart

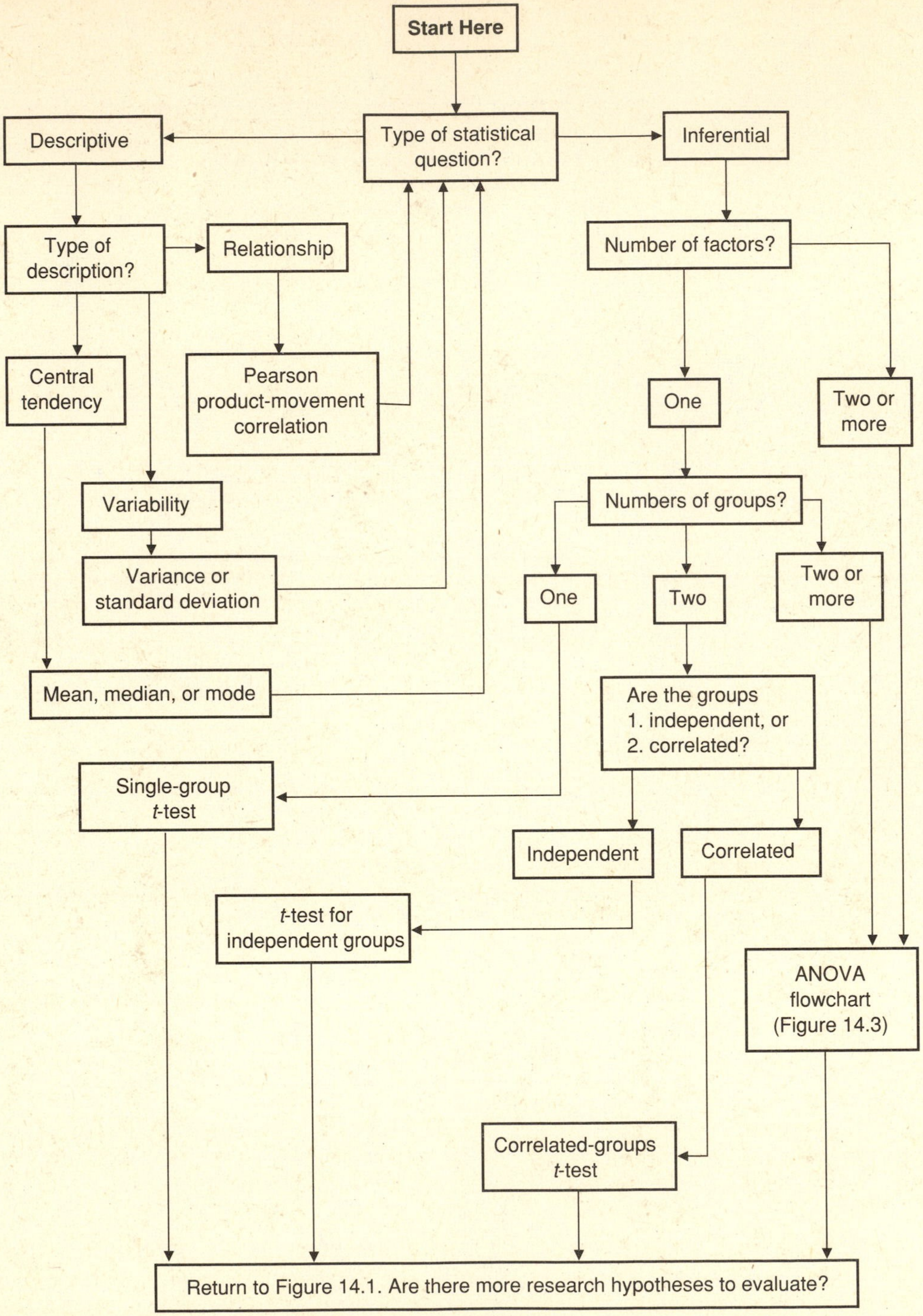

Figure 14.3   Selecting Statistical Analyses: ANOVA Flowchart

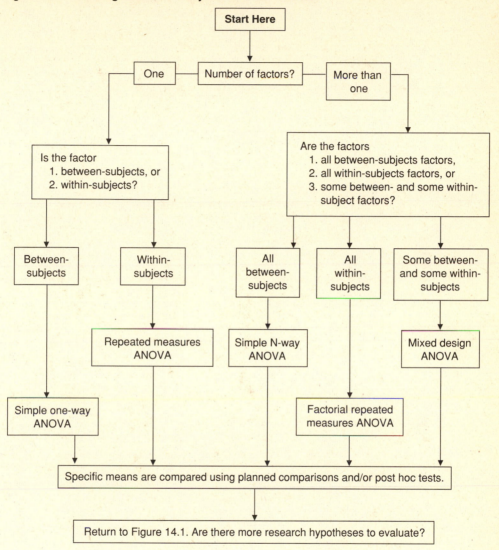

Note: Most formulas for the various ANOVAs and related statistical tests can be found in Appendix C. For additional computational procedures, consult an advanced statistics text (e.g., Myers, 1972; Winer, 1971).

To use the model the researcher begins by describing the research, asking questions to identify the major characteristics of the research, and proceeds through the flowcharts, until the appropriate statistical procedures are determined. As we move through the flowcharts, each decision moves us closer to a particular statistical procedure. The questions to be answered in the decision tree are discussed in

Figure 14.4   Selecting Statistical Analyses: Ordered Data Flowchart

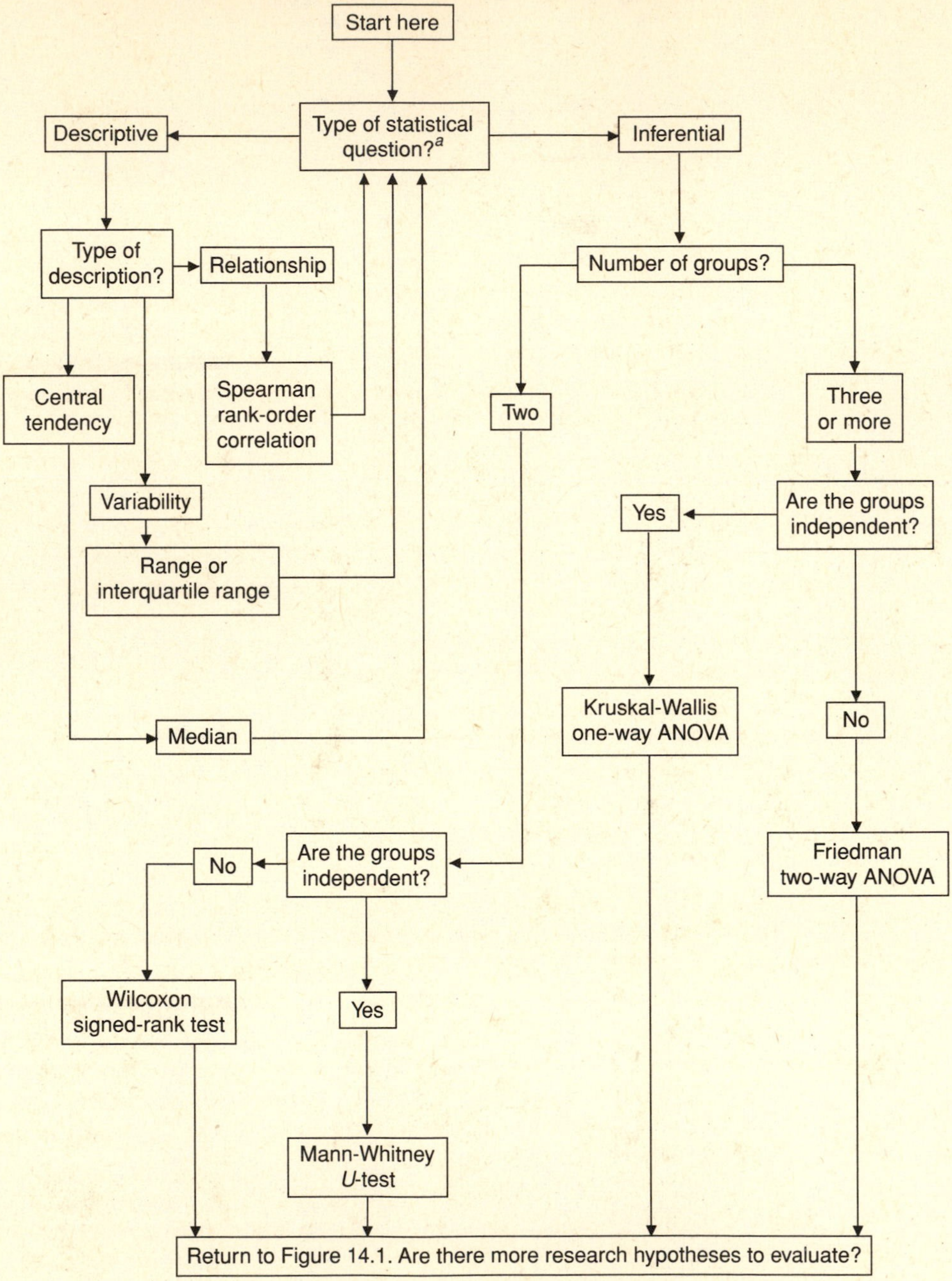

[a] It is best to start with descriptive statistics.

Note: Computational formulas for the statistical procedures described here can be found in Siegel (1956).

Figure 14.5   Selecting Statistical Analyses: Nominal Data Flowchart

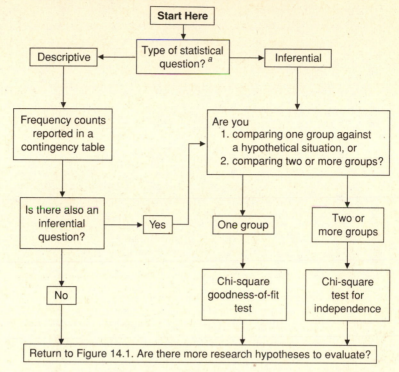

[a]It is best to start with descriptive statistics.

detail in earlier chapters. There are no new concepts in this chapter; rather, this chapter makes the decision process more formal and systematic.

Decision-Tree Flowcharts   The *decision-tree flowcharts* organized the sequence of ideas through which the decision-making process flows. Because the procedures discussed may not be clear after a first reading, we recommend that you reread them and complete the exercises at the end of the chapter until you thoroughly understand the procedures. In the next section we present an example of research and proceed through the flowcharts to determine the appropriate statistical procedures.

Most studies test more than one research hypothesis and include more than one dependent measure. Therefore, several statistical procedures may be required. Descriptive statistics are first computed for all variables in the study. If there are separate groups, the descriptive statistics are computed for each group. In lower-constraint research, descriptive statistics may be all that are needed. In higher-constraint research, however, we generally have refined the questions and designed the study to answer specific questions about differences between groups. Therefore, at the higher-constraint levels, we want to use the power of inferential statistics to determine answers to questions. In most cases, we cycle through the flowcharts several times to determine appropriate statistical procedures before all questions are answered.

Figures 14.1 through 14.5 present the flowcharts for determining the appropriate statistical procedure. Figure 14.1 shows the overall structure of the decision tree;

it is the initial flowchart. Figures 14.2 through 14.5 present specific sections of the overall flowchart given in Figure 14.1. Although the flowcharts may look imposing, they are easy to follow. To illustrate the process we will use the flowcharts to determine the set of statistical analyses for a hypothetical study of social problem-solving skills in young children.

Identifying Research Variables To use the decision-tree flowcharts, we need to identify and organize key aspects of the research design as we did in the preceding example. This list of research design characteristics helps to organize the analysis of data from the study.

Our hypothetical research study focuses on social problem-solving skills in sixth-grade children. We will compare boys and girls in their problem-solving skills using several different measures. The research is more complex than the animal-learning study presented earlier because several research hypotheses are being tested. Thus, we need to determine several statistical analyses. No matter how complex the study may be, the procedures for determining an appropriate statistical analysis are the same as in the simpler example.

1. Describe the study.
2. Identify its major characteristics.
3. Make systematic decisions using the flowcharts.

Sex Differences in Children's Social Problem-Solving Skills

The study compares sixth-grade boys and girls on their problem-solving skills in social situations. From the sixth grade of a local grammar school, 20 boys and 20 girls are randomly selected. Three different measures are taken in the study. In the first measure, subjects are tested individually. Ten social situations are described to each subject. In each of these situations, one or more social problems or conflicts will be included (e.g., another student pushes ahead in line). Three ways to solve the conflict are described for each situation, and the subject is asked to choose one of the three solutions (i.e., a multiple-choice test). For each problem, one solution is clearly most socially appropriate and, therefore, is considered to be the correct answer. Each subject's score is the number of correct choices for the ten social situations. The task is presented to the children on audiotape with a coordinated filmstrip to standardize the presentation and to maximize the children's attention. The second dependent measure is the teacher's ranking of the children on social competence. The ranking is based on observations of the children's behavior in three settings—the structured classroom, an unstructured social activity within the classroom, and recess. For the third dependent measure, an independent rater classifies each of the children as either "above average in social competence" or "below average in social competence" based on standardized information provided by the teachers.

The research focuses on sex differences in problem-solving skills. The statement of the problem is: "Is there a sex difference in problem-solving skills for sixth-grade students?" The problem statement combined with operational definitions leads to three research hypotheses:

1. Sixth-grade boys and girls differ in the identification of the correct social response in a multiple-choice task.
2. Sixth-grade boys and girls differ in their ranking on social competence based on observations in three behavior settings.
3. Sixth-grade boys and girls differ in the proportion classified as either "above average on social competence" or "below average on social competence."

Identifying the Study's Major Characteristics   Having described the study, the next step is to identify its major characteristics.

1. **Level of constraint?** Differential (i.e., differences between two preexisting groups).
2. **Independent variables?** There is one independent variable—the sex of subjects. It is a nonmanipulated independent variable.
3. **Levels of the independent variable?** There are two levels of the independent variable—boys and girls.
4. **Type of design?** Independent-groups, differential design.

5–8. **Dependent variable(s)?** There are three dependent variables (5). Their measures are listed below (6), along with the level of measurement for each (7), and the type of data generated by each measure (8).

Dependent Measure	Level of Measurement	Type of Data
Score on the social-skills multiple-choice test	Ratio	Score
Ranking of subjects on social competence	Ordinal	Ordered
Independent classification of social competence	Nominal	Nominal

9. **Research hypotheses?** There are three research hypotheses:
   a. Sixth-grade boys and girls differ in the identification of the correct social response in a multiple-choice task.
   b. Sixth-grade boys and girls differ in their ranking on social competence based on observations in three behavior settings.
   c. Sixth-grade boys and girls differ in the proportion classified as either "above average on social competence" or "below average on social competence."
10. **What kind of test is needed?** For each hypothesis, a test of differences between independent groups is needed.

As we can see, the study is a differential, independent-groups design with two levels of the nonmanipulated independent variable. The dependent measures generate three different levels of data. Therefore, we suspect that different statistical procedures will be used to analyze data from each dependent measure. We are interested in testing for group differences.

Selecting Appropriate Descriptive and Inferential Statistics   After the major characteristics of the study are identified, the next step is to determine the appropriate procedures for descriptive statistics and inferential statistics for each of the three hypotheses. It is useful to begin with descriptive statistics.

The first hypothesis uses a multiple-choice test as the dependent measure. We start by calculating *descriptive statistics* and do so separately for each of the two groups (boys and girls). The flowcharts help us select the appropriate statistics. We have already accomplished the first task outlined in the initial flowchart (Figure 14.1)—identifying the major characteristics of the study. Therefore, we move down the flowchart and begin with the first research hypothesis. The first hypothesis is: "Sixth-grade boys and girls differ in the identification of the correct social response in a multiple-choice task." The dependent variable for the hypothesis is the social skills multiple-choice test. We follow Figure 14.1 to the point where the flowchart inquires, "For the Dependent Variable: Type of Data?" As we have already determined, this dependent variable produces score data. Therefore, following the flowchart, we are directed to use the score data flowchart (Figure 14.2).

We are interested in descriptive statistics at this point, so we move to the left branch of Figure 14.2. Here we are asked, "Type of Description?" Normally for score data we want both a measure of central tendency and a measure of variability. The flowchart tells us that the mean, median, and mode are appropriate measures of central tendency and the variance and standard deviation are appropriate measures of variability for score data. We ordinarily compute only the mean as the measure of central tendency. Thus, the mean, variance, and standard deviation are computed as the descriptive statistics for each of the two groups.

Now that we have determined the appropriate descriptive statistics for the first hypothesis, we turn to *inferential statistics* for the first hypothesis. The score data flowchart (Figure 14.2) directs us back to the box asking, "Type of Statistical Question?" We are interested in an inferential question, so we branch to the right in Figure 14.2, where it asks for the number of factors. Because we have one factor (the independent variable—biological sex), we follow that branch to where it asks for the number of groups. Because we have two groups (boys and girls), we can go in either of two directions. The rightmost branch takes us to a simple one-way analysis of variance (see Figure 14.3). The middle branch leads to a *t*-test (for independent groups). Both are correct procedures and will lead to the same conclusions about differences between the groups. Having selected an inferential statistical procedure for the first research hypothesis, we return to Figure 14.1. Thus, we determine that for Hypothesis 1 we calculate means, variances, and standard deviations as descriptive statistics and use an independent-groups *t*-test or a simple one-way ANOVA for the inferential statistic.

As we move down the initial flowchart (Figure 14.1), we are asked whether there are more research hypotheses to evaluate. Because there are, we look to the middle portion of the flowchart where it asks, "What Is the Dependent Variable in the Research Hypothesis?" We identify the variable and move down to where it asks what type of data it represents. For the second research hypothesis, the dependent measure is the teacher's rankings of the children's social competence (ordered data). The flowchart tells us to consult Figure 14.4—the ordered data flowchart. We are interested in descriptive statistics, so we branch to the left and are informed that the median is an appropriate measure of central tendency and the range or the interquartile range is the appropriate measure of variability for ordered data. Having determined the appropriate descriptive statistics for the second research hypothesis, we now turn to the inferential statistics. We follow the flowchart back to the box asking, "Type of Statistical Question?" We branch right to find an appropriate inferential statistical procedure. If we follow the flowchart correctly (for two independent groups), it will suggest a Mann-Whitney U-test.

The third research hypothesis uses a dependent variable that is measured on a nominal scale, and we are therefore directed by the initial flowchart to use Figure 14.5—the nominal data flowchart. If we follow the flowchart correctly, we determine that frequency counts in a contingency table is an appropriate descriptive statistic. Likewise, an appropriate inferential procedure is a chi-square test for independence.

If our study were a larger one with more research hypotheses, we would continue this process of using the flowcharts to find the correct descriptive and inferential statistics and compute the statistics for all remaining dependent measures in the study. The example illustrates the need to be well organized during the work because of the many different decisions to be made. Carefully labeling the results will minimize errors during later analyses and report writing. Most research studies employ more than one measure and test more than one research hypothesis. Although computers can simplify the task of computation, the researcher still needs to decide what statistics to compute, and to label and organize the computer output carefully to avoid later confusion or error.

We recommend that you use these flowcharts with other research examples. With practice, you will become familiar with the rules in the flowcharts and eventually will not need to refer to them. Indeed, that is a goal. But initially, when learning to make decisions, the flowcharts provide a convenient way to organize necessary information when selecting a statistical procedure.

Secondary Analyses

After completing descriptive and inferential analyses, we often carry out secondary analyses. *Secondary analyses* typically fall into three categories: (1) *post hoc analyses* or planned comparisons to look at specific mean differences after conducting an overall ANOVA; (2) analyses designed to help explain the pattern of results; or (3) unplanned exploratory analyses (sometimes referred to as data snooping).

Post Hoc Analyses   When doing an ANOVA with more than two groups, specific mean comparisons are the logical next step in the interpretation of significant F-ratios. The significant F in a one-way ANOVA, for example, tells us only that at least one of the means is significantly different from at least one other mean. It does not tell us which means are different from which other means. Most often, the interpretation requires this more specific information, which can be provided by a variety of post hoc tests or planned comparisons.

Secondary Analyses to Help Explain Results   Another set of secondary analyses involves looking at variables that may help to explain the observed set of results.

Suppose that differences are found but that they are difficult to interpret because we cannot be sure that some confounding variable was adequately controlled. This kind of problem is less common in experimental research because the high level of control minimizes potential confounding. In lower-constraint research, particularly in differential research, these issues can be real problems, and secondary analyses are often essential to interpret data adequately.

A set of secondary analyses that should be included in the report of any research project regardless of its level of constraint are descriptive statistics on the demographic characteristics of the sample of subjects (e.g., age, social class, level of education, and so on). These statistics allow us to compare different studies in terms of the populations studied. They also give us information needed to determine the limits of generalizability of the findings.

These are only some of the uses of secondary statistical analyses to help interpret findings of a primary analysis. Some of the analyses in this category are quite sophisticated and beyond the scope of this text. It is important to realize, however, that in many lower-constraint research studies the secondary analyses may outnumber the primary analyses and be critical in the interpretation of the results.

Data Snooping   The third set of secondary analyses are what we have called *data snooping.* Here researchers can play their hunches and see whether, for example, there are any relationships, differences, or interactions that were not predicted. Data snooping is useful in large-scale, lower-constraint studies, where clues to many potential relationships between variables may be buried in the mass of data. Good data snooping is as much an art as a science. However, it is important to note that we must be cautious in interpreting relationships discovered in such a post hoc treasure hunt. If we are appropriately cautious, data snooping can be a rich source of hypotheses for later research, and it should not be overlooked. At least one high-level text is devoted entirely to this art (Tukey, 1977).

Caveats and Disclaimers

The flowchart system outlined in this chapter is designed as a teaching device—a way to organize and formalize what is often a difficult task for students. The inferential statistics portion of this system focuses on the kinds of questions asked most often in psychological hypotheses—specifically, are there mean differences between groups on the dependent measure? There are other kinds of questions—such as, "Are there differences in the variability between the groups?"—that are not covered by the set of flowcharts. For such questions, other reference sources need to be consulted (Keppel, 1991; Myers & Well, 1991). However, for a large majority of the typical questions investigated in psychological research the flowcharts will identify an appropriate statistical procedure to use.

The statistical procedures suggested by the flowcharts are not the only appropriate procedures for answering a specific question. In almost all cases, there are alternative data-analysis approaches available. The statistical procedures given in Figures 14.1 through 14.5 are the ones most commonly used in these situations, but other procedures may also be appropriate. Therefore, the flowcharts are more helpful in finding a statistical procedure to use in a study than in evaluating whether a particular statistical approach used by some other researcher is appropriate.

Box 14.1   **The Robust Nature of Parametric Statistics**

At several points in the text, we note that statistical tests make assumptions about the data. For example, an implicit assumption of parametric statistics (e.g., *t*-test, ANOVA) is that data are on at least an interval level of measurement (score data). But most parametric tests make other assumptions about data, which are not highlighted in the text because they are not critical. Sometimes an assumption on which an inferential statistical procedure is based can be violated without threatening the validity of the conclusion drawn from the statistical test. In such a case, we say that the statistical procedure is *robust* to violations of the assumption. For example, many statistical tests assume that scores in the population are distributed normally (i.e., they form a symmetric bell-shaped distribution). If the population of scores is actually skewed, we have violated an assumption of the statistical test. If that statistical procedure is not robust to this assumption, the violation distorts the procedure, making conclusions drawn from the statistical analysis suspect. Fortunately, most parametric statistics are robust to violations of assumptions about population distributions. We can use them confidently regardless of the shape of the distributions.

As it turns out, most parametric statistics are robust to violations of almost all assumptions on which they are based if the sample size in each of the groups is approximately equal (Glass, Peckham, & Sanders, 1972). This conclusion is based on a series of computer simulation studies known as Monte Carlo studies (named after the famous gambling resort). In a *Monte Carlo study* the computer is used to simulate sampling of subjects from populations with known characteristics. In this way the researcher can see what effect violations of assumptions have on the accuracy of decisions. The approach has been used to investigate the effects of violations of single assumptions or violations of more than one assumption at the same time (Levy, 1980). Monte Carlo studies continue to show the remarkable robustness of most statistics to assumption violations when sample sizes are equal. Consequently, these assumptions are not emphasized in the text and are not built into the decision rules of the flowcharts.

Note the emphasis above on equal sample sizes. Unless sample sizes of groups are approximately equal, violations of assumptions may affect the validity of statistical procedures. Hence, from a design perspective, particularly for the novice researcher, it is beneficial to try to have approximately equal sample sizes.

PRE-DATA CHECK

At some point the researcher is ready to make the observations that will yield data—the empirical component of the research. Making the observations involves recording subjects' responses in either natural settings or in more controlled laboratory settings. The data from the subjects will be analyzed, interpreted, and communicated. Research plans are complex, and if not constructed carefully, then all the work of collecting data might be compromised and the value of the data seriously impaired. Thus, the researcher must be sure that all of the preliminary planning has been completed before beginning to gather data. This is somewhat like the airline pilot who makes a pre-flight check to ensure that all parts of the complicated machinery are functioning properly—in that case to be sure that the plane is ready to fly. Likewise, the researcher should carry out a *pre-data check* to see if the research "is ready to fly."

Let us assume that you have developed your hypotheses, designed your study, and have made all preparations for data collection. Now, stop. Now is the time to go through the pre-data checklist to make sure you are ready to begin data collection. The steps in the pre-data check are briefly discussed below and summarized in Table 14.1.

I. Initial Problem Definition

Go back to the very beginning of your project. By now you must have completed your literature review based on your initial ideas. In that process you have refined your statement of the problem and identified the major variables you will be studying. Now you must check to see that those variables have been operationally defined appropriately.

1. Has a literature review of initial ideas been completed?
2. Has the problem statement been clearly developed?
3. Are variables identified and operationally defined?

II. Clarity of the Research Hypothesis (or Hypotheses)

Having completed the check in part I, now move on to check your research hypotheses. In order to proceed with the study, the research hypothesis must be clearly stated as a prediction of relationship between two or more variables. The relationship may be differential, correlational, or causal, but must be clearly indicated in the research hypothesis. Further, the research hypothesis should indicate the type and, if appropriate, the direction of the relationship.

4. Does the research hypothesis clearly state the type and direction of relationship among the variables?

III. Statistical Analysis Procedures

Statistical analysis procedures should be selected before you gather data. Know what descriptive statistical procedures you are going to run. Double-check your inferential statistical procedures—know what statistical procedures will be used for each research hypothesis (here you can use the flowcharts presented earlier in this chapter).

5. Are all descriptive statistical procedures planned?
6. For each hypothesis, are inferential statistical procedures planned?
7. Are you planning post hoc or secondary analyses? If so, what are they?

IV. Theoretical Basis and Operational Definitions

You know that near the end of your work, after you have obtained and analyzed your data, you will have the all-important task of interpreting and communicating the results. These rational processes provide meaning to your research, its discoveries, and implications for theory. These processes can also stimulate further research and influence practical applications. Thus, it is critical that you have a clear understanding of the theoretical bases for your research. Make sure that your hypotheses and your procedures in fact do address the issues you raised initially, so your results can be related to those issues.

8. Is the theoretical base for your study clear?
9. Do your hypotheses and procedures address the issues?

V. Adequacy of the Independent Variable Manipulation (for Experimental Research)

The essence of experimentation is the creation and protection of internal validity, and that means the experimental manipulations must be carefully selected and carried out. Have the manipulations (the operational definitions of the experimental and control groups) been clearly defined and pretested for feasibility?

10. Have the independent variable manipulations been carefully planned (experimental and control groups clearly operationally defined)?
11. Have the manipulations been pretested? Are changes needed?
12. Has a manipulation check been planned?

VI. Adequacy of the Dependent Measures

It is critical that the dependent measures be adequate. They must be clearly defined—both conceptually and operationally. They should be pretested for feasibility (i.e., ease and smoothness of presentation). You should evaluate reliability and validity data, if available. If these are new measures, they should have been pretested and reliability and validity data obtained. In either event, be sure you have included procedures to measure their reliability in your current research. Know how the responses are to be recorded and scored. Your piloting of the procedures should tell you about how long the subjects will require to complete the tasks, and at what points there may be some difficulties for them. Problems in administration of the procedures should all be solved before you test a single subject. Be sure you know the level of measurement and type of data for each dependent measure. These measures will constitute your data—be careful and precise in obtaining them.

13. Are all dependent measures operationally defined?
14. Have they been pretested or piloted?
15. Do you have prior reliability and validity data?
16. Did you include procedures to measure reliability?

VII. Are All Controls in Place?

Now is the time for the final check to see that you have carefully anticipated threats to internal and external validity. Double check to see that all your controls are in place. You do not want to complete your data collection only to find out that some uncontrolled factor provides an alternative explanation of your results.

17. Are controls for threats to internal validity in place?
18. Are controls for external validity in place?

VIII. Subjects

A. Subject Selection and Representativeness of the Sample   The researcher must be sure that the subjects adequately represent the target population. You should know the type of sample you have (a random sample, a stratified random sample, an ad hoc sample). You must have confidence that you will be able to make inferences with confidence about the target population.

Adequate demographic measures must be included to define the sample, especially if this is an ad hoc sample. Measures of age, sex, socioeconomic class, and so on are necessary if (a) any generalizations are to be made beyond the research sample and (b) any replication is to be attempted.

19. Will the sampling procedures select a sample that adequately represent the target population?
20. Have demographic measures been included to describe the sample and evaluate how well it represents the population?

B. Sample Size   We must be sure that we have a sufficient number of subjects to meet all of the conditions of the study (i.e., to fill all cells of the design and to provide enough data to meet needs of the statistical analyses).

21. Is the sample sufficiently large?[2]

C. Subject Assignment   If the research involves group comparison and an experimental manipulation, then subjects will have to be properly assigned to conditions. The researcher must check to see that all subject assignments have been carried out according to the research design.

22. Have subjects been properly assigned to conditions according to the research design?
23. If it is a differential design, have the groups been carefully defined?
24. If it is a matched-subjects design, has the information on the matching been preserved to allow its use in the analysis?

D. Subject Availability   The researcher must be sure that all subjects have been contacted and scheduled for the procedures and have agreed to participate and funding is available if subjects fees for participation are to be paid?

25. Are subjects available?
26. Have subjects been scheduled or a procedure for scheduling them set up?
27. Are subject-fee payment procedures, if required, in place?

E. Research Ethics Considerations   We must be sure that all ethical issues have been anticipated and corrected and subject safeguards are in place.

---

[2]This is a complex question having to do with statistical power. The mathematical procedures for defining "sufficiently large" are beyond the scope of this text. The interested student is referred to Cohen (1988).

28. Has IRB ethics approval been obtained?
29. For human research, are the informed consent forms available?
30. Are debriefing and/or feedback procedures ready?
31. For animal research, have all of the ethical guidelines been checked and followed?

IX. Preparation of the Setting

A. Space and Equipment   The researcher must be sure the research space is available for use when needed, that it has been prepared appropriately for the research, and that all needed equipment is in place and functioning correctly.

32. Is adequate space available?
33. Is it free of distracting conditions?
34. Has all equipment been checked out?

B. Personnel (e.g., Research Assistants)   Proper training of research assistants is critical to ensure the data will be collected as planned by the researcher and that subjects will not be unintentionally influenced by the assistant.

35. Is there a sufficient number of research assistants?
36. Are the assistants adequately trained for emergencies?
37. Are the assistants adequately trained in the research procedures?
38. Are single- or double-blind procedures necessary and in place?

X. Adequacy of Subject Preparation, Instruction, and Procedures

All instructions to the subjects, procedures, tests, etc. should prepared and piloted. There should be no surprises for the experimenter—you do not want to "waste" a single subject.

39. Are all instructions to subjects clear?
40. Have the instructions and procedures been piloted?

SUMMARY

Selecting an appropriate statistical procedure is often one of the most confusing steps in the research process for beginning students. A flowchart system is presented that organizes for students a process of selecting appropriate statistical procedures. The flowchart system requires that students begin by describing the major characteristics of the research study—a process with which students should be familiar. Information from the summary is used to answer a series of questions which lead students step-by-step toward the selection of appropriate statistical procedures. The flowcharts help to organize this task. A major goal is for students to learn the decision-making procedures so that eventually the flowcharts will not be needed.

TABLE 14.1 SUMMARY OF PRE-DATA CHECKLIST

I. Initial Problem Definition

1. Literature review completed?
2. Problem statement developed?
3. Variables identified and operationally defined?

II. Research Hypothesis

4. Research hypothesis clearly state expected relationship among the variables?

III. Statistical Analysis

5. Descriptive statistics planned?
6. Inferential statistics planned?
7. Post hoc or secondary analyses planned?

IV. Theoretical Basis

8. Theoretical base for study clear?
9. Do hypotheses and procedures address the issues?

V. Independent Variable Manipulation (experimental research)

10. Independent variable manipulations planned?
11. Manipulations pretested?
12. Manipulation check planned?

VI. Dependent Measures

13. Dependent measures operationally defined?
14. Dependent measures piloted?
15. Reliability and validity data available?
16. Did you include procedures to measure reliability?

VII. Controls

17. Controls for threats to internal validity in place?
18. Controls for threats to external validity in place?

VIII. Subjects

A. Subject Selection

19. Sample adequately represent target population?
20. Demographic variables measured?

B. Sample Size

21. Sample sufficiently large?

C. Subject Assignment

22. Subjects properly assigned to conditions (experimental research)?
23. Groups carefully defined (differential research)?
24. Information on the matching preserved for analysis (matched-subjects design)?

D. Subject Availability

25. Subjects available?
26. Subjects scheduled?
27. Subject-fee procedures ready?

Continued

TABLE 14.1   *Continued*

E. Research Ethics

28. IRB approval obtained (human research)?
29. Informed consent forms available (human research)?
30. Debriefing and/or feedback procedures ready (human research)?
31. Ethical guidelines checked and research approved (animal research)?

IX. Preparation of the Setting

A. Space and Equipment

32. Adequate space available?
33. Free of distractions?
34. Equipment checked?

B. Personnel

35. Sufficient research staff?
36. Assistants adequately trained for emergencies?
37. Assistants adequately trained in procedures?
38. Blind procedures in place?

X. Adequacy of Subject Preparation, Instruction, Procedures

39. Instructions to subjects clear?
40. Instructions and procedures piloted?
If all check out, then you are ready to "fly."

We also present in the chapter a pre-data checklist similar to the preflight checklist used by pilots. After the study is designed, the procedures determined, and everything is set to go, the pre-data check provides a final verification that you are ready to collect the data.

REVIEW EXERCISES

14.1   **Define the following key terms. Be sure you understand them. They are discussed in the chapter and defined in the glossary.**

decision tree
decision-tree flowcharts
descriptive statistics
inferential statistics
secondary analyses

post hoc analyses
data snooping
robust
Monte Carlo study
pre-data check

14.2   **Answer each of the following. Check your answers in the chapter.**

1. What does it mean when we say that a statistical test is robust to a particular assumption?
2. What measures are available to quantify relationships among variables? When should each of the measures be used?
3. What are the major measures of central tendency and variability?

4. What is the difference between a planned comparison and a post hoc test? (If necessary, refer to Chapter 10.)
5. In what situation can the researcher use either a t-test or an ANOVA to compare group means?

14.3 **Think about and work the following problems. For each of the following situations, study the research plan and identify:**

  a. Level of constraint
  b. Independent variable(s)
  c. Levels of independent variables
  d. Type of design
  e. Dependent variable(s)
  f. Dependent measure(s)
  g. Level of measurement for each dependent measure
  h. Type of data generated from each dependent measure
  i. Research hypotheses
  j. Kind of statistical test that is appropriate for the research hypothesis

  Use the flowcharts to identify the following for each hypothesis:

  k. Appropriate descriptive statistic(s)
  l. Appropriate inferential statistic(s)

1. A researcher randomly assigns 30 hypertensive subjects to three groups of 10 each. Group 1 is taught muscle relaxation training; Group 2 is taught cognitive relaxation training; Group 3 is a no-treatment control. After the manipulation, blood pressure readings are taken on all subjects. Blood pressure is represented by two numbers. The systolic blood pressure represents the maximum blood pressure at the point that the heart is actually beating. The diastolic blood pressure represents the minimum blood pressure between beats. Both are measured in terms of the number of millimeters of mercury that can be pushed up in a column by the pressure. The researcher wants to know (i) whether relaxation training reduces hypertension and (ii) whether one type of relaxation training is more effective than the other.

2. A researcher has the hypothesis that (i) people with phobias are particularly sensitive to minor levels of stimulation and (ii) females with phobias are particularly sensitive. A fear survey questionnaire is given to 300 college freshmen. Of the 300, 50 students have high phobia scores. From the nonphobic subjects, 30 females and 20 males are randomly selected. Thus, a group of 50 (30 female, 20 male) phobics and a group of 50 (30 female, 20 male) nonphobic subjects are constructed. All subjects are tested on their sensitivity to minimal stimuli, a task that yields a simple score of the number of correct responses.

3. In a study of the effects of teacher feedback on accuracy of performance, ten children (five males and five females) are tested under three different conditions: immediate feedback, delayed feedback, and no feedback. All ten children are included in each condition. The order of presentation of feedback conditions is counterbalanced. The children are tested on their reading accuracy (i.e., the number of reading errors is counted).

4. The study focuses on the effects of smiling on children's evaluation of adults and on accuracy of learning and recall. A total of 30 children (15 males and 15 females) are randomly assigned to three conditions. Each condition is presented a videotape showing a teacher reading a story. The same teacher and the same story are used in each condition. In the first condition, the teacher smiles 60 percent of the time; in the second condition, the teacher smiles 30 percent of the

time; and in the third condition, the teacher does not smile. After viewing the tape, the children are given (i) a learning test scored on the number of correct answers to questions about the story, and (ii) a rating on a 1–5 scale of how much they like the teacher (assume an ordinal scale). Two weeks later, the children are tested for retention of material from the story (i.e., scored on the number of correct answers to questions about the story).

5. A psychiatric survey is conducted in a large metropolitan area. A random sample of 2000 residents is chosen. Each resident is interviewed and diagnosed into one of six categories as follows: (i) well—no psychiatric symptoms; (ii) mild— mild psychiatric symptoms but person is functioning adequately; (iii) moderate— some symptoms but little apparent interference with life adjustment; (iv) impaired—moderate symptoms with some interference in life adjustment; (v) severe—serious symptoms, functioning but with great difficulty; (vi) incapacitated—seriously impaired, unable to function. The number of people from each social class is calculated for each category.

6. A research study focusing on fear involves 30 parent/child pairs. Three hypotheses are tested in the study: (i) the number of fears reported by the parent is correlated with the number of fears reported by the child; (ii) the degree of fear reported by the parent is correlated with the degree of fear reported by the child; (iii) the number of fears and the degree of fear reported by both the parent and the child are reduced by the introduction of a fear-reduction program. Both parent and child are given a fear survey schedule, which measures the number of fears reported. In addition, both parent and child are rated on an index of fear severity with a range of 1–7 (assume the rating scale is an ordinal scale). After the initial measures, parents are randomly assigned to one of two groups: one group receives a fear-reduction program whereas the other group receives no treatment. At the end of this part of the study, the fear survey schedule and the rating scale of fear intensity are administered again to all parents.

Chapter
15

Research Methodology:
An Evolving Discipline

We have presented research as an active thinking process of asking and answering questions, in which there is a constant interplay between inductive and deductive thinking. We presented few rules because we believe that rules tend to oversimplify the tasks of designing, conducting, evaluating, and interpreting research findings. Research is a process of inquiry. The methods selected to answer a question depend on many factors, including practical and ethical constraints and the desire to get the most precise answer possible. Many traditional methods of research used in psychology and in other biological and social sciences were presented. Basic concepts such as validity, threats to validity, and control have been presented from a conceptual perspective, and designs have been explained in terms of these concepts.

The research strategies discussed in this text are by no means all-inclusive. Other strategies have been and continue to be used in answering questions about behavior. As noted earlier, there is no single "best way" of answering a question in science. The most effective approaches for answering a question depend on the kind of question asked. However, regardless of the kinds of questions asked or the procedures used to answer them, there are defined phases in every research project. The research begins with a general idea that is carefully refined into a specific question or problem. Procedures are selected, modified, and adapted to answer the question(s). Observations are made, and data are analyzed. Finally, data are interpreted, and results and conclusions are communicated to other professionals. Regardless of the level of sophistication of the research method or the type of question asked, the phases of research remain the same.

Another idea emphasized throughout the text is the concept of levels of constraint. It is argued that good research can be conducted at many different levels of constraint. In this respect, we differ from some of our colleagues who argue that the best and most effective way of answering a question is always with experimental research. We agree that experimental research does provide a more unambiguous answer to a causal question than do other levels of research. However, many questions of interest to psychologists cannot be answered with experimental research. Under some conditions, manipulating variables may be outside the practical control of the experimenter or may be ethically unacceptable. These restrictions, however, make the question no less worthwhile. Therefore, a significant portion of the text is devoted to the concepts and procedures of what is labeled low-constraint research. It should be emphasized again that low-constraint research methods are not considered sloppy research; they are appropriate and useful procedures for answering certain kinds of questions. Low-constraint research procedures are especially important in the early stages of a research program, in which the flexibility of such methods makes it more likely that we will be able to gather the breadth of data needed to understand the broad conceptual issues being addressed by the project.

NEW DIRECTIONS IN RESEARCH METHODOLOGY

Science is continually evolving as new questions are raised and new people become involved in the process of finding answers to these questions. As science evolves, so does its methodology. New research methods are developed in *every* science, and old methods are revised and updated to meet the needs and curiosity of scientists. New perspectives on a question create new problems, and the various disciplines search for techniques to find the answers.

The Evolution of Research Questions and Methods

Changes in methods used to study a problem evolve as questions change. As answers to questions are found, new issues and new questions arise, which may require new methodologies. Therefore, the methods used in a research area change as original questions are answered and new questions are formulated.

An example is the historical sequence of the study of genetic influences on schizophrenia. One of the initial questions asked whether genetic factors contribute to schizophrenia. Subsequent clinical observations suggested that schizophrenia runs in families, but the observations were informal and less than systematic. In time, more precisely controlled research was carried out which verified the initial clinical observations. Verification was accomplished through differential research in which the rates of schizophrenia were measured in samples of families of patients with schizophrenia and control families. But, as you may have recognized, a major confounding variable (environmental influences) was uncontrolled in the studies. That is, the higher frequency of schizophrenia in the families of patients with schizophrenia might have been caused by either genetic influences or environmental conditions. Research methods were needed to separate the influences of genetics and environment. One of the ways developed was to study patients who had been adopted as infants and who later developed schizophrenia. The patients had a set of relatives who shared their genetic heritage (their biological relatives) and a set of relatives who shared their environment (their adoptive relatives). The rates of schizophrenia in each of these sets of relatives indicated the contributions of genetics and environment to the development of schizophrenia. The studies showed that schizophrenia is more likely in the biological relatives than in the adoptive relatives of patients with schizophrenia who had been adopted at birth. Data from such studies answered the initial question and made it clear that genetics plays an important role in the development of schizophrenia.

With that question answered, new questions were raised. For example, if genetics plays a role, what role is it and what is the role of other factors in the eventual development of the disorder? The new question was addressed by looking back into the developmental histories of schizophrenics for clues. But this is an ex post facto approach to research, and it does not allow us to test causal hypotheses. A better method was needed. Because it was known that genetics strongly influenced schizophrenia, Mednick and Schulsinger (1968) suggested studying individuals who are genetically related to schizophrenics—the offspring of mothers with schizophrenia. The approach was called "high-risk research" because the subjects identified for study had a much higher risk of developing schizophrenia than did an unselected sample. However, 95 percent of all patients with schizophrenia do not have a parent with schizophrenia. Therefore, this research approach produced a biased sample of potential schizophrenic patients. A behavioral high-risk approach was proposed (Chapman, Chapman, Raulin, & Edell, 1978) which identified people at risk for schizophrenia on the basis of personality characteristics. The current functioning of these subjects could be studied (e.g., Levin & Raulin, 1991; Silverstein, Raulin, Pristach, & Pomerantz, 1992), and the subjects could be followed over time to determine their risk for schizophrenia and other disorders (Chapman, Chapman, Kwapil, Eckblad, Zinser, 1994).

With the genetic risk factor established for schizophrenia, researchers began to look for the mechanisms responsible for the disorder. Careful measurement of performance known to be related to specific brain functioning has given us considerable insight into the underlying neurological mechanism for schizophrenia (Gupta et al., 1995; Sanders, Keshanavan, & Schooler, 1994). CAT scans and MRIs allowed researchers to look at the structure of the brain of patients with schizophrenia and compare it with the structure of brains of controls (e.g., Benson & Stuss, 1990; Lewine, Gulley, Risch, Jewart, & Houpt, 1990; Nasrallah, Schwartzkopf, Olson, & Coffman, 1990). PET scans (e.g., Bench, Dolan, Friston, & Frackowiak, 1990; Buchsbaum, 1990), rCBF records (e.g., Wood & Flowers, 1990), and EEGs (e.g., Gattaz et al., 1992; Josiassen, Roemer, Johnson, & Shagass, 1990) allowed researchers to look at the functioning of a schizophrenic patient's brain. Computer models of brain functioning have built in various hypothesized schizophrenic brain dysfunctions to see if the models would create the symptoms seen in patients with schizophrenia (Cohen & Servan-Schreiber, 1989, 1992). Careful study of key subjects (e.g., identical twins—one of whom has schizophrenia while the other does not) has has helped to identify environmental factors contributing to the disorder (Cantor-Graae et al., 1994; Torrey et al., 1994). The nature of the risk factors has been probed with mathematical procedures developed for that specific purpose by Meehl and his colleagues (e.g., Meehl, 1995; Meehl & Yonce, 1994). Several investigators (Korfine & Lenzenweger, 1995; Lenzenweger & Korfine, 1992; Lowrie & Raulin, 1995), using these techniques, have found evidence for a taxonic category of risk—that is, for a risk factor that is all or nothing. The information gained from all these lines of research and a dozen other research approaches has fueled a renewed attack on this devastating emotional disorder.

The example illustrates how questions help shape research designs. Studies designed to answer one question often raise other questions in the process. The new questions sometimes require new research approaches, which often are created by scientists as a by-product of a "need to know" the answer. We cannot predict what the next major research approach in the study of schizophrenia will be. It will be selected and/or created as the need develops, and the need to do so will be shaped by answers to current questions. But the principles behind any new research approach in this area will be the same ones underlying the designs discussed in the current text.

The Impact of Other Disciplines

Developments in related disciplines can have a significant positive impact on the discipline of psychology. One of the best examples is the study of neurological influences on human behavior.

Developments in the field of biochemistry, which permitted much finer analyses of organic chemicals, made possible the discovery that there are many more neurotransmitters involved in the functioning of the central nervous system than previously believed. This explosion in the number of known chemical transmission agents required scientists to rethink the role of neurotransmitters. The concept of specific transmitter influences in precise locations within the brain and other parts of the central nervous system became a much more intellectually appealing theory. But how do we study specific influences of specific neurotransmitters in specific locations in the brain? Much of the previous research on neurotransmitters operated under the assumption that there are general levels of the chemicals in the system, and the procedures used for measuring the chemicals were usually nonspecific with respect to the location of the action of each transmitter. There was a need to develop techniques to sample from specific locations within the brain. Because brain-functioning processes are part of the living organism and not only a matter of the organism's structure, it was necessary to accomplish the sampling without damaging the organism. A sampling of brain tissue at autopsy would provide little useful information. It would also be enormously helpful to be able to experimentally manipulate specific neurotransmitters at specific locations. A procedure known as "micro-iontophoresis" (Curtis & Crawford, 1969) was developed, which allowed the researcher to inject specific amounts of certain substances into the synapses of neurons while the animal was awake and functioning. For the first time, this new technology offered the possibility of using experimental methods to investigate the relationship between neurotransmitters functioning at specific locations of the brain and their effect on the behavior of living organisms.

The research of Elaine Hull and her students illustrates some of these techniques as well as even newer technologies. Dr. Hull has been studying the neuro-mechanisms controlling the sexual behavior of rats. Presumably similar mechanisms control the sexual behavior of humans. She and her students have refined techniques to implant surgically microcannulae (tiny tubes) into specific locations of a rat's brain. With such an implant the animal is able to function normally without discomfort, but the researcher is able to influence the functioning of specific regions of the brain by injecting substances through the cannula. It is important to note that the techniques must not cause pain to the animal, because even a rat is less likely to engage in sex if it has a headache. Her research (e.g., Hull et al., 1991; Warner et al., 1991) systematically identified the brain mechanisms that control sexual motivation, motor behavior related to sexual activity, and sexual reflexes. Her work is now incorporating a new, even more amazing technique. Being able to inject specific neurotransmitter agonists (substances that enhance the action of specific neurotransmitters) or antagonists (substances that block the action of specific neurotransmitters) gives considerable information about the functional mechanisms of a system. However, it is useful to observe the normal functioning of a system. Crude methods sampled specific locations of a rat's brain at key points in sexual behavior, but the techniques involved immediate removal of the section of the brain and a chemical fixing of that section for analysis. An alternative is to sample the chemical composition in an alert and active animal using a technique called "microdialysis." This technique implants a cannula in a specific location; but the cannula has a tube within a tube, with the outer tube having a chemically porous tip. Neurotransmitters diffuse across this tip into the fluid that is pumped slowly through the cannula. The levels of neurotransmitters in the fluid can then be measured. Also, drugs can be added to the fluid and diffused into the brain. This technique will not only verify earlier findings, but can also give clues about the temporal sequence of brain actions involved in sexual activity. As is always the case in science, these new techniques are providing the answers to some important questions, and in the process are raising yet more questions that demand still newer techniques. Using these and other techniques, Hull and her colleagues have confirmed through a series of studies (Hull, Du, Lorrain, & Matuszewich, in press) an earlier theory that a specific brain region (the medial preoptic area) seems to control sexual motivation. Here the developments in other scientific disciplines—biochemistry and neuroscience—have affected research in another science, psychology.

Multidisciplinary Research

As a science grows, there is increasing specialization so that researchers seem to work in ever more narrow areas. Such specialization is important as it focuses the researcher's efforts on specific problems and allows the development of sophisticated approaches to problems. With such specific details established, researchers can then turn to integrating the information into a broader understanding. In this endeavor, we find researchers from different disciplines coming together to pool their knowledge in interdisciplinary research projects.

An example of this interdisciplinary approach is the newly emerging area of behavioral medicine. The field has brought together physicians, researchers in neurology, physiology, and several different areas of psychology. Another example is the interdisciplinary research integrating sociology, law, and psychology (Levine, 1974, 1980; Levine & Howe, 1985). Still another example is the rapidly growing field of artificial intelligence. In this interdisciplinary field, mathematicians, psychologists, and computer scientists developed models of thinking that can be programmed on computers to solve complex problems. Interdisciplinary fields such as neuroscience and cognitive science are now growing at phenomenal rates as the value of these interdisciplinary partnerships becomes more apparent. We expect interdisciplinary research to continue to increase and to provide greater integrations in the understanding of human functioning.

Moving Research Out of the Laboratory

Many psychologists are rediscovering old methods as a result of their concern for external validity in current research approaches. For example, naturalistic and case-study research is becoming more common in many areas that previously relied almost exclusively on higher-constraint research. Mark Freeman (1984) argues that understanding the development of a person requires that we take a historical perspective, noting the developmental influences that color his or her current perspective on life. The more individualized approach to developmental psychology is different from what has been the tradition over the last few decades. It reinforces the point made throughout the text—lower-constraint research is a legitimate way of looking at certain research questions and, from some perspectives, may even be the best way to study a phenomenon.

Well-controlled experiments can be carried out in natural settings. For example, the work of Ramey and his colleagues (e.g., Ramey, 1995) with severely disadvantaged children in real-world settings demonstrate that early, vigorous interventions can have permanent and powerful effects on a child's development. In response to demands for such real-world information, researchers have increased their research efforts in natural settings. Conducting research in natural settings is difficult and challenging, but the reward of good generalization of results to other real-world settings makes the effort worthwhile.

The Impact of Computers

In a relatively short period of time, computers have had a major impact on research. Perhaps not since the Industrial Revolution has so much changed so quickly. One reason that the computer has had such an impact is the monumental growth of computer technology. Today's typical notebook computer can perform all the functions of a 1950s computer that had to be housed in several floors of a large building—and today's computer will do the work far more rapidly and more reliably. Since the introduction of personal computers in the late 1970s, the power of these machines has more than doubled every two years (Rupley & Clyman, 1995). Today you can buy a PC that is 1000 times more powerful than the original PC for less than half the cost (in inflation-corrected dollars).

Computers have dramatically increased the efficiency of the laboratory. Tasks that once took an enormous amount of time can now be done in seconds. The most obvious benefactor of this improved efficiency is the data-analysis phase. Students who have worked through something as complex as a two-way ANOVA on a pocket calculator can appreciate the time savings of computer analyses. The computer can run a million analyses in less time than it takes most people to compute a simple mean from their data. The increased efficiency has allowed the development of complex and labor-intensive analysis procedures, such as multivariate ANOVAs and factor analyses, which use complex computational techniques to obtain precise estimates of population parameters. This has created an explosion in the number and sophistication of analysis procedures. We may be reaching the limit of this growth in data analysis, however, not because computers cannot do the computations but because humans may not be able to comprehend the results. For example, the computer can easily analyze a factorial study with a dozen or more factors. The mathematical formulas for computation are easily generalized to more complex designs, and computers can perform the computations quickly. But few people can actually visualize and understand the meaning of, for example, a five-way interaction—five different factors combining in a unique way to affect the dependent variable.

Such developments in computerized data analysis may also have created some problems. Perhaps data analysis has become too easy, and some of the care that used to be exercised on the design and execution of studies may have been lost. One of our colleagues worked her way through graduate school in the early 1950s by conducting factor analyses. The analyses were carried out using the most modern calculating instruments of the time, mechanical calculators. To complete a typical analysis required nine months of working 20 hours per week. Today, the same analysis is completed by a computer in less than a second and costs a few pennies. The entire analysis can be set up by a knowledgeable student in a few minutes. When an analysis takes nine months to complete and costs thousands of dollars, one makes sure that the data being analyzed are as precise and accurate as possi-

After years of working on the project, Professor Gronski discovers there are practical limits to miniaturization.

ble and that the analysis is appropriate for the data available and the question(s) being asked. It is not clear that the same care goes into these aspects of the research now that the analyses are so easy and inexpensive to accomplish.

Despite such potential problems, there are other ways in which the computer can improve the efficiency and quality of psychological research. Laboratories now often use computers to interact with and to gather data from subjects. This may reduce the number of mistakes, which can result in lost or distorted data. The computer can carry out complex procedures flawlessly for one subject after another. This also has the potential of minimizing experimenter bias. Computers can take and record measures in a completely objective manner, they can present stimuli to different groups of subjects in exactly the same way, and they can perform all of these tasks in a perfectly replicated manner in study after study. The software to run studies or carry out analyses can be shared with other researchers, increasing the precision in the replication of laboratory procedures.

Some common laboratory paradigms in use today would not be possible without the aid of computers. The computer is not limited to presenting stimuli in a single predetermined sequence. Rather, it is capable of recording the responses of subjects, evaluating the responses, and choosing the next stimulus to present based on subjects' responses. This permits us to test much more complex hypotheses than are possible with a static presentation of a given set of stimuli. Of course, mechanical equipment that is responsive to the subject in a study has been available for years. The Skinner box is the best-known example. What the computer adds is an expansion of the range and level of complexity of response. It also dramatically simplifies the task of modifying procedures to test new hypotheses. With the old mechanical equipment, modifying procedures often meant physically changing the equipment or designing and building new equipment. With computer-controlled studies, often little more than software changes are required. In many computer-controlled laboratories, new studies can be up and running in a few hours instead of weeks or months.

The computer also offers us some totally new ways of understanding phenomena. An example of such a new approach is the computer modeling of cognitive processes (Marr, 1982). Computer modeling is an idea that is borrowed and adapted from the artificial intelligence field. In artificial intelligence, computers are programmed to behave intelligently, to solve problems, and to react to stimuli. When building artificial intelligence systems, we are not particularly interested in duplicating human functioning. However, when building computer models of cognitive functions, we do attempt to duplicate human functions. Instead of developing complex abstract models of cognitive processes and designing factorial studies that are too complicated for anyone to understand, we create a computer model of functioning that we can manipulate to observe the effects of manipulation.

A class of computer models that has received considerable attention recently is called "parallel distributed processing (PDP)" or "connectionist" models (Bechtel & Abrahamsen, 1991; Rumelhart, McClelland, & the PDP Research Groups, 1986; McClelland, Rumelhart et al., 1986). These models simulate mathematically the interconnection characteristics of networks of neurons. For this reason, these models are sometimes called "neuro-networks," although many researchers in this field are uncomfortable with this term, believing that it overstates the similarity of the computer-based models to the way a real brain functions. We know that neurons in the brain are heavily interconnected. We know that the brain uses parallel processing to accomplish its remarkable feats in very little time. In contrast, the current generation of computers process material serially, one task after another, using very fast electronic circuits. You can visualize these two models of operation by imagining two small companies. One company has one employee who does everything. This lone employee has to work very hard and very fast to be competitive. The other company has several employees, each doing their own work and coordinating their efforts with the other employees. The one-employee company is the way a modern computer works, whereas the brain is more like the company with several employees.

PDP models have been developed to mimic several human processes including perception, learning, language use, and memory retrieval. The models are intriguing for many reasons. First, the models learn to function correctly—not by being programmed with a set of rules, but rather by being exposed to input and output data and by dynamically adjusting the strength of the interconnections to give more accurate responses. In other words, these models learn by experience. In theory, extremely complex behavior can be learned by these PDP models with sufficient exposure to relevant situations. PDP computer chips are now being produced for research purposes and are now being used in robotlike devices to test their limits. This area of research not only promises a new perspective on brain functioning and perhaps some insights into how our own brain operates, but also has the potential to be a major technological breakthrough as well.

What is interesting from a psychological perspective about PDP models is that they often perform much as humans do. When learning to respond correctly, these models often make the same kinds of mistakes that human beings make. For example, a model designed to learn how to form plural nouns from singular nouns seems to learn quickly that many nouns add an "*s*" (e.g., toy; toys), but that there are exceptions (e.g., mouse; mice). During the learning process the model is apt to produce *mices* as the plural of *mouse* much as a child might. These models seem to produce behavior that is rule-based, but no rules were ever given to the program (Rumelhart, McClelland et al., 1986). Human behavior often appears to be rule-based, but theorists have often wondered how we acquired the rules.

In Chapter 15 of the second edition of this text, we introduced parallel distributed processing models as one of the cutting edge areas of psychology. At the time there was only a handful of books and just over 100 published papers. In the fours years since that edition was written over, 1000 articles, chapters, and books have been published on the topic—an explosion of research and theory almost unmatched in psychology. These models have been used to give us a new perspective on cognitive functions such as reasoning (e.g., Kasabov, & Shishkov, 1993), learning (e.g., Dennett, 1993), language processing, (e.g., Collier, 1994), and visual processing (Mousavi & Schalkoff, 1994), to name but a few. In addition, a variety of pathological conditions have been modeled with PDP procedures including obsessive-compulsive disorder (e.g., Stein & Hollander, 1994), dyslexia (e.g., Plaut, & Shallice, 1993; Seidenberg, 1993; Snowling, Hulme, & Goulandris, 1994), aphasia (e.g., Harley, 1993), and schizophrenia (e.g., Cohen & Servan-Schreiber, 1992; Hoffman & McGlashan, 1993; Raulin & Brenner, 1993). There does not seem to be any area where previous theories have not been challenged by the PDP models.

The goal in computer modeling is to find a model that can reproduce exactly what we see in human behavior in comparable situations. The idea is directly analogous to using scale models of airplanes and testing them in wind tunnels. We have theories and formulas that predict how certain factors will affect the aerodynamics of an airplane. However, so many factors come into play in real-life situations that we can make only educated guesses about what would happen to a real airplane. But with a model and the wind tunnel to simulate flight conditions, we can actually test our guesses and fine-tune a system that has become so complex it strains the limits of human understanding. We may soon be able to accomplish similar goals with computer models of cognitive functioning.

Computers have even had an impact on the way we collaborate. Electronic mail (E-Mail) has made it possible for researchers at distant universities to collaborate easily, passing messages and information back and forth in seconds. Electronic mail networks encourage this collaboration by providing this communication option to faculty and students at little or no cost. Computer technology is now being used to enhance even more direct collaboration regardless of the distance between researchers (Schrage, 1991). With modern software, researchers in different cities can be working on the same document at the same time, sharing ideas as if they were gathered around a table writing a draft of an article. This new computer technology allows collaborators to be spread all over the country or even the world and still be able to work closely together. The explosion in this technology was discussed earlier in the text (see Box 2.1).

The impact of computers on psychological research is only beginning to be felt. The directions for the future will be shaped by the inventiveness of today's scientists. Computers are becoming so inexpensive that every active laboratory in the country will have computing power available. There are many who believe that computers will offer whole new ways of looking at questions and will permit new research paradigms that will answer questions yet to be imagined. It is an exciting period for science. But we must not forget that it is the scientist's imagination and not the silicon of the computer chips that is fueling this explosion. The computer is a powerful resource, but human thought and creativity harness this resource. Basic science is unlikely to be changed by the computer. The computer will add efficiency but the scientist will still ask the questions, decide the best ways to search for the answers, set up the studies, and evaluate the results.

SCIENCE: AN INTERACTION BETWEEN EMPIRICISM AND RATIONALISM

It is important to restate a point made in Chapter 1: new technologies used in the research laboratory do not define a science. Rather, any scientific discipline is defined by its subject matter and by the processes that are used to answer the questions of interest to that discipline.

In Chapter 1, *science* is defined as a combination of empiricism and rationalism. By requiring that scientific theories conform to both logical restrictions and to the realities of the world about us, we demand more of scientific theories than of any other system of knowing. Few scientific theories stand up to this kind of double scrutiny. Theories are constantly being rejected because they are either logically inconsistent (a rational criterion) and/or they do not accurately predict data (an empirical criterion). Science progresses by rejecting inadequate theories and proposing and testing new theories that will stand up better to the rigorous demands of rationalism and empiricism. Initially, students may find this process to be negativistic—researchers always try to criticize and reject theories rather than prove them. However, it is not negativism but rather *skepticism* that characterizes science. We use theories, but we never really accept them—we constantly question their validity. A good scientist expects that all theories eventually will be shown to be false or not completely true and will be replaced by better theories. In science, we accept little on faith except for the method of science itself.

Science has become a major enterprise in today's world. Millions of people work in and around scientific laboratories. Scientific disciplines have become more specialized as their knowledge base grows. As the discipline develops, the research techniques it uses will evolve to handle the specific questions of that discipline.

Therefore, different scientific disciplines appear to be using different research methods. In this text, we cover many of the most commonly used research techniques in the discipline of psychology. Although the techniques covered differ somewhat from those used in other sciences, the differences are more surface differences than conceptual differences. A research biologist would have no trouble conceptually understanding the research methodology of chemistry or psychology, and vice versa. In this text, we try to present concepts and build specific research techniques on them. If students understand the concepts that underlie the techniques, it will be relatively easy to understand new research techniques—whether they are from the discipline of psychology or some other science.

New research techniques are an almost inevitable result of a developing science. New scientific disciplines are also inevitable as the knowledge base of science builds and increased specialization is required. What was once philosophy is now a dozen different basic sciences. What was once physics is now physics, astronomy, and chemistry. Specialization is necessary given the incredible complexity of many disciplines, but it tends to isolate disciplines from the ideas and discoveries of other sciences. Organizations such as the American Association for the Advancement of Science (AAAS) strive to unite the many subdisciplines of science and maintain a healthy level of communication among disciplines. Support for this effort comes from the belief that the method of science (empiricism coupled with rationalism) is a strong bond between apparently diverse areas. It is hoped that students gain from this text a good understanding of research approaches in psychology, as well as a good understanding of science and scientific thought and how the specific research approaches in psychology are applications of basic scientific processes to a particular subject matter—the behavior of organisms.

It is appropriate to end the text by repeating an idea that is stressed throughout: the essence of science is its *way of thinking.* The important tools of scientists are their skills in systematically combining rational thinking and empirical findings to ask and answer questions about nature. The scientist's enthusiasm, skepticism, and creativity are essential components in the process of scientific thinking, as are the technologies of each discipline. But mostly, it is the *thinking process that constitutes the essence of science.* To emphasize this point, recall the imagery used in Chapter 1: a scientist can operate scientifically while sitting under a tree in the woods, thinking through a problem, and using apparatus no more technical than a pad and pencil.

REVIEW EXERCISE

Think of the scientist sitting under the tree "being scientific." Your task as teaching assistant for the course is to explain to students how a person can be scientific in these surroundings—apparently so inactive and so far away from the laboratory. How can you explain it in enough detail to answer students' questions?

Appendix
A

Writing a Research Report:
APA Publication Style

Publication is a critical part of the research process. Literally, *publication* means "to make public." Making science a public discipline serves two purposes. First, it facilitates building on old knowledge by making the knowledge accessible to everyone. Second, it subjects each finding to the scrutiny of many scientists who can independently review the logic, procedures, results, and conclusions.

There is much to communicate in a research report, yet space restrictions demand that a report be concise. Thus, guidelines are necessary to aid communication while minimizing the journal space used. The publication manual prepared by the American Psychological Association (1994) is used as a guide by most psychology journals and journals in several other disciplines. Psychology majors, particularly those planning to attend graduate school, should purchase a copy of the manual.[1]

STRUCTURE OF A RESEARCH ARTICLE

Organization is one key to a good research article. The American Psychological Association recommends that the body of a research article be organized into four parts: introduction, method, results, and discussion. In addition, the report should have a title page and a short (100–150 word) abstract, a reference section, and if necessary, figures and tables. The *abstract* briefly describes the study and its findings, permitting readers to ascertain what the article is about so as to decide whether it is of interest and should be read more thoroughly. The abstract is also published in one or more journals that specialize in abstracts (e.g., *Psychological Abstracts*). These journals are cross-referenced to make it easier for a researcher to identify relevant research. The *reference section* provides details on where the reports of previous research can be found. There are specific standards on how to record that information so that it can be presented in a concise and complete manner. Occasionally, additional attachments are included at the end of an article in the form of appendices. These can contain extended information, materials, or scales that are not readily available elsewhere. The major sections of a journal article are shown in Table A.1.

WRITING THE RESEARCH REPORT

This section covers the preparation of each section of a research report. Clarity and precision in the presentation of research results are important. Where appropriate, specific information on APA publication style is given.

---

[1]The *Publication Manual of the American Psychological Association* can be purchased directly from the American Psychological Association at nominal cost [Book Orders; 750 First St., N.E.; Washington, D.C. 20002-4242; (202) 336-5510; FAX (202) 336-5502]. The American Psychological Association also publishes a workbook to help students learn APA style (Gelfand & Walker, 1994). There are also other inexpensive texts available (e.g., Rosnow & Rosnow, 1992) that focus exclusively on writing reports in APA style.

TABLE A.1   MAJOR SECTIONS AND SUBSECTIONS OF A MANUSCRIPT

1. Title Page
2. Abstract
3. Introduction
4. Method
   a. Subjects
   b. Apparatus
   c. Procedure
5. Results
6. Discussion
7. References
8. Appendices
9. Footnotes
10. Tables
11. Figure captions
12. Figures

TABLE A.2   FIVE LEVELS OF HEADINGS

THIS IS A CENTERED UPPERCASE HEADING (LEVEL 5)

This is a Centered Upper- and Lowercase Heading (Level 1)

This is a Centered, Underlined, Uppercase and Lowercase Heading (Level 2)

This is an Uppercase and Lowercase Side Heading (Level 3)

This is a paragraph heading (level 4). The paragraph heading is in lowercase, is underlined, and should end with a period as shown.

Note: If only one level of heading is needed in a report, use level 1; if two levels are needed, use levels 1 and 3; if three levels are needed, use levels 1, 3, and 4; if four levels are needed, use levels 1, 2, 3, and 4; if 5 levels are needed, use all of the above with the level 5 heading subordinating the other four levels as shown above.

Using Levels of Headings to Organize

An *outline* is one of the best ways to organize any report. The familiar indentation pattern of the outline makes it easy to see the overall structure of the report. A well-written article follows the organization of an outline. In the article, however, different *levels of headings* are used instead of indentation to indicate the outline organization. Table A.2 presents examples of five different levels of headings that can be used in a research report.

Sections of a Research Report

Title Page   The *title page* includes the title of the article, the list of authors, the institutional affiliations of the authors, and a running head. The title should be concise while still describing the focus of the study. Phrases such as "a report on" or "a study of" add little information and should be avoided. A running head is placed at the top of the title page. It is an abbreviated title with no more than 50 characters and spaces. When the article is printed in a journal, part of the running head (called a header) will appear at the top of each page. Note that page numbering begins with the title page (page number 1) and continues serially for all the pages except the artwork (i.e., figures).

Abstract   The *abstract* must summarize the research paper in no more than 960 characters and spaces (about 120 words). It must include all elements of the research report. Enough information should be given so that anyone who reads the research study after reading the abstract will not be surprised by what they find in the article. Even though the abstract appears first, it is usually written last because it essentially summarizes the work. Although the abstract is one of the shortest sections of the study, it is often the most difficult to write because so much must be said in limited space. The abstract is published by abstracting services such as *Psychological Abstracts.*

Introduction   The *introduction* states the research problem and discusses prior research. It begins with a broad or general statement of the research problem and proceeds to narrow the focus to the specific research being reported. A good introduction need not be long but it must be well organized. One should focus only on those prior research studies directly relevant to the current research study and should not attempt to review all of the research in a broad area. The introduction usually ends with a specific statement of the research hypotheses to be investigated. A good rule of thumb is if the hypotheses seem to follow naturally from everything that precedes them, then the introduction is well organized and well structured. If, on the other hand, a reader finds some or all of the hypotheses to be surprising in light of what is stated previously, then the introduction is not well focused and fails to provide the rationale for the current research study.

In the introduction, other research is referred to by naming the researcher(s) and the date when the research was published. With this information, the reader can turn to the reference list and find where the work was published. There are two standard forms for referring to published work, as shown in the following examples:

> In previous research, most subjects found the situation to be realistic (Johnson & Hall, 1979).
> Johnson and Hall (1979) found that most subjects considered the procedure to be realistic.

For citing several studies, we can use the following format:

> Several investigators have found this situation to be realistic for their subjects (Johnson & Hall, 1979, 1980a, 1980b; Kelley, 1976; Michaels, Johnson, & Smith, 1981; Smith & Rodick, 1977).

The forms tell the reader what was found, which researchers made the observation, and when. You may have noticed that the APA referencing conventions were used throughout this text. Each reference that appears in a research article must appear in the reference section, and all references that appear in the reference list must appear in the paper.

Method   The purpose of the *method section* is to describe exactly how the research was carried out. We describe the subjects and how they were selected, the apparatus, equipment and/or materials, and the procedures used. These are typically discussed in separate subsections.

The *subjects subsection* describes how subjects were selected and their demographic characteristics (such as age, education, and sex), from where subjects were obtained (from a college student subject pool, a psychiatric hospital, or a local shopping mall), and what inducements were used to obtain their cooperation (money, experimental credit for students, and so on). In addition, the researcher should describe how subjects were assigned to groups. If it is a differential research study, where the assignment is based on classifying the subjects, the procedures used to classify the subjects should be described. If subjects drop out of the experiment or decline to participate, the number of such subjects and the groups they were in should be reported. There should be enough information to allow a researcher to compare the sample with samples from similar research projects.

The next subsection will depend on the study. It might be called the *apparatus or equipment subsection, materials, instruments,* or *measures subsection,* or some combination of these terms. In this subsection all physical aspects of the research study are described. If the study involves equipment, the type of equipment used and the settings of the equipment should be reported. If psychological tests are used, we describe them and give a reference to where they can be obtained. If the test forms are unique or custom-made for the study, they should either be included as an appendix or made available to any reader on request. The goal of the apparatus or equipment subsection is to provide readers with sufficient information to allow them to replicate the study.

The *procedure subsection* describes how the study was carried out. If additional manipulation of data was carried out after the subject has left the experiment, it should be described in the procedure section. For example, if particular scoring procedures were used, they should be described. If specific instructions were given to the subject, the instructions should be included. In other words, the procedure subsection should tell the reader everything that the subject and the researcher did during the course of the study.

Results   The purpose of the *results section* is to tell the reader what was found in the study. A statistical description of the results is usually needed as well as appropriate statistical tests. Reporting statistical findings in a concise yet understandable way requires that the writer follow certain conventions. The usual convention is to present the descriptive statistics first followed by the results of the inferential statistical tests. When reporting inferential statistics one should report what statistic was used, the number of degrees of freedom, the computed value of the statistic, and the probability of obtaining the computed value of the statistic by chance. Each of these is organized in a precise order (see Table A.3). All non-Greek, single-letter terms used in reporting statistical results (e.g., F, t, p) should be underlined in the manuscript. With this format, readers can easily interpret the importance of certain

TABLE A.3   REPORTING STATISTICS IN THE TEXT OF A RESEARCH REPORT

Reporting *t*-tests

Boys were found to be significantly more aggressive than girls in the playground situation, $t(28) = 2.33$, $p < 0.05$.

Reporting ANOVAs

There was a significant difference in performance between the three distraction conditions, $F(2, 27) = 3.69$, $p < 0.05$.

Reporting chi-squares

Psychology majors were significantly more likely to classify themselves as "humanistic" than were engineering majors, $X^2(1, N = 60) = 4.47$, $p < 0.05$.

TABLE A.4   A TYPICAL TABLE IN A RESEARCH REPORT

Table 1

Posttreatment Measures for the Three Treatment Approaches

Measures	Type of Therapy		
	Behavioral	Cognitive	Analytic
Number of activities[a]	4.6	3.8	2.1
Beck scores[b]	16.7	15.3	17.5
Insight ratings[c]	2.0	3.1	3.7

[a] The mean number of recreational activities in a one-week period.
[b] Mean Beck Depression Inventory scores—higher scores indicate greater depression.
[c] Rating based on an independent interview—ratings range from 1 (no insight) to 5 (maximum insight).

results even if they are not familiar with the statistical procedure used because the probability value at the end of the report will mean the same thing. Anytime *p* is less than 0.05 (a traditional value of alpha), we would conclude the findings are unusual enough that it is unlikely they could have occurred as a result of chance. Although it is important to express the statistical significance of comparisons made in the study, it is equally important to give the reader the information needed to interpret the results, such as the actual mean scores or frequencies.

Often the most effective way of presenting statistical information is to organize it in a table or figure. Tables and figures should be carefully labeled for the reader. Tables should give the reader enough information so they can be interpreted without information from the text. Each table should be numbered using Arabic numerals starting with number 1. The first line of the table should read "Table" and the number. The next line of the table should be a brief title. An example of a typical table title might be "Mean Reaction Times for Distracted and Nondistracted Subjects." The title should be underlined. If the title is more than one line long, it should be double-spaced. The actual values in the table will be arranged in columns and rows with the columns and rows clearly labeled. The columns should be labeled at the top of each column and the rows at the far left-hand side of the table. If additional information is necessary to interpret the table, it should be included at the bottom in the form of a footnote. An example of a typical table format is in Table A.4.

Figure A.1

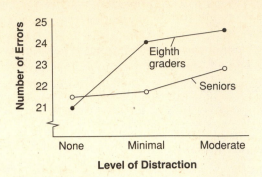

Figures can also be an effective way of presenting information. It is important, however, to label a figure completely. Both the *x*- and the *y*-axis should be labeled, and each figure should have a title. Figures should be numbered sequentially starting with number 1 and should be numbered independently of tables. When submitting a paper for publication each figure should be professionally drawn and submitted as a glossy print. The figures are numbered on the back of the print, and the figure numbers and titles appear on a separate sheet. Figure A.1 presents an example.

In preparing a manuscript for publication tables and figures are assembled and placed at the end of the manuscript. Each table or figure should be referred to in the manuscript.

There is no one correct way of presenting the results of a study. It is often useful for the researcher to try to organize results in various ways—testing both tables and figures to determine which method is most effective.

Discussion   You interpret and evaluate the results in the *discussion section.* It is helpful to begin the discussion section by briefly summarizing the results in nontechnical language. Then the reader should be told what you believe the results mean. The interpretation of the results should follow logically from the actual data obtained in the study. It is useful in the discussion section to focus on the future directions that research might take. If there are weaknesses in the current study, we should describe ways that they may be overcome in future studies. If the study suggests new hypotheses, we should suggest ways in which the hypotheses might be adequately tested. The goal of any research project is to find answers to questions. But the outcome of most good research projects is to suggest new and important questions that still need to be answered. Suggesting directions for future research is a natural part of any well-designed, well-executed research project.

References   The *reference list* provides the reader with the information needed to seek out the original source of information. Each study discussed in the paper is listed in alphabetical order by the last name of the author(s). Works by the same author are arranged chronologically according to publication date. In addition to the author(s) and the title of the research study, a complete reference to the research report is included. The most common reference is to an article in a research journal. The format for such a reference is to list (1) the author(s), last name first, (2) the year the paper was published listed in parentheses, (3) the title of the article, (4) the journal title, (5) the volume of the journal, and (6) the pages of the article. The journal title and the volume number are underlined, but nothing else in the reference should be underlined. The typesetter will set any underlined material in italics. Here are two examples of references to *journal articles:*

> Beck, A. T. (1970). Role of fantasies in psychotherapy and psychopathology. Journal of Nervous and Mental Disease, *150,* 3–17.
> Benbow, C. P., & Stanley, J. C. (1980). Sex differences in mathematical ability: Fact or artifact? Science, *210,* 1262–1264.

A similar format is used for a reference to a book. Again, we list (1) the author(s), (2) the year the book was published in parentheses, (3) the title of the book, which should be underlined, (4) the city in which the book was published, and (5) the publisher. Here are examples of references to *books:*

> Johnson, R. N. (1972). Aggression in man and animals. Philadelphia: Saunders.
> Welkowitz, J., Ewen, R. B., & Cohen, J. (1982). Introductory statistics for the behavioral sciences (3rd ed.). San Diego: Harcourt Brace Jovanovich.

The reference section of this text provides many other examples of the final typeset form for references. Remember, what appears as italicized in the published form is material that is underlined in the manuscript.

WRITING STYLE

Good writing is important whether you are writing a journal article or a letter home. It is one of the most difficult things to teach, and it can be learned only through practice. However, there are different kinds of writing. Writing a journal article requires technical writing. Precision, conciseness, and organization are important in technical writing. Flowery adjectives and a poetic style are best left to the creative writer.

The primary purpose of writing a research report is communication, and anything that obscures communication should be avoided. Pronouns should be used sparingly and should never be ambiguous. Abbreviations should also be used sparingly and should always be explained to the reader. Using active voice and simple sentence structure can help a writer avoid numerous communication pitfalls (such as dangling or misplaced modifiers). Traditionally, the research report is written in the past tense and primarily in the third person (e.g., "The experimenter assigned each subject. . . ."), although there is a current trend to use more first person in research reports. A good way to improve a research report is to have someone who was not involved in the research read the report. Anything that is unclear to your reader will probably also be unclear to other readers. Writing manual such as Strunk and White's (1979) *Elements of Style* or Zinsser's (1994) *On Writing Well* are a valuable resources for any writer.

Although some researchers find the writing phase to be challenging and rewarding, for many researchers writing a good research report is a demanding task. It is made somewhat easier if the research itself is carefully planned and well organized. For all researchers, however, telling people about something that they discovered can be truly exciting.

SUMMARY

The final stage of any research project is the communication of the results. Appendix A lists some of the basic features of the APA writing style for research reports. A journal article is a carefully organized presentation of the research and its findings. The body of the article is divided into introduction, method, results, and discussion sections, which help to organize the entire paper. In addition, the article should have an abstract that summarizes the study and a complete list of references.

Appendix B

Random Numbers

To use the table of random numbers, select any starting point and any direction (up, down, left, right). For example, if we want to assign subjects randomly to each of five groups, we might start at the beginning of row 85 and move left to right. We number the groups 1 through 5. We assign the first subject to the group designated by the first digit we encounter that is between 1 and 5; the second subject is assigned to the group designated by the next suitable digit encountered, and so on. By this method, the first ten subjects are randomly assigned to the following groups: 1, 3, 1, 1, 2, 2, 4, 2, 1, 3.

It is also possible to randomize within blocks so that the same number of subjects is in each condition. For example, if we want to assign the first five subjects—one to each of the five groups—and we use the same starting point (beginning of row 85), we get the following assignment: 1, 3, 2, 4, 5. Our second block of five subjects are assigned to the following groups: 3, 2, 5, 4, 1. Variations of these procedures can be used for random selection of subjects from an accessible population, assignment of groups to conditions, or in some form of stratified random sampling.

Row Number										
00000	10097	32533	76520	13586	34673	54876	80959	09117	39292	74945
00001	37542	04805	64894	74296	24805	24037	20636	10402	00822	91665
00002	08422	68953	19645	09303	23209	02560	15953	34764	35080	33606
00003	99019	02529	09376	70715	38311	31165	88676	74397	04436	27659
00004	12807	99970	80157	36147	64032	36653	98951	16877	12171	76833
00005	66065	74717	34072	76850	36697	36170	65813	39885	11199	29170
00006	31060	10805	45571	82406	35303	42614	86799	07439	23403	09732
00007	85269	77602	02051	65692	68665	74818	73053	85247	18623	88579
00008	63573	32135	05325	47048	90553	57548	28468	28709	83491	25624
00009	73796	45753	03529	64778	35808	34282	60935	20344	35273	88435
00010	98520	17767	14905	68607	22109	40558	60970	93433	50500	73998
00011	11805	05431	39808	27732	50725	68248	29405	24201	52775	67851
00012	83452	99634	06288	98033	13746	70078	18475	40610	68711	77817
00013	88685	40200	86507	58401	36766	67951	90364	76493	29609	11062
00014	99594	67348	87517	64969	91826	08928	93785	61368	23478	34113
00015	65481	17674	17468	50950	58047	76974	73039	57186	40218	16544
00016	80124	35635	17727	08015	45318	22374	21115	78253	14385	53763
00017	74350	99817	77402	77214	43236	00210	45521	64237	96286	02655
00018	69916	26803	66252	29148	36936	87203	76621	13990	94400	56418
00019	09893	20505	14225	68514	46427	56788	96297	78822	54382	14598
00020	91499	14523	68479	27686	46162	83554	94750	89923	37089	20048
00021	80336	94598	26940	36858	70297	34135	53140	33340	42050	82341
00022	44104	81949	85157	47954	32979	26575	57600	40881	22222	06413
00023	12550	73742	11100	02040	12860	74697	96644	89439	28707	25815
00024	63606	49329	16505	34484	40219	52563	43651	77082	07207	31790
00025	61196	90446	26457	47774	51924	33729	65394	59593	42582	60527
00026	15474	45266	95270	79953	59367	83848	82396	10118	33211	59466
00027	94557	28573	67897	54387	54622	44431	91190	42592	92927	45973
00028	42481	16213	97344	08721	16868	48767	03071	12059	25701	46670
00029	23523	78317	73208	89837	68935	91416	26252	29663	05522	82562
00030	04493	52494	75246	33824	45862	51025	61962	79335	65337	12472
00031	00549	97654	64051	88159	96119	63896	54692	82391	23287	29529
00032	35963	15307	26898	09354	33351	35462	77974	50024	90103	39333
00033	59808	08391	45427	26842	83609	49700	13021	24892	78565	20106
00034	46058	85236	01390	92286	77281	44077	93910	83647	70617	42941
00035	32179	00597	87379	25241	05567	07007	86743	17157	85394	11838
00036	69234	61406	20117	45204	15956	60000	18743	92423	97118	96338
00037	19565	41430	01758	75379	40419	21585	66674	36806	84962	85207

Row
Number

00038	45155	14938	19476	07246	43667	94543	59047	90033	20826	69541
00039	94864	31994	36168	10851	34888	81553	01540	35456	05014	51176
00040	98086	24826	45240	28404	44999	08896	39094	73407	35441	31880
00041	33185	16232	41941	50949	89435	48581	88695	41994	37548	73043
00042	80951	00406	96382	70774	20151	23387	25016	25298	94624	61171
00043	79752	49140	71961	28296	69861	02591	74852	20539	00387	59579
00044	18633	32537	98145	06571	31010	24674	05455	61427	77938	91936
00045	74029	43902	77557	32270	97790	17119	52527	58021	80814	51748
00046	54178	45611	80993	37143	05335	12969	56127	19255	36040	90324
00047	11664	49883	52079	84827	59381	71539	09973	33440	88461	23356
00048	48324	77928	31249	64710	02295	36870	32307	57546	15020	09994
00049	69074	94138	87637	91976	35584	04401	10518	21615	01848	76938
00050	09188	20097	32825	39527	04220	86304	83389	87374	64278	58044
00051	90045	85497	51981	50654	94938	81997	91870	76150	68476	64659
00052	73189	50207	47677	26269	62290	64464	27124	67018	41361	82760
00053	75768	76490	20971	87749	90429	12272	95375	05871	93823	43178
00054	54016	44056	66281	31003	00682	27398	20714	53295	07706	17813
00055	08358	69910	78542	42785	13661	58873	04618	97553	31223	08420
00056	28306	03264	81333	10591	40510	07893	32604	60475	94119	01840
00057	53840	86233	81594	13628	51215	90290	28466	68795	77762	20791
00058	91757	53741	61613	62669	50263	90212	55781	76514	83483	47055
00059	89415	92694	00397	58391	12607	17646	48949	72306	94541	37408
00060	77513	03820	86864	29901	68414	82774	51908	13980	72893	55507
00061	19502	37174	69979	20288	55210	29773	74287	75251	65344	67415
00062	21818	59313	93278	81757	05686	73156	07082	85046	31853	38452
00063	51474	66499	68107	23621	94049	91345	42836	09191	08007	45449
00064	99559	68331	62535	24170	69777	12830	74819	78142	43860	72834
00065	33713	48007	93584	72869	51926	64721	58303	29822	93174	93972
00066	85274	86893	11303	22970	28834	34137	73515	90400	71148	43643
00067	84133	89640	44035	52166	73852	70091	61222	60561	62327	18423
00068	56732	16234	17395	96131	10123	91622	85496	57560	81604	18880
00069	65138	56806	87648	85261	34313	65861	45875	21069	85644	47277
00070	38001	02176	81719	11711	71602	92937	74219	64049	65584	49698
00071	37402	96397	01304	77586	56271	10086	47324	62605	40030	37438
00072	97125	40348	87083	31417	21815	39250	75237	62047	15501	29578
00073	21826	41134	47143	34072	64638	85902	49139	06441	03856	54552
00074	73135	42742	95719	09035	85794	74296	08789	88156	64691	19202

Row
Number

00075	07638	77929	03061	18072	96207	44156	23821	99538	04713	66994
00076	60528	83441	07954	19814	59175	20695	05533	52139	61212	06455
00077	83596	35655	06958	92983	05128	09719	77433	53783	92301	50498
00078	10850	62746	99599	10507	13499	06319	53075	71839	06410	19362
00079	39820	98952	43622	63147	64421	80814	43800	09351	31024	73167
00080	59580	06478	75569	78800	88835	54486	23768	06156	04111	08408
00081	38508	07341	23793	48763	90822	97022	17719	04207	95954	49953
00082	30692	70668	94688	16127	56196	80091	82067	63400	05462	69200
00083	65443	95659	18238	27437	49632	24041	08337	65676	96299	90836
00084	27267	50264	13192	72294	07477	44606	17985	48911	97341	30358
00085	91307	06991	19072	24210	36699	53728	28825	35793	28976	66252
00086	68434	94688	84473	13622	62126	98408	12843	82590	09815	93146
00087	48908	15877	54745	24591	35700	04754	83824	52692	54130	55160
00088	06913	45197	42672	78601	11883	09528	63011	98901	14974	40344
00089	10455	16019	14210	33712	91342	37821	88325	80851	43667	70883
00090	12883	97343	65027	61184	04285	01392	17974	15077	90712	26769
00091	21778	30976	38807	36961	31649	42096	63281	02023	08816	47449
00092	19523	59515	65122	59659	86283	68258	69572	13798	16435	91529
00093	67245	52670	35583	16563	79246	86686	76463	34222	26655	90802
00094	60584	47377	07500	37992	45134	26529	26760	83637	41326	44344
00095	53853	41377	36066	94850	58838	73859	49364	73331	96240	43642
00096	24637	38736	74384	89342	52623	07992	12369	18601	03742	83873
00097	83080	12451	38992	22815	07759	51777	97377	27585	51972	37867
00098	16444	24334	36151	99073	27493	70939	85130	32552	54846	54759
00099	60790	18157	57178	65762	11161	78576	45819	52979	65130	04860
00100	03991	10461	93716	16894	66083	24653	84609	58232	88618	19161
00101	38555	95554	32886	59780	08355	60860	29735	47762	71299	23853
00102	17546	73704	92052	46215	55121	29281	59076	07936	27954	58909
00103	32643	52861	95819	06831	00911	98936	76355	93779	80863	00514
00104	69572	68777	39510	35905	14060	40619	29549	69616	33564	60780
00105	24122	66591	27699	06494	14845	46672	61958	77100	90899	75754
00106	61196	30231	92962	61773	41839	55382	17267	70943	78038	70267
00107	30532	21704	10274	12202	39685	23309	10061	68829	55986	66485
00108	03788	97599	75867	20717	74416	53166	35208	33374	87539	08823
00109	48228	63379	85783	47619	53152	67433	35663	52972	16818	60311
00110	60365	94653	35075	33949	42614	29297	01918	28316	98953	73231
00111	83799	42402	56623	34442	34994	41374	70071	14736	09958	18065

Row
Number

00112	32960	07405	36409	83232	99385	41600	11133	07586	15917	06253
00113	19322	53845	57620	52606	66497	68646	78138	66559	19640	99413
00114	11220	94747	07399	37408	48509	23929	27482	45476	85244	35159
00115	31751	57260	68980	05339	15470	48355	88651	22596	03152	19121
00116	88492	99382	14454	04504	20094	98977	74843	93413	22109	78508
00117	30934	47744	07481	83828	73788	06533	28597	20405	94205	20380
00118	22888	48893	27499	98748	60530	45128	74022	84617	82037	10268
00119	78212	16993	35902	91386	44372	15486	65741	14014	87481	37220
00120	41849	84547	46850	52326	34677	58300	74910	64345	19325	81549
00121	46352	33049	69248	93460	45305	07521	61318	31855	14413	70951
00122	11087	96294	14013	31792	59747	67277	76503	34513	39663	77544
00123	52701	08337	56303	87315	16520	69676	11654	99893	02181	68161
00124	57275	36898	81304	48585	68652	27376	92852	55866	88448	03584
00125	20857	73156	70284	24326	79375	95220	01159	63267	10622	48391
00126	15633	84924	90415	93614	33521	26665	55823	47641	86225	31704
00127	92694	48297	39904	02115	59589	49067	66821	41575	49767	04037
00128	77613	19019	88152	00080	20554	91409	96277	48257	50816	97616
00129	38688	32486	45134	63545	59404	72059	43947	51680	43852	59693
00130	25163	01889	70014	15021	41290	67312	71857	15957	68971	11403
00131	65251	07629	37239	33295	05870	01119	92784	26340	18477	65622
00132	36815	43625	18637	37509	82444	99005	04921	73701	14707	93997
00133	64397	11692	05327	82162	20247	81759	45197	25332	83745	22567
00134	04515	25624	95096	67946	48460	85558	15191	18782	16930	33361
00135	83761	60873	43253	84145	60833	25983	01291	41349	20368	07126
00136	14387	06345	80854	09279	43529	06318	38384	74761	41196	37480
00137	51321	92246	80088	77074	88722	56736	66164	49431	66919	31678
00138	72472	00008	80890	18002	94813	31900	54155	83436	35352	54131
00139	05466	55306	93128	18464	74457	90561	72848	11834	79982	68416
00140	39528	72484	82474	25593	48545	35247	18619	13674	18611	19241
00141	81616	18711	53342	44276	75122	11724	74627	73707	58319	15997
00142	07586	16120	82641	22820	92904	13141	32392	19763	61199	67940
00143	90767	04235	13574	17200	69902	63742	78464	22501	18627	90872
00144	40188	28193	29593	88627	94972	11598	62095	36787	00441	58997
00145	34414	82157	86887	55087	19152	00023	12302	80783	32624	68691
00146	63439	75363	44989	16822	36024	00867	76378	41605	65961	73488
00147	67049	09070	93399	45547	94458	74284	05041	49807	20288	34060
00148	79495	04146	52162	90286	54158	34243	46978	35482	59362	95938
00149	91704	30552	04737	21031	75051	93029	47665	64382	99782	93478

Row
Number

00150	94015	46874	32444	48277	59820	96163	64654	25843	41145	42820
00151	74108	88222	88570	74015	25704	91035	01755	14750	48968	38603
00152	62880	87873	95160	59221	22304	90314	72877	17334	39283	04149
00153	11748	12102	80580	41867	17710	59621	06554	07850	73950	79552
00154	17944	05600	60478	03343	25852	58905	57216	39618	49856	99326
00155	66067	42792	95043	52680	46780	56487	09971	59481	37006	22186
00156	54244	91030	45547	70818	59849	96169	61459	21647	87417	17198
00157	30945	57589	31732	57260	47670	07654	46376	25366	94746	49580
00158	69170	37403	86995	90307	94304	71803	26825	05511	12459	91314
00159	08345	88975	35841	85771	08105	59987	87112	21476	14713	71181
00160	27767	43584	85301	88977	29490	69714	73035	41207	74699	09310
00161	13025	14338	54066	15243	47724	66733	47431	43905	31048	56699
00162	80217	36292	98525	24335	24432	24896	43277	58874	11466	16082
00163	10875	62004	90391	61105	57411	06368	53856	30743	08670	84741
00164	54127	57326	26629	19087	24472	88779	30540	27886	61732	75454
00165	60311	42824	37301	42678	45990	43242	17374	52003	70707	70214
00166	49739	71484	92003	98086	76668	73209	59202	11973	02902	33250
00167	78626	51594	16453	94614	39014	97066	83012	09832	25571	77628
00168	66692	13986	99837	00582	81232	44987	09504	96412	90193	79568
00169	44071	28091	07362	97703	76447	42537	98524	97831	65704	09514
00170	41468	85149	49554	17994	14924	39650	95294	00556	70481	06905
00171	94559	37559	49678	53119	70312	05682	66986	34099	74474	20740
00172	41615	70360	64114	58660	90850	64618	80620	51790	11436	38072
00173	50273	93113	41794	86861	24781	89683	55411	85667	77535	99892
00174	41396	80504	90670	08289	40902	05069	95083	06783	28102	57816
00175	25807	24260	71529	78920	72682	07385	90726	57166	98884	08583
00176	06170	97965	88302	98041	21443	41808	68984	83620	89747	98882
00177	60808	54444	74412	81105	01176	28838	36421	16489	18059	51061
00178	80940	44893	10408	36222	80582	71944	92638	40333	67054	16067
00179	19516	90120	46759	71643	13177	55292	21036	82808	77501	97427
00180	49386	54480	23604	23554	21785	41101	91178	10174	29420	90438
00181	06312	88940	15995	69321	47458	64809	98189	81851	29651	84215
00182	60942	00307	11897	92674	40405	68032	96717	54244	10701	41393
00183	92329	98932	78284	46347	71209	92061	39448	93136	25722	08564
00184	77936	63574	31384	51924	85561	29671	58137	17820	22751	36518
00185	38101	77756	11657	13897	95889	57067	47648	13885	70669	93406
00186	39641	69457	91339	22502	92613	89719	11947	56203	19324	20504

Row Number										
00187	84054	40455	99396	63680	67667	60631	69181	96845	38525	11600
00188	47468	03577	57649	63266	24700	71594	14004	23153	69249	05747
00189	43321	31370	28977	23896	76479	68562	62342	07589	08899	05985
00190	64281	61826	18555	64937	13173	33365	78851	16499	87064	13075
00191	66847	70495	32350	02985	86716	38746	26313	77463	55387	72681
00192	72461	33230	21529	53424	92581	02262	78438	66276	18396	73538
00193	21032	91050	13058	16218	12470	56500	15292	76139	59526	52113
00194	95362	67011	06651	16136	01016	00857	55018	56374	35824	71708
00195	49712	97380	10404	55452	34030	60726	75211	10271	36633	68424
00196	58275	61764	97586	54716	50259	46345	87195	46092	26787	60939
00197	89514	11788	68224	23417	73959	76145	30342	40277	11049	72049
00198	15472	50669	48139	36732	46874	37088	63465	09819	58869	35220
00199	12120	86124	51247	44302	60883	52109	21437	36786	49226	77837

Source: RAND Corporation (1955). A million random digits. Glencoe, IL: Free Press of Glencoe.

Appendix C

Statistical Computation Procedures

Appendix C lists the computational formulas for frequently used statistics. Interpretation of statistical findings are covered in Chapters 5, 10, 11, and 12. We are not including computational examples because computer analyses have virtually replaced hand computations.

DESCRIPTIVE STATISTICS

Measures of Central Tendency

Mean   The *mean* is the arithmetic average of all scores. The mean is computed by adding the scores and dividing by the number of scores, as shown in Equation C.1.

$$\overline{X} = \frac{\sum X}{N} \tag{C.1}$$

Median   The *median* is the middle score or the score at the 50th percentile. To compute the median, order the scores from lowest to highest. If there is an odd number of scores, the median is the $(N + 1)/2$ score (where N is the number of scores). If there is an even number of scores, the median is the average of the $N/2$ score and the $(N/2) + 1$ score.

Mode   The *mode* is the most frequently occurring score. With large data sets it is advisable to prepare a frequency distribution to simplify the task of finding the most frequent score. It is possible to have more than one mode, in which case each mode is reported.

Measures of Variability

Variance   Equation C.2 presents the formula for the *variance* (s^2).

$$s^2 = \frac{SS}{df} = \frac{\sum (X - \overline{X})^2}{N - 1} \tag{C.2}$$

Standard Deviation   The *standard deviation* (s) is the square root of the variance.

$$s = \sqrt{s^2} \tag{C.3}$$

Measures of Relationship

Pearson Product-Moment Correlation   Equation C.4 gives the formula for the *Pearson product-moment correlation*. X and Y in Equation C.4 represent the two variables, and r is the correlation coefficient. The subscript $_{xy}$ is included to clarify exactly what variables are being correlated.

$$r_{xy} = \frac{\sum XY - \dfrac{(\sum X)(\sum Y)}{N}}{\sqrt{\left[\sum X^2 - \dfrac{(\sum X)^2}{N}\right]\left[\sum Y^2 - \dfrac{(\sum Y)^2}{N}\right]}} \tag{C.4}$$

Spearman Rank-Order Correlation The formula for the *Spearman rank-order correlation* is given in Equation C.5. The variable *d* represent the difference in the rank of *X* and *Y* for each subject.

$$r_s = 1 - \frac{6\sum d^2}{N(N^2 - 1)} \tag{C.5}$$

INFERENTIAL STATISTICS

Inferential statistics are used to draw conclusions about population characteristics on the basis of information from samples drawn from the population. In this section we assume that the student is familiar with the concepts of hypothesis testing. We present only the computational formulas for some of the most widely used inferential statistics. [For more information, consult Howell (1987), Runyon and Haber (1991), Shavelson (1988), and Welkowitz, Ewen and Cohen (1990).]

Parametric Statistics

In this section, we list the computational formulas for parametric tests of differences in population means.

Independent Samples *t*-Test The *independent samples* t-*test* is used to compare the means from two independent samples of subjects. The samples are independent if different subjects appear in each sample and the subjects in the two samples are not matched in any way. The subscripts $_1$ and $_2$ in the computational formula (Equation C.6) are used to designate the two groups.

$$t = \frac{(\overline{X}_1 - \overline{X}_2)}{\sqrt{\left[\dfrac{SS_1 + SS_2}{N_1 + N_2 - 2}\right]\left[\dfrac{1}{N_1} + \dfrac{1}{N_2}\right]}} \tag{C.6}$$

Correlated *t*-Test A *correlated* t-*test* is used to analyze the results of either a within-subjects study with two groups or a matched-pairs study with two groups. The computational formula is given as Equation C.7.

$$t = \frac{(\overline{X}_1 - \overline{X}_2)}{\sqrt{\dfrac{s_1^2}{N_1} + \dfrac{s_2^2}{N_2} - 2r\left(\dfrac{s_1}{\sqrt{N_1}}\right)\left(\dfrac{s_2}{\sqrt{N_2}}\right)}} \tag{C.7}$$

Analysis of Variance (ANOVA)   ANOVA procedures are used to test for differences in means between two or more groups. In this section we list the computational formulas for some of the more frequently used ANOVA models.

The results of an analysis of variance are summarized in a table, the structure of which is the same regardless of the complexity of the model. The first column lists the source of variance; the second, the degrees of freedom; the third, the sums of squares; the fourth, the mean squares; and the fifth, the F-ratios. Often a sixth column is included that lists the p value for each F. In all cases the mean square for a particular source is computed by dividing the sum of squares for the source by the degrees of freedom for the source. The F is always a ratio of two mean squares. In the sections that follow, we summarize the computational formulas for everything but the sums of squares in a summary table format. The computational procedures for each of the sums of squares are listed as part of the discussion of the ANOVA model.

A *simple one-way ANOVA* is used to compare the group means of two or more independent groups. There are three sources of variance—between, within, and total. The computational formulas for everything except the sums of squares are given in Table C-1.

The computational formulas for the sum of squares within (abbreviated SS_w), the sum of squares between (SS_b) and the total sum of squares (SS_T) are given in Equations C.8–C.10. To clarify the notation, $\left(\sum X\right)_i$ refers to the sum of all the scores in the ith group and n_i refers to the sample size in the ith group. The term $\left(\sum X\right)_T$ refers to the total sum of X. SS_i is the sum of squares for the ith group. k refers to the number of groups.

$$SS_b = \sum_{i=1}^{k} \frac{\left(\left(\sum X\right)_i\right)^2}{n_i} - \frac{\left(\left(\sum X\right)_T\right)^2}{N} \tag{C.8}$$

$$SS_w = \sum_{i=1}^{k} SS_i \tag{C.9}$$

$$SS_T = \left(\sum X^2\right)_T - \frac{\left(\left(\sum X\right)_T\right)^2}{N} \tag{C.10}$$

A significant F-ratio indicates that at least one mean is different from at least one other mean. Additional procedures are needed to evaluate which means are different from which other means. If we have a specific prediction about certain means, a *planned comparison* can be used to test that prediction. The planned comparison

TABLE C.1   COMPUTATIONAL FORMULAS FOR A ONE-WAY ANOVA SUMMARY TABLE

Source	df	SS	MS	F
Between	$k-1$	SS_b	SS_b/df_b	MS_b/MS_w
Within	$N-k$	SS_w	SS_w/df_w	
Total	$N-1$	SS_T		

computes a *contrast,* which is a weighted sum of the means, and then compares that contrast with an error term, which is a function of the MS_w. Equation C.11 shows how to compute the contrast and Equation C.13 shows how to compute the test statistic.

$$\hat{c} = \sum_{i=1}^{k} w_i \, X_i \tag{C.11}$$

where

$$\sum_{i=1}^{k} w_i = 0 \tag{C.12}$$

$$t = \frac{\hat{c}}{\sqrt{MS_w\left[\sum_{i=1}^{k} \frac{w_i^2}{n_i}\right]}} \tag{C.13}$$

A *repeated-measures ANOVA* is used to analyze within-subjects designs with two or more groups. The error term in this analysis takes into account the correlation between conditions. Three sums of squares are computed: sum of squares for the subjects (SS_s), sum of squares between conditions (SS_b), and the error term sum of squares (SS_E). Equations C.14–C.16 show the computational formulas for each of these. Table C-2 shows the remaining computational formulas for the ANOVA summary table.

$$SS_s = \frac{\sum_{i=1}^{n}\left(\sum_{j=1}^{k} X_{ij}\right)^2}{k} - \frac{\left(\sum_{i=1}^{n}\sum_{j=1}^{k} X_{ij}\right)^2}{(n)(k)} \tag{C.14}$$

$$SS_b = \frac{\sum_{j=1}^{k}\left(\sum_{i=1}^{n} X_{ij}\right)^2}{n} - \frac{\left(\sum_{i=1}^{n}\sum_{j=1}^{k} X_{ij}\right)^2}{(n)(k)} \tag{C.15}$$

$$SS_E = \sum_{i=1}^{n}\sum_{j=1}^{k} X_{ij}^2 - \frac{\left(\sum_{i=1}^{n}\sum_{j=1}^{k} X_{ij}\right)^2}{(n)(k)} - SS_s - SS_b \tag{C.16}$$

In a *simple two-way ANOVA* the SS_b is partitioned into three terms. Two of the terms represent the two factors (labeled *A* and *B*) and the third term represents the interaction of these factors (labeled *AB*). Because there are several terms, slightly more complex notation is needed. We use *a* as the number of levels of factor *A* and

TABLE C.2   COMPUTATIONAL FORMULAS FOR A ONE-WAY REPEATED-MEASURES ANOVA SUMMARY TABLE

Source	df	SS	MS	F
Subjects	$n-1$	SS_s	SS_s/df_s	
Between	$k-1$	SS_b	SS_b/df_b	MS_b/MS_E
Error	$(n-1)(k-1)$	SS_E	SS_E/df_E	

b as the number of levels of factor *B*. We use the subscripts $_i$ and $_j$ for the *A* and *B* factors, respectively. We use the subscripts $_A$, $_B$, $_{AB}$, $_w$ and $_T$ to identify the source of variance.

The SS_T is computed by treating the data as if it came from one group. The SS_w is computed by summing the individual SSs from each of the $a \times b$ groups (i.e., treating it as if it were a one-way ANOVA with $a \times b$ groups). Equation C.17 looks more complicated than Equation C.9 because we have to sum across two factors instead of one. The term SS_{ij} refers to the sum of squares for the cell represented by the *i*th level of factor *A* and the *j*th level of factor *B*.

$$SS_w = \sum_{i=1}^{a} \sum_{j=1}^{b} SS_{ij} \tag{C.17}$$

Computing the sums of squares for factors *A* and *B* involves ignoring (or collapsing across) the one factor while doing the computation for the other factor. The formulas for SS_A and SS_B are given in Equations C.18 and C.19. The notation is an extension of the notation used earlier. The term $(\Sigma X)_{ij}$ refers to the sum of scores from the cell formed by the *i*th level of *A* and the *j*th level of *B*. Therefore, the numerator in the first term of Equation C.18 represents the sum of scores collapsed across *B* for each level of *A*. The denominator represents the sample size for each level of *A*.

$$SS_A = \sum_{i=1}^{a} \frac{\left(\sum_{j=1}^{b} (\Sigma X)_{ij}\right)^2}{\sum_{j=1}^{b} n_{ij}} - \frac{\left((\Sigma X)_T\right)^2}{N} \tag{C.18}$$

$$SS_B = \sum_{j=1}^{b} \frac{\left(\sum_{i=1}^{a} (\Sigma X)_{ij}\right)^2}{\sum_{i=1}^{a} n_{ij}} - \frac{\left((\Sigma X)_T\right)^2}{N} \tag{C.19}$$

Computing the sum of squares for the interaction (SS_{AB}) requires the computation of four terms (Equation C.20), but three of them are familiar.

$$SS_{AB} = \sum_{i=1}^{a} \sum_{j=1}^{b} \frac{\left((\Sigma X)_{ij}\right)^2}{n_{ij}} - \sum_{i=1}^{a} \frac{\left(\sum_{j=1}^{b} (\Sigma X)_{ij}\right)^2}{\sum_{j=1}^{b} n_{ij}} - \sum_{j=1}^{b} \frac{\left(\sum_{i=1}^{a} (\Sigma X)_{ij}\right)^2}{\sum_{i=1}^{a} n_{ij}} - \frac{\left((\Sigma X)_T\right)^2}{N} \tag{C.20}$$

Table C-3 presents the computational formulas for the remainder of the summary table. For computation of more complex ANOVA models, consult Myers and Well (1991).

Nonparametric Statistics

Chi-Square Goodness-of-Fit Test   With nominal data each subject is categorized. The appropriate summary statistic is the frequencies in each of the categories. The

TABLE C.3 COMPUTATIONAL FORMULAS FOR A TWO-WAY ANOVA SUMMARY TABLE

Source	df	SS	MS	F
Factor A	$(a - 1)$	SS_A	SS_A / df_A	MS_A / MS_w
Factor B	$(b - 1)$	SS_B	SS_B / df_B	MS_B / MS_w
AB interaction	$(a - 1)(b - 1)$	SS_{AB}	SS_{AB} / df_{AB}	MS_{AB} / MS_w
Within-groups	$N - ab$	SS_w	SS_w / df_w	
Total	$N - 1$	SS_T		

chi-square (written χ^2) *goodness-of-fit* test evaluates the pattern of these frequencies against a specified hypothesis. The hypothesis is converted into expected frequencies (E in the formula) and then compared with the observed frequencies (*O*).

$$\chi^2 = \sum_{i=1}^{k} \frac{(O_i - E_i)^2}{E_i}$$

(C.21)

Chi-Square Test for Independence The *chi-square test for independence* is used for comparing two or more groups to determine if different patterns of frequencies exist in the groups. The chi-square formula is unchanged in the test for independence. The only change is in the way the expected cell frequencies are computed. In the test for independence, we compute the expected cell frequencies based on the overall pattern of frequencies in the groups. The expected cell frequency is computed by multiplying the row and column totals for that cell together and dividing by the grand total (total number of subject across all cells).

Cautions Regarding Chi-Square Chi-square is an often misused statistical procedure. Caution is necessary. The data for chi-square are always frequencies—percentages are never used in the computations. Individual events or measures must be independent of one another. It is not legitimate to have a person contribute more than one data point. Every subject or event must appear once and only once in the summary table. The most common violation of this principle is excluding nonoccurrences from the table.

It should be noted that many statistics texts, especially older textbooks, argue that chi-square should not be used if any expected cell frequencies are too small (usually a cutoff of 5 is used). More recent work (Camilli & Hopkins, 1978) suggests that such a rule is overly restrictive and that chi-square gives accurate results even when expected cell frequencies are quite small. Many older textbooks suggest using the Yates correction for continuity whenever there is one degree of freedom. Again, recent research suggests that such a procedure is unnecessarily restrictive and actually leads to less accurate conclusions.

Other Nonparametric Statistics Nonparametric statistics have been developed to test almost any statistical hypothesis. Although once quite popular, nonparametric statistics are used today only when the dependent measure generates nominal or ordered data. Siegel (1956) is still one of the best summaries of the many nonparametric statistical procedures available to researchers.

REGRESSION

A correlation coefficient can provide the basis for a *linear regression* equation. Equation C.22 gives the formula for predicting Y (termed Y') from X written as a traditional linear equation (i.e., $bX + a$).

$$Y' = \left[(r_{xy})\left(\frac{s_y}{s_x}\right) \right] X + \left[\overline{Y} - (r_{xy})\left(\frac{s_y}{s_x}\right) \overline{X} \right] \qquad \text{(C.22)}$$

SUMMARY

Statistics are tools that help us interpret the results of studies. The appropriate statistic(s) depend on the nature of data and of the question being asked. This appendix listed the computational formulas for some of the more commonly used statistics. For a more detailed description of these procedures and other procedures not described here, consult any entry-level textbooks on statistics [e.g., Howell (1987) or Shavelson (1988)].

Appendix D

Statistical Analyses Using SPSS for Windows

This appendix outlines the basic principles needed to organize, prepare, and conduct statistical analyses. We will be using one of the most popular statistical analysis packages—*SPSS for Windows*—but the principles we describe apply to virtually any statistical analysis package. *SPSS for Windows* is designed to run on IBM-compatible personal computers running the Windows operating system.[1] A variety of other statistical packages exist—some designed to run on mainframe computers (e.g., BMDP, SPSS-X, & Minitab) and others designed to run on personal computers (e.g., SPSS-PC+). Although each statistical package uses different commands, they tend to operate similarly. Programs designed to run on mainframe computers (large, centralized computers that you access from remote terminals) usually operate in batch mode. This means that you set up a series of command statements describing the data and the analyses you want and send these statements to the computer in one batch to be run. Some statistical analysis packages designed for personal computers (e.g., SPSS-PC+) can also be run in batch mode. However, most packages running on personal computers take advantage of the fact that you have exclusive access to the computer and are therefore structured to conduct one step at a time, giving immediate feedback of results before you select the next step or analysis. The *SPSS for Windows* program is documented in a series of manuals (Norusis, 1994a, 1994b, 1994c), which can be purchased at most university book stores. Many university computer centers sponsor low-cost courses on using particular statistical packages. The trend is to make statistical analysis packages increasingly easier to operate. That is as it should be. However, even modern statistical analysis packages cannot decide what statistical procedures are appropriate and how to interpret the results of the analysis. There is no substitute for solid training in statistics and research design.

ORGANIZING AND ENTERING THE DATA

The first step in any data analysis is to organize and enter the data onto a file accessible to the data-analysis program. Most statistical packages designed to run on personal computers have an integrated data entry system. Statistical analysis packages written to run on mainframe computers typically require that the data be entered into a computer file in a specified format. We will not be covering the process of entering data for mainframe computers in this appendix, but the manuals for any of statistical package that runs on a mainframe will describe the procedures. Before you begin the process of data entry, always consult the manual for the statistical package that you intend to use to see what restrictions on data organization and entry apply.

---

[1]This text went into production just days before the release of Windows 95. We used the current version of *SPSS for Windows* (Version 6.1), but we anticipate that a version of *SPSS for Windows* optimized for the Windows 95 operating system will be out by the time this text is released. The Windows 95 screens have a different look and feel than the Windows (Version 3.1) screens. Therefore, we expect that there will be superficial differences in the appearance of newer editions of *SPSS for Windows*. We have been assured by the SPSS corporation that the operating principles will be unchanged in the anticipated upgrade.

Virtually all statistical analysis packages follow the same conventions for data entry. For example, the order of the variables has to be identical for each subject. If you have six variables measured on each subject (age, sex, IQ score, the condition the subject was assigned to, and pretest and posttest measures on your dependent variable), those six variables must appear in the same order for each subject. In addition, each line (called a record) contains data from a single subject.[2] The only exception to this principle is that data from matched-subject designs will place the data from the set of matched subjects on a single record. Statistical analysis packages usually arrange data by *field* and *record,* although a given package may use different terms for these concepts. A *record* consists of all the data for a given subject and is represented as rows in your data entry sheet. Within each record are individual *fields,* which contain the scores for a subject on a given variable. In our previous example, there are six fields (age, sex, IQ, condition, pretest, posttest) in each record. Actually, we often add a seventh field to provide an identification number (ID #) for each subject.

It is best to organize the data before you begin data entry. One way to do this is to construct a data matrix table that resembles the data file. Another way to organize the data is to have data sheets for each subject, which organize the variables and have a place for the subject's score on each variable. A data sheet for a rather complex hypothetical study is illustrated in Figure D.1. This example is for a treatment study of severe depression. A properly constructed data sheet will not only organize the data entry process, but can also help in the coding of the data (discussed below).

Coding Data Before Entry

Many variables produce numerical scores, which require no coding before data entry. Examples are reaction times, scores on psychological tests, the number of responses in a given time interval, and so on. Other variables require some kind of coding or scoring before the data are suitable for analysis. Sometimes the codes are simple. For example, the sex of the subject can be coded as M or F for male and female, respectively. Some statistical analysis programs operate more efficiently with numerical codes than alphabetic codes, so you may want to use 1 and 2 as the codes for male and female, respectively. The numerical code in this case is arbitrary. When arbitrary codes are used, special care must be exercised to label the output so that the codes are easily identifiable. Most statistical analysis packages have routine procedures for incorporating such labels.

In some situations, coding the data is an involved process that needs to be carefully thought out if the data analysis is to go smoothly. Suppose that you are coding a diagnostic interview for indications of psychopathology. To give an overly simplified example, suppose you asked four questions: (1) Do you experience obsessions? (2) Do you experience compulsions? (3) If obsessions and/or compulsions are experienced, do they seem unreasonable to you? (4) Do they cause marked distress

---

[2]When you have large data sets on a mainframe computer, the record may contain several lines of data because of limitations on the length of a line. Each subject will have the same number of lines of data organized in exactly the same manner. This constraint rarely applies to statistical packages set up to run on personal computers, where the package has its own built-in data entry procedures.

TABLE D.1   AN EXAMPLE OF A DATA SHEET FOR A SINGLE SUBJECT

Data Sheet

Subject # _____   Condition _____   Age _____

Sex (1) male (2) female   Education_____   IQ Score _____

Age of onset _____   # of Episodes (> 1 month)_____

Family History? (1) yes (2) no   Hospitalized? (1) yes (2) no

Pretest scores:

Beck_____   Item Scores (1)_____   (2)_____   (3)_____   (4)_____   (5)_____
(6)_____   (7)_____   (8)_____   (9)_____   (10)_____   (11)_____   (12)_____
(13)_____   (14)_____   (15)_____   (16)_____   (17)_____   (18)_____   (19)_____
(20)_____   (21)_____   Depressive Cognitions Score_____
Energy Rating_____   Activity Score_____   Anxiety Score_____

Posttest scores:

Beck_____   Item Scores (1)_____   (2)_____   (3)_____   (4)_____   (5)_____
(6)_____   (7)_____   (8)_____   (9)_____   (10)_____   (11)_____   (12)_____
(13)_____   (14)_____   (15)_____   (16)_____   (17)_____   (18)_____   (19)_____
(20)_____   (21)_____   Depressive Cognitions Score_____
Energy Rating_____   Activity Score_____   Anxiety Score_____

Three-month followup:

Beck_____   Item Scores (1)_____   (2)_____   (3)_____   (4)_____   (5)_____
(6)_____   (7)_____   (8)_____   (9)_____   (10)_____   (11)_____   (12)_____
(13)_____   (14)_____   (15)_____   (16)_____   (17)_____   (18)_____   (19)_____
(20)_____   (21)_____   Depressive Cognitions Score_____
Energy Rating_____   Activity Score_____Anxiety Score_____

and/or are excessively time-consuming (over one hour per day)? Of course the questions would be worded differently to define for the subject exactly what you mean by each term, and some of these questions would actually involve a series of questions. The information for these four basic questions is sufficient to decide whether the subject suffers from obsessive-compulsive disorder—OCD for short (DSM-IV, American Psychiatric Association, 1994). How could you code such data to give yourself maximum flexibility in the data analysis? You could take the information from the four questions, make the diagnosis, and code your diagnosis directly (e.g., 1 for OCD present; 2 for OCD not present). To get a 1 code (OCD present) you would have to have a yes to either or both questions 1 and 2 as well as a yes to both question 3 and 4. That means that there are several patterns of responses that would receive a diagnosis code of 1 (yes, yes, yes, yes; yes, no, yes, yes; and no, yes, yes, yes). There are also several ways in which you could get a diagnosis code of 2. By coding only the diagnosis (OCD either present or absent), you have lost information that might have been useful in an analysis. For example, unless you go back and recode, you no longer know which subjects reported obsessions and which reported compulsions. A carefully constructed coding scheme allows you to record the original data with all of the detail intact and still be able to simplify the data if you wish.

Principles of the Windows Environment[3]

Before we can proceed, we need to take a couple of paragraphs to cover the operation of computer programs run from the Windows environment. Windows gets its name because program operations are illustrated on the screen by boxes (called windows). There may be several windows on the screen at the same time, but only one will be operational at a time. The top line of each window has the name of the program running in that window (and often the name of the file in use by that program). The top line will be dark (usually blue on color monitors) if the program is active and dimmed (white on color monitors) if the program is not active. Windows is a visual interface between you and the computer. Much of the operation of Windows-based computer programs is accomplished by "pointing and clicking." You point a cursor (usually an arrow) by moving a device called a mouse.[4] When the arrow is pointing to the correct place on the screen, you click a button. Most devices for pointing (e.g., a mouse) have two buttons, although a few have more than two buttons. Virtually all normal operations involve clicking the left button—either once or twice depending on the type of operation.

Windows-based programs are represented on the computer screen by small pictures called icons. You start a program by pointing at its icon and clicking the left button twice in rapid succession. Figure D.1 illustrates several icons for frequently used programs arranged on one of your author's computers.[5] The third icon in the third row is the icon for *SPSS for Windows.*

One advantage of the Windows environment is that programs are organized so that each program operates in a similar manner. The second line of a window identifies a series of menus with a single word (e.g., File, Edit, Format, Help, etc.). Clicking with the left button on any of these words will open the menu, showing a list of submenus of tasks that can be accomplished by the program. In complex programs, many of the submenus have menus of their own. Clicking a submenu will either start a task or give you another window where you specify the parameters of the task you want done. This similarity between programs often permits an experienced Windows user to move easily from one program to another, sometimes without needing to consult the manual for the program. Most Windows programs have their own on-line help through the Help Menu (always the rightmost term on the menu line).

The statistical analysis program that we will be using in this appendix and throughout the text is *SPSS for Windows.* This program follows all of the Windows programming conventions described above. Starting *SPSS for Windows* requires nothing more than clicking twice on the SPSS icon.[6] The result will be the initial *SPSS for Windows* screen shown in Figure D.2

---

[3]Experienced Windows users can skip this section.
[4]Portable computers often move the pointer with a tracker ball or a small joystick device, which are easier to build into small computers.
[5]You might note the presence of some games among the computer programs. After all, you can't work all the time!
[6]From now on, unless we specify otherwise "clicking" means clicking the left mouse button and "double clicking" means clicking the left mouse button twice in quick succession.

Figure D.1   An Example of a Windows Screen Showing Several Program Icons in a Program Group Called "Textbook"

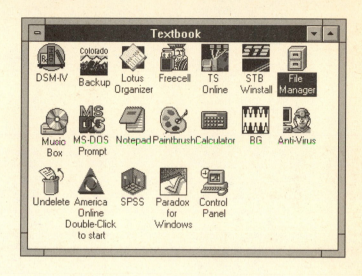

Figure D.2   The Opening Screen for *SPSS for Windows*

Entering the Data and Defining the Variables

In the remainder of this appendix we will be using *SPSS for Windows* exclusively in our examples. However, the principles apply equally well to most computer analysis packages.

Computers work with files. Traditionally, files use an 8.3 naming convention, where there are up to eight characters (termed the *filename*), followed by a period,

Figure D.3 Data Entry Example for *SPSS for Windows*

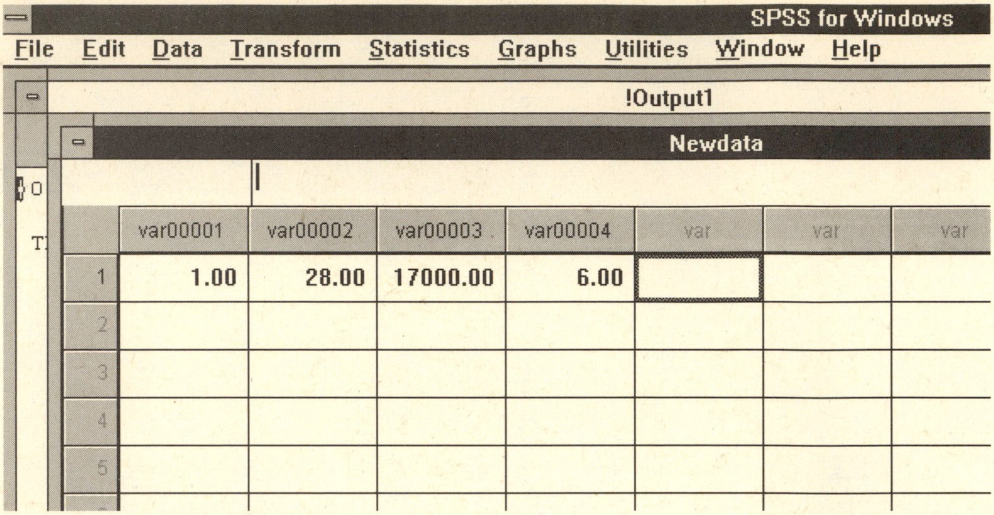

followed by up to three additional characters (termed the *extension*).[7] The extension is often used to identify the type of file. For example, *SPSS for Windows* uses ".sav" to indicate a data file and ".lst" to indicate an output file. *SPSS for Windows* automatically applies these extensions to the appropriate file for you. The .sav files in *SPSS for Windows* are written to your disk in a particular structure that the program controls. Therefore, it is best to do all of your editing of data files from the *SPSS for Windows* data screen. Notice in Figure D.2 that when you first start the *SPSS for Windows* program, you get the Newdata screen in the foreground. This is a matrix with columns representing fields and rows representing records. This structure is referred to as a *spreadsheet.* Each record typically corresponds to one subject, and each field corresponds to a variable.

To illustrate the process of data entry, we will enter the data in Table 5.2 and label the variables.[8] We will structure the data exactly as it is shown in Table 5.2. When you first open the Newdata window, the first cell (upper left) is highlighted. You can use the mouse to move to any cell (a plus sign is the cursor when you are working in the spreadsheet) and can select that cell by clicking the mouse. Anything you type will go into the selected cell as soon as you hit either the enter key or one of the arrow keys. Starting in the upper left corner, we will enter the data for the first subject by typing "1" (do not type the quotation marks) and hitting the right arrow key to move to the next cell in that row. When you do that you will notice that the column title (which had read "var") changes to var00001. This is the default name for that variable. In a minute, we will show you how to change the default names as well as the way the numbers are displayed. To continue the data entry for the first subject, type the following: 28→17000→6→. The result should be what you see in Figure D.3.

---

[7] The Windows 95 operating system will allow longer filenames, and Macintosh computers have allowed long filenames for many years.
[8] The best way to understand this section is to work along, following the steps on your computer as you read.

Figure D.4   The Define Variable Screen from *SPSS for Windows*

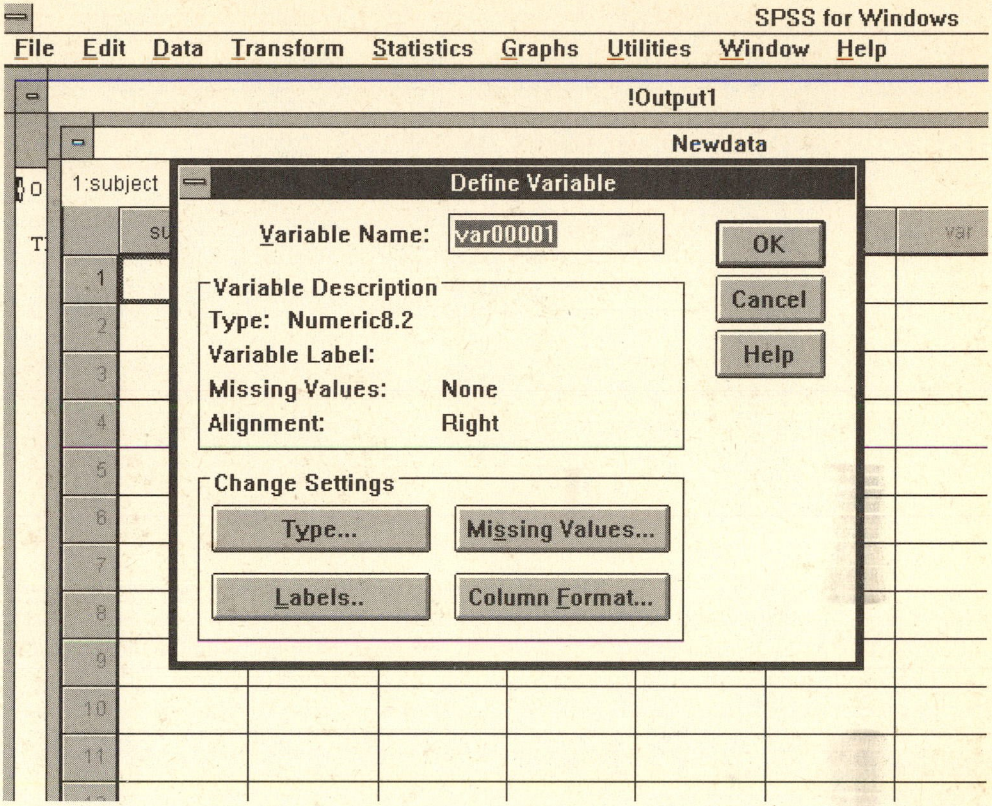

			SPSS for Windows
File	**Edit**	**Data**	**Transform** **Statistics** **Graphs** **Utilities** **Window** **Help**

!Output1

Newdata

1:subject

Define Variable

Variable Name: var00001   OK

Cancel

Variable Description
Type: Numeric8.2   Help
Variable Label:
Missing Values: None
Alignment: Right

Change Settings

Type...   Mi**s**sing Values...

Labels..   Column Format...

If you tried to enter "M" in column 5, you probably discovered that it did not work. Unless you define the variable differently, *SPSS for Windows* will only accept numeric input. We will now define the variables, give them names, and set up the sex and political affiliation variables to accept letter codes.

To define a variable we first highlight one of the cells in that variable's column. Move the cursor with the mouse to any cell in the first column and click the left button. Then select the "Data" menu and the "Define Variable" option, which will give you what you see in Figure D.4. The Define Variable box lists the current values for the first variable. We will change many of these settings starting with the variable name. Move the cursor to variable name at the top of the box and click the left button. Delete the default name of var00001 and replace it with "subject." Then move the cursor down to the button labeled "Type. . . " and click, which will give you the screen shown in Figure D.5. You will want to change the number of Decimal Places from 2 to 0 by moving the cursor to the Decimal Places box, clicking, delete the number 2, insert 0, and click on the Continue button. This returns you to the previous screen, where you click the OK button to complete the definition of the first variable. Notice that the subject number, which had read 1.00, now reads 1.

We will be defining each of the remaining variables in much the same way. We will name the remaining variables "age," "income," "voted," "sex," and "poliffil." With the

Figure D.5   The Define Variable type Subscreen of the Define Variable Screen from *SPSS for Windows*

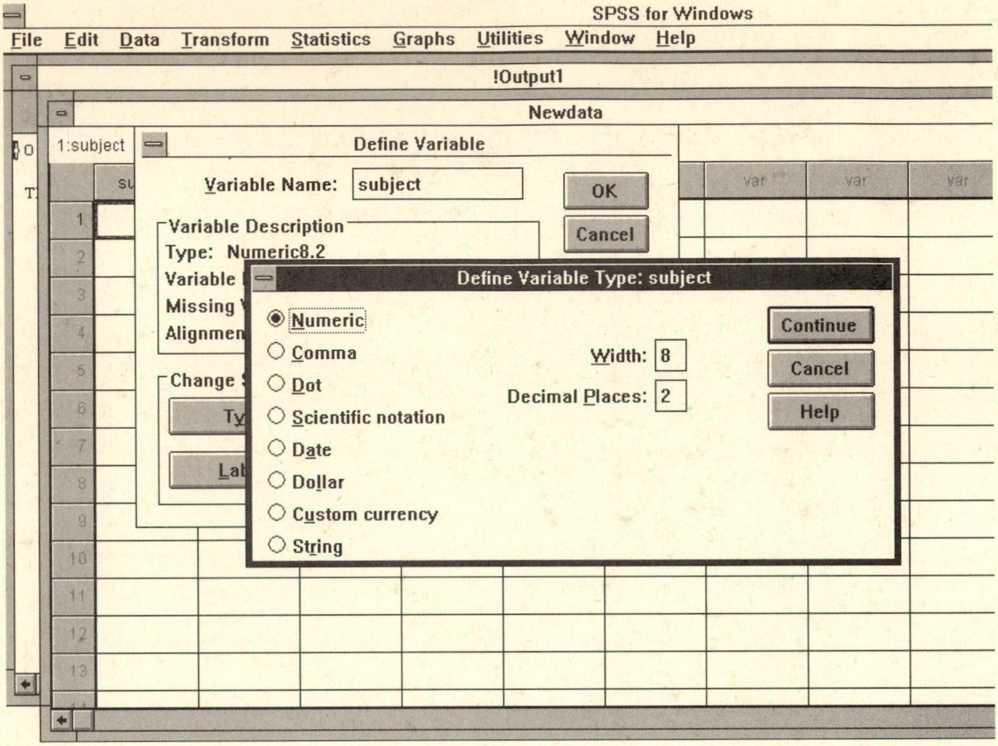

variables "age" and "voted," we will set the number of decimal places to zero as we did for the first variable ("subject"). For income, we will also change the type, but this time we will select the Dollar option on the left by clicking on the small circle preceding the word *dollar* and then selecting the format that shows no decimal places and room for up to six figures (plus the comma and the dollar sign). When you select that option you will see that the width and decimal places readings below automatically change to 8 and 0, respectively. The variables "sex" and "polaffil" require a new wrinkle. After changing the name of these variables and clicking on the Type button, we will select the String option on the left, set the number of characters to 1, and click on the Continue button. A *string variable* is any variable that contains nonnumeric characters. We are using letter codes in our example for the variables "sex" and "polaffil." Although our letter codes for these variables are reasonably self-explanatory, it is best to provide explicit labels for each of these codes. We do that by clicking on the "Labels. . ." button of the Define Variables box, which will give us the screen shown in Figure D.6. We then give a more detailed description of our variable. Here we are not restricted to just eight characters as we were with the variable name. We should also list each value that the variable can take and its associated label below. For example, Figure D.6 shows that the value "F" is associated with the value label "female." We click the Add button (which is now highlighted since we have put values in the Value and Value Labels boxes) to add this value label. Do the same for male:

Figure D.6   The Define Labels Subscreen from the Define Variable Screen from *SPSS for Windows*

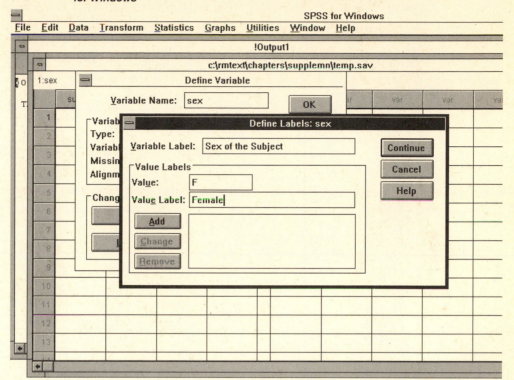

click on Continue to return to the Define Label box, and click on OK to complete this variable. A similar process can be used to define the "polaffil" variable and its three value labels ("Democrat," "Republican," and "Other").

Now we can enter the code letters for these two variables. We enter "M" and "R" (without the quotations) in columns 5 and 6, respectively. We then move the cursor to the beginning of the second line and enter the data for the second subject. We continue this process until all of the data from the 24 subjects in Table 5.2 have been entered. At this point the screen looks like Figure D.7. Our last step is to save that file by selecting the File menu and the Save As option, which will give us the screen shown in Figure D.8. We name the file using a name that ends with the extension ".sav" to indicate it is an *SPSS for Windows* data file. We also tell the program where on our disk we want the file saved.[9]

The level of detail in the preceding paragraph may have been unnecessary. The advantage of *SPSS for Windows* is that it is so intuitive that most students with a basic knowledge of statistics can figure the program out by playing with it for a short

---

[9]We are assuming that you have some familiarity with subdirectories in this saving-the-file operation. If you are not familiar with this terminology, you should consult a basic Windows manual for these concepts.

Figure D.7 Completed Entry of the Data from Table 5.2

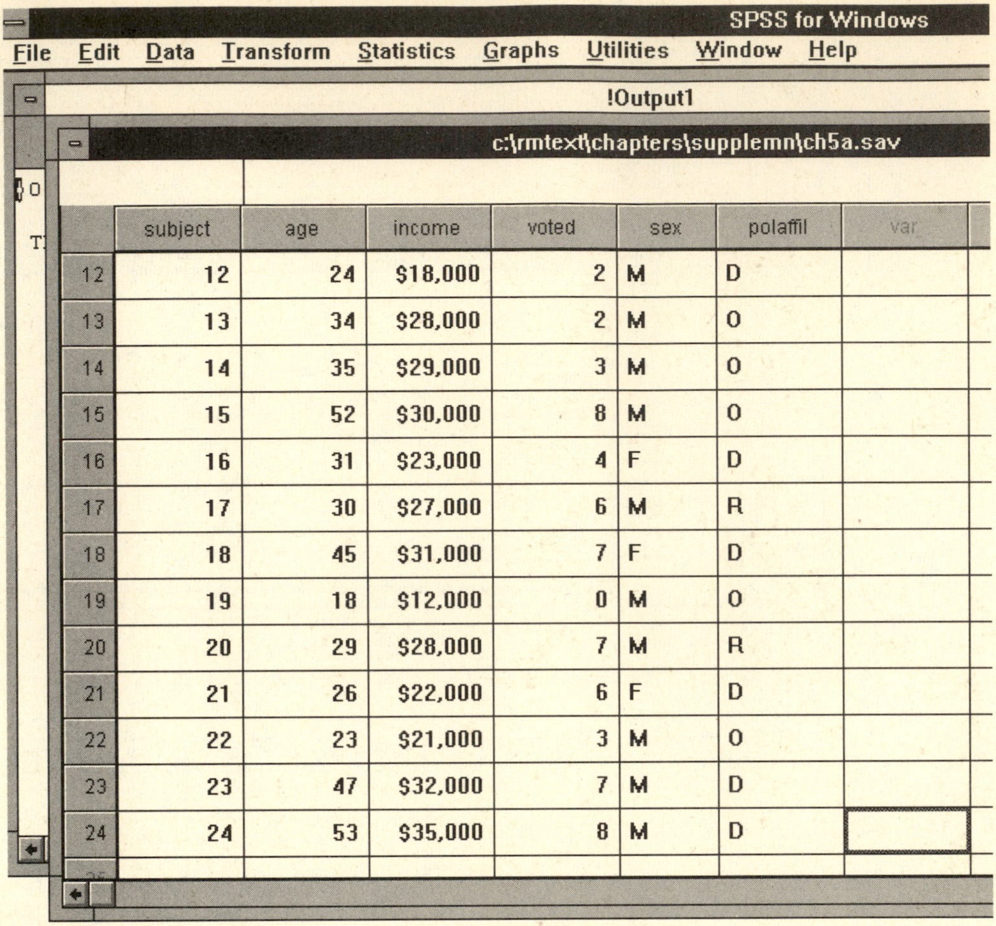

	SPSS for Windows
File Edit Data Transform Statistics Graphs Utilities Window Help	

!Output1

c:\rmtext\chapters\supplemn\ch5a.sav

	subject	age	income	voted	sex	polaffil	var
12	12	24	$18,000	2	M	D	
13	13	34	$28,000	2	M	O	
14	14	35	$29,000	3	M	O	
15	15	52	$30,000	8	M	O	
16	16	31	$23,000	4	F	D	
17	17	30	$27,000	6	M	R	
18	18	45	$31,000	7	F	D	
19	19	18	$12,000	0	M	O	
20	20	29	$28,000	7	M	R	
21	21	26	$22,000	6	F	D	
22	22	23	$21,000	3	M	O	
23	23	47	$32,000	7	M	D	
24	24	53	$35,000	8	M	D	

while. On this first task, however, we wanted to list explicitly every step. In the sections that follow, we will move through the procedures more quickly. Do not be afraid to simply try something to see how it works. It is very hard to do anything that you cannot undo. The worst that is likely to happen is that you will have to start over.

To summarize data entry principles:

1. Always give each variable a descriptive name (up to eight characters) and a more extended name if the eight characters are not self-explanatory.
2. Be sure to give value labels to any variable that uses codes so that the output will be readily interpretable.
3. Remember that each row represents one subject and each column represents one variable.
4. Save the data file with a name that is descriptive enough that you will be able to identify the file easily.

Figure D.8   The Save Data Screen from *SPSS for Windows*

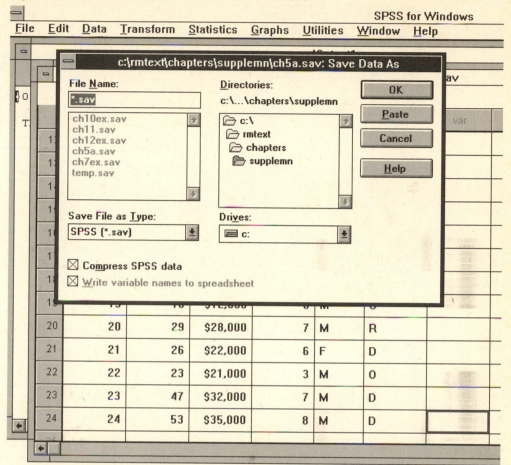

DATA ANALYSIS USING *SPSS FOR WINDOWS*

Descriptive Statistics

In a computerized statistical analysis, descriptive statistics serve two purposes. The first purpose is to describe the data, especially on those variables that will not be a part of the inferential statistical analyses. These might include the demographic characteristics of the sample, correlations of dependent variables with other variables measured, and the characteristics of the dependent variables themselves. The second purpose is to find evidence of errors in the data entry process. No matter how diligent you are in checking your data during the entry process, it is relatively easy to input a data point incorrectly. In order to be successful at spotting these data entry errors before doing the inferential statistics, you must be familiar with the data and the variables being measured. Checking the maximum and minimum scores will often help you spot errors, because you will find a score that is out of range (i.e.,

Figure D.9 The Open Data File Screen from *SPSS for Windows*

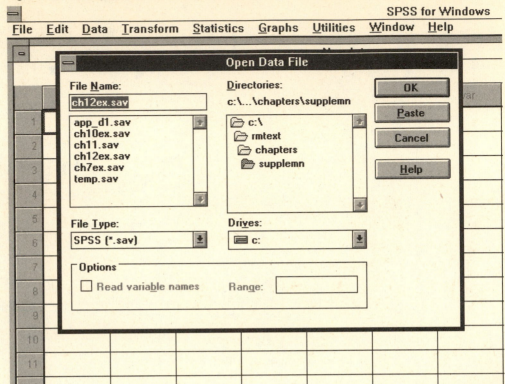

larger or smaller than it could possibly be). Of course, you must know what the largest and smallest possible scores could be to make this strategy work. Also look for scores that are highly unlikely although technically possible. If they show up, check the original data to make sure that such scores actually exist. Check to see that the mean is close to the middle of the numbers you remember seeing for a variable during the data collection and entry processes. Be particularly careful in checking variables that you may have computed—either before data entry or as part of the statistical analyses. Errors in the computations or the formulas given to the computer program are easy to make and will often result in clearly wrong answers that can be easily spotted if you are looking for them.

We will divide our overview of descriptive statistics into three sections: (1) descriptions of categorical data; (2) descriptions of score data; and (3) correlations. In each section, we will show how to generate both descriptive statistics and appropriate graphs. Our examples will draw heavily on the data set entered previously and shown in Table 5.2. Before we do the analyses, we must select the data file that was previously prepared and saved by selecting the File menu, the Open submenu, and the Data choice on the Open submenu, which will give us the screen shown in Figure D.9. We then select the file and click on OK to open it for the *SPSS for Windows* program.

Figure D.10   The Frequencies Procedure Screen from *SPSS for Windows*

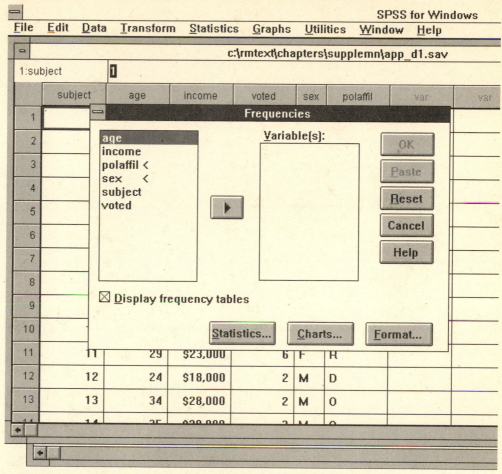

Categorical Data   Categorical data represents a classification of subjects, and the appropriate summary statistics are frequencies. We compute summary statistics for categorical data in *SPSS for Windows* by selecting the Statistics menu, the Summarize submenu, and the Frequencies choice, which gives us the screen shown in Figure D.10. We want to compute frequencies for the two categorical variables ("sex" and "polaffil"). To do so, we highlight each of these variables in turn by clicking on them in the left box and move them to the right box by clicking on the arrow button between the boxes. If we change our mind, we can move the variable back to the left box in the same manner. Once both variables have been moved, we click on OK and the analysis is run, producing the output shown in Table D.1. This output lists both the frequency and percent of subjects in each category.

Sometimes we want to tabulate frequencies for joint categories (e.g., female independents). To do this we use a procedure called crosstabs (short for cross tabulation). We select the Statistics menu, the Summarize submenu, and the Crosstabs option, which will give us the screen shown in Figure D.11. To do a cross tabulation

TABLE D.2   OUTPUT FROM THE FREQUENCIES PROCEDURE OF *SPSS FOR WINDOWS*

POLAFFIL   Political Affiliation (expressed)

Value Label	Value	Frequency	Percent	Valid Percent	Cum Percent
Democrat	D	9	37.5	37.5	37.5
Other	O	8	3.3	33.3	70.8
Republican	R	7	29.2	29.2	100.0
	Total	24	100.0	100.0	

Valid cases 24   Missing cases 0

SEX   Subject s Gender

Value Label	Value	Frequency	Percent	Valid Percent	Cum Percent
Female	F	7	29.2	29.2	29.2
Male	M	17	70.8	70.8	100.0
	Total	24	100.0	100.0	

Valid cases 24   Missing cases 0

of sex by polaffil, we move one of these variables to the box marked "row(s)" and the other the box marked "column(s)" and press the OK button. This will produce the output shown in Table D.3.

Finally, if we wanted to graph the data with a histogram, we select the Graph menu, the Bar submenu, and then click on the Simple icon and the Define button (in that order), which gives us the screen shown in Figure D.12. To produce a graph of the frequencies of political affiliations, we move the variable polaffil to the Category Axis box and click on OK. This produces the Bar graph shown in Figure D.13

Score Data   Descriptive statistics for score data involve more than just the frequencies of each score. We can produce such a frequency distribution if we desire by using the procedure described above for obtaining the frequency counts for our categorical variables. If we want additional summary statistics, such as mean and variance, we must use the Descriptives option (under Statistics menu and Summarize submenu). Selecting the Descriptives option will give us the screen shown in Figure D.14. Notice that not all the variables are listed in the left box. Descriptives cannot be run on categorical data, and our alphabetical code for the "sex" and "polaffil" variables implied that these were categorical variables. Hence, they were excluded from the list. We will produce descriptive statistics for the variables "age," "income," and "voted" by moving them from the left box to the right box in the same manner as described above. We could do the same for the "subject" variable, but since that variable is simply an identification number for each subject, the analysis would have no purpose. The Descriptives option will compute by default the mean,

Figure D.11   The Crosstabs Procedure Screen from *SPSS for Windows*

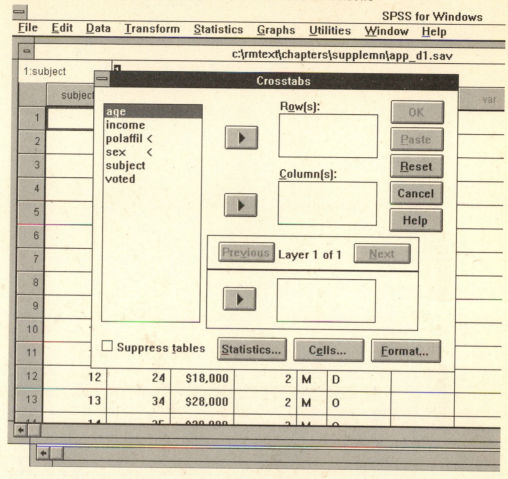

standard deviation, and minimum and maximum scores for each variable that we select. If we want to compute additional summary statistics, we click on the Options
button and select the additional summary statistics we want. When we have identified the variables and selected the summary statistics, clicking on OK will run the
analyses, producing the output shown in Table D.4.[10]

Correlations   To compute the Pierson product-moment correlation between age
and income, we select the Statistics menu, the Correlate submenu, and the Bivariate
option (which literally means two variables). These selections will give us the screen
shown in Figure D.15. We select the variables "age" and "income" and move them to
the right box. The default options in this procedure are to compute a Pierson product-
moment correlation and a two-tail *p*-value. Since these are the options we want, we
only need to click on OK to run the correlations. The resulting output is shown in Table
D.5. Notice that *SPSS for Windows* actually gives us four correlations. The program is

---

[10]If you run several analyses, *SPSS for Windows* will append the output of each analysis to the output file
from the first analysis.

POLAFFIL Political Affiliation (expressed) by SEX Subject's Gender

```
                   SEX      Page 1 of 1
           Count
                   Female   Male
                                         Row
                     F        M          Total
           ................................................
POLAFFIL
                   D   5      4             9
Democrat                                  37.5
           ................................................
                   0   1      7             8
Other                                     33.3
           ................................................
                   R   1      6             7
Republican                                29.2
           ................................................
           Column      7       17          24
           Total     29.2     70.8       100.0
```

Number of Missing Observations: 0

Figure D.12   The Define Simple Bar Screen from the Graph Procedure in *SPSS for Windows*

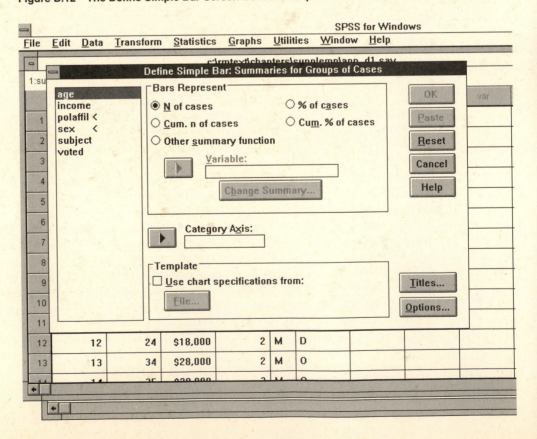

Figure D.13   A Simple Bar Graph from *SPSS for Windows*

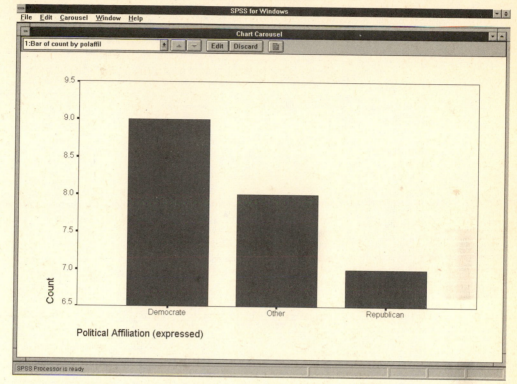

set up to compute an intercorrelation matrix (i.e., the correlation of each variable with every other variable that was selected) for as many variables as you select. If you select 10 variables, there would be a 10×10 matrix of intercorrelations. The diagonal (from the upper left to the lower right) of that matrix will list the correlation of each variable with itself, which will always be equal to 1.00 (a perfect correlation). The correlational matrix above and below this diagonal will be mirror images of one another because the correlation of variable x with variable y is the same as the correlation of variable y with variable x. In our simplified example of only two variables, the correlation between age and income is .8870 and the probability of getting that correlation or a larger correlation by chance if the population correlation were actually zero (the *p*-value) is listed as .000. Actually, no correlation will give you a *p*-value of zero; but since only three digits are printed, a value listed as .000 actually means that the probability is less than .001. If we assume the traditional decision criteria (termed alpha level) of .05, we would conclude that these two variables are significantly correlated with one another because our *p*-value is less than the alpha level of .05 (see Chapter 5 for a more detailed explanation of this terminology).

Inferential Statistics

This section will set up several common inferential statistics, but will also reference analyses that were described earlier in the text. The previous section on correlations

Figure D.14 The Descriptives Procedure Screen from *SPSS for Windows*

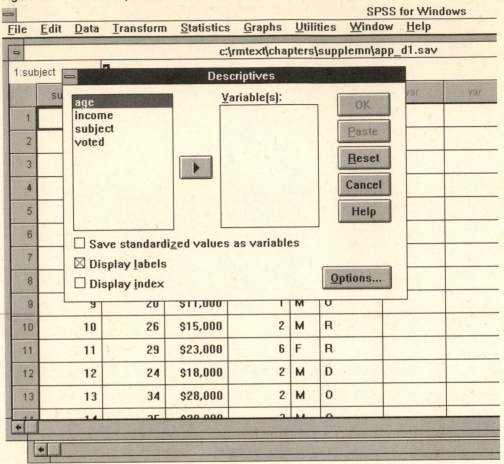

TABLE D.4 OUTPUT FROM THE DESCRIPTIVES PROCEDURE OF *SPSS FOR WINDOWS*

Number of valid observations (listwise) = 24.00

Variable	Mean	Std Dev	Minimum	Maximum	Valid N	Label
VOTED	3.92	2.76	0	8	24	# of times voted in 1
AGE	32.42	10.19	18	53	24	
INCOME	23708.33	7061.71	$11,000	$35,000	24	

Figure D.15   The Bivariate Correlations Screen from *SPSS for Windows*

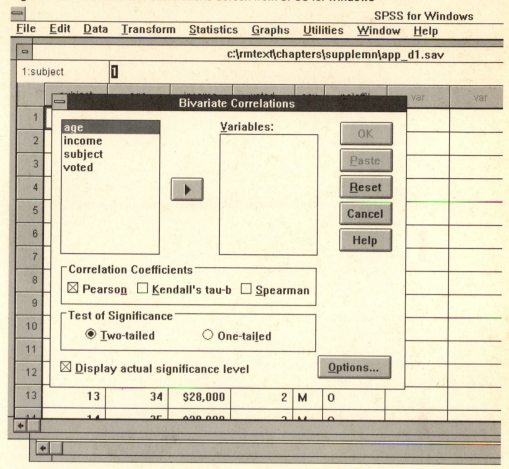

TABLE D.5   OUTPUT FROM THE BIVARIATE CORRELATION PROCEDURE OF *SPSS FOR WINDOWS*

```
           - - Correlation Coefficients - -

                              AGE              INCOME

AGE                        1.0000               .8870
                           ( 24)                ( 24)
                           P= .              P = .000

INCOME                      .8870             1.0000
                           ( 24)                ( 24)
                        P = .000                P= .

(Coefficient / (Cases) / 2-tailed Significance)

"." is printed if a coefficient cannot be computed
```

provided a nice introduction to inferential statistics. In addition to computing the correlation between two variables, *SPSS for Windows* also computed the probability of obtaining that correlation or a larger one (the *p*-value) if the correlation in the population was zero. In effect, this was testing the null hypothesis that there is a zero correlation in the population. All of the inferential statistics that we will compute in this section will be interpreted the same way. If the *p*-value is less than the alpha we set, then we reject the null hypothesis being tested with that analysis.

Independent Samples *t*-test   For this analysis we will compare the income level of males and females in our sample of 24 subjects from our Chapter 5 example. We select the Statistics menu, the Compare Means submenu, and the Independent Samples *t*-test option, which will give us the screen shown in Figure D.16. We then select the variable that defines our groups—in this case, "sex"—and move it from the left box to the box labeled Grouping Variable. We then click the Define Groups button and define Group 1 as "M" and Group 2 as "F" (do not put in the quotation marks). Clicking on Continue returns us to the Independent Samples *t*-Test box, where we now must define the dependent variable. We highlight our dependent variable, "income," in the left box and move it to the box labeled Test Variable(s).[11] Clicking on OK runs the test, producing the output shown in Table D.6. This output is a bit complex. The first part of the output gives summary statistics for the two groups; the second part lists the inferential statistics. *SPSS for Windows* computes two *t*-values and their associated *p*-values—one based on the assumption of equal variances in the two groups and the other not requiring that assumption. Just above the *t*-tests in Table D.6 is a statistical test for the equality of the variances in the group. We consult the test for equality of variances to determine which *t*-test to use. In this case, the variances show a statistically significant difference ($p = .029$), so we use the *t*-test for unequal variances (the second one). The *t* is well short of significance ($p > .05$), so we fail to reject the null hypothesis that there is a sex difference in salary levels.

One-Way ANOVA   We set up a one-way ANOVA in Chapter 10 using the data from our hypothetical study of typing speed and room temperature. The key to this analysis is to remember that each subject's data appears on a different line and that there must be a variable that defines which group the subject was in. The details of setting up this analysis and the output can be found in Chapter 10 (Figures 10.1 and 10.2; output in Table 10.10).

Repeated Measures ANOVA   We set up a repeated measures ANOVA in Chapter 11 (Figures 11.1 through 11.4; output in Table 11.3). This analysis used the data shown in Table 11.2 from a within-subjects design. Each subject contributed three scores in this hypothetical study, and the three scores for a subject appear on the same line (or record). Please note that each of the six subjects in this hypothetical study would have been tested with a different order for the three conditions. However, for the analyses we must organize the data so that each column represents a condition under which the subject was tested, regardless of what order the conditions were presented to that particular subject.

[11]Note that we could move more than one dependent variable into this box, simultaneously testing for sex differences in age, income, and the number of times the person voted in the last five years in one run if we chose.

Figure D.16 The Independent Samples *t*-Test Screen from *SPSS for Windows*

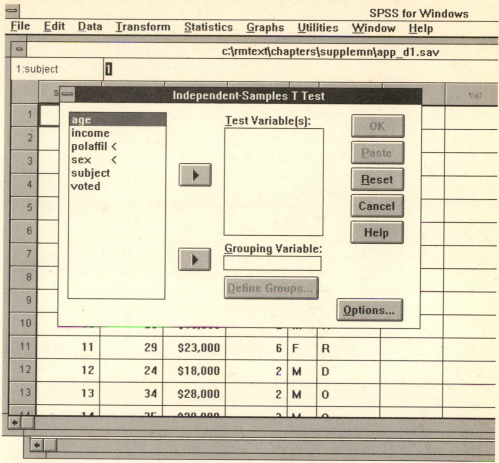

A repeated-measures ANOVA can also be used to test data from a matched-subjects design (as discussed in Chapter 11). The procedures for the analysis are identical to those used in a within-subjects design with one exception; the data on each line of a matched-subjects design represents the scores from a set of matched subjects, each assigned to a different group. It is critical in this design to maintain a record of who the subjects were matched with because this information is required to set up the data file and conduct the analysis.

Factorial ANOVA We will use the data from the Children's Dark Fears study introduced in Chapter 12 (data in Table 12.4) to illustrate a factorial ANOVA. This study had two factors—level of illumination and type of images—each with two levels of the factor. Both were between-subjects factors (i.e., each subject was tested in only one of the four possible cells). The key to this analysis is coding the data properly for the analysis. At a minimum, we need three variables to code the data. For each of the 40 subjects we need to code whether they were in the light or dark condition (level of illumination factor), whether they viewed fearful or neutral images (type of images factor), and their pulse rate during testing (the dependent measure). Figure D.17 illus-

TABLE D.6   OUTPUT FROM THE INDEPENDENT SAMPLES *T*-TEST PROCEDURE
            OF *SPSS FOR WINDOWS*

```
t-tests for independent samples of SEX Subject's Gender
```

Variable	Number of Cases	Mean	SD	SE of Mean
INCOME				
Male	17	23882.3529	7920.561	1921.018
Female	7	23285.7143	4855.042	1835.033

```
Mean Difference = 596.6387

Levene's Test for Equality of Variances: F = 5.448 P = .029
```

t-test for Equality of Means

Variances	t-value	df	2-Tai Sig	SE of Diff	95% CI for Diff
Equal	.18	22	.856	3240.113	(-6124.56,7317.835)
Unequal	.22	18.17	.825	2656.625	(-4986.09,6179.367)

Figure D.17   Data Input for a Two-Factor ANOVA with Two Between-Subjects Factors

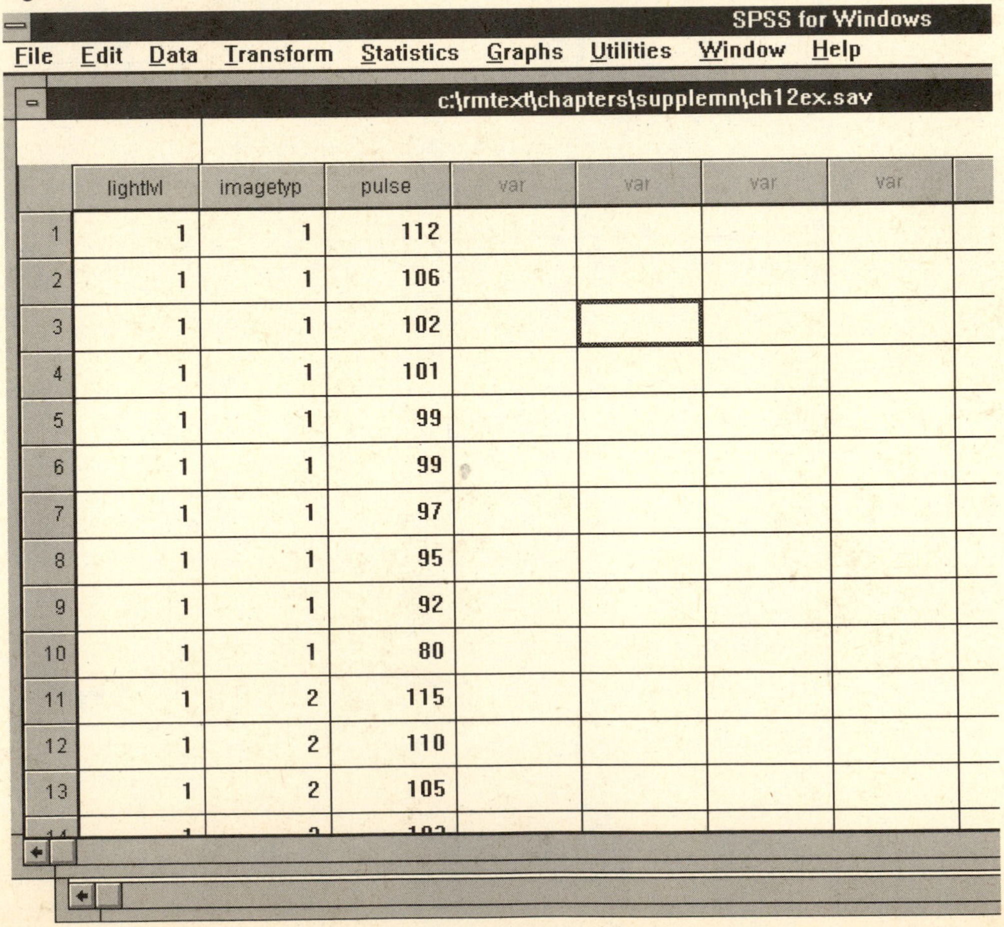

	lightlvl	imagetyp	pulse	var	var	var	var	
1	1	1	112					
2	1	1	106					
3	1	1	102					
4	1	1	101					
5	1	1	99					
6	1	1	99					
7	1	1	97					
8	1	1	95					
9	1	1	92					
10	1	1	80					
11	1	2	115					
12	1	2	110					
13	1	2	105					
14	1	2	103					

SPSS for Windows

c:\rmtext\chapters\supplemn\ch12ex.sav

File Edit Data Transform Statistics Graphs Utilities Window Help trates the data matrix as it was entered into *SPSS for Windows*. We used the Define Variables submenu from the Data menu to name each of the variables and to label the meaning of the codes for the two factors (lightlvl: 1 = lighted; 2 = dark/imagetyp: 1 = fearful; 2 = neutral). *We must have separate variables to define the level of each factor in our data structure in order to run a factorial analysis correctly.*

To run a factorial, we select the Statistics menu, the ANOVA Models submenu, and the General Factorial option, which gives us the screen shown in Figure D.18. We then move the dependent variable (pulse) from the left box to the dependent variable box and the two factors ("lightlvl" and "imagetyp") to the Factor(s) box. For each factor, we must define the range (i.e., tell how many levels). Once those tasks are accomplished, we run the analysis by clicking the OK button. The output was shown in Table 12.5.

The General Factorial option is an enormously powerful option, capable of not only running the basic ANOVA, but also running the specific means comparisons (either as planned comparisons or as post hoc tests). Most of the modules for *SPSS for Windows* have multiple capabilities. Exploring all of these capabilities is beyond the

Figure D.18   The General Factorial ANOVA Screen from *SPSS for Windows*

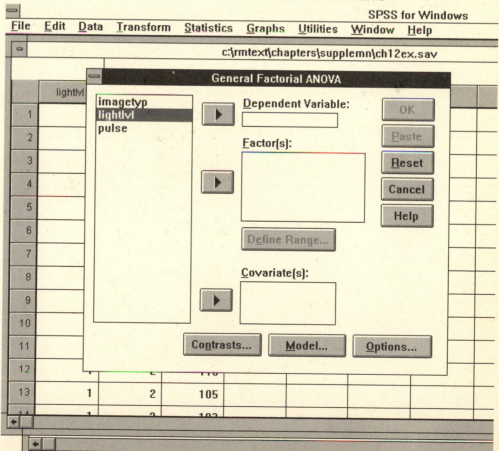

scope of this brief appendix, but the manuals for *SPSS for Windows,* or for any other statistical package for that matter, will detail the full range of the program's power.

SUMMARY

This appendix summarized basic concepts and procedures used in setting up and running statistical analyses computer packages. Specific examples using *SPSS for Windows* were included, with sample output provided. Some of the procedures presented would generalize easily to use of other statistical packages. To fully utilize *SPSS for Windows* or any other statistical package, you will need to consult the program's manual(s) for setup and interpretational details. You also need to be familiar with the basic operation of the computer on which the package runs.

Appendix E

Selected Answers to Exercises

These selected answers to exercises should serve as basic ideas around which more complete answers could be elaborated.

CHAPTER 1

1.3.1   Knowledge obtained through science is always tentative because any idea may change in light of new knowledge.

1.3.2   Both science and art seeks to represent parts of the universe, and there is considerable similarity in the observation, abstraction, and representation processes.

1.3.3   Like all sciences, social science combines logic and empirical observation. Science is not defined by its equipment, technology, or its level of development, but by its way of thinking.

1.3.4   Science is defined by its way of thinking. This scientist thus could be operating in an eminently scientific manner.

CHAPTER 2

2.3.2   Useful information can be obtained at all levels of research, and it is important to know when to use each level.

2.3.4   (a) Case-study. (b) Experimental. (c) Experimental. (d) Differential. (e) Naturalistic. (f) Correlational.

2.3.5   Science is defined by its way of thinking.

CHAPTER 3

3.3.2   (a) Variables are ethnic prejudices and socioeconomic status. Both are organismic variables. Potential extraneous variables are age and sex of children. (b) Variables are amount of alcohol consumed (a stimulus variable) and number of driving errors (a behavioral variable). Potential extraneous variables are the person's age and weight, alcohol history, driving skill, and so on. (c) Variables include the laundry products to be compared and the condition under which the comparison is made (stimulus variables) and the subject's response (a behavioral variable). Possible confounding variables are the behavior of the interviewer and past history with the particular product. (d) Variables are size and peer status (subject variables). Possible extraneous variables include the child's appearance, intellect, personality, social class, and differential behavior of the teacher toward the children.

3.3.3   (a) Children in research are subjects at risk because, as minors, they are unable to give informed consent. The safeguard is to obtain informed consent from some responsible adult. (b) The ethical issue is the mild deception in not telling subjects that some of the other subjects are actually assistants of the experimenter. The usual safeguards are to obtain consent (even though complete information is not given) and to do a debriefing once the experiment is completed. (c) There are two issues here. The first is that information is obtained from files of patients and it is not clear who should give permission for this. Second, information is obtained from these files about other people (i.e., the family), and it is not clear who should give permission. The safeguard is to obtain permission from a responsible administrator in the hospital and, if possible, from the patient and family.

CHAPTER 4

4.3.1   (a) IQ score; interval; score. (b) Number of disruptive outbursts; ratio; score. (c) The time for a response to occur; ratio; score. (d) Position at end of race; ordinal; ordered. (e) Speed of each runner; ratio; score. (f) Income of subjects; ratio; score. (g) Number of people in each category of car preference; nominal; nominal.

4.3.2   (a) Television violence; manipulated; number of aggressive acts; ratio/score; rating of aggression; ordinal/ordered. (b) What subjects are told about being paid; manipulated; time to solve the problems; ratio/score.

4.3.3   IQ is based on an interval scale of measurement with no true zero point.

CHAPTER 5

5.3.2   (a) Hours of food deprivation; manipulated; number of trials to learn the maze; ratio/score. (b) Age of the child; nonmanipulated; rating of enjoyment; ordinal/ordered. (c) Diagnosis; nonmanipulated; frequency of birth complications; nominal/nominal.

CHAPTER 6

6.3.1   Freud's work is case-study research with no manipulation of independent variables and no controls to rule out extraneous sources of variation. Consequently, one cannot be sure of the causal relationship between variables.

6.3.2 Useful information can be obtained from all levels of research. Every level of research has advantages and disadvantages. High-constraint research can establish causal relationships but lacks the flexibility of lower-constraint research.

6.3.3 The ex post facto fallacy is acceptance of a causal inference when such an inference cannot be properly made because no variable is manipulated. Alternative hypotheses cannot be ruled out, and consequently, causal relationships cannot be inferred.

CHAPTER 7

7.3.1 (a) Significant; 17 percent; age and height show a modest but significant relationship in grade-school females. (b) Not significant; 10 percent; there appears to be no relationship between depression and level of activity in hospitalized psychiatric patients. (c) Significant; 4 percent; there is a small but statistically significant relationship between the two assertiveness measures.

7.3.2 (a) One possible group is a nondelinquent group of boys of the same age. Confounding variables are social class, IQ, effects of labeling, family size, siblings, etc. This group controls for the subject's sex and age but probably not for most of the other variables mentioned. A second control group could be nondelinquent boys of the same age who are matched with the experimental group on variables such as social class and IQ. This group controls for age, sex, social class, and IQ but not other variables. A third group could be boys of the same age and social class who had emotional difficulties other than juvenile delinquency. This group controls for factors such as a "deviant" label. (b) One possible group might be loading dock personnel from the same company. However, this group would not be a good control because there are a number of differences between the experimental and control groups, such as sex, schooling, job tasks, lifestyle, and so on. A better control group might be other clerks whose work does not include CRT work. This control group would control for most variables, although the possibility exists that there are differences between CRT clerks and other clerks in terms of their level of responsibility, degree of tension, and age. The best possible control group would be a group of clerks from the same or similar companies that are matched on age, social class, sex, education, etc., but who do not work on CRTs. (c) One possible control group would be people randomly selected from an uncontaminated neighborhood. However, unless the neighborhood is selected to be of the same socioeconomic class, there are likely to be differences in health care. Another possible control group might be a group of individuals who had lived in that neighborhood for a short period of time relative to the subjects in the experimental group. (d) One possible control group would be randomly selected individuals of the same age who are not depressed. Possible confounding variables might be sex, social class, and the roles that the individuals are in (e.g., parents, students, and so forth).

7.3.3 In both correlational and differential research we are interested in quantifying the degree of relationship between two or more variables.

CHAPTER 8

8.3.3 The statement of a problem identifies the major variables; operational definitions describe how the variables will be measured or manipulated. For example, anxiety may be operationally defined as a rating of anxiety level by the subject. The operational definition would lead to specific procedures for the conduct of the study. In another study anxiety might be operationally defined in a different way (e.g., pulse rate). The different operational definitions lead to a different sets of procedures, but the research would be focused on the same conceptual variable (anxiety). The two studies focus on the same construct but from different vantage points, and thus they give us new information about the same general phenomena.

CHAPTER 9

9.3.1 The target population includes all children in elementary schools throughout the country. The accessible population is the 473 students enrolled in this particular elementary school (i.e., a nonrandom subsample of the target population). Generalizing to the target population is risky. The researcher draws the sample from the accessible population. If the sample is random, generalizing to the accessible population should be no problem. However, the researcher must be careful when extending the generalization to the target population.

9.3.2 Representativeness refers to the degree to which the sample is similar to the population from which it is drawn. It is not an absolute, and it is possible for a sample to be representative of a population on some variables while not being representative of the same population on other variables.

9.3.3 (a) Two levels; bright and dark illumination. (b) Four levels; different levels of noise. (c) Three levels; no clues, one clue, five clues. (d) Five levels; five different pain relief medications.

CHAPTER 10

10.3.1 (a) Randomly assigning subjects to conditions increases confidence that there is no bias in subject assignment. Random assignment is a good control for many threats to internal validity. (b) Adding a control group controls for specific threats to validity, such as maturation, history, and instrumentation. Because the control and the experimental groups are treated in the same manner and in the same time frame, any specific effect (such as maturation) should affect each group equally and hence not contribute to the comparison between groups.

10.3.2 Human variability is part of nature; without variability, we could not make comparisons between subjects. The degree of variability can be quantified. One widely used measure of variability is the variance.

10.3.3 Error variance is random variation, which sometimes produces scores that are too large or too small. It is as likely that the scores will be too large as that they will be too small. In contrast, systematic variation tends to move the scores in only one direction. Because all scores are affected in that one direction, the result is that the mean score is shifted. Error variation does not affect the mean score but can mask systematic variance. Therefore, it is important to maximize the systematic variance due to the experimental manipulation and to minimize the error variance.

10.3.5 The *F*-ratio evaluates the effects of one variable on another by examining the ratio of two variances. The mean square between is a function of the error variance and the systematic variance and is the numerator of the ratio; the mean square within is a function of the error variance and is the denominator of the ratio. If there is no systematic effect of the independent variable on the dependent variable, both the mean square between and the mean square within will be estimates of the error variance only. In this case, the expected F will be 1. If there is a systematic effect of the independent variable on the dependent variable, the numerator will be larger than the denominator and the F-ratio will be greater than 1.

CHAPTER 11

11.3.3   With three conditions, 6 orders are possible; five conditions, 120 orders; six conditions, 720 orders. Because there are so many possible orders with five and six conditions, counterbalancing is not a feasible control for order effects.

11.3.4   Matching on a large number of variables is difficult. Therefore, we match only on relevant variables. Relevant variables (a) are strongly related to the dependent measure and (b) show a great deal of natural variability in the population sampled.

11.3.5   A major advantage of matched-subjects designs over within-subject designs is that there are no sequencing effects in the matched-subjects designs (such as practice and carry-over effects).

CHAPTER 12

12.3.1   When you have a factorial design, there are many possible effects to be evaluated. Each of the independent variables can have an effect on the dependent variables by itself (a main effect). In addition, interactions of two or more independent variables can produce a joint effect—one that is more than the additive effect of the independent variables. It is an enhancement created by the combination of two or more variables. Our focus in factorial studies is usually on the interactions.

12.3.3   There is no main effect for Factor A, but there is a main effect for Factor B and an interaction of A and B. As always, we interpret the interaction first. The matrix of cell means illustrates the effect of the interaction. In condition B_1, scores decrease from condition A_1 through A_4. The opposite trend is observed under the B_2 condition (scores tend to increase from A_1 through A_4). The main effect for B is reflected in the generally higher scores for B_2 as compared with B_1, regardless of the level of A.

12.3.4   (a) An A main effect; no B main effect; no interaction. (b) An A main effect; a B main effect; no interaction. (c) No A main effect; a B main effect; an interaction. (It always helps to draw the graphs.)

CHAPTER 13

13.3.1   (a) Both groups change in the same way and to the same degree. Therefore, we say there is no effect. (b) This is the classic crossover where the control group does not change but the experimental group, which was initially lower, is considerably higher at posttest. In this case, we assume that the experimental condition did have an effect. (c) Both groups changed but the control group changed more. Therefore, it seems unlikely that the manipulation had an effect.

13.3.2   (a) There appears to be no effect of the manipulation. (b) There does appear to be an effect of the manipulation; scores that tended to be low prior to the manipulation increased after the manipulation.

13.3.3   Single-subject designs allow each subject to serve as his or her own control. Hence, internal validity is protected and causality can be inferred for the particular subject in the study. The weakness of the single-subject design is that external validity may be weak.

13.3.4   Controls available in the laboratory control threats to internal validity, and, consequently, we are able to draw causal inferences between variables. In natural settings it is difficult to apply these controls and, therefore, it is difficult to draw causal inferences. The trade-off is that laboratory control is achieved by simplifying real-life variables. Such simplification may or may not accurately represent the real world, and one must be careful in generalizing laboratory studies to the real world.

CHAPTER 14

14.3.1   (a) Experimental. (b) Type of training. (c) Muscle relaxation; cognitive relaxation; no training. (d) Independent groups. (e) Blood pressure. (f) Systolic and diastolic blood pressure. (g) Ratio for both. (h) Score data for both. (i) "Relaxation training reduces hypertension" and "The two relaxation procedures will be differentially effective in reducing blood pressure." (j) For each hypothesis, a test of differences. (k) For each hypothesis, mean, variance, and standard deviation. (l) For the first hypothesis, a one-way ANOVA; for the second hypothesis, either a one-way ANOVA or a *t*-test.

14.3.3   (a) Experimental. (b) Type of feedback. (c) Immediate feedback, delayed feedback, and no feedback. (d) Correlated-groups, within-subjects design. (e) Reading accuracy. (f) Number of reading errors. (g) Ratio. (h) Score. (i) "The type of feedback will affect reading accuracy." (j) A test of differences between correlated groups. (k) Mean, standard deviation, and variance. (l) Repeated measures ANOVA.

Appendix F

Conducting Library Research

USING THE LIBRARY

In research, we always want to relate our ideas and research findings to the ideas of other researchers and the results of their studies. University libraries accumulate these bodies of knowledge to facilitate the research of the university faculty and students. Research ideas and findings can be found in books, journals, technical reports, and a variety of other media. A small college library often will have 250,000 or more books and journals. A major university library may contain 5,000,000 or more books, often housed in a dozen or more specialized libraries, and will subscribe to more than 10,000 journals, each journal publishing a hundred or more individual articles per year. In addition, almost any university library in the country will have electronic and mail access to the collections in virtually all other libraries through interlibrary loan. When you enter the modern university library you are in touch with nearly all of the information that has ever been published! (You should be impressed by that thought, and properly respectful of the library and of the professionals who operate it.) Fortunately, you will need only a small fraction of that information for your own research. How to find what you need is the focus of this appendix.

The Reference Librarian

The reference librarian is one of the researcher's best friends—a professional who knows the smoothest routes through the maze of reference information. A good reference librarian can help you track down almost any information you need, and then ten minutes later will be helping someone else track down information in an entirely different field. Whether you need to find a particular book or to learn how to use the library's computer search resources, the reference librarian is a valuable consultant. Most university libraries also have courses or documentation to help you to master the resources of the library. Although we will be outlining in this appendix many of the basic sources and strategies for library research, we cannot stress enough the importance of utilizing the expertise available in your own library. A university library is much more than just a collection of books.

HOW RESEARCH MATERIALS ARE ORGANIZED

When we talk about research literature, we make a distinction between primary and secondary sources. *Primary sources* publish the details of research studies. Research journals are the main primary sources, although dissertations also fall into this category. *Secondary sources* publish integrative reviews of broad areas of research. Some journals specialize in such review articles. Other secondary sources include books and chapters in edited books. We will describe each of these sources of information below.

Primary Sources

Journal Articles   Journals provide both primary and secondary sources of information, although the majority of journals are considered primary sources (i.e., they report the results of original research studies). Research reports include a brief literature review, a statement of the problem and the hypotheses to be tested, a detailed account of the procedures, the results and statistical analyses, and a discussion of how the researchers interpret the results. In the discussions of their findings, researchers relate their results to the prevailing models or theories, thus helping to integrate new information and add to the base on which further research and theory development will rest.

Dissertations   Dissertations are another source that reports the results of research studies. Dissertations are research studies conducted by advanced graduate students as part of the requirements for a Ph.D. Many of these studies are eventually published in journals, but are also available in their original form to researchers interested in the same or similar questions. Universities will include the dissertations conducted at their own institutions as part of their library collection, but a copy of virtually any dissertation can be obtained in a few days through an organization called University Microfilms, which maintains copies of each dissertation from hundreds of universities.

Secondary Sources

Secondary sources provide reviews of entire areas of research—organizing and discussing many research reports. However, they are not intended to provide the detail you will find in the original sources such as research reports in journal articles. Furthermore, the newest research discussed in a secondary source is at least one to two years older than the paper's date of publication because of the normal publication lag. You will still have to search current journals to find the most recent research. These secondary sources provide important information; they summarize, organize, critique, and integrate research areas and identify further directions for research and theory development. They also list the critical studies in the area in their reference sections. They are an invaluable source in your literature review and are particularly useful when you need a broad, integrated view of your topic.

Review Articles in Journals   Although most journals report the results of original research studies, other journals specialize in integrating the results of many studies in reviews that attempt to organize and make sense out of a broad area of research. There are several journals in psychology that are devoted completely or primarily to reviews. Some examples are *Psychological Bulletin, Psychological Review, Behavioral Science,* and *Clinical Psychology Reviews.*

Books and Chapters in Books   Reviews of research areas are also published in books and chapters in books. In fact, edited books are becoming a major secondary source of information in psychology. Fortunately, *Psychological Abstracts* now includes both books and book chapters in its database.

Annual Reviews   This series—published by Annual Review, Inc.—provides an annual volume in each of many scientific disciplines, including psychology. The *Annual Review of Psychology* is a good example of a secondary source of information. It contains comprehensive review articles of psychological research in defined areas. You should check recent volumes of the *Annual Review of Psychology* to see if there is a review of your topic. If it is there, you will find a wealth of information about research in that field and many references to other work.

FINDING THE RELEVANT RESEARCH

Abstracting Services

Psychological Abstracts   The *Psychological Abstracts*—updated and published monthly by the American Psychological Association (APA)—lists not only titles, authors, dates, and source (i.e., journals, books) for virtually everything relevant to the field of psychology, but also an abstract of each work. The *Psychological Abstracts* are organized by keywords, which are summarized in a separate publication—the *Thesaurus of Psychological Index Terms* (described later). The APA also publishes a series of journals called *PsycSCAN,* which are quarterly compilations of references organized under several topics (e.g., clinical, applied, developmental).

In addition to the bound volumes of *Psychological Abstracts* that you will find on your library reference shelves, the APA also has several computer search programs (*PsycINFO, PsycLIT, PsycFILE,* and *PASAR*). *PsycLit* is the most commonly used and probably the most convenient for students. It covers virtually the same material as the bound volumes of *Psychological Abstracts.* All of the literature search programs published by the APA (bound volumes and computerized) are subsumed under the general heading *PsycINFO Services.*

Educational Resource Information Center (ERIC)   *ERIC* indexes and abstracts research in education and related areas such as psychology. If your topic is related to educational research you should consult *ERIC* as well as *Psychological Abstracts.*

Subject or Keyword Services

There are a number of sources that reference materials by title, author, and keywords, but do not include the abstract. Even without the abstract, these indexes can be a valuable source for identifying relevant materials. Several examples are given below.

Library Catalogs   The most familiar index to most students is the library card catalog. This is actually a misnomer because most of the actual card catalogs have been replaced by computerized versions of the same index, which can be accessed through terminals in the library or elsewhere on campus or even from your own computer at home via a modem. The library catalog lists all of the books available to you in the library's collection. You can search by author, title, or subject. In computerized libraries you may even be able to see if the book is available to be checked out.

Books in Print   *Books in Print* is a quarterly publication listing all books that are currently in print. Most libraries have hard-cover volumes of *Books in Print,* with books indexed by author, subject, and title. Many libraries now have this index available through computer searches, which can be conducted from either library or remote terminals.

Index Medicus   Just as *Psychological Abstracts* provides a citation index for literature of interest to psychologists, *Index Medicus* provides an index to biomedical literature. It does not, however, provide abstracts of the literature but does include full references (author, title, date, source). When your topic has biomedical aspects, you should also consult *Index Medicus*. The computerized version of *Index Medicus* is called *Medline*.

Readers' Guide to Periodical Literature   This is a general index, which covers a wide area of popular literature. It provides citations, but not abstracts.

Literature Citation Indexes

The abstract and keyword services above are helpful in finding material by topic or author. There are times when you want to find literature through another means—the citations to previous work that each publication makes. Certain lines of research are so indebted to one or two early publications on the topic that one can find virtually every article on the topic by identifying those articles that cite these early publications. There are several important indexes that permit citation searches. The *Science Citation Index* and the *Social Science Citation Index* are two examples of this kind of reference. These indexes publish citation information in physical sciences (e.g., biology, chemistry, physics) and in the social sciences (e.g., sociology, psychology, economics), respectively. One can find references to work in psychology in both indexes.

Table F.1 lists the major indexes for psychological research.

TABLE F.1   MAJOR CITATION REFERENCE INDEXES FOR PSYCHOLOGICAL RESEARCH

1. **Review Articles and Chapters**

   Annual Review of Psychology
   Psychological Bulletin
   Psychological Review
   Behavioral Science
   Clinical Psychology Reviews

2. **Abstract Services and Citation Indexes (both Bound and Computer Formats)**

   Psychological Abstracts (bound volumes)
   PsycLIT (psychological abstracts on computer programs)
   ERIC (Educational Resource Information Center)
   Books in Print (bound volumes and computer format)
   Index Medicus and *Medline* (computer index)
   Social Science Citation Index
   Science Citation Index

3. **Other Important Information Sources**

   Thesaurus of Psychological Index Terms
   Library Catalog
   Readers' Guide to Periodical Literature

SEARCH STRATEGIES

Searching by Topic

How do you search through this mass of information in the various indexes to find what you need for your project? Like all research, library research needs a clear problem statement. Before you begin your library research, be sure you know what you are looking for. You will need both a clear statement of the problem and a list of the *key terms* that would identify relevant research papers. These key terms will be used in your search to enter the various indexes and to guide you through journals and annual reviews. The *Thesaurus of Psychological Index Terms,* published by the American Psychological Association, can be very helpful here. It not only lists the index terms that are used in *Psychological Abstracts,* but also lists the cross-referenced terms that might also identify relevant literature on a topic. Look up your topic in the *Thesaurus,* and it will list the index terms under which you will find appropriate references. Use those as your key terms to conduct your search through the various citation indexes. Similar publications listing index terms are available for other abstract services such as *ERIC.*

Computer Searches   Fortunately, many libraries now have extensive facilities for computer searches, saving a great deal of time and making your search more complete and systematic. *PsycLit, Books in Print, ERIC, Index Medicus,* and dozens of other indexes can be accessed through computer terminals in the library and elsewhere. Consult your reference librarian to learn how to use these systems. The procedures for doing computer searches vary from one system to another, but most systems operate under the same general principles. All systems have records (containing all of the information about a publication) and fields within each record. Each field contains specific information about a publication (e.g., title, author, journal, keywords, and abstract). You can search a specific field or all fields to find information. For example, if you know that relevant research was published by "John Smith," you can search the author field for that name.

There are many strategies for computer searches of the research literature, but most people start by searching for keywords. Most indexes will have a keyword field, where a small number of descriptive terms summarize the main content of the paper. Searching this field for certain topics is adequate for many searches. But computers are so powerful and fast that it is easy to search everything (title, keywords, abstract, etc.) to find potentially relevant papers. Entering keywords to narrow a search is an art that requires considerable logic and some practice. In most systems, entering the term "child" will identify any article that has the terms child, childhood, children, and child's.[1] Similarly, entering the term "schizophren" will identify articles that have the terms schizophrenia or schizophrenic. A term like "schizo" will identify the same articles, but will also include articles that have terms like schizotypal, schizotaxia, or schizotype. Some keywords will identify several thousand potential articles, while other keywords identify no articles. If the list is too large, you

---

[1]All of these terms have the root "child" in them.

will have to reduce it to make it manageable. You might refine the list by limiting it to only those papers published in a given time period—perhaps the last five or ten years. But you probably want to also narrow the list by further restricting the topic. To do this you must understand two Boolean operators—AND and OR. If you are interested in childhood fears, you could use the term "childhood fears" in your search. However, such a search would miss any article that did not use that specific phrase (perhaps using a phrase like "fears common in childhood" instead). Using the Boolean operator AND to search for "fear AND child" would likely give you a more complete search. Any article that had both the term "fear" and the term "child" in its record would be identified.[2] The operator AND will narrow a search by requiring that two conditions be met. In contrast, the operator OR will broaden a search by identifying articles that meet one of several specified conditions. For example, searching for "frontal OR parietal OR occipital OR temporal" would identify any article that mentions one of these lobes of the brain anywhere in the record.

Once you have narrowed the search to an appropriate size list you can enter commands to display not only titles, authors, and sources, but also abstracts of each article if they are available in your database. By reading these abstracts you can select those that appear to be most appropriate for your topic and eliminate the rest. At this point you will have a screen display of a fairly refined list of appropriate articles. Using the print command will give you a printout of your selected references and their abstracts.

Now the real work begins. Your list of references is just that—a list. What remains is locating each of the papers, books, and chapters, reading them, integrating the information, and writing your paper. As you proceed with this part of your task you will eliminate more of the cited work as not appropriate or useful, and you will also find more references in the various reference sections of each paper you read. Listed below are a couple of useful strategies for identifying other relevant papers.

Searching Backward

Every article, chapter, or book will review relevant research and give you the references for each of those studies in their reference section. This is an invaluable source of relevant material. Of course, not every paper referenced in articles that you identified as relevant will be relevant to your topic, but some will be. Recently published articles and review articles are especially useful with this strategy because they will likely list more relevant research studies. Inspecting the reference list from appropriate articles will help identify other investigators doing work on your topic. Searching the author field for the names of these investigators is often a useful supplementary strategy. These strategies are not a substitute for the topic search described above, but can be valuable in identifying additional relevant papers.[3]

---

[2]Each computer index has its own rules for specifying searches with Boolean operators. Be sure to check the documentation or talk with a reference librarian for details of the system you are using.

[3]A note of caution is warranted here. It is bad form to cite a paper that you have not read based on information that you obtained from another researcher's citation of that source. It is entirely possible that the other researcher misunderstood the paper and therefore cited the material incorrectly.

TABLE F.2   A SUMMARY OF THE LITERATURE SEARCH PROCESS

1. Have a clear statement of the literature search problem.
2. From the problem statement identify the key terms for your topic. Use the *Thesaurus of Psychological Index Terms* to help determine your key terms.
3. Consult with your reference librarian and determine which citation indexes are most likely to include the information you seek.
4. Search the citation indexes using your key terms. *PsycLIT* is probably the most useful for you. Look for secondary as well as primary sources. Read the titles and abstracts of the papers and chapters; narrow your list by deleting those that seem least relevant.
5. Print out the list of remaining references; find the original articles, books, and chapters; read them.
6. As you gain information from your reading you will refine your ideas, gain new ideas, and will further refine your problem statement.
7. Consult other citation indexes (*ERIC, Social Science Citation Index, Readers' Guide,* etc.).
8. At any point in this search process you can consult your reference librarian!

Searching Forward

The searching forward strategy is possible because of the existence of citation indexes. If virtually all articles on a topic cite one or more classic articles, then one can identify these later articles by using an appropriate citation index. Again, this strategy is not a substitute for searching by topic, but can be a useful supplement.

Table F.2 summarizes the literature search process.

SUMMARY OF LIBRARY RESEARCH

The importance of library research cannot be overestimated. Without library resources, each investigator would effectively be "reinventing the wheel" with every research study. Fortunately, the modern university library not only has the relevant past research on virtually any topic, but also has the complex indexing necessary to find the material you need. This appendix summarized briefly the library resources available to the student researcher and described briefly some of the strategies one might use to find appropriate background material for a study. Our discussion was very brief, however, and only touched the surface of this topic. We strongly encourage you to use the services of the reference librarian to learn more about the specific resources available at your institution. We also recommend Reed and Baxter (1992), which outlines in more detail the resources and strategies covered in this appendix.

Glossary

a posterior comparison See *post hoc test*.

a priori comparison See *planned comparison*.

ABA design See *reversal design*.

abscissa The *x*-axis on a graph.

abstract A brief description of a research study that appears at the beginning of the research paper and is included in abstract journals such as *Psychological Abstracts*. The length of an abstract is restricted to a specified number of characters because abstracts of research articles are now routinely transferred to computerized databases.

accessible population That subset of a target population that is available to the researcher and from which the sample is drawn.

ad hoc sample Sample of subjects drawn from an accessible population. Characteristics of the ad hoc sample must be described to define the limits of generalizability.

alpha level Level of Type I error (the probability of rejecting the null hypothesis when the null hypotheses is true).

analysis of covariance (ANCOVA) Statistical procedure similar to analysis of variance, used to evaluate whether two or more groups have different population means. Analysis of covariance statistically removes the effects of extraneous variables on the dependent variable and hence increases the power of the statistical test.

analysis of variance (ANOVA) Statistical procedure used to analyze for mean differences between two or more groups. ANOVAs compare the variability between groups with the variability within groups. Many variations of analysis of variance are possible, including repeated measures ANOVAs and factorial ANOVAs.

ANOVA summary table Table that organizes the results of an analysis of variance computation. For each source of variation the appropriate degrees of freedom, sums of squares, mean squares, and *F*-ratios are listed. (Examples are given in Chapters 10–12.)

apparatus subsection That section of a research report in which physical aspects of the study (apparatus, measuring instruments, etc.) are described.

applied psychology Any use of psychological principles, theories, or technologies to deal with existing problems or concerns. In research, *applied psychology* refers to research that is specifically aimed at understanding and correcting problems faced by people.

applied research Research to provide solutions to practical problems. Applied research is contrasted with basic research.

archival records Any source of data (such as census data) for events that have already occurred.

artifact In research, any apparent effect of a major conceptual variable that is actually the result of a confounding variable not properly controlled. Artifacts threaten the validity of research conclusions.

association Relationship or correlation.

assumptions of science Basic tenets that form the bases for more complex scientific theory and research.

attrition Potential confounding variable in research. Attrition is the loss of subjects before or during the research. The subjects who remain may not be representative of the population. Hence, any conclusions drawn may not generalize to the entire population.

authority A way of acquiring knowledge. New ideas are accepted as valid because some respected authority has declared the idea to be true.

automation Use of equipment to conduct most or all aspects of presenting stimuli and recording subjects' responses. Automation can minimize the work required of the researcher, increase precision in data gathering, and minimize experimenter bias in gathering and recording data.

average deviation The sum of the deviations from the mean divided by the number of scores.

balanced placebo design A 2 × 2 research design developed in alcohol research in which the factors are (1) what the subject actually consumes (alcohol or no alcohol) and (2) what the person is told they are consuming (alcohol or no alcohol). This design permits the separation of the pharmacological effects of alcohol from the expectation effects. See *deception.*

base rates Naturally occurring frequency of events (i.e., before any manipulations to alter the rates have been carried out).

basic research Fundamental or pure research. Basic research is carried out to add to knowledge but without applied or practical goals. Basic research is often contrasted with applied research.

behavior Any observable act from any living organism. Behavior is the subject matter of psychology.

behavioral medicine See *health psychology.*

behavioral variable Variable representing an organism's behavior.

behaviorism A philosophical perspective in psychology that argues that a scientific psychology should base its theories on observable events only (such as behavior). This perspective challenged the introspective methodologies that dominated the early discipline of psychology.

beta The probability of making a Type II error. See *Type II error.*

between-groups variance Index of the variability among group means.

between-subject factors Independent variables in factorial designs in which subjects are assigned to conditions so that each subject appears only in one condition.

between-subjects design Research design using two or more groups in which each subject appears in only one of the groups.

bimodal A distribution of scores that has two modes (most frequently occurring score).

Biomedical Programs (BMDP) Computer package of statistical data-analysis procedures.

blind When the researcher and/or subject is not aware of information that would, if available, increase the likelihood of biasing the experimental results. See *single-blind procedure.*

canonical correlation A correlation between two sets of variables. The first canonical correlation is derived by computing the linear combination of each set of variables that will give the highest possible correlation. Additional canonical correlations can be computed using different linear combinations of the variables in each set. This technique helps scientists to understand complex relationships between constructs that cannot be easily tapped by a single measure.

carry-over effects These are the effects of a subject participating in one condition on his or her performance in all subsequent conditions. Carry-over effects occur only when subjects appear in more than one experimental condition (i.e., in within-subjects designs).

case-study level of constraint Research in which a few constraints are placed on subjects' behavior. Case-study research usually focuses on the behavior of a single subject.

categorical data Synonymous with *nominal data.*

categorical variable Synonymous with *discrete variable*. A categorical variable can have only a finite number of values.

causal hypothesis Usual form of the research hypothesis in experimental research. It states that the independent variable has a causal relationship to the dependent variable. To accept this hypothesis, one must have rejected the null hypothesis and all confounding-variable hypotheses.

causal inference Conclusion that the change in the independent variable resulted in a change in the dependent variable. It may be drawn only if all potential confounding variables are properly controlled.

causally related Two variables are causally related if a change in one variable results in a predictable change in the other variable and the change occurs as a direct result of the action of the first variable.

ceiling effects See *scale attenuation effects*.

central tendency Average or typical score in a distribution. Three measures of central tendency are the mean, median, and mode.

chi-square A statistical distribution that forms the basis for inferential statistics used with *nominal data*.

classification variables Organismic or subject variables used to classify subjects into discrete groups. Classification variables are used for assigning subjects to groups in differential research.

coding data Process by which numerical or classification scores are assigned to a set of responses from a subject. The coded data are usually in a form that can be more easily analyzed statistically.

coefficient of determination The square of the Pearson product-moment correlation. It represents the proportion of variability in one variable that can be predicted on the basis of information about the other variable.

cognitive psychology The subdiscipline of psychology that studies perceptual processing and basic thought processes.

cognitive science A broad field that encompasses several disciplines (behavioral neuroscience, neuroanatomy, neurophysiology, computer science, linguistics, etc.), all of which are interested in modeling and understanding the basic brain processes behind thought and behavior.

cohort effect The concept that people of a given chronological age in a given culture may behave similarly throughout their lives and different from people of other ages because of shared life experiences.

column means In factorial designs, one factor is usually illustrated as separate columns of data where each column represents a different level of the factor. A second factor might be illustrated as rows of data, where the different rows represent levels of the second factor. Column means are computed by taking the mean of all subjects who appear in a given column regardless of their level on the second factor.

communication phase of research Research phase in which the rationale, hypotheses, methods, results, and interpretations of the study are presented in oral or written form to other researchers.

computer-analysis programs Sophisticated computer programs for many different statistical analyses of data sets. See also *Biomedical Programs (BMDP); Minitab; Statistical Analysis System (SAS)*.

conceptual replication See *systematic replication*.

confounded Two variables are said to be confounded if they vary simultaneously during a study, thus not allowing us to determine which of these variables was responsible for the observed change in the dependent variable.

confidence interval An interval in which we predict the population parameter to fall with a specified level of confidence (e.g., a 95 percent confidence interval will contain the population parameter 95 percent of the time).

confidentiality An ethical requirement in most research; information, particularly sensitive and personal information, provided by subjects as part of a research study should be protected and made unavailable to anyone other than the researchers.

confounding variable Any uncontrolled variable that might affect the outcome of a study. A potential confounding variable exists only if (1) there is a mean difference between the groups on the variable and (2) there is a correlation between the variable and the dependent measure.

confounding-variable hypothesis Actually, a set of hypotheses. Each confounding-variable hypothesis states that a particular confounding variable is responsible for the observed changes in the dependent measure. Each of the hypotheses must be rejected before one can safely conclude a causal relationship between the independent and dependent variables.

constraints Restrictions placed on the researcher in an effort to increase the precision of the research and enhance the validity of the conclusions drawn from the research.

constants Variables that are prevented from varying (i.e., held constant by the researcher).

construct An idea constructed by the researcher to explain events observed in a particular situation. Constructs are not necessarily direct representations of reality; they are not facts. They are explanatory fictions because, in most cases, we do not know the real reason for a particular event. Once formulated, constructs are used *as if* they are true (i.e., analogically) to predict relationships between variables in situations that had not previously been observed.

construct validity   Validity of a theory. Most theories in science present broad conceptual explanation of relationships between variables and make many different predictions about the relationships between particular variables in certain situations. Construct validity is established by verifying the accuracy of each possible prediction that might be made from the theory. Because the number of predictions is usually infinite, construct validity can never be fully established. However, the more independent predictions from the theory verified as accurate, the stronger will be the construct validity of the theory.

contingency   A particular relationship between two or more variables where, given that the first event occurs, the second event is highly probable. The relationship between the variables is a probabilistic one and does not necessarily imply a causal connection between them.

continuous variable   Any variable that can theoretically take on an infinite number of values. Continuous variables are often contrasted with discrete or categorical variables.

contrast   See *planned comparison*.

control   See *control in research*.

control group   A group of subjects used in either differential or experimental research that serves as a basis of comparisons for other (experimental) groups. The ideal control group is similar to the experimental group on all variables except the variable that defines the group (independent variable).

control in research   Any procedure that is designed to block the possibility of confounding the effects of the independent variable with other variables.

controlled research   Any research that employs adequate control procedures to rule out competing hypotheses. Well-controlled research permits scientists to draw causal conclusions about the relationships between the variables studied.

correlation coefficient   The index of the degree of relationship between two or more variables.

correlated-groups design   Research design in which the subjects in each of the groups are related to the subjects in the other groups. Two variations of the correlated-groups design are (1) the within-subjects design and (2) the matched-subjects design. Correlated-groups designs provide more powerful tests of the hypotheses because they control for individual differences between subjects. They are contrasted with independent-groups design.

correlated *t*-test (or direct-difference *t*-test or matched-pairs *t*-test)   Statistical procedure used to test for mean differences between two groups in a within-subjects or matched-subjects design.

correlation   Degree of relationship between two or more variables.

correlation coefficient   Statistic that quantifies the degree of relationship between two or more variables. There are many kinds of correlation coefficients, depending on the type of data and relationship predicted.

correlational level of constraint   Research designed to quantify the relationship between two or more variables. At this level there is no manipulation of variables and no attempt to draw causal inferences.

correlational research   Research that seeks to measure the relationship between variables without trying to determine causality. The term is sometimes used broadly to include any nonexperimental research design (such as differential research and quasi-experimental designs).

counterbalancing   Control procedure used in within-subjects designs to control for sequencing effects. It is most practical when there is a small number of conditions in the study.

criterion   In a regression analysis, the criterion is the variable that one is attempting to predict.

criterion measure   The variable that we want to predict in *regression*.

crossover effects   In quasi-experimental research, a finding where two nonequivalent groups show one pattern of scores before the manipulation and the reverse pattern of scores after the manipulation. The name derives from the crossing of the lines when such a result is graphed.

cross-sectional design   A design that compares the performance, attitudes, or histories of people of different ages or at different times in history. The groups are defined by the age range of the people in the groups or the historical time in which subjects were tested. In a cross-sectional study, subjects appear in only one group. This design is often contrasted with longitudinal designs.

cross-sectional research   Research in which a cross-sectional research design is used.

cross-tabulation   Procedure for organizing frequency data that displays the relationship between two or more nominal variables. A cross-tabulation table contains individual cells, with the number in each cell representing the frequency of subjects who show that particular combination of characteristics.

data   Plural noun that refers to information gathered in research. Research conclusions are drawn on the basis of an evaluation of the data gathered as part of a study.

data-analysis phase of research Research phase in which data gathered from observing subjects are analyzed, usually with statistical procedures.

data snooping Type of secondary analysis of data to help generate hypotheses for further study.

deception Procedures used in research to hide from the subject the true nature of the study. Many studies require deception to prevent subject expectancy effects, but the use of deception raises ethical issues that must be addressed by the researcher. Ethical use of deception requires complete debriefing of the subjects at the end of the study.

decision tree An organized pathway of ideas leading to a defined goal, in which at various points a decision is made about which of two "branches" of ideas to follow to the next decision point.

decision-tree flowcharts Flowchart model in which answers to specific questions lead to branching to a new set of questions or procedures. (Chapter 14 presents a decision-tree model designed to help students select appropriate statistical tests in a given research situation.)

deductive reasoning Reasoning from the general to the particular. In deductive reasoning, specific predictions are made about future events.

deductive theory A theory that emphasizes constructs and the relationship between constructs and seeks to make from the theory predictions that can be tested with empirical research. Often contrasted with *inductive theory* and *functional theory*.

degrees of freedom (df) Statistical concept. One degree of freedom is lost each time a population parameter is estimated on the basis of a sample of data from the population. The distribution of most statistics (*t, F,* and so on) are tabled by degrees of freedom (df).

demand characteristics Any aspect of the situation created by the researcher that suggests to the subject what behavior is expected.

dependent variable Variable that is hypothesized to have a relationship with the independent variable.

descriptive statistics Those statistics or statistical procedures that summarize and/or describe the characteristics of a sample of scores.

design notation (e.g., 2×2; 3×2; $2 \times 4 \times 3$) In factorial designs a way of indicating the number of factors and how many levels of each factor. For example, a $2 \times 4 \times 3$ design has three factors where the first factor has two levels, the second has four levels, and the third has three levels, for a total of 24 combinations.

difference score Arithmetic difference between scores on the dependent measure at two points in time for a particular subject.

differential level of constraint Research in which two or more groups defined on the basis of some preexisting organismic variables are compared on a dependent measure.

differential research Research that involves comparing two or more existing groups on a dependent variable.

diffusion of treatment Potential confounding variable that occurs when subjects in one condition communicate information to subjects in another condition. This can be a particular problem in research settings where subjects are in close communication with one another (such as in a school or hospital or in the undergraduate psychology subject pool of a university).

direct differences t-test See *correlated t-test*.

discrete variable A discrete variable can take on only a finite number of values. Often contrasted with *continuous variable*.

discussion section The final substantive section of a research report where we interpret our findings in light of other research and theory.

dispersion Variability; how spread out the scores are in a sample.

double-blind procedure Research procedure in which neither the researcher nor the subject knows in which condition the subject is tested. The purpose is to minimize the possibility of experimenter bias and of subject expectancies.

ecological validity Experiments achieve ecological validity when they reproduce accurately the real-life situations, thus allowing easy generalization of their findings to the real world. See *external validity*.

effective range Characteristic of any dependent measure; the range expressed in score units over which the dependent measure accurately reflects the level of the dependent variable.

electronic mail A mechanism for sending messages via computers to anyone who has an electronic mail address. Electronic mail utilizes the Internet, which is a collection of mainframe computers around the world that are interconnected via high-speed phone lines.

e-mail See *electronic mail*.

empirical Based on observed data. A relationship between variables is empirically established if it has been observed to occur.

empiricism System of knowing about the world that is based solely on observation of the events around us.

enumerative data Synonymous with *nominal data.*

equipment subsection see *apparatus subsection.*

error term Generic term used in many different statistics, it provides a basis for comparing observed differences between groups. The error term is usually based on a measure of the variability of scores within each group.

error variance Type of error term that is a function of the variability of scores within groups.

ethical checks A series of questions that a researcher must ask about the research and the specific procedures included to safeguard subjects.

ex post facto design Nonexperimental research design in which the current situation of the subject is observed and related to previous events. Because there are no manipulations of variables and confounding variables cannot be controlled, alternative hypotheses cannot be ruled out. Therefore, it is a weak design and causal inferences cannot be drawn from it.

ex post facto fallacy Error in reasoning where one assumes that the observed relationship between current events and some historical events represents a causal relationship.

exact replication Repeating a study by using exactly the same procedure used in the original study. See also *replication.*

experiment High-constraint research procedure in which subjects in two or more conditions are compared on a dependent measure, with subjects assigned without bias to each of the conditions. These may be either within-subjects or between-subjects designs. Experimental designs provide adequate control over virtually all possible confounding variables.

experimental design Set of procedures that defines a research study at the experimental level of constraint. In experimental design, subjects are assigned to groups or conditions without bias (such as with random assignment), and all appropriate control procedures are used.

experimental group Group of subjects assigned to one or more conditions in an experiment where a specified level of the independent variable exists. The experimental group(s) is (are) usually contrasted with a control group.

experimental level of constraint Research in which two or more groups or conditions (where subjects are assigned to groups or conditions without bias) are compared on at least one dependent measure. At the experimental level of constraint, the research design provides adequate controls for most confounding variables and, therefore, allows the researcher to draw causal inferences.

experimental variance Degree of variability among the group means in a research study.

experimentation Process by which a researcher studies the relationship between independent and dependent variables by systematically manipulating the independent variable, assigning subjects without bias to each level of the independent variable, and observing the effects of the independent variable on the dependent variable.

experimenter bias Any effect that the expectations of the researcher might have on the measurement and recording of the dependent variable. Uncontrolled experimenter bias threatens the validity of research.

experimenter effects Any behavior of a researcher that might affect the behavior of the subject or the measurement of the dependent variable. Experimenter expectancies can create powerful experimenter effects.

experimenter expectancies Expectations of the researcher about the relationship between the variables being studied. Experimenter expectancies may affect the accuracy of the observations, especially in situations that require judgment on the part of the researcher.

experimenter reactivity Any action by the researcher other than the manipulation of the independent variable that tends to influence the response of the subjects. A type of experimenter bias.

external validity Extent to which the results of a study accurately indicate the true nature of a relationship between variables in the real world. If a study has external validity, the results are said to be generalizable to the real world.

extraneous variable Any variable other than the independent variable that might affect the dependent measure in a study. Extraneous variables are potentially confounding and must be controlled.

extraneous variance Variability in scores on the dependent measure that can be accounted for by the effects of extraneous variables.

factorial ANOVA Analysis of variance procedure for evaluating factorial designs.

factorial design Research designs employing more than one independent variable simultaneously. The major advantage of a factorial design is that it can measure the joint (interactive) effects of two or more independent variables.

factors In a factorial design, each of the independent variables is a factor.

facts Empirically observed events.

field research Research conducted outside the laboratory in natural settings. Field research might include low-constraint research (such as naturalistic or case-study research) or may include higher-constraint procedures applied to natural settings. An advantage of field research is that results more easily generalize to the real world because observations are made in a real-world setting.

filler items Any questions or items that are asked along with items that make up the dependent measure in a study. Filler items are typically not scored as part of the dependent measure. Their purpose is to distract subjects from the true purpose of the study by making it unclear exactly what the dependent measure is.

floor effects See *scale attenuation effects.*

flowcharts Organizational device that allows one to reach a decision by following a path defined by answers to particular questions. (Chapter 14 illustrates the use of flowcharts to select the appropriate statistical test for any given research procedure.)

F-ratio (or *F*-test) A test statistic computed by taking the ratio of two variances. *F*-ratios are used most often in analysis of variance where the two variance estimates are an estimate based on (1) the difference between group means and (2) the difference among subjects within groups.

F-test See *F-ratio.*

free random assignment Assignment of subjects to groups on a completely random basis so that the assignment of any given subject has no effect on the assignment of any other subject.

frequencies The number of objects (e.g., subjects in a study) that fall into a specified category. Frequencies represent *nominal data.*

frequency data Synonymous with *nominal data.*

frequency distribution Organizational device used to simplify large data sets.

frequency polygon Graph that illustrates a frequency distribution. It is constructed by putting a dot above each possible score (which are listed on the *x*-axis) at a height that indicates the appropriate frequency of that score (which is indicated on the *y*-axis). The dots are then connected to form a graph of the frequency distribution.

functional theory Functional theories tend to emphasize equally the inductive and deductive aspects of theory building. Often contrasted with *inductive theory* and *deductive theory.*

functionalism A philosophical perspective that stresses the need to study how the mind functions. Often contrasted with *structuralism.*

general control procedures Control achieved through preparation of settings, careful response measurement, and replication.

general population See *population.*

generalizability Extent to which the findings from a research study are applicable to the outside world.

generalize Assuming that the findings of a particular research study will be found for other subjects or in other settings.

generalization The process of assuming that the findings from one's study will also apply to other situations, places, or times. See *generalize.*

Gestalt psychology A philosophical perspective in the field of perception that rests on the concept that the whole is greater than the sum of its parts. Gestalt psychology seeks to find broad principles describing how people process complex sensory input.

graphs A means of presenting data visually. Some examples of graphs are histograms and frequency polygons.

graphs of factorial data Graphs that provide a visual illustration of interaction effects and main effects in factorial studies.

grouped frequency distribution Frequency distribution that provides the frequency of scores in intervals of equal size. Grouped frequency distributions are used with continuous data or in situations where there is a large range of possible scores.

health psychology A relatively new applied discipline in psychology that focuses on understanding and modifying behavior that is related to the physical health of the person.

heterogeneous A group is said to be heterogeneous if there is considerable variability within the group.

histogram A bar graph in which the frequency of any given score or the mean for any given group is represented by the height of the bar. Histograms allow one to see the shape of a distribution or compare the performance of subjects tested under various conditions.

history Potential confounding variable. History represents any change in the dependent variable over the course of a research study that is a function of events other than the manipulation of the independent variable.

homogeneous Any grouping of events that share the same characteristics. A population is said to be homogeneous if the subjects in the population are similar to one another.

humanistic psychology A philosophical perspective that grew out of existential philosophies. Humanistic psychologists emphasize subjective experience and the distinctively human qualities of choice and self-realization.

idea-generating phase of research First step in any research project during which the researcher selects a topic to study.

incidental comparison See *post hoc test*.

incidental learning Learning that occurs without specific reinforcement, usually while learning a different task.

independent-groups design See *between-subjects design*.

independent samples Samples that include different subjects in each group and where the selection of subjects for one sample does not influence the selection of subjects for any other sample.

independent variable Any variable in research that defines separate groups of subjects on which the dependent measure is taken. Subjects may be assigned to these groups on the basis of either (1) some preexisting characteristics (differential research) or (2) some form of random assignment (experimental research).

individual differences Natural differences between people on any variable. Individual differences between people on a dependent measure tend to obscure effects of an independent variable on the dependent measure(s).

inductive reasoning Reasoning from the particular to the general. Used to generate theories or models based on particular observations or ideas.

inductive theory Inductive theories are built on a strong empirical base and tend not to stray far from that empirical base. Often contrasted with *deductive theory* and *functional theory*.

inference Any conclusion drawn on the basis of some set of information. In research we draw inferences on the basis of empirical data we collect and ideas we construct.

inferential statistics Statistical procedures that compute the probability of obtaining the particular pattern of data in a study if all subjects were actually drawn from the same population. If the probability of obtaining such a pattern of scores is low, we reject the hypothesis that all subjects were drawn from the same population (null hypothesis) and conclude that there were meaningful differences between groups or conditions.

informed consent Critical principle in the ethical treatment of subjects. Subjects have the rights to know exactly what they are getting into and to refuse to participate.

informed consent form A form that is designed specifically for each research project and is signed by each human subject prior to the beginning of the study. The informed consent form must present enough detail about the study and its risks to permit subjects to make informed decisions about their participation. The consent form should be reviewed and approved by the *Institutional Review Board* as part of their evaluation of the research proposal.

Institutional Review Board (IRB) Formal body that operates in most institutions where research is conducted. The IRB reviews all research proposals to determine if they meet ethical guidelines.

instrumentation Potential confounding variable involving any change in the measuring instrument over time that causes the instrument to give different readings when no change has occurred in the subject.

instruments subsection See *apparatus subsection*.

interaction Combined effect of two or more independent variables on the dependent variable. Interactions can be measured only in factorial designs.

internal consistency reliability Index of how homogeneous the individual items of a measure are. If the individual items are homogeneous, they will tend to correlate strongly with one another, suggesting that all items are measuring the same characteristic.

internal validity Accuracy of the research study in determining the relationship between the independent and the dependent variables. Internal validity can be assured only if all potential confounding variables have been properly controlled.

interpretation phase of research Research phase in which the results of statistical analyses of data are interpreted in light of (1) the adequacy of control procedures in the research design, (2) previous research, and (3) existing theories about the behavior under study.

interrater reliability Index of the consistency between two or more ratings made by separate raters. It is indexed by the correlation between the ratings of two raters.

interrater reliability coefficient A correlation coefficient expressing the degree of agreement of observations made by two or more raters. See *reliability*.

interrupted time-series design Type of research design suitable for either single subjects or groups in which multiple measures of the dependent variable are taken before and after some experimental manipulation. Time-series designs provide some control for history and maturation, even without the inclusion of a control group.

interval scale Scale of measurement in which the distance between any two adjacent scores is the same as the distance between any other two adjacent scores but zero is not a true zero. An example of an interval scale is temperature measured in either Centigrade or Fahrenheit.

interview schedule A standardized interview, with each question and procedures spelled out for the interviewer. Interview schedules provide consistency in interviews that are a part of research projects.

introduction The first substantive section of a research paper, where the authors review previous research and theory relevant to the study being reported to provide the framework and rationale for the study.

intuition A way of acquiring knowledge. In intuition, ideas come to people supposedly without intellectual effort or sensory processes.

invasion of privacy Ethical issue in research. Researchers should avoid invading the privacy of subjects. When impossible, every effort should be made to protect subjects' privacy by maintaining confidentiality of records.

Kappa An index in interrater agreement that factors into the index the probability of chance agreement. As a consequence, Kappa coefficients are comparable across a wide range of base rates and conditions.

knowledge Any information we have about the world around us. Knowledge may be achieved in different ways including the use of scientific research.

Laboratory Animal Care Committee A formalized committee that reviews every research proposal that involves animal subjects for appropriate and ethical treatment of the animals involved. Every research center (e.g., a university) that conducts animal research must have a local Laboratory Animal Care Committee.

Latin square design A procedure used to provide a measure of counterbalancing in a within-subjects design. Instead of using all possible orders of presentation (as in counterbalancing), a Latin square design uses a set of orders that ensure that every experimental condition appears equally often in every position in the order.

levels of constraint Degree of systematic control applied in research. Research methods can range from low to high constraint. The labels assigned to these levels of constraint are *naturalistic, case-study, correlational, differential,* and *experimental.*

levels of headings The mechanism used in published research articles for organizing the report. Levels of headings are similar to an outline, with the various sections and subsections of the report representing different levels of the outline. The APA publication guidelines specify how levels of headings should be used to organize research articles.

linear relationship Relationship between two or more variables which, when plotted in a standard coordinate system, tend to cluster around a straight line. Most correlation coefficients are sensitive only to linear relationships between variables.

list server A mechanism that permits continuous electronic conversations between people who may be spread all over the world. Electronic mail messages sent to a list server are distributed to everyone on a distribution list, allowing the easy exchange of ideas among large groups of people. Replies to messages are also distributed to everyone on the list.

logic Set of operations that can be applied to statements and conclusions drawn from those statements to determine the internal accuracy of the conclusions.

longitudinal (panel) design A research design in which a group of subjects is followed over time, with the dependent measures repeated during follow-up testings. Longitudinal designs are frequently used in developmental psychology. This design is often contrasted with cross-sectional designs.

longitudinal research Research in which a longitudinal research design is used.

main effects In a factorial design, *main effects* refer to the individual effects of the independent variables. In contrast, *interaction effects* are the combined effects of two or more independent variables on the dependent variable.

manipulated factors Independent variables in a factorial design in which the levels of the factors are determined by active manipulation by the experimenter.

manipulated independent variable Type of independent variable found in an experimental research study. When manipulated independent variables are used, subjects are assigned to groups or conditions without bias.

manipulation The explicit control of the independent variable by the researcher.

manipulation check Procedure designed to verify that the independent variable did occur at different levels in the different groups or conditions. A manipulation check is independent of any evaluation of the effect of the independent variable on the dependent variable.

Mann-Whitney *U-test* A nonparametric inferential statistic used to test the difference between two groups when the dependent measure produces ordinal data.

matched-pairs t-test See *correlated* t-*test*.

matched random assignment Experimental procedure used to help ensure that groups are equivalent at the beginning of the study. In matched random assignment, subjects are matched in small groups (size is determined by the number of conditions in the study) on relevant variables and each member of the group is randomly assigned to one of the conditions of the study until all members have been assigned to one condition. Matched random assignment can be difficult if we attempt to match on more than one variable or if there are several conditions in the research study. Matched random assignment is an alternative to a within-subjects design and should be used whenever significant sequencing effects can be expected in a within-subjects design.

matched-subjects design Research design in which subjects are matched on a variable that is highly correlated with the dependent measure. Once matched, each subject is randomly assigned to each of the groups defined by the independent variable. The design helps control for individual differences without introducing the sequencing problems inherent in a within-subjects design.

materials subsection See *apparatus subsection*.

matrix of cells Structure of cells in a factorial design.

maturation Potential confounding factor involving changes in subjects on the dependent measure during the course of the study that results from normal growth processes.

mean Arithmetic average of scores. The mean is the most commonly used measure of central tendency but should be computed only for score data.

mean square In analysis of variance (ANOVA), the mean square is a variance estimate. Several different mean squares are computed in any ANOVA. It is the ratio of mean squares that is the F-ratio and constitutes the inferential statistical test.

measurement error Any inaccuracy found in the measurement of a variable. Although it is impossible to determine the precise degree and direction of measurement error for a given subject, it is possible to specify the average error associated with a particular measure.

measurement reactivity Any effect on the subject's behavior that results from the subject being aware that he or she is being observed and measured. When measurement reactivity is excessive, a researcher may want to consider using unobtrusive measures to minimize the effect.

measures subsection See *apparatus subsection*.

median Middle score in a distribution.

method section The section of the research report that details the nature of the sample and the procedures used in the study.

Minitab Computer package for statistical analysis of data.

mixed designs (between- and within-subjects variables) Factorial design in which at least one of the factors is a between-subjects factor and at least one of the factors is a within-subjects factor. The pattern of between- and within-subjects factors affects the selection of the statistical analysis.

mixed designs (manipulated and nonmanipulated variables) Factorial design in which at least one of the factors represents a nonmanipulated independent variable and at least one of the factors represents a manipulated independent variable. The distinction between manipulated and nonmanipulated variables does not affect the data analysis. However, the interpretation of the results must take into account the fact that at least some of the factors are nonmanipulated factors and, therefore, represent differential research.

mode Most frequent score in a distribution.

models In science, models are representations of the complex reality of the real world.

moderator variable Any variable that has an effect on the observed relationship between two or more other variables. When a moderator variable is operating, it is best to measure the relationship between variables separately in subgroups defined by the moderator variable. For example, relationships between variables are often evaluated separately in males and females (a commonly used moderator variable).

Monte Carlo studies A procedure that evaluates the effectiveness of statistical tests by simulating with a computer the repeated sampling of subjects from a population with known parameters. The characteristics of the populations can be systematically varied to see what effect these variations have on the accuracy of the statistical decision. This process allows one to determine empirically the probability of Type I and Type II errors to see the strength of the impact of violations of the assumptions of statistical procedures.

multilevel, completely randomized, between-subjects design A research design using more than two groups, in which subjects are randomly assigned to groups, and each subject appears in only one group.

multiple baseline design Research design often used with single subjects when one wants to infer a causal relationship between the independent and dependent variables. Baselines on several different behaviors are taken, and treatment strategies are applied at different points in time to each behavior being monitored.

multiple correlation A correlation where one variable (we will call it *X*) is correlated with a set of variables. The correlation is computed by finding the linear combination of the set that will provide the highest possible correlation with the *X* variable.

multiple observers Control used to evaluate the accuracy of observations made by two or more independent observers.

multivariable designs See *factorial designs*.

multivariate analysis of variance (MANOVA) Extension of analysis of variance where two or more dependent measures are simultaneously evaluated.

multivariate techniques Advanced statistical procedures used to evaluate complex relationships between variables.

naturalistic level of constraint Research carried out in natural settings where the researcher makes no attempt to manipulate the environment as part of the research.

negative correlation Relationship between two variables in which an increase in one variable predicts a decrease in the other.

nominal data Data produced when a nominal scale of measurement is used. Nominal data are frequencies of subjects in each of the specific categories.

nominal scale Scale of measurement in which only categories are produced as scores. Examples are diagnostic classification, sex of the subject, and political affiliation.

nonequivalent control-group design Quasi-experimental design used in field settings. In this design two or more groups, which may not be equivalent at the beginning of the study, are compared on the dependent measure.

nonexperimental designs Any research design that fails to provide adequate controls for typical confounding.

nonlinear relationship Any relationship between two or more variables that is characterized by a scatter plot where the points tend to cluster around a curved instead of a straight line. Most correlations coefficients are insensitive to nonlinear relationships.

nonmanipulated factors Independent variables in a factorial design in subjects are assigned to groups on the basis of some preexisting factor. See *differential research*.

nonmanipulated independent variable The preexisting variable that determines group membership in a differential research study.

nonparametric statistics Inferential statistical procedures that do not rely on estimating population parameters such as the mean and variance.

nonprobability sampling Any sampling procedure in which some subjects have a higher probability of being selected than other subjects or where the selection of a given subject changes the probability of selecting other subjects. Often contrasted with *probability sampling*.

nonreactive measure Any dependent measure that provides consistent scores regardless of whether the subject is aware or unaware of being measured.

normal distribution Distribution of scores that is characterized by a bell-shaped curve in which the probability of a score drops off rapidly from the midpoint to the tails of the distribution. A true normal curve is defined by a mathematical equation and is a function of two variables (the mean and variance of the distribution). Normal distributions are useful in psychology because psychological variables tend to show distributions that are close to normal.

null hypothesis States that the subjects from each group are drawn from populations with identical population parameters. The null hypothesis is tested by inferential statistics.

objective measure Any measure that requires little or no judgment on the part of the person making the measurement. Objective measures are more resistant to experimenter biases than *subjective measures*.

observation Empirical process in which data about the phenomenon of interest are gathered and reported. Careful observation is a central task in all research.

observation phase of research Research phase in which the actual data are gathered.

observational variable Any variable that is observed and not manipulated in research. The term is usually used in low-constraint research where the independent and dependent variable distinction does not apply.

observed organismic variable Any characteristic of the subject that can be measured and used for classification.

one-way ANOVA Statistical procedure that evaluates differences in mean scores of two or more groups where the groups are defined by a single independent variable.

operational definition Detailed set of procedures used to measure or manipulate the level of a variable.

ordered data Data produced by ordinal scales of measurement.

orderliness belief Belief dating from ancient artisans that events in nature are predictable.

ordinal scale Scale of measurement where the scores can be rank ordered but the distance between any two adjacent scores will not necessarily be the same as the distance between any other two adjacent scores.

ordinate The *y*-axis on a graph.

organismic variable Any characteristic of the subject that can be used for classification. An organismic variable may be either directly observed (*observed organismic variable*) or may be inferred on the basis of the responses of the subject (*response-inferred organismic variable*).

outline The essential features or main aspects of ideas under discussion, organized under headings and subheadings, and serving as the guidelines for fuller discussion or development.

panel design See *longitudinal design*.

parametric statistics Inferential statistical procedures that rely on sample statistics to draw inferences about population parameters such as the mean and variance.

parsimony A guiding principle in science where you prefer a simple theory to a more complex theory if both theories will explain the data equally well.

partial correlation A correlation between two variables (we will call them X and Y) where the effects of a third variable (Z) are statistically removed from one of the two original variables before computing the correlation. Conceptually, it is the correlation between X and Y if Z were constant.

participant-observer Any researcher gathering data in a setting in which the researcher is an active part. Participant observation tends to be less obtrusive than other observational procedures. However, the possibility for experimenter reactivity in participant observation is quite high.

path analysis A procedure that seeks to unravel causal links between variables from strictly correlational data by hypothesizing detailed causal models and factoring the correlation matrix to see how closely the pattern of observed relationships fits the hypothesized causal model.

Pearson product-moment correlation Index of the degree of linear relationship between two variables where each variable represents score data.

percent agreement A measure of interrater reliability in which the percentage of times the raters agree is computed.

percentile Normative score that converts the raw score earned by a subject into a number from 0 to 100, which reflects the percentage of subjects who score lower than the subject in question.

percentile rank See *percentile*.

perfect correlation Correlation of a +1.00 or a −1.00. When two variables are perfectly correlated, knowing the score on one variable permits perfect prediction of the score on the other. In a scatter plot, a perfect correlation is shown by all points falling on a straight line (but not a horizontal or vertical line).

phase of research Every research project develops through phases in which certain types of questions are asked and answered. These phases are: idea-generating, problem-definition, procedures-design, observation, data-analysis, interpretation, and communication.

placebo effect In a treatment study, any observed improvement in response to a sham treatment. Placebo effects are probably the result of subjects' expectations for treatment effectiveness.

planned comparison Sometimes called a contrast; a specific comparison of mean performance between groups in a research study. Planned comparisons must be planned before data collection and should be based on theoretical considerations.

population Any clearly defined set of objects or events (people, occurrences, animals, and so on). Populations usually represent all events in a particular class (e.g., all college students, all boys between the ages of 10 and 12, all headache sufferers).

population parameters Any summary statistic computed on the entire population.

positive correlation Relationship between two variables where one variable increases as the other variable increases.

post hoc tests (or comparisons or analyses) Secondary analyses that evaluate relationships between variables not specifically hypothesized by the researcher prior to the study.

power See *power of a statistical test.*

power of a statistical test Ability of an inferential statistical procedure to detect differences between groups when such differences actually exist.

practice effects Any change in performance on a dependent measure that results from previous exposure of the subject to the measurement procedure.

practical significance Often contrasted with *statistical significance.* Practical significance refers to whether the observed difference between two groups or conditions in a study is large enough to have a meaningful impact on the life and functioning of the subject.

pre-data check A careful and systematic assessment of each point in a research design prior to data collection.

predictor measure The variable in regression that is used to predict the scores on the *criterion measure.* For example, a test score (the predictor measure) might be used to predict future performance in a job.

preexisting variable Any characteristic of the subjects that existed prior to the research study. If preexisting variables are not controlled, they can confound the results of a study, leading to incorrect conclusions. Preexisting variables are particularly problematic in differential research.

pretest-posttest design Set of research designs in which subjects are tested at two points in time—before and after the administration of the independent variable.

pretest-posttest, natural control-group design Nonexperimental research design in which preexisting groups are each measured before and after the manipulation of an independent variable. These naturally occurring groups are assigned to different levels of the independent variable.

probability sampling A sampling procedure in which all subjects have an equal probability of being selected and the selection of any subject does not change the probability of selecting any other subject. Often contrasted with *nonprobability sampling.*

probe Refers to the process of comparing the mean performance among groups of subjects in a research study to see which groups are statistically different from one another.

problem-definition phase of research Research phase where vague and general research ideas are converted into precise questions to be studied.

procedures-design phase of research Research phase where the specific procedures to be used in the gathering of data are developed.

procedure subsection That section of a research report that describes in detail how the study was carried out.

process of inquiry The perspective taken by this text that views research as a dynamic process focused on formulating questions and systematically answering those questions through carefully controlled studies.

program evaluation research Specific area of field research for evaluating the effectiveness of a program in meeting its stated goals.

psychoanalysis The psychological treatment approach that is based on the psychodynamic theories of Freud and his followers.

psychology Scientific study of the behavior of organisms.

psychophysics One of the earliest approaches to the study of behavior. Psychophysics involves the presentation of precise stimuli to subjects under controlled conditions and the recording of the subjects' responses.

***p*-value** The probability of obtaining the statistic (e.g., *t* or *F*) or a larger statistic by chance if the *null hypothesis* is true. Statistical analysis programs routinely compute *p*-values in addition to the test statistic.

quasi-experimental design Research designs that, although not true experimental designs with all experimental controls built in, provide experiment-like controls to minimize threats to internal validity. (Several quasi-experimental designs are discussed in Chapter 13.)

questionnaire A psychological instrument that lists questions to be asked of subjects.

random number generator A computer function that generates an endless sequence of random numbers.

random order of presentation This is a way of controlling for carry-over effects in within-subjects designs. Each subject is tested under all conditions, but the order of the conditions is randomly determined for each subject.

random sampling Procedure for the selection of subjects to be included in a research study, where each subject in the population has an equal chance of being selected and where the selection of any one subject will not affect the probability of selecting any other subject. In most research, random sampling from the population is not carried out because the procedure is not feasible. Instead, researchers rely on sampling from an accessible population.

randomization Any procedure that assigns a value or order in an unpredictable or random way, such as by use of tables of random numbers. Randomization procedures may be used for selecting subjects, assigning subjects to groups or conditions, or assigning the order in which a subject will experience a number of successive conditions.

randomized, posttest-only, control-group design Experimental design in which subjects are randomly assigned to two groups on the independent variable. Each group is tested on the dependent variable after the independent variable manipulation.

randomized, pretest-posttest, control-group design Experimental design in which subjects are randomly assigned to two groups and each subject is tested on the dependent variable both before and after the manipulation of the independent variable.

range Distance between the lowest score and the highest score inclusive of the scores.

ratio scale Scale of measurement in which the intervals between scores are equal (as in the interval scale) and the zero point on the scale represents none of the quality being measured (a true zero). Examples of ratio scales are height, weight, and frequency of an event.

rationalism One of many ways of knowing about the universe. Relies on systematic logic and a set of premises from which logical inferences are made.

reactive measure Any measurement procedure that produces different scores depending on whether subjects are aware they are being measured.

reference list The listing of a source of information (e.g., research article, book, chapter, etc.) that contributed to a research paper. The APA Publication Manual lists specifications for how to list a reference so that others can quickly retrieve it for review.

reference section The section of a research report that follows the substantive sections of the report and lists each of the papers and articles (and where they might be found) that contributed to the ideas and procedures of the study described in the report.

regression A mathematical procedure that produces an equation for predicting a variable (the *criterion measure*) from one or more other variables (the *predictor measures*). The procedures for determining the regression equation are designed to maximize the accuracy of the prediction. Linear (i.e., straight line) regression equations are usually used, although it is possible to develop nonlinear regression equations.

regression equation The mathematical equation that predicts the value of one variable from one or more other variables. Most regression equations are linear regression equations.

regression to the mean Potential confounding variable that occurs whenever subjects are selected because of extreme scores (either very high or very low) on some variable. When retested on the same or similar variable the original extreme sample tends to be less extreme on average (scores will be generally closer to the mean).

reification of a construct Incorrectly accepting a construct as a fact.

relationship Any connection between two or more variables. In research there are many types of relationships, from simple contingencies to established causal relationships.

relative score See *standard score*.

reliability Index of the consistency of a measuring instrument in repeatedly providing the same score for a given subject. There are many different types of reliability, each referring to a different aspect of consistency. Types of reliability include interrater reliability, test-retest reliability, and internal consistency reliability.

repeated-measures ANOVA Statistical procedure to evaluate the mean differences between two or more conditions where the same subjects contribute scores under each condition. The repeated measures ANOVA takes into account the fact that the same subjects appear in all conditions.

repeated-measures design Any research design in which subjects are tested more than once. Examples of such designs are pretest-posttest designs, within-subjects designs, and time-series designs.

repeated-measures factorials Factorial design in which all factors are within-subjects factors. Each subject is tested under every possible combination of conditions in the design.

replication To repeat a study with either no changes at all in the procedure (exact replication) or carefully planned changes in the procedure (systematic or conceptual replication).

representative sample Sample of subjects that adequately reflects the characteristics of the population from which the sample is drawn.

representativeness Degree to which a sample is representative of the population from which the sample is drawn.

research data See *data*.

research ethics Set of guidelines designed to protect human and nonhuman subjects from the risks of participating in research.

research hypothesis Precise and formal statement of a research question. The research hypothesis is constructed by adding operational definitions for each of the variables to the statement of the problem.

research setting Any characteristics of the situation and/or surroundings in which a research project is carried out. Settings may vary from natural, real-world settings to highly constrained and carefully controlled laboratory situations.

response-inferred organismic variable Construct referring to some hypothesized internal attribute of the organism that cannot be directly observed but, instead, is inferred on the basis of some observed behavior. Examples are intelligence, anxiety, anger, and love.

response-set biases Any tendency for a subject to distort their response to a dependent measure. A powerful response-set bias is social desirability. Response-set biases create measurement errors.

results section The section of a research report that describes the findings and reports on the statistical analyses of the data.

reversal (ABA) design Research design often used with single subjects, where the effects of an independent variable on a dependent variable are inferred from observations made first without the independent variable present, then with the independent variable present, and again without the independent variable present. If an effect is noticed both when the independent variable is added and when it is later removed, it is likely that the independent variable is causally related to the dependent measure.

rival hypothesis Any feasible alternative hypothesis to the causal hypothesis.

robust Used in reference to statistical procedures. A statistical test is said to be robust to violations of the assumptions on which the test is based if the test consistently leads to accurate conclusions in spite of the assumption violations.

row means In factorial designs, one factor is usually illustrated as separate rows of data where each row represents a different level of the factor. A second factor is illustrated as columns of data where the different columns represent various levels of the second factor. Row means are computed by taking the mean of all subjects who appear in a given row regardless of their level on the second factor.

sample Any subset drawn from a population. Researchers work with samples of subjects and draw inferences about the larger population.

sample statistic Descriptive index of some characteristic of the sample of subjects. Population parameters are estimated on the basis of statistics.

sampling Process of drawing a sample from a population. Many sampling techniques are available including random sampling, stratified random sampling, and various nonrandom sampling techniques.

sampling error Chance variation among different samples drawn from the same population.

sampling frame In survey research a sampling frame is a list of all subjects from an available population. The sampling frame is a subset of a larger population from which a representative sample is drawn.

scale attenuation effects Any limitation on the measuring instrument that limits the ability of the instrument to make discriminations at the top of the scale (ceiling effects) or the bottom of the scale (floor effects).

scales of measurement Characteristics of the scores produced by a particular measurement instrument. Scales of measurement vary on how closely scores match the real number system. There are four generally recognized scales of measurement: nominal scale, ordinal scale, interval scale, and ratio scale.

scatter plot Graphic technique that illustrates the relationship between two or more variables. In a two-variable situation, the scatter plot is constructed by labeling the *x*-axis with one of the variables and the *y*-axis with the other variable and plotting each subject's pair of scores in the *xy* coordinate system. The scatter plot will illustrate the type of relation present (no relationship, linear relationship, or nonlinear relationship), the direction of the relationship, and the strength of the relationship.

science Way of knowing about the universe around us, which combines rationalism and empiricism to form a system that places great demands on procedures, data, and theories.

Scientific Revolution Period of time (the 15th through the 17th centuries) in which scientific methods and applications became independent from theology and developed rapidly into a generally recognized way of understanding nature.

scientist Anyone who utilizes the methods of science (i.e., a combined rational and empirical approach) to study a phenomenon.

scientist-practitioner model A model for the training of clinical psychologists. Students are taught both research skills and diagnosis and treatment skills in an integrated manner. The rationale is that clinical psychology is an emerging discipline in which practitioners need to learn from new research and contribute to the knowledge base by conducting their own research. This approach is also known as the Boulder model, named after the conference held in Boulder, Colorado, in which these principles were endorsed.

score data Data produced by interval or ratio scales of measurement.

secondary analyses In the analysis of research data, secondary analyses look at questions that are not directly stated in the original research hypothesis but that may be relevant to understanding some of the primary analyses.

selection Potential confounding variable in any research project. Selection represents any process that may create groups not equivalent at the beginning of the study.

sequencing effects Potential confounding variable in research involving repeated or multiple measures. Sequencing effects are the effects on the performance of subjects in later conditions as a consequence of their having previously participated in other conditions.

simple random sampling See *random sampling*.

single-blind procedure Research procedure in which the researcher is unaware of the condition to which each subject is assigned. The purpose of the single-blind procedure is to minimize measurement biases.

single-group, posttest-only design Nonexperimental research design in which the researcher manipulates the independent variable and then takes a postmanipulation measure on the dependent variable. The difference between this design and an ex post facto design is the actual manipulation of the independent variable by the researcher.

single-group, pretest-posttest design Nonexperimental design in which a group of subjects is measured on a dependent variable, the independent variable is manipulated, and a second measure on the dependent variable is taken. The design does allow comparison between pretest and posttest scores, but because no control group exists, confounding variables are not adequately controlled.

single-subject design Research design that seeks information sufficient to draw with a reasonable degree of confidence causal inferences about the relationship between an independent and dependent variable. The various types of single-subject design all have some form of built-in control to compensate for the fact that no control group exists. Typical examples of single-subject designs include ABA design, single-subject, randomized time-series design, and multiple baseline design.

single-subject, randomized, time-series designs Designs frequently used in naturalistic settings where multiple measures on the dependent variable are taken both before and after some manipulation of an independent variable. This type of design provides partial control of many potential confounding variables by allowing the researcher to see patterns in the movement of the dependent measure over time and specific changes in the dependent measure that appear to be a function of the manipulation of the independent measure.

single-variable designs Any research design that includes just one independent variable.

skepticism Unwillingness to accept information as valid knowledge without some documentation to confirm the information. Skepticism is one of the strongest tools available to a scientist.

skewed distribution Any distribution of scores in which the majority of scores bunch up at the end of the distribution. Skewed distribution is often contrasted with *symmetric distribution*.

skewed negatively Distribution in which scores are concentrated near the top of the scale with few scores near the lower end of the scale.

skewed positively Distribution in which scores are concentrated near the bottom of the scale with few scores near the top of the scale.

social desirability Response set that can have a powerful influence on information gathered from human subjects. Subjects showing a social desirability response set will tend to say what they believe is expected of them (i.e., they tend to present themselves in a socially desirable light).

Solomon's four-group design Sophisticated experimental design that combines the randomized, posttest-only, control-group design and the randomized, pretest-posttest, control-group design.

Spearman rank-order correlation Correlation coefficient that indexes the degree of relationship between two variables, each of which is measured on an ordinal scale of measurement.

spread Synonymous with *variability*.

specific means comparisons The process of evaluating differences in group performance in a research study with more than one level of the independent variable to see which groups are statistically different from which other groups. Specific means comparisons can be carried out as either *planned comparisons or post hoc tests*.

standard deviation Square root of variance. The standard deviation is an index of variability in the distribution of scores.

standard error of the differences between means In statistics, the denominator in a *t*-test.

standard score A score that gives the relative standing in a distribution. A standard score is computed by subtracting the distribution mean from the score and dividing that value by the standard deviation from the distribution.

statement of the problem First major refinement of initial research ideas, in which a clear statement of the expected relationship between conceptual variables is made. The statement of the problem is refined into one or more research hypotheses by specifying the operational definitions of each conceptual variable in the statement.

Statistical Analysis System (SAS) Computer package for statistical data analysis.

statistical hypothesis Synonymous with *null hypothesis.*

Statistical Package for the Social Sciences (SPSS) Computer package for statistical data analysis.

statistical power See *power of a statistical test.*

statistical significance A finding is said to achieve statistical significance if it is unlikely that such a finding would have occurred by chance alone. See *statistically significant differences.*

statistical validity Accuracy of conclusions drawn from a statistical test. To enhance statistical validity, one must meet critical assumptions and requirements of a statistical procedure.

statistically significant correlation A correlation large enough that one would conclude that there is a nonzero relationship between the variables.

statistically significant differences A difference between two or more means large enough that it is unlikely to be a chance occurrence (i.e., the observed difference between the means appears to be reliable).

statistics Mathematical procedures used to evaluate the results of a research study. Some statistical procedures describe data (descriptive statistics), whereas others help draw conclusions about data (inferential statistics).

status survey A simple survey designed to provide a description of the current status of some population characteristic.

stimulus variable Any variable part of the environment to which an organism reacts. A stimulus variable may be a natural part of the environment and observed by the researcher or may be actively manipulated by the researcher.

strata Subpopulations within populations from which we draw samples based on the base rates in the population of the factor(s) that determine the strata.

stratified random sampling Variation of the random sampling procedure in which a population is divided in narrow strata along some critical dimension. Subjects are then selected randomly from each of the strata in the same proportion that the strata are represented in the population. Stratified random sampling can increase the representativeness of the sample and is used extensively in sophisticated survey research.

structuralism A philosophical perspective in which the scientist seeks to identify the structure of the underlying mechanisms that control behavior, such as consciousness. This approach was popularized by Wundt. Often contrasted with *functionalism.*

subject assignment Procedure of assigning subjects to a group or condition. Subject assignment may be made on the basis of some random procedure (experimental research) or on the basis of some preexisting condition in the subjects (differential research).

subject effects Any response by subjects in a study that does not represent the way they would normally behave if not under study. Two powerful subject effects are the placebo effect and a subject's response to the demand characteristics of the study.

subject selection The procedures by which potential subjects for a research study are identified. Subject selection procedures have a major impact on the external validity of a study. Subject selection may include random sampling, stratified random sampling, or designation of an ad hoc sample.

subject variable Synonymous with *organismic variable.*

subjective measures Measures based primarily on subjects' uncorroborated opinions, feelings, biases, or judgments. Subjective measures, as contrasted with *objective measures,* are more prone to distortions due to subject or experimenter effects.

subjects at risk Subjects involved in a research project that poses some potential risk to them. When subjects are at risk, the researcher is responsible for informing them of the risks and minimizing those risks.

subjects' rights Guarantees of proper treatment that subjects can justly expect in research.

subjects subsection That section of a research report in which the subjects and the methods of subject selection are described.

summary statistics Descriptive statistics that provide, in a single number, some general characteristic of the sample. Typical summary statistics are the mean, median, variance, and standard deviation.

sum of squares   Sum of the squared differences from the mean. The sum of squares is the numerator in the variance formula.

survey   A set of one or more questions posed to a group of subjects about their attitudes, beliefs, plans, lifestyles, or any other variable of interest. Surveys may be conducted over the phone, in person, or through the use of a written form.

survey research   Research that seeks to use survey procedures to identify relationships among the variables being surveyed.

symmetric distribution   Graphical representation of any distribution in which the right half of the distribution is a mirror image of the left half. Symmetric distribution is often contrasted with *skewed distribution*.

systematic replication   (or conceptual replication) Situation where a study is repeated with small, theory-based changes in the procedures. Systematic replication is more common than exact replication because it verifies original findings while also expanding knowledge of the phenomena.

table   Organizational device where information (often statistical information) is summarized briefly.

table of random numbers   A table containing a long list of randomly generated numbers. Such tables are used frequently in research for random selection and assignment of subjects. A table of random numbers is included in Appendix B of this text.

target population   Population to which we hope to generalize the findings of a research study. In most research, the entire target population is not accessible to the researcher.

technology   Physical instruments or tools used by researchers. Note that technology does not define science; it merely provides tools for scientists to make and record observations, analyze data, and simplify their work.

tenacity   Way of knowing about the universe. Tenacity is accepting an idea as true because it has been accepted as true for a long period of time.

testing   Potential confounding variable in research. Testing represents any change in a subject's score on a dependent measure that is a function of the subject having been tested previously in the research project.

test-retest reliability   Index of the consistency in scores over time. Test-retest reliability is computed by calculating the *Pearson's product-moment correlation* between scores from two testings separated by some specified time interval.

theoretical concept   Abstraction (thought or idea) that defines the relationship between two or more variables.

theory   In science, theory is the collection of ideas about how and why variables are related to one another. Theory is usually built on empirical observations and is validated by making predictions deduced from the theory, which are then empirically tested.

time-series design   See *interrupted time-series design*.

title page   The first page of a research report manuscript. The title page lists the authors and their affiliations, the title of the paper, and a running head (a brief title which will appear at the top of each page in the published paper).

treatment   See *manipulation*.

trimodal   A distribution that has three modes (most frequently occurring score).

true experiment   See *experiment*.

true zero   Characteristic of a measurement scale where zero represents none of the concept being measured.

t-test   Statistical procedure designed to test for mean differences between two groups of subjects.

t-test for independent groups   Statistical procedure designed to test for mean differences between two groups of subjects where all subjects in the study appear in one and only one group.

two-group posttest-only design   A design where two groups of subjects are compared once after some manipulation of the independent variable.

two-way ANOVA   Statistical procedure for the analysis of a factorial design with two independent variables.

Type I error   Probability of rejecting the null hypothesis when the null hypothesis is true.

Type II error   Probability of not rejecting the null hypothesis when the null hypothesis is false.

univariate   Having to do with one variable. For example, a univariate distribution would provide the distribution for a single variable.

univariate designs   See *single-variable designs*.

unobtrusive measure Any measure that can be taken on subjects without their being aware they are being measured.

unobtrusive observer Anyone who is able to observe the behavior of subjects without their being aware they are being observed.

validity Major concept in research that has several specific meanings (internal validity, external validity, construct validity, statistical validity). In a general sense, *validity* refers to the methodological and/or conceptual soundness of research (e.g., in the case of an experiment, a question regarding validity is "Does this experiment really test what it is supposed to test?").

variability Differences among subjects on any given variable.

variable Any characteristic that can take on different values. Variables are sets of events measured in research. Research is aimed at defining the relationships between variables.

variance Summary statistic that indicates the degree of variability among subjects for a given variable. The variance is essentially the average squared deviation from the mean and is the square of the standard deviation.

within-group variance Variability among subjects within a particular group or condition. Provides a basis for comparing mean differences between groups in most statistical procedures.

within-subjects design Research design in which individual differences are controlled by having the same subjects tested under all conditions.

within-subjects factorial A factorial design in which each subject appears in each condition.

within-subjects factors Independent variables in factorial designs in which each subject is tested under all conditions.

***x*-axis (abscissa)** In a graph the *x*-axis is the horizontal axis.

***y*-axis (ordinate)** In a graph the *y*-axis is the vertical axis.

Z-score See *standard score*.

References

Abramson, L. Y., Seligman, M. E. P., Teasdale, J. D. (1978). Learned helplessness in humans: Critique and reformulation. *Journal of Abnormal Psychology, 87,* 49–74.

American Psychological Association. (1981). Ethical principles of psychologists. *American Psychologist, 36,* 633–638.

American Psychological Association. (1986). *Guidelines for ethical conduct in the care and use of animals.* Washington, DC: Author.

American Psychiatric Association. (1994). *Diagnostic and statistical manual of mental disorders* (4th ed.). Washington, DC: Author.

American Psychological Association. (1994). *Publication manual of the American Psychological Association* (4th ed.). Washington, DC: Author.

American Psychological Association (1995). Call for comments on the revision of APA's Ethical Principles in the Conduct of Research with Human Participants. *Trends in Education, 2,* 16.

Anastasi, A. (1988). *Psychological testing* (6th ed.). New York: Macmillan.

Arnett, J. (1995). The young and the restless: Adolescent reckless behavior. *Current Directions in Psychological Science, 4,* 67–71.

Bachrach, A. J. (1981). *Psychological research: An introduction.* New York: Random House.

Bandura, A. I. (1969). *Principles of behavior modification.* New York: Holt, Rinehart and Winston.

Barber, T. X., & Silver, M. J. (1968). Fact, fiction and the experimenter bias effect. *Psychological Bulletin Monograph Supplement, 70,* 1–29.

Barlow, D. H., & Hersen, M. (1984). *Single case experimental designs: Strategies for studying behavior change* (2nd ed.) New York: Pergamon.

Bartlett, J. (1980). *Bartlett's familiar quotations.* Boston: Little, Brown.

Bass, E., & Davis, L. (1988). *The courage to heal: A guide for women survivors of sexual abuse.* New York: Harper & Row.

Bechtel, W., & Abrahamsen, A. (1991). *Connectionism and the mind: An introduction to parallel processing in networks.* Cambridge, MA: Basil Blackwell.

Benbow, C. P., & Stanley, J. C. (1980). Sex differences in mathematical ability: Fact or artifact? *Science, 210,* 1262–1264.

Bench, C. J., Dolan, R. J., Friston, K. J., & Frackowiak, R. S. (1990). Positron emission tomography in the study of brain metabolism in psychiatric and neuropsychiatric disorders. *British Journal of Psychiatry, 157,* 82–95.

Benson, D. F., & Stuss, D. T. (1990). Frontal lobe influences on delusions: A clinical perspective. *Schizophrenia Bulletin, 16,* 403–411.

Bergin, A. E. (1966). Some implications of psychotherapy research for therapeutic practice. *Journal of Abnormal Psychology, 71,* 235–246.

Bergin, A. E., & Strupp, H. H. (1970). New directions in psychotherapy research. *Journal of Abnormal Psychology, 76,* 13–26.

Bernstein, J. (1980). *Experiencing science.* New York: Dutton.

Bleuler, E. (1950). The fundamental symptoms. In E. Bleuler (Ed.), *Dementia praecox; or the group of schizophrenias* (J. Ziskin, Trans.) (pp. 14–54). New York: International University Press. (Original work published 1911.)

Boesch, C., & Boesch-Acherman, H. (1991). Dim forest, bright chimps. *Natural History, September,* 50–56.

Boring, E. G. (1950). *A history of experimental psychology.* New York: Appleton-Century-Crofts.

Bornstein, P. H., & Quevillon, R. P. (1976). The effects of a self-instructional package on overactive preschool boys. *Journal of Applied Behavior Analysis, 9,* 179–188.

Brotemarkle, R. A. (1966). Fifty years of clinical psychology: Clinical psychology, 1896–1946. In I. N. Mensh (Ed.), *Clinical psychology: Science and profession* (pp. 63–68). New York: Macmillan.

Buchsbaum, M. S. (1990). The frontal lobes, basal ganglia, and temporal lobes as sites for schizophrenia. *Schizophrenia Bulletin, 16,* 379–389.

Busch, L. (1991). Science under wraps in Prince William Sound. *Science, 252,* 772–773.

Camilli, G., & Hopkins, K. D. (1978). Applicability of chi square to 2×2 contingency tables with small expected cell frequencies. *Psychological Bulletin, 85,* 163–167.

Campbell, A., Converse, P. E., & Rodgers, W. L. (1976). *The quality of American life: Perceptions, evaluations and satisfactions.* New York: Russell Sage Foundation.

Campbell, D. T. (1969). Reforms as experiments. *American Psychologist, 24,* 409–429.

Campbell, D. T., & Stanley, J. C. (1966). *Experimental and quasi-experimental designs for research on teaching.* Chicago: Rand McNally.

Canadian Council on Animal Care. (1993) *Guide to the care and use of experimental animals.* 151 Slater, Ottawa, Ont. K1P 5H3, Canada.

Cantor-Graae, E., McNeil, T. F., Torrey, E. F., Quinn, P., Bowler, A., Sjöström, K., & Rawlings, R. (1994). Are neurological abnormalities in well discordant monozygotic co-twins of schizophrenic subjects the result of perinatal trauma? *American Journal of Psychiatry, 151,* 1194–1199.

Caporaso, J. A. (1974). *The structure and function of European integration.* Pacific Palisades, CA: Goodyear.

Chapman, L. J., & Chapman, J. P. (1969). Illusory correlation as an obstacle to the use of valid psychodiagnostic signs. *Journal of Abnormal Psychology, 74,* 271–287.

Chapman, L. J., & Chapman, J. P. (1973). *Disordered thought in schizophrenia.* Englewood Cliffs, NJ: Prentice Hall.

Chapman, L. J., Chapman, J. P., Kwapil, T. R., Eckblad, M., & Zinser, M. C. (1994). Putatively psychosis-prone subjects 10 years later. *Journal of Abnormal Psychology, 103,* 171–183.

Chapman, L. J., Chapman, J. P., Raulin, M. L., & Edell, W. S. (1978). Schizotypy and thought disorder as a high risk approach to schizophrenia. In G. Serban (Ed.) *Cognitive defects in the development of mental illness.* (pp. 351–360) New York: Brunner-Mazel.

Clagett, M. (1948). The medieval heritage: Religious, philosophic, scientific. In J. L. Blau, J. Buchler, & G. T. Matthews (Eds.), *Chapters in western civilization* (Vol. 1, pp. 74–122). New York: Columbia University Press.

Cohen, J., & Cohen, P. (1983). *Applied Multiple Regression/Correlation Analysis for the Behavioral Sciences* (2nd ed.). Hillsdale, NJ: Lawrence Erlbaum Associates.

Cohen, J. A. (1960). A coefficient of agreement for nominal scales. *Educational and Psychological Measurement, 20,* 37–46.

Cohen, J. A. (1988). *Statistical power analyses for the behavioral sciences* (2nd ed.). Hillsdale, NJ: Erlbaum.

Cohen, J. D., & Servan-Schreiber, D. (1989). *A parallel distributed processing approach to behavior and biology in schizophrenia.* (Tech. Rep. No. AIP-100), Pittsburgh: Carnegie Mellon University, The Artificial Intelligence and Psychology Project.

Cohen, J. D., & Servan-Schreiber, D. (1992). Context, cortex, and dopamine: A connectionist approach to behavior and biology in schizophrenia. *Psychological Review, 99,* 34–77.

Collier, R. (1994). An historical overview of natural language processing systems that learn. *Artificial Intelligence Review, 8,* 17–54.

Cook, T. D., & Campbell, D. T. (1979). *Quasi-experimentation: Design and analysis issues for field studies.* Chicago: Rand McNally.

Coombs, C. H., Raiffa, H. & Thrall, R. M. (1954). Some views on mathematical models and measurement theory. *Psychological Review, 61,* 132–144.

Copi, I. M., & Cohen, C. (1990). *Introduction to logic* (8th ed.). New York: Macmillan.

Correa, V. I., Poulson, C. L., & Salzberg, C. L. (1984). Training and generalization of reach-grasp behavior in blind, retarded young children. *Journal of Applied Behavior Analysis, 17,* 57–69.

Crown, S. (1975). "On being sane in insane places": A comment from England. *Journal of Abnormal Psychology, 84,* 453–455.

Curtis, D. R., & Crawford, J. M. (1969). Central synaptic transmission-microelectrophoretic studies. *Annual Review of Pharmacology, 9,* 209–240.

Daniken, E. von (1970). *Chariots of the gods.* New York: Putnam.

Daniken, E. von (1972). *Gods from outer space.* New York: Bantam Books.

Darley, J. M., & Latane, B. (1968). Bystander intervention in emergencies: Diffusion of responsibility. *Journal of Personality and Social Psychology, 8,* 377–383.

Darwin, C. (1859). *On the origin of species by means of natural selection, or the preservation of favored races in the struggle for life.* London: John Murray. (New York: Modern Library, 1967).

Dawis, R. (1987). Scale construction. *Journal of Counseling Psychology, 39,* 481–489.

Dennett, D. C. (1993). Learning and labeling. *Mind and Language, 8,* 540–548.

Dennett, D. C. (1995). *Darwin's dangerous idea: Evolution and the meaning of life.* New York: Simon & Schuster.

Dollard, J., & Miller, N. E. (1950). *Personality and psychotherapy.* New York: McGraw-Hill.

Edge, H. L., Morris, R. L., Rush, J. H., & Palmer, J. (1986). *Foundations of parapsychology: Exploring the boundaries of human capability.* Boston: Rutledge & Kegan Paul.

Epstein, L. H., Valosky, A., Wing, R., & McCurley, J. (1994). Ten-year outcomes of behavioral family-based treatment for childhood obesity. *Health Psychology, 13,* 373–383.

Fancher, R. E. (1990). *Pioneers of psychology* (2nd ed.). New York: W. W. Norton.

Farrington, B. (1949a). *Greek science: 1. Thales to Aristotle.* Harmondsworth: Pelican Books.

Farrington, B. (1949b). *Greek science: 2. Theophrastus to Galen.* Harmondsworth: Pelican Books.

Federal Register. (1991). Federal policy for the protection of human subjects: Notices and rules. *Federal Register, 56,* 117, 28002–28007.

Festinger, L. (1957). *A theory of cognitive dissonance.* Stanford, CA: Stanford University Press.

Fisher, R. A. (1935). *The design of experiments.* London: Oliver & Boyd.

Fossey, D. (1983). *Gorillas in the mist.* Boston, MA: Houghton Mifflin.

Fowler, R. D. (1995). *Report of the chief executive officer and executive vice president.* Washington, DC: American Psychological Association.

Freeman, M. (1984). History, narrative, and life-span developmental knowledge. *Human Development, 27,* 1–9.

Gaito, J. (1980). Measurement scales and statistics: Resurgence of an old misconception. *Psychological Bulletin, 87,* 564–567.

Gattaz, W. F., Mayer, S., Zielger, P. Platz, M., et al. (1992). Hypofrontality on topographic EEG in schizophrenia: Correlations with neuropsychological and psychopathological parameters. *European Archives of Psychiatry and Clinical Neuroscience, 241,* 328–332.

Gelfand, H., & Walker, C. J. (1994). *Mastering APA style: Student's workbook and training guide* (2nd ed.). Washington, DC: American Psychological Association.

Glass, G. V., Peckham, P. D., & Sanders, J. R. (1972). Consequences of failure to meet assumptions underlying the fixed effects analyses of variance and covariance. *Review of Educational Research, 42,* 237–288.

Glass, G. V., Willson, V. L., & Gottman, J. M. (1975). *Design and analysis of time series.* Boulder, CO: Laboratory of Educational Research Press.

Gleick, J. (1987). *Chaos: Making a new science.* New York: Penguin Books.

Goodall, J. (1971). *In the shadow of man.* Boston: Houghton-Mifflin.

Goodall, J. (1978). Chimp killings: Is it the man in them? *Science News, 113,* 276.

Goodall, J. (1986). *The Chimpanzees of Gombe.* Cambridge, MA: Belknap Press/Harvard University Press.

Graziano, A. M. (1974). *Child without tomorrow.* Elmsford, NY: Pergamon Press.

Graziano, A. M., Hamblen, J. L., & Plante, W. A. (1995, July). *The use of corporal punishment in 320 middle class American families.* Paper presented at the Fourth International Family Violence Conference, Durham, NH.

Graziano, A. M., & Kean, J. (1968). Programmed relaxation and reciprocal inhibition with psychotic children. *Behaviour Research and Therapy, 6,* 433–437.

Graziano, A. M., Lindquist, C. M., Kunce, L. J., & Munjal, K. (1992). Physical punishment in childhood and current attitudes: An exploratory comparison of college students in the United States and India. *Journal of Interpersonal Violence, 7,* 147–155.

Graziano, A. M., & Mooney, K. C. (1982). Behavioral treatment of "nightfears:" A 2½ to 3 year follow-up. *Journal of Consulting and Clinical Psychology, 50,* 598–599.

Graziano, A. M., & Namaste, K. A. (1990). Parental use of physical force in child discipline: A survey of 679 college students. *Journal of Interpersonal Violence, 5,* 449–463.

Guerin, D., & MacKinnon, D. P. (1985). An assessment of the California Child Passenger Restraint Requirement. *American Journal of Public Health, 75,* 142–144.

Gupta, S., Andreasen, N. C., Arndt, S., Flaum, M., Schultz, S. K., Hubbard, W. C., & Smith, M. (1995). Neurological soft signs in neuroleptic-naive and neuroleptic-treated schizophrenic patients and in normal comparison subjects. *American Journal of Psychiatry, 152,* 191–196.

Harley, T. A. (1993). Connectionist approaches to language disorders. *Aphasiology, 7,* 221–249.

Helmstadter, G. C. (1970). *Research concepts in human behavior.* New York: Appleton-Century-Crofts.

Heron, W., Doane, B. K., & Scott, T. H. (1956). Visual disturbance after prolonged perceptual isolation. *Canadian Journal of Psychology, 10,* 13–18.

Hoffman, R. E., & McGlashan, T. H. (1993). Parallel distributed processing and the emergence of schizophrenic symptoms. *Schizophrenia Bulletin, 19,* 119–140.

Holden, C. (1995). Etheric Archives. *Science, 267,* 1764.

Hothersall, D. (1984). *History of psychology.* Philadelphia, PA: Temple University Press.

Howell, D. C. (1987). *Statistical methods for psychology* (2nd ed.). Boston: Duxbury.

Hull, C. L. (1943). *Principles of behavior.* New York: Appleton-Century-Crofts.

Hull, E. M., Du, J., Lorrain, D. S. & Matuszewich, L. (in press). Extracellular dopamine in the medial preoptic area: Implications for sexual motivation and hormonal control of copulation. *Journal of Neuroscience.*

Hull, E. M., Weber, M. S., Eaton, R. C., Dua, R., Markowski, V. P., Lumley, L., & Moses, J. (1991). Dopamine receptors in the ventral tegmental area affect motor, but not motivational or reflexive, components of copulation in male rats. *Brain Research, 554,* 72–76.

Hyman, R. (1964). *The nature of psychological inquiry.* Englewood Cliffs, NJ: Prentice Hall.

Josiassen, R. C., Roemer, R. A., Johnson, M. M., & Shagass, C. (1990). Are gender differences in schizophrenia reflected in brain event-related potentials. *Schizophrenia Bulletin, 16,* 229–246.

Kasabov, N. K., Shishkov, S. I. (1993). A connectionist production system with partial match and its use for approximate reasoning. Special Issue: Architectures for integrating neural and symbolic processes. *Connection Science Journal of Neural Computing, Artificial Intelligence, and Cognitive Research, 5,* 275–305.

Kazdin, A. E. (1992). *Research design in clinical psychology* (2nd ed.). New York: Macmillan.

Keith, A. (1954). Darwin and the "Origin of Species." In H. Shapley, S. Rapport, & H. Wright (Eds.), *A treasury of science* (pp. 437–446). New York: Harper and Brothers.

Kendler, H. H. (1993). Psychology and the ethics of social policy. *American Psychologist, 48,* 1046–1053.

Keppel, G. (1991). *Design and analysis: A research handbook.* Englewood Cliffs, NJ: Prentice Hall.

Kerlinger, F. N. (1986). *Foundations of behavioral research* (3rd ed.). New York: Holt, Rinehart and Winston.

Kety, S. S., Rosenthal, D., Wender, P. H., & Schulsinger, F. (1968). The types and prevalence of mental illness in the biological and adoptive families of adopted schizophrenics. In D. Rosenthal & S. S. Kety (Eds.), *The transmission of schizophrenia* (pp. 345–362). Oxford: Pergamon.

Kimmel, M. J., Pruitt, D. G., Magenau, J. M., Konar-Goldband, E., & Carnevale, P. J. D. (1980). Effects of trust, aspiration, and gender on negotiation tactics. *Journal of Personality and Social Psychology, 38,* 9–22.

Kitto, H. D. F. (1951). *The Greeks.* Harmondsworth, England. Pelican Books.

Koegel, R. L., O'Dell, M. C., & Koegel, I. Y. (1987). A natural language teaching paradigm for nonverbal autistic children. *Journal of Autism and Developmental Disorders, 17,* 187–200.

Korfine, L., & Lenzenweger, M. F. (1995). The taxonicity of schizotypy: A replication. *Journal of Abnormal Psychology, 104,* 26-31.

Kraemer, D. L., Hastrup, J. L., Sobota, M., & Bornstein, R. F. (1985, April). *Adolescent crying: Norms and self-control.* Paper presented at the meeting of the Eastern Psychological Association, Boston, MA.

Kratochwill, T. R. (Ed.). (1978). *Single-subject research: Strategies for evaluating change.* New York: Academic Press.

Krumenaker, L. (1993). Virtual libraries, complete with journals, get real. *Science, 260,* 1066–1067.

Lang, A. R., & Sibrel, P. A. (1989). Psychological perspectives on alcohol consumption and interpersonal aggression: The potential role of individual differences in alcohol-related criminal violence. *Criminal Justice and Behavior, 16,* 299–324.

Lawler, E. E., III, & Hackman, J. R. (1969). Impact of employee participation in the development of pay incentive plans: A field experiment. *Journal of Applied Psychology, 53,* 467–471.

Lenzenweger, M. F., & Korfine, L. (1992). Confirming the latent structure and base rate of schizotypy: A taxometric analysis. *Journal of Abnormal Psychology, 101,* 567–571.

Levin, R., & Raulin, M. L. (1991). Preliminary evidence for the proposed relationship between frequent nightmares and schizotypal symptomatology. *Journal of Personality Disorders, 3,* 8–14.

Levine, A. G. (1982). *The Love Canal: Science, politics and people.* Lexington, MA: D. C. Heath.

Levine, M. (1974). Scientific method in the adversary model. *American Psychologist, 29,* 661–677.

Levine, M. (1980). Investigative reporting as a research method: An analysis of Bernstein and Woodward's *All the President's Men. American Psychologist, 35,* 626–638.

Levine, M., & Howe, B. (1985). The penetration of social science into legal culture. *Law and Policy, 7,* 173–198.

Levy, K. (1980). A Monte Carlo study of analysis of covariance under violations of the assumptions of normality and equal regression slopes. *Educational and Psychological Measurement, 40,* 835–840.

Lewine, R. R. J., Gulley, L. R., Risch, S. C., Jewart, R., & Houpt, J. L. (1990). Sexual dimorphism, brain morphology, and schizophrenia. *Schizophrenia Bulletin, 16,* 195–203.

Loehlin, J. C. (1992). *Latent variable models: An introduction to factor, path, and structural analyses* (2nd ed.). Hillsdale, NJ: Lawrence Erlbaum Associates.

Loftus, E. F., & Hoffman, H. G. (1989). Misinformation and memory: The creation of new memories. *Journal of Experimental Psychology: General, 118,* 100–104.

Loftus, E. F., & Ketcham, K. (1991). *Witness for the defense: The accused, the eye witness, and the expert who puts memory on trial.* New York: St. Martin's Press.

Loftus, E. F., & Ketcham, K. (1994). *The myth of repressed memory: False memories and allegations of sexual abuse.* New York: St. Martin's Press.

Lord, F. M. (1967). A paradox in the interpretation of group differences. *Psychological Bulletin, 68,* 304–305.

Lovaas, O. I. (1973). *Behavioral treatment of autistic children.* Morristown, NJ: General Learning Press.

Lovaas, O. I. (1987). Behavioral treatment and normal educational and intellectual functioning in young autistic children. *Journal of Consulting and Clinical Psychology, 55,* 3–9.

Lowrie, G., & Raulin, M. L. (1995, April). *Schizotypy: Taxonic or Dimensional?* Paper presented at the Annual Convention of the Eastern Psychological Association, Boston.

Lubinski, D., & Benbow, C. P. (1992). Gender differences in abilities and preferences among the gifted: Implications for the math-science pipeline. *Current Directions in Psychological Science, 1,* 61–66.

Madsen, K. B. (1988). *A history of psychology in metascientific perspective.* Amsterdam: North Holland Publishers.

Marlatt, G. A., Demming, B., & Reid, J. B. (1973). Loss of control drinking in alcoholics: An experimental analogue. *Journal of Abnormal Psychology, 81,* 233–241.

Marr, D. (1982). *Vision: A computational investigation into the human representation and processing of visual information.* San Francisco: W. H. Freeman.

Martin, P., & Bateson, P. (1986). *Measuring behavior: An introductory guide.* London: Cambridge University Press.

Marx, M. H. (Ed.). (1963). *Theories in contemporary psychology.* New York: Macmillan.

Masling, J. M., & Bornstein, R. F. (1994). *Empirical perspectives on object relations theory: Empirical studies of psychoanalytic theory* (Vol. 5). Washington, DC: American Psychological Association.

Masters, W. H., & Johnson, V. E. (1966). *Human sexual response.* Boston: Little, Brown.

Mazur-Hart, S. F., & Berman, J. J. (1977). Changing from fault to no-fault divorce: An interrupted time-series analysis. *Journal of Applied Social Psychology, 7,* 300–312.

McClelland, J. L., Rummelhart, D. E., & the PDP Research Group. (1986). *Parallel distributed processing: Explorations in the microstructure of cognitions. Volume 2: Psychological and biological models.* Cambridge, MA: MIT Press.

McGillicuddy, N. B., Welton, G. L., & Pruit, D. G. (1987). Third-party intervention: A field experiment comparing three different models. *Journal of Personality and Social Psychology, 53,* 104–112.

McSweeny, A. J. (1978). The effects of response cost on the behavior of a million persons: Charging for directory assistance in Cincinnati. *Journal of Applied Behavior Analysis, 11,* 47–51.

Meacham, J. A. (1994). Discussions by e-mail: Experiences from a large class on multiculturalism. *Liberal Education, 80,* 36–39.

Meacham, J. A. (1995). E-mail discussions in a large class. *Interface (UB Computing and Information Technology Newsletter), 26*(6, January/February). Accessible through e-mail by sending the following message to: listserv@uvbm.cc.buffalo.edu:Get meacham.v26i0al Interfac

Mednick, S. A., & Schulsinger, F. (1968). Some powerful characteristics related to breakdown in children with schizophrenic mothers. In D. Rosenthal & S. S. Kety (Eds.), *The transmission of schizophrenia* (pp. 267–291). Oxford: Pergamon.

Meehl, P. E. (1990). Toward an integrated theory of schizotaxia, schizotypy, and schizophrenia. *Journal of Personality Disorders, 4,* 1–99.

Meehl, P. E. (1995). Bootstraps taxometrics: Solving the classification problem in psychopathology. *American Psychologist, 50,* 266–275.

Meehl, P. E., & Yonce, L. J. (1994). Taxometric analysis: I. Detecting taxonicity with two quantitative indicators using means above and below a sliding cut (MAMBAC procedure). *Psychological Reports, 74,* 1059–1274.

Michell, J. (1986). Measurement scales and statistics: A clash of paradigms. *Psychological Bulletin, 87,* 564–567.

Milbrath, L. W., Hausbeck, K. M., & Enright, S. M. (1991). *An inquiry into environmental education: Levels of knowledge, awareness and concern among New York State high school students.* Unpublished technical report. Buffalo: State University of New York.

Miller, N. E. (1971). *Neal E. Miller: Selected papers.* Chicago: Aldine Atherton.

Miller, N. E. (1985). The value of behavioral research with animals. *American Psychologist, 40,* 423–440.

Mousavi, M. S., & Schalkoff, R. J. (1994). An implementation of stereo vision using a multi-layer feedback architecture. *IEEE Transactions on Systems, Man, and Cybernetics, 24,* 1220–1238.

Myers, J. L., & Well, A. D. (1991). *Research design and statistical analysis.* New York: HarperCollins.

Nagel, E. (1948). The development of modern science. In J. L. Blau, J. Buchler, & G. T. Matthews (Eds.), *Chapters in western civilization* (Vol. 1, pp. 241–284). New York: Columbia University Press.

Nasrallah, H. A., Schwartzkopf, S. B., Olson, S. C., & Coffman, J. A. (1990). Gender differences in schizophrenia on MRI brain scans. *Schizophrenia Bulletin, 16,* 205–210.

National Institutes of Health. (1991). *Preparation and Maintenance of Higher Mammals During Neuroscience Experiments.* NIH Publication No. 91-3207. National Eye Institute, Building 31, Room 6A47, Bethesda, MD.

National Institutes of Health. (1986). *OPPR Public Health Service Policy on Humane Care and Use of Laboratory Animals.* Office of Protection from Research Risks, NIH, 6100 Executive Blvd., Suite 3B01-MSC 7509, Rockville, MD. 20892-7509.

National Institutes of Health. (1985). *Guide for the Care and Use of Laboratory Animals.* NIH Publication No. 85-23. NIH, Bldg. 14-A, Room 100, 9000 Rockville Pike, Bethesda, MD 20892.

Neale, J. M., & Oltmanns, T. F. (1981). Assessment of schizophrenia. In D. H. Barlow (Ed.), *Behavioral assessment of adult disorders* (pp. 87–128). New York: Guilford.

Neisser, U., & Harsch, N. (1992). Phantom flashbulbs: False recollection of hearing the news about Challenger. In E. Winograd & U. Neisser (Eds.), *Affect and accuracy in recall: Studies of "flashbulb" memories* (pp. 9–31). New York: Cambridge University Press.

Nelson, G. (1970). [Interview.] In S. Rosner & I. E. Abt (Eds.), *The creative experience* (pp. 251–268). New York: Grossman.

Norusis, M. J. (1994a). *SPSS for Windows: Advanced statistics (Release 6.0).* Chicago: SPSS.

Norusis, M. J. (1994b). *SPSS for Windows: Base manual (Release 6.0).* Chicago: SPSS.

Norusis, M. J. (1994c). *SPSS for Windows: Statistics (Release 6.0).* Chicago: SPSS.

Nunnally, J. C., & Bernstein, I. H. (1993). *Psychometric theory* (3rd ed.). New York: McGraw-Hill.

Oppel, F. (Ed.). (1987). *Early flight: From balloons to biplanes.* Secaucus, NJ: Castle Publishers.

Oppenheimer, J. R. (1956). Analogy in science. *American Psychologist, 11,* 127–135.

Orne, M. T. (1962). On the social psychology of the psychological experiment: With particular reference to demand characteristics and their implications. *American Psychologist, 17,* 776–783.

Osberg, T. M., & Raulin, M. L. (1989). Networking as a tool for career advancement among academic psychologists. *Teaching of Psychology, 16,* 26–28.

Parsons, J. E. (Ed.). (1980). *The psychology of sex differences and sex roles.* New York: McGraw-Hill.

Pauling, L. (1981). Cited in A. J. Bachrach, *Psychological research: An introduction* (4th ed., p. 3). New York: Random House.

Pelham, W. E. (1994). *Attention Deficit Hyperactivity Disorder.* Colloquium presented at the State University of New York at Buffalo (November 3, 1994).

Pelham, W. E., Murphy, D. A., Vannatta, K., Milich, R., Licht, B. G., Gnagy, E. M., Greenslade, K. E., Greiner, A. R., & Vodde-Hamilton, M. (1992). Methylphenidate and attributions in boys with attention-deficit hyperactivity disorder. *Journal of Consulting and Clinical Psychology, 60,* 282–292.

Phillips, D. P. (1983). The impact of mass media violence on U.S. homicides. *American Sociological Review, 48,* 560–568.

Plaut, D. C., & Shallice, T. (1993). Deep dyslexia: A case study of connectionist neuropsychology. *Cognitive Neuropsychology, 10,* 377–500.

Prilleltensky, I. (1994). Psychology and social ethics. *American Psychologist, 49,* 966–967.

Ramey, C. T. (1995, June). *Biology and experience codetermine intellectual development: Beyond additive models.* Part of the Presidential Symposium entitled "Beyond the Bell Curve: Genes, Intelligence and Achievement in Perspective" presented at the Annual Convention of the American Psychological Society, New York.

Raulin, M. L. (1984). Development of a scale to measure intense ambivalence. *Journal of Consulting and Clinical Psychology, 52,* 63–72.

Raulin, M. L., & Brenner, V. (1993). Ambivalence. In C. G. Costello (Ed.), *Symptoms of schizophrenia* (pp. 201–226). New York: Wiley.

Raulin, M. L., & Graziano, A. M. (1995). Quasi-experiments and correlational studies. In A. M. Coleman (Ed.), *Psychological research methods and statistics.* London: Longman. 1122–1141

Raulin, M. L., Brenner, V., deBeaumont, S. M., & Vetter, C. J. (1995, November). *The impact of managed care on treatment outcome: Initial findings.* Poster presented at the annual convention of the Association for the Advancement of Behavior Therapy, Washington, DC.

Raulin, M. L., deBeaumont, S. M., Brenner, V., & Vetter, C. J. (1995, June). *Comparing outcome of psychological/psychiatric intervention in managed care and traditional health insurance environments.* Poster presented at the Annual Convention of the Association of Applied and Preventive Psychology, whose Convention is held jointly with the American Psychological Society, New York.

Reed, J. G., & Baxter, P. M. (1992). *Library use: A handbook of psychology* (2nd ed). Washington, DC: American Psychological Association.

Reese, W. L. (1980). *Dictionary of philosophy and religion: Eastern and Western thought.* Atlantic Highlands, NJ: Humanities Press.

Roberts, F. S. (1979). *Measurement theory with applications to decision-making utility and the social sciences.* Reading, MA: Addison-Wesley.

Rohsenow, D. J., & Marlatt, G. A. (1981). The balanced placebo design: Methodological considerations. *Addictive Behavior, 6,* 107–122.

Rosenhan, D. L. (1973). On being sane in insane places. *Science, 179,* 250–258.

Rosenthal, R. (1976). *Experimenter effects in behavioral research.* New York: Halsted Press.

Rosenthal, R. (1994). Science and ethics in conducting, analyzing, and reporting psychological research. *Psychological Science, 5,* 127–134.

Rosenthal, R., & Fode, K. L. (1963a). The effect of experimenter bias on the performance of the albino rat. *Behavioral Science, 8,* 183–189.

Rosenthal, R., & Fode, K. L. (1963b). Three experiments in experimenter bias. *Psychological Reports, 12,* 491–511.

Rosnow, R. L., & Rosenthal, R. (1995). Some things you learn aren't so: Cohen's paradox, Asch's paradigms, and the interpretation of interaction. *Psychological Science 6,* 3–9.

Rosnow, R. L., & Rosnow, M. (1992). *Writing papers in psychology: A study guide.* (2nd ed.). Belmont, CA: Brooks/Cole.

Rossi, P. H., Wright, J. D., & Anderson, A. B. (1985). *Handbook of survey research.* New York: Academic Press.

Rubin, J. Z., Pruitt, D. G., & Kim, S. (1994). *Social conflict, escalation, stalemate, and settlement.* New York: McGraw-Hill.

Rummelhart, D. E., McClelland, J. L., & the PDP Research Group. (1986). *Parallel distributed processing: Explorations in the microstructure of cognitions. Volume 1:* Foundations. Cambridge, MA: MIT Press.

Runyon, R. P., & Haber, A. (1991). *Fundamentals of behavioral statistics* (7th ed). Reading, MA: Addison-Wesley.

Rupley, S., & Clyman, J. (1995). P6: The next step. *PC Magazine, 14*(15), 102–118. September 12, 1995.

Sanders, R. D., Keshavan, M. S., Schooler, N. R. (1994). Neurological examination abnormalities in neuroleptic-naive patients with first-break schizophrenia: Preliminary results. *American Journal of Psychiatry, 151,* 1231–1233.

Schrage, M. (1991). Computer tools for thinking in tandem. *Science, 253,* 505–507 (August 2, 1991).

Schultz, D. (1987). *A history of modern psychology* (4th ed.). New York: Harcourt Brace College Publishers.

Schuman, H., & Kalton, G. (1985). Survey methods. In G. Lindzey & E. Aronson (Eds.), *The handbook of social psychology* (3rd ed., Vol. 1, pp. 635–698). New York: Random House.

Seidenberg, M. S. (1993). A connectionist modeling approach to word recognition and dyslexia. *Psychological Science, 4,* 299–304.

Seigel, S. (1956). *Nonparametric statistics for the behavioral sciences.* New York: McGraw-Hill.

Seligman, M. E. P. (1974). Depression and learned helplessness. In R. J. Friedman & M. J. Katz (Eds.), *The psychology of depression: Contemporary theory and research.* Washington, DC: Winston-Wiley.

Shavelson, R. J. (1988). *Statistical reasoning for the behavioral sciences* (2nd ed.). Boston: Allyn & Bacon.

Sidman, M. (1960). *Tactics of scientific research: Evaluating scientific data in psychology.* New York: Basic Books.

Silverstein, S. M., Raulin, M. L., Pristach, E. A., & Pomerantz, J. R. (1992). Perceptual organization and schizotypy. *Journal of Abnormal Psychology, 101,* 265–270.

Simner, M. (1995). Report of the membership committee chair. Ottawa, Canada: Canadian Psychological Association.

Skinner, B. F. (1938). *The behavior of organisms.* New York: Appleton-Century-Crofts.

Skinner, B. F. (1953). *Science and human behavior.* New York: Macmillan.

Skinner, B. F. (1956). A case history in scientific method. *American Psychologist, 11,* 221–233.

Skinner, B. F. (1972). *Cumulative record: A selection of papers* (3rd ed.). New York: Appleton-Century-Crofts.

Skinner, B. F. (1990, August). Skinner's keynote address: Lifetime scientific contribution remarks. Presentation at the annual convention of the American Psychological Association, Boston. (Available on audio- or videocassette from the American Psychological Association Continuing Education Section)

Snowling, M., Hulme, C., & Goulandris, N. (1994). Word recognition in developmental dyslexia: A connectionist interpretation. *Quarterly Journal of Experimental Psychology: Human Experimental Psychology, 47,* 895–916.

Society for Neuroscience (1991). *Handbook of the use of animals in research.* Society for Neuroscience, 11 Dupont Circle, N.W., Suite 500 WA D.C., 20036.

Society for Neuroscience. (1995). *Membership directory.* Washington, D.C.: Author.

Solomon, R. L. (1949). An extension of control group design. *Psychological Bulletin, 46,* 137–150.

Spearman, C. (1904). "General intelligence" objectively determined and measured. *American Journal of Psychology, 15,* 201–293.

Spitzer, R. L. (1975). On pseudoscience in science, logic in remission, and psychiatric diagnoses: A critique of Rosenhan's "On being sane in insane places." *Journal of Abnormal Psychology, 84,* 442–452.

Staddon, J. E. R., & Bueno, J. L. O. (1991). On models, behaviorism, and the neural basis of learning. *Psychological Science, 2,* 3–11.

Stein, D., J., & Hollander, E. (1994). A neural network approach to obsessive-compulsive disorder. *Journal of Mind and Behavior, 15,* 223–237.

Sternberg, R. I., & Lubart, T. I. (1992). Buy low and sell high: An investment approach to creativity. *Current Directions in Psychological Science, 1,* 1–15.

Stevens, S. S. (1946). On the theory of scales of measurement. *Science, 103,* 677–680.

Stevens, S. S. (1957). On the psychophysical law. *Psychological Review. 64,* 153–181.

Strain, P. S. (1983). Generalization of autistic children's social behavior change: Effects of developmentally integrated and segregated settings. *Analysis and Intervention in Developmental Disabilities, 3,* 23–34.

Strain, P. S. (1984). Social behavior patterns of non-pairs in mainstream schools. *Analysis and Intervention in Developmental Disabilities, 4,* 15–28.

Strunk, W., Jr., & White, E. B. (1979). *The elements of style* (3rd ed.). New York: Macmillan.

Szent-Gyorgi, A. (1971). Looking back. *Perspectives in Biology and Medicine, 13,* 1.

Taubes, G. (1993). Publication by electronic mail takes physics by storm. *Science, 259,* 1246–1248.

Tinbergen, N. (1951). *The study of instinct.* London: Oxford University Press.

Tinbergen, N. (1963). *The Herring Gull's world.* London: Collins.

Tomlinson, T. (1990). *Case study: conceiving children to use for tissue transplantation.* Medical Humanities Report, Spring Center for Ethics and Humanities in the Life Sciences, Michigan State University.

Torrey, E. F., Taylor, E. H., Bracha, H. S., Bowler, A. E., McNeil, T. F., Rawlings, R. R., Quinn, P. O., Bigelow, L. B., Rickler, K., Sjöström, K., Higgins, E. S., & Gottesman, I. I. (1994). Prenatal origin of schizophrenia in a subgroup of discordant monozygotic twins. *Schizophrenia Bulletin, 20,* 423–432.

Tufte, E. R. (1983). *The visual display of quantitative information.* Cheshire, CT: Graphics Press.

Tukey, J. W. (1977). *Exploratory data analysis.* Reading, MA: Addison-Wesley.

Ulrich, R. E. (1991). Animal rights, animal wrongs and the question of balance. *Psychological Science, 2,* 197–201.

Wang, Z. M., Heshka, S., Pierson, R. N., & Heynsfield, S. B. (1995). Systematic organization of body-composition method. An overview with emphasis on component-based methods. *American Journal of Clinical Nutrition, 61,* 457–465.

Warner, R. K., Thompson, J. T., Markowski, V. P., Loucks, J. A., Bazzett, T. J., Eaton, R. C., & Hull, E. M. (1991). Microinjection of the dopamine antagonist cis-flupenthixol into the MPOA impairs copulation, penile reflexes and sexual motivation in male rats. *Brain Research, 540,* 177–182.

Webb, E. J., Campbell, D. T., Schwartz, R. D., & Sechrest, L. (1966). *Unobtrusive measures: Nonreactive research in the social sciences.* Chicago: Rand McNally.

Weiner, B. (1975). "On being sane in insane places": A process (attributional) analysis and critique. *Journal of Abnormal Psychology, 84,* 433–441.

Welkowitz, J., Ewen, R. B., & Cohen, J. (1990). *Introductory statistics for the behavioral sciences* (4th ed.). San Diego: Harcourt Brace Jovanovich.

Welton, G. L., Pruitt, D. G., & McGillicuddy, N. B. (1988). The role of caucusing in community mediation. *Journal of Conflict Resolution, 32,* 181–202.

Wender, P. H., Kety, S. S., Rosenthal, D., Schulsinger, F., Ortmann, J., & Lunde, I. (1986). Psychiatric disorder in the biological and adoptive families of adopted individuals with affective disorders. *Archives of General Psychiatry, 43,* 923–929.

Whitehead, A. B. (1925). *Science and the modern world.* New York: Macmillan.

Wolpe, J. (1958). *Psychotherapy by reciprocal inhibition.* Stanford, CA: Stanford University Press.

Wolpe, J. (1990). *The practice of behavior therapy* (4th ed.). New York: Pergamon Press.

Wood, F. B., & Flowers, D. L. (1990). Hypofrontal vs. hypo-sylvian blood flow in schizophrenia. *Schizophrenia Bulletin, 16,* 413–424.

Zinsser, W. (1994). *On writing well* (5th ed). New York: HarperCollins.

Name Index

Subject Index

Note: Page numbers in *italics* indicate figures; page numbers followed by *n* indicate footnotes; page numbers followed by *t* indicate tables.